D0781865

Rationality in action
Contemporary approaches

Rationality in action
Contemporary approaches

Edited by
Paul K. Moser
Loyola University of Chicago

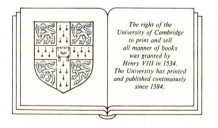

The right of the
University of Cambridge
to print and sell
all manner of books
was granted by
Henry VIII in 1534.
The University has printed
and published continuously
since 1584.

Cambridge University Press

Cambridge
New York   Port Chester   Melbourne   Sydney

Published by the Press Syndicate of the University of Cambridge
The Pitt Building, Trumpington Street, Cambridge CB2 1RP
40 West 20th Street, New York, NY 10011, USA
10 Stamford Road, Oakleigh, Melbourne 3166, Australia

© Cambridge University Press 1990

First published 1990

Printed in the United States of America

Library of Congress Cataloging-in-Publication Data

Rationality in action : contemporary approaches / [edited by] Paul K.
Moser.

p.   cm.

Includes bibliographical references.

1. Decision-making.   I. Moser, Paul K., 1957–
BF448.R37   1990   90-31391
153.8′3 – dc20   CIP

British Library Cataloguing in Publication Data

Moser, Paul K. *1957–*

Rationality in action : contemporary approaches.

1. Rationality
I. Title
153.43

ISBN 0 521 38572 5 hard covers
ISBN 0 521 38598 9 paperback

Contents

Contributors

Maurice Allais   *Centre d'Analyse Economique, Ecole Nationale Supérieure des Mines de Paris, Centre National de la Recherche Scientifique*
Kenneth Arrow   *Department of Economics, Stanford University*
Robert Audi   *Department of Philosophy, University of Nebraska – Lincoln*
Robert Axelrod   *Department of Political Science, University of Michigan*
Richard Brandt   *Department of Philosophy, University of Michigan*
Donald Davidson   *Department of Philosophy, University of California – Berkeley*
Daniel Ellsberg   *The Rand Corporation, Santa Monica**
David Gauthier   *Department of Philosophy, University of Pittsburgh*
John Harsanyi   *Department of Economics, University of California – Berkeley*
Daniel Kahneman   *Department of Psychology, University of British Columbia*
David Lewis   *Department of Philosophy, Princeton University*
R. Duncan Luce   *Department of Psychology and Social Relations, Harvard University*
Robert Nozick   *Department of Philosophy, Harvard University*
Howard Raiffa   *Department of Economics, Harvard University*
Leonard Savage   *Department of Statistics, Yale University**
Amartya Sen   *Department of Philosophy, Harvard University*
Herbert Simon   *Department of Philosophy, Carnegie-Mellon University*
Michael Slote   *Department of Philosophy, University of Maryland*
Amos Tversky   *Department of Psychology, Stanford University*
Bernard Williams   *Department of Philosophy, University of California – Berkeley*

*Asterisk indicates affiliation when item was first published.

Preface

The rationality of action is practical, in contrast to merely theoretical, rationality. Such rationality is a longstanding subject of interdisciplinary importance. Philosophers and psychologists, as well as economists, political scientists, and sociologists, among varying other theorists, pursue general accounts of practical rationality. Their common quarry promises to elucidate at least these major topics: (a) the nature of successful practical deliberation, (b) the conditions for effective goal-satisfaction, (c) the relation of reasons to motives, preferences, and values, (d) the connections, if any, between rationality and impartiality and between rationality and social cooperation, and (e) the essence of irrational decision making. The importance of these topics is obviously not limited to the concerns of any single discipline.

This book includes twenty-one selections that will be of long-term importance to theoretical work on practical rationality. Most of the selections are essentially nontechnical and accessible to a wide range of readers, including advanced undergraduates, from varying disciplines. The book's selections fall under three main categories: (I) Individual Decision Theory: Concepts and Foundations, (II) Game Theory and Group Decision Making, and (III) Reasons, Desires, and Irrationality. Given the interdisciplinary prominence and the diversity of these categories, this book can serve as the main text for advanced undergraduate and graduate courses on practical rationality from a range of disciplines.

I am grateful to Bradley Owen and Dwayne Mulder, my research assistants at Loyola University of Chicago, for their fine help in the preparation of the book's manuscript. I am grateful also to Terry Moore, Executive Editor for Humanities at Cambridge University Press, and to several anonymous referees for helpful advice on the book's selections. Finally, I thank Marilyn Prudente of Comprehensive Graphics for her excellent copyediting.

Chicago, Illinois   Paul K. Moser

Rationality in action: general introduction

Paul K. Moser

Questions about rational action have recently attracted broad interdisciplinary interest from philosophers, psychologists, sociologists, economists, political scientists, and anthropologists, among others. But such theorists do not share anything like a uniform account of rational action. The selections in this collection highlight many of the fundamental disagreements among theorists of rationality: for instance, disagreements over (a) the formulation and the significance of decision theory, (b) the relevance of game theory to rational decision making, (c) the roles of desires and values in rational action, and (d) the conditions for irrational action. Various other topics have generated controversy, but topics (a)–(d) receive primary attention in the following selections.

In the light of traditional decision theory, many theorists, from each of the wide ranges of disciplines indicated, take rationality to be a minister without portfolio. On their view, rationality does not require any particular substantive ends or goals of its own; it consists simply in the optimal pursuit of one's preferred ends, whatever those ends happen to be. This is the familiar *instrumentalist* conception of rational action, versions of which appear in many economic and decision-theoretic approaches to rational decision making.

An opposing view states that certain ends are essential to rationality, that rationality is a minister with portfolio. This is the *substantialist* conception of rationality that originated with Aristotle, held sway among Western philosophers in medieval times, but lost influence with the rise of modern decision theory. Which view is correct, instrumentalism or substantialism? This is one of the main controversial issues highlighted by some of the subsequent selections (e.g., the chapters by Simon, Williams, Brandt, and Audi). Some of the other main issues will be outlined in the remainder of this introduction and in the introductions to the three main parts of this book.

1. Individual decision theory: basic themes

Individual decision theory characterizes rational action in terms of an optimal choice under certain specified conditions. The latter conditions involve (a) the set of alternative actions available to the decision maker, (b) the decision maker's degree of certainty about the outcomes of each of the members of (a), and (c) the decision maker's ranking of the members of (a) on the basis of his or her ranking of the presumed outcomes of those members. Conditions (a)–(c) are essential to a *decision-situation* for a decision maker. Simply characterized, rational decision making consists in one's choosing the best member from the set of available alternative actions. In cases where one is certain of outcomes, the best member will be simply the highest-ranked member in the set of available alternative actions.

One's ranking of the available alternatives and their presumed outcomes, according to individual decision theory, derives ultimately from one's preferences, or one's desires. If a person's preferences satisfy certain consistency and completeness requirements, they will be characterizable by a well-defined utility function that enables rational decision making to be construed as *utility maximization* of a sort that will be explained. On instrumentalist approaches, the utility of an outcome is a function ultimately of a person's ranked preferences. So, on these approaches, we can understand talk of "maximizing utility" as talk of optimizing relative to personal ranked preferences. An individual's ranking of his or her preferences regarding outcomes is, thus, on instrumentalist approaches, a fundamental determinant of the rationality of that individual's decisions.

Before pursuing the ranking of preferences and outcomes further, we should clarify the notion of a *decision-situation*. A rational decision must take account of various possible states of the world, and of the consequences (or outcomes) of each available action relative to each of the relevant possible states of the world. A well-known example from Leonard Savage (1972, pp. 13–14) will help:

Your wife has just broken five good eggs into a bowl when you come in and volunteer to finish making the omelet. A sixth egg, which for some reason must either be used for the omelet or wasted altogether, lies unbroken beside the bowl. You must decide what to do with this unbroken egg. Perhaps it is not too great an oversimplification to say that you must decide among three acts only, namely, to break it into the bowl containing the other five, to break it into a saucer for inspection, or to throw it away without inspection. Depending on the state of the egg, each of these three acts will have some consequence of concern to you.

Savage provides a table (shown at the top of page 3) to represent the decision-matrix involved in his example.

We can construct such a decision-matrix for a wide range of decision-situations. Savage's example illustrates that our available actions have different outcomes that depend on what the actual states of the world are. It

Act	State	
	Good	Rotten
Break into bowl	Six-egg omelet	No omelet, and five good eggs destroyed
Break into saucer	Six-egg omelet, and a saucer to wash	Five-egg omelet, and a saucer to wash
Throw away	Five-egg omelet, and one good egg destroyed	Five-egg omelet

also illustrates, more generally, that a decision-situation includes a set of available actions, a set of possible states of the world, and a set of outcomes for each of the available actions.

The central question for a theory of rationality concerns, of course, how someone is rationally to assess the available actions in a decision-situation. According to decision theory, an individual's preferences toward the possible outcomes of available actions determine, at least in part, what actions are rational for him or her. The preferability (or desirability) of an outcome for a decision maker determines, as suggested, the personal *utility* of that outcome. An *ordinal* scale for possible outcomes is just a ranking of those outcomes in order of preference. Such a ranking does not indicate, however, the *extent* or *degree* to which a decision maker prefers one outcome to another. When a decision maker is certain about the outcomes of his or her actions relative to actual states of the world, an ordinal ranking is typically adequate. Given such certainty, a rational decision maker need only invoke his or her ordinal ranking of outcomes based on personal preferences; the decision maker need only choose the action that has the highest utility on his or her ranking. (See Chapter 1 by Luce and Raiffa for some relevant discussion.)

Problems arise, however, when a decision maker does not have certainty about outcomes. Decision theorists distinguish two such general situations. In decisions under *risk,* a person has complete information about his or her available actions, their outcomes, and relevant states of the world, but can only assign various definite probabilities less than one to the possible outcomes of available actions. (*Bayesian* decision theory, represented for example by Ramsey (1931) and Savage (1972), assumes that the relevant probabilities are subjective in that they are determined by the decision maker's beliefs about states of the world; for critical discussion, see Kyburg (1968), Kahneman and Tversky (1972), and Mellor (1983).) In decisions under *uncertainty,* a person lacks information about relevant states of the world, and so cannot even assign definite probabilities to the various possible outcomes of his or her available actions. (See Chapter 3 by Luce and Raiffa for discussion of various decision criteria for cases of uncertainty.) Bayesian decision theorists, however, typically construe all decision making as decision making under risk, on the assumption that a decision maker can use his or her beliefs to generate subjective probabilities regarding relevant states of the world and outcomes of available actions.

Given the usual absence of certainty about the future for us, we might consider ourselves to be ordinarily in situations of decision making under risk or under uncertainty. The simplicity of decision making under certainty seems rarely ours to enjoy. But some theorists have argued that we often find ourselves in situations somewhere between the domains of risk and uncertainty. In such situations, apparently, we have partial information about outcomes, but this information does not enable us to formulate determinate probabilities about all relevant states of the world. (See Chapter 4 by Daniel Ellsberg, on this matter.)

When the outcomes of our actions are calculable with definite numerical probabilities less than one, we need some way of measuring preferences quantitatively. In such cases we need some determinate way to relate our preferences to the numerical probabilities attached to the possible outcomes of our available actions. We need, in other words, *quantities* or *units* of utility; we need something like a *cardinal* ranking of utilities. Clearly, money does not give us a general invariant measure of utility; the marginal utility of money can vary depending on how much money one has. John von Neumann and Oskar Morgenstern (1953, Chap. 1) have proposed that we could find the desired measurability of preferences in an *interval* scale provided by the odds we accept in a presumed lottery. On this view, measurements of preference do not rely on an independent zero point, but only compare the intervals between the various points on a preference scale. Von Neumann and Morgenstern have shown how this approach enables us to represent preference measurements arithmetically. (See Chapter 1 by Luce and Raiffa and Chapter 2 by Savage for some relevant discussion; see also Savage (1972, pp. 73–6).)

Supposing then that preferences, and thus utilities, are numerically measurable, we still need to identify conditions for optimal decision making under risk. Clearly we cannot simply recommend that a person should always choose the action whose outcome has the highest personal utility. Such a recommendation is not sensitive to the amount of risk that may be involved in choosing the optimal outcome. It may be imprudently risky to pursue an optimal outcome. Thus a *maximax* policy of maximizing the maximum prospective utility from one's alternative actions will appeal only to those who are unmoved by considerations of risk. At the other extreme, a *maximin* policy of maximizing the minimum prospective utility (i.e., choosing the best of the worst) from one's alternatives will appeal only to those who are pessimistic about taking risks based on probabilities. (See Chapter 3 by Luce and Raiffa for a discussion of maximin policies.)

To accommodate considerations of risk *and* utility, many decision theorists have proposed that the rational decision maker should choose an action that maximizes *expected utility*. In general, the expected utility of an action is calculated as follows: (a) multiply the utility of each possible outcome of that action by the probability of that outcome occurring, (b) add up the results of the former, and (c) subtract from the resulting sum the initial cost, in terms of utility, of performing the action. The calculations of (a) enable the decision maker to discount the utilities of possible outcomes by their associated probabilities of occurring; that is, the calculations factor risks into the decision-making situation.

For simplicity, let's use money to represent utility, and let's suppose that we will bet five dollars on the throw of a pair of dice. We can play for either

(a) five hundred dollars if a pair of twos is rolled, otherwise no payoff, or

(b) thirty dollars if the dice add up to an odd number, otherwise no payoff.

The probability of rolling a pair of twos is, of course, 1/36, and the probability of rolling the dice to add up to an odd number is 1/2. So the probability of not rolling a pair of twos is 35/36, and the probability of the dice not adding up to an odd number is 1/2. Thus:

the expected utility of (a) $= 1/36(\$500) + 35/36(-\$5) = \$13.89 - \$4.86 = \$9.03$, and

the expected utility of (b) $= 1/2(\$30) + 1/2(-\$5) = \$15 - \$2.50 = \$12.50$.

If we follow the policy of maximizing expected utility, we therefore should go with (b). This example assumes that the expected utility of the gamble is the main concern for us; it assumes that we do not prefer high-risk gambles, in general, to gambles recommended by expected utility.

But of course we could have preferences favoring high risk. We could, for example, prefer the excitement of risky gambles, and this could prompt us to go for the big wins while neglecting probabilities. Would such a violation of maximizing expected utility necessarily be irrational, and if so, why? A similar question is raised by the possibility of risk-averse decision makers who prefer not to take risks at all when they stand to lose a great deal. These are controversial questions about the *normative* significance of maximizing expected utility. Basically, the key issue is whether, and if so why, a rational decision maker *should* always maximize expected utility. A related issue is whether decision makers generally *do* actually maximize expected utility. The latter issue concerns the *descriptive* significance of the policy of maximizing expected utility. (Chapter 6 by Kahneman and Tversky presents a number of decision problems where people's preferences systematically violate the policy of maximizing expected utility; see also Chapter 5 by Allais, Chapter 8 by Simon, and the essays in Kahneman, Slovic, and Tversky (1982).)

Decision theorists do not always sharply distinguish the normative and the descriptive significance of the policy of maximizing expected utility. But in general we may assume that concerns to use that policy to explain how people *actually* make decisions are basically descriptive, whereas concerns to use that policy as a criterion for *rational* decision making are fundamentally normative. So when economists invoke a maximization policy to determine a rational market decision, their concerns are essentially normative; and when psychologists use such a policy to account for actual human behavior, their concerns are essentially descriptive. Yet decision theorists generally seem to agree that adequate principles of rational decision making should be psychologically realistic relative to actual human decision making. After all, we are concerned with *human* rational decision making.

2. Beyond traditional decision theory

Individual decision theory does not account in any straightforward way for *competitive* decision-situations. In such situations, the outcome of one's actions depends on the decisions of another decision maker who, given interests that conflict with one's own, can be expected to take one's own decision-strategy into account. These situations receive focal attention in game theory, the discipline founded by von Neumann and Morgenstern (1953) and surveyed by Luce and Raiffa (1957) and by Davis (1983). (See Chapter 11 by Harsanyi for discussion of game theory.) Game theorists distinguish between two-person and *n*-person games, and between zero-sum and non-zero-sum games. In a zero-sum game between you and me, any loss for either one of us is a gain for the other; the outcomes of any combination of our strategies for action will sum up to zero. In a non-zero-sum game between you and me, in contrast, we both could gain something under a certain combination of strategies.

However, if you and I are in a competitive situation with conflicting interests, my having evidence for thinking that you have a reason to do something could give you a reason to avoid performing the action in question. For, given the conflict of interests, you may want to deprive me of the success available from my conforming to my evidence about your reasons. In such a competitive situation, decision makers will have considerable difficulty in assigning definite probabilities to the outcomes of their actions, and so they will have considerable difficulty in maximizing expected utility.

Let's illustrate a case of competitive decision making with the famous prisoner's dilemma. Suppose you and I are prisoners charged with having committed a crime. We are awaiting trial in separate cells, unable to communicate with each other. The prosecuting attorney wants more evidence against us in her effort to convict both of us. So she offers each of us the following deal: If you confess to the crime, and help us to convict your unconfessing partner, you will receive only one year in prison, whereas your partner will receive five years. If neither of us confesses, she promises, we each will be convicted on a lesser charge and spend two years in prison. And if both of us confess, we will each get a three-year sentence.

We can summarize the situation as follows *from your standpoint:*

	I don't confess	I do confess
You don't confess	Two years	Five years
You do confess	One year	Three years

Naturally the main goal for each of us is to spend as few years in prison as possible. We will of course be better off if neither of us confesses than if both of us confess. But I don't care as much about what happens to you as I care about what happens to me; nor do you care as much about what happens to me as you care about what happens to you. You care mainly about reducing your own sentence, and I care mainly about reducing mine. Finally, each of us knows that the other is in an identical, exactly symmetrical situation. And if each of us is unable to assign a definite probability to what the other will do, we are both faced with decision making under considerable uncertainty.

What then is the rational thing for you to do in the imagined situation? Clearly you cannot guarantee the outcome you prefer most; you cannot prevent me from confessing while you do confess. The next best outcome for both of us would have both of us refrain from confessing. This option seems to involve some cooperation between us; it apparently involves my trusting you not to confess and your trusting me not to confess. Such cooperation is clearly preferable, for both of us, to the noncooperative option where both of us confess. Yet the latter noncooperative option could be recommended to you by these considerations: Either I will confess or I won't. If I do confess, then your confessing will be better for you than your not confessing. On the other hand, if I do not confess, then your confessing will, again, be better for you than your not confessing. So it seems that you should confess. Similarly, it seems that I should confess, too, for reasons directly analogous to yours.

But on the foregoing line of reasoning, we both will confess and get a three-year sentence. This sentence, of course, is not preferable to the two years each of us will get if we don't confess. So maybe we should cooperate after all. But what exactly does rationality recommend here: cooperation or noncooperation? This is the controversial issue that receives focal attention in Chapters 11, 12, and 13 by Harsanyi, Axelrod, and Gauthier, respectively. Issues about the role of cooperation in rationality lead naturally to questions about the rationality of morality and to questions about a sort of rationality that is not utility-maximizing in the familiar sense. (See Chapter 13 by

Gauthier on the notion of "constrained maximizing"; see also the essays in Campbell and Sowden (1985).)

The prisoner's dilemma, as argued by David Lewis (1979), seems to be a version of what is called "Newcomb's problem," a problem formulated by the physicist William Newcomb. (See Chapter 9 by Robert Nozick and Chapter 10 by Lewis.) Suppose a highly reliable predictor of your behavior offers you a choice between the two boxes before you. You can see that one box contains one thousand dollars. You cannot see the contents of the second box, but you are told by the trustworthy predictor that it contains either one million dollars or nothing. You have the choice of taking either just the second box or both boxes. But the predictor has determined the contents of the second box on this strategy: If his prediction is that you will take only the second box, he puts one million dollars in it; and if his prediction is that you will take both boxes, he puts nothing in the second box. The predictor has determined the contents of the second box prior to your decision. Further, you know that the predictor is almost perfect in his predictions about your behavior. What then is the rational choice for you?

Many decision theorists, so-called one-boxers, recommend that you take only the second box. And many other decision theorists, so-called two-boxers, recommend that you take both boxes. One-boxers emphasize that the conditional probability that the predictor predicts that you take only the second box, given that you do take only the second box, is nearly one. And these theorists stress that the conditional probability that the predictor predicts that you take both boxes, given that you do take both boxes, is also nearly one. If we take dollars to be utilities, the conditional expected utility of your taking only the second box will be much higher than that of taking both boxes. So the one-boxers can rely on a principle of maximizing expected utility to support their recommendation.

Two-boxers have a different rationale. They emphasize that by the time of your choice, the predictor will have already made his prediction and determined what is in the second box. Your choice thus will not determine the contents of the second box. If the predictor is to place one million dollars in the second box, he has already done so. So, the recommendation goes, you should take both boxes, as this choice will put you one thousand dollars ahead of taking only the second box. Taking both boxes will guarantee a better outcome than taking only the second. Thus a consideration of *dominance,* where a certain action comes out better than any available alternative, would seem to support the two-boxers' recommendation.

Causal decision theorists, in accord with the two-boxer rationale, use Newcomb's problem to illustrate that standard Bayesian decision theory is insufficiently sensitive to causal factors in decision making. They emphasize that in Newcomb's problem one's decision is *causally* independent of the predictor's prediction, even though there is a relation of *probabilistic* dependence between the two. Further, these theorists propose that, whenever possible, we should use relations of causal dependence, instead of conditional probabilistic dependence, as a basis for assessing expected utility. On their view, an adequate decision theory must allow for the priority of relations of causal dependence to relations of merely probabilistic dependence. But the details of an adequate causal decision theory are a subject of continuing controversy. (See Chapter 10 by Lewis for some contrasting approaches to causal decision theory.)

In sum, then, the prisoner's dilemma and Newcomb's problem raise important questions about the roles of cooperation and of causation in rational decision making. Decision theorists continue to debate these and other issues about rational choice, as the following selections illustrate in detail. The subsequent introductions to the book's three main parts identify some of the other matters of continuing controversy, including the Allais paradox and the Ellsberg paradox for decision theory. The section introductions also introduce some controversial issues about rational choice, including social choice, that are independent of traditional decision theory.

3. Conclusion

If this general introduction has a central lesson, it is that traditional decision theory cannot plausibly be thought to give us an uncontroversial account of rational action. Decision theory seems to generate at least as many controversial questions as it answers. The subsequent selections should enable us to make progress on the important question of the exact role of decision theory in a comprehensive account of rational action. These selections should also improve understanding of the roles of cooperation, causation, desires, and values in rational action.

References

Campbell, Richmond, and Lanning Sowden, eds. *Paradoxes of Rationality and Co-operation.* Vancouver: University of British Columbia Press, 1985.

Davis, Morton. *Game Theory.* 2d ed. New York: Basic Books, 1983.

Kahneman, Daniel, and Amos Tversky. "Subjective Probability: A Judgment of Representativeness." *Cognitive Psychology* 3 (1972): 430–54.

Kahneman, Daniel, Paul Slovic, and Amos Tversky, eds. *Judgment Under Uncertainty: Heuristics and Biases.* Cambridge: Cambridge University Press, 1982.

Kyburg, Henry. "Bets and Beliefs." *American Philosophical Quarterly* 5 (1968): 63–78.

Lewis, David. "Prisoners' Dilemma is a Newcomb Problem." *Philosophy and Public Affairs* 8 (1979): 235–40.

Luce, R. D., and Howard Raiffa. *Games and Decisions.* New York: Wiley, 1957.

Mellor, D. H. "Objective Decision Making." *Social Theory and Practice* 9 (1983): 289–309.

Ramsey, F. P. "Truth and Probability." In *The Foundations of Mathematics,* 156–98. London: Routledge and Kegan Paul, 1931.

Savage, Leonard. *The Foundations of Statistics.* 2d ed. New York: Dover, 1972.

von Neumann, John, and Oskar Morgenstern. *Theory of Games and Economic Behavior.* 3d ed. Princeton: Princeton University Press, 1953.

Part I

Individual decision theory: concepts and foundations

This part of the book consists of three main sections: A. Decisions Under Certainty, Risk, and Uncertainty, B. Problems and Revisions, and C. Newcomb's Problem and Causal Decision Theory. The essays in Sections B and C require, at least for the most part, an understanding of the main general themes of the essays in Section A.

A. Decisions under certainty, risk, and uncertainty

This section consists of three essays that introduce some notions and themes essential to individual decision theory. In "Utility Theory," R. Duncan Luce and Howard Raiffa explain how utility theory fits into decision theory. They distinguish between decisions under *certainty,* decisions under *risk,* and decisions under *uncertainty,* and then explain how considerations of utility figure in individual decision making under certainty and risk. Luce and Raiffa outline a standard approach to decision making under risk, and then give an axiomatic treatment of utility to elucidate some key components of that approach. They also correct some common misinterpretations of modern utility theory, and identify some important empirical issues about the applicability of utility theory to actual decision making.

In "Historical and Critical Comments on Utility," Leonard Savage reviews and assesses some prominent notions of utility. He outlines some objections from Daniel Bernoulli (1700–82) against the universal applicability of the principle of mathematical expectation: the principle that the gamble with the highest expected winnings is best (or, in other terms, that wealth measured in cash is a utility function). Savage also defends modern utility theory against several objections. He is especially concerned to defend his "sure-thing principle," which he states as follows (*The Foundations of Statistics,* 2d ed., p. 21):

If the person would not prefer [act] f to [act] g, either knowing that the event B obtained, or knowing that the event $-B$ obtained, then he does not prefer f to g. Moreover (provided he does not regard B as virtually impossible) if he would definitely prefer g to f, knowing that B obtained, and if he would not prefer f to g, knowing that B did not obtain, then he definitely prefers g to f.

Roughly put, the main idea here is that if two acts have the same outcome in a particular situation, then the act one prefers should be independent of what that shared outcome is. Savage replies to an objection from Maurice Allais against his sure-thing principle. (See Chapter 5 on the objection from Allais.) The key issue of dispute is whether a rational choice between alternative actions can be affected by the values of outcomes that are not a function just of expected utility in terms of utilities of outcomes.

In "Individual Decision Making Under Uncertainty," Luce and Raiffa pursue the issue of what constitutes reasonable criteria for optimality in cases of decision making under uncertainty, or under what some call "complete ignorance." They assess such decision criteria as maximin utility or minimax loss, minimax regret (suggested by Leonard Savage), the principle of insufficient reason, and the pessimism–optimism index (suggested by Leonid Hurwicz). In addition, they aim to specify some "reasonable desiderata" that an adequate decision criterion should fulfill. They also assess cases of "partial ignorance" that seem to fall between the extremes of complete ignorance and risk.

B. Problems and revisions

This section consists of five essays that identify fundamental problems facing traditional decision theory. In "Risk, Ambiguity, and the Savage Axioms," Daniel Ellsberg asks whether we can always describe our states of uncertainty in terms of definite probabilities. He aims to characterize a class of situations where reasonable people "neither wish nor tend to conform" to axioms prescribing the maximization of expected utility on the basis of numerical probabilities. Ellsberg considers an urn that is known to contain thirty red balls and sixty black and yellow balls (the latter two colors in unknown proportion). You are to draw one ball at random from the urn. In the first choice situation, you have two alternatives: If you choose alternative 1, you will receive one hundred dollars if you draw a red ball, but nothing if you draw a black ball or a yellow ball; if you choose alternative 2, you will receive one hundred dollars if you draw a black ball, but nothing if you draw a red ball or a yellow ball. The second choice situation is similar, but gives you two different alternatives: If you choose alternative 3, you will receive one hundred dollars if you draw either a red or a yellow ball, otherwise nothing; if you choose alternative 4, you will receive one hundred dollars if you draw either a black or a yellow ball, otherwise nothing.

So we have this matrix:

		Red	Black	Yellow
I.	1	$100	$0	$0
	2	$0	$100	$0
II.	3	$100	$0	$100
	4	$0	$100	$100

A very frequent pattern of response to these decision-situations is that alternative 1 is preferred to alternative 2, and alternative 4 is preferred to alternative 3. But this pattern violates Savage's sure-thing principle.

The pattern of preferences here is explainable by the following consideration. We know that the proportion of red balls in the urn is one-third, but we do not know the proportion of black balls. Ellsberg proposes that the present decision-situation falls between the extremes of decision making under risk and decision making under uncertainty. In such a situation, according to Ellsberg, what is at issue is the "ambiguity" of one's information concerning the relative likelihood of events. This ambiguity, in the given example, consists in one's not knowing enough to rule out a number of possible distributions of the balls in the urn. As Ellsberg emphasizes, "if 'complete ignorance' is rare or nonexistent, 'considerable' ignorance is surely not."

In "Criticism of the Postulates and Axioms of the American School," Maurice Allais critically assesses certain basic assumptions of the decision theories formulated by von Neumann and Morgenstern, Savage, Samuelson, and others. In criticizing Savage's sure-thing principle, Allais appeals to two decision-situations. (For simplicity my example alters the numbers used in Allais's example.) In the first situation, you have a choice between (a) receiving one million dollars for certain and (b) a lottery that gives you a 10 percent chance of winning five million dollars, an 89 percent chance of winning one million dollars, and a 1 percent chance of winning nothing. In the second situation, you have a choice between two lotteries. In one lottery, you have a 10 percent chance of winning five million dollars and a 90% percent chance of winning nothing; in the other lottery, you have an 11 percent chance of winning one million dollars and an 89 percent chance of winning nothing. So you face this matrix:

		state 1 Pr(state 1) = 1%	state 2 Pr(state 2) = 10%	state 3 Pr(state 3) = 89%
I.	1	$1,000,000	$1,000,000	$1,000,000
	2	$0	$5,000,000	$1,000,000
II.	3	$0	$5,000,000	$0
	4	$1,000,000	$1,000,000	$0

In situation I, most people prefer alternative 1 to alternative 2. Apparently most people don't find the 10 percent chance of winning five million dollars, joined with the 89 percent chance of winning one million dollars, sufficiently decisive to compensate for the 1 percent chance of winning nothing. In situation II, most people prefer alternative 3 to alternative 4. Evidently since the chance of winning is almost the same in alternatives 3 and 4, people generally prefer the alternative with the bigger payoff. Such patterns of preference conflict with Savage's sure-thing principle and with the policy of maximizing expected utility. (See Chapter 2 by Savage for a reply to Allais.)

In "Prospect Theory: An Analysis of Decision Under Risk," Daniel Kahneman and Amos Tversky describe a number of decision-situations in which people's preferences generally violate key assumptions of expected utility theory. They use such situations to argue that expected utility theory is not an adequate descriptive model for human decision making under risk. Kahneman and Tversky use Allais's example to illustrate that people generally overweight outcomes that are presumed certain, relative to outcomes that are merely probable; they call this phenomenon the *certainty effect*. Kahneman and Tversky also present an alternative descriptive model of decision making under risk. Called *prospect theory,* their model distinguishes two phases in a decision-situation: an initial stage of editing and a subsequent phase of evaluation. The editing stage is a preliminary analysis of the available prospects, where a simplified representation of alternatives and outcomes is often made. The second phase involves evaluation of the edited prospects and a choice of the prospect of highest value. The evaluation in this phase replaces probabilities with more general decision weights, and uses values involving gains and losses based on deviations from a certain reference point. Kahneman and Tversky present their model as more adequate than standard expected utility theory as a descriptive account of human decision making.

In "Judgment Under Uncertainty: Heuristics and Biases," Kahneman and Tversky argue that people generally rely on heuristic principles that reduce complex tasks of assessing probabilities and predicting values to simpler operations. Such heuristics can be useful, but often lead to serious errors and biases. Kahneman and Tversky identify three heuristics for assessing probabilities and predicting values, and discuss biases to which these heuristics lead. They first identify a *representativeness heuristic* where the probabilities that an item A belongs to a class B, or originates from a process B, are evaluated by the degree to which an A is representative of, or resembles, B. On this heuristic, when A is highly representative of B, the probability that A originates from B is judged to be high. Next they identify an *availability heuristic* where one assesses the frequency of a class or the probability of an event by the ease with which instances or occurrences can be brought to mind. Support for this heuristic comes from the fact that instances of large classes are typically reached faster than instances of less frequent classes. And finally they identify an *adjustment-from-an-anchor heuristic* where estimates are made by starting from an initial value that is adjusted to yield a final estimate. This heuristic typically is used in numerical prediction when an initial numerical value is available to the decision maker. Kahneman and Tversky conclude that a better understanding of such heuristics and their resulting biases will improve decision making under uncertainty.

In "Alternative Visions of Rationality," Herbert Simon begins with an argument that reason is altogether instrumental. On his view, reason can tell us how to achieve our goals, but it cannot tell us what our ultimate goals should be. So far as considerations of rationality go, according to Simon, even Hitler's Nazi goals cannot be faulted. Simon objects to expected utility theory on the ground that humans have at their disposal neither the facts nor the consistent structure of values nor the reasoning power needed to apply the principles of utility theory. Simon presents, as an alternative, a "behavioral model" according to which human rationality is "bounded." Rational decision making on this view is not determined by a comprehensive utility function. It doesn't require optimization or even consistency. Basically it involves the application of a certain range of personal values to resolve fairly specific problems a person faces, in a way that is satisfactory (rather than optimal) for that person. Simon's model thus gives up many of the formal properties of traditional utility theory.

C. Newcomb's problem and causal decision theory

This section consists of two essays that focus on the role of causal factors in rational decision making. In "Newcomb's Problem and Two Principles of Choice," Robert Nozick presents Newcomb's predictor paradox (which was previously outlined in the general introduction), and approaches it indirectly by examining the following two decision principles:

Expected Utility Theory. *Perform, from the actions available to you, an action with maximal expected utility.*

Dominance Principle. *If there is a partition of states of the world such that relative to it, action A weakly dominates action B for you, perform A rather than B.*

Weak dominance is defined as follows: *A* weakly dominates *B* for you if and only if (i) for each state of the world, you either prefer the outcome of *A* to the outcome of *B* or are indifferent between those outcomes, and (ii) for some state of the world, you prefer the outcome of *A* to the outcome of *B*. Nozick examines some situations where the two foregoing principles conflict, where one of those principles recommends one action while the other recommends another action. He argues that in situations like that of Newcomb's problem, one should choose the dominant action, and ignore the conditional probabilities that do not indicate an influence of one's actions on the relevant states of the world. Thus Nozick sides with two-boxers and gives a nod to causal decision theory.

In "Causal Decision Theory," David Lewis proposes that, in light of Newcomb's problem (of which Lewis presents a few versions), we need a decision theory sensitive to causal distinctions. He examines various formulations of causal decision theory to show that they share an important thesis about rational choice and differ mainly on matters of emphasis and formulation. Lewis defines a *dependency hypothesis* as a maximally specific proposition about how the things an agent cares about do and do not depend causally on the agent's present actions. On Lewis's explanation, causal decision theory is causal in two ways: "The dependency hypotheses are causal in their content: they class worlds together on the basis of likenesses of causal dependence. But also the dependency hypotheses themselves are causally independent of the agent's actions. They specify his influence over other things, but over them he has no influence." Lewis examines the causal decision theory of Brian Skyrms and of Allan Gibbard and William Harper to explain how his own conditions for causal decision theory figure in their approaches. In conclusion, Lewis defends causal decision theory against a general objection.

A. *Decisions under certainty, risk, and uncertainty*

1. Utility theory

R. Duncan Luce and Howard Raiffa

1. A classification of decision making

The modern theory of utility is an indispensable tool for the remainder of this book, and so it is imperative to have a sound orientation toward it. Apparently this is not easy to achieve, judging by the many current misconceptions about the nature of "utility." It is, perhaps, unfortunate that von Neumann and Morgenstern employed this particular word for the concept they created – unfortunate because there have been so many past uses and misuses of various concepts called utility that many people view anything involving that word with a jaundiced eye, and because others insist on reading into the modern concept meanings from the past. We certainly are not going to assert that there are no serious limitations to the von Neumann–Morgenstern theory, but it can be frustrating to hear devastating denunciations which, although relevant to theories of the past, are totally irrelevant to – or incorrect for – the modern theory.

Pedagogically, it might be wise to defer this discussion until it is forced upon us in the context of game theory. Certainly, the needs of game theory would provide excellent reason to study the concept; however, it would also necessitate a sizeable digression in what will prove to be an already long argument. Furthermore, utility theory is not a part of game theory. It is true that it was created as a pillar for game theory, but it can stand apart and it has applicability in other contexts. So we have elected to present it first. As background, we shall describe in this section how the problems of decision making have been classified, in this way showing where utility theory fits into the overall picture. In the next section we shall discuss the classical notion of utility and indicate how, through its defects, it led up to the modern

Reprinted with permission from Luce and Raiffa, *Games and Decisions* (New York: Dover, 1989), 12–38.

concept. No attempt is made to trace the history of the concept in detail; an excellent history can be found in Savage (1954).[1] In sections 4 and 5 we shall present a version of the theory itself, and in 6 and 7 some of the more common fallacies surrounding it. The chapter closes with a brief discussion of the experimental problems. . . .

The field of decision making is commonly partitioned according to whether a decision is made by (i) an individual or (ii) a group, and according to whether it is effected under conditions of (a) certainty, (b) risk, or (c) uncertainty. To this last classification we really must add (d) a combination of uncertainty and risk in the light of experimental evidence. This is the province of statistical inference.

The distinction between an individual and a group is not a biological-social one but simply a functional one. Any decision maker – a single human being or an organization – which can be thought of as having a unitary interest motivating its decisions can be treated as an individual in the theory. Any collection of such individuals having conflicting interests which must be resolved, either in open conflict or by compromise, will be considered to be a group. These are not clearly defined formal words in the theory; rather they are vague classificatory concepts suggesting the identifications one might make in applications. Depending upon one's viewpoint, an industrial organization may be considered as an individual in conflict with other similar organizations or as a group composed of competing departments.

As to the certainty-risk-uncertainty classification, let us suppose that a choice must be made between two actions. We shall say that we are in the realm of decision making under:

(a)   *Certainty* if each action is known to lead invariably to a specific outcome (the words prospect, stimulus, alternative, etc., are also used).

(b)   *Risk* if each action leads to one of a set of possible specific outcomes, each outcome occurring with a known probability. The probabilities are assumed to be known to the decision maker. For example, an action might lead to this risky outcome: a reward of $10 if a "fair" coin comes up heads, and a loss of $5 if it comes up tails. Of course, certainty is a degenerate case of risk where the probabilities are 0 and 1.

(c)   *Uncertainty* if either action or both has as its consequence a set of possible specific outcomes, but where the probabilities of these outcomes are completely unknown or are not even meaningful.

. . . [W]e may now say a few words about decision making under certainty and about the backgrounds of modern utility theory. For more comprehensive surveys of utility theory see Adams (1954), Edwards (1954c), and Savage (1954).

---

[1] [See Chapter 2 for the relevant discussion.]

2. Individual decision making under certainty

Decision making under certainty is a vast area! The bulk of formal theory in economics, psychology, and management sciences can be classed under this heading. Until quite recently, the mathematical tools used were largely the calculus to find maxima and minima of functions and the calculus of variations to find functions, production schedules, inventory schedules, and so on which optimize performance over time – dynamic programing, so to speak. We will not discuss these topics, for their connection with game theory is remote, but we shall sketch some of the ideas which led to utility theory.

Typically, decision making under certainty boils down to this: Given a set of possible acts, to choose one (or all) of those which maximize (or minimize) some given index. Symbolically, let x be a generic act in a given set F of feasible acts and let $f(x)$ be an index associated to (or appraising) x; then find those $x^{(0)}$ in F which yield the maximum (or minimum) index, i.e., $f(x)$ for all x in F.

Very often the heart of the problem is the appropriate choice of the associated index. In many economic contexts profit and loss are suitable indices, but in other contexts no such quantities are readily available. Consider, for example, a person who wishes to purchase one of several paintings. In a sense, we can assert that the essence of the problem is: How should the subject select an index function so that his choice reduces to finding the alternative with the maximum index?

Operationally, of course, we can suppress this problem, for all we need to do is observe his purchase. Alternatively, we can observe his behavior in a host of more restricted situations and from this predict his purchase. For example, in an experimental study one might instruct him as follows. "Here are ten valuable reproductions. We will present these to you in pairs and you will tell us which one of each pair you would prefer to own. After you have given your answers to all paired comparisons, we will actually choose a pair at random and present you with the choice you have previously made. Hence, it is to your advantage to record, as best as you are able, your own true tastes." Now, it may be possible to account for all his choices by assuming that he has a simple ranking of the paintings, from the least liked to the most liked, such that the subject always chooses, in any paired comparison, the one with the higher ranking. If so, his choices can be pithily summarized by assigning numbers to the paintings in such a way that their magnitudes reflect this preference ranking. For example, 1 to the least liked, 2 to the next, ... and 10 to the best liked. This can be done provided his preferences satisfy the one condition of *transitivity:* if A is preferred in the paired comparison (A, B) and B is preferred to the paired comparison (B, C), then A is preferred in the paired comparison (A, C), and this holds for all possible triples of alternatives A, B, and C. This concept of transitivity is extremely important and should be well understood. It is a completely natural notion in much of our language: if A is larger than B and B is larger than C, then A is larger than C (or substitute "heavier," "better," etc.).

If we are able to rank the alternatives and if we assign a numerical index, then in a totally *tautological* sense we can assert that the subject has behaved as if he always chooses the painting with the higher index. From this it is easy to slip into saying that one was preferred to another because it has a larger latent index of "satisfaction" or "utility." This is an unrewarding slip – indeed, it is a trap one must be careful to avoid. This usage was once a burning issue in the economic literature, but it has been totally discredited. One of the reasons is the striking non-uniqueness of the index. For example, suppose we have only the three alternatives A, B, and C, where A is the most preferred, B the next, and C the least. Then, one may summarize this by saying that they are worth 3, 2, and 1 "utiles" respectively. Of course, had the associated "utiles" been 30, 20.24, and 3.14, the same manifest response pattern of preference would be observed. Indeed, any numbers a, b, and c such that $a > b > c$ would lead to the same manifest data. When it was conclusively shown that large segments of economic thought could be maintained by postulating merely an ordinal preference pattern – an ordering – for alternatives without including an underpinning of latent "utiles," the utility notion was not worth philosophizing about. Still, one may contend that introducing the numbers does no harm, that they summarize the ordinal data in a compact way, and that they are mathematically convenient to manipulate. But, in part, their very manipulative convenience is a source of trouble, for one must develop an almost inhuman self-control not to read into these numbers those properties which numbers usually enjoy. For example, one must keep in mind that it is meaningless to add two together or to compare magnitudes of differences between them. If they are used as indices in the way we have described, then the only meaningful numerical property is order. We may compare two indices and ask which is the larger, but we may not add or multiply them. . . .

4. Individual decision making under risk

The problems of making decisions under risk first appeared in the analysis of a fair gamble, and here again the desire for a utility concept arose. Consider a gamble in which one of n outcomes will occur, and let the possible outcomes be worth $a_1, a_2, \ldots, a_n$ dollars, respectively. Suppose that it is known that the respective probabilities of these outcomes are $p_1, p_2, \ldots, p_n$, where each p_i lies between 0 and 1 (inclusive) and their sum is 1. How much is it worth to participate in this gamble?

The monetary expected value is

$$b = a_1 p_1 + a_2 p_2 + \cdots + a_n p_n,$$

and, so one argument goes, the "fair price" for the gamble is its expected value b. However, the famous St. Petersburg paradox, due to D. Bernoulli, casts serious doubt that for most people the money expectation formulates what they consider to be the "fair price." The paradox is this: A "fair" coin, which is defined by the property that the probability of heads is ½, is tossed until a head appears. The gambler receives 2^n dollars if the first head occurs on trial n. The probability of this occurrence is simply the probability of a sequence of tails on the first $n-1$ trials and a head on the nth, which is ½ multiplied n times, i.e., $(½)^n$. Thus, one receives 2 dollars with probability ½, 4 dollars with probability ¼, 8 dollars with probability ⅛, and so on. Therefore, the expected value is

$$2(½)+4(¼)+8(⅛)+16(\tfrac{1}{16})+\cdots = 1+1+1+1+\cdots,$$

which does not sum to any finite number. It follows, then, that one should be willing to pay any sum, however large, for the privilege of participating in such a gamble. As a description of behavior, this is silly! As Bernoulli emphasized, people do not, and will not, behave in accord with the monetary expected value of this gamble.

Bernoulli suggested the following modification of the analysis in order to rescue the principle that people behave according to an expected value. The pertinent variable to be averaged, he argued, is not the actual monetary worth of outcomes, but rather the intrinsic worths of their monetary values. It is plausible to suppose that the intrinsic worth of money increases with money, but at a diminishing rate. A function having this property is the logarithm. Thus, if the "utility" of m dollars is $\log_{10} m$, then the fair price would not be the monetary expected value but the monetary equivalent of the utility expected value

$$b = (½)\log_{10} 2 + (¼)\log_{10} 4 + (⅛)\log_{10} 8 + \cdots.$$

It can be shown that this sum does, in the limit, approach a finite value, which we have called b. Then the "monetary fair price" of the gamble is a dollars, where $\log_{10} a = b$.

There are certain obvious criticisms of Bernoulli's tack, and these suggest some of the ideas involved in von Neumann and Morgenstern's approach to risk. First, the utility association to money is completely *ad hoc*. There are an infinity of functions which increase at a decreasing rate, and, certainly, the association may vary from person to person – but how? Second, why should a decision be based upon the expected value of these utilities? The rationale generally given for using expected value involves an argument as to what will happen in the long run when the gamble is repeated many times. Although it is easy to see the merit of such a frequency interpretation for a gambling house, it is by no means clear that it should apply to an individual who participates in the gamble only once.

Thus, what we want is a construction of a utility function for each individual which, in some sense, represents his choices among gambles and which has as a consequence the fact that the expected value of utility represents the utility of the corresponding gamble. We know from our previous examination of utility that this would be a hopeless aim if we considered only a finite number of certain alternatives, but, once we admit all possible gambles among a set of alternatives, we are dealing with an infinite set and by its very size there will be many more constraints on the utility function. *Very roughly,* von Neumann and Morgenstern have shown the following: If a person is able to express preferences between every possible pair of gambles, where the gambles are taken over some basic set of alternatives, then one *can* introduce utility associations to the basic alternatives in such a manner that, if the person is guided solely by the utility expected value, *he is acting in accord with his true tastes* – provided only that there is an element of consistency in his tastes. For the moment, let us ignore the exact statement of this proviso, which is important; we will return to it in the next section where we present a formal statement of one form of their result.

There are two points to be emphasized about this result. First, the utility function so constructed reflects preferences about the alternatives in a certain given situation, and so it will reflect not only how the subject feels about the alternatives (prizes, outcomes, or stimuli) in the abstract, but how he feels about them in the particular situation. For example, the resulting function will incorporate his attitude towards the whole gambling situation. Second, the utility associations are introduced in such a manner as to justify the central role of expected value without any further argument, specifically, without any discussion of long run effects.

The essence of their idea can be illustrated simply. Suppose that our subject prefers alternative A to B, B to C, and A to C. Any three numbers a, b, and c which decrease in magnitude are suitable indices to reflect this ordinal preference. But, remember, we are admitting gambles. Suppose we ask his preference between: (i) obtaining B for certain, and (ii) a gamble with A or C as the outcome, where the probability that it is A is p and the probability that it is C is $1-p$. We refer to these as the "certain option" and the "lottery option." It seems plausible that if p is sufficiently near to 1, so that the outcome of the lottery option is very likely to be A, the lottery will be preferred. But, if p is near 0, then the certain option will be preferred. As p changes continuously from 1 to 0 the preference for the lottery option must change into preference for the certain option. We idealize this preference pattern by supposing that there is one and only one point of change and that at this point the two options are indifferent. Let us suppose that it is the point $\frac{2}{3}$. If we arbitrarily associate the number 1 to alternative A and 0 to C, then what number should we associate to B to summarize our information about his preferences when this one gamble is allowed? Naturally, $\frac{2}{3}$. If this choice is made, then B is a "fair equivalent" for the gamble with A and C as outcomes with probabilities $\frac{2}{3}$, $\frac{1}{3}$, respectively, in the sense that the utility of B equals the utility expected value of the gamble,

$$1(\tfrac{2}{3}) + 0(\tfrac{1}{3}) = \tfrac{2}{3}.$$

There are triples of numbers other than $(1, \frac{2}{3}, 0)$ which also can serve to summarize the information we have about our subject's tastes, but not nearly so many as when all outcomes were certain. Adding the information of just this one gamble restricts the triples to those of the form

$$a+b, \; \frac{2}{3}a+b, \; b,$$

where the number a must be positive.

We note that in all such triples the numerical difference between the utility assignments to B and C is twice that between A and B. Does this permit us to say that going from B to C is twice as (or even just more) desirable than going from A to B? We think not! The number $\frac{2}{3}$ was determined by choices among risky alternatives, and it reflects attitudes toward gambling, not toward the two intervals. Suppose, for example, that, because of his aversion to gambling, our subject reported he would be indifferent between paying out $9 and having a 50–50 chance of paying out $10 or nothing. His response could then be summarized by saying that his utilities for $0, −$9, and −$10 are 1, $\frac{1}{2}$, and 0. We would be unwilling, however, to say that going from −$10 to −$9 is "just as enjoyable" as going from −$9 to $0.

In this theory it is extremely important to accept the fact that the subject's preferences among alternatives and lotteries came prior to our numerical characterization of them. We do not want to slip into saying that he preferred A to B because A has the higher utility; rather, because A is preferred to B, we assign A the higher utility.

If we add more gambles to the collection and try to assign utilities as we have done, it is clear that to be successful the subject's preferences will have to satisfy some consistency requirements. For example, if he prefers A to B, B to C, and a lottery which yields A with probability $\frac{2}{3}$ and C with probability $\frac{1}{3}$ to a lottery which yields A with probability $\frac{3}{4}$ and C with probability $\frac{1}{4}$, then we are in trouble. Or if he prefers A to B, B to C, and B to *any* lottery involving A and C as prizes so long as it is a bona fide gamble, i.e., $p \neq 1$, we are again in trouble.

Once one has this idea of utility, then the task is to develop a set of consistency requirements which, on the one hand, seem plausible as an idealized model of human preferences, and which, on the other, allow one to prove that the utility assignments can be made. In the next section we shall present such a set of axioms, but let us first suggest the general nature of these consistency demands by a few descriptive and intuitive words:

    i.   Any two alternatives shall be comparable, i.e., given any two, the subject will prefer one to the other or he will be indifferent between them.

   ii.   Both the preference and indifference relations for lotteries are transitive, i.e., given any three lotteries A, B, and C, if he prefers A to B and B to C, then he prefers A to C; and if he is indifferent between A and B and between B and C, then he is indifferent between A and C.

iii.   In case a lottery has as one of its alternatives (prizes) another lottery, then the first lottery is decomposable into the more basic alternatives through the use of the probability calculus.

iv.   If two lotteries are indifferent to the subject, then they are interchangeable as alternatives in any compound lottery.

v.   If two lotteries involve the same two alternatives, then the one in which the more preferred alternative has a higher probability of occurring is itself preferred.

vi.   If A is preferred to B and B to C, then there exists a lottery involving A and C (with appropriate probabilities) which is indifferent to B.

5. An axiomatic treatment of utility

The purpose of this section is to make precise both the consistency requirements and the theorem which we discussed informally in the last section. We shall adopt a set of axioms which are a bit different from those already available in the literature. At some, but relatively unimportant, expense in generality, we can employ axioms which are extremely simple and which lead to the utility numbers quite directly. For other axiom systems the reader is referred to von Neumann and Morgenstern (1947), Herstein and Milnor (1953), and Hausner (1954).

As we present these axioms, it is well to have some interpretation of them in mind. We suggest the following: Suppose that one has to make a choice between a pair of lotteries which are each composed of complicated risky alternatives. Because of their complexity it may be extremely difficult to decide which one is preferable. A natural procedure, then, is to analyze each lottery by decomposing it into simpler alternatives, to make decisions as to preference among these alternatives, and to agree upon some consistency rules which relate the simpler decisions to the more complicated ones. In this way, a consistent pattern is imposed upon the choices between complicated alternatives. Our analysis will follow these lines. At the outset we will not require that a subject choose consistently between all pairs of risky alternatives – just between some of the simpler ones. In the end, we shall show that consistency among the simpler alternatives, plus a commitment to certain rules of composition, implies overall consistency, in the sense that utility numbers can be introduced to summarize choices.

At the same time, as we introduce each assumption (i.e., axiom), we shall view it critically to see just how it will restrict the applicability of the model. Such a model must, inevitably, be a compromise between wider and wider applicability through less restrictive assumptions and richer and more elegant mathematical representation through stronger assumptions.

There is little practical loss of generality if we suppose that all lotteries are built up from a finite set of basic alternatives or prizes, which we denote by $A_1, A_2, ..., A_r$. A lottery ticket is a chance mechanism which yields the prizes $A_1, A_2, ..., A_r$ as outcomes with certain known probabilities. If the probabilities are $p_1, p_2, ..., p_r$, where each $p_i \geq 0$ and the sum is 1, then the corresponding lottery is denoted by $(p_1 A_1, p_2 A_2, ..., p_r A_r)$. We interpret this expression to mean only this: One and only one prize will be won and the probability that it will be A_i is p_i. Operationally, one can think of a lottery as the following experiment: A circle having unit circumference is subdivided into arcs of lengths $p_1, p_2, ..., p_r$, and a "fair" pointer is spun which if it comes to rest in the arc of length p_i means that prize A_i is the outcome.

The meaning of such a lottery bears some consideration. We are definitely assuming that there is no conceptual difficulty in assigning objective probabilities to the events in question by using symmetries of the experiment and past experience with it. That is to say, we are quite willing to admit a frequency interpretation of probability when assigning probabilities to the events. We do not, however, view the lottery itself from a frequency point of view; it is a single entity that will be conducted *once and only once,* not something to be repeated many times. This restriction to events having known objective probabilities will permit us to deal with most of the conceptual problems of game theory. . . .

We shall now be concerned with an individual's choice between a pair of lottery tickets $L = (p_1 A_1, p_2 A_2, ..., p_r A_r)$ and $L' = (p_1' A_1, p_2' A_2, ..., p_r' A_r)$. If L is preferred to L', this means that the individual prefers the experiment associated with L to that associated with L'.

Among the basic prizes, we use the symbolism $A_i \gtrsim A_j$ to denote that A_j is not preferred to A_i. Equivalently, we say that A_i is preferred or indifferent to A_j.

Assumption 1 (ordering of alternatives). *The "preference or indifference" ordering, $\gtrsim$, holds between any two prizes, and it is transitive. Formally, for any A_i and A_j, either $A_i \gtrsim A_j$ or $A_j \gtrsim A_i$; and if $A_i \gtrsim A_j$ and $A_j \gtrsim A_k$ then $A_i \gtrsim A_k$.*

These assumptions can be criticized on the grounds that they do not correspond to manifest behavior when people are presented with a sequence of paired comparisons. This can happen even over time periods when it is reasonable to suppose individual tastes remain stationary. There are several possible rationalizations for such intransitivities. For one, people have only vague likes and dislikes and they make "mistakes" in reporting them. Often when one is made aware of intransitivities of this kind he is willing to admit inconsistency and to realign his responses to yield a transitive ordering. See Savage (1954, pp. 100–104) [reprinted in Chapter 2] for a penetrating discussion of an example due to Allais which traps people, including Savage, into inconsistencies. Once the inconsistency is pointed out, Savage claims that he is grateful to the theory for indicating his inconsistency and he promptly reappraises his evaluations.

A second rationalization asserts that intransitivities often occur when a subject forces choices between inherently incomparable alternatives. The idea is that each alternative invokes "responses" on several different "attribute" scales and that, although each scale itself may be transitive, their amalgamation need not be. This is the sort of thing which psychologists cryptically summarize by terming it a multidimensional phenomenon.

No matter how intransitivities arise, we must recognize that they exist, and we can take only little comfort in the thought that they are an anathema to most of what constitutes theory in the behavioral sciences today. We may say that we are only concerned with behavior which is transitive, adding hopefully that we believe this need not always be a vacuous study. Or we may contend that the transitive description is often a "close" approximation to reality. Or we may limit our interest to "normative" or "idealized" behavior in the hope that such studies will have a metatheoretic impact on more realistic studies. In order to get on, we shall be flexible and accept all of these as possible defenses, and to them add the traditional mathematician's hedge: transitive relations are far more mathematically tractable than intransitive ones.

Since the labeling of the prizes is immaterial, we lose no generality in assuming that they have been numbered so that $A_1 \gtrsim A_2 \gtrsim \cdots \gtrsim A_r$ and that A_1 is strictly preferred to A_r. The latter condition is added only to keep things from being trivial.

Suppose that $L^{(1)}, L^{(2)}, \ldots, L^{(s)}$ are s lotteries which each involve $A_1, A_2, \ldots, A_r$ as prizes. If $q_1, q_2, \ldots, q_s$ are any s non-negative numbers which sum to 1, then $(q_1 L^{(1)}, q_2 L^{(2)}, \ldots, q_s L^{(s)})$ denotes a compound lottery in the following sense: one and only one of the given s lotteries will be the prize, and the probability that it will be $L^{(i)}$ is q_i.

Assumption 2 (reduction of compound lotteries). *Any compound lottery is indifferent to a simple lottery with $A_1, A_2, \ldots, A_r$ as prizes, their probabilities being computed according to the ordinary probability calculus. In particular, if*

$$L^{(i)} = (p_1^{(i)} A_1, p_2^{(i)} A_2, \ldots, p_r^{(i)} A_r), \quad for \ i = 1, 2, \ldots, s,$$

then

$$(q_1 L^{(1)}, q_2 L^{(2)}, \ldots, q_s L^{(s)}) \sim (p_1 A_1, p_2 A_2, \ldots, p_r A_r),$$

where

$$p_i = q_1 p_i^{(1)} + q_2 p_i^{(2)} + \cdots + q_s p_i^{(s)}.$$

This assumption is deceptively simple. It seems to state that any complex lottery can be reduced to a simple one by operating with the probabilities in what appears to be the obvious way. However, consider the lottery $L^{(1)}$, which we have assumed is described by an experiment $\mathbf{p}^{(1)} = (p_1^{(1)}, p_2^{(1)}, \ldots, p_r^{(1)})$, and the more complex lottery which is described by the experiment $\mathbf{q} =$

$(q_1, q_2, ..., q_s)$. It is perfectly possible that these two experiments might not be statistically independent; for example, it might happen that, if the first alternative comes up in experiment **q**, then the third alternative in experiment $\mathbf{p}^{(1)}$ is bound to occur. If so, the reduction given in assumption 2 makes no sense at all. It must, therefore, be interpreted as implicitly requiring one of two things: either that the experiments involved are statistically independent or that such a symbol as $p_j^{(i)}$ actually denotes the conditional probability of prize j in experiment $\mathbf{p}^{(i)}$ given that lottery i arose from experiment **q**.

Once this interpretation is made, the assumption seems quite plausible. Nonetheless, it is not empty for it abstracts away all "joy in gambling," "atmosphere of the game," "pleasure in suspense," and so on, for it says that a person is indifferent between a multistage lottery and the single stage one which is related to it by the probability calculus. (One neat example of multistage lotteries is found in Paris, as was pointed out to us by Harold Kuhn. Throughout that city are wheels of chance having as prizes tickets in the National Lottery.)

Assumption 3 (continuity). *Each prize A_i is indifferent to some lottery ticket involving just A_1 and A_r. That is to say, there exists a number u_i such that A_i is indifferent to $[u_i A_1, 0A_2, ..., 0A_{r-1}, (1-u_i)A_r]$. For convenience, we write $A_i \sim [u_i A_1, (1-u_i)A_r] = \tilde{A}_i$, but note well that A_i and $\tilde{A}_i$ are two quite different entities.*

This is a continuity assumption. If $A_1 > A_i > A_r$, it is plausible that $[pA_1, (1-p)A_r]$ is preferred to A_i if p is near 1, and that the preference is inverted if p is near 0, so it is also plausible that as p is shifted from 1 to 0 there is a point of inversion when the two are indifferent.

Although this assumption seems plausible, at least as a criterion of consistency, there are examples where it does not seem universally applicable. It is safe to suppose that most people prefer $1 to $0.01 and that to death. Would, however, one be indifferent between one cent and a lottery, involving $1 and death, that puts any positive probability on death? When put in such bald form, some, whom we would hesitate to charge with being "irrational," will say No. At the same time, there are others who would argue that the lottery is preferable provided that the chance of death is as low as, say, one in 10^{1000}, for such an event is a virtual impossibility. Even though the universality of the assumption is suspect, two thoughts are consoling. First, in few applications are such extreme alternatives as death present. Second, even if assumption 3 is neither explicitly assumed nor a consequence of other assumptions, a utility calculus can be derived. A single number will no longer suffice; rather, an n-tuple is needed; nonetheless, a good deal of game theory can be constructed on this more complicated utility foundation. We will not describe this theory of n-dimensional utilities; the interested reader can consult Hausner (1954).

Assumption 4 (substitutibility). *In any lottery L, $\tilde{A}_i$ is substitutable for A_i, that is, $(p_1 A_1, \ldots, p_i A_i, \ldots, p_r A_r) \sim (p_1 A_1, \ldots, p_i \tilde{A}_i, \ldots, p_r A_r)$.*

This assumption, taken with the third, is reminiscent of what is known in other work as the assumption of the *independence of irrelevant alternatives.* . . . If one asserts $A_i \sim \tilde{A}_i$, then in view of assumption 4 we also assert that not only are they indifferent when considered alone but also when substituted in any lottery ticket. Thus, the other possible alternatives must be irrelevant to the decision that they are indifferent.

Assumption 5 (transitivity). *Preference and indifference among lottery tickets are transitive relations.*

The comments following assumption 1 apply here even more strongly.

From these first five assumptions it is possible to find for any lottery ticket one to which it is indifferent and which only involves A_1 and A_r. Let $(p_1 A_1, p_2 A_2, \ldots, p_r A_r)$ be the given ticket. Replace each A_i by $\tilde{A}_i$. Assumption 3 states that these indifferent elements exist, and assumption 4 says they are substitutable. So by using the transitivity of indifference serially,

$$(p_1 A_1, \ldots, p_r A_r) \sim (p_1 \tilde{A}_1, \ldots, p_r \tilde{A}_r).$$

If now we sequentially apply the probability reduction assumption 2, it is easy to see that we get

$$(p_1 A_1, p_2 A_2, \ldots, p_r A_r) \sim [p A_1, (1-p) A_r],$$

where

$$p = p_1 u_1 + p_2 u_2 + \cdots + p_r u_r.$$

A numerical example illustrating this calculation is given at the end of the section.

We now introduce our final assumption:

Assumption 6 (monotonicity). *A lottery $[p A_1, (1-p) A_r]$ is preferred or indifferent to $[p' A_1, (1-p') A_r]$ if and only if $p \geq p'$.*

This seems eminently reasonable: between two lotteries involving only the most and least preferred alternatives one should select the one which renders the most preferred alternative more probable. But is it always? A mountain climber certainly prefers the alternative "life" to "death," yet when climbing he prefers some lottery of life and death to life itself, i.e., not climbing. Our trouble here appears to be not so much the assumption but the alternatives we have chosen in the example. A successful climb does not just mean life but also the thrill of the climb, publicity, etc. The real alternative is this "gestalt" which is completely dependent upon there being the risk of death to be attractive.

As this point is important, let us cite another example where the psychological reaction to an outcome of an experiment depends upon the probabilities in the experiment as well as on the actual outcome. Suppose X and Y are two people who are forced to exchange sums of money depending upon the outcome of an experiment. If X is sensitive to Y's feeling, he may prefer that no money be transferred and his preference may decrease with the amount to be transferred (up to some limit, say \$100) regardless of who pays. Thus, if

   A_1 means X pays \$5 to Y

and

   A_2 means Y pays \$10 to X,

X may well exhibit the following preferences:

$$(\tfrac{2}{3}A_1, \tfrac{1}{3}A_2) > (1A_1, 0A_2) > (0A_1, 1A_2).$$

Such a pattern would violate assumption 6. In other words, X prefers A_2 when it occurs by chance to having it outright.

   Although these examples may be a bit strained, they do suggest that, if there is a psychological interaction between the basic alternatives and the probabilities, it may be necessary to use a richer set of basic alternatives in order for assumption 6 to be approximately valid.

   With these six assumptions we are done, for if two lotteries L and L' are given, the first five assumptions permit us to reduce them to the form of lotteries in assumption 6, and then we decide between them on the basis of assumption 6. That is, for lotteries $L = (p_1 A_1, \ldots, p_r A_r)$ and $L' = (p_1' A_1, \ldots, p_r' A_r)$, we compute

$$p_1 u_1 + p_2 u_2 + \cdots + p_r u_r \quad \text{and} \quad p_1' u_1 + p_2' u_2 + \cdots + p_r' u_r,$$

and if the former is larger we prefer L to L', if the latter L' to L, and if they are equal L and L' are indifferent. Put as a formal theorem:

If the preference or indifference relation $\gtrsim$ satisfies assumptions 1 through 6, there are numbers u_i associated with the basic prizes A_i such that for two lotteries L and L' the magnitudes of the expected values

$$p_1 u_1 + p_2 u_2 + \cdots + p_r u_r \quad \text{and} \quad p_1' u_1 + p_2' u_2 + \cdots + p_r' u_r$$

reflect the preference between the lotteries.

   Let us introduce the following terms.... If a person imposes a transitive preference relation $\gtrsim$ over a set of lotteries and if to each lottery L there is assigned a number $u(L)$ such that the magnitudes of the numbers reflect the preferences, i.e., $u(L) \geq u(L')$ if and only if $L \gtrsim L'$, then we say there exists a *utility function* u over the lotteries. If, in addition, the utility function has the property that $u[qL, (1-q)L'] = qu(L) + (1-q)u(L')$, for all probabilities q and lotteries L and L', then we say the utility function is *linear.*[2] The above result can then be stated: if assumptions 1 through 6 are met, then there is a linear utility function over the set of risky alternatives arising from a finite set of basic alternatives.

Specifically, such a utility function u is given by:

$$u(A_1) = 1,$$

$$u(A_i) = u_i, \qquad \text{for } 1 < i < r \text{ (see assumption 3)},$$

$$u(A_r) = 0,$$

and

$$u(p_1 A_1, \ldots, p_r A_r) = p_1 u_1 + p_2 u_2 + \cdots + p_r u_r,$$

where $u_1 = 1$ and $u_r = 0$ by definition.

If a and b are any two constants such that $a > 0$, then the function u', where

$$u'(L) = au(L) + b$$

for any lottery L, is also a linear utility function, as is easily shown. Technically, we call u' a positive linear transformation of u. It can also be shown that, if u^* as well as u is a linear utility function representing the ordering $\gtrsim$, then there exist constants a^* and b^*, $a^* > 0$, such that

$$u^*(L) = a^* u(L) + b^*$$

for all lotteries L. That is, if u^* is a linear utility function, then it is a positive linear transformation of u.

A concrete numerical example may clarify the whole procedure. Consider a person choosing among lotteries involving the four alternatives A_1, A_2, A_3, and A_4, which he prefers in the order given. Of the two lotteries,

$$L = (0.25A_1, 0.25A_2, 0.25A_3, 0.25A_4),$$

$$L' = (0.15A_1, 0.50A_2, 0.15A_3, 0.20A_4),$$

which should he choose? Suppose that we determine that he is indifferent between A_2 and $\tilde{A}_2 = (0.6A_1, 0.4A_4)$ and between A_3 and $\tilde{A}_3 = (0.2A_1, 0.8A_4)$. We know by assumption 3 that some such lotteries involving A_1 and A_4 must exist. Now, by assumptions 4 and 5 it follows that

$$L \sim [0.25A_1, 0.25(0.6A_1, 0.4A_4), 0.25(0.2A_1, 0.8A_4), 0.25A_4],$$

which according to assumption 2 simplifies to

$$L \sim (0.45A_1, 0.55A_4).$$

---

[2] Sometimes this property is referred to as the *expected utility hypothesis* since it asserts that the utility of a lottery is equal to the expected utility of its component prizes. Not only is this terminology more explicit (if less brief), but it would help to avoid confusion. The much overworked word "linear" will also arise later with a different meaning. We will sometimes assume that the utility of money is linear with money meaning that a plot of utility versus money forms a straight line.

A similar calculation shows that

$$L' \sim (0.48A_1, 0.52A_4).$$

Thus, if this person is to be consistent with our six assumptions and at the same time have the stated indifferences between A_2 and $\tilde{A}_2$ and between A_3 and $\tilde{A}_3$, then he must prefer L' to L.

Two possible linear utility indicators are given in the following table:

Lottery	A_1	A_2	A_3	A_4	$(p_1A_1, p_2A_2, p_3A_3, p_4A_4)$
u	1.0	0.6	0.2	0.0	$p_1(1) + p_2(0.6) + p_3(0.2) + p_4(0)$
u'	1.6	0.8	0.0	−0.4	$p_1(1.6) + p_2(0.8) + p_3(0) + p_4(-0.4)$

The first of these is the one described above, and the second one is the linear transformation of it obtained by using the constants $a = 2$ and $b = -0.4$.

Given that a subject's preferences can be represented by a linear utility function, then *he behaves as if he were a maximizer of expected values of utility*. It is important to recognize that a subject's manifest behavior may be summarized by a linear utility function without his being consciously aware of making his choices in this manner. About his subconscious awareness we will not comment.

The general theory of utility is not confined to a finite set of basic alternatives nor to cases where a least or a most preferred alternative exists. We have only examined a simple special case, but one with sufficient complexity so that we can see just what is involved when we use utility theory in game theory. If one is interested in the more general theories, which are correspondingly more complicated, see the papers referred to at the beginning of this section.

6. Some common fallacies

Newcomers to modern utility theory tend to be critical of the idea, and, to be sure, there are valid reasons, but as criticisms are so often based on a fallacious understanding of the construct we have elected to point out some of the more common misinterpretations.

Fallacy 1. $(p_1A_1, \ldots, p_rA_r)$ *is preferred to* $(p_1'A_1, \ldots, p_r'A_r)$ *because the utility of the former,* $p_1u_1 + \cdots + p_ru_r$, *is larger than the utility of the latter,* $p_1'u_1 + \cdots + p_r'u_r$.

Some care must be taken to see why this is a fallacy, for there are two quite distinct ways of interpreting utility theory. First, we may think of the theory as a description of preference, in which case the causal relationship of the fallacy is the exact opposite of the truth; the preferences among lottery tickets logically precede the introduction of a utility function. Second, we may think of the theory as a guide to consistent action. Here, again, certain (simple) preferences come first and certain rules of consistency are accepted in order to reach decisions between more complicated choices. Given these, it turns out that it is possible to summarize both the preferences and the rules of consistency by means of utilities, and this makes it very easy to calculate what decisions to make when the alternatives are complex. The point is that there is no need to assume, or to philosophize about, the existence of an underlying subjective utility function, for we are not attempting to account for the preferences or the rules of consistency. We only wish to devise a convenient way *to represent* them.

Fallacy 2. *Suppose that $A > B > C > D$ and that the utilities of these alternatives satisfy $u(A) + u(D) = u(B) + u(C)$, then $(\frac{1}{2}B, \frac{1}{2}C)$ should be preferred to $(\frac{1}{2}A, \frac{1}{2}D)$ because, although they have the same expected utility, the former has the smaller utility variance.*

This is a completely wrong interpretation of the utility notion, and again it results from a failure to accept that preferences precede utilities. It misses the point of utility theory. The principal result of utility theory for risk is that a linear utility index can be defined which reflects completely a person's preferences among the risky alternatives. If the fallacy actually made sense, then it would be a beautiful example to show that a utility function is impossible. This is not to say that, if the prizes are money, we will not find a person preferring the gamble with the smaller money variance when the expected values of money are the same. We probably will, but this only goes to show that the utility of money (if the concept is meaningful) cannot be linear with money.

Fallacy 3. *Suppose that $A > B > C > D$ and that the utility function has the property that $u(A) - u(B) > u(C) - u(D)$, then the change from B to A is more preferred than the change from D to C.*

Again, if we consider how the utility function is constructed from preferences between pairs of alternatives, not between pairs of pairs of alternatives, it is clear that the above statement is not justified. Indeed, empirically, it may well be false. This does not mean that one should not consider constructing a theory of utility which is able to compare utility differences. We only want to emphasize that the present theory does not permit such comparisons. . . .

Our fourth fallacy is so important, and in many ways really an unresolved problem, that we shall treat it separately in the next section.

7. Interpersonal comparisons of utility

There is one thing which we stressed when discussing the classical attempts to devise a numerical utility for decision making under certainty which we have not adequately discussed for utility functions when there is risk: the uniqueness of the function. Under certainty, one of the difficulties was the almost complete lack of uniqueness – any order-preserving transformation of the numbers was equally acceptable. It is also true in the risky situations that any order-preserving transformation of a utility function is again a utility function, but such a transformation of a *linear* utility function does not generally result in a *linear* utility function. One must, therefore, keep in mind the class of transformations which take a linear utility function into one of the same type. As we pointed out before, the appropriate class consists of those transformations known as the positive linear ones, i.e., if u is a linear utility function over a set of risky alternatives and if a and b are any constants so long as a is positive, then $u' = au + b$ is again a linear utility function over the set. Conversely, if u and u' are two linear utility functions for a preference relation over the same set of alternatives, then there exist constants a and b, where a is positive, such that $u' = au + b$.

Another way of stating this uniqueness result is that the consistency axioms (such as assumptions 1 through 6 of section 5) determine a linear utility function which is unique up to its zero point and its unit. If we choose any two alternatives which are not indifferent, then we can always set the utility of the less preferred to be zero and the utility of the more preferred to be one. As we shall come to see, the non-uniqueness of the zero point is of no real concern in any of the applications of utility theory, but the arbitrary unit of measurement gives trouble. The trouble may be illustrated most easily by a fictitious example in the measurement of distances. Suppose two people are isolated from each other and each is given a measuring stick marked off in certain and possibly different arbitrary units. The one subject is given full-scale plans for an object to be constructed to the same size by the other, and he is permitted to send only messages stating angles and lengths (in his units) of the object. With such limited communication it is clearly possible for the second man to construct a scale model of the object, but it will only be of the correct size if it happens that both measuring rods are marked in the same units. Clearly, once the barriers on communication are dropped, the two men can determine with fair accuracy the relationship between their two units by measuring things they each have and which are known to have about the same size, e.g., the span of a hand, or width of a trouser leg, etc.

In utility theory, if we should want to compare utilities between two people much the same problem exists: we do not know the relationship between the two units. The big difference between utility and length measurement is that we do not seem to have any "outside thing" which can be measured by both persons to ascertain the relation between the units. Certain proposals for an "outside" standard of unit utility have been offered; for example, it has been suggested that for each person in the situation his most preferred alternative be assigned the value 1 and his least preferred the value 0. Often, however, this seems to fail to capture one's intuitive idea of an interpersonal comparison of utility: in a gamble between a rich man and a poor one which involves money in the range of $-\$1$ to $+\$1$, it is hard to believe that a gain of $1 should have the same utility for each of them. In some sense, the poor man is far more "sensitive" to a fixed monetary change than is the rich one, and his preference for it is correspondingly more "intense." Just exactly what this means we do not know, but it seems to mean something to each of us. We are forever trying to decide whether one outcome means more or less to another person than a different outcome means to us. . . .

Thus, the fact that a linear utility function is defined only up to a linear transformation leads to the problem of interpersonal comparisons of utility when there is more than one person in the situation. Since it is not solved, one can either assume that such comparisons are possible, knowing that this creates (at least at present) an Achilles' heel in the theory, or one can attempt to devise theories in which comparisons are not made. Both approaches have been taken in game theory.

8. Experimental determinations of utility

Given such an axiomatic theory as that presented in section 5, can we find the utility function for an individual in a given situation? If the question is meant naively, the answer is surely No. If it is refined in various ways, the answer is Maybe – at least several people have tried. We do not propose to examine such work in detail but rather to discuss the general problem very briefly and to guide the reader to the (limited) literature on such problems. For a more detailed guide to this literature, plus some of the purely theoretical work, up to the beginning of 1954, see Edwards (1954c).

The most obvious difficulty in attempting to confirm the theory is that it rests upon an infinity of paired comparisons, but there are others too. Obviously, in an experiment one will only make a relatively few paired comparisons, so one way or another the verification will have to be based upon these. One procedure is to determine the utilities of a few alternatives experimentally, using the assumption that a utility function exists and that it is linear. Suppose we arbitrarily assign utilities of 0 and 1 to two alternatives and then we determine the utility of a third by finding the lottery of the first two which is indifferent to it. For example, suppose $C \sim [pA, (1-p)B]$; then by linearity $u(C) = u[pA, (1-p)B] = pu(A) + (1-p)u(B) = p$. If this is done for several more points, then one soon knows enough values on the utility scale (assuming it exists) to make predictions. For example, suppose it was found that $u(D) = q$. Then we could predict whether the lottery $[rA, (1-r)C]$ is preferred or not to the lottery $[sD, (1-s)B]$ for a particular choice of r and s. If these predictions are confirmed experimentally, we then have some confidence that we have obtained a portion of the utility function. This is the method which was used by Mosteller and Nogee (1951).

A more elegant, if more difficult, alternative to starting with a model having an infinity of comparisons is to devise one in which only a finite number are to be made. Such a model must be quite different from the one we have described if it is to lead to a linear utility function which is unique up to a linear transformation. However, such axiom systems are possible as has been shown by Suppes and Winet (1955) and for this case Davidson, Siegel, and Suppes (1955) have devised an experimental setup in which it can be checked. This work is probably the most experimentally elegant in the area, and the results have been very encouraging.

A second difficulty in attempting to ascertain a utility function is the fact that the reported preferences almost never satisfy the axioms, e.g., there are usually intransitivities. Furthermore, if the same pair is offered several times, then in some cases the subject will not be consistent in his reports. One cannot expect the data to fit the model perfectly, but how does one determine which model they fit most closely and how does one measure how good the agreement is? Such problems pose the following intriguing and important statistical problem: to formulate a model which assumes that a subject is actually (or latently or genotypically) a von Neumann–Morgenstern utilitist in the sense of "having" a linear utility function, but that his responses yield this underlying order confounded by random disturbances and errors. We need not consider the question whether or not a true utility function exists, for we may take the pragmatic approach that such a postulate makes more precise what we shall mean by a "reasonable," or "approximate," or "realistic" fit of the data to theory. To date, little has been published on this problem.

A third, and possibly the most puzzling, difficulty arises from the basic probabilities in the model. We have, in our discussion, identified them with certain physical experiments, and certainly in a normative theory this is what one would want to do. But, if we are trying to describe behavior, it may be unreasonable to suppose that people deal with objective probabilities as if they satisfy the axioms of the calculus of probabilities or that they only cope with situations in which objective probabilities are defined. This leads one to consider introducing the idea of subjective probabilities, on the basis of which people are assumed to act. If such exist, little is known about them – how they combine with one another, how they interact with the utility values, how they are related to the objective probabilities, etc. Edwards (see references 1953, 1954) has run a series of experiments on this question, and he has considerable evidence to support the view that people react in, shall we say, strange ways to objective probabilities. In their experimental work, Davidson, Siegel, and Suppes had to work with an event having subjective probability ½ and they found that many of the obvious things having objective probability ½ would not do.

While writing this book one of us became intrigued with these last two problems – the probabilistic nature of preferences and the role of subjective probability – and devised a probabilistic theory of utility which closely parallels some models of psychophysical discrimination. For example, subjective probability is axiomatized by properties somewhat similar to those of objective probabilities, but it is then shown that subjective probability possesses the defining property of a subjective (Fechnerian) sensation scale as the term is used in psychophysics. . . .

There can be no question that it is extremely difficult to determine a person's utility function even under the most ideal and idealized experimental conditions; one can almost say that it has yet to be done. Indeed, should it be done? Since we think it should, let us consider it carefully.

If it is so difficult to determine utility functions under the best of conditions, there is certainly no hope at all that it can be done under field conditions for situations of practical interest. Thus, if the theories built upon utility theory really demand such measurements, they are doomed practically; if they can be useful without making such measurements, then why go to the trouble of learning how? As in the physical sciences, we would claim that a theory may very well postulate quantities which cannot be measured in general, and yet that it will be possible to derive some conclusions from them which are of use. To be sure, if the measurements could be made, more could be concluded; but this is not the same as saying that, if the measurements cannot be made, nothing can be concluded. We therefore move on to the second part of our conditional question: why, then, make any measurements in the laboratory? The main purpose is to see if under any conditions, however limited, the postulates of the model can be confirmed and, if not, to see how they may be modified to accord better at least with those cases. It will still be an act of faith to postulate the general existence of these new constructs, but somehow one feels less cavalier if he knows that there are two or three cases where the postulates have actually been verified.

Every indication now is that the utility model, and possibly therefore the game model, will have to be made more complicated if experimental data are to be handled adequately. . . . [T]he utility model's . . . domain of applicability is limited and it is completely unclear how it can be utilized in game theory. Furthermore, neither it nor any of the present utility models take into account the intuition, now bolstered by a staggering amount of empirical data for a wide variety of psychological dimensions (see Miller 1956 for a partial survey), that people rarely categorize a single dimension into more than seven or so distinct levels. The major exceptions seem to be cases where the culture provides a simple, fine, and unambiguous scale, such as money. Since, however, most decisions, even when money is a factor, are not based entirely on monetary considerations, discrete categorization of preferences may be the basic case to study. . . .

9. Summary

The primary purpose of this chapter was to introduce the central ideas of modern utility theory, which is a cornerstone of much decision theory. As background, we classified decision making according to whether a decision is reached by an individual or a group, and whether it is effected under conditions of certainty, risk, uncertainty, or a mixture of uncertainty and risk in the light of experimental evidence. . . .

Decision making under certainty encompasses much of formal theory in social science. This problem can be viewed as follows: given a set of possible acts, to choose those which maximize (or minimize) a given index. In many traditional applications, the solution can be formulated in the language of the calculus, but some of the more interesting modern problems require more sophisticated techniques. . . .

[We were] led to the question whether any individual decision problem can be represented by a numerical index called utility. This is not only possible but also possible in a great many ways, provided the preference relations are transitive. Historically there have been so many misuses of this representation that it has been totally discredited. However, once decision making under risk became an issue the idea of a numerical utility reappeared. Since numbers would have to be attached to the infinity of possible gambles, it seemed conceivable that there might be sufficient constraints on the index to make it unique, or nearly so, thus avoiding some of the troubles usually associated with utility.

To achieve such a result, it is necessary that the preference relation meet certain more or less plausible consistency requirements. A set of axioms, closely related to those given by von Neumann and Morgenstern, were stated and discussed. Among the more important requirements were these: preference shall be transitive, i.e., if A is preferred to B, and B to C, then A is preferred to C; any gamble shall be decomposed into its basic alternatives according to the rules of the probability calculus; and if A is preferred to B and B to C, then there shall exist a gamble involving A and C which is judged indifferent to B. From these and other axioms it was shown that numbers can be assigned to the basic alternatives in such a fashion that one gamble is preferred to another if and only if the expected utility of the former is larger than the expected utility of the latter. If u is such an index, any other is related to it by a linear transformation, i.e., there is a positive constant a and a constant b such that $au + b$ is the second index. Such an index u is called a *linear utility function,* where "linear" means that the utility of a gamble is the expected value of the utilities of its components.

Certain cautions must be maintained in interpreting this concept: One alternative possesses a larger utility than another because it is more preferred, not the other way round. All the preference information is summarized by the expected value of utility – in particular, utility variance has no meaning. The fact that one utility difference is larger than another does not permit us to say that the one change is subjectively larger than the other, for the utility function was constructed in terms of subjective responses to gambles, not in terms of the subjective evaluation of two different changes.

Since neither the zero nor the unit of a utility scale is determined, it is not meaningful in this theory to compare utilities between two people.

The chapter closed with a brief sketch of some of the experimental problems associated with utility theory, and references were given to several experimental studies. It was suggested that a less idealized theory is needed, one more amenable to empirical study.

References

Adams, E. W., "A survey of Bernoullian utilities and applications," Behavioral Models Project, *Technical Report* 9, Columbia University, 1954.

Davidson, Donald, Sidney Siegel, and Patrick Suppes, "Some experiments and related theory on the measurement of utility and subjective probability," Applied Mathematics and Statistics Laboratory, *Technical Report* 1, Stanford University, Stanford, 1955.

Edwards, Ward, "Experiments on economic decision-making in gambling situations," *Econometrica,* 21, 349–350, 1953 (abstract).

"Probability preferences among bets with differing expected values," *American Journal of Psychology,* 67, 56–67, 1954(*a*).

"The theory of decision making," *Psychological Bulletin,* 5, 380–417, 1954(*c*).

Hausner, Melvin, "Multidimensional utilities," in Thrall, R. M., C. H. Coombs, and R. L. Davis, eds., *Decision Processes,* pp. 167–180, John Wiley & Sons, New York, 1954.

Herstein, I. N., and J. W. Milnor, "An axiomatic approach to measurable utility," *Econometrica,* 21, 291–297, 1953.

Miller, G. A., "The magical number seven, plus or minus two: some limits on our capacity for processing information," *Psychological Abstracts,* 63, 81–97, 1956.

Mosteller, Fredrick, and Philip Nogee, "An experimental measurement of utility," *Journal of Political Economy,* 59, 371–404, 1951.

Savage, L. J., *The Foundations of Statistics,* John Wiley & Sons, New York, and Chapman & Hall, London, 1954.

Suppes, Patrick, and Muriel Winet, "An axiomatization of utility based on the notion of utility differences," *Management Science,* 1, 259–270, 1955.

Von Neumann, John, and Oskar Morgenstern, *Theory of Games and Economic Behavior,* first edition, second edition, Princeton University Press, Princeton, 1944, 1947.

2. Historical and critical comments on utility

Leonard J. Savage

A casual historical sketch of the concept of utility will perhaps have some interest as history. At any rate, most of the critical ideas pertaining to utility that I wish to discuss find their places in such a sketch as conveniently as in any other organization I can devise. Much more detailed material on the history of utility, especially insofar as the economics of risk bearing is concerned, is to be found in Arrow's review article [A6]. Stigler's historical study [S18] emphasizes the history of the now almost obsolete economic notion of utility in riskless situations, a notion still sometimes confused with the one under discussion.

[T]he earliest mathematical studies of probability were largely concerned with gambling, particularly with the question of which of several available cash gambles is most advantageous. Early probabilists advanced the maxim that the gamble with the highest expected winnings is best or, in terms of utility, that wealth measured in cash is a utility function. Some sense can be seen in that maxim, which will here be called by its traditional though misleading name, the *principle of mathematical expectation*. First, it has often been argued that the principle follows for the long run from the weak law of large numbers, applied to large numbers of independent bets, in each of which only sums that the gambler considers small are to be won or lost. Second, Daniel Bernoulli, who, in [B10], was one of the first to introduce a general idea of utility corresponding to that developed in [my *The Foundations of Statistics*], made the following analysis of the principle, which justifies its application in limited but important contexts. If the consequences f to be considered are all quantities of cash, it is reasonable to suppose that $U(f)$ will change smoothly with changes in f. Therefore, if a person's present wealth is f_0, and he contemplates various gambles, none of which can greatly

Reprinted with permission from Savage, *The Foundations of Statistics,* 2d ed. (New York: Dover, 1972), 91–104.

change his wealth, the utility function can, for his particular purpose, be approximated by its tangent at f_0, that is,

$$U(f) \simeq U(f_0) + (f - f_0) U'(f_0), \tag{1}$$

a linear function of f. Since a constant term is irrelevant to any comparison of expected values, the approximation amounts to regarding utility as proportional to wealth, that is, to following the principle of mathematical expectation. So far as I know, the only other argument for the principle that has ever been advanced is one concerning equity between two players. As Bernoulli says, that argument is irrelevant at best; and neither of the relevant arguments justifies categorical acceptance of the principle. None the less, the principle was at first so categorically accepted that it seemed paradoxical to mathematicians of the early eighteenth century that presumably prudent individuals reject the principle in certain real and hypothetical decision situations.

Daniel Bernoulli (1700–1782), in the paper [B10], seems to have been the first to point out that the principle is at best a rule of thumb, and he there suggested the maximization of expected utility as a more valid principle. Daniel Bernoulli's paper reproduces portions of a letter from Gabriel Cramer to Nicholas Bernoulli, which establishes Cramer's chronological priority to the idea of utility and most of the other main ideas of Bernoulli's paper. But it is Bernoulli's formulation together with some of the ideas that were specifically his that became popular and have had widespread influence to the present day. It is therefore appropriate to review Bernoulli's paper in some detail.

Being unable to read Latin, I follow the German edition [B11].

Bernoulli begins by reminding his readers that the principle of mathematical expectation, though but weakly supported, had theretofore dominated the theory of behavior in the face of uncertainty. He says that, though many arguments had been given for the principle, they were all based on the irrelevant idea of equity among players. It seems hard to believe that he had never heard the argument justifying the principle for the long run, even though the weak law of large numbers was then only in its mathematical infancy. *Ars Conjectandi* [B12], then a fairly up-to-date and most eminent treatise on probability, does seem to give only the argument about equity, and that in countless forms. This treatise by Daniel's uncle, Jacob (= James) Bernoulli (1654–1705), incidentally, contains the first mathematical advance toward the weak law, proving it for the special case of repeated trials.

Many examples show that the principle of mathematical expectation is not universally applicable. Daniel Bernoulli promptly presents one: "To justify these remarks, let us suppose a pauper happens to acquire a lottery ticket by which he may with equal probability win either nothing or 20,000 ducats. Will he have to evaluate the worth of the ticket as 10,000 ducats; and would he be acting foolishly, if he sold it for 9,000 ducats?"

Other examples occur later in the paper as illustrations of the use of the utility concept. Thus a prudent merchant may insure his ship against loss at sea, though he understands perfectly well that he is thereby increasing the insurance company's expected wealth, and to the same extent decreasing his own. Such behavior is in flagrant violation of the principle of mathematical expectation, and to one who held that principle categorically it would be as absurd to insure as to throw money away outright. But the principle is neither obvious nor deduced from other principles regarded as obvious; so it may be challenged, and must be, because everyone agrees that it is not really insane to insure.

Bernoulli cites a third, now very famous, example illustrating that men of prudence do not invariably obey the principle of mathematical expectation. This example, known as the St. Petersburg paradox (because of the journal in which Bernoulli's paper was published) had earlier been publicized by Nicholas Bernoulli, and Daniel acknowledges it as the stimulus that led to his investigation of utility.[1] Suppose, to state the St. Petersburg paradox succinctly, that a person could choose between an act leaving his wealth fixed at its present magnitude or one that would change his wealth at random, increasing it by $(2^n - f)$ dollars with probability 2^{-n} for every positive integer n. No matter how large the admission fee f may be, the expected income of the random act is infinite, as may easily be verified. Therefore, according to the principle of mathematical expectation, the random act is to be preferred to the status quo. Numerical examples, however, soon convince any sincere person that he would prefer the status quo if f is at all large. If f is $128, for example, there is only 1 chance in 64 that a person choosing the random act will so much as break even, and he will otherwise lose at least $64, a jeopardy for which he can seek compensation only in the prodigiously improbable winning of a prodigiously high prize.

Appealing to intuition, Bernoulli says that the cash value of a person's wealth is not its true, or moral, worth to him. Thus, according to Bernoulli, the dollar that might be precious to a pauper would be nearly worthless to a millionaire – or, better, to the pauper himself were he to become a millionaire. Bernoulli then postulates that people do seek to maximize the expected value of moral worth, or what has been called moral expectation.

Operationally, the moral worth of a person's wealth, so far as it concerns behavior in the face of uncertainty, is just what I would call the utility of the wealth, and moral expectation is expectation of utility. It seems mystical, however, to talk about moral worth apart from probability and, having done so, doubly mystical to postulate that this undefined quantity serves as a utility. These obvious criticisms have naturally led many to discredit the very idea of utility, but §§2–4 [of my *The Foundations of Statistics*] show

---

[1] Daniel refers to this Nicholas Bernoulli as his uncle, but, in view of dates mentioned in the last section of Daniel's paper and the genealogy in Chapter 8 of [B9], I think he must have meant his elder cousin (1687–1759), perhaps using "uncle" as a term of deference.

(following von Neumann and Morgenstern) that there is a more cogent, though not altogether unobjectionable, path to that concept.

Bernoulli argued, elaborating the example of the pauper and the millionaire, that a fixed increment of cash wealth typically results in an ever smaller increment of moral wealth as the basic cash wealth to which the increment applies is increased. He admitted the possibility of examples in which this law of diminishing marginal utility, as it has come to be called in the literature of economics, might fail. For example, a relatively small sum might be precious to a wealthy prisoner who required it to complete his ransom. But Bernoulli insisted that such examples are unusual and that as a general rule the law may be assumed. In mathematical terms, the law says that utility as a function of money is a concave (i.e., the negative of a convex) function.[2] It follows from the basic inequality concerning convex functions... that a person to whom the law of diminishing marginal utility applies will always prefer the status quo to any fair gamble, that is, to any random act for which the change in his expected wealth is zero, and that he will always be willing to pay something in addition to its actuarial, or expected, value for insurance against any loss to himself. The law of diminishing marginal utility has been very popular, and few who have considered utility since Bernoulli have discarded it, or even realized that it was not necessarily part and parcel of the utility idea. Of course, the law has been embraced eagerly and uncritically by those who have a moral aversion to gambling.

Bernoulli went further than the law of diminishing marginal utility and suggested that the slope of utility as a function of wealth might, at least as a rule of thumb, be supposed, not only to decrease with, but to be inversely proportional to, the cash value of wealth. This, he pointed out, is equivalent to postulating that utility is equal to the logarithm (to any base) of the cash value of wealth. To this day, no other function has been suggested as a better prototype for Everyman's utility function. Nonetheless, as Cramer pointed out in his aforementioned letter, the logarithm has a serious disadvantage; for, if the logarithm were the utility of wealth, the St. Petersburg paradox could be amended to produce a random act with an infinite expected utility (i.e., an infinite expected logarithm of income) that, again, no one would really prefer to the status quo. To take a less elaborate example, suppose that a man's total wealth, including an appraisal of his future earning power, were a million dollars. If the logarithm of wealth were actually his utility, he would as soon as not flip a coin to decide whether his wealth should be changed to ten thousand dollars – roughly $500 per year – or a hundred million dollars. This seems preposterous to me. At any rate, I am sure you can construct an example along the same lines that will seem preposterous

[2] Often the meanings of "convex" and "concave" as applied to functions are interchanged. A function is here called convex if it appears convex, in the ordinary sense of the word, when viewed from below. Such a function is, of course, also concave from above, whence the confusion.

to you. Cramer therefore concluded, and I think rightly, that the utility of cash must be bounded, at least from above. It seems to me that a good argument can also be adduced for supposing utility to be bounded from below, for, however wealth may be interpreted, we all subject our total wealth to slight jeopardy daily for the sake of a large probability of avoiding more moderate losses. But the logarithm is unbounded both from above and from below; so, though it might be a reasonable approximation to a person's utility in a moderate range of wealth, it cannot be taken seriously over extreme ranges.

Bernoulli's ideas were accepted wholeheartedly by Laplace [L1], who was very enthusiastic about the applications of probability to all sorts of decision problems. It is my casual impression, however, that from the time of Laplace until quite recently the idea of utility did not strongly influence either mathematical or practical probabilists.

For a long period economists accepted Bernoulli's idea of moral wealth as the measurement of a person's well-being apart from any consideration of probability. Though "utility" rather than "moral worth" has been the popular name for this concept among English-speaking economists, it is my impression that Bernoulli's paper is the principal, if not the sole, source of the notion for all economists, though the paper itself may often have been lost sight of. Economists were for a time enthusiastic about the principle of diminishing marginal utility, and they saw what they believed to be reflections of it in many aspects of everyday life. Why else, to paraphrase Alfred Marshall (pp. 19, 95 of [M2]), does a poor man walk in a rain that induces a rich man to take a cab?

During the period when the probability-less idea of utility was popular with economists, they referred not only to the utility of money, but also to the utility of other consequences such as commodities (and services) and combinations (or, better, patterns of consumption) of commodities. The theory of choice among consequences was expressed by the idea that, among the available consequences, a person prefers those that have the highest utility for him. Also, the idea of diminishing marginal utility was extended from money to other commodities.

The probability-less idea of utility in economics has been completely discredited in the eyes of almost all economists, the following argument against it – originally advanced by Pareto in pp. 158–159 and the Mathematical Appendix of [P1] – being widely accepted. If utility is regarded as controlling only consequences, rather than acts, it is not true – as it is when acts, or at least gambles, are considered and the formal definition in §3 [of *The Foundations of Statistics*], is applied – that utility is determined except for a linear transformation. Indeed, confining attention to consequences, any strictly monotonically increasing function of one utility is another utility. Under these circumstances there is little, if any, value in talking about utility at all, unless, of course, special economic considerations should render one utility, or say a linear family of utilities, of particular interest. That possibility remains academic to date, though one attempt to exploit it was made by Irving Fisher, as is briefly discussed in the paragraph leading to Footnote 155 of [S18]. In particular, utility as a function of wealth can have any shape whatsoever in the probability-less context, provided only that the function in question is increasing with increasing wealth, the provision following from the casual observation that almost nobody throws money away. The history of probability-less utility has been thoroughly reported by Stigler [S18].

What, then, becomes of the intuitive arguments that led to the notion of diminishing marginal utility? To illustrate, consider the poor man and the rich man in the rain. Those of us who consider diminishing marginal utility nonsensical in this context think it sufficient to say simply that it is a common observation that rich men spend money freely to avoid moderate physical suffering whereas poor men suffer freely rather than make corresponding expenditures of money; in other terms, that the rate of exchange between circumstances producing physical discomfort and money depends on the wealth of the person involved.

In recent years there has been revived interest in Bernoulli's ideas of utility in the technical sense of §§2–4 [of *The Foundations of Statistics*], that is, as a function that, so to speak, controls decisions among acts, or at least gambles. Ramsey's essays in [R1], which in spirit closely resemble the first five chapters of [*The Foundations of Statistics*], present a relatively early example of this revival of interest. Ramsey improves on Bernoulli in that he defines utility operationally in terms of the behavior of a person constrained by certain postulates. Ramsey's essays, though now much appreciated, seem to have had relatively little influence.

Between the time of Ramsey and that of von Neumann and Morgenstern there was interest in breaking away from the idea of maximizing expected utility, at least so far as economic theory was concerned (cf. [T1a]). This trend was supported by those who said that Bernoulli gives no reason for supposing that preferences correspond to the expected value of some function, and that therefore much more general possibilities must be considered. Why should not the range, the variance, and the skewness, not to mention countless other features, of the distribution of some function join with the expected value in determining preference? The question was answered by the construction of Ramsey and again by that of von Neumann and Morgenstern...; it is simply a mathematical fact that, almost any theory of probability having been adopted and the sure-thing principle having been suitably extended, the existence of a function whose expected value controls choices can be deduced. That does not mean that as a theory of actual economic behavior the theory of utility is absolutely established and cannot be overthrown. Quite the contrary, it is a theory that makes factual predictions many of which can easily be observed to be false, but the theory may have some value in making economic predictions in certain contexts where the departures from it happen not to be devastating. Moreover, as I have been arguing, it may have value as a normative theory.

Von Neumann and Morgenstern initiated among economists and, to a lesser extent, also among statisticians an intense revival of interest in the technical utility concept by their treatment of utility, which appears as a digression in [V4].

The von Neumann–Morgenstern theory of utility has produced this reaction, because it gives strong intuitive grounds for accepting the Bernoullian utility hypothesis as a consequence of well-accepted maxims of behavior. To give readers...some idea of the von Neumann–Morgenstern theory, I may repeat that the treatment of utility as applied to gambles presented in §3 [of *The Foundations of Statistics*] is virtually copied from their book [V4]. Indeed, their ideas on this subject are responsible for almost all of my own. One idea now held by me that I think von Neumann and Morgenstern do not explicitly support, and that so far as I know they might not wish to have attributed to them, is the normative interpretation of the theory.

Of course, much of the new interest in utility takes the form of criticism and controversy. The greater part of this discussion that has come to my attention has not yet been published. A list of references leading to most of that which has is [B7], [W14], [S1], [C4], [F13], [A2].

I shall successively discuss each of the recent major criticisms of the modern theory of utility known to me. My method in each case will be first to state the criticism in a form resembling those in which it is typically put forward, regardless of whether I consider that form well chosen. I will then discuss the criticism, elaborating its meaning and indicating its rebuttal, when there seems to me to be one.

(a) Modern economic theorists have rigorously shown that there is no meaningful measure of utility. More specifically, if any function **U** fulfills the role of a utility, then so does any strictly monotonically increasing function of **U**. It must, therefore, be an error to conclude that every utility is a linear function of every other.

This argument has been advanced with a seriousness that is surprising, considering that it concedes little intelligence or learning to the proponents of the utility theory under discussion and considering that it results, as will immediately be explained, from the baldest sort of a terminological confusion. To be fair, I must go on to say that I have never known the argument to be defended long in the presence of the explanation I am about to give.

In ordinary economic usage, especially prior to the work of von Neumann and Morgenstern, a utility associated with gambles would presumably be simply a function **U** associating numbers with gambles in such a way that $f \leq g$, if and only if $U(f) \leq U(g)$; though economic discussion of utility was, prior to von Neumann and Morgenstern, almost exclusively confined to consequences rather than to gambles or to acts. It is unequivocally true, as I have already brought out, that any monotonic function of a utility in this wide classical sense is itself a utility. What von Neumann and Morgenstern have shown is that, granting certain hypotheses, there exists at least one classical utility **V** satisfying the very special condition

$$V(\alpha f + \beta g) = \alpha V(f) + \beta V(g), \tag{2}$$

where f and g are any gambles and α, β are non-negative numbers such that $\alpha + \beta = 1$. Furthermore, if I may for the moment call a classical utility satisfying (2) a von Neumann–Morgenstern utility, every von Neumann–Morgenstern utility is an increasing linear function of every other. To put the point differently, the essential conclusion of the von Neumann–Morgenstern utility theory is that (2) can be satisfied by a classical utility, but not by very many. The confusion arises only because von Neumann and Morgenstern use the already pre-empted word "utility" for what I here call "von Neumann–Morgenstern utility." In retrospect, that seems to have been a mistake in tactics, but one of no long-range importance.

(b) The postulates leading to the von Neumann–Morgenstern concept of utility are arbitrary and gratuitous.

Such a view can, of course, always be held without the slightest fear of rigorous refutation, but a critic holding it might perhaps be persuaded away from it by a reformulation of the postulates that he might find more appealing than the original set, or by illuminating examples.... Incidentally, the main function of the von Neumann–Morgenstern postulates themselves is to put the essential content of Daniel Bernoulli's "postulate" into a form that is less gratuitous in appearance. At least one serious critic, who had at first found the system of von Neumann and Morgenstern gratuitous, changed his mind when the possibility of deriving certain aspects of that system from the sure-thing principle was pointed out to him.

(c) The sure-thing principle goes too far.[3] For example, if two lotteries with cash prizes (not necessarily positive) are based on the same set of lottery tickets and so arranged that the prize that will be assigned to any ticket by the second lottery is at least as great as the prize assigned to that ticket by the first lottery, then there is no doubt that virtually any person would find a ticket in the first lottery not preferable to the same ticket in the second lottery. If, however, the prizes in each lottery are themselves lottery tickets, such that the prize associated with any ticket in the first lottery is not preferred by the person under study to the prize associated with the same ticket

---

[3] [On page 21 Savage states the sure-thing principle as follows: "If the person would not prefer f to g, either knowing that the event B obtained, or knowing that the event $-B$ obtained, then he does not prefer f to g. Moreover (provided he does not regard B as virtually impossible) if he would definitely prefer g to f, knowing that B obtained, and if he would not prefer f to g, knowing that B did not obtain, then he definitely prefers g to f."]

by the second lottery, the conclusion that the person will not prefer a ticket in the first lottery to the same ticket in the second is no longer compelling.

This point resembles the preceding one in that the intuitive appeal of an assumption can at most be indicated, not proved. I do think it cogent, however, to stress in connection with this particular point that a cash prize is to a large extent a lottery ticket in that the uncertainty as to what will become of a person if he has a gift of a thousand dollars is not in principle different from the uncertainty about what will become of him if he holds a lottery ticket of considerable actuarial value.

Perhaps an adherent to the criticism in question would think it relevant to reply thus: Though cash sums are indeed essentially lottery tickets, a sum of money is worth at least as much to a person as a smaller sum, in a peculiarly definite and objective sense, because money can, if one desires, always be quickly and quietly thrown away, thereby making any sum available to a person who already has a larger sum. But I have never heard that reply made, nor do I here plead its cogency.

(d) An actual systematic deviation from the sure-thing principle and, with it, from the von Neumann–Morgenstern theory of utility, can be exhibited. For example, a person might perfectly reasonably prefer to subsist on a packet of Army K rations per meal than on two ounces of the best caviar per meal. It is then to be expected, according to the sure-thing principle, that the person would prefer the K rations to a lottery ticket yielding the K rations with probability 9/10 and the caviar diet with probability 1/10. That expectation is no doubt fulfilled, if the lottery is understood to determine the person's year-long diet once and for all. But, if the person is able to have at each meal a lottery ticket offering him the K rations or the caviar with the indicated probabilities, it is not at all unlikely, granting that he likes caviar and has some storage facilities, that he will prefer this "lottery diet." This conclusion is in defiance of the principle that "the theory of consumer demand is a static theory." (Cf. [W14].)

I admit that the theory of utility is not static in the indicated sense, as the foregoing example conclusively shows. But there is not the slightest reason to think of a lottery producing either a steady diet of caviar or a steady diet of K rations as being the same lottery as one having a multitude of different prizes almost all of which are mixed chronological programs of caviar and K rations. The fact that a theory of consumer behavior in riskless situations happens to be static in the required sense (under certain special assumptions about storability and the linearity of prices) is no argument at all that the theory of consumer behavior in risky circumstances should be static in the same sense (as I mention in a note appended to [W14]).

(e) If the von Neumann–Morgenstern theory of utility is not static, it is not subject to repeated empirical observation and is therefore vacuous. (Cf. [W14].)

I think the discussion in §3.1 [of *The Foundations of Statistics*] of how to determine the preferences of a hot man for a swim, a shower, and a glass of beer, and the discussion in §5 of the practicality of identifying pseudo-microcosms are steps toward showing how the theory can be put to empirical test without making repeated trials on any one person.

(f) Casual observation shows that real people frequently and flagrantly behave in disaccord with the utility theory, and that in fact behavior of that sort is not at all typically considered abnormal or irrational.

Two different topics call for discussion under this heading. In the first place, it is undoubtedly true that the behavior of people does often flagrantly depart from the theory. None the less, all the world knows from the lessons of modern physics that a theory is not to be altogether rejected because it is not absolutely true. It seems not unreasonable to suppose, and examples could easily be cited to confirm, that in the extremely complicated subject of the behavior of people very crude theory can play a useful role in certain contexts.

Second, many apparent exceptions to the theory can be so reinterpreted as not to be exceptions at all. For example, a flier may be observed doing a stunt that risks his life, apparently for nothing. That seems to be in complete violation of the theory; but, if in addition it is known that the flier has a real and practical need to convince certain colleagues of his courage, then he is simply paying for advertising with the risk of his life, which is not in itself in contradiction to the theory. Or, suppose that it were known more or less objectively that the flier has a need to demonstrate his own courage to himself. The theory would again be rescued, but this time perhaps not so convincingly as before. In general, the reinterpretation needed to reconcile various sorts of behavior with the utility theory is sometimes quite acceptable and sometimes so strained as to lay whoever proposes it open to the charge of trying to save the theory by rendering it tautological. The same sort of thing arises in connection with many theories, and I think there is general agreement that no hard-and-fast rule can be laid down as to when it becomes inappropriate to make the necessary reinterpretation. For example, the law of the conservation of energy (or its atomic age variant, the law of the conservation of mass *and* energy) owes its success largely to its being an expression of remarkable and reliable facts of nature, but to some extent also to certain conventions by which new sorts of energy are so defined as to keep the law true. A stimulating discussion of this delicate point in connection with the theory of utility is given by Samuelson in [S1].

(g) Introspection about certain hypothetical decision situations suggests that the sure-thing principle and, with it, the theory of utility are normatively unsatisfactory. Consider an example based on two decision situations each involving two gambles.[4]

---

[4] This particular example is due to Allais [A2]. Another interesting example was presented somewhat earlier by Georges Morlat [C4].

Situation 1. Choose between

Gamble 1. $500,000 with probability 1; and

Gamble 2. $2,500,000 with probability 0.1,
$500,000 with probability 0.89,
status quo with probability 0.01.

Situation 2. Choose between

Gamble 3. $500,000 with probability 0.11,
status quo with probability 0.89; and

Gamble 4. $2,500,000 with probability 0.1,
status quo with probability 0.9.

Many people prefer Gamble 1 to Gamble 2, because, speaking qualitatively, they do not find the chance of winning a *very* large fortune in place of receiving a large fortune outright adequate compensation for even a small risk of being left in the status quo. Many of the same people prefer Gamble 4 to Gamble 3; because, speaking qualitatively, the chance of winning is nearly the same in both gambles, so the one with the much larger prize seems preferable. But the intuitively acceptable pair of preferences, Gamble 1 preferred to Gamble 2 and Gamble 4 to Gamble 3, is not compatible with the utility concept or, equivalently, the sure-thing principle. Indeed that pair of preferences implies the following inequalities for any hypothetical utility function.

$$U(\$500,000) > 0.1U(\$2,500,000) + 0.89U(\$500,000) + 0.1U(\$0),$$

$$0.1U(\$2,500,000) + 0.9U(\$0) > 0.11U(\$500,000) + 0.89U(\$0);$$

(3)

and these are obviously incompatible.

Examples like the one cited do have a strong intuitive appeal; even if you do not personally feel a tendency to prefer Gamble 1 to Gamble 2 and simultaneously Gamble 4 to Gamble 3, I think that a few trials with other prizes and probabilities will provide you with an example appropriate to yourself.[5]

If, after thorough deliberation, anyone maintains a pair of distinct preferences that are in conflict with the sure-thing principle, he must abandon, or modify, the principle; for that kind of discrepancy seems intolerable in a normative theory. Analogous circumstances forced D. Bernoulli to abandon the theory of mathematical expectation for that of utility [B10]. In general, a person who has tentatively accepted a normative theory must conscientiously study situations in which the theory seems to lead him astray; he must decide for each by reflection – deduction will typically be of little relevance – whether to retain his initial impression of the situation or to accept the implications of the theory for it.

To illustrate, let me record my own reactions to the example with which this heading was introduced. When the two situations were first presented,

---

[5] Allais has announced (but not yet published) an empirical investigation of the responses of prudent, educated people to such examples [A2]. [Cf. Maurice Allais and Ole Hagen, eds., *Expected Utility Hypotheses and the Allais Paradox* (Dordrecht: D. Reidel, 1979), 611–654.]

Table 1. *Prizes in units of $100,000 in a lottery realizing gambles 1–4*

		Ticket number		
		1	2–11	12–100
Situation 1 {	Gamble 1	5	5	5
	Gamble 2	0	25	5
Situation 2 {	Gamble 3	5	5	0
	Gamble 4	0	25	0

I immediately expressed preference for Gamble 1 as opposed to Gamble 2 and for Gamble 4 as opposed to Gamble 3, and I still feel an intuitive attraction to those preferences. But I have since accepted the following way of looking at the two situations, which amounts to repeated use of the sure-thing principle.

One way in which Gambles 1–4 could be realized is by a lottery with a hundred numbered tickets and with prizes according to the schedule shown in Table 1.

Now, if one of the tickets numbered from 12 through 100 is drawn, it will not matter, in either situation, which gamble I choose. I therefore focus on the possibility that one of the tickets numbered from 1 through 11 will be drawn, in which case Situations 1 and 2 are exactly parallel. The subsidiary decision depends in both situations on whether I would sell an outright gift of $500,000 for a 10-to-1 chance to win $2,500,000 – a conclusion that I think has a claim to universality, or objectivity. Finally, consulting my purely personal taste, I find that I would prefer the gift of $500,000 and, accordingly, that I prefer Gamble 1 to Gamble 2 and (contrary to my initial reaction) Gamble 3 to Gamble 4.

It seems to me that in reversing my preference between Gambles 3 and 4 I have corrected an error. There is, of course, an important sense in which preferences, being entirely subjective, cannot be in error; but in a different, more subtle sense they can be. Let me illustrate by a simple example containing no reference to uncertainty. A man buying a car for $2,134.56 is tempted to order it with a radio installed, which will bring the total price to $2,228.41, feeling that the difference is trifling. But, when he reflects that, if he already had the car, he certainly would not spend $93.85 for a radio for it, he realizes that he has made an error.

One thing that should be mentioned before this chapter is closed is that the law of diminishing marginal utility plays no fundamental role in the von Neumann–Morgenstern theory of utility, viewed either empirically or normatively. Therefore the possibility is left open that utility as a function of wealth may not be concave, at least in some intervals of wealth. Some economic-theoretical consequences of recognition of the possibility of non-concave segments of the utility function have been worked out by Friedman and myself [F12], and by Friedman alone [F11]. The work of Friedman and myself on this point is criticized by Markowitz [M1].

References

Allais, Maurice
   [A2] "Le comportement de l'homme rationnel devant le risque: Critique des postulats et axioms de l'école Americaine," *Econometrica,* 21 (1953), 503–546.
Arrow, Kenneth J.
   [A6] "Alternative approaches to the theory of choice in risk-taking situations," *Econometrica,* 19 (1951), 404–437.
Baumol, William J.
   [B7] "The Neumann–Morgenstern utility index – an ordinalist view," *Journal of Political Economy,* 59 (1951), 61–66.
Bell, E. T.
   [B9] *Men of Mathematics,* New York, Simon and Schuster, 1937.
Bernoulli, Daniel
   [B10] "Specimen theoriae novae de mensura sortis," *Commentarii academiae scientiarum imperialis Petropolitanae* (for 1730 and 1731), 5 (1738), 175–192.
   [B11] *Die Grundlage der modernen Wertlehre. Versuch einer neuen Theorie der Wertbestimmung von Glücksfällen* (German translation of [B10] by Alfred Pringsheim, with introduction by Ludwig Frick), Leipzig, Duncker V. Humblot, 1896.
Bernoulli, Jacob (= James)
   [B12] *Ars conjectandi,* Basel, 1713.
Centre National de Recherche Scientifique
   [C4] *Fondements et applications de la théorie du risque en économetrie,* Paris, Centre National de la Recherche Scientifique, 1954. (Report of an international econometric colloquium on risk, in which there was much discussion of utility, held in Paris, May 12–17, 1952.)
Friedman, Milton
   [F11] "Choice, chance, and personal distribution of income," *Journal of Political Economy,* 61 (1953), 277–290.
Friedman, Milton, and L. J. Savage
   [F12] "The utility analysis of choices involving risk," *Journal of Political Economy,* 56 (1948), 279–304.
   [F13] "The expected-utility hypothesis and the measurability of utility," *Journal of Political Economy,* 60 (1952), 463–474.
Laplace, Pierre Simon de
   [L1] *Essai philosophique sur les probabilités* (First edition), Paris, 1814.
Markowitz, Harry
   [M1] "The utility of wealth," *Journal of Political Economy,* 60 (1952), 151–158.

Marshall, Alfred
[M2] *Principles of Economics* (First edition), London, Macmillan, 1890.
Pareto, Vilfredo
[P1] *Manuel d'économie politique* (Second edition), Paris, Giard, 1927. (First edition 1909. Based on a still earlier book in Italian.)
Ramsey, Frank P.
[R1] "Truth and probability" (1926), and "Further considerations" (1928), in *The Foundations of Mathematics and Other Logical Essays,* London, Kegan Paul, and New York, Harcourt, Brace and Co., 1931....
Samuelson, Paul A.
[S1] "Probability, utility, and the independence axiom," *Econometrica,* 20 (1952), 670–678.
Stigler, George J.
[S18] "The development of utility theory," *Journal of Political Economy,* Part I, 58 (1950), 307–327: Part II, 58 (1950), 378–396.
Tintner, Gerhard
[T1*a*] "A contribution to the non-static theory of choice," *Quarterly Journal of Economics,* 56 (1942), 274–306.
von Neumann, John, and Oskar Morgenstern
[V4] *Theory of Games and Economic Behavior* (Second edition), Princeton, Princeton University Press, 1947....
Wold, H.
[W14] "Ordinal preferences or cardinal utility," *Econometrica,* 20 (1952), 661–664.

3. Individual decision making under uncertainty

R. Duncan Luce and Howard Raiffa

1. Introduction and statement of problem

In a game the uncertainty is due entirely to the unknown decisions of the other players, and, in the model, the degree of uncertainty is reduced through the assumption that each player knows the desires of the other players and the assumption that they will each take whatever actions appear to gain their ends. Traditionally, the game model is not called decision making under uncertainty; that title is reserved for another special class of problems which lie in the domain of uncertainty. These problems, which we shall discuss presently, have for the most part grown up and been examined in the statistical literature, for they are very much involved in an understanding of experimental evidence and in drawing appropriate inferences from data.

The gist of the problem is simple to state. A choice must be made from among a set of acts $A_1, A_2, ..., A_m$, but the relative desirability of each act depends upon which "state of nature" prevails, either $s_1, s_2, ..., s_n$. The term "state of nature" will be more fully explicated later, but we hope the idea is intuitively clear. As the decision maker, we are aware that one of several possible things is true; which one it is is relevant to our choice, but we do not even know the relative probabilities of their truth – or, indeed, if it is even meaningful to talk about probabilities – let alone which one obtains. A simple example will illustrate the dilemma; this one is due to Savage (1954):

Your wife has just broken five good eggs into a bowl when you come in and volunteer to finish making the omelet. A sixth egg, which for some reason must be either used for the omelet or wasted altogether, lies unbroken beside the bowl. You must

Reprinted with permission from Luce and Raiffa, *Games and Decisions* (New York: Dover, 1989), 275–306.

decide what to do with this unbroken egg. Perhaps it is not too great an oversimplification to say that you must decide among three acts only, namely, to break it into the bowl containing the other five, to break it into a saucer for inspection, or to throw it away without inspection. Depending on the state of the egg, each of those three acts will have some consequence of concern to you, say that indicated by Table 1.

Table 1.

Act	State	
	Good	Rotten
Break into bowl	Six-egg omelet	No omelet, and five good eggs destroyed
Break into saucer	Six-egg omelet and a saucer to wash	Five-egg omelet and a saucer to wash
Throw away	Five-egg omelet, and one good egg destroyed	Five-egg omelet

In general, to each pair (A_i, s_j), consisting of an act and a state, there will be a consequence or outcome. We assume that our subject's preferences among these outcomes, and among hypothetical lotteries with these outcomes as prizes, are consistent in the sense that they may be summarized by means of a utility function [see Chapter 1]. If we arbitrarily choose some specific utility function, in other words, choose the origin and a unit of measurement, then we can summarize the decision problem under uncertainty (d. p. u. u.) as in Table 2. Here u_{ij} is the utility associated to the consequence of the pair (A_i, s_j). So the problem reduces to: Given an m by n array of numbers u_{ij}, to choose a row (act) which is optimal in some sense – or, more generally, to rank the rows (acts) according to some optimality criterion.

Somewhat more must be said about the states of nature. With respect to any decision problem, the set of "states of nature" is assumed to form a mutually exclusive and exhaustive listing of those aspects of nature which are relevant to this particular choice problem and about which the decision maker is uncertain. Although this characterization is quite vague, often there is a natural enumeration of the possible, pertinent, states of the world in particular contexts. We assume that there is a "true" state of the world which is unknown to the decision maker at the time of choice.

One extreme possibility we know how to treat – namely, risk. In that case a probability distribution over the set of states is known – or, better yet, the decision maker deems it suitable to act as if it were known. For example, suppose in the omelet problem described above, the husband – a scientifically minded farmer – "knows" that in a random sample of six eggs the conditional probability of the sixth egg's being rotten when the other five are

Table 2.

Acts	States					
	s_1	s_2	$\cdots$	s_j	$\cdots$	s_n
A_1	u_{11}	u_{12}	$\cdots$	u_{1j}	$\cdots$	u_{1n}
A_2	u_{21}	u_{22}	$\cdots$	u_{2j}	$\cdots$	u_{2n}
$\vdots$	$\vdots$	$\vdots$		$\vdots$		$\vdots$
A_i	u_{i1}	u_{i2}	$\cdots$	u_{ij}	$\cdots$	u_{in}
$\vdots$	$\vdots$	$\vdots$		$\vdots$		$\vdots$
A_m	u_{m1}	u_{m2}	$\cdots$	u_{mj}	$\cdots$	u_{mn}

good is 0.008. Thus, he may view breaking the sixth egg into the bowl as the lottery: 0.992 probability of the six-egg-omelet prize and 0.008 probability of the no-omelet-and-five-good-eggs-destroyed prize. In other words, an *a priori* probability distribution over the states "good" and "rotten" allows one to structure the problem as one of decision making under risk – as a choice among lotteries.

In general, if an *a priori* probability distribution over the states of nature exists, or is assumed as meaningful by the decision maker, then the problem can be transformed into the domain of decision making under risk. In particular, if the probabilities of states $s_1, s_2, \ldots, s_n$ are $p_1, p_2, \ldots, p_n$, respectively, (where $\sum_{j=1}^{n} p_j = 1$, $p_j \geq 0$), then the utility index for act A_i is its expected utility, i.e., $u_{i1}p_1 + u_{i2}p_2 + \cdots + u_{in}p_n$. The act having the maximum utility index is chosen, and we say that this act is "best against the given *a priori* probability distribution." (Equivalently, we can think of the decision problem as a game: the decision maker is player 1 who has strategies $A_1, A_2, \ldots, A_m$; "nature" is player 2 who has strategies $s_1, s_2, \ldots, s_n$; the payoff to 1 for the strategy pair (A_i, s_j) is u_{ij}; and, if 1 knows that 2 is employing the mixed strategy $(p_1 s_1, p_2 s_2, \ldots, p_n s_n)$, 1 should adopt a strategy (act) which is best against this mixed strategy, i.e., against the given *a priori* probability distribution.)

Thus, one extreme assumption leads us to a problem we have already examined in detail. Let us, therefore, turn to the other extreme in which we assume that the decision maker is "completely ignorant" as to which state of nature prevails. This phrase "completely ignorant" is vague, we know, and it has led to much philosophical controversy. The vagueness will be considerably diminished when later we attempt to cope axiomatically with decision making under uncertainty; however, perhaps it can now be reduced some by an illustration. Let us again examine the omelet problem, but with the cast changed. Instead of a scientific farmer, suppose the omelet is completed by a city boy unaccustomed to the ways of eggs. Furthermore, assume that the five eggs already broken were white, whereas the sixth is speckled brown and (to the city boy!) of unusual size. He doesn't have the faintest idea what to expect, having had no previous experience in matters of this kind. Nonetheless, he must make a decision, which leads to the question of criteria for decision making when the states are completely uncertain.

2. Some decision criteria

We shall now list, but only partially discuss, certain criteria which have been offered to resolve the decision problem under uncertainty, which we shall abbreviate as d. p. u. u. A criterion is well-defined if and only if it prescribes a precise algorithm which, for any d. p. u. u., unambiguously selects the act(s) which is (are) tautologically termed "optimal according to the criterion."

In each of the following criteria we shall suppose that we are given a d. p. u. u. having acts $A_1, A_2, ..., A_m$, states $s_1, s_2, ..., s_n$, and utility payoffs u_{ij}, $i = 1, ..., m$ and $j = 1, ..., n$.

The maximin criterion

To each act assign its security level as an index. Thus, the index for A_i is the minimum of the numbers $u_{i1}, u_{i2}, ..., u_{in}$. Choose that act whose associated index is maximum – i.e., choose the act which maximizes the minimum payoff. Thus, each act is appraised by looking at the worst state for that act, and the "optimal choice" is the one with the best worst state.

We have seen in the theory of games that the optimal security level often can be raised by allowing randomizations over acts. Consider, for example:

$$\begin{array}{c} \\ A_1 \\ A_2 \end{array} \begin{array}{cc} s_1 & s_2 \\ \left[\begin{array}{cc} 0 & 1 \\ 1 & 0 \end{array}\right]. \end{array}$$

In this case, the security level for each act is 0, but if we permit randomization between A_1 and A_2 the security level can be raised to ½ by using $(\frac{1}{2}A_1, \frac{1}{2}A_2)$. This is the hedging principle....

The maximin principle can be given another interpretation which, although often misleading in our opinion, is sufficiently prevalent to warrant some comment. According to this view the decision problem is a two-person zero-sum game where the decision maker plays against a diabolical Miss Nature.[1] The maximin strategy is then a best retort against nature's minimax strategy, i.e., against the "least favorable" *a priori* distribution nature can employ. We recall that in a two-person zero-sum game the maximin strategy makes

---

[1] In a recent lecture to statisticians one of the authors spoke of "diabolical Mr. Nature." The audience reaction was so antagonistic that we have elected the path of least resistance.

good sense from various points of view: it maximizes 1's security level; and it is good against player 2's minimax strategy, which there is reason to suspect 2 will employ since it optimizes his security level and, in turn, it is good against 1's maximin strategy. In a game against nature, however, such a cyclical reinforcing effect is completely lacking.

Nonetheless, just because a close conceptual parallelism between a d. p. u. u. and a zero-sum game is lacking, it does not follow that the maximin procedure is not a wise criterion to adopt. It has the merit that it is extremely conservative in a context where conservatism *might* make good sense. We will have more to say about this later.

(It is customary in the literature to consider negative utility, disutility, or loss, as an index appraising consequences. With that orientation the decision maker, therefore, attempts to minimize the maximum loss he runs from adopting an act – i.e., he "minimaxes" instead of "maximining." Consequently, the principle described above is usually called the *minimax principle*.)

The following simple example exhibits a possible objection to the maximin principle:

$$\begin{array}{c} \\ A_1 \\ A_2 \end{array} \begin{array}{cc} s_1 & s_2 \\ \left[\begin{array}{cc} 0 & 100 \\ 1 & 1 \end{array}\right]. \end{array}$$

Since A_1 and A_2 have security levels of 0 and 1 respectively, A_2 is preferred to A_1 relative to the maximin criterion. This remains true even if randomized acts are considered. Some consider this unreasonable, and to emphasize their objection they point out that this criterion would still select A_2 even if the 1 were reduced to 0.00001 and the 100 increased to 10^6. These critics agree that act A_2 is reasonable *if* player 2 is a conscious adversary of 1, for then 2 should choose s_1, and A_2 is best against s_1; but, they emphasize, nature does not behave in that way, and if we are completely ignorant about the true state of nature, then they claim A_1 is manifestly better.

The minimax risk criterion

This criterion (suggested by Savage (1951) as an improvement over the maximin (utility) criterion) can be suggested by continuing the analysis of the above d. p. u. u. If s_1 is the true state, then we have no "risk" or "regret" if we choose A_2, but some "risk" if we choose A_1; if s_2 is the true state, then we have no risk if we choose A_1 and a good deal of risk if we choose A_2. Schematically:

$$\begin{array}{cc} \text{Utility Payoffs} & \text{"Risk" Payoffs} \end{array}$$

$$\begin{array}{c} \\ A_1 \\ A_2 \end{array} \begin{array}{cc} s_1 & s_2 \\ \left[\begin{array}{cc} 0 & 100 \\ 1 & 1 \end{array}\right] \end{array} \rightarrow \begin{array}{c} \\ A_1 \\ A_2 \end{array} \begin{array}{cc} s_1 & s_2 \\ \left[\begin{array}{cc} 1 & 0 \\ 0 & 99 \end{array}\right]. \end{array}$$

In terms of "risk" payoffs, A_1 has a possible maximum risk of 1, whereas A_2 has a possible maximum risk of 99. Consequently, A_1 minimizes the maximum risk. However, if randomization is permitted, neither A_1 nor A_2 is optimal.

The general procedure goes as follows:

i.   To a d. p. u. u. with utility entries u_{ij}, associate a new table with risk payoffs r_{ij}, where r_{ij} is defined as the amount that has to be added to u_{ij} to equal the maximum utility payoff in the jth column.

ii. Choose that act which minimizes the maximum risk index for each act.

To illustrate the "reasonableness" of a criterion based upon risk payoffs rather than utility payoffs, consider some d. p. u. u. with money payoffs and a decision maker whose utility function is linear with money. Now suppose this d. p. u. u. is modified by giving a $10 bonus to the decision maker, regardless of his choice, provided a particular state, say s_3, turns out to be the true state. This bonus, so it is argued, cannot alter the strategic aspects of the decision problem, hence the preference pattern among acts should be identical for both the original and the modified problem. This amounts to saying that adding a constant to any column of the payoff array should not change the preference ordering of acts. In particular, then, the arrays

$$\begin{bmatrix} 0 & 100 \\ 1 & 1 \end{bmatrix} \quad \text{and} \quad \begin{bmatrix} 0+a & 100+b \\ 1+a & 1+b \end{bmatrix}$$

should be strategically equivalent for any a and b. By setting a equal to -1 and b equal to -100, we get

$$\begin{bmatrix} -1 & 0 \\ 0 & -99 \end{bmatrix},$$

which is the negative of the risk payoff array. Therefore, the maximin criterion for this payoff array is the same as the minimax criterion for the risk array.

In criticism of this proposal, we quote from Chernoff (1954):

Unfortunately, the minimax regret [risk] criterion has several drawbacks. First, it has never been clearly demonstrated that differences in utility do in fact measure what one may call regret [risk]. In other words, it is not clear that the "regret" of going from a state of utility 5 to a state of utility 3 is equivalent in some sense to that of going from a state of utility 11 to one of utility 9. Secondly, one may construct examples where an arbitrarily small advantage in one state of nature outweighs a considerable advantage in another state. Such examples tend to produce the same feelings of uneasiness which led many to object to the [maximin utility] criterion.

A third objection which the author considers very serious is the following. In some examples the minimax regret criterion may select a strategy [act] A_3 among the available strategies[2] A_1, A_2, A_3, and A_4. On the other hand, if for some reason A_4 is made unavailable, the minimax regret criterion will select A_2 among A_1, A_2, and A_3. The author feels that for a reasonable criterion the presence of an undesirable strategy A_4 should not have an influence on the choice among the remaining strategies.

Chernoff's third objection to the minimax risk principle is a variation on our old theme of the "independence of irrelevant alternatives." There is an obvious modification of the minimax risk principle which copes with the problem of non-independence of irrelevant alternatives – but, unfortunately, it has its own, more serious fault. Roughly, the idea is: instead of comparing an act with all others to ascertain the risk, which introduces the difficulties when new acts are added, simply make paired comparisons between acts. *Relative to the universe of any two acts,* and for each state, determine the risk of taking each act. Of the two acts, choose the one whose maximum risk is least. An optimal act is then defined as one which is preferred or indifferent, when compared in this way, to every other act. This procedure is unsatisfactory because there are d. p. u. u.'s in which intransitivities occur, and so for these cases it fails to lead to an unambiguous optimal act. An example is the d. p. u. u.

$$
\begin{array}{c}
\\
A_1 \\
A_2 \\
A_3
\end{array}
\begin{array}{ccc}
s_1 & s_2 & s_3 \\
\left[\begin{array}{ccc}
10 & 5 & 1 \\
0 & 10 & 4 \\
5 & 2 & 10
\end{array}\right]
\end{array}
\quad \text{(payoff in utility units).}
$$

The procedure outlined yields the following:

(i) A_1 over A_2 for: A_1 has a maximum risk of 5 (from s_2) whereas A_2 has a maximum risk of 10 (from s_1).

(ii) A_2 over A_3 for: A_2 has a maximum risk of 6 (from s_3) whereas A_3 has a maximum risk of 8 (from s_2).

(iii) A_3 over A_1 for: A_3 has a maximum risk of 5 (from s_1) whereas A_1 has a maximum risk of 9 (from s_3).

Consequently, none of the three acts can be optimal since each is less preferred (in a paired comparison) than one of the others.

This same example also illustrates Chernoff's third objection to the minimax risk criterion. Restricting ourselves to acts A_2 and A_3, that criterion selects A_2 as optimal and A_3 *as non-optimal.* When A_1 is added, the risk matrix is

$$
\begin{array}{c}
\\
A_1 \\
A_2 \\
A_3
\end{array}
\begin{array}{ccc}
s_1 & s_2 & s_3 \\
\left[\begin{array}{ccc}
0 & 5 & 9 \\
10 & 0 & 6 \\
5 & 8 & 0
\end{array}\right]
\end{array}
\quad \text{(payoff in risk units).}
$$

[2] Chernoff uses letters d_1, d_2, d_3, and d_4.

and A_3 *is then optimal* since its maximum risk is a minimum among the maximum risks.

The pessimism-optimism index criterion of Hurwicz

The maximin utility and the minimax risk criteria are each ultraconservative (or pessimistic) in that, relative to each act, they concentrate upon the state having the worst consequence. Why not look at the best state, or at a weighted combination of the best and worst? This, in essence, is the Hurwicz (1951a) criterion.

For act A_i, let m_i be the minimum and M_i the maximum of the utility numbers $u_{i1}, u_{i2}, ..., u_{in}$. Let a fixed number α between 0 and 1, called the pessimism-optimism index, be given. To each A_i associate the index $\alpha m_i + (1-\alpha)M_i$, which we shall term the α-index of A_i. Of two acts, the one with higher α-index is preferred.

Note that, if $\alpha = 1$, the above procedure is the maximin (utility) criterion, whereas if $\alpha = 0$, it is the maximax (utility) criterion. If neither of these are satisfactory, then how does one decide what α to use? One way is to see what seems reasonable in certain simple classes of d. p. u. u.'s, for example, in the class:

$$
\begin{array}{c} & \begin{array}{cc} s_1 & s_2 \end{array} \\ \begin{array}{c} A_1 \\ A_2 \end{array} & \left[\begin{array}{cc} 0 & 1 \\ x & x \end{array} \right] \end{array} \quad \text{(utility payoff).}
$$

The α-indices of A_1 and A_2 are $1-\alpha$ and x respectively. Consequently, if one can choose an x such that A_1 and A_2 are indifferent, then one can impute an α-level to oneself. For example, if A_1 and A_2 are indifferent for $x = \frac{3}{8}$, then α must be $\frac{5}{8}$. Thus, by resolving a simple decision problem an α-level can be chosen empirically, which, in turn, can be employed in more complicated decisions.

But there are also objections to this criterion; one may be illustrated by the following example:

$$
\begin{array}{c} & \begin{array}{ccc} s_1 & s_2 & s_3 \end{array} \\ \begin{array}{c} A_1 \\ A_2 \\ (\frac{1}{2}A_1, \frac{1}{2}A_2) \end{array} & \left[\begin{array}{ccc} 0 & 1 & 0 \\ 1 & 0 & 0 \\ \frac{1}{2} & \frac{1}{2} & 0 \end{array} \right] \end{array} \quad \text{(utility payoff).}
$$

Suppose the α-level of $\frac{1}{4}$ is chosen. The α-indices of A_1 and A_2 are each $\frac{1}{4} \cdot 0 + (1-\frac{1}{4}) \cdot 1 = \frac{3}{4}$, whereas the index of $(\frac{1}{2}A_1, \frac{1}{2}A_2)$ is $\frac{1}{4} \cdot 0 + (1-\frac{1}{4}) \cdot \frac{1}{2} = \frac{3}{8}$. Consequently, although A_1 and A_2 are each optimal, the procedure of tossing a fair coin and taking A_1 if heads and A_2 if tails is not optimal. Critics of the Hurwicz criterion claim that any randomization over optimal acts (according to a particular criterion) should itself also be optimal according to that criterion. Remember that a randomization which uses only optimal acts will ultimately cause the decision maker to adopt one of these optimal acts!

A second possible criticism of the Hurwicz criterion is that it resolves the following d. p. u. u. counter to one's best intuitive judgment:

$$
\begin{array}{c}
\begin{array}{cccccc} s_1 & s_2 & s_3 & \cdots & s_i & \cdots & s_{100} \end{array} \\
\begin{array}{c} A_1 \\ A_2 \end{array}
\left[\begin{array}{cccccc}
0 & 1 & 1 & \cdots & 1 & \cdots & 1 \\
1 & 0 & 0 & \cdots & 0 & \cdots & 0
\end{array}\right].
\end{array}
$$

According to any α-level Hurwicz criterion, both acts A_1 and A_2 have an α-index of $1-\alpha$, and so they are considered indifferent; however, if one is "completely ignorant" concerning which is the true state, then, the critics argue, A_1 is manifestly better than A_2. But, in defense of Hurwicz, *is A_1 clearly better than A_2*? What seems to be implied here is that the "true" state is "more likely" to be one of the states s_2 to s_{100} than s_1. This, however, is not what Hurwicz intuits about the notion of "complete ignorance," for he would assert that "complete ignorance" implies the above d. p. u. u. is strategically equivalent to

$$
\begin{array}{c}
\begin{array}{cc} s_1' & s_2' \end{array} \\
\begin{array}{c} A_1 \\ A_2 \end{array}
\left[\begin{array}{cc}
0 & 1 \\
1 & 0
\end{array}\right].
\end{array}
$$

A complete characterization of what he means by the term "complete ignorance" can best be given in axiomatic form (see section 4).

The criterion based on the "principle of insufficient reason"

The criterion of insufficient reason asserts that, if one is "completely ignorant" as to which state among $s_1, s_2, \ldots, s_n$ obtains, then one should behave as if they are equally likely. Thus, one is to treat the problem as one of risk with the uniform *a priori* probability distribution over states, and to each act A_i assign its expected utility index,

$$
\frac{u_{i1}+u_{i2}+\cdots+u_{in}}{n}
$$

and choose the act with the largest index.

At this juncture, it would be apropos to digress into the philosophical foundations of probability and to review the special role of the principle of insufficient reason in relation to these foundations. But we shall resist this temptation, for to do the topic justice would require a sizable digression, and there are already excellent expository accounts of this material. (See, for instance, Arrow (1951), Nagel (1939), and Savage (1954); each of these references, in turn, gives a relatively complete bibliography.) We will confine ourselves to a few simple remarks.

The principle of insufficient reason, first formulated by Jacob Bernoulli (1654–1705), states in boldest terms that, if there is no evidence leading one to believe that one event from an exhaustive set of mutually exclusive events is more likely to occur than another, then the events should be judged equally probable. This principle is extremely vague, and its indiscriminate use has led to many nonsensical results. Writers since Bernoulli's time have attempted to add qualifications to the principle and to specify limited interpretations so as to avoid some of the more blatant contradictions.

From an empirical point of view, one difficulty with the principle is this: Suppose we are confronted with a real problem in decision making under uncertainty, then our first task is to give a mutually exclusive and exhaustive listing of the possible states of nature. The rub is that many such listings are possible, and in general these different abstractions of the same problem will, when resolved by the principle of insufficient reason, yield different real solutions. For instance, in one listing of the states we might have: s_1, the organism remains fixed; s_2, the organism moves. In another equally good listing we might have: s_1, the organism remains fixed; s_2, the organism moves to the left; s_3, the organism moves to the right. We can further complicate our description of the possible states of nature by noting which leg first moves, whether the animal raises its head or not, etc.

There is a counterargument to this objection. Although it may be true that there are various acceptable interpretations as to what constitutes a state in a given real problem, it is not true that we will feel that the states are "equally likely" in each interpretation. In other words, care must be exerted in the choice of states if one wishes to use this principle. As it stands, this defense is weak in that there is a crying need for an empirical clarification of the term "equally likely." Eventually, we shall examine two suggested clarifications. The first, an axiomatic treatment due to Chernoff (1954), characterizes his notion of "complete ignorance" in such a manner as to justify logically the principle of insufficient reason. This will be described in section 4. In the second, the equally likely assignment gains empirical meaning through the "practical" suggestions for probability assignments offered by the personalistic school of probability (see section 5).

Incidentally, the arguments against the principle of insufficient reason become even more cogent when there are an infinite set of pertinent states of nature, for then it is difficult to single out a natural parametrization, or enumeration, of the states for which a suitable generalization of the "equally likely" criterion is appropriate.

Before we turn to the axiomatic studies of decision criteria, what of the poor decision maker who is now totally confused by the pros and cons of the above criteria? Can he, in desperation, compromise by adopting some sort of arbitrary composite of the criteria? Subsequently, we will suggest some plausible composites; however, for the present, the following example must be included as a note of caution, for some *apparently* acceptable compromises may not be so acceptable after all.

Take the case of a decision maker who cannot crystallize his preferences among the maximin criterion, the Hurwicz criterion with $\alpha = \frac{3}{4}$, and the principle of insufficient reason. He thus decides to define one act as preferable to another if and only if a majority of these three criteria register this preference. The following d. p. u. u. establishes that this compromise procedure is not well defined:

$$
\begin{array}{c}
\begin{array}{ccc} s_1 & s_2 & s_3 \end{array} \\
\begin{array}{c} A_1 \\ A_2 \\ A_3 \end{array}
\left[\begin{array}{ccc}
2 & 12 & -3 \\
5 & 5 & -1 \\
0 & 10 & -2
\end{array} \right]
\end{array}
\qquad \text{(utility payoff).}
$$

Preferences according to:

Maximin criterion	A_2 over A_3 over A_1
Hurwicz criterion[3] ($\alpha = \frac{3}{4}$)	A_3 over A_1 over A_2
Principle of insufficient reason	A_1 over A_2 over A_3

A majority of the criteria select A_1 over A_2, A_2 over A_3, and A_3 over A_1 – an intransitivity. The majority decision principle applied in social welfare contexts leads to the same embarrassing intransitivities of preference. The reasons are analogous.

3. Axiomatic treatment: the axioms not referring to "complete ignorance"

Instead of applying specific proposed decision criteria to carefully selected decision problems, thereby determining whether or not each criterion complies with our intuitive criteria (which we deem to be reasonable), let us, as so often before, invert the procedure. Let us cull from our intuitions certain reasonable desiderata for decision criteria to fulfill, which we can then investigate both as to compatibility with one another and as to their logical implications. Our axiomatic presentation mainly follows Chernoff (1954), but it is also a curious mixture of the works of Milnor (1954), Hurwicz (1951a), Savage (1954), Arrow (1953), and unpublished comments by Rubin.

There are two distinct types of axiomatic approaches in the literature. In one the criterion must establish for each d. p. u. u. a complete ordering of the available acts. As in the four criteria we have previously mentioned, this is usually effected by attaching a numerical index to each act. In the other approach, a criterion isolates an "optimal" subset of acts, but it does not attempt to rank non-optimal ones. Of course, this can be thought of as a complete ordering of all acts – but into just two categories: optimal and non-optimal! We will follow the latter procedure, for it is closer to the natural demands of the problem area.

---

[3] The α-indices of A_3, A_1, and A_2 are $\frac{1}{4}(10) + (\frac{3}{4})(-2) = 1$, $\frac{1}{4}(12) + (\frac{3}{4})(-3) = \frac{3}{4}$, and $(\frac{1}{4})(5) + (\frac{3}{4})(-1) = \frac{2}{4}$, respectively.

Let A' and A'' be two arbitrary but specific acts in a decision problem. We define the following preliminary notions.

    i. $A' \sim A''$: means that the acts are *equivalent* in the sense that they yield the same utilities for each state of nature.

    ii. $A' > A''$: means that A' *strongly dominates* A'' in the sense that A' is preferred to A'' for each state of nature.

    iii. $A' \gtrsim A''$: means that A' *weakly dominates* A'' in the sense that A' is preferred to A'' for at least one state and is preferred or indifferent to A'' for all other states.

Since any d. p. u. u. is characterized by a class of acts $\mathcal{A}$, a set of states of nature S, and a utility function u, we may symbolically identify the d. p. u. u. with the triple $(\mathcal{A}, S, u)$. A decision criterion associates to each d. p. u. u., i.e., to each $(\mathcal{A}, S, u)$, a subset $\hat{\mathcal{A}}$ of $\mathcal{A}$; the acts in $\hat{\mathcal{A}}$ are called *optimal* for $(\mathcal{A}, S, u)$ relative to the given criterion. $\hat{\mathcal{A}}$ is called the *choice* or *optimal* set.

Desiderata for criteria

Axiom 1. *For any d. p. u. u. $(\mathcal{A}, S, u)$, the set $\hat{\mathcal{A}}$ is non-empty, i.e., every problem can be resolved.*

Axiom 2. *The choice set for d. p. u. u. does not depend upon the choice of origin and unit of the utility scale used to abstract the problem.*

Axiom 3. *The choice set is invariant under the labeling of acts, i.e., the real acts singled out as optimal should not depend upon the arbitrary labeling of acts used to abstract the problem.*

Axiom 4. *If A' belongs to $\hat{\mathcal{A}}$ and $A'' \gtrsim A'$ or $A'' \sim A'$, then A'' belongs to $\hat{\mathcal{A}}$.*

Axioms 1 through 4 are quite innocuous in the sense that, if a person takes serious issue with them, then we would contend that he is not really attuned to the problem we have in mind.

An act A' is said to be *admissible* if there is no act A in $\mathcal{A}$ such that $A \gtrsim A'$, i.e., A' is admissible if A' is not weakly dominated by any other act.

Axiom 5. *If A' belongs to $\hat{\mathcal{A}}$, then A' is admissible.*

Axiom 5 is equivalent to:

Given A', if there exists an A such that $A \gtrsim A'$ (that is, if A' is not admissible), then A' does not belong to $\hat{\mathcal{A}}$.

It should be noted that as they were originally stated neither the maximin principle nor the Hurwicz α-criteria satisfy axiom 5; however, both can be appropriately modified in a trivial manner. To see the problem, consider the following d. p. u. u.:

$$
\begin{array}{c c c c}
 & s_1 & s_2 & s_3 \\
A_1 & \left[\begin{array}{c} 0 \end{array}\right. & 1 & \left.\begin{array}{c} \frac{3}{4} \end{array}\right] \\
A_2 & \left[\begin{array}{c} 0 \end{array}\right. & 1 & \left.\begin{array}{c} \frac{1}{2} \end{array}\right]
\end{array}.
$$

The strategy A_2 is not admissible, since $A_1 \gtrsim A_2$; however, A_1 and A_2, and all randomizations between them, have the same security level, 0, and the same Hurwicz α-index. Consequently, any randomized act is optimal according to these criteria. We can modify them to meet axiom 5 either by deleting all acts which are not admissible, or by deleting from the class of optimal acts those which are not admissible. This point suggests the next axiom.

Axiom 6. *Adding new acts to a d. p. u. u., each of which is weakly dominated by or is equivalent to some old act, has no effect on the optimality or non-optimality of an old act.*

Example. A gentleman wandering in a strange city at dinner time chances upon a modest restaurant which he enters uncertainly. The waiter informs him that there is no menu, but that this evening he may have either broiled salmon at $2.50 or steak at $4.00. In a first-rate restaurant his choice would have been steak, but considering his unknown surroundings and the different prices he elects the salmon. Soon after the waiter returns from the kitchen, apologizes profusely, blaming the uncommunicative chef for omitting to tell him that fried snails and frog's legs are also on the bill of fare at $4.50 each. It so happens that our hero detests them both and would always select salmon in preference to either, yet his response is "Splendid, I'll change my order to steak." Clearly, this violates the seemingly plausible axiom 6. Yet can we really argue that he is acting unreasonably? He, like most of us, has concluded from previous experience that only "good" restaurants are likely to serve snails and frog's legs, and so the risk of a bad steak is lessened in his eyes.

This illustrates the important assumption implicit in axiom 6, namely, that adding new acts to a d. p. u. u. *does not alter one's a priori information as to which is the true state of nature.* In what follows, we shall suppose that this proviso is satisfied. In practice this means that, if a problem is first formulated so that the availability of certain acts influences the plausibility of certain states of nature, then it must be reformulated by redefining the states of nature so that the interaction is eliminated.

Axiom 6 can be strengthened to the following form of the principle of the independence of irrelevant alternatives:

Axiom 7. *If an act is non-optimal for a d. p. u. u., it cannot be made optimal by adding new acts to the problem.*

A typical violation of axiom 7 is this incongruous exchange.

DOCTOR: Well, Nurse, that's the evidence. Since I must decide whether or not he is tubercular, I'll diagnose tubercular.

NURSE: But, Doctor, you do not have to decide one way or the other, you can say you are undecided.

DOCTOR: That's true, isn't it? In that case, mark him not tubercular.

NURSE: Please repeat that!

The example given at the end of the discussion of the minimax risk criterion shows that axiom 7 rules out the minimax risk principle.

Note that axiom 7 does not prevent an optimal act from being changed into a non-optimal one by adding new acts; this is true even if none of the new acts is optimal. Therefore, one might wish to strengthen axiom 7 to:

Axiom 7′. *The addition of new acts does not transform an old, originally non-optimal act into an optimal one, and it can change an old, originally optimal act into a non-optimal one only if at least one of the new acts is optimal.*

A further strengthening of axiom 7 is:

Axiom 7″. *The addition of new acts to a d. p. u. u. never changes old, originally non-optimal acts into optimal ones and, in addition, either*

(i)   *All the old, originally optimal acts remain optimal, or*
(ii) *None of the old, originally optimal acts remain optimal.*

The all-or-none feature of axiom 7″ may seem a bit too stringent, but one can offer this rationalization for it. Suppose that the merit of each act can be summarized by a single numerical index which is independent of the other acts available. Then the optimal set of the original problem is composed of all the acts with the highest index. Now, among the new acts either there is one with a higher index, which therefore annihilates all the old optimal acts, or there is not and the original optimal set is left intact. A severe criticism of axiom 7″ is that it yields unreasonable results when it is coupled with either of the more palatable axioms 5 and 6. Take, for example, the following d. p. u. u.:

$$A_1 \begin{bmatrix} s_1 & s_2 & s_3 & s_4 \\ 0 & 4 & 2 & 2 \\ 4 & 0 & 0 & 4 \end{bmatrix}.$$

It is reasonable that some criterion should allow both A_1 and A_2 in the optimal set. Now add an A_3 whose utilities are

$$A_3 [4 \quad 0 \quad 0.1 \quad 4]$$

Since A_2 is weakly dominated by A_3, axiom 5 implies that act A_2 cannot remain optimal. But one may very well want also to keep A_1 as optimal, in violation of 7″. The rationalization of axiom 7″ (namely, that each act can be fully appraised by a single index) is apparently not suitable. This is suggested by the fact that acts A_2 and A_3 have the same indices according to the maximin (utility), minimax risk or regret, and Hurwicz (for any α-index) criteria. The criterion based on the principle of insufficient reason, however, does satisfy axiom 7″.

There is still another variation on the theme of the independence of irrelevant alternatives, which is especially suited to finding the logical consequences of some combinations of these axioms.

Axiom 7‴. *An act A' is optimal only if it is optimal in the paired comparisons between A' and A, for all A in $\mathcal{Q}$.*

This axiom enables us to transform the decision problem into a series of paired comparisons between acts and to eliminate those acts which are not optimal in any one of these comparisons. We will not, however, use this condition.

Axiom 7 and its different versions are somewhat controversial. Each of these rules out the minimax risk or regret principle. We are most sympathetic to axioms 7 and 7‴. The others, 7′ and 7″, are slightly harder to see through (i.e., they are a little less intuitive), so let us suspend judgment until some of their consequences are stated.

The next axiom is due to Rubin. To suggest it, suppose a decision maker is given two decision problems having the same sets of available acts and states but differing in payoffs. Suppose the second problem is trivial in the sense that the payoff depends only upon the state and not upon the act adopted. In other words, in the array representing problem 2, all entries in the same column are the same. If the decision maker knows only that he is playing problem 1 with probability p and problem 2 with probability $1 - p$ when he has to adopt an act, then he should adopt an act which is optimal for problem 1, since problem 2, which enters with probability $1 - p$, is irrelevant as far as his choice is concerned. It is straightforward to formalize this requirement into an axiom, but we will be content merely with the following suggestive formulation.

Axiom 8. *Consider a probability mixture of two d. p. u. u.'s with the same sets of actions and states. If the second d. p. u. u. has payoffs which do not depend upon the act chosen, then the optimal set of the mixture problem should be the same as the optimal set of the first d. p. u. u.*

Axiom 8 can be shown to imply that *adding a constant to each entry of a column of a d. p. u. u. does not alter the optimal set.* Instead of Rubin's axiom, perhaps it would have been simpler to take the italicized consequence as the axiom; however, we feel, as do Rubin and Chernoff, that this property is not as intuitively compelling as the axiom given.

Axiom 8 goes a long way towards selecting a criterion. For example, it rules out the maximin criterion and all the Hurwicz α-criteria. Therefore, we should be careful before we accept or reject it. First, to argue against the axiom, these points may be raised.

i.   As stated, the axiom is not intuitive enough to be given the status of a basic desideratum.

ii. Consider the following problems:

	Problem 1			Problem 2			Problem 3	
	s_1	s_2		s_1	s_2		s_1	s_2

$$A_1 \begin{bmatrix} 0 & -9 \\ A_2 \\ -10 & 0 \end{bmatrix},$$

Problem 1:
$$\begin{array}{c} A_1 \\ A_2 \end{array} \begin{bmatrix} 0 & -9 \\ -10 & 0 \end{bmatrix},$$

Problem 2:
$$\begin{array}{c} A_1 \\ A_2 \end{array} \begin{bmatrix} 1000 & 0 \\ 1000 & 0 \end{bmatrix},$$

Problem 3:
$$\begin{array}{c} A_1 \\ A_2 \end{array} \begin{bmatrix} 500 & -\frac{9}{2} \\ 495 & 0 \end{bmatrix},$$

where, it will be noted, problem 3 is a mixture of the other two in which each is played with probability ½. Intuitively, a plausible method for analyzing these d. p. u. u.'s is to be somewhat pessimistic and to behave as if the less desirable state is somewhat more likely to arise. The extreme example of this rule is the maximiner who focuses entirely on the undesirable state, but our point holds equally well for one who emphasizes the undesirable state only slightly. In problem 1, s_1 is less desirable, and so one is led to choose A_1. In problem 3, s_2 is less desirable, and so one might be led to choose A_2. But if one subscribes to axiom 8, the same alternative must be chosen in both cases, and so we are led to doubt the axiom.

iii. Axiom 8, when added to axiom 3 (i.e., the choice set is invariant under labeling of acts) and to axiom 7 (i.e., the addition of acts cannot make a non-optimal act optimal), both of which are extremely reasonable, yields the following result: *If an optimal act of a given d. p. u. u. is equivalent to a probability mixture of two other acts, then each of these acts is also optimal.*[4] For example, in the d. p. u. u.

$$\begin{array}{c} A_1 \\ A_2 \\ A_3 \end{array} \begin{bmatrix} 0 & 2 \\ 1 & 0 \\ \frac{1}{2} & 1 \end{bmatrix},$$

with columns s_1 and s_2,

if A_3 is optimal, so are A_1 and A_2, since A_3 is equivalent to ($\frac{1}{2}A_1$, $\frac{1}{2}A_2$). This also implies the result that one need *never resort to randomized acts* in this type of decision problem. Since, it is contended, this consequence is absurd, one should discard the weakest link in the argument leading to it. Therefore, axiom 8 should go.

Now, to argue against these arguments point by point:

i.   Rubin's axiom is not only intuitively meaningful but it seems perfectly reasonable. This is a matter of taste!

ii. The very compelling *a priori* quality of Rubin's axiom argues against the analysis which led us to choose A_1 in problem 1 and A_2 in prob-

---

[4] This proposition is referred to as the anticonvexity property of the optimal set.

lem 3. Certainly, the intuitive analysis cannot be used without restriction, for it would also lead us to choose A_2 again in

$$
\begin{array}{cc}
 & s_1 \quad\; s_2 \\
\begin{array}{c} A_1 \\ A_2 \end{array} & \left[\begin{array}{cc} 500 & -0.01 \\ 100 & 0 \end{array}\right].
\end{array}
$$

and that seems counterintuitive. We suspect that most people who are unaware of axiom 8 would find it difficult to resolve problem 3 above and that they could easily be persuaded to choose either A_1 or A_2; however, once they become aware of the axiom they will find it acceptable and will use it to decide upon A_1 in that problem.

iii.   Is the assertion that one need never resort to randomized strategies in a d. p. u. u. so absurd? Maybe not, for one can cite many "reasonable" criteria which lead to an optimal non-randomized act for any d. p. u. u. Furthermore, there are arguments against randomization; for example, part of the discussion found in section 4.10 [of *Games and Decisions*], where we examined the operational interpretation of randomized strategies and cast some doubt upon their applicability, can be taken over almost verbatim. Finally, Chernoff (1954, p. 438) argues as follows:

> It would seem that the need for randomization depends on the statistician's need to oversimplify the statement of his problem because with limited computational ability he cannot take full advantage of the actual relationships involved. Generally, the simplification has the effect of *combining states of nature which are equivalent when random samples are insisted upon.* [Italics ours.]

This discussion leads naturally to the next axiom.

Axiom 9. *If A' and A'' are both optimal for a d. p. u. u., a probability mixture of A' and A'' is also optimal, i.e., the optimal set is convex.*

Remember that a probability mixture using A' or A'' will in fact choose either A' or A'', and, if they are both optimal, certainly any mixture should be. This seems very palatable; however, it rules out all Hurwicz's criteria with $\alpha < 1$. Put in another fashion, if we are committed to using some one of the criteria of the Hurwicz family, and if we impose axiom 9, then we must choose $\alpha = 1$, that is, the maximin (utility) criterion.

Hurwicz would argue, facetiously perhaps, that it does not grieve him too much to be forced into the $\alpha = 1$ camp, for that is where he started from in the first place. He only invented the pessimism–optimism index as a modification of the maximin criterion in order to appease those souls who were unwilling to endorse its pessimistic approach. However, he would continue, axiom 9 is not as innocuous as it seems. If axiom 9 were a consequence of some other more basic axioms, he would not object too much, but it does not seem to him to warrant the status of an axiom. Suppose A_1 and A_2 are both optimal acts. It is true that a mixture such as $(\frac{1}{2}A_1, \frac{1}{2}A_2)$ will, operationally, result in a selection of one of the two optimal acts. Nonetheless, the mixture may evoke a psychological response in its own right, and, before it is known which optimal act is adopted, there is no compelling reason why the anticipation of the mixture must be as good as either A_1 or A_2. For example, an optimist might like both A_1 and A_2 because in each case he can look forward to very desirable returns if certain states obtain; however, with the randomization all expected returns will be mitigated, and so the anticipation is not nearly so pleasant. Of course, the counterargument is that the apparent reasonableness of the axiom simply demonstrates the irrationality of the optimist's wishful thinking. So the battle is joined. The present authors are very partial to the axiom and believe the argument against it is rather weak.

So far we have not tried to characterize the notion of "complete ignorance." Our purpose in postponing this discussion is obvious: Axioms 1 through 9 are pertinent to decision making where one is not "completely ignorant" of the true state. It is interesting that, even without committing ourselves on the notion of "complete ignorance," acceptance of axioms 1 through 9 serves to eliminate the maximin criterion (eliminated by axiom 8), the minimax risk or regret (eliminated by axiom 7 or any of its variations), and the Hurwicz α-criteria (eliminated by axiom 8 and, for $\alpha < 1$, by axiom 9). Nonetheless, axioms 1 through 9 are compatible: the criterion based on the principle of insufficient reason, for example, satisfies all of them.

The following theorem is basic:

To each criterion which resolves all d. p. u. u.'s in such a manner as to satisfy axioms 1, 3, 4, 5, 7', 8, and 9, there is an appropriate a priori distribution over the states of nature which is independent of any new acts which might be added, such that an act is optimal (according to the criterion) only if it is best against this a priori distribution.

Note, this theorem does *not* say that if an act is best against this *a priori* distribution then it is optimal according to the criterion. It only says the converse. The theorem indicates that, if we are committed to axioms 1, 3, 4, 5, 7', 8, and 9, our first step should be to search for a suitable *a priori* distribution. What distribution is chosen will, naturally, depend upon the information we possess concerning the true state of nature.

4. Axiomatic treatment: the axioms referring to "complete ignorance"

Now we turn to the question of "complete ignorance." Consider the following axiom:

Axiom 10. *For any d. p. u. u., the optimal set should not depend upon the labeling of the states of nature.*

Obviously, if we have reason to suspect that a given state of nature is quite likely the true state whereas another state is quite likely not the true state, then in any abstraction of the problem we wish to distinguish between these two states. Or, if we number the states of nature in a given problem in such a manner that the lower the number the more likely we feel that it is the "true" state, then certainly we want to keep the labeling of the states in mind and axiom 10 would not be at all appropriate. Loosely speaking, whenever axiom 10 is not appropriate, we are not in the realm of "complete ignorance."

There is a tendency to read too much into this axiom. Some hold that adopting axiom 10 is essentially equivalent to assuming that each state is equally likely. Although this is true when a suitable collection of the other axioms is added to 10 (see below), it is not true for 10 alone, or for 10 and certain of the other axioms. For example, if axiom 7''' is accepted (i.e., A' is optimal only if it is optimal in each paired comparison), then axiom 10 has the following interpretation: If A' is optimal and if the utilities for A'', $[u(A'', s_1), u(A'', s_2), ..., u(A'', s_n)]$, are a permutation of those for A', $[u(A', s_1), u(A', s_2), ..., u(A', s_n)]$, then A'' is also optimal. This does not require that the states of nature be equally likely, since the maximin criterion, for example, satisfies this requirement.

It is very easy to see the role that axiom 10 plays when appended to axioms 1, 3, 4, 5, 7', 8, and 9. As a consequence of these other axioms, almost everything hinges on an *a priori* probability distribution over the states of nature. Yet, if we must be indifferent to the labeling of the states, it can be shown that the only possible *a priori* distribution must make each state equally likely, i.e., it must be the one which assigns the probability $1/n$ to each state if there are n states in all.

Thus, by coupling axiom 10 with the theorem we stated for these seven axioms, we know that an act is optimal only if it yields the highest average utility (the average being taken over all n utilities associated with the act and where each utility number is given weight $1/n$). But with axiom 10 added it can be shown that the "only if" assertion can be strengthened to "if and only if," i.e., *if an act has the highest average utility, then it is indeed optimal.* To round out the picture, the same result holds if for axiom 7' one substitutes axioms 6 and 7. (Note that 7' implies 7 directly, and when it is bolstered by 4 and 5 it also implies 6.)

In summary, then, axioms 1 through 10 (actually 2 is not needed) characterize the criterion based on the principle of insufficient reason, i.e., it is the unique criterion which satisfies them. This result is due to Chernoff (1954).

The maximiners and minimaxers, however, argue that, although axiom 10 is all right, it does not go far enough in characterizing the notion of "complete ignorance." For example, consider the two d. p. u. u.'s

D. P. U. U. 1   D. P. U. U. 2

$$
\begin{array}{c}
\begin{array}{cccc} s_1 & s_2 & s_3 & s_4 \end{array}\\
\begin{array}{c} A_1 \\ A_2 \end{array}
\left[\begin{array}{cccc}
6 & 2 & 2 & 2 \\
0 & 5 & 5 & 5
\end{array}\right]
\end{array}
\quad \text{and} \quad
\begin{array}{c}
\begin{array}{cc} s_1 & s_2 \end{array}\\
\begin{array}{c} A_1 \\ A_2 \end{array}
\left[\begin{array}{cc}
6 & 2 \\
0 & 5
\end{array}\right].
\end{array}
$$

According to the criterion based on the principle of insufficient reason, A_2 is optimal for d. p. u. u. 1 and A_1 for d. p. u. u. 2. But *if one is truly completely ignorant* about the true state in each problem aren't these problems identical? In d. p. u. u. 1, s_2, s_3, and s_4 can be strategically lumped into one state – call it s^*. True, s^* is "not less likely" to be true than either s_2, s_3, or s_4, but if we are completely ignorant we cannot say anything about s_1 versus s^*. The principle of insufficient reason interprets complete ignorance as "each state being equally likely," so s^* must be treated as if it were "three times as likely" as s_1, and, therefore, this criterion chooses A_2. But, in considering s^* as more likely than s_1, one admits that he is *not completely ignorant*. According to some, the very essence of complete ignorance is to treat d. p. u. u.'s 1 and 2 as equivalent. They would add that one is almost never in a state of *complete* ignorance, but they would insist that, if one wants to list reasonable desiderata for criteria which purport to handle this case, the following axiom is indispensable.

Axiom 11. *If a d. p. u. u. is modified by deleting a repetitious column (i.e., collapsing two states which yield identical payoffs for all acts into one), then the optimal set is not altered.*

Axiom 11 can be strengthened to:

Axiom 11'. *If a d. p. u. u. is modified by deleting a column which is equivalent to a probability mixture of other columns, then the optimal set is not altered.*

If one feels strongly about the criterion based on the principle of insufficient reason and also wants to endorse axiom 11, the two can be combined into this criterion: In any d. p. u. u. delete all repetitious columns, and in this modified d. p. u. u. choose those acts having the highest average payoff (equal weights). This criterion fails to satisfy axiom 7 or any of its variations. For example, consider the following d. p. u. u.:

$$
\begin{array}{c}
\begin{array}{ccc} s_1 & s_2 & s_3 \end{array}\\
\begin{array}{c} A_1 \\ A_2 \\ A_3 \end{array}
\left[\begin{array}{ccc}
11 & 0 & 0 \\
0 & 10 & 10 \\
9 & 9 & 0
\end{array}\right].
\end{array}
$$

If the choice is confined to A_1 or A_2, A_1 is optimal (since by axiom 11 s_3 is deleted). If A_3 is added to A_1 and A_2, then s_3 cannot be deleted, and according to this criterion A_2 is changed from non-optimal to optimal whereas A_1 is changed from optimal to non-optimal. Thus, any variant of axiom 7 is contradicted.

Axioms 10 and 11 together are said to characterize "complete ignorance." Although axioms 10 and 11 are compatible, and axioms 1 to 9 are compatible, all eleven obviously are not. Something will have to be deleted, and one possible candidate is Rubin's axiom 8 – which amounts to saying that the addition of a constant to a column has no effect on the optimal set. The Hurwicz α-criteria, modified to the extent of deleting all weakly dominated acts before applying the criteria, satisfy axioms 1 through 6, plus any version of 7, plus 10 and 11. The maximin (utility) criterion, modified in the same way, satisfies these and axiom 9 in addition.

Arrow (1953), modifying a result due to Hurwicz (1951a), has proved the following result: If a criterion satisfies axioms 1, 3, 4, 7″, 10, 11, then it takes into account only the minimum and maximum utility associated with each act. However, the particular way these maxima and minima are to be used to select a specific act as best is left unresolved by the group of axioms. For example, all the Hurwicz α-criteria are compatible with this axiom set. Another compatible criterion is: An act is optimal if and only if either its minimum is larger than the minimum of any other act or, when there are ties for the largest minimum, it has the largest maximum among those acts with the largest minimum.

Suppose that we let m denote the minimum utility associated with an act and M the maximum, then if we accept this axiom set (1, 3, 4, 7″, 10, 11) the crux of the problem is to decide upon an ordering between pairs (m', M') and (m'', M''). If we also demand that axiom 2 be met, the criterion must yield the same ordering when we change the utilities by a linear transformation. Thus, if the criterion selects (m', M') over (m'', M'') then it must also select $(am'+b, aM'+b)$ over $(am''+b, aM''+b)$, where $a > 0$. In this connection, the following can be shown: If, for the d. p. u. u.

$$
\begin{array}{c@{}c}
 & \begin{array}{cc} s_1 & s_2 \end{array} \\
\begin{array}{c} A_1 \\ A_2 \end{array} & \left[\begin{array}{cc} 0 & 1 \\ x & x \end{array} \right],
\end{array}
$$

there exists a number α such that we would say A_1 is optimal for all $x \le 1 - \alpha$, and A_2 is optimal for all $x \ge 1 - \alpha$, and if we demand that a criterion yielding this decision also satisfy axioms 1, 2, 3, 4, 7″, 10, and 11, then it must be Hurwicz's with index α.

The approach just used, which will be employed again in the next section, warrants a comment. We first commit ourselves to a class of axioms, thereby restricting the class of potential criteria. Second, we consider a simple class of d. p. u. u.'s for which we feel able to make subjective commitments as to the optimal sets. If our choice of axioms and special cases is clever, then by using the axioms we can logically extend the consistent decisions given for a simple class of d. p. u. u.'s to a precise formula which resolves all d. p. u. u.'s.

▶ Milnor (1954) states a set of requirements for reasonable decision criteria, where the criteria do not select an optimal set of acts but yield a complete (transitive) ordering for all acts. The analysis is much simpler in these terms. We outline his work here with a minimum of comments. In parentheses after each axiom we give the nearest corresponding statement in terms of optimal sets.

1. **Ordering.** *All acts must be completely ordered.* (1.)
2. **Symmetry.** *The ordering is independent of labeling of rows and columns.* (3 and 10.)
3. **Strong domination.** *Act A' is preferred to A" if A' strongly dominates A".* (4 and 5.)
4. **Continuity.** *If A' is preferred to A" in a sequence of d. p. u. u.'s, then A" is not preferred to A' in the limit d. p. u. u.* [A sequence of d. p. u. u.'s converge to a limiting d. p. u. u. if the utility numbers for each (act, state) pair converge to the utility number of the (act, state) pair of the limit d. p. u. u.] (No correlate.)
5. **Linearity.** *The ordering is not changed by linear utility transformations.* (2.)
6. **Row adjunction.** *The ordering between old rows is not changed by adding a new row.* (7, 7', 7", 7"'.)
7. **Column linearity.** *The ordering is not changed by adding a constant to a column.* (8.)
8. **Column duplication.** *Adding an identical column does not change the ordering.* (11.)
9. **Convexity.** *If A' and A" are indifferent in the ordering, then neither A' nor A" is preferred to* ($\frac{1}{2}A'$, $\frac{1}{2}A''$). (9.)
10. **Special row adjunction.** *Adding a weakly dominated act does not change the ordering of old acts.* (6.)

Milnor summarizes his results in the table.

Axiom	Laplace	Wald	Hurwicz	Savage
1. Ordering	⊗	⊗	⊗	⊗
2. Symmetry	⊗	⊗	⊗	⊗
3. Str. dom.	⊗	⊗	⊗	⊗
4. Continuity	x	⊗	⊗	⊗
5. Linearity	x	x	⊗	x
6. Row adj.	⊗	⊗	⊗	⋯
7. Col. lin.	⊗	⋯	⋯	⊗
8. Col. dup.	⋯	⊗	⊗	⊗
9. Convexity	x	⊗	⋯	⊗
10. Sp. row adj.	x	x	x	⊗

In this tabulation Laplace refers to the criterion based on the principle of insufficient reason, Wald to the maximin utility criterion, Hurwicz to the α optimism-pessimism criteria, and Savage to the minimax risk or regret criterion. An x means the criterion and the axiom are compatible. Each criterion is characterized by the axioms marked ⊗.

Note that, unlike Chernoff's characterization of the Laplace criterion, Milnor's does not require the convexity axiom. This discrepancy seems strange until it is recalled that Milnor's axioms 1 and 6 are stronger than their correlates in Chernoff's system. Milnor demands a complete ordering, not just an optimal set, and his sixth axiom corresponds to axiom 7", which is stronger than axiom 7 used by Chernoff.

Another point of discrepancy is Milnor's use of strong domination and continuity. All four of the criteria satisfy these conditions, but they would not if weak domination (i.e., axiom 5) were employed instead of strong domination. To see this, consider the d. p. u. u.

$$\begin{array}{c} \quad s_1 \quad s_2 \\ \begin{array}{c} A_1 \\ A_2 \end{array} \left[\begin{array}{cc} 0 & 4 \\ 1/n & 3 \end{array} \right]. \end{array}$$

By the maximin utility criterion, A_2 is preferred to A_1 for all n, but in the limit as n increases we obtain

$$\begin{array}{c} \quad s_1 \quad s_2 \\ \begin{array}{c} A_1 \\ A_2 \end{array} \left[\begin{array}{cc} 0 & 4 \\ 0 & 3 \end{array} \right], \end{array}$$

so by weak domination A_1 is preferred to A_2. Thus, that criterion cannot satisfy both weak domination and continuity.   ◀

5. The case of "partial ignorance"

A common criticism of such criteria as the maximin utility, minimax regret, Hurwicz α, and that based on the principle of insufficient reason is that they are rationalized on some notion of *complete* ignorance. In practice, however, the decision maker usually has some vague partial information concerning the true state. No matter how vague it is, he may not wish to endorse any characterization of complete ignorance (e.g., axiom 10 or 11), and so the heart is cut out of criteria based on this notion. The present section is devoted to suggestions for coping with this hiatus between complete ignorance and risk.

As background for this discussion, consider a contestant on the famous $64,000 quiz show who has just answered the $32,000 question correctly. His problem is whether to choose act A_1, to try for $64,000, or to choose act A_2, to stop at $32,000. His d. p. u. u. takes the form:

| | The $64,000 question is one that the contestant | |
	s_1 = could answer	s_2 = could not answer
A_1 = try for $64,000	Obtain $64,000 (taxable) plus prestige, publicity, etc.	Obtain a consolation prize of a Cadillac, plus knowledge that $32,000 (taxable) was lost
A_2 = stop	Obtain $32,000 (taxable), get less prestige and publicity than for the (A_1, s_1) pair	Same as (A_2, s_1) pair

We assume that in utility terms the problem reduces to the form:

$$
\begin{array}{c c}
 & \begin{array}{c c} s_1 & s_2 \end{array} \\
\begin{array}{c} A_1 \\ A_2 \end{array} & \left[\begin{array}{c c} 1 & 0 \\ x & x \end{array} \right].
\end{array}
$$

Let us suppose further that no other contestant has ever tried for the $64,000 question. For all our contestant knows, the difficulty of the question can run the gamut from the impossible to "What was the color of Washington's white horse?" Everything hinges on his appraisal of the relative possibilities of s_1 and s_2. He might take the point of view that he is completely ignorant of the true state, but it is much more likely that he would take into consideration such intangibles as: (*a*) the public reaction against the sponsor if the question were too difficult; (*b*) the bad precedent that would be set if the question were too easy; and (*c*) the trend in question difficulty in going from $4,000 to $8,000, from $8,000 to $16,000, and from $16,000 to $32,000. Although the problem surely is not in the realm of complete ignorance, it is not obvious how this vague information can be systematically processed.

Suppose, after due deliberation, the contestant chooses A_1. We can then assert that he behaved as if it were meaningful to assign an *a priori* probability to s_1 of x or greater.[5] Conversely, one is tempted to say that, if the "subjective probability" of s_1 is x or greater, then A_1 should be chosen. It is this net of ideas which will be partially formulated now.

We shall first report on the school led by Savage (1954), which holds the view that by processing one's partial information (as evidenced by one's responses to a series of simple hypothetical questions of the Yes-No variety) one can generate an *a priori* probability distribution over the states of nature which is appropriate for making decisions. This reduces the decision problem from one of uncertainty to one of risk. The *a priori* distribution obtained in this manner is called a *subjective* probability distribution.

Savage, in his *The Foundations of Statistics,* "develops, explains, and defends a certain abstract theory of behavior of a highly idealized person faced with uncertainty." The theory is based on a synthesis of the works of Bruno de Finetti on a personalistic view of probability and of the modern theory of utility due to von Neumann and Morgenstern. Since Savage expounds his position with vigor and clarity, we shall merely attempt to capture what, to our minds, is the most salient contribution of his school. Furthermore, we shall not follow Savage's development of the subject; rather we shall graft the new concepts onto the development given in the two previous sections.

Let $s_1, s_2, \ldots, s_n$ be a labeling of the possible states of nature for some concrete decision problem. Each of these labels refers to specific real world phenomena and we (in the role of a decision maker) might feel that some states are more plausible than others. Suppose, furthermore, that after reflection

---

[5] An equally valid interpretation of this single choice is that the subject applied a Hurwicz criterion with index $\alpha \leq 1 - x$.

we are convinced that we want to be consistent when facing problems of this type – consistent in the sense that our adopted decision criterion should satisfy axioms 1, 3, 4, 5, 7', 8, and 9. Since these axioms do not in any way refer to our state of ignorance concerning the true state of nature, we are free to commit ourselves to them independent of any information we possess or subjective feelings we have as to the relative plausibility of the different states. Now, as we previously noted, any criterion which satisfies these axioms must select as optimal a subset of the acts which are best against some specific *a priori* distribution. Furthermore, this *a priori* distribution is independent of the particular acts available in a given problem (as long as the states $s_1, s_2, \ldots, s_n$ are involved) since adding new acts does not change nonoptimal acts into optimal ones. Thus, it is reasonable to assert that if there exists an "appropriate" *a priori* probability distribution over the states, then this distribution depends solely upon our state of information concerning $s_1, s_2, \ldots, s_n$. The strategy now is to consider a series of simple hypothetical d. p. u. u.'s with these states of nature, to resolve them according to our best intuitive judgement, and then to use these commitments to infer a plausible *a priori* distribution.

Let us illustrate the procedure by a case which involves three specific states $s_1, s_2,$ and s_3. In order to generate an "appropriate" *a priori* distribution over these states let us introduce two hypothetical acts, A_1 and A_2, such that their consequences for the various states have the following monetary equivalences:

$$
\begin{array}{c}
 \quad s_1 \quad\ \ s_2 \quad\ \ s_3 \\
A_1 \left[\begin{array}{ccc} \$0 & \$0 & \$100 \\ \$y & \$y & \$y \end{array} \right]. \\
A_2
\end{array}
$$

Adjust act A_2, i.e., y, until we are indifferent between A_1 and A_2. Suppose the point of indifference (which is assumed to exist) is at \$65. Suppose, further, that we are indifferent between obtaining \$65 for certain and getting \$100 with an objective probability of 0.8 and \$0 with an objective probability of 0.2. Hence the utilities of \$0, \$65, and \$100 can be taken as 0, 0.8, and 1. In utility payoffs we have

$$
\begin{array}{c}
 \quad s_1 \quad\ \ s_2 \quad\ \ s_3 \\
A_1 \left[\begin{array}{ccc} 0 & 0 & 1 \\ 0.8 & 0.8 & 0.8 \end{array} \right]. \\
A_2
\end{array}
$$

Now, indifference between A_1 and A_2 is compatible with an *a priori* distribution only if the *a priori* probability of s_3 is 0.8. If we have no preferences about the states themselves then, as a check and possible short cut, we could ask ourselves: "If we were given the alternative (*a*) of obtaining a prize of x dollars if s_3 turns out to be true and nothing if s_1 or s_2 were true, versus the alternative (*b*) of obtaining a prize of x dollars with objective probability p and nothing with objective probability $1-p$, for what p would we be indifferent?" To check, we would require that indifference come at $p = 0.8$

independent of the value of x, so long as it is positive! In a similar manner, we could force ourselves to accept a probability assignment for s_2 and for s_1. In practice, however, one's choices for a series of problems – no matter how simple – usually are not consistent. For example, the *a priori* probability assignments for s_1, s_2, s_3 may not add up to 1. Once confronted with such inconsistencies, one should, so the argument goes, modify one's initial decisions in such a manner as to be consistent. Let us assume that this jockeying – making snap judgments, checking on their consistency, modifying them, again checking on consistency, etc. – leads ultimately to a bona fide *a priori* distribution. Now, if we wish our decision criterion both to satisfy the axioms stated above and to yield results that agree with our by now consistent set of preferences for simple hypothetical problems, then we are committed to a criterion which selects as optimal only acts which are best against this *a priori* distribution.

▶ To describe precisely what Savage means by a consistent set of preferences, we must outline briefly his postulates for a personalistic theory of decision. The assumed ingredients of the decision problem are:

    i.   The set of *states* of the world – a set S with (an infinite number of) elements $s, s', \ldots$ and with subsets $E, E', \ldots$ called *events*.

    ii.   The set of *consequences* – a set C with elements $c, c', \ldots$.

    iii.   The set of *acts* – set $\mathcal{Q}$ with elements $A, A', \ldots$.

    iv.   An assignment to each act-state pair (A, s) of a consequence from C which is denoted by $A(s)$.

    v.   A binary relation $\succeq$ between pairs of acts which is interpreted to mean "is preferred or indifferent to."

Savage then postulates and defines the following:

Postulate 1. *The relation $\succeq$ is a weak ordering of the acts, i.e., every pair of acts is comparable and the relation is transitive.*

Definition: The expression "$A \succeq A'$ given E" means that, if acts A and A' are modified so that their consequences are the same for every state not included in the event E, but if they are not changed for the states in E, then the modification of A is preferred or indifferent to the modification of A'.

This definition is not well defined unless the preference relation between modified acts is required not to depend upon the particular agreement selected for states not in E. The next postulate makes this assumption indirectly.

Postulate 2. *Conditional preference, as defined above, is well defined.*

Definition: If $A(s) = c$ and $A'(s) = c'$ for every s in S, then we define $c \succeq c'$ if and only if $A \succeq A'$.

The given A and A' of this definition are called "constant" acts since their consequences are independent of which state holds. The relation $\succeq$ is extended to the set of consequences by identifying each consequence with the constant act which yields it for each state.

Definition: An event ϕ is called *null* if every pair of acts are indifferent given ϕ, i.e., for every A and A', $A \gtrsim A'$ given ϕ and $A' \gtrsim A$ given ϕ.

Postulate 3. *If E is a non-null event and $A(s) = c$ and $A'(s) = c'$ for all s in E, then $A \gtrsim A'$ given E if and only if $c \gtrsim c'$.*

This asserts that conditional preferences do not affect consequence preferences.

Definition: The event E is said to be *not more probable than* the event E' if, whenever

   (i) c and c' are any two consequences such that $c > c'$,
  (ii) $A(s) = c$ for s in E and $A(s) = c'$ for s not in E, and
 (iii) $A'(s) = c$ for s in E' and $A'(s) = c'$ for s not in E',

then $A' \gtrsim A$.

Postulate 4. *Probabilitywise, any two events are comparable.*

Postulate 5. *There is at least one pair of acts which are not indifferent.*

Postulate 6. *Suppose $A > A'$. For each consequence c, no matter how desirable or undesirable it may be, there exists a sufficiently fine partitioning of S into a finite number of events such that if either A or A' is modified to yield c for any single event of the partition the preference for A over A' is not changed.*

Postulate 7. *Let A' be an act and let A_s' be the constant act which agrees with A' for the state s. Then,*

   (i) $A \gtrsim A_s'$ *given E for all s in E implies $A \gtrsim A'$ given E, and*
  (ii) $A_s' \gtrsim A$ *given E for all s in E implies $A' \gtrsim A$ given E.*

From these seven postulates Savage is able to show (among other things) the following two theorems.

Theorem. *There exists a unique real-valued function P defined for the set of events (subsets of S) such that*

   (i) $P(E) \geq 0$ *for all E,*
  (ii) $P(S) = 1$,
 (iii) *If E and E' are disjoint, then $P(E \cup E') = P(E) + P(E')$, and*
 (iv) *E is not more probable than E' if and only if $P(E) \leq P(E')$.*

P is called the *personalistic probability* measure reflecting the individual's reported feelings as to which of a pair of events is more likely to occur.

Theorem. *There exists a real-valued function u defined over the set of consequences having the following property: If E_i, where $i = 1, 2, \ldots, n$, is a partition of S and A is an act with consequence c_i on E_i, and if E_i', where $i = 1, 2, \ldots, m$, is another partition of S and A' is an act with consequence c_i' on E_i', then $A \gtrsim A'$ if and only if*

$$\sum_{i=1}^{n} u(c_i) P(E_i) \geq \sum_{i=1}^{m} u(c_i') P(E_i').$$

The function u is called a *utility* function. As in the von Neumann–Morgenstern theory, it is unique up to a positive linear transformation.   ◄

A primary, and elegant, feature of Savage's theory is that no concept of objective probability is assumed; rather a subjective probability measure arises as a consequence of his axioms. This in turn is used to calibrate utilities, and it is established that it can be done in such a way that expected utilities correctly reflect preferences. Thus, Savage's contribution – a major one in the foundations of decision making – is a synthesis of the von Neumann–Morgenstern utility approach to decision making and de Finetti's calculus of subjective probability.

To transform vague information concerning the states of nature into an explicit *a priori* probability distribution, the decision maker has had to register consistent choices in a series of simple hypothetical problems involving these states. No one claims that this is an easy task, but some go so far as to assert that in some contexts even these preliminary choices are too difficult to make with any confidence. They hold, further, that, if consistent responses are forced, the results are not very reliable and to build upon them is a mistake. They feel, introspectively, that, if one could instantaneously wipe out the memory of one's past choices and if the process for obtaining a subjective *a priori* distribution were immediately repeated, the new *a priori* distribution could easily be quite different from the old one.

There are two suggestions in the literature, Hurwicz (1951*b*) and Hodges and Lehman (1952), designed to cope partially with this problem. Let A be a generic act in $\mathcal{C}$ (the decision maker's strategy set); let $\mathbf{x}$ denote the generic randomized act in X (the set of all randomized acts); let s be a generic state of nature in S (nature's state set); let $\mathbf{y}$ denote an *a priori* probability distribution over S; and let Y be the set of all *a priori* probability distributions. As we have seen, Savage suggests that partial knowledge can be utilized to find a unique *a priori* distribution $\mathbf{y}^{(0)}$, and the decision maker is to choose an A which is best against $\mathbf{y}^{(0)}$. Hurwicz goes in the other direction: he suggests that *partial ignorance* over S can be effectively processed to yield *complete ignorance* over some subset $Y^{(0)}$ of Y. That is, although our knowledge may be insufficient to choose a specific *a priori* distribution in Y, it may be adequate to eliminate certain *a priori* distributions – let the remaining class be $Y^{(0)}$. Hurwicz proposes that the *a priori* distributions in $Y^{(0)}$ should be treated as new states of nature about which one is totally ignorant, and that a criterion based on complete ignorance over these states should be utilized. For example, let $M(\mathbf{x}, \mathbf{y})$ be the utility payoff when the decision maker chooses the randomized act $\mathbf{x}$ and when $\mathbf{y}$ is the *a priori* distribution. To apply the Hurwicz α-criterion, associate to each act $\mathbf{x}$ the α-index,

$$\alpha m_{\mathbf{x}} + (1 - \alpha) M_{\mathbf{x}},$$

where $m_{\mathbf{x}}$ and $M_{\mathbf{x}}$ are, respectively, the minimum and maximum payoffs[6] which result from $\mathbf{x}$ as the *a priori* distribution $\mathbf{y}$ runs over its domain $Y^{(0)}$. Choose an act which yields the highest α-index.

[6] There is some question here of the existence of the minimum and maximum; however, from a mathematical point of view, this can be taken care of easily.

The spirit of Hurwicz's proposal is quite clear, and there are contexts[7] where we feel his specific proposal can be employed. In general, however, we feel that his suggestions are too vague to resolve the problem. Operationally, how does one characterize the elements of $Y^{(0)}$? Even if all "reasonable" **y** are included in $Y^{(0)}$, can't some **y**'s be "more reasonable" than others? Maybe one could capture this differential plausibility for **y**'s in $Y^{(0)}$ by an *a priori* distribution on $Y^{(0)}$. But why stop there? There is a next level, and a next, etc. Of course, expedient compromises can be made, and Hurwicz's original hope still has merit: that from a lot of special decisions about $Y^{(0)}$, one will come closer to extracting faithfully one's partial information about the states than by a forced choice of an *a priori* distribution.

Independently of Hurwicz, Good (1950) has offered much the same suggestion for processing information; however, he subsequently used the maximin criterion rather than the α-criteria.

Hodges and Lehmann (1952) also take the position that, in practice, information about states of nature often lies somewhere between complete ignorance and a precise specification of an *a priori* distribution. For example, an *a priori* distribution $\mathbf{y}^{(0)}$ might seem likely and yet not be sufficiently reliable to base decisions on. An act which is best against $\mathbf{y}^{(0)}$ might involve a large risk if some state actually turns out to be true. (Note that Hodges and Lehmann, like most statisticians, phrase their results in terms of risk payoffs rather than in utility payoffs.) So they propose that: (*a*) An act (maybe randomized) be found which minimizes the maximum risk; let its maximum risk be C. (*b*) On the basis of the quantity C and the context of the problem, choose a quantity C_0, greater than C, to serve as the maximum tolerable risk. (*c*) Choose an act **x** which is best against $\mathbf{y}^{(0)}$ *subject to the condition that the act has a maximum risk not greater than C_0*.[8] Naturally, the choice of C_0 will depend upon how much confidence we have in $\mathbf{y}^{(0)}$.

6. Games as decision making under uncertainty

The problem of individual decision making under uncertainty can be considered as a one-person game against a neutral nature. Some of these ideas

---

[7] Let the two states of nature be whether a subject does or does not have tuberculosis, and suppose that from medical statistics the proportion of people having T.B. is known to be π. Because the subject is self-selected, we may be unwilling to say that the *a priori* probability of T.B. is π; but we may find it acceptable to say that it is anything greater than or equal to π, and, conceivably, we might behave as if we were completely ignorant as to which value it has in this interval.

[8] Once $\mathbf{y}^{(0)}$ is chosen, the payoff for **x** is a linear function. Mathematically, then, the problem is one of minimizing a linear function subject to linear inequalities – i.e., a linear-programing problem.... Because of the equivalence between linear programing and two-person zero-sum game theory, it is reasonable that game theory should be pertinent in proving theorems in this area. It is!

can be applied indirectly to individual decision making under conflict, i.e., where the adversary is not neutral but a true adversary. In a two-person non-zero-sum, non-cooperative game, let us refer to player 1 as "the decision maker" and to 2 as "the adversary." The decision maker wishes to choose an "optimal" set from the set of possible strategies (acts) available to him. One *modus operandi* for the decision maker is to generate an *a priori* probability distribution over the states (pure strategies) of his adversary by taking into account both the strategic aspects of the game and what "psychological" information is known about his adversary, and to choose an act which is best against this *a priori* distribution. To determine such a subjective *a priori* distribution, the decision maker might imagine a series of simple hypothetical side bets whose payoffs depend upon the strategy his adversary employs. This is easier said than done, however, since the decision maker cannot ignore the possibility that his adversary will attempt to hypothecate such a procedure for him and will adjust his choice of strategy accordingly. In other words, the decision maker's very selection of an *a priori* distribution for his adversary sets up indirect forces to alter this initial choice. If such is the case, one can argue that the decision maker should keep on modifying the *a priori* distribution until this alleged indirect feedback no longer produces any change – until there exists an equilibrium in the decision maker's mind. We suspect that, roughly, this is the way games of strategy are actually played. If in a given situation the theory is clear cut and if a decision maker knows that his adversary will comply with the theory, then, in a sense, the theory defines the decision maker's choice of an *a priori* distribution for his adversary.

Of course, a decision maker may not feel very confident in his subjective appraisals of his adversary, and so he might want to compromise in some way. For example, he might use the compromise suggested by Hodges and Lehmann (1952) and discussed in the preceding section. They state:

> The formulations given here may be applicable also to games played against an opponent rather than against Nature. This would be the case (in the two-person zero-sum game) if one believed from past experience that the opponent is likely to make certain mistakes. One could then take advantage of these and still protect oneself in case the opponent has improved.

Or, the decision maker might use the Hurwicz proposal and maximin, or he might use an α-index over some suitably chosen restricted class of *a priori* distributions. . . .

References

Arrow, K. J., "Hurwicz's optimality criterion for decision-making under ignorance," *Technical Report* 6, Department of Economics and Statistics, Stanford University, 1953.

"Alternative approaches to the theory of choice in risk-taking situations," *Econometrica,* 19, 404–437, 1951.

Chernoff, Herman, "Rational selection of decision functions," *Econometrica,* 22, 422–443, 1954.

Good, I. J., *Probability and the Weighing of Evidence,* Charles Griffin and Company, London, and Hafner Publishing Company, New York, 1950.

Hodges, J. L., Jr., and E. L. Lehmann, "The uses of previous experience in reaching statistical decisions," *Annals of Mathematical Statistics,* 23, 396–407, 1952.

Hurwicz, Leonid, *Optimality Criteria for Decision Making Under Ignorance,* Cowles Commission Discussion Paper, Statistics, No. 370, 1951 (mimeographed) (*a*).

"Some specification problems and applications to econometric models," *Econometrica,* 19, 343–344, 1951 (abstract) (*b*).

Milnor, J. W., "Games against nature," in Thrall, R. M., C. H. Coombs, and R. L. Davis, eds., *Decision Processes,* pp. 49–60, John Wiley & Sons, New York, 1954.

Nagel, Ernest, "Principles of the theory of probability," *International Encyclopedia of Unified Science,* Vol. I, No. 6, University of Chicago Press, Chicago, 1939.

Savage, L. J., "The theory of statistical decision," *Journal of the American Statistical Association,* 46, 55–67, 1951.

The Foundations of Statistics, John Wiley & Sons, New York, and Chapman & Hall, London, 1954.

B. *Problems and revisions*

4.   Risk, ambiguity, and the Savage axioms

Daniel Ellsberg

1. Are there uncertainties that are not risks?

There has always been a good deal of skepticism about the behavioral significance of Frank Knight's distinction between "measurable uncertainty" or "risk," which may be represented by numerical probabilities, and "unmeasurable uncertainty" which cannot. Knight maintained that the latter "uncertainty" prevailed – and hence that numerical probabilities were inapplicable – in situations when the decision-maker was ignorant of the statistical frequencies of events relevant to his decision; or when a priori calculations were impossible; or when the relevant events were in some sense unique; or when an important, once-and-for-all decision was concerned.[1]

Yet the feeling has persisted that, even in these situations, people tend to *behave* "as though" they assigned numerical probabilities, or "degrees of belief," to the events impinging on their actions. However, it is hard either to confirm or to deny such a proposition in the absence of precisely-defined procedures for *measuring* these alleged "degrees of belief."

What might it mean operationally, in terms of refutable predictions about observable phenomena, to say that someone behaves "as if" he assigned

Research for this paper was done as a member of the Society of Fellows, Harvard University, 1957. It was delivered in essentially its present form, except for Section 3, at the December meetings of the Econometric Society, St. Louis, 1960. In the recent revision of Section 3, I have been particularly stimulated by discussions with A. Madansky, T. Schelling, L. Shapley, and S. Winter.

Reprinted with permission from *Quarterly Journal of Economics* 75 (1961), 643–69. Copyright © 1961, John Wiley & Sons, Inc.

[1] F. H. Knight (1921). But see Arrow's comment: "In brief, Knight's uncertainties seem to have surprisingly many of the properties of ordinary probabilities, and it is not clear how much is gained by the distinction. . . . Actually, his uncertainties produce about the same reactions in individuals as other writers ascribe to risk." K. J. Arrow (1951, pp. 417, 426).

quantitative likelihoods to events: or to say that he does not? An intuitive answer may emerge if we consider an example proposed by Shackle, who takes an extreme form of the Knightian position that statistical information on frequencies within a large, repetitive class of events is strictly irrelevant to a decision whose outcome depends on a single trial. Shackle not only rejects numerical probabilities for representing the uncertainty in this situation; he maintains that in situations where all the potential outcomes seem "perfectly possible" in the sense that they would not violate accepted laws and thus cause "surprise," it is impossible to distinguish meaningfully (i.e., in terms of a person's behavior, or any other observations) between the relative "likelihoods" of these outcomes. In throwing a die, for instance, it would not surprise us at all if an ace came up on a single trial, nor if, on the other hand, some other number came up. So Shackle concludes:

Suppose the captains in a Test Match have agreed that instead of tossing a coin for a choice of innings they will decide the matter by this next throw of a die, and that if it shows an ace Australia shall bat first, if any other number, then England shall bat first. Can we now give any meaningful answer whatever to the question, "Who will bat first?" except "We do not know?"[2]

Most of us might think we could give better answers than that. We could say, "England will bat first," or more cautiously: "I think England will probably bat first." And if Shackle challenges us as to what we "mean" by that statement, it is quite natural to reply: "We'll *bet* on England; and we'll give you good odds."

It so happens that in this case statistical information (on the behavior of dice) is available and does seem relevant even to a "single shot" decision, our bet; it will affect the odds we offer. As Damon Runyon once said, "The race is not always to the swift nor the battle to the strong, but that's the way to bet." However, it is our bet itself, and not the reasoning and evidence that lies behind it, that gives operational meaning to our statement that we find one outcome "more likely" than another. And we may be willing to place bets – thus revealing "degrees of belief" in a quantitative form – about events for which there is no statistical information at all, or regarding which statistical information seems in principle unobtainable. If our pattern of bets were suitably orderly – if it satisfied certain postulated constraints – it would be possible to infer for ourselves numerical subjective probabilities for events, in terms of which some future decisions could be predicted or described. Thus a good deal – perhaps all – of Knight's class of "unmeasurable uncertainties" would have succumbed to measurement, and "risk" would prevail instead of "uncertainty."

A number of sets of constraints on choice-behavior under uncertainty have now been proposed, all more or less equivalent or closely similar in

[2] G. L. S. Shackle (1955, p. 8). If this example were not typical of a number of Shackle's works, it would seem almost unfair to cite it, since it appears so transparently inconsistent with commonly-observed behavior. Can Shackle really believe that an Australian captain who cared about batting first would be *indifferent* between staking this outcome on "heads" or on an ace?

spirit, having the implication that – for a "rational" man – *all* uncertainties can be reduced to *risks*.[3] Their flavor is suggested by Ramsey's early notions that, "The degree of a belief is...the extent to which we are prepared to act upon it," and "The probability of ⅓ is clearly related to the kind of belief which would lead to a bet of 2 to 1" (Ramsey, 1931, p. 171). Starting from the notion that gambling choices are influenced by, or "reflect," differing degrees of belief, this approach sets out to *infer* those beliefs from the actual choices. Of course, in general those choices reveal not only the person's relative expectations but his relative preferences for outcomes; there is a problem of distinguishing between these. But if one picks the right choices to observe, and if the Savage postulates or some equivalent set are found to be satisfied, this distinction can be made unambiguously, and either qualitative, or, ideally, numerical probabilities can be determined. The propounders of these axioms tend to be hopeful that the rules *will* be commonly satisfied, at least roughly and most of the time, because they regard these postulates as normative maxims, widely-acceptable principles of rational behavior. In other words, people should tend to behave in the postulated fashion, because that is the way they would *want* to behave. At the least, these axioms are believed to predict certain choices that people will make when they take plenty of time to reflect over their decision, in the light of the postulates.

In considering only deliberate decisions, then, does this leave any room at all for "unmeasurable uncertainty": for uncertainties *not* reducible to "risks," to quantitative or qualitative probabilities?

A side effect of the axiomatic approach is that it supplies, at last (as Knight did not), a useful operational meaning to the proposition that people do *not* always assign, or act "as though" they assigned, probabilities to uncertain events. The meaning would be that with respect to certain events they did not obey, nor did they wish to obey – *even on reflection* – Savage's postulates or equivalent rules. One could emphasize here either that the postulates failed to be acceptable in those circumstances as normative rules, or that they failed to predict reflective choices; I tend to be more interested in the latter aspect, Savage no doubt in the former. (A third inference, which H. Raiffa favors, could be that people need more drill on the importance of conforming to the Savage axioms.) But from either point of view, it would follow that *there would be simply no way to infer meaningful probabilities for those events from their choices,* and theories which purported to describe their uncertainty in terms of probabilities would be quite inapplicable in that area (unless quite different operations for measuring probability were devised). Moreover, such people could not be described as maximizing the mathematical expectation of utility on the basis of numerical probabilities

<hr />

[3] Ramsey (1931)...; Savage (1954); de Finetti (1951, pp. 217–226); Suppes, Davidson, and Siegel (1957). Closely related approaches, in which individual choice behavior is presumed to be stochastic, have been developed by Luce (1959) and Chipman (1960). Although the argument in this paper applies equally well to these latter stochastic axiom systems, they will not be discussed explicitly.

for those events derived on *any* basis. Nor would it be possible to derive numerical "von Neumann–Morgenstern" utilities from their choices among gambles involving those events.

I propose to indicate a class of choice-situations in which many otherwise reasonable people neither wish nor tend to conform to the Savage postulates, nor to the other axiom sets that have been devised. But the implications of such a finding, if true, are not wholly destructive. First, both the predictive and normative use of the Savage or equivalent postulates might be improved by avoiding attempts to apply them in certain, specifiable circumstances where they do not seem acceptable. Second, we might hope that it is precisely in such circumstances that certain proposals for alternative decision rules and nonprobabilistic descriptions of uncertainty (e.g., by Knight, Shackle, Hurwicz, and Hodges and Lehmann) might prove fruitful. I believe, in fact, that this is the case.

2. Uncertainties that are not risks

Which of two events, α, β, does an individual consider "more likely"? In the Ramsey–Savage approach, the basic test is: *On which event would he prefer to stake a prize, or to place a given bet?* By the phrase, "to offer a bet *on* α" we shall mean: to make available an action with consequence a if α occurs (or, as Savage puts it, if α "obtains") and b if α does not occur (i.e., if $\bar{\alpha}$, or "not-α" occurs), where a is preferable to b.

Suppose, then, that we offer a subject alternative bets "on" α and "on" β (α, β need not be either mutually exclusive or exhaustive, but for convenience we shall assume in all illustrations that they are mutually exclusive).

		Events		
		α	β	$\bar{\alpha} \cap \bar{\beta}$
Gambles	I	a	b	b
	II	b	a	b

The Ramsey–Savage proposal is to interpret the person's preference between I and II as revealing the relative likelihood he assigns to α and β. If he does not definitely prefer II to I, it is to be inferred that he regards α as "not less probable than" β, which we will write: $\alpha \geq \beta$.

For example, in the case of Shackle's illustration, we might be allowed to bet either that England will bat first or that Australia will (these two events being complementary), staking a $10 prize in either case:

	England first	Australia first
I	$10	$0
II	$0	$10

If the event were to be determined by the toss of a die, England to bat first if any number but an ace turned up, *I* would strongly prefer gamble I (and if Shackle should really claim indifference between I and II, I would be anxious to make a side bet with him). If, on the other hand, the captains were to toss a coin, I would be indifferent between the two bets. In the first case an observer might infer, on the basis of the Ramsey–Savage axioms, that I regarded England as more likely to bat first than Australia (or, an ace as less likely than not to come up); in the second case, that I regarded heads and tails as "equally likely."

That inference would, in fact, be a little hasty. My indifference in the second case would indeed indicate that I assigned equal probabilities to heads and tails, *if I assigned any probabilities at all to those events;* but the latter condition would remain to be proved, and it would take further choices to prove it. I might, for example, be a "minimaxer," whose indifference between the two bets merely reflected the fact that their respective "worst outcomes" were identical. To rule out such possibilities, it would be necessary to examine my pattern of preferences in a number of well-chosen cases, in the light of certain axiomatic constraints.

In order for any relationship $\geqq$ among events to have the properties of a "qualitative probability relationship," it must be true that:

(a) $\geqq$ is a complete ordering over events; for any two events α, β either α is "not less probable than" β, or β is "not less probable than" α, and if $\alpha \geq \beta$ and $\beta \geq \gamma$, then $\alpha \geq \gamma$.

(b)   If α is more probable than β, then "not-α" (or, $\bar{\alpha}$) is less probable than not-β ($\bar{\beta}$); if α is equally probable to $\bar{\alpha}$, and β is equally probable to $\bar{\beta}$, then α is equally probable to β.

(c)   If α and γ are mutually exclusive, and so are β and γ (i.e., if $\alpha \cap \gamma = \beta \cap \gamma = 0$), and if α is more probable than β, then the union $(\alpha \cup \gamma)$ is more probable than $(\beta \cup \gamma)$.

Savage proves that the relationship $\geqq$ among events, inferred as above from choices among gambles, will have the above properties if the individual's pattern of choices obeys certain postulates. To indicate some of these briefly:

P1: Complete ordering of gambles, or "actions," In the example below either I is preferred to II, II is preferred to I, or I and II are indifferent. If I is preferred to II, and II is preferred or indifferent to III, then I is preferred to III (not shown).

	α	β	$\bar{\alpha} \cap \bar{\beta}$
I	a	b	b
II	b	a	b

P2: The choice between two actions must be unaffected by the value of pay-offs corresponding to events for which both actions have the *same* payoff (i.e., by the value of pay-offs in a constant column). Thus, if the subject preferred I to II in the example above, he should prefer III to IV, below, when a and b are unchanged and c takes any value:

	α	β	$\bar{\alpha} \cap \bar{\beta}$
III	a	b	c
IV	b	a	c

This corresponds to Savage's Postulate 2, which he calls the "Sure-thing Principle" and which bears great weight in the analysis. One rationale for it amounts to the following: Suppose that a person would not prefer IV to III if he *knew* that the third column would not "obtain"; if, on the other hand, he knew that the third column *would* obtain, he would still not prefer IV to III, since the pay-offs (whatever they are) are equal. So, since he would not prefer IV to III "in either event," he should not prefer IV when he does not know *whether or not* the third column will obtain.

"Except possibly for the assumption of simple ordering," Savage asserts, "I know of no other extralogical principle governing decisions that finds such ready acceptance."[4]

P4: The choice in the above example must be independent of the values of a and b, given their ordering. Thus, preferring I to II, the subject should prefer V to VI below, when $d > e$:

	α	β	$\bar{\alpha} \cap \bar{\beta}$
V	d	e	e
VI	e	d	e

This is Savage's Postulate 4, the independence of probabilities and pay-offs. Roughly, it specifies that the choice of event on which a person prefers to stake a prize should not be affected by the size of the prize.

In combination with a "noncontroversial" Postulate P3 (corresponding to "admissibility," the rejection of dominated actions), these four postulates,

---

[4] Savage notes that the principle, in the form of the rationale above, "cannot appropriately be accepted as a postulate in the sense that P1 is, because it would introduce new undefined technical terms referring to knowledge and possibility that would render it mathematically useless without still more postulates governing these terms." . . . He substitutes for it a postulate corresponding to P2 above as expressing the same intuitive constraint. Savage's P2 corresponds closely to "Rubin's Postulate" (Luce & Raiffa, 1957, p. 290) [this volume p. 69] or Milnor's "Column Linearity" postulate, (Luce & Raiffa, 1957, p. 297) [this volume p. 76], which implies that adding a constant to a column of pay-offs should not change the preference ordering among acts.

If numerical probabilities were assumed known, so that the subject were dealing explicitly with known "risks," these postulates would amount to Samuelson's (1952) "Special Independence Assumption," on which Samuelson relies heavily in his derivation of "von Neumann–Morgenstern utilities."

if generally satisfied by the individual's choices, imply that his preference for I over II (or III over IV, or V over VI) may safely be interpreted as sufficient evidence that he regards α as "not less probable than" β; the relationship "not less probable than" *thus operationally defined,* will have all the properties of a "qualitative probability relationship." (Other postulates, which will not be considered here, are necessary in order to establish *numerical* probabilities.) In general, as one ponders these postulates and tests them introspectively in a variety of hypothetical situations, they do indeed appear plausible. That is to say that they do seem to have wide validity as normative criteria (for me, as well as for Savage); they are probably[5] roughly accurate in predicting certain aspects of actual choice behavior in many situations and better yet in predicting reflective behavior in those situations. To the extent this is true, it should be possible to infer from certain gambling choices in those situations at least a qualitative probability relationship over events, corresponding to a given person's "degrees of belief."

Let us now consider some situations in which the Savage axioms do *not* seem so plausible: circumstances in which none of the above conclusions may appear valid.

Consider the following hypothetical experiment. Let us suppose that you confront two urns containing red and black balls, from one of which a ball will be drawn at random. To "bet on Red_I" will mean that you choose to draw from Urn I; and that you will receive a prize a (say $100) if you draw a red ball ("if Red_I occurs") and a smaller amount b (say, $0) if you draw a black ("if not-Red_I occurs").

You have the following information. Urn I contains 100 red and black balls, but in a ratio entirely unknown to you; there may be from 0 to 100 red balls. In Urn II, you confirm that there are exactly 50 red and 50 black balls. An observer – who, let us say, is ignorant of the state of your information about the urns – sets out to measure your subjective probabilities by interrogating you as to your preferences in the following pairs of gambles:

1. "Which do you prefer to bet on, Red_I or $Black_I$: or are you indifferent?" That is, drawing a ball from Urn I, on which "event" do you prefer the $100 stake, red or black: or do you care?
2. "Which would you prefer to bet on, Red_{II} or $Black_{II}$?"
3. "Which do you prefer to bet on, Red_I or Red_{II}?"[6]
4. "Which do you prefer to bet on, $Black_I$ or $Black_{II}$?"[7]

---

[5] I bet.

[6] Note that in no case are you invited to choose both a color and an urn freely; nor are you given any indication beforehand as to the full set of gambles that will be offered. If these conditions were altered (as in some of H. Raiffa's experiments with students), you could employ randomized strategies, such as flipping a coin to determine what color to bet on in Urn I, which might affect your choices.

[7] See immediately preceding note.

Let us suppose that in both the first case and the second case, you are indifferent (the typical response).[8] Judging from a large number of responses, under absolutely nonexperimental conditions, your answers to the last two questions are likely to fall into one of three groups. You may still be indifferent within each pair of options. (If so, you may sit back now and watch for awhile.) But if you are in the majority, you will report that you prefer to bet on Red_{II} rather than Red_I, and $Black_{II}$ rather than $Black_I$. The preferences of a small minority run the other way, preferring bets on Red_I to Red_{II}, and $Black_I$ to $Black_{II}$.

If you are in either of these latter groups, you are now in trouble with the Savage axioms.

Suppose that, betting on red, you preferred to draw out of Urn II. An observer, applying the basic rule of the Ramsey–Savage approach, would infer tentatively that you regarded Red_{II} as "more probable than" Red_I. He then observes that you also prefer to bet on $Black_{II}$ rather than $Black_I$. Since he cannot conclude that you regard Red_{II} as more probable than Red_I and, at the same time, not-Red_{II} as more probable than not-Red_I – this being inconsistent with the essential properties of probability relationships – he must conclude that your choices are not revealing judgments of "probability" at all. So far as these events are concerned, it is *impossible* to infer probabilities from your choices; you must inevitably be violating some of the Savage axioms (specifically, P1 and P2, complete ordering of actions or the Sure-thing Principle).[9]

---

[8] Here we see the advantages of purely hypothetical experiments. In "real life," you would probably turn out to have a profound color preference that would invalidate the whole first set of trials, and various other biases that would show up one by one as the experimentation progressed inconclusively.

However, the results in Chipman's almost identical experiment (1960, pp. 87–88) do give strong support to this finding; Chipman's explanatory hypothesis differs from that proposed below.

[9] In order to relate these clearly to the postulates, let us change the experimental setting slightly. Let us assume that the balls in Urn I are each marked with a I, and the balls in Urn II with a II; the contents of both urns are then dumped into a single urn, which then contains 50 Red_{II} balls, 50 $Black_{II}$ balls, and 100 Red_I and $Black_I$ in unknown proportion (or in a proportion indicated only by a small random sample, say, one red and one black). The following actions are to be considered:

	100		50	50
	R_I	B_I	R_{II}	B_{II}
I	a	b	b	b
II	b	a	b	b
III	b	b	a	b
IV	b	b	b	a
V	a	a	b	b
VI	b	b	a	a

Let us assume that a person is indifferent between I and II (between betting on R_I or B_I), between III and IV and between V and VI. It would then follow from Postulates 1 and 2, the

The same applies if you preferred to bet on Red_I and $Black_I$ rather than Red_{II} or $Black_{II}$. Moreover, harking back to your earlier (hypothetical) replies, any *one* of these preferences involves you in conflict with the axioms. For if one is to interpret from your answers to the first two questions that Red_I is "equally likely" to not-Red_I, and Red_{II} is equally likely to not-Red_{II}, then Red_I (or $Black_I$) should be equally likely to Red_{II} (or to $Black_{II}$), and any preference for drawing from one urn over the other leads to a contradiction.[10]

It might be objected that the assumed total ignorance of the ratio of red and black balls in Urn I is an unrealistic condition, leading to erratic decisions. Let us suppose instead that you have been allowed to draw a random sample of two balls from Urn I, and that you have drawn one red and one black. Or a sample of four: two red and two black. Such conditions do not seem to change the observed pattern of choices appreciably (although the reluctance to draw from Urn I goes down somewhat, as shown for example, by the amount a subject will pay to draw from Urn I; this still remains well below what he will pay for Urn II). The same conflicts with the axioms appear.

Long after beginning these observations, I discovered recently that Knight had postulated an identical comparison, between a man who knows that there are red and black balls in an urn but is ignorant of the numbers of each, and another who knows their exact proportion. The results indicated above directly contradict Knight's own intuition about the situation: "It must

assumption of a complete ordering of actions and the Sure-thing Principle, that, I, II, III and IV are all indifferent to each other.

To indicate the nature of the proof, suppose that I is preferred to III (the person prefers to bet on R_I rather than R_{II}). Postulates 1 and 2 imply that certain transformations can be performed on this pair of actions *without affecting their preference ordering*; specifically, one action can be replaced by an action indifferent to it (P1 – complete ordering) and the value of a constant column can be changed (P2 – Sure-thing Principle).

Thus starting with I and III and performing such "admissible transformations" it would follow from P1 and P2 that the *first* action in *each* of the following pairs should be preferred:

	R_I	B_I	R_{II}	B_{II}	
I	a	b	b	b	
III	b	b	a	b	
I′	a	b	b	a	P2
III′	b	b	a	a	
I″	a	b	b	a	P1
III″	a	a	b	b	
I‴	b	b	b	a	P2
III‴	b	a	b	b	
I⁗	b	b	a	b	P1
III⁗	a	b	b	b	

Contradiction: I preferred to III, and I⁗ (equivalent to III) preferred to III⁗ (equivalent to I).

[10] See immediately preceding note.

be admitted that practically, if any decision as to conduct is involved, such as a wager, the first man would have to act on the supposition that the chances are equal." (Knight, 1921, p. 219). If indeed people were compelled to act on the basis of some Principle of Insufficient Reason when they lacked statistical information, there would be little interest in Knight's own distinctions between risk and uncertainty so far as conduct was involved. But as many people predict their own conduct in such hypothetical situations, they do *not* feel obliged to act "as if" they assigned probabilities at all, equal or not, in this state of ignorance.

Another example yields a direct test of one of the Savage postulates. Imagine an urn known to contain 30 red balls and 60 black and yellow balls, the latter in unknown proportion. (Alternatively, imagine that a sample of two drawn from the 60 black and yellow balls has resulted in one black and one yellow.) One ball is to be drawn at random from the urn; the following actions are considered:

	30 Red	60 Black	Yellow
I	$100	$0	$0
II	$0	$100	$0

Action I is "a bet on red," II is "a bet on black." Which do you prefer?

Now consider the following two actions, under the same circumstances:

	30 Red	60 Black	Yellow
III	$100	$0	$100
IV	$0	$100	$100

Action III is a "bet on red or yellow"; IV is a "bet on black or yellow." Which of these do you prefer? Take your time!

A very frequent pattern of response is: action I preferred to II, and IV preferred to III. Less frequent is: II preferred to I, and III preferred to IV. Both of these, of course, violate the Sure-thing Principle, which requires the ordering of I to II to be preserved in III and IV (since the two pairs differ only in their third column, constant for each pair).[11] The first pattern, for

---

[11] Kenneth Arrow has suggested the following example, in the spirit of the above one:

	100 R_I	B_I	50 R_{II}	50 B_{II}
I	*a*	*a*	*b*	*b*
II	*a*	*b*	*a*	*b*
III	*b*	*a*	*b*	*a*
IV	*b*	*b*	*a*	*a*

Assume that I is indifferent to IV, II is indifferent to III. Suppose that I is preferred to II; what is the ordering of III and IV? If III is not preferred to IV, P2, the Sure-thing Principle,

example, implies that the subject prefers to bet "on" red rather than "on" black; and he also prefers to bet "against" red rather than "against" black. A relationship "more likely than" inferred from his choices would fail condition (b) above of a "qualitative probability relationship," since it would indicate that he regarded red as more likely than black, but also "not-red" as more likely than "not-black." Moreover, he would be acting "as though" he regarded "red or yellow" as less likely than "black or yellow," although red were more likely than black, and red, yellow and black were mutually exclusive, thus violating condition (c) above.

Once again, it is impossible, on the basis of such choices, to infer even qualitative probabilities for the events in question (specifically, for events that include yellow or black, but not both). Moreover, for any values of the pay-offs, it is impossible to find probability numbers in terms of which these choices could be described – even roughly or approximately – as maximizing the mathematical expectation of utility.[12]

You might now pause to reconsider your replies. If you should repent of your violations – if you should decide that your choices implying conflicts with the axioms were "mistakes" and that your "real" preferences, upon reflection, involve no such inconsistencies – you confirm that the Savage postulates are, if not descriptive rules for you, your *normative criteria* in these situations. But this is by no means a universal reaction; on the contrary, it would be exceptional.

Responses do vary. There are those who do *not* violate the axioms, or say they won't, even in these situations (e.g., G. Debreu, R. Schlaifer, P. Samuelson); such subjects tend to apply the axioms rather than their intuition, and when in doubt, to apply some form of the Principle of Insufficient Reason. Some violate the axioms cheerfully, even with gusto (J. Marschak, N. Dalkey); others sadly but persistently, having looked into their hearts, found conflicts with the axioms and decided, in Samuelson's phrase,[13] to satisfy their preferences and let the axioms satisfy themselves. Still others (H. Raiffa)

is violated. If IV is not preferred to III, P1, complete ordering of actions, is violated. (If III is indifferent to IV, both P1 and P2 are violated.)

[12] Let the utility pay-offs corresponding to $100 and $0 be 1, 0; let P_1, P_2, P_3 be the probabilities corresponding to red, yellow, black. The expected value to action I is then P_1; to II, P_2; to III, $P_1 + P_3$; to IV, $P_2 + P_3$. But there are no P's, $P_i \geq 0$, $\Sigma P_i = 1$, such that $P_1 > P_2$ and $P_1 + P_3 < P_2 + P_3$.

[13] P. Samuelson (1950).

To test the predictive effectiveness of the axioms (or of the alternative decision rule to be proposed in the next section) in these situations, controlled experimentation is in order. (See Chipman's ingenious experiment (1960).) But, as Savage remarks ([*Foundations of Statistics*], p. 28), the mode of interrogation implied here and in Savage's book, asking "the person not how he feels, but what he would do in such and such a situation" and giving him ample opportunity to ponder the implications of his replies, seems quite appropriate in weighing "the theory's more important normative interpretation." Moreover, these nonexperimental observations can have at least negative empirical implications, since there is a presumption that people whose instinctive choices violate the Savage axioms, and who claim upon further reflection that they do not *want* to obey them, do not *tend* to obey them normally in such situations.

tend, intuitively, to violate the axioms but feel guilty about it and go back into further analysis.

The important finding is that, after rethinking all their "offending" decisions in the light of the axioms, a number of people who are not only sophisticated but reasonable decide that they wish to persist in their choices. This includes people who previously felt a "first-order commitment" to the axioms, many of them surprised and some dismayed to find that they wished, in these situations, to violate the Sure-thing Principle. Since this group included L. J. Savage, when last tested by me (I have been reluctant to try him again), it seems to deserve respectful consideration.

3. Why are some uncertainties not risks?

Individuals who would choose I over II and IV over III in the example above (or, II over I and III over IV) are simply not acting "as though" they assigned numerical or even qualitative probabilities to the events in question. There are, it turns out, other ways for them to act. But what *are* they doing?

Even with so few observations, it is possible to say some other things they are *not* doing. They are not "minimaxing"; nor are they applying a "Hurwicz criterion," maximizing a weighted average of minimum pay-off and maximum for each strategy. If they were following any such rules they would have been indifferent between each pair of gambles, since all have identical minima and maxima. Moreover, they are not "minimaxing regret," since in terms of "regrets" the pairs I–II and III–IV are identical.[14]

Thus, *none* of the familiar criteria for predicting or prescribing decision-making under uncertainty corresponds to this pattern of choices. Yet the choices themselves do not appear to be careless or random. They are persistent, reportedly deliberate, and they seem to predominate empirically; many of the people who take them are eminently reasonable, and they insist that they *want* to behave this way, even though they may be generally respectful of the Savage axioms. There are strong indications, in other words, not merely of the existence of reliable patterns of blind behavior but of the operation of definite normative criteria, different from and conflicting with the familiar ones, to which these people are trying to conform. If we are talking about you, among others, we might call on your introspection once again. What did *you* think you were doing? What were you trying to do?

One thing to be explained is the fact that you probably would *not* violate the axioms in certain other situations. In the urn example, although a person's choices may not allow us to infer a probability for yellow, or for (red or black), we may be able to deduce quite definitely that he regards (yellow or black) as "more likely than" red; in fact, we might be able to arrive at

---

[14] No one whose decisions were based on "regrets" could violate the Sure-thing Principle, since all constant columns of pay-offs would transform to a column of 0's in terms of "regret"; on the other hand, such a person would violate P1, complete ordering of strategies.

quite precise numerical estimates for his probabilities, approximating ⅔, ⅓. What is the difference between these uncertainties, that leads to such different behavior?

Responses from confessed violators indicate that the difference is not to be found in terms of the two factors commonly used to determine a choice situation, the relative desirability of the possible pay-offs and the relative likelihood of the events affecting them, but in a third dimension of the problem of choice: the nature of one's information concerning the relative likelihood of events. What is at issue might be called the *ambiguity* of this information, a quality depending on the amount, type, reliability and "unanimity" of information, and giving rise to one's degree of "confidence" in an estimate of relative likelihoods.

Such rules as minimaxing, maximaxing, Hurwicz criteria or minimaxing regret are usually prescribed for situations of "complete ignorance," in which a decision-maker lacks any information whatever on relative likelihoods. This would be the case in our urn example if a subject had no basis for considering any of the possible probability distributions over red, yellow, black – such as $(1, 0, 0)$, $(0, 1, 0)$, $(0, 0, 1)$ – as a better estimate, or basis for decision, than any other. On the other hand, the Savage axioms, and the general "Bayesian" approach, are unquestionably appropriate when a subject is willing to base his decisions on a definite and precise choice of a particular distribution: His uncertainty in such a situation is unequivocally in the form of "risk."

But the state of information in our urn example can be characterized neither as "ignorance" nor "risk" in these senses. Each subject does know enough about the problem to *rule out* a number of possible distributions, including all three mentioned above. He *knows* (by the terms of the experiment) that there are red balls in the urn; in fact, he knows that exactly ⅓ of the balls are red. Thus, in his "choice" of a subjective probability distribution over red, yellow, black – if he wanted such an estimate as a basis for decision – he is limited to the set of potential distributions between $(⅓, ⅔, 0)$ and $(⅓, 0, ⅔)$; i.e., to the infinite set $(⅓, \lambda, ⅔ - \lambda)$, $0 \le \lambda \le ⅔$. Lacking any observations on the number of yellow or black balls, he may have little or no information indicating that one of the remaining, infinite set of distributions is more "likely," more worthy of attention than any other. If he should accumulate some observations, in the form of small sample distributions, this set of "reasonable" distributions would diminish, and a particular distribution might gather increasing strength as a candidate; but so long as the samples remain small, he may be far from able to select one from a number of distributions, or one composite distribution, as a unique basis for decision.

In some situations where two or more probability distributions over the states of nature seem reasonable, or possible, it may still be possible to draw on different sorts of evidence, establishing probability weights in turn to these different distributions to arrive at a final, composite distribution. Even in our examples, it would be misleading to place much emphasis on the notion that a subject has *no* information about the contents of an urn on which no observations have been made. The subject can always ask himself: "What is the likelihood that the experimenter has rigged this urn? Assuming that he has, what proportion of red balls did he probably set? If he is trying to trick me, how is he going about it? What other bets is he going to offer me? What sort of results is he after?" If he has had a lot of experience with psychological tests before, he may be able to bring to bear a good deal of information and intuition that seems relevant to the problem of weighting the different hypotheses, the alternative reasonable probability distributions. In the end, these weights, and the resulting composite probabilities, may or may not be equal for the different possibilities. In our examples, actual subjects do tend to be indifferent between betting on red or black in the unobserved urn, in the first case, or between betting on yellow or black in the second. This need not at all mean that they felt "completely ignorant" or that they could think of no reason to favor one or the other; it does indicate that the reasons, if any, to favor one or the other balanced out subjectively so that the possibilities entered into their final decisions weighted equivalently.

Let us assume, for purposes of discussion, that an individual can always assign relative weights to alternative probability distributions reflecting the relative support given by his information, experience and intuition to these rival hypotheses. This implies that he can always assign relative likelihoods to the states of nature. But how does he *act* in the presence of his uncertainty? The answer to that may depend on another sort of judgment, about the reliability, credibility, or adequacy of his information (including his relevant experience, advice and intuition) as a whole: not about the relative support it may give to one hypothesis as opposed to another, but about its ability to lend support to any hypothesis at all.

If all the information about the events in a set of gambles were in the form of sample-distributions, then ambiguity might be closely related, inversely, to the size of the sample.[15] But sample-size is not a universally useful index of this factor. Information about many events cannot be conveniently described in terms of a sample distribution; moreover, sample-size seems to focus mainly on the quantity of information. "Ambiguity" may be high (and the confidence in any particular estimate of probabilities low) even where

---

[15] See Chipman (1960, pp. 75, 93). Chipman's important work in this area, done independently and largely prior to mine, is not discussed here since it embodies a stochastic theory of choice; its spirit is otherwise closely similar to that of the present approach, and his experimental results are both pertinent and favorable to the hypotheses below (though Chipman's inferences are somewhat different).

See also the comments by N. Georgescu-Roegen on notion of "credibility," a concept identical to "ambiguity" in (1958, pp. 24–26) and (1954). These highly pertinent articles came to my attention only after this paper had gone to the printer, allowing no space for comment here.

there is ample quantity of information, when there are questions of reliability and relevance of information, and particularly where there is *conflicting* opinion and evidence.

This judgment of the ambiguity of one's information, of the over-all credibility of one's composite estimates, of one's confidence in them, cannot be
expressed in terms of relative likelihoods of events (if it could, it would simply affect the final, compound probabilities). Any scrap of evidence bearing
on relative likelihood should already be represented in those estimates. But
having exploited knowledge, guess, rumor, assumption, advice, to arrive at
a final judgment that one event is more likely than another or that they are
equally likely, one can still stand back from this process and ask: "How
much, in the end, is all this worth? How much do I really know about the
problem? How firm a basis for choice, for appropriate decision and action,
do I have?" The answer, "I don't know very much, and I can't rely on that,"
may sound rather familiar, even in connection with markedly unequal estimates of relative likelihood. If "complete ignorance" is rare or nonexistent,
"considerable" ignorance is surely not.

Savage himself alludes to this sort of judgment and notes as a difficulty
with his approach that no recognition is given to it:

there seem to be some probability relations about which we feel relatively "sure"
as compared with others.... The notion of "sure" and "unsure" introduced here
is vague, and my complaint is precisely that neither the theory of personal probability, as it is developed in this book, nor any other device known to me renders the
notion less vague.... A second difficulty, perhaps closely associated with the first
one, stems from the vagueness associated with judgments of the magnitude of personal probability.[16]

Knight asserts what Savage's approach tacitly denies, that such overall
judgments may influence decision:

The action which follows upon an opinion depends as much upon the amount of
confidence in that opinion as it does upon the favorableness of the opinion itself....
Fidelity to the actual psychology of the situation requires, we must insist, recognition
of these two separate exercises of judgment, the formation of an estimate and the
estimation of its value. (Knight, 1921, p. 227)

Let us imagine a situation in which so many of the probability judgments
an individual can bring to bear upon a particular problem are either "vague"
or "unsure" that his confidence in a particular assignment of probabilities,
as opposed to some other of a set of "reasonable" distributions, is very low.
We may define this as a situation of high ambiguity. The general proposition

16 Savage (1954, pp. 57, 58, 59). Savage later goes so far as to suggest that the "aura of vagueness" attached to many judgments of personal probability might lead to systematic violations of his axioms although the decision rule he discusses as alternative – minimaxing
regret – cannot, as mentioned in footnote 14, account for the behavior in our examples.

to be explored below is that it is precisely in situations of this sort that self-consistent behavior violating the Savage axioms may commonly occur.

Ambiguity is a subjective variable, but it should be possible to identify "objectively" some situations likely to present high ambiguity, by noting situations where available information is scanty or obviously unreliable or highly conflicting; or where expressed expectations of different individuals differ widely; or where expressed confidence in estimates tends to be low. Thus, as compared with the effects of familiar production decisions or well-known random processes (like coin flipping or roulette), the results of Research and Development, or the performance of a new President, or the tactics of an unfamiliar opponent are all likely to appear ambiguous. This would suggest a broad field of application for the proposition above.

In terms of Shackle's cricket example: Imagine an American observer who had never heard of cricket, knew none of the rules or the method of scoring, and had no clue as to the past record or present prospects of England or Australia. If he were confronted with a set of side bets as to whether England would bat first – this to depend on the throw of a die or a coin – I expect (unlike Shackle) that he would be found to obey Savage's axioms pretty closely, or at least, to want to obey them if any discrepancies were pointed out. Yet I should not be surprised by quite different behavior, at odds with the axioms, if that particular observer were forced to gamble heavily on the proposition that England would *win the match.*

Let us suppose that an individual must choose among a certain set of actions, to whose possible consequences we can assign "von Neumann–Morgenstern utilities" (reflecting the fact that in choosing among *some* set of "unambiguous" gambles involving other events and these same outcomes, he obeys the Savage axioms). We shall suppose that by compounding various probability judgments of varying degrees of reliability he can eliminate certain probability distributions over the states of nature as "unreasonable," assign weights to others and arrive at a composite "estimated" distribution y^o that represents all his available information on relative likelihoods. But let us further suppose that the situation is ambiguous for him. Out of the set Y of all possible distributions there remains a set Y^o of distributions that still seem "reasonable," reflecting judgments that he "might almost as well" have made, or that his information – perceived as scanty, unreliable, *ambiguous* – does not permit him confidently to rule out.

In choosing between two actions, I and II, he can compute their expected utilities in terms of their pay-offs and the "estimated" probability distribution y^o. If the likelihoods of the events in question were as unambiguous as those in the situations in which his von Neumann–Morgenstern utilities were originally measured, this would be the end of the matter; these pay-offs embody all his attitudes toward "risk," and expected values will correspond to his actual preferences among "risky" gambles. But in this case, where his final assignment of probabilities is less confident, that calculation may leave him uneasy. "So I has a lower expectation than II, on the basis of *these* estimates of probabilities," he may reflect; "How much does that tell me? That's not much of a reason to choose II."

In this state of mind, searching for additional grounds for choice, he may try new criteria, ask new questions. For any of the probability distributions in the "reasonably possible" set Y^o, he can compute an expected value for each of his actions. It might now occur to him to ask: "What might happen to me if my best estimates of likelihood don't apply? What is the *worst* of the reasonable distributions of pay-off that I might associate with action I? With action II?" He might find he could answer this question about the lower limit of the reasonable expectations for a given action much more confidently than he could arrive at a single, "best guess" expectation; the latter estimate, he might suspect, might vary almost hourly with his mood, whereas the former might look much more solid, almost a "fact," a piece of evidence definitely worth considering in making his choice. In almost no cases (excluding "complete ignorance" as unrealistic) will the *only* fact worth noting about a prospective action be its "security level": the "worst" of the expectations associated with reasonably possible probability distributions. To choose on a "maximin" criterion alone would be to ignore entirely those probability judgments for which there is evidence. But in situations of high ambiguity, such a criterion may appeal to a conservative person as deserving *some* weight, when interrogation of his own subjective estimates of likelihood has failed to disclose a set of estimates that compel exclusive attention to his decision-making.

If, in the end, such a person chooses action I, he may explain:

In terms of my best estimates of probabilities, action I has almost as high an expectation as action II. But if my best guesses should be rotten, which wouldn't surprise me, action I gives me better protection; the worst expectation that looks reasonably possible isn't much worse than the "best guess" expectation, whereas with action II it looks possible that my expectation could really be terrible.

An advocate of the Savage axioms as normative criteria, foreseeing where such reasoning will lead, may interject in exasperation:

Why are you double-counting the "worst" possibilities? They're already taken into account in your over-all estimates of likelihoods, weighted in a reasoned, realistic way that represents – by your own claim – your best judgment. Once you've arrived at a probability distribution that reflects everything you know that's relevant, don't fiddle around with it, use it. Stop asking irrelevant questions and whining about how little you really know.

But this may evoke the calm reply:

It's no use bullying me into taking action II by flattering my "best judgment." *I* know how little that's based on; I'd back it if we were betting with pennies, but I want to know some other things if the stakes are important, and "How much might I expect to lose, without being unreasonable?" just strikes me as one of those things. As for the reasonableness of giving extra weight to the "bad" likelihoods, my test for that is pragmatic; in situations where I really can't judge confidently among a whole range of possible distributions, this rule steers me toward actions whose expected values are relatively *insensitive* to the particular distribution in that range, without giving up too much in terms of the "best guess" distribution. That strikes me as a sensible, conservative rule to follow. What's wrong with it?

"What's wrong with it" is that it will lead to violations of Savage's Postulate 2, and will make it impossible for an observer to describe the subject's choices as though he were maximizing a linear combination of pay-offs and probabilities over events. Neither of these considerations, even on reflection, may pose to our conservative subject overwhelming imperatives to change his behavior. It will *not* be true that this behavior is erratic or unpredictable (we shall formalize it in terms of a decision rule below), or exhibits intransitivities, or amounts to "throwing away utility" (as would be true, for example, if it led him occasionally to choose strategies that were strongly "dominated" by others). There is, in fact, no obvious basis for asserting that it will lead him in the long run to worse outcomes than he could expect if he reversed some of his preferences to conform to the Savage axioms.

Another person, or this same person in a different situation, might have turned instead or in addition to some other criteria for guidance. One might ask, in an ambiguous situation: "What is the *best* expectation I might associate with this action, without being unreasonable?" Or: "What is its average expectation, giving all the reasonably possible distributions equal weight?" The latter consideration would not, as it happens, lead to behavior violating the Savage axioms. The former would, in the same fashion though in the opposite direction as the "maximin" criterion discussed above; indeed, this "maximaxing" consideration could generate the minority behavior of those who, in our urn example, prefer II to I and III to IV. Both these patterns of behavior could be described by a decision rule similar to the one below, and their respective rationales might be similar to that given above. But let us continue to focus on the particular pattern discussed above, because it seems to predominate empirically (at least, with respect to our examples) and because it most frequently corresponds to *advice* to be found on decision-making in ambiguous situations.

In reaching his decision, the relative weight that a conservative person will give to the question, "What is the worst expectation that might appear reasonable?" will depend on his confidence in the judgments that go into his estimated probability distribution. The less confident he is, the more he will sacrifice in terms of estimated expected pay-off to achieve a given increase in "security level"; the more confident, the greater increase in "security level" he would demand to compensate for a given drop in estimated expectation. This implies that "trades" are possible between security level and estimated expectation in his preferences, and that does seem to correspond to observed responses. Many subjects will still prefer to bet on R_{II} than R_I in our first example even when the proportion of red to black in Urn II is lowered to 49:51, or will prefer to bet on red than on yellow in the second example even when one red ball is removed from the urn. But at *some* point, as the "unambiguous" likelihood becomes increasingly unfavorable, their choices will switch.[17]

Assuming, purely for simplicity that these factors enter into his decision rule in linear combination, we can denote by ρ his degree of confidence, in a given state of information or ambiguity, in the estimated distribution y^o, which in turn reflects all of his judgments on the relative likelihood of distributions, including judgments of equal likelihood. Let $\min_x$ be the minimum expected pay-off to an act x as the probability distribution ranges over the set Y^o; let est_x be the expected pay-off to the act x corresponding to the estimated distribution y^o.

The simplest decision rule reflecting the above considerations would be:[18] *Associate with each x the index:*

$$\rho \cdot \text{est}_x + (1 - \rho) \cdot \min_x$$

Choose that act with the highest index.

An equivalent formulation would be the following, where y^o is the estimated probability vector, $y_x^{\min}$ the probability vector in Y^o corresponding to $\min_x$ for action x and (X) is the vector of pay-offs for action x: *Associate with each x the index:*

$$[\rho \cdot y^o + (1 - \rho) y_x^{\min}](x)$$

Choose that act with the highest index.

In the case of the red, yellow, and black balls, supposing no samples and no explicit information except that $\frac{1}{3}$ of the balls are red, many subjects might lean toward an estimated distribution of $(\frac{1}{3}, \frac{1}{3}, \frac{1}{3})$: if not from "ignorance," then from counterbalancing considerations. But many of these would find the situation ambiguous; for them the "reasonable" distributions Y^o might be all those between $(\frac{1}{3}, \frac{2}{3}, 0)$ and $(\frac{1}{3}, 0, \frac{2}{3})$. Assuming for purposes of illustration $\rho = \frac{1}{4}$ (Y^o, y^o, X and ρ are all subjective data to be inferred by an observer or supplied by the individual, depending on whether

---

[17] This contradicts the assertions by Chipman (1960, p. 88) and Georgescu-Roegen (1954, pp. 527–530, 1958, p. 25) that individuals order uncertainty-situations lexicographically in terms of estimated expectation and "credibility" (ambiguity); ambiguity appears to influence choice even when estimated expectations are not equivalent.

[18] This rule is based upon the concept of a "restricted Bayes solution" developed by J. L. Hodges, Jr., and E. L. Lehmann (1952). The discussion throughout Section 3 of this paper derives heavily from the Hodges and Lehmann argument, although their approach is motivated and rationalized somewhat differently.

See also, L. Hurwicz (1951a). This deals with the same sort of problem and presents a "generalized Bayes-minimax principle" equivalent, in more general form, to the decision rule I proposed in an earlier presentation of this paper (December, 1960), but both of these lacked the crucial notions developed in the Hodges and Lehmann approach of a "best estimate" distribution y^o and a "confidence" parameter ρ.

the criterion is being used descriptively or for convenient decision-making), the formula for the index would be:

$$\tfrac{1}{4} \cdot \text{est}_x + \tfrac{3}{4}\min_x.$$

The relevant data (assigning arbitrary utility values of 6 and 0 to the money outcomes \$100 and \$0) would be:

	Red	Yellow	Black	Min_x	Est_x	Index
I	6	0	0	2	2	2
II	0	6	0	0	2	.5
III	6	0	6	2	4	2.5
IV	0	6	6	4	4	4

A person conforming to this rule with these values would prefer I to II and IV to III, in violation of the Sure-thing Principle: as do most people queried. In justifying this pattern of behavior he might reproduce the rationale quoted above (*q.v.*); but most verbal explanations, somewhat less articulately, tend to be along these lines:

The expected pay-off for action I is definite: 2. The risks under action II may be no greater, but I know what the risk is under action I and I don't under action II. The expectation for action II is ambiguous, it might be better or it might be worse, anything from 0 to 4. To be on the safe side, I'll assume that it's closer to 0; so action I looks better. By the same token, IV looks better than III; I *know* that my expected pay-off with IV is 4, whereas with III it might be as low as 2 (which isn't compensated by the chance that it could be 6). In fact, I know the whole *probability distribution of pay-offs* (though not the distribution over *events*) for I and IV, but I don't for II and III. I know that a pay-off of 6 is *twice as likely* as 0 under IV, whereas 6 *may* be only half as likely as 0 under III.

Leaving the advocate of the Savage axioms, if he is still around to hear this, to renew his complaints about the silliness and irrelevance of such considerations, let us note a practical consequence of the decision rule which the above comment brings into focus. It has already been mentioned that the rule will favor – other things (such as the estimated expectation) being roughly equal – actions whose expected value is less sensitive to variation of the probability distribution within the range of ambiguity. Such actions may frequently be those definable as "status quo" or "present behavior" strategies. For these, ρ may be high, the range of Y_o small.

A familiar, ongoing pattern of activity may be subject to considerable uncertainty, but this uncertainty is more apt to appear in the form of "risk"; the relation between given states of nature is known precisely, and although the random variation in the state of nature which "obtains" may be considerable, its stochastic properties are often known confidently and in detail. (Actually, this confidence may be self-deceptive, based on ignoring some treacherous possibilities; nevertheless, it commonly exists.) In contrast, the ambiguities surrounding the outcome of a proposed *innovation,* a departure from current strategy, may be much more noticeable. Different sorts of events are relevant to its outcome, and their likelihoods must now be estimated, often with little evidence or prior expertise; and the effect of a given state of nature upon the outcome of the new action may itself be in question. Its variance may not appear any higher than that of the familiar action when computed on the basis of "best estimates" of the probabilities involved, yet the meaningfulness of this calculation may be subject to doubt. The decision rule discussed will not preclude choosing such an act, but it will definitely bias the choice away from such ambiguous ventures and toward the strategy with *"known* risks." Thus the rule is "conservative" in a sense more familiar to everyday conversation than to statistical decision theory; it may often favor traditional or current strategies, even perhaps at high risk, over innovations whose consequences are undeniably ambiguous. This property may recommend it to some, discredit it with others (some of whom might prefer to reverse the rule, to emphasize the more hopeful possibilities in ambiguous situations); it does not seem irrelevant to one's attitude toward the behavior.

In the equivalent formulation in terms of $y_x^{\min}$ and y^o, the subject above could be described "as though" he were assigning weights to the respective pay-offs of actions II and III, whose expected values are ambiguous, as follows (assuming $y^o = (\frac{1}{3}, \frac{1}{3}, \frac{1}{3})$ in each case):

	$y_x^{\min}$	$\rho \cdot y^o + (1-\rho) y_x^{\min}$
II	$(\frac{1}{3}, 0, \frac{2}{3})$	$(\frac{1}{3}, \frac{1}{12}, \frac{7}{12})$
III	$(\frac{1}{3}, \frac{2}{3}, 0)$	$(\frac{1}{3}, \frac{7}{12}, \frac{1}{12})$

Although the final set of weights for each set of pay-offs resemble probabilities (they are positive, sum to unity, and represent a linear combination of two probability distributions), they differ for each action, since $y_x^{\min}$ will depend on the pay-offs for x and will vary for different actions. If these weights were interpreted as "probabilities," we would have to regard the subject's subjective probabilities as being dependent upon his pay-offs, his evaluation of the outcomes. Thus, this model would be appropriate to represent cases of true pessimism, or optimism or wishfulness (with $y_x^{\min}$ substituting for $y_x^{\min}$). However, in this case we are assuming *conservatism,* not pessimism; our subject does not actually expect the worst, but he chooses to act *"as though" the worst were somewhat more likely than his best estimates of likelihood would indicate.* In either case, he violates the Savage axioms; it is impossible to infer from the resulting behavior a set of probabilities *for events* independent of his payoffs. In effect, he "distorts" his best estimates of likelihood, in the direction of increased emphasis on the less favorable outcomes and to a degree depending on ρ, his confidence in his best estimate.[19]

Not only does this decision model account for "deviant" behavior in a particular, ambiguous situation, but it covers the observed shift in a subject's behavior as ambiguity decreases. Suppose that a sample is drawn from the urn, strengthening the confidence in the best estimates of likelihood, so that ρ increases, say, to ¾. The weights for the pay-offs to actions II and III would now be:

$$\rho \cdot y^o + (1-\rho) y_x^{min}$$

II   (⅓, ¼, ⁵⁄₁₂)
III   (⅓, ⁵⁄₁₂, ¼)

and the over-all index would be:

Index
I   2
II   1.5
III   3.5
IV   4

In other words, the relative influence of the consideration, "What is the worst to be expected?" upon the comparison of actions is lessened. The final weights approach closer to the "best estimate" values, and I and II approach closer to indifference, as do III and IV. This latter aspect might show up behaviorally in the amount a subject is willing to pay for a given bet on yellow, or on (red or black), in the two situations.

In the limit, as ambiguity diminishes for one reason or another and ρ approaches 1, the estimated distribution will come increasingly to dominate decision. With confidence in the best estimates high, behavior on the basis of the proposed decision rule will roughly conform to the Savage axioms, and it would be possible to infer the estimated probabilities from observed choices. But prior to this, a large number of information states, distinguishable from each other and all far removed from "complete ignorance," might

[19] This interpretation of the behavior pattern contrasts to the hypothesis or decision rule advanced by Fellner (1961). Fellner seems unmistakably to be dealing with the same phenomena discussed here, and his proposed technique of measuring a person's subjective probabilities and utilities in relatively "unambiguous" situations and then using these measurements to calibrate his uncertainty in more ambiguous environments seems to me a most valuable source of new data and hypotheses. Moreover, his descriptive data and intuitive conjectures lend encouraging support to the findings reported here. However, his solution to the problem supposes a single set of weights determined independently of pay-offs (presumably corresponding to the "best estimates" here) and a "correction factor," reflecting the degree of ambiguity or confidence, which operates on these weights in a manner independent of the structure of pay-offs. I am not entirely clear on the behavioral implications of Fellner's model or the decision rule it implies, but in view of these properties I am doubtful whether it can account adequately for all the behavior discussed above.

all be sufficiently ambiguous as to lead many decision-makers to conform to the above decision rule with $\rho < 1$, in clear violation of the axioms.

Are they foolish? It is not the object of this paper to judge that. I have been concerned rather to advance the testable propositions: (1) certain information states can be meaningfully identified as highly ambiguous; (2) in these states, many reasonable people tend to violate the Savage axioms with respect to certain choices; (3) their behavior is deliberate and not readily reversed upon reflection; (4) certain patterns of "violating" behavior can be distinguished and described in terms of a specified decision rule.

If these propositions should prove valid, the question of the optimality of this behavior would gain more interest. The mere fact that it conflicts with certain axioms of choice that at first glance appear reasonable does not seem to me to foreclose this question; empirical research, and even preliminary speculation, about the nature of actual or "successful" decision-making under uncertainty is still too young to give us confidence that these axioms are not abstracting away from vital considerations. It would seem incautious to rule peremptorily that the people in question should not allow their perception of ambiguity, their unease with their best estimates of probability, to influence their decision: or to assert that the manner in which they respond to it is against their long-run interest and that they would be in some sense better off if they should go against their deep-felt preferences. If their rationale for their decision behavior is not uniquely compelling (and recent discussions with T. Schelling have raised questions in my mind about it), neither, it seems to me, are the counterarguments. Indeed, it seems out of the question summarily to judge their behavior as irrational: I am included among them.

In any case, it follows from the propositions above that for their behavior in the situations in question, the Bayesian or Savage approach gives wrong predictions and, by their lights, bad advice. They act in conflict with the axioms deliberately, without apology, because it seems to them the sensible way to behave. Are they clearly mistaken?

References

Arrow, K. J. "Alternative approaches to the theory of choice in risk-taking situations," *Econometrica, 19* (1951), 404–437.

Chipman, J. S. "Stochastic choice and subjective probability," in *Decisions, Values and Groups,* ed. by D. Willner, Pergamon Press, New York, 1960.

de Finetti, B. "Recent suggestions for reconciliation of theories of probability," in *Proceedings of the Second Berkeley Symposium on Mathematical Statistics and Probability,* Berkeley, 1951, 217–226.

Fellner, W. "Distortion of subjective probabilities as a reaction to uncertainty," *Quarterly Journal of Economics, 75* (1961), 670–689.

Georgescu-Roegen, N. "Choice, expectation and measurability," *Quarterly Journal of Economics, 68* (1954).

"The Nature of Expectation and Uncertainty," in *Expectation, Uncertainty and Business Behavior,* ed. by M. Bowman, Social Science Research Council, New York, 1958.

Hurwicz, L. "Optimality criteria for decision making under ignorance," *Cowles Commission Discussion Paper, Statistics,* no. 370, 1951a (mimeographed).

"Some specification problems and applications to econometric models," (abstract) *Econometrica, 19* (1951b), 343–344.

Hodges, J. L., and Lehmann, E. L. "The uses of previous experience in reaching statistical decisions," *Annals of Mathematical Statistics, 23* (1952), 396–407.

Knight, F. H. *Risks, Uncertainty and Profit,* Houghton Mifflin, Boston, 1921.

Luce, R. D. *Individual Choice Behavior,* Wiley, New York, 1959.

Luce, R. D., and Raiffa, H. *Games and Decisions,* Wiley, New York, 1957.

Ramsey, F. P. "Truth and probability," in *The Foundations of Mathematics and Other Logical Essays,* ed. by R. B. Braithwaite, Routledge and Kegan Paul, London, 1931, 156–198, and in *Foundations: Essays in Philosophy, Mathematics and Economics,* ed. by D. H. Mellor, Routledge and Kegan Paul, London 1978, 58–100.

Samuelson, P. "Probability and the attempts to measure utility," *The Economic Review* (July 1950), 169–70.

"Probability, utility and the independence axiom," *Econometrica, 20* (1952), 670–678.

Savage, L. J. *The Foundations of Statistics,* John Wiley, New York, 1954; 2nd revised edition, Dover, New York, 1972.

Shackle, G. L. S. *Uncertainty in Economics,* Cambridge University Press, Cambridge, 1955.

Suppes, P., Davidson, D., and Siegel, S. *Decision-Making,* Stanford University Press, Stanford, 1957.

5. Criticism of the postulates and axioms of the American School

Maurice Allais

The historical development of the theoretical concept of the pure psychology of risk

46. The theoretical view of the pure psychology of risk has passed through four successive stages.[1]

(a) In a *first stage,* it was thought that the value V of a random prospect is equal to its mathematical expectation

$$V = p_1 g_1 + p_2 g_2 + \cdots + p_n g_n, \tag{I}$$

i.e. the average value of the possible gains weighted by their objective probabilities.

(b) In a *second stage,* psychological values were introduced to replace the monetary values in the initial formulation. This led to

$$\bar{s}(V) = p_1 \bar{s}(g_1) + p_2 \bar{s}(g_2) + \cdots + p_n \bar{s}(g_n), \tag{II}$$

in which the p_i are objective probabilities.

In this formulation, the rule of probable values is used to combine the utility attaching to different possible gains rather than the gains themselves. This is the hypothesis that Bernoulli naturally came to develop to explain the St. Petersburg paradox, and it was later adopted by Laplace in his theory of *moral expectancy.*[2] More recently, von Neumann and Morgenstern were led to develop a formula corresponding to this approach in their *Theory of Games.*[3]

Reprinted with permission from M. Allais and O. Hagen, eds., *Expected Utility Hypotheses and the Allais Paradox* (Dordrecht: D. Reidel, 1979), 67–95.

[1] In point of fact, some authors do not seem to have got beyond the third. There are even a few who refuse to go beyond the third.

[2] [In French: *espérances morales.*]

[3] In our opinion the same can no doubt be said of Marschak (*Rational Behaviour, Uncertain Prospects and Measurable Utility,* 1950) despite his claim that his indicator $B(g)$ also takes account of the dispersion of psychological values.

(c) In a *third stage,* the idea took root that the individual does not take account of objective probabilities as such, but acts in terms of his psychological perception of these probabilities, i.e., in terms of subjective probabilities. This leads to the formulation

$$\bar{s}(V) = \overline{p_1}\bar{s}(g_1) + \overline{p_2}\bar{s}(g_2) + \cdots + \overline{p_n}\bar{s}(g_n), \qquad \text{(III)}$$

in which the $\bar{p}$ are subjective probabilities. This is still the neo-Bernoullian formulation, but allowing for the replacement of objective by subjective probabilities.[4]

(d) The *fourth stage* consists of the realisation that it is not enough to consider the probability-weighted average psychological value $\gamma = \bar{s}(g)$; the distribution of the probabilities must also be allowed for. This produces the formula

$$\bar{s}(V) = h[\psi(\gamma)], \qquad \text{(IV)}$$

in which h is a functional of the probability density $\psi(\gamma)$ of the psychological values.

The present author's thinking is in terms of this fourth stage, whose implication is that the *dispersion* of the psychological values about their mean is at least as important a factor as the psychological distortion of monetary values and objective probabilities, so that *even in a first approximation,* it is necessary to take account of the shape of the distribution of psychological values, and in particular of the second-order moments of this distribution.

Actual behaviour of man and the psychology of the rational man

47. There seems to be general agreement that the neo-Bernoullian formulation does not successfully represent actual behaviour, and that...various factors...are relevant and should be introduced. However, difficulties arise in specifying how a rational person would be expected to behave under conditions of risk.

To simplify the discussion, the secondary factors...can be neglected in a first approximation; examination will be limited to appraising the characteristics which the pure psychology of risk should possess in order to be rational.

In the first instance an accurate definition must be given of what is meant by the adjective "rational."

The author considers that a person's conduct can be considered rational if it satisfies the general principle of not being self-contradictory. This, in

---

[4] Savage seems to find his place in this stage, although he, like Marschak, claims that his indicator allows for the dispersion of psychological values.

turn, implies two conditions. The first is that the ends pursued should be logically consistent; the second, that the means employed should be appropriate to these ends.

As regards the pure psychology of risk, the first condition implies, on the one hand, that the various random prospects can be classified to constitute an ordered set, and on the other hand, that the axiom of absolute preference is verified. Both are necessary for logical consistency.

The second condition implies that the individual takes account of objective probabilities; from a scientific point of view, this is necessary for action to be efficient.

The author further considers that these two conditions are both necessary and sufficient for the psychology considered to be viewed as rational.

Using the notation presented above, rational psychology can be described in the most general case by

$$\bar{s}(V) = f[\psi(\gamma)], \tag{1}$$

in which f is a functional of the objective frequency function $\psi(\gamma)$ of the psychological values $\gamma = \bar{s}(g)$ under the single constraint that this function must satisfy the axiom of absolute preference.

In particular, there is no reason to consider that where an individual's conduct fails to satisfy the relation

$$\bar{s}(V) = \sum p_i \bar{s}(g_i), \tag{2}$$

it must necessarily be irrational, since an attitude which takes account of the *dispersion* of psychological values, could not be considered as irrational.

In point of fact, it would be improper to brand a cautious man irrational because he is willing to accept a lower psycho-mathematical expectation as the price of lower dispersion. Nor can a person who enjoys risk as such be labelled as irrational, merely because he accepts a lower psycho-mathematical expectation as the counterpart of the availability of some chance of extremely high psychological gain. He may be felt to be imprudent – this is as may be – but it seems impossible to say that he is irrational.[5]

It cannot be too strongly emphasized *that there are no criteria for the rationality of ends as such other than the condition of consistency.* Ends are completely arbitrary. To prefer highly dispersed random outcomes may seem irrational to the prudent, but for somebody with this penchant, there is nothing irrational about it. This area is like that of tastes: they are what they are, and differ from one person to the next.[6]

---

[5] Although again, there are cases in which a cautious, rational subject could well prefer dispersion to mathematical expectation.

[6] This is a real truism, but in an epoch in which totalitarian tendencies are rife, no language is too strong to denounce the propensity of many of our contemporaries for branding as *irrational* any behaviour that is not to their taste. In Calvin's day, it was considered irrational to play cards, and this activity was therefore forbidden in Geneva.

The neo-Bernoullian formulation and the law of large numbers

48. Basically, the intuitive justification of formulations founded on the mathematical expectation of psychological values is the law of large numbers.

Consideration of monetary values

(A) *To simplify the discussion, first assume that psychological gain is equal to monetary gain.* This assumption is approximately true over any region of the cardinal utility curve in which the curve and its tangent are practically indistinguishable.

The law of large numbers tells us that in the long run, the average gain will tend, in the sense of the statistical theory, to its mathematical expectation. In other words, there is always a number of trials or events, n, which is large enough for the probability of a deviation between the average gain and the mathematical expectation to become smaller than any pre-selected number ϵ. The conclusion drawn is that the rule of mathematical expectation holds.

This rule has already generated much heated debate, and in all likelihood, there is still more to come.[7] The following points are worth making:

(1) *If I am able to participate in a long series of games, but could be ruined early on, possibly even in the first round, it is obvious that the justification of the rule of mathematical expectation by the law of large numbers is invalid.* There would be little consolation for me in the knowledge that, had I been able to hold on, my winnings would probably have tended to the value of their mathematical expectation.

(2) *At all events, there is a limit to the number of rounds in which I can participate,* if only because my life span is limited. Thus there is always some dispersion of the average gain to be allowed for. In practice, the concept of a very long series of trials is not realistic, and the dispersion of the average gain is never negligible in practice.[8]

(3) *Even if I were genuinely able to participate in an extremely large number of trials, it is by no means evident that my optimum strategy would be to rely on the rule of mathematical expectation.* What matters to the player is not the average gain but the cumulative gain and its distribution.

Let us assume for example, that the gain in a unit round of a game is distributed according to the Laplace–Gauss law, with an average value of m_1 and a standard deviation of σ_1. In a series of n rounds, the mathematical expectation will be

$$M = nm_1, \tag{1}$$

---

[7] The best analysis, to the author's knowledge, is that of Paul Lévy, 1925, *Calcul des probabilités,* pp. 111–133.

[8] If it were to become negligible, there would no longer be any problem.

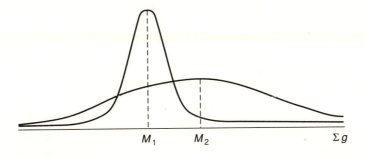

Figure 1

and the standard deviation

$$\Sigma_1 = \sqrt{n}\,\sigma_1. \tag{2}$$

If I have a choice between the strategy (m_1, σ_1) and the strategy (m_2, σ_2) (see Figure 1) with $m_1 < m_2$, $\sigma_1 < \sigma_2$, there is no reason for me necessarily to prefer the second. It is true that for n rounds, my mathematical expectancy would be

$$M_2 - M_1 = n(m_2 - m_1),$$

but at the same time,

$$\Sigma_2 - \Sigma_1 = \sqrt{n}(\sigma_2 - \sigma_1)$$

would hold, and there is no difficulty in finding examples in which a prudent, rational man should clearly prefer the first strategy, even though it is associated with a lower mathematical expectancy and the number of rounds is high.[9,10]

(4) Finally, it is clear that *in the case of an isolated event or trial which is not to be repeated, the justification based on the law of large numbers does not apply at all.*

At the same time, *the specific characteristic of most of the cases in which random decisions are taken is that they in fact relate to isolated events.* In the author's view, the law of large numbers is utterly without relevance here. Everything depends on the special circumstances involved.

The governing factor here is personal psychology. Some will prefer to rely on mathematical expectation, others will attach greater importance to the

---

[9] It would be enough to consider cases in which σ_1 is very small and σ_2 very large.

[10] It must nevertheless be noted that the mathematical expectation formulation is, in general, justified in the sense that it is *generally* advantageous to participate for an *infinite* period in a game whose mathematical expectation is positive, and disadvantageous if it is not.

This does not contradict the hypothesis discussed above, namely, that if two games have positive mathematical expectations, the more advantageous of the two may still be that with the lower expectation.

form of the distribution. No one rule of conduct can be considered as more rational than another.

(5) *The only value of the rule of mathematical expectation is that it provides an overall indication.* In this context, as has already been noted, its service is exactly that yielded by the use of a mean value to summarise a set of numbers. No less, and no more.

Consideration of psychological values

(B) If allowance is now made for the psychological values $\bar{s}(g)$ rather than for the monetary values g, *all the foregoing statements can be transposed without difficulty,* providing the probability distribution of g is replaced by that of $\bar{s}(g)$. Here again, the justification of the rule of mathematical expectation provided by the law of large numbers is a sheer *illusion*.

It is precisely to avoid all these difficulties, which *needlessly and uselessly* complicate the study of the psychology of risk, that we have based all our reasoning on the case of an isolated choice.

Moreover, it is essential to stress here that *it would be wrong to consider that a strategy of maximising the mathematical expectation*

$$\sum p_i \bar{s}(g_i)$$

would be a good first approximation rule in all circumstances, when we have to take a decision concerning a random choice.[11]

> #### Criticism of the neo-Bernoullian formulation as a behavioural rule for rational man

1. The state of the discussion

> #### The views of the supporters of the neo-Bernoullian formulation

49. As far as can be judged, the neo-Bernoullian formulation, as originally presented by von Neumann and Morgenstern,[12] has three characteristics:

(1) It applies to *anybody* whose field of choice is ordered.
(2) It results in *an index $B(g)$ which is identified with cardinal utility* $\bar{s}(g)$.[13] By observing actual random choices it should be possible to

---

[11] This error is especially well demonstrated by the behaviour of a businessman or a gambler who balances the mathematical expectation of the outcome against the probability of ruin (see §65...below). *In this case, the rule of mathematical expectation is, in general, a poor guide, even as a first approximation*.

[12] von Neumann and Morgenstern, 1947, *Theory of Games and Economic Behavior*, pp. 8–31 and 617–632.

[13] Subject, of course, to a linear transformation, a point which must be underlined once for all.

determine cardinal utility. This thesis naturally implies that the neo-Bernoullian formulation is capable of providing a suitable portrayal of the behaviour of real man, and therefore of forecasting it.[14]

(3)   It uses *objective probabilities* as weighting coefficients.

Marschak's formulation[15] has the three following characteristics:

(1)   It relates not to the actual behaviour of real man, but to what a *rational* man's behaviour ought to be.[16]
(2)   It yields *an index B(g) which,* according to the statements of the proponents of this formulation (Marschak, Samuelson, Friedman), is claimed to be *distinct from cardinal utility $\bar{s}(g)$.*[17]
(3)   Like the preceding formulation, it uses *objective probabilities* for weighting.

The third formulation is that given by Savage, and it also has three distinguishing features:

(1)   Like the second, it applies only to *rational* behaviour.
(2)   It yields an index $B(g)$ which, like the second formulation, is claimed to be *distinct from cardinal utility $\bar{s}(g)$.*
(3)   It uses *subjective probabilities.*

As can be seen, *these three positions are very different.* In particular, the American School has in fact put forward two claims:

(1)   Actual behaviour can be represented by the neo-Bernoullian formulation, and in conjunction with the observation of choices involving risk, this formulation provides a means of determining cardinal utility.
(2)   The neo-Bernoullian formulation is capable of portraying only the behaviour of rational man.

The questions presently under discussion

50. *At present,* the following points seem to be accepted by all proponents[18] of the neo-Bernoullian formulation:

---

[14] This is the position taken by Friedman and Savage in their 1948 paper "The Utility Analysis of Choices Involving Risk," and by Frederick Mosteller and Philip Nogee in their 1951 paper "Experimental Measurement of Utility."

[15] Marschak, 1950, op. cit.

[16] It should be noted that the von Neumann–Morgenstern analysis *nowhere* makes any mention of a rationality condition, at least explicitly.

[17] Milton Friedman initially argued that the two indexes B and $\bar{s}$ were identical subject only to a linear transformation, a point of view similar to that of von Neumann–Morgenstern. He subsequently felt constrained to adopt this fallback position.

[18] Who participated in the 1952 Colloquium in Paris, i.e. de Finetti, Friedman, Marschak, Samuelson and Savage.

(1) The formulation does not apply to actual behaviour. It is used only to describe the behaviour of a "rational" man.

(2) The index $B(g)$ is distinct from the indicator of cardinal utility $\bar{s}(g)$.

The view that the two indexes $B(g)$ and $\bar{s}(g)$ would be one and the same has gradually had to be abandoned,[19] and there is currently no support[20] for the thesis that cardinal utility can be measured by examining empirical data on choices involving risk, a thesis which would imply that real behaviour can be suitably portrayed by the neo-Bernoullian formulation.

It is easy to see why this view had to be abandoned. *If the identity*

$$B(g) \equiv \bar{s}(g)$$

were accepted, the neo-Bernoullian formulation would clearly ignore the dispersion of psychological values . . ., and this would lead to considering as irrational the attitude of a careful person who attaches weight to this dispersion. Such a position is manifestly untenable.[21]

Thus the original contention of the Bernoullian school has been laid aside, and at present the only difference in viewpoint relates to the definition of the concept of probability. Savage and de Finetti claim that only subjective probabilities exist, whereas Marschak uses objective probabilities. However, as regards the behaviour of a rational man, Savage would no doubt agree that it is proper to consider objective probabilities defined with reference to experimentally observed frequencies.

If this can be taken as so, the central argument of the proponents of the neo-Bernoullian formulation[22] is that an index $B(g)$ necessarily exists for any rational individual such that the value V of any random prospect is given by the relation

$$B(V) = \sum_i p_i B(g_i) \tag{1}$$

with

$$\sum p_i = 1, \tag{2}$$

the p_i being objective probabilities.

From this standpoint, the index $B(g)$ is considered to include allowance both for the psychological distortion of monetary values and the utility (or

---

[19] In their 1948 article, "The Utility Analysis of Choices Involving Risk," Friedman and Savage interpreted the Bernoulli formula as relating to cardinal utility. They no longer argue this, and speak only of a choice-generating index. However, in a number of papers, Friedman still seems to be identifying the two concepts.

[20] Among the participants in the 1952 Colloquium (see Note [18] above).

[21] [This paragraph was Note 66 of the original French text.]

[22] In particular Baumol, de Finetti, Friedman, Marschak, von Neumann–Morgenstern, Samuelson and Savage. It should be noted that Samuelson, whose point of view was similar to the present author's as recently as two years ago (i.e., 1950) has now gone over to the other camp.

disutility) associated with the shape of the probability distribution of the psychological values....

It may be noted in passing that these two elements are not considered to be "irrational." It is accepted that a rational individual's scale of psychological values may differ from the monetary scale, and that he may have a greater or lesser propensity for safety or for risk. There seems to be agreement that this is an issue of psychology and not of "rationality."

The argument developed below *casts doubt on the validity of relation (1) for a rational man.* It will be argued that the neo-Bernoullian formulation is not only incapable of representing the behaviour of real man properly, or of determining cardinal utility, but more, that *even for a rational man,* the linkage between the value V and gains g_i is in general of much more complex form:

$$\bar{s}(V) = f(g_1, g_2, ..., g_n, p_1, p_2, ..., p_n), \tag{3}$$

a relation which, in the case of the pure psychology of risk can be written in the form

$$\bar{s}(V) = \sum_i \alpha_i(g_1, g_2, ..., g_n, p_1, p_2, ..., p_n)\bar{s}(g_i), \tag{4}$$

in which

$$\sum_i \alpha_i(g_1, g_2, ..., g_n, p_1, p_2, ..., p_n) = 1, \tag{5}$$

but the α_i are in general distinct from the probabilities p_i so that in general *no index $B(g)$ exists which satisfies the neo-Bernoullian formulation.*

The author accepts that a rational man may well act according to the Bernoulli formulation, but in this case, his index $B(g)$ will necessarily be identical to his cardinal utility, and we will have[23] $B(g) \equiv \bar{s}(g)$ so that if he does follow the Bernoulli formulation, this is because of his specific psychology vis-à-vis risk, which renders him indifferent to the dispersion of psychological values. But in general, there is no reason for this to be so; rather the opposite.

In the light of the remarks made earlier on the dispersion of psychological values..., our point of view is that *the American School's psychological theory of risk neglects the specific feature of this psychology, namely the dispersion of psychological values, which is omitted in its initial axioms.*

The sophisticated mathematical deductions with which the American School has conducted its analysis should not mislead us. Only the initial premises and the interpretation of the results are of real significance. However complex the mathematical development of the deductions, it has no intrinsic value beyond its purely mathematical interest, which is irrelevant from the standpoint of economic analysis that concerns us here. *The complexity or*

---

[23] Possibly subject to a linear transformation it is recalled once again.

scientific value of the deductive process can never confer scientific value on the premisses.

Definition of rationality

51. To derive the neo-Bernoullian formulation, the American School starts from various systems of axioms or postulates. But in fact it is clear – and this is an important point – that it is not relevant to define rationality in terms of obedience to any of these systems, for, in this case, *there could not possibly be any discussion.*

The neo-Bernoullian formulation is in fact rigorously equivalent to any one whatsoever of these systems of axioms, and there is clearly *no interest at all* in discussing the view that a rational man should behave according to the neo-Bernoullian formulation when rationality is itself defined in terms of obedience to one of the systems of axioms from which that principle is deduced. *This is a tautological proposition, and therefore useless scientifically.*

To discuss the proposition "should a rational man act according to the neo-Bernoullian formulation" is meaningful *only if rationality is defined other than by direct or indirect reference to that formulation.*

It is therefore necessary to define what is meant by "rationality." In practice, two definitions are possible, depending whether the standpoint taken is that of abstract reasoning or that of experience.

(a) Abstract definition of rationality

52. Other than the pseudo-definition of rationality in terms of respect of their systems of axioms, the proponents of the neo-Bernoullian formulation offer nothing by way of a precise statement. Given this gap, and as we have already indicated,[24] we must have recourse to the definition which is suggested by scientific logic: a man will be deemed to act rationally

- (a) if he pursues ends that are mutually consistent (i.e. not contradictory),
- (b) if he employs means that are appropriate to these ends.

As has been noted, the only consequences which these two conditions entail are:

- (1) that the field of choice is ordered;
- (2) that the axiom of absolute preference is satisfied;
- (3) that objective probabilities are considered.

Points (1) and (2) are contested by nobody. As regards point (3) it seems hard to dispute that it would be of advantage to replace the objective probabilities by subjective probabilities which would be distinct from them.

---

[24] §47 above.

It is important to underline that the three points listed are the *only* consequences of the consistency condition. In particular, it cannot be accepted that either Savage's fifth axiom of independence[25] or Samuelson's substitution axiom[26] constitute conditions of consistency.

So far as Savage's fifth axiom is concerned, if...two equivalent prospects share a common component, there is no necessary reason for this equivalence to subsist if the common component undergoes a shift. To the contrary: it is clear that this shift will alter the form of the probability distribution of the psychological values.[27]

Similarly, it is impossible to take Samuelson's substitution axiom as absolutely indispensable from the standpoint of rationality. Let (P_1) and (P_2) be two equivalent prospects, whose equivalence is expressed by the symbolic relation $(P_1) = (P_2)$.

The substitution axiom signifies that if (P_3) is any random prospect whatever, then, for any α, we should have

$$\alpha(P_1) + (1-\alpha)(P_3) = \alpha(P_2) + (1-\alpha)(P_3),$$

where the symbol $[\alpha(P_1) + (1-\alpha)(P_3)]$ stands for a lottery ticket which offers the probability α of prospect (P_1) and the probability $(1-\alpha)$ of prospect (P_3). This axiom is justified, it is claimed, because whether or not the event whose probability is α occurs, the individual concerned will ultimately be in possession of two equivalent prospects. In reality, this claim is unacceptable, for it assumes that the first drawing, corresponding to the probabilities $[\alpha, (1-\alpha)]$ is *neutral*. In fact *it is not*. This is an *ex post* conclusion, whereas the problem must be viewed *ex ante*.[28]

If the above definition of rationality is not accepted, another must be put forward. So far, none has, and it seems idle to discuss what might be proposed in its place. Actually, it is hard at this stage to see what could be.[29]

(b) Experimental definition of rationality

53. If it is not felt possible or desirable to use an abstract definition of rationality, the only option is to rely on experience, *and to observe the behaviour of men whom one has reason in other respects to believe act rationally.*

In the author's view, *the adherents of the neo-Bernoullian school should be asked to reply clearly to the three following questions:*

[25] Savage, ["An Axiomatization of Reasonable Behavior in the Face of Uncertainty," *Colloques Internationaux XL, Econométrie* (1953), 29–33].

[26] Samuelson, ["Utility, Preference, and Probability," *Colloques Internationaux XL, Econométrie* (1953), 141–50].

[27] See §63 below for a detailed criticism of Savage's fifth axiom.

[28] See §64...below.

[29] It may be noted in passing that no objection to the proposed definition was raised in the discussion of the present paper during the 1952 Paris Colloquium.

(1)   Do you directly or indirectly define rationality as meaning obedience to your axioms?

(2)   If not, do you accept an abstract definition, and if so, which one?

(3)   In the absence of an abstract definition other than one couched in terms of obedience to your axioms, do you accept that rationality can be defined by having regard to the behaviour of persons who are commonly considered as rational?[30]

2. Refutation of the neo-Bernoullian formulation

Conditions for refutation of the neo-Bernoullian formulation

54. As the neo-Bernoullian formulation is claimed to be general, it may be refuted by providing as little as *one example* of rational behaviour which does not correspond either to the final formulation or any of the systems of postulates to which it is equivalent.

This having been stated clearly, the refutation presented below comprises two parts. In the first, using the abstract definition of rationality, we show that the rational man will not necessarily follow the neo-Bernoullian formulation. The second part is an analysis of the behaviour of persons who are generally considered as rational, and which is absolutely incompatible with the neo-Bernoullian formulation.

For reasons set forth earlier,[31] the discussion will deal with...the case of a single choice involving risk.[32]

A. Refutation of the neo-Bernoullian formulation based on the abstract definition of rationality

1. The neo-Bernoullian formulation is more restrictive than the axiom of absolute preference

55. It will first be shown that the axiom of absolute preference does not suffice in itself to entail the existence of an index $B(x)$ which satisfies the neo-Bernoullian relation.[33]

This can be seen as follows. Let (P_1), (P_2) and (P_3) be random prospects which can take material shape as three lottery tickets, and assume that (P_3) is preferred to (P_1) and (P_2). Using $>$ to denote preference, we have

$$(P_1) < (P_3), \qquad (P_2) < (P_3). \tag{1}$$

---

[30] The end of §53 was Note 72 of the original French text.

[31] § ...48 above.

[32] This same frame is admitted by the American School.

[33] This demonstration is due to MM. Massé and Morlat.

It can be shown [34] that if the inequalities (1) necessarily entail the inequality

$$[\alpha(P_1) + (1-\alpha)(P_2)] < (P_3), \tag{2}$$

(using the symbol $[\alpha(P_1) + (1-\alpha)P_2]$ to denote a lottery ticket with a probability α of winning the ticket (P_1) as prize and $(1-\alpha)$ of winning the ticket (P_2), α having any value whatever,[35] then there necessarily exists an index $B(x)$ which satisfies the neo-Bernoullian formulation. Conversely, if the neo-Bernoullian formulation is verified, the conditions (1) imply condition (2).

However, if it is assumed only that the axiom of absolute preference is verified it cannot in general be affirmed that conditions (1) imply condition (2). All that can be said is that the conditions

$$(P_1) \ll (P_3), \qquad (P_2) \ll (P_3), \tag{3}$$

necessarily entail

$$\lceil \alpha(P_1) + (1-\alpha)(P_2)] \ll (P_3), \tag{4}$$

using the sign $\ll$ to denote absolute preference, and this in turn implies

$$[\alpha(P_1) + (1-\alpha)P_2] < (P_3). \tag{5}$$

Let P be the total probability that the outcome will be some figure between $-\infty$ and x. Then, from the principle of compound probabilities

$$P_{12} = \alpha P_1 + (1-\alpha)P_2, \tag{6}$$

where P_{12} is the probability P that the compound lottery ticket

$$[\alpha(P_1) + (1-\alpha)(P_2)]$$

will yield a gain exceeding g. Thus we have in Figure 2 the geometric equality

$$P_1 P_{12} = (1-\alpha)P_1 P_2. \tag{7}$$

In this figure, the curve representing the random prospect P_{12} lies between the curves of the prospects P_1 and P_2, so that geometrically, and in the light of the earlier analysis, it can be verified immediately that the conditions (3) do indeed imply condition (4) and therefore condition (5).

At the same time, it can be verified that the axiom of absolute preference is less restrictive than the neo-Bernoullian formulation or any of the equivalent systems of axioms.

---

[34] See the works of the American School, especially the investigations of Marschak (1950), Samuelson (1953) and Savage ([*The Foundations of Statistics,* Wiley, New York,] 1954).

[35] This property, taken as an axiom by the American School, is merely a variant of the substitutability axiom which considers two equivalent prospects (P_1) and (P_2) as substitutable in a compound prospect, implying

$$\alpha(P_1) + (1-\alpha)(P_3) = \alpha(P_2) + (1-\alpha)(P_3),$$

where (P_3) is any prospect whatsoever.

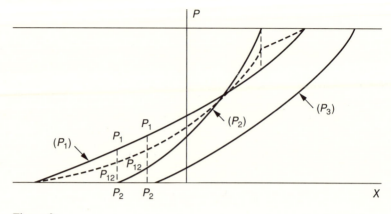

Figure 2

2. Rationality in no way implies the neo-Bernoullian formulation

56. The foregoing yields an immediate refutation of the neo-Bernoullian formulation as the rational man's guide to behaviour, using an abstract definition of rationality.

Such a definition was given earlier.[36] If it is accepted – and no other has been put forward apart from some pseudo-definitions which can only lead to tautological propositions in the areas that concern us here – then the *only implications* of rational conduct are:

(a)   use of an ordered field of choice;
(b)   use of objective probabilities;
(c)   conformity with the axiom of absolute preference.[37]

Now, these three properties are insufficient to deduce the existence of an index $B(g)$ such that[38]

$$B(V) = \sum_i p_i B(g_i),$$

where V is the value of the random prospect

$$(g_1, g_2, ..., g_n, p_1, p_2, ..., p_n).$$

---

[36] §52 above.

[37] A very important point in the context of the present discussion is that we have not defined rationality by referring to the axiom of absolute preference. To have done so would have been to fall into the same trap as the American School.

    The axiom of absolute preference (so-called in order to align our terminology on that of Massé and Morlat) is merely a *consequence* of the mutual consistency that ought to characterise the ends pursued by a rational individual.

[38] To see this, it is enough to verify, as was done above (§55), that the axiom of absolute preference is much less restrictive than any of the systems of axioms that imply the neo-Bernoullian formulation.

It follows that:

(1)   To be rational, an individual's behaviour need not necessarily be what the neo-Bernoullian formulation would have it be.

(2)   In reality, given that the consequences of the abstract definition of rationality are less restrictive than the axioms of the neo-Bernoullian school, the latter contain one or more additional constraints which *may* actually be *irrational*.

3. Examples of rational behaviour satisfying the axiom of absolute preference without satisfying the neo-Bernoullian formulation

It is easy to find a number of particularly simple examples of a psychology that meets the criterion of absolute preference without satisfying the neo-Bernoullian formulation.

(1) The choice between different gains g of probability p.   **57.** Consider an individual having to choose between random prospects each consisting of a gain g_i whose probability is p_i, and assume that his ordinal preference function is given by

$$S = f(g, p). \tag{1}$$

This function satisfies the criterion of absolute preference if we have

$$\partial f/\partial g > 0, \qquad \partial f/\partial p > 0. \tag{2}$$

But in general it does not satisfy the neo-Bernoullian formulation, which would require

$$S = f[pB(g)], \tag{3}$$

where f and B are increasing functions. In other words, according to the neo-Bernoullian formulation, the preference index should be an increasing function of the product $pB(g)$.

This verifies the markedly greater restrictiveness of the neo-Bernoullian formulation.[39]

(2) The choice between prospects distributed according to the normal law.
58. Consider an individual having to choose between a number of random prospects (P) that can be described by *normal distributions* of mean M and standard deviation Σ, and assume that in order to make this particular choice,[40] his preference index is of the form

---

[39] It should be stressed at this point that there seem no particularly good grounds for considering an individual's psychology as irrational if his preference index is given by relation (1) subject to the conditions (2) of §57.

[40] For this purpose, it is enough to assume that the functional ... $S = h[\varphi(g)]$ of the subject reduces to expressions (1) of §58 when the density $\varphi(g)$ is distributed according to the normal law.

$$S = f(M, \Sigma).$$ (1)

For the axiom of absolute preference to be satisfied, it is necessary and sufficient that *for given* Σ, the index S should be an increasing function of M, i.e. that

$$\partial f / \partial M > 0.$$ (2)

It is easy to see that in general no index $B(x)$ exists such that we could have

$$f(M, \Sigma) = \int_{-\infty}^{+\infty} B(x) \frac{\exp[-(x-M)^2/2\Sigma^2]}{\sqrt{2\pi}\,\Sigma}\, dx,$$ (3)

with

$$B'_x > 0.$$ (4)

This further example again shows that the neo-Bernoullian formulation is much more restrictive than it need be in terms of rationality alone.[41]

(3) The choice between alternative prospects with an average gain of M and a probability P of a loss exceeding X.   **59.** Now consider an individual who has to choose between various prospects each of which is characterized by an average gain M and a probability P of experiencing a loss in excess of a given value X.[42]

Any field of choice

$$S = f(M, P)$$ (1)

satisfies the axiom of absolute preference providing that it is true simultaneously that

$$\partial S / \partial M > 0, \qquad \partial S / \partial P < 0.$$ (2)

Consider the two curves C_1 and C_2 of Figure 3. If the curve C_2 lies about the curve C_1, the two conditions

$$M_1 < M_2, \qquad P_1 > P_2,$$ (3)

hold (Figure 3). Figure 4 shows that these conditions indeed imply the conditions (2), and vice-versa.[43]

But it can also be shown that in general, the psychological pattern (1) does not satisfy the neo-Bernoullian formulation, which requires a function of the type

$$S = f(M - aP),$$ (4)

in which a is a positive constant.

---

[41] It is again hard to see how an individual whose behaviour when choosing among various Gaussian i.e. normal distributions is represented by relation (1) of §58, the distribution being normal, could be considered as irrational.

[42] If X is the player's fortune, P represents the probability of his ruin.

[43] [The last paragraph is Note 87 of the original French text of 1952.]

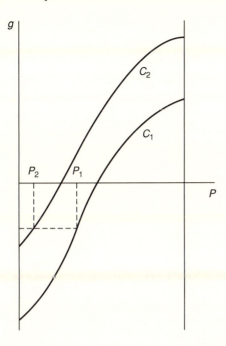

Figure 3

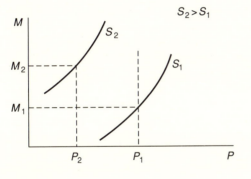

Figure 4

Thus it is verified that in general a field of choice of the type (1) and (2) satisfies the axiom of absolute preference without verifying the neo-Bernoullian formulation.

Finally, it should be observed that the neo-Bernoullian formula's general inability to portray the psychology of an individual who balances the mathematical expectation of his monetary gains against his probability of losing more than a certain sum is repeated in the case in which the balance concerns

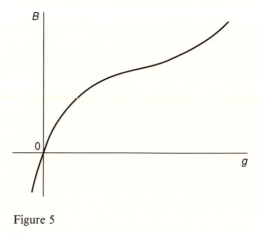

Figure 5

the mathematical expectation of the psychological values and the probability of a loss exceeding a certain threshold.

B. *Refutation of the neo-Bernoullian formulation using the experimental definition of rationality*

60. In the absence of an abstract definition of rationality that leads to anything but tautological propositions, recourse must be had to the experimental definition yielded by *observation of the behaviour of men who may be considered as rational and who are fully familiar with the calculus of probabilities.* It is then possible to cite the following *facts indicated by experience* as being in opposition to the neo-Bernoullian formulation or any of the corresponding sets of axioms or postulates:

1. *The simultaneous purchase of lottery tickets and insurance policies*

61. In order to make the neo-Bernoullian formulation cover the fact that lottery tickets and insurance policies can be and are bought concurrently, Friedman and Savage[44] were obliged to endow their index with a complicated shape, the second derivative d^2B/dg^2 being initially positive and then becoming negative (see Figure 5).

To the extent that one accepts, *as they did in 1948,* that

$$\bar{s}(g) \equiv B(g), \tag{1}$$

the conclusion must be that in some cases the marginal utility of money could be an increasing function of the gain, which I consider to be in flagrant contradiction to introspective data. Any tests that could be invented in this area would lead to the same conclusion.

[44] *The Utility Analysis of Choices Involving Risk,* 1948.

The objection evidently vanishes if it is claimed, *as Friedman and Savage now do,* that the index $B(g)$ is distinct from the utility function;[45] but as will be seen below, this claim is difficult to maintain.

2. The behaviour of the very prudent in choices with risk involving small sums

62. In the local domain, for *small values* of gains g, changes in the index $B(g)$ may be considered as practically linear, and in this case the component producing its curvature is eliminated. Thus if a neo-Bernoullian index exists, it implies in this case that $V = \Sigma\, p_i g_i$, i.e. the value of a random prospect is equal to its mathematical expectation.

Nevertheless, experience shows that very cautious people who are commonly considered as rational may prefer \$4 to one chance in two of winning \$10; or a gain of \$400 to one chance in two of winning \$1000, etc. In formulating this question, it should be made clear that this is a *once-only offer,* not to be repeated, i.e. a single choice.[46]

This is an incontestable experimental observation, and it is hard to see how, from the standpoint of rationality, a person with a marked preference for safety could be open to criticism. *However this type of behaviour undermines the fundamental position of the American School.*[47]

3. Choices in the neighbourhood of certainty undermining Savage's principle of independence

63. Under Savage's fifth axiom,[48] the order of preference of two random prospects (1) and (2) having a part in common is left unchanged by any displacement of this part. This can be called the independence principle, for it brings out an essential aspect of the neo-Bernoullian formulation (see Figure 6).

It is easy to build up many examples in which the answer given by reputedly rational people would run counter to Savage's fundamental axiom.[49] One

---

[45] Although even here, the shape of the index $B(g)$ should be assumed to be complicated enough.

[46] See what we have already said on this point in... §48 above.

[47] Savage has objected that marked curvature of the index could serve to explain such behaviour. A priori, this explanation is not very convincing (although it is of course theoretically possible). *In practice, it is invalidated by the fact that the index determined by the analysis of other random prospects is necessarily only slightly curved for small sums.* This is a decisive proof that, in general, no index exists which is capable of explaining choices involving risk by the neo-Bernoullian formulation.

    The sample taken subsequently in 1952 provided *decisive confirmation of the views expressed above.*

[48] Savage, 1952, *An Axiomatisation of Reasonable Behavior in the Face of Uncertainty.*

[49] After the May 1952 symposium, a sample was run using many similar examples (see Allais, 1953, "La psychologie de l'homme rationnel devant le risque").

    The results will be published as soon as possible. The subjects were all people who are generally considered as eminently rational, and all in all, the results provided very strong support of the author's views. All the tests used were based on the fundamental idea that the psychological value of a gain with which a given probability is associated is not independent

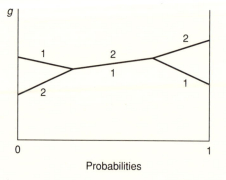

Figure 6

need only, as a general rule, choose extreme cases in which the advantages (or drawbacks) of complementarity may be particularly strong. This is particularly true of the choice between certain and uncertain gains whose value is high by comparison with the player's fortune. It is easy here to show the considerable psychological importance attaching to the advantage of certainty as such. Figures 7(a) and (b) present the geometrical portrayal of two following questions: [50]

(1) *Do you prefer Situation A to Situation B?*
     Situation A:
       – *certainty* of receiving 100 million.
     Situation B:
       – *a 10% chance* of winning 500 million,
       – *an 89% chance* of winning 100 million,
       – *a 1% chance* of winning nothing.
(2) *Do you prefer Situation C to Situation D?*
     Situation C:
       – *an 11% chance* of winning 100 million,
       – *an 89% chance* of winning nothing.
     Situation D:
       – *a 10% chance* of winning 500 million,
       – *a 90% chance* of winning nothing.

If Savage's postulate were justified, the preference $A > B$ should entail $C > D$.

What one finds, however, is that the pattern for most highly prudent persons, the curvature of whose satisfaction curves is not very marked, and

of the gains attaching to the other probabilities, although according to the neo-Bernoullian formulation, it should be.

[50] [All the examples which follow were given in French francs at 1952 prices. 100 French francs in 1952 were worth about the same as 10 dollars in 1975.]

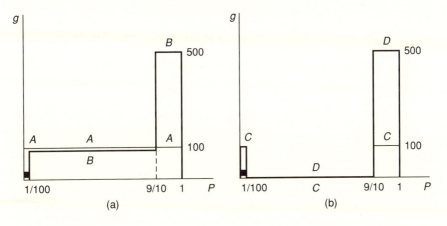

Figure 7

who are considered generally as rational, is the pairing $A > B$ and $C < D$. This contradicts Savage's fifth axiom.

It should be noted that the mathematical expectations attaching to the four situations are (in millions of units)

$$a = 100, \qquad b = 139, \qquad c = 11, \qquad d = 50.$$

Given the curvature of their cardinal utility function and the advantages of safety, most prudent persons prefer A, even though its mathematical expectancy is some 40% below that of B. However, this curvature is not generally marked enough for them to prefer D to C, although the ratio of mathematical expectations is 1 to 5. It will be remarked that for questions C and D, the complementarity effect corresponding to the 1% chance of a zero win is small.

This example is a good illustration of the *pseudo-evident* character of Savage's axiom V. *That it is accepted by so many is due to the fact that not all its implications are perceived, although far from being rational; some of them are in certain psychological situations wholly irrational* (as for example, in the case described above of the highly prudent individual whose personal assessment of value continues to increase perceptibly in the neighbourhood of 100 million).

4. Choices in the neighbourhood of certainty undermining Samuelson's principle of substitutability

64. Samuelson's substitutability principle asserts that if, in the notation of §52

$$(P_1) < (P_2), \tag{1}$$

then

$$(P_1') \equiv \alpha(P_1) + (1-\alpha)(P_3) < (P_2') \equiv \alpha(P_2) + (1-\alpha)(P_3), \qquad (2)$$

where (P_3) and α are respectively any prospect and any probability.

As a result, the order of preference for (P_1) and (P_2) is not reversed by compounding them with any other outcome whatsoever (P_3). *This clearly implies that there is no complementarity effect capable of upsetting this order.*[51]

This being so, examples of rational persons' behaviour invalidating this axiom are easy to find. *All that is needed is to find cases in which the complementarity relations of (P_3) with (P_1) and (P_2) (or the absence of such relations) may change the order of preference.*

To illustrate this, let (P_2) be a certain gain, and (P_1) an uncertain one. Any compound prospect (P_1') removes the certainty (i.e. the advantage of complementarity) attaching to the right-hand member of the inequality (1), whereas the left hand member is not affected in this way. Thus, . . . consider the following case:

$$P_1 \begin{cases} 98\%: & 500 \text{ million} \\ 2\%: & 0 \end{cases} \qquad P_2 \begin{cases} 100 \text{ million} \\ \text{certain} \end{cases} \qquad P_3 \begin{cases} 1 \text{ certain} \end{cases}$$

Experience shows that the acknowledgedly rational but prudent will prefer the *certainty* of 100 million to be received to a 98% chance of winning 500 million, associated with a 2% chance of not winning anything. For them we will have:

$$(P_1) < (P_2). \qquad (1)$$

But *at the same time,* they may prefer a 0.98% chance of winning 500 million (mathematical expectation: 4.9 million) to a 1% chance of winning 100 million (mathematical expectation: 1 million) because, *once far away from certainty, they weight psychological values by probabilities,* i.e. according

---

[51] A parallel with certainly available goods shows this particularly well. Suppose I am appraising three pieces of furniture (M_1), (M_2) and (M_3), and prefer (M_2) to (M_1), then

$$(M_1) < (M_2). \qquad (1)$$

It does not follow that

$$(M_1) + (M_3) < (M_2) + (M_3), \qquad (2)$$

for (M_3) may be *complementary* to (M_1), but not to (M_2), which can upset the preference ordering. Condition (1) can entail (2) *only if the items considered are independent.*

The consequence of the independence hypothesis for certainly available goods is the relation

$$\bar{S}(A, B, ..., C) = \varphi_A(A) + \varphi_B(B) + \cdots + \varphi_C(C) \qquad (3)$$

in which $\bar{S}$ is cardinal utility, or the relation

$$S(A, B, ..., C) = F[\varphi_A(A) + \varphi_B(B) + \cdots + \varphi_C(C)] \qquad (4)$$

in which S is ordinal utility and F any increasing function, which shows how utterly close is the connection between this independence hypothesis and the neo-Bernoullian formulation.

to the rule $\bar{s}(V) = \sum p_i \bar{s}(g_i)$ and their $\bar{s}(g)$ functions may attach a markedly higher psychological value to 500 million than to 100 million.

For such persons, this second preference pattern yields:

$$(P_1') = \frac{1}{100}(P_1) + \frac{99}{100}(P_3) > (P_2') \equiv \frac{1}{100}(P_2) + \frac{99}{100}(P_3).$$

We have the following:

$$(P_1') = \frac{1}{100}(P_1) + \frac{99}{100}(P_3) \equiv \begin{cases} 0.98\%: & 500 \text{ million} \\ 99\%: & 1 \\ 0.02\%: & 0 \end{cases}$$

or approximately

$$\begin{cases} 0.98\%: & 500 \text{ million} \\ 99.02\%: & 0 \end{cases}$$

and

$$(P_2') = \frac{1}{100}(P_2) + \frac{99}{100}(P_3) \equiv \begin{cases} 1\%: & 100 \text{ million} \\ 99\%: & 1 \end{cases}$$

or practically

$$\begin{cases} 1\%: & 100 \text{ million} \\ 99\%: & 0 \end{cases}$$

This is *an observation from experience* which invalidates Samuelson's substitution principle.

In the author's opinion, *nobody could say that persons acting in this way are behaving irrationally* because they attach a high value to certainty, but, where the outcome is far from certain, weight psychological values by their probabilities. If somebody does wish to argue the contrary, it would be quite fascinating to hear his grounds!

5. Entrepreneurial behaviour when large losses may be incurred
65. Observation shows that prudent businessmen act as though they were balancing the probable gain g against the probability P of a loss exceeding X.[52] In other words, their ordinal preference index is of the form

$$S = f(M, P), \tag{1}$$

with [53]

$$\partial S/\partial M > 0, \qquad \partial S/\partial P < 0. \tag{2}$$

Once the probability P attaching to an activity becomes at all significant its potential yield must be substantial, or it will not be undertaken. The

[52] See Note [42] above.
[53] As for the player...who must balance his probable winnings after n plays against the corresponding probability of ruin.

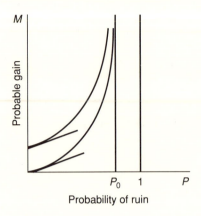

Figure 8

ultra-cautious will purely and simply eliminate all random prospects for which the probability of ruin exceeds a certain threshold value.

As we have seen earlier, a preference of type (1) and (2) satisfies the axiom of absolute preference, but can only satisfy the neo-Bernoullian formulation if it is of the form [54]

$$S = f(M - aP). \tag{3}$$

If it is accepted (*as seems psychologically very natural and at all events highly rational*) that M increases more quickly than P for a given level of the preference index, this linear structure of preference curves is absolutely excluded.

Is it really possible to consider as irrational a person who, for each choice among random prospects, takes his decision by weighing the probable gain M against the probability P of losing more than a certain sum X which he wishes not to exceed in any circumstances, acting according to the neo-Bernoullian formulation *for small values* of M and P (parallel lines), but abstaining completely from any project which he judges has a 90% or greater probability of losing X? His indifference function would be of the form shown in Figure 8, and this is, in general, absolutely incompatible with the neo-Bernoullian formulation.

If, as seems psychologically admissible, the psychology of uncertainty is continuous, a linear form of the type (3) is absolutely impossible.

Consider a sum M_0 whose psychological value is great, for instance $M_0 = \$1$ million. On the same indifference line we would have

$$1 = M - aP,$$

---

[54] §59 above.

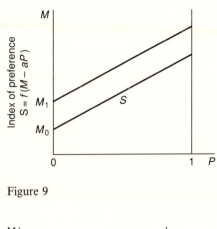

Figure 9

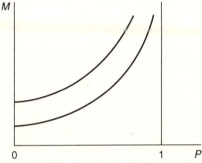

Figure 10

which relation intimates that any random prospect providing a probable gain of M million with a probability P of ruin is worth 1 million. Now, if $P = 1$, ruin is certain, and the value of the certainty of the ruin cannot be valued at \$1 million. This is inadmissible and in fact no indifference curve can cut the vertical axis $P = 1$. Figure 9 is really impossible and reality corresponds to Figure 8 or 10.[55]

At all events, any form of behaviour corresponding to $S = f(M, P)$ functions, which satisfy the general conditions (2), seems to be perfectly possible psychologically, and there seems no reason for branding it as irrational.[56,57]

---

[55] [These two paragraphs are Notes 98 and 99 of the original French text of 1952.]

[56] In this regard, see also the very interesting remarks by Massé and Morlat on the behaviour of the insurers described in Dubourdieu's mathematical theory of insurance (Massé et Morlat, 1952, "Sur le Classement Economique des Perspectives Aléatoires").

[57] It is of interest to note that if the behavioural rule was such that any random prospect is eliminated if its probability P of a loss more than X exceeds a threshold of ϵ, while the principle of selection among the remaining random prospects is to maximise the probable value of the

It is easy to show, using an example, how the neo-Bernoullian formulation leads to *unacceptable* conclusions. Consider a person with a capital of 5 million units who:

(a) states that his choice between various random prospects is based on arbitrage between the average gain M and the probability of ruin P;

(b) agrees to take part in a game in which his chance of winning 100 million is $(1-10^{-6})$, with a probability of ruin of 10^{-6};

(c) refuses steadfastly to take part in any game, *whatever the potential winnings,* in which his probability of ruin is $(1-10^{-6})$, and the probability of winning 10^{-9}.

It can hardly be claimed that he is irrational. He accepts the first alternative because it offers *the virtual certainty of winning 100 million,*[58] and refuses the second because he is *virtually certain to be ruined.* Yet it can easily be seen that this behavioural pattern stands in total contradiction with the neo-Bernoullian formulation.[59]

---

psychological gain, this would be compatible with the neo-Bernoullian formulation, by taking $\bar{s}(g)$ as equal to $-\infty$ for all gains below $-X$.

However, observed behaviour indicates that there is some dependence between this probable value and the probability of ruin P. Where this is so, the neo-Bernoullian formulation is of course not verified.

[58] Borel considers that a probability of 10^{-6} is considered as negligible by human agents (*Le jeu, la chance, et les théories scientifiques modernes,* 1941, p. 108).

[59] From condition (a), if the neo-Bernoullian formulation is valid, then, for the individual considered, we have

$$S = f(M - aP), \tag{1}$$

S being the ordinal index of preference.

To say that he will play if the game offers a probability $(1-p_0)$ of winning n_0 million and a probability p_0 of being ruined, i.e. of losing his fortune F, is to say that

$$0 < (1-p_0)n_0 - p_0 F - ap_0, \tag{2}$$

with the notation of §...55 above and taking (1) into account.

To say that he will abstain from participating in another game, whatever the potential winnings n_1, if his probability of ruin is $(1-q_1)$ is to say that according to (1)

$$0 > q_1 n_1 - (1-q_1)F - a(1-q_1), \tag{3}$$

for any value of n_1.

From (2) and (3) we deduce

$$\frac{q_1}{1-q_1}n_1 - F < a < \frac{1-p_0}{p_0}n_0 - F, \tag{4}$$

whence

$$n_1 < \frac{1-p_0}{p_0}\frac{1-q_1}{q_1}n_0. \tag{5}$$

This condition is independent of F and cannot be satisfied whatever the value of n_1.

In the example given in the text ($p_0 = q_1 = 10^{-6}$, $n_0 = 10^8$), the inequality (5), implied by the neo-Bernoullian formulation for the considered subject, is equivalent for practical pur-

It may, of course, be objected that this is an extreme case. But if the absurdity of the conclusions stemming from a theory is to be demonstrated, the only way is to pick cases whose absurdity is painfully evident – in other words, extreme cases. As was noted earlier, the critic can select his own ground here, for it is enough to find *one* example in which the neo-Bernoullian formulation is manifestly erroneous to rebut it in general.

In the case of individual choices among random prospects similar behaviour is often observed when the persons concerned are both rational and prudent. People of this ilk start by laying down the *maximum* loss they are willing to suffer in any circumstances, and then choose by balancing the mathematical expectation against their probability of ruin. Here, the arbitrage relates not to the mathematical expectation M of the monetary values g, but to the mathematical expectation μ of the psychological values γ, so that $S = S(\mu, P)$.

As was shown above, this behaviour pattern is incompatible with the neo-Bernoullian formulation, apart from the exceptional case in which the psychological value is linearly dependent on the monetary gain and in which S is of the form[60]

$$S = S(M - aP).$$

The behaviour of rational man and the existence of a neo-Bernoullian index

66. To summarise, whether one proceeds from the abstract definition of rationality or from actual observation of the behaviour of persons whom it is reasonable to consider as rational, the conclusion reached is that for a rational man, in general no index $B(x)$ exists such that the optimum situation can be defined by maximising the expectation $\sum p_i B(x_i)$.

poses to the inequality,

$$n_1 < 10^{20}.$$

To upset it, the value of n_1, must of course be taken fabulously high, *but there is no reason for not doing so,* since the subject considered is assumed to maintain his choice (c) *whatever the value of n_1.*

Clearly there is a close connection between this example and the statement above regarding the impossibility of conceiving of indifference curves which intersect the vertical $q = 1$ other than at infinity.

[The 1952 analysis of the example was partially erroneous. It has been corrected in 1977.]

[60] §59 above *in fine.*

6.   Prospect theory: an analysis of decision under risk

Daniel Kahneman and Amos Tversky

1. Introduction

Expected utility theory has dominated the analysis of decision making under risk. It has been generally accepted as a normative model of rational choice (Keeney and Raiffa, 1976), and widely applied as a descriptive model of economic behavior (e.g., Friedman and Savage, 1948, and Arrow, 1971). Thus, it is assumed that all reasonable people would wish to obey the axioms of the theory (von Neumann & Morgenstern, 1944, and Savage, 1954), and that most people actually do, most of the time.

The present paper describes several classes of choice problems in which preferences systematically violate the axioms of expected utility theory. In the light of these observations we argue that utility theory, as it is commonly interpreted and applied, is not an adequate descriptive model and we propose an alternative account of choice under risk.

2. Critique

Decision making under risk can be viewed as a choice between prospects or gambles. A prospect $(x_1, p_1; \ldots; x_n, p_n)$ is a contract that yields outcome x_i with probability p_i, where $p_1 + p_2 + \cdots + p_n = 1$. To simplify notation, we omit null outcomes and use (x, p) to denote the prospect $(x, p; 0, 1-p)$ that yields x with probability p and 0 with probability $1-p$. The (riskless) prospect

This work was supported in part by grants from the Harry F. Guggenheim Foundation and from the Advanced Research Projects Agency of the Department of Defense and was monitored by Office of Naval Research under Contract N00014-78-C-0100 (ARPA Order No. 3469) under Subcontract 78-072-0722 from Decisions and Designs, Inc. to Perceptronics, Inc. We also thank the Center for Advanced Study in the Behavioral Sciences at Stanford for its support. Reprinted with permission from *Econometrica* 47 (1979), 263–91.

that yields x with certainty is denoted by (x). The present discussion is restricted to prospects with so-called objective or standard probabilities.

The application of expected utility theory to choices between prospects is based on the following three tenets.

   i   Expectation: $U(x_1, p_1; \ldots; x_n, p_n) = p_1 u(x_1) + \cdots + p_n u(x_n)$.

That is, the overall utility of a prospect, denoted by U, is the expected utility of its outcomes.

   ii   Asset Integration: $(x_1, p_1; \ldots; x_n, p_n)$ is acceptable at asset position w if $U(w + x_1, p_1; \ldots; w + x_n, p_n) > u(w)$.

That is, a prospect is acceptable if the utility resulting from integrating the prospect with one's assets exceeds the utility of those assets alone. Thus, the domain of the utility function is final states (which include one's asset position) rather than gains or losses.

Although the domain of the utility function is not limited to any particular class of consequences, most applications of the theory have been concerned with monetary outcomes. Furthermore, most economic applications introduce the following additional assumption.

   iii   Risk Aversion: u is concave ($u'' < 0$).

A person is risk averse if he prefers the certain prospect (x) to any risky prospect with expected value x. In expected utility theory, risk aversion is equivalent to the concavity of the utility function. The prevalence of risk aversion is perhaps the best known generalization regarding risky choices. It led the early decision theorists of the eighteenth century to propose that utility is a concave function of money, and this idea has been retained in modern treatments (Pratt, 1964, Arrow, 1971).

In the following sections we demonstrate several phenomena which violate these tenets of expected utility theory. The demonstrations are based on the responses of students and university faculty to hypothetical choice problems. The respondents were presented with problems of the type illustrated below.

Which of the following would you prefer?

     A: 50% chance to win 1000,   B: 450 for sure.
        50% chance to win nothing;

The outcomes refer to Israeli currency. To appreciate the significance of the amounts involved, note that the median net monthly income for a family is about 3000 Israeli pounds. The respondents were asked to imagine that they were actually faced with the choice described in the problem, and to indicate the decision they would have made in such a case. The responses were anonymous, and the instructions specified that there was no "correct" answer to such problems, and that the aim of the study was to find out how people choose among risky prospects. The problems were presented in question-naire form, with at most a dozen problems per booklet. Several forms of each questionnaire were constructed so that subjects were exposed to the problems in different orders. In addition, two versions of each problem were used in which the left–right position of the prospects was reversed.

The problems described in this paper are selected illustrations of a series of effects. Every effect has been observed in several problems with different outcomes and probabilities. Some of the problems have also been presented to groups of students and faculty at the University of Stockholm and at the University of Michigan. The pattern of results was essentially identical to the results obtained from Israeli subjects.

The reliance on hypothetical choices raises obvious questions regarding the validity of the method and the generalizability of the results. We are keenly aware of these problems. However, all other methods that have been used to test utility theory also suffer from severe drawbacks. Real choices can be investigated either in the field, by naturalistic or statistical observa-tions of economic behavior, or in the laboratory. Field studies can only pro-vide for rather crude tests of qualitative predictions, because probabilities and utilities cannot be adequately measured in such contexts. Laboratory experiments have been designed to obtain precise measures of utility and probability from actual choices, but these experimental studies typically in-volve contrived gambles for small stakes, and a large number of repetitions of very similar problems. These features of laboratory gambling complicate the interpretation of the results and restrict their generality.

By default, the method of hypothetical choices emerges as the simplest procedure by which a large number of theoretical questions can be inves-tigated. The use of the method relies on the assumption that people often know how they would behave in actual situations of choice, and on the fur-ther assumption that the subjects have no special reason to disguise their true preferences. If people are reasonably accurate in predicting their choices, the presence of common and systematic violations of expected utility theory in hypothetical problems provides presumptive evidence against that theory.

Certainty, probability, and possibility

In expected utility theory, the utilities of outcomes are weighted by their probabilities. The present section describes a series of choice problems in which people's preferences systematically violate this principle. We first show that people overweight outcomes that are considered certain, relative to out-comes which are merely probable – a phenomenon which we label the *cer-tainty effect*.

The best known counter-example to expected utility theory which exploits the certainty effect was introduced by the French economist Maurice Allais in 1953. Allais's example has been discussed from both normative and descriptive standpoints by many authors (MacCrimmon and Larsson, 1979, and Slovic and Tversky, 1974). The following pair of choice problems is a variation of Allais's example, which differs from the original in that it refers to moderate rather than to extremely large gains. The number of respondents who answered each problem is denoted by N, and the percentage who chose each option is given in brackets.

Problem 1: Choose between
A: 2500 with probability   .33,   B: 2400 with certainty.
     2400 with probability   .66,
     0 with probability   .01;
$N = 72$ [18]   [82]*

Problem 2: Choose between
C: 2500 with probability   .33,   D: 2400 with probability   .34,
     0 with probability   .67;   0 with probability   .66.
$N = 72$ [83]*   [17]

The data show that 82 percent of the subjects chose B in Problem 1, and 83 percent of the subjects chose C in Problem 2. Each of these preferences is significant at the .01 level, as denoted by the asterisk. Moreover, the analysis of individual patterns of choice indicates that a majority of respondents (61 percent) made the modal choice in both problems. This pattern of preferences violates expected utility theory in the manner originally described by Allais. According to that theory, with $u(0) = 0$, the first preference implies

$$u(2400) > .33u(2500) + .66u(2400) \quad \text{or} \quad .34u(2400) > .33u(2500)$$

while the second preference implies the reverse inequality. Note that Problem 2 is obtained from Problem 1 by eliminating a .66 chance of winning 2400 from both prospects under consideration. Evidently, this change produces a greater reduction in desirability when it alters the character of the prospect from a sure gain to a probable one, than when both the original and the reduced prospects are uncertain.

A simpler demonstration of the same phenomenon, involving only two-outcome gambles is given below. This example is also based on Allais (1953).

Problem 3:
A: (4000, .80),   or   B: (3000).
$N = 95$ [20]   [80]*

Problem 4:
C: (4000, .20),   or   D: (3000, .25).
$N = 95$ [65]*   [35]

In this pair of problems as well as in all other problem-pairs in this section, over half the respondents violated expected utility theory. To show that the modal pattern of preferences in Problems 3 and 4 is not compatible with the theory, set $u(0) = 0$, and recall that the choice of B implies $u(3000)/u(4000) > 4/5$, whereas the choice of C implies the reverse inequality. Note that the prospect $C = (4000, .20)$ can be expressed as $(A, .25)$, while the prospect $D = (3000, .25)$ can be rewritten as $(B, .25)$. The substitution axiom of utility theory asserts that if B is preferred to A, then any (probability) mixture (B, p) must be preferred to the mixture (A, p). Our subjects did not obey this axiom. Apparently, reducing the probability of winning from 1.0 to .25 has a greater effect than the reduction from .8 to .2. The following pair of choice problems illustrates the certainty effect with non-monetary outcomes.

Problem 5:
A: 50% chance to win a three-week tour of England, France, and Italy;
$N = 72$ [22]

B: A one-week tour of England, with certainty.

[78]*

Problem 6:
C: 5% chance to win a three-week tour of England, France, and Italy;
$N = 72$ [67]*

D: 10% chance to win a one-week tour of England.

[33]

The certainty effect is not the only type of violation of the substitution axiom. Another situation in which this axiom fails is illustrated by the following problems.

Problem 7:
A: (6000, .45),   or   B: (3000, .90).
$N = 66$ [14]   [86]*

Problem 8:
C: (6000, .001),   or   D: (3000, .002).
$N = 66$ [73]*   [27]

Note that in Problem 7 the probabilities of winning are substantial (.90 and .45), and most people chose the prospect where winning is more probable. In Problem 8, there is a *possibility* of winning, although the probabilities of winning are minuscule (.002 and .001) in both prospects. In this situation where winning is possible but not probable, most people choose the prospect that offers the larger gain. Similar results have been reported by MacCrimmon and Larsson (1979).

The above problems illustrate common attitudes toward risk or chance that cannot be captured by the expected utility model. The results suggest the following empirical generalization concerning the manner in which the substitution axiom is violated. If (y, pq) is equivalent to (x, p), then (y, pqr) is

Table 1. *Preferences between positive and negative prospects*

	Positive prospects				Negative prospects		
Problem 3:	(4000, .80)	<	(3000)	Problem 3′:	(−4000, .80)	>	(−3000)
N = 95	[20]		[80]*	N = 95	[92]*		[8]
Problem 4:	(4000, .20)	>	(3000, .25)	Problem 4′:	(−4000, .20)	<	(−3000, .25)
N = 95	[65]*		[35]	N = 95	[42]		[58]
Problem 7:	(3000, .90)	>	(6000, .45)	Problem 7′:	(−3000, .90)	<	(−6000, .45)
N = 66	[86]*		[14]	N = 66	[8]		[92]*
Problem 8:	(3000, .002)	<	(6000, .001)	Problem 8′:	(−3000, .002)	>	(−6000, .001)
N = 66	[27]		[73]*	N = 66	[70]*		[30]

preferred to (x, pr), $0 < p, q, r < 1$. This property is incorporated into an alternative theory, developed in the second part of the paper.

The reflection effect

The previous section discussed preferences between positive prospects, i.e., prospects that involve no losses. What happens when the signs of the outcomes are reversed so that gains are replaced by losses? The left-hand column of Table 1 displays four of the choice problems that were discussed in the previous section, and the right-hand column displays choice problems in which the signs of the outcomes are reversed. We use $-x$ to denote the loss of x, and > to denote the prevalent preference, i.e., the choice made by the majority of subjects.

In each of the four problems in Table 1 the preference between negative prospects is the mirror image of the preference between positive prospects. Thus, the reflection of prospects around 0 reverses the preference order. We label this pattern the *reflection effect.*

Let us turn now to the implications of these data. First, note that the reflection effect implies that risk aversion in the positive domain is accompanied by risk seeking in the negative domain. In Problem 3′, for example, the majority of subjects were willing to accept a risk of .80 to lose 4000, in preference to a sure loss of 3000, although the gamble has a lower expected value. The occurrence of risk seeking in choices between negative prospects was noted early by Markowitz (1952). Williams (1966) reported data where a translation of outcomes produces a dramatic shift from risk aversion to risk seeking. For example, his subjects were indifferent between (100, .65; −100, .35) and (0), indicating risk aversion. They were also indifferent between (−200, .80) and (−100), indicating risk seeking. A recent review by Fishburn and Kochenberger (1979) documents the prevalence of risk seeking in choices between negative prospects.

Second, recall that the preferences between the positive prospects in Table 1 are inconsistent with expected utility theory. The preferences between the corresponding negative prospects also violate the expectation principle in the same manner. For example, Problems 3′ and 4′, like Problems 3 and 4, demonstrate that outcomes which are obtained with certainty are over-weighted relative to uncertain outcomes. In the positive domain, the certainty effect contributes to a risk averse preference for a sure gain over a larger gain that is merely probable. In the negative domain, the same effect leads to a risk seeking preference for a loss that is merely probable over a smaller loss that is certain. The same psychological principle – the over-weighting of certainty – favors risk aversion in the domain of gains and risk seeking in the domain of losses.

Third, the reflection effect eliminates aversion for uncertainty or variability as an explanation of the certainty effect. Consider, for example, the prevalent preferences for (3000) over (4000, .80) and for (4000, .20) over (3000, .25). To resolve this apparent inconsistency one could invoke the assumption that people prefer prospects that have high expected value and small variance (see, e.g., Allais, 1953; Markowitz, 1959; and Tobin, 1958). Since (3000) has no variance while (4000, .80) has large variance, the former prospect could be chosen despite its lower expected value. When the prospects are reduced, however, the difference in variance between (3000, .25) and (4000, .20) may be insufficient to overcome the difference in expected value. Because (−3000) has both higher expected value and lower variance than (−4000, .80), this account entails that the sure loss should be preferred, contrary to the data. Thus, our data are incompatible with the notion that certainty is generally desirable. Rather, it appears that certainty increases the aversiveness of losses as well as the desirability of gains.

Probabilistic insurance

The prevalence of the purchase of insurance against both large and small losses has been regarded by many as strong evidence for the concavity of the utility function for money. Why otherwise would people spend so much money to purchase insurance policies at a price that exceeds the expected actuarial cost? However, an examination of the relative attractiveness of various forms of insurance does not support the notion that the utility function for money is concave everywhere. For example, people often prefer insurance programs that offer limited coverage with low or zero deductible over comparable policies that offer higher maximal coverage with higher deductibles – contrary to risk aversion (see, e.g., Fuchs, 1976). Another type of insurance problem in which people's responses are inconsistent with the concavity hypothesis may be called probabilistic insurance. To illustrate this concept, consider the following problem, which was presented to 95 Stanford University students.

Problem 9: Suppose you consider the possibility of insuring some property against damage, e.g., fire or theft. After examining the risks and the premium you find that you have no clear preference between the options of purchasing insurance or leaving the property uninsured.

It is then called to your attention that the insurance company offers a new program called *probabilistic insurance*. In this program you pay half of the regular premium. In case of damage, there is a 50 percent chance that you pay the other half of the premium and the insurance company covers all the losses; and there is a 50 percent chance that you get back your insurance payment and suffer all the losses. For example, if an accident occurs on an odd day of the month, you pay the other half of the regular premium and your losses are covered; but if the accident occurs on an even day of the month, your insurance payment is refunded and your losses are not covered.

Recall that the premium for full coverage is such that you find this insurance barely worth its cost.

Under these circumstances, would you purchase probabilistic insurance:

	Yes,	No.
$N = 95$	[20]	[80]*

Although Problem 9 may appear contrived, it is worth noting that probabilistic insurance represents many forms of protective action where one pays a certain cost to reduce the probability of an undesirable event – without eliminating it altogether. The installation of a burglar alarm, the replacement of old tires, and the decision to stop smoking can all be viewed as probabilistic insurance.

The responses to Problem 9 and to several other variants of the same question indicate that probabilistic insurance is generally unattractive. Apparently, reducing the probability of a loss from p to $p/2$ is less valuable than reducing the probability of that loss from $p/2$ to 0.

In contrast to these data, expected utility theory (with a concave u) implies that probabilistic insurance is superior to regular insurance. That is, if at asset position w one is just willing to pay a premium y to insure against a probability p of losing x, then one should definitely be willing to pay a smaller premium ry to reduce the probability of losing x from p to $(1-r)p, 0 < r < 1$. Formally, if one is indifferent between $(w-x, p; w, 1-p)$ and $(w-y)$, then one should prefer probabilistic insurance $(w-x, (1-r)p; w-y, rp; w-ry, 1-p)$ over regular insurance $(w-y)$.

To prove this proposition, we show that

$$pu(w-x) + (1-p)u(w) = u(w-y)$$

implies

$$(1-r)pu(w-x) + rpu(w-y) + (1-p)u(w-ry) > u(w-y).$$

Without loss of generality, we can set $u(w-x)=0$ and $u(w)=1$. Hence, $u(w-y)=1-p$, and we wish to show that

$$rp(1-p)+(1-p)u(w-ry)>1-p \quad \text{or} \quad u(w-ry)>1-rp$$

which holds if and only if u is concave.

This is a rather puzzling consequence of the risk aversion hypothesis of utility theory, because probabilistic insurance appears intuitively riskier than regular insurance, which entirely eliminates the element of risk. Evidently, the intuitive notion of risk is not adequately captured by the assumed concavity of the utility function for wealth.

The aversion for probabilistic insurance is particularly intriguing because all insurance is, in a sense, probabilistic. The most avid buyer of insurance remains vulnerable to many financial and other risks which his policies do not cover. There appears to be a significant difference between probabilistic insurance and what may be called contingent insurance, which provides the certainty of coverage for a specified type of risk. Compare, for example, probabilistic insurance against all forms of loss or damage to the contents of your home and contingent insurance that eliminates all risk of loss from theft, say, but does not cover other risks, e.g., fire. We conjecture that contingent insurance will be generally more attractive than probabilistic insurance when the probabilities of unprotected loss are equated. Thus, two prospects that are equivalent in probabilities and outcomes could have different values depending on their formulation. Several demonstrations of this general phenomenon are described in the next section.

The isolation effect

In order to simplify the choice between alternatives, people often disregard components that the alternatives share, and focus on the components that distinguish them (Tversky, 1972). This approach to choice problems may produce inconsistent preferences, because a pair of prospects can be decomposed into common and distinctive components in more than one way, and different decompositions sometimes lead to different preferences. We refer to this phenomenon as the *isolation effect*.

Problem 10: Consider the following two-stage game. In the first stage, there is a probability of .75 to end the game without winning anything, and a probability of .25 to move into the second stage. If you reach the second stage you have a choice between

$$(4000, .80) \quad \text{and} \quad (3000).$$

Your choice must be made before the game starts, i.e., before the outcome of the first stage is known.

Note that in this game, one has a choice between $.25 \times .80 = .20$ chance to win 4000, and a $.25 \times 1.0 = .25$ chance to win 3000. Thus, in terms of

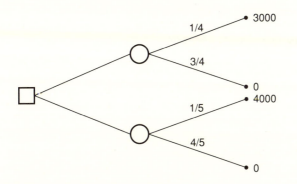

Figure 1. The representation of Problem 4 as a decision tree (standard formulation).

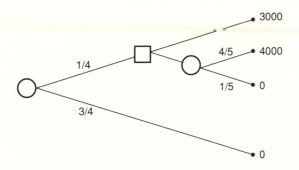

Figure 2. The representation of Problem 10 as a decision tree (sequential formulation.

final outcomes and probabilities one faces a choice between (4000, .20) and (3000, .25), as in Problem 4 above. However, the dominant preferences are different in the two problems. Of 141 subjects who answered Problem 10, 78 percent chose the latter prospect, contrary to the modal preference in Problem 4. Evidently, people ignored the first stage of the game, whose outcomes are shared by both prospects, and considered Problem 10 as a choice between (3000) and (4000, .80), as in Problem 3 above.

The standard and the sequential formulations of Problem 4 are represented as decision trees in Figures 1 and 2, respectively. Following the usual convention, squares denote decision nodes and circles denote chance nodes. The essential difference between the two representations is in the location of the decision node. In the standard form (Figure 1), the decision maker faces a choice between two risky prospects, whereas in the sequential form (Figure 2) he faces a choice between a risky and a riskless prospect. This is accomplished by introducing a dependency between the prospects without changing either probabilities or outcomes. Specifically, the event "not winning 3000" is included in the event "not winning 4000" in the sequential formulation, while the two events are independent in the standard formulation. Thus, the outcome of winning 3000 has a certainty advantage in the sequential formulation, which it does not have in the standard formulation.

The reversal of preferences due to the dependency among events is particularly significant because it violates the basic supposition of a decision-theoretical analysis, that choices between prospects are determined solely by the probabilities of final states.

It is easy to think of decision problems that are most naturally represented in one of the forms above rather than in the other. For example, the choice between two different risky ventures is likely to be viewed in the standard form. On the other hand, the following problem is most likely to be represented in the sequential form. One may invest money in a venture with some probability of losing one's capital if the venture fails, and with a choice between a fixed agreed return and a percentage of earnings if it succeeds. The isolation effect implies that the contingent certainty of the fixed return enhances the attractiveness of this option, relative to a risky venture with the same probabilities and outcomes.

The preceding problem illustrated how preferences may be altered by different representations of probabilities. We now show how choices may be altered by varying the representation of outcomes.

Consider the following problems, which were presented to two different groups of subjects.

Problem 11: In addition to whatever you own, you have been given 1000. You are now asked to choose between

A: (1000, .50)   and   B: (500).
$N = 70$ [16]   [84]*

Problem 12: In addition to whatever you own, you have been given 2000. You are now asked to choose between

C: (−1000, .50)   and   D: (−500).
$N = 68$ [69]*   [31]

The majority of subjects chose B in the first problem and C in the second. These preferences conform to the reflection effect observed in Table 1, which exhibits risk aversion for positive prospects and risk seeking for negative ones. Note, however, that when viewed in terms of final states, the two choice problems are identical. Specifically,

A = (2000, .50; 1000, .50) = C,   and   B = (1500) = D.

In fact, Problem 12 is obtained from Problem 11 by adding 1000 to the initial bonus, and subtracting 1000 from all outcomes. Evidently, the subjects did not integrate the bonus with the prospects. The bonus did not enter into the comparison of prospects because it was common to both options in each problem.

The pattern of results observed in Problems 11 and 12 is clearly inconsistent with utility theory. In that theory, for example, the same utility is assigned to a wealth of $100,000, regardless of whether it was reached from a prior wealth of $95,000 or $105,000. Consequently, the choice between a total wealth of $100,000 and even chances to own $95,000 or $105,000 should be independent of whether one currently owns the smaller or the larger of these two amounts. With the added assumption of risk aversion, the theory entails that the certainty of owning $100,000 should always be preferred to the gamble. However, the responses to Problem 12 and to several of the previous questions suggest that this pattern will be obtained if the individual owns the smaller amount, but not if he owns the larger amount.

The apparent neglect of a bonus that was common to both options in Problems 11 and 12 implies that the carriers of value or utility are changes of wealth, rather than final asset positions that include current wealth. This conclusion is the cornerstone of an alternative theory of risky choice, which is described in the following sections.

3. Theory

The preceding discussion reviewed several empirical effects which appear to invalidate expected utility theory as a descriptive model. The remainder of the paper presents an alternative account of individual decision making under risk, called prospect theory. The theory is developed for simple prospects with monetary outcomes and stated probabilities, but it can be extended to more involved choices. Prospect theory distinguishes two phases in the choice process: an early phase of editing and a subsequent phase of evaluation. The editing phase consists of a preliminary analysis of the offered prospects, which often yields a simpler representation of these prospects. In the second phase, the edited prospects are evaluated and the prospect of highest value is chosen. We next outline the editing phase, and develop a formal model of the evaluation phase.

The function of the editing phase is to organize and reformulate the options so as to simplify subsequent evaluation and choice. Editing consists of the application of several operations that transform the outcomes and probabilities associated with the offered prospects. The major operations of the editing phase are described below.

Coding. The evidence discussed in the previous section shows that people normally perceive outcomes as gains and losses, rather than as final states of wealth or welfare. Gains and losses, of course, are defined relative to some neutral reference point. The reference point usually corresponds to the current asset position, in which case gains and losses coincide with the actual amounts that are received or paid. However, the location of the reference point, and the consequent coding of outcomes as gains or losses, can be affected by the formulation of the offered prospects, and by the expectations of the decision maker.

Combination. Prospects can sometimes be simplified by combining the probabilities associated with identical outcomes. For example, the prospect (200, .25; 200, .25) will be reduced to (200, .50) and evaluated in this form.

Segregation. Some prospects contain a riskless component that is segregated from the risky component in the editing phase. For example, the prospect (300, .80; 200, .20) is naturally decomposed into a sure gain of 200 and the risky prospect (100, .80). Similarly, the prospect (−400, .40; −100, .60) is readily seen to consist of a sure loss of 100 and of the prospect (−300, .40).

The preceding operations are applied to each prospect separately. The following operation is applied to a set of two or more prospects.

Cancellation. The essence of the isolation effects described earlier is the discarding of components that are shared by the offered prospects. Thus, our respondents apparently ignored the first stage of the sequential game presented in Problem 10, because this stage was common to both options, and they evaluated the prospects with respect to the results of the second stage (see Figure 2). Similarly, they neglected the common bonus that was added to the prospects in Problems 11 and 12. Another type of cancellation involves the discarding of common constituents, i.e., outcome-probability pairs. For example, the choice between (200, .20; 100, .50; −50, .30) and (200, .20; 150, .50; −100, .30) can be reduced by cancellation to a choice between (100, .50; −50, .30) and (150, .50; −100, .30).

Two additional operations that should be mentioned are simplification and the detection of dominance. The first refers to the simplification of prospects by rounding probabilities or outcomes. For example, the prospect (101, .49) is likely to be recoded as an even chance to win 100. A particularly important form of simplification involves the discarding of extremely unlikely outcomes. The second operation involves the scanning of offered prospects to detect dominated alternatives, which are rejected without further evaluation.

Because the editing operations facilitate the task of decision, it is assumed that they are performed whenever possible. However, some editing operations either permit or prevent the application of others. For example, (500, .20; 101, .49) will appear to dominate (500, .15; .99, .51) if the second constituents of both prospects are simplified to (100, .50). The final edited prospects could, therefore, depend on the sequence of editing operations, which is likely to vary with the structure of the offered set and with the format of the display. A detailed study of this problem is beyond the scope of the present treatment. In this paper we discuss choice problems where it is reasonable to assume either that the original formulation of the prospects leaves no room for further editing, or that the edited prospects can be specified without ambiguity.

Many anomalies of preference result from the editing of prospects. For example, the inconsistencies associated with the isolation effect result from the cancellation of common components. Some intransitivities of choice are explained by a simplification that eliminates small differences between prospects (see Tversky, 1969). More generally, the preference order between prospects need not be invariant across contexts, because the same offered prospect could be edited in different ways depending on the context in which it appears.

Following the editing phase, the decision maker is assumed to evaluate each of the edited prospects, and to choose the prospect of highest value. The overall value of an edited prospect, denoted V, is expressed in terms of two scales, π and v.

The first scale, π, associates with each probability p a decision weight $\pi(p)$, which reflects the impact of p on the over-all value of the prospect. However, π is not a probability measure, and it will be shown later that $\pi(p) + \pi(1-p)$ is typically less than unity. The second scale, v, assigns to each outcome x a number $v(x)$, which reflects the subjective value of that outcome. Recall that outcomes are defined relative to a reference point, which serves as the zero point of the value scale. Hence, v measures the value of deviations from that reference point, i.e., gains and losses.

The present formulation is concerned with simple prospects of the form $(x, p; y, q)$, which have at most two non-zero outcomes. In such a prospect, one receives x with probability p, y with probability q, and nothing with probability $1 - p - q$, where $p + q \leq 1$. An offered prospect is strictly positive if its outcomes are all positive, i.e., if $x, y > 0$ and $p + q = 1$; it is stricly negative if its outcomes are all negative. A prospect is regular if it is neither strictly positive nor strictly negative.

The basic equation of the theory describes the manner in which π and v are combined to determine the over-all value of regular prospects.

If $(x, p; y, q)$ is a regular prospect (i.e., either $p + q < 1$, or $x \geq 0 \geq y$, or $x \leq 0 \leq y$), then

$$V(x, p; y, q) = \pi(p)v(x) + \pi(q)v(y) \tag{1}$$

where $v(0) = 0$, $\pi(0) = 0$, and $\pi(1) = 1$. As in utility theory, V is defined on prospects, while v is defined on outcomes. The two scales coincide for sure prospects, where $V(x, 1.0) = V(x) = v(x)$.

Equation (1) generalizes expected utility theory by relaxing the expectation principle. An axiomatic analysis of this representation is sketched in the Appendix, which describes conditions that ensure the existence of a unique π and a ratio-scale v satisfying equation (1).

The evaluation of strictly positive and strictly negative prospects follows a different rule. In the editing phase such prospects are segregated into two components: (i) the riskless component, i.e., the minimum gain or loss which is certain to be obtained or paid; (ii) the risky component, i.e., the additional gain or loss which is actually at stake. The evaluation of such prospects is described in the next equation.

If $p+q=1$ and either $x>y>0$ or $x<y<0$, then

$$V(x, p; y, q) = v(y) + \pi(p)[v(x) - v(y)]. \tag{2}$$

That is, the value of a strictly positive or strictly negative prospect equals the value of the riskless component plus the value-difference between the outcomes, multiplied by the weight associated with the more extreme outcome. For example, $V(400, .25; 100, .75) = v(100) + \pi(.25)[v(400) - v(100)]$. The essential feature of equation (2) is that a decision weight is applied to the value-difference $v(x) - v(y)$, which represents the risky component of the prospect, but not to $v(y)$, which represents the riskless component. Note that the right-hand side of equation (2) equals $\pi(p)v(x) + [1 - \pi(p)]v(y)$. Hence, equation (2) reduces to equation (1) if $\pi(p) + \pi(1-p) = 1$. As will be shown later, this condition is not generally satisfied.

Many elements of the evaluation model have appeared in previous attempts to modify expected utility theory. Markowitz (1952) was the first to propose that utility be defined on gains and losses rather than on final asset positions, an assumption which has been implicitly accepted in most experimental measurements of utility (see, e.g., Davidson et al., 1957, and Mosteller and Nogee, 1951). Markowitz also noted the presence of risk seeking in preferences among positive as well as among negative prospects, and he proposed a utility function which has convex and concave regions in both the positive and the negative domains. His treatment, however, retains the expectation principle; hence it cannot account for the many violations of this principle; see, e.g., Table 1.

The replacement of probabilities by more general weights was proposed by Edwards (1962), and this model was investigated in several empirical studies (e.g., Anderson and Shanteau, 1970, and Tversky, 1967). Similar models were developed by Fellner (1965), who introduced the concept of decision weight to explain aversion for ambiguity, and by van Dam (1975) who attempted to scale decision weights. For other critical analyses of expected utility theory and alternative choice models, see Allais (1953), Coombs (1975), Fishburn (1977), and Hansson (1975).

The equations of prospect theory retain the general bilinear form that underlies expected utility theory. However, in order to accommodate the effects described in the first part of the paper, we are compelled to assume that values are attached to changes rather than to final states, and that decision weights do not coincide with stated probabilities. These departures from expected utility theory must lead to normatively unacceptable consequences, such as inconsistencies, intransitivities, and violations of dominance. Such anomalies of preference are normally corrected by the decision maker when he realizes that his preferences are inconsistent, intransitive, or inadmissible. In many situations, however, the decision maker does not have the opportunity to discover that his preferences could violate decision rules that he wishes to obey. In these circumstances the anomalies implied by prospect theory are expected to occur.

The value function

An essential feature of the present theory is that the carriers of value are changes in wealth or welfare, rather than final states. This assumption is compatible with basic principles of perception and judgment. Our perceptual apparatus is attuned to the evaluation of changes or differences rather than to the evaluation of absolute magnitudes. When we respond to attributes such as brightness, loudness, or temperature, the past and present context of experience defines an adaptation level, or reference point, and stimuli are perceived in relation to this reference point (Helson, 1964). Thus, an object at a given temperature may be experienced as hot or cold to the touch depending on the temperature to which one has adapted. The same principle applies to non-sensory attributes such as health, prestige, and wealth. The same level of wealth, for example, may imply abject poverty for one person and great riches for another – depending on their current assets.

The emphasis on changes as the carriers of value should not be taken to imply that the value of a particular change is independent of initial position. Strictly speaking, value should be treated as a function in two arguments: the asset position that serves as reference point, and the magnitude of the change (positive or negative) from that reference point. An individual's attitude to money, say, could be described by a book, where each page presents the value function for changes at a particular asset position. Clearly, the value functions described on different pages are not identical: they are likely to become more linear with increases in assets. However, the preference order of prospects is not greatly altered by small or even moderate variations in asset position. The certainty equivalent of the prospect (1000, .50), for example, lies between 300 and 400 for most people, in a wide range of asset positions. Consequently, the representation of value as a function in one argument generally provides a satisfactory approximation.

Many sensory and perceptual dimensions share the property that the psychological response is a concave function of the magnitude of physical change. For example, it is easier to discriminate between a change of 3° and a change of 6° in room temperature, than it is to discriminate between a change of 13° and a change of 16°. We propose that this principle applies in particular to the evaluation of monetary changes. Thus, the difference in value between a gain of 100 and a gain of 200 appears to be greater than the difference between a gain of 1100 and a gain of 1200. Similarly, the difference between a loss of 100 and a loss of 200 appears greater than the difference between a loss of 1100 and a loss of 1200, unless the larger loss is intolerable. Thus, we hypothesize that the value function for changes of wealth is normally concave above the reference point ($v''(x) < 0$, for $x > 0$) and often convex below it ($v''(x) > 0$, for $x < 0$). That is, the marginal value of both gains and losses generally decreases with their magnitude. Some support for this hypothesis has been reported by Galanter and Pliner (1974), who scaled the perceived magnitude of monetary and non-monetary gains and losses.

The above hypothesis regarding the shape of the value function was based on responses to gains and losses in a riskless context. We propose that the value function which is derived from risky choices shares the same characteristics, as illustrated in the following problems.

Problem 13:

$$(6000, .25), \quad \text{or} \quad (4000, .25; 2000, .25).$$
$$N = 68 \quad [18] \qquad\qquad [82]^*$$

Problem 13′:

$$(-6000, .25), \quad \text{or} \quad (-4000, .25; -2000, .25).$$
$$N = 64 \quad [70]^* \qquad\qquad [30]$$

Applying equation (1) to the modal preference in these problems yields

$$\pi(.25)\,v(6000) < \pi(.25)\,[v(4000) + v(2000)] \quad \text{and}$$
$$\pi(.25)\,v(-6000) > \pi(.25)\,[v(-4000) + v(-2000)].$$

Hence, $v(6000) < v(4000) + v(2000)$ and $v(-6000) > v(-4000) + v(-2000)$. These preferences are in accord with the hypothesis that the value function is concave for gains and convex for losses.

Any discussion of the utility function for money must leave room for the effect of special circumstances on preferences. For example, the utility function of an individual who needs $60,000 to purchase a house may reveal an exceptionally steep rise near the critical value. Similarly, an individual's aversion to losses may increase sharply near the loss that would compel him to sell his house and move to a less desirable neighborhood. Hence, the derived value (utility) function of an individual does not always reflect "pure" attitudes to money, since it could be affected by additional consequences associated with specific amounts. Such perturbations can readily produce convex regions in the value function for gains and concave regions in the value function for losses. The latter case may be more common since large losses often necessitate changes in life style.

A salient characteristic of attitudes to changes in welfare is that losses loom larger than gains. The aggravation that one experiences in losing a sum of money appears to be greater than the pleasure associated with gaining the same amount (Galanter and Pliner, 1974). Indeed, most people find

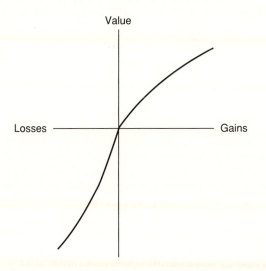

Figure 3. A hypothetical value function.

symmetric bets of the form $(x, .50; -x, .50)$ distinctly unattractive. Moreover, the aversiveness of symmetric fair bets generally increases with the
size of the stake. That is, if $x > y \geq 0$, then $(y, .50; -y, .50)$ is preferred to
$(x, .50; -x, .50)$. According to equation (1), therefore,

$$v(y) + v(-y) > v(x) + v(-x) \quad \text{and} \quad v(-y) - v(-x) > v(x) - v(y).$$

Setting $y = 0$ yields $v(x) < -v(-x)$, and letting y approach x yields $v'(x) <$
$v'(-x)$, provided v', the derivative of v, exists. Thus, the value function for
losses is steeper than the value function for gains.

In summary, we have proposed that the value function is (i) defined on
deviations from the reference point; (ii) generally concave for gains and
commonly convex for losses; (iii) steeper for losses than for gains. A value
function which satisfies these properties is displayed in Figure 3. Note that
the proposed S-shaped value function is steepest at the reference point, in
marked contrast to the utility function postulated by Markowitz (1952) which
is relatively shallow in that region.

Although the present theory can be applied to derive the value function
from preferences between prospects, the actual scaling is considerably more
complicated than in utility theory, because of the introduction of decision
weights. For example, decision weights could produce risk aversion and risk
seeking even with a linear value function. Nevertheless, it is of interest that the
main properties ascribed to the value function have been observed in a detailed analysis of von Neumann-Morgenstern utility functions for changes of
wealth (Fishburn and Kochenberger, 1979). The functions had been obtained
from thirty decision makers in various fields of business, in five independent

studies (Barnes and Reinmuth, 1976; Grayson, 1960; Green, 1963; Halter & Dean, 1971; and Swalm, 1966). Most utility functions for gains were concave, most functions for losses were convex, and only three individuals exhibited risk aversion for both gains and losses. With a single exception, utility functions were considerably steeper for losses than for gains.

The weighting function

In prospect theory, the value of each outcome is multiplied by a decision weight. Decision weights are inferred from choices between prospects much as subjective probabilities are inferred from preferences in the Ramsey-Savage approach. However, decision weights are not probabilities: they do not obey the probability axioms and they should not be interpreted as measures of degree or belief.

Consider a gamble in which one can win 1000 or nothing, depending on the toss of a fair coin. For any reasonable person, the probability of winning is .50 in this situation. This can be verified in a variety of ways, e.g., by showing that the subject is indifferent between betting on heads or tails, or by his verbal report that he considers the two events equiprobable. As will be shown below, however, the decision weight $\pi(.50)$ which is derived from choices is likely to be smaller than .50. Decision weights measure the impact of events on the desirability of prospects, and not merely the perceived likelihood of these events. The two scales coincide (i.e., $\pi(p) = p$) if the expectation principle holds, but not otherwise.

The choice problems discussed in the present paper were formulated in terms of explicit numerical probabilities, and our analysis assumes that the respondents adopted the stated values of p. Furthermore, since the events were identified only by their stated probabilities, it is possible in this context to express decision weights as a function of stated probability. In general, however, the decision weight attached to an event could be influenced by other factors, e.g., ambiguity (Ellsberg, 1961, Chapter 4, this volume; Fellner, 1961).

We turn now to discuss the salient properties of the weighting function π, which relates decision weights to stated probabilities. Naturally, π is an increasing function of p, with $\pi(0) = 0$ and $\pi(1) = 1$. That is, outcomes contingent on an impossible event are ignored, and the scale is normalized so that $\pi(p)$ is the ratio of the weight associated with the probability p to the weight associated with the certain event.

We first discuss some properties of the weighting function for small probabilities. The preferences in Problems 8 and 8' suggest that for small values of p, π is a subadditive function of p, i.e., $\pi(rp) > r\pi(p)$ for $0 < r < 1$. Recall that in Problem 8, (6000, .001) is preferred to (3000, .002). Hence

$$\frac{\pi(.001)}{\pi(.002)} > \frac{v(3000)}{v(6000)} > \frac{1}{2} \quad \text{by the concavity of } v.$$

The reflected preferences in Problem 8' yield the same conclusion. The pattern of preferences in Problems 7 and 7', however, suggests that subadditivity need not hold for large values of p.

Furthermore, we propose that very low probabilities are generally overweighted, that is, $\pi(p) > p$ for small p. Consider the following choice problems.

Problem 14:

$$\begin{array}{ccc} (5000, .001), & \text{or} & (5). \\ N = 72 \quad [72]^* & & [28] \end{array}$$

Problem 14':

$$\begin{array}{ccc} (-5000, .001), & \text{or} & (-5). \\ N = 72 \quad [17] & & [83]^* \end{array}$$

Note that in Problem 14, people prefer what is in effect a lottery ticket over the expected value of that ticket. In Problem 14', on the other hand, they prefer a small loss, which can be viewed as the payment of an insurance premium, over a small probability of a large loss. Similar observations have been reported by Markowitz (1952). In the present theory, the preference for the lottery in Problem 14 implies $\pi(.001)v(5000) > v(5)$, hence $\pi(.001) > v(5)/v(5000) > .001$, assuming the value function for gains is concave. The readiness to pay for insurance in Problem 14' implies the same conclusion, assuming the value function for losses is convex.

It is important to distinguish overweighting, which refers to a property of decision weights, from the overestimation that is commonly found in the assessment of the probability of rare events. Note that the issue of overestimation does not arise in the present context, where the subject is assumed to adopt the stated value of p. In many real-life situations, overestimation and overweighting may both operate to increase the impact of rare events.

Although $\pi(p) > p$ for low probabilities, there is evidence to suggest that, for all $0 < p < 1$, $\pi(p) + \pi(1-p) < 1$. We label this property subcertainty. It is readily seen that the typical preferences in any version of Allais's example (see, e.g., Problems 1 and 2) imply subcertainty for the relevant value of p. Applying equation (1) to the prevalent preferences in Problems 1 and 2 yields, respectively,

$$v(2400) > \pi(.66)v(2400) + \pi(.33)v(2500), \quad \text{i.e.,}$$
$$[1 - \pi(.66)v(2400) > \pi(.33)v(2500) \quad \text{and}$$
$$\pi(.33)v(2500) > \pi(.34)v(2400); \quad \text{hence,}$$
$$1 - \pi(.66) > \pi(.34), \quad \text{or} \quad \pi(.66) + \pi(.34) < 1.$$

Applying the same analysis to Allais' original example yields $\pi(.89) + \pi(.11) < 1$, and some data reported by MacCrimmon and Larsson (1979) imply subcertainty for additional values of p.

The slope of π in the interval $(0, 1)$ can be viewed as a measure of the sensitivity of preferences to changes in probability. Subcertainty entails that π is regressive with respect to p, i.e., that preferences are generally less sensitive to variations of probability than the expectation principle would dictate. Thus, subcertainty captures an essential element of people's attitudes to uncertain events, namely that the sum of the weights associated with complementary events is typically less than the weight associated with the certain event.

Recall that the violations of the substitution axiom discussed earlier in this paper conform to the following rule: If (x, p) is equivalent to (y, pq) then (x, pr) is not preferred to (y, pqr), $0 < p, q, r \le 1$. By equation (1),

$$\pi(p)v(x) = \pi(pq)v(y) \quad \text{implies} \quad \pi(pr)v(x) \le \pi(pqr)v(y); \quad \text{hence,}$$

$$\frac{\pi(pq)}{\pi(p)} \le \frac{\pi(pqr)}{\pi(pr)}.$$

Thus, for a fixed ratio of probabilities, the ratio of the corresponding decision weights is closer to unity when the probabilities are low than when they are high. This property of π, called subproportionality, imposes considerable constraints on the shape of π: it holds if and only if $\log \pi$ is a convex function of $\log p$.

It is of interest to note that subproportionality together with the overweighting of small probabilities imply that π is subadditive over that range. Formally, it can be shown that if $\pi(p) > p$ and subproportionality holds, then $\pi(rp) > r\pi(p)$, $0 < r < 1$, provided π is monotone and continuous over $(0, 1)$.

Figure 4 presents a hypothetical weighting function which satisfies overweighting and subadditivity for small values of p, as well as subcertainty and subproportionality. These properties entail that π is relatively shallow in the open interval and changes abruptly near the end-points where $\pi(0) = 0$ and $\pi(1) = 1$. The sharp drops or apparent discontinuities of π at the endpoints are consistent with the notion that there is a limit to how small a decision weight can be attached to an event, if it is given any weight at all. A similar quantum of doubt could impose an upper limit on any decision weight that is less than unity. This quantal effect may reflect the categorical distinction between certainty and uncertainty. On the other hand, the simplification of prospects in the editing phase can lead the individual to discard events of extremely low probability and to treat events of extremely high probability as if they were certain. Because people are limited in their ability to comprehend and evaluate extreme probabilities, highly unlikely events are either ignored or overweighted, and the difference between high probability and certainty is either neglected or exaggerated. Consequently, π is not well-behaved near the end-points.

The following example, due to Zeckhauser, illustrates the hypothesized nonlinearity of π. Suppose you are compelled to play Russian roulette, but are given the opportunity to purchase the removal of one bullet from the

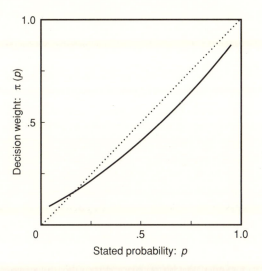

Figure 4. A hypothetical weighting function.

loaded gun. Would you pay as much to reduce the number of bullets from four to three as you would to reduce the number of bullets from one to zero? Most people feel that they would be willing to pay much more for a reduction of the probability of death from $\frac{1}{6}$ to zero than for a reduction from $\frac{4}{6}$ to $\frac{3}{6}$. Economic considerations would lead one to pay more in the latter case, where the value of money is presumably reduced by the considerable probability that one will not live to enjoy it.

An obvious objection to the assumption that $\pi(p) \neq p$ involves comparisons between prospects of the form $(x, p; x, q)$ and $(x, p'; x, q')$, where $p + q = p' + q' < 1$. Since any individual will surely be indifferent between the two prospects, it could be argued that this observation entails $\pi(p) + \pi(q) = \pi(p') + \pi(q')$, which in turn implies that π is the identity function. This argument is invalid in the present theory, which assumes that the probabilities of identical outcomes are combined in the editing of prospects. A more serious objection to the nonlinearity of π involves potential violations of dominance. Suppose $x > y > 0$, $p > p'$, and $p + q = p' + q' < 1$; hence $(x, p; y, q)$ dominates $(x, p'; y, q')$. If preference obeys dominance, then

$$\pi(p)v(x) + \pi(q)v(y) > \pi(p')v(x) + \pi(q')v(y),$$

or

$$\frac{\pi(p) - \pi(p')}{\pi(q') - \pi(q)} > \frac{v(y)}{v(x)}.$$

Hence, as y approaches x, $\pi(p) - \pi(p')$ approaches $\pi(q') - \pi(q)$. Since $p - p' = q' - q$, π must be essentially linear, or else dominance must be violated.

Direct violations of dominance are prevented, in the present theory, by the assumption that dominated alternatives are detected and eliminated prior to the evaluation of prospects. However, the theory permits indirect violations of dominance, e.g., triples of prospects so that A is preferred to B, B is preferred to C, and C dominates A. For an example, see Raiffa (1968, p. 75).

Finally, it should be noted that the present treatment concerns the simplest decision task in which a person chooses between two available prospects. We have not treated in detail the more complicated production task (e.g., bidding) where the decision maker generates an alternative that is equal in value to a given prospect. The asymmetry between the two options in this situation could introduce systematic biases. Indeed, Lichtenstein and Slovic (1971) have constructed pairs of prospects A and B, such that people generally prefer A over B, but bid more for B than for A. This phenomenon has been confirmed in several studies, with both hypothetical and real gambles, e.g., Grether and Plott (1979). Thus, it cannot be generally assumed that the preference order of prospects can be recovered by a bidding procedure.

Because prospect theory has been proposed as a model of choice, the inconsistency of bids and choices implies that the measurement of values and decision weights should be based on choices between specified prospects rather than on bids or other production tasks. This restriction makes the assessment of v and π more difficult because production tasks are more convenient for scaling than pair comparisons.

4. Discussion

In the final section we show how prospect theory accounts for observed attitudes toward risk, discuss alternative representations of choice problems induced by shifts of reference point, and sketch several extensions of the present treatment.

Risk attitudes

The dominant pattern of preferences observed in Allais's example (Problems 1 and 2) follows from the present theory iff

$$\frac{\pi(.33)}{\pi(.34)} > \frac{v(2,400)}{v(2,500)} > \frac{\pi(.33)}{1-\pi(.66)}.$$

Hence, the violation of the independence axiom is attributed in this case to subcertainty, and more specifically to the inequality $\pi(.34) < 1 - \pi(.66)$. This analysis shows that an Allais-type violation will occur whenever the v-ratio of the two non-zero outcomes is bounded by the corresponding π-ratios.

Problems 3 through 8 share the same structure, hence it suffices to consider one pair, say Problems 7 and 8. The observed choices in these problems are implied by the theory iff

$$\frac{\pi(.001)}{\pi(.002)} > \frac{v(3,000)}{v(6,000)} > \frac{\pi(.45)}{\pi(.90)}.$$

The violation of the substitution axiom is attributed in this case to the subproportionality of π. Expected utility theory is violated in the above manner, therefore, whenever the v-ratio of the two outcomes is bounded by the respective π-ratios. The same analysis applies to other violations of the substitution axiom, both in the positive and in the negative domain.

We next prove that the preference for regular insurance over probabilistic insurance, observed in Problem 9, follows from prospect theory – provided the probability of loss is overweighted. That is, if $(-x, p)$ is indifferent to $(-y)$, then $(-y)$ is preferred to $(-x, p/2; -y, p/2; -y/2, 1-p)$. For simplicity, we define for $x \geq 0$, $f(x) = -v(-x)$. Since the value function for losses is convex, f is a concave function of x. Applying prospect theory, with the natural extension of equation (2), we wish to show that

$$\pi(p) f(x) = f(y) \quad \text{implies}$$

$$f(y) \leq f(y/2) + \pi(p/2)[f(y) - f(y/2)] + \pi(p/2)[f(x) - f(y/2)]$$
$$= \pi(p/2) f(x) + \pi(p/2) f(y) + [1 - 2\pi(p/2)] f(y/2).$$

Substituting for $f(x)$ and using the concavity of f, it suffices to show that

$$f(y) \leq \frac{\pi(p/2)}{\pi(p)} f(y) + \pi(p/2) f(y) + f(y)/2 - \pi(p/2) f(y)$$

or

$$\pi(p)/2 \leq \pi(p/2), \quad \text{which follows from the subadditivity of } \pi.$$

According to the present theory, attitudes toward risk are determined jointly by v and π, and not solely by the utility function. It is therefore instructive to examine the conditions under which risk aversion or risk seeking are expected to occur. Consider the choice between the gamble (x, p) and its expected value (px). If $x > 0$, risk seeking is implied whenever $\pi(p) > v(px)/v(x)$, which is greater than p if the value function for gains is concave. Hence, overweighting $(\pi(p) > p)$ is necessary but not sufficient for risk seeking in the domain of gains. Precisely the same condition is necessary but not sufficient for risk aversion when $x < 0$. This analysis restricts risk seeking in the domain of gains and risk aversion in the domain of losses to small probabilities, where overweighting is expected to hold. Indeed these are the typical conditions under which lottery tickets and insurance policies are sold. In prospect theory, the overweighting of small probabilities favors both gambling and insurance, while the S-shaped value function tends to inhibit both behaviors.

Although prospect theory predicts both insurance and gambling for small probabilities, we feel that the present analysis falls far short of a fully adequate account of these complex phenomena. Indeed, there is evidence from both experimental studies (Slovic et al., 1977), survey research (Kunreuther et al., 1978), and observations of economic behavior, e.g., service and medical insurance, that the purchase of insurance often extends to the medium range of probabilities, and that small probabilities of disaster are sometimes entirely ignored. Furthermore, the evidence suggests that minor changes in the formulation of the decision problem can have marked effects on the attractiveness of insurance (Slovic et al., 1977). A comprehensive theory of insurance behavior should consider, in addition to pure attitudes toward uncertainty and money, such factors as the value of security, social norms of prudence, the aversiveness of a large number of small payments spread over time, information and misinformation regarding probabilities and outcomes, and many others. Some effects of these variables could be described within the present framework, e.g., as changes of reference point, transformations of the value function, or manipulations of probabilities or decision weights. Other effects may require the introduction of variables or concepts which have not been considered in this treatment.

Shifts of reference

So far in this paper, gains and losses were defined by the amounts of money that are obtained or paid when a prospect is played, and the reference point was taken to be the status quo, or one's current assets. Although this is probably true for most choice problems, there are situations in which gains and losses are coded relative to an expectation or aspiration level that differs from the status quo. For example, an unexpected tax withdrawal from a monthly pay check is experienced as a loss, not as a reduced gain. Similarly, an entrepreneur who is weathering a slump with greater success than his competitors may interpret a small loss as a gain, relative to the larger loss he had reason to expect.

The reference point in the preceding examples corresponded to an asset position that one had expected to attain. A discrepancy between the reference point and the current asset position may also arise because of recent changes in wealth to which one has not yet adapted (Markowitz, 1952). Imagine a person who is involved in a business venture, has already lost 2000 and is now facing a choice between a sure gain of 1000 and an even chance to win 2000 or nothing. If he has not yet adapted to his losses, he is likely to code the problem as a choice between $(-2000, .50)$ and (-1000) rather than as a choice between $(2000, .50)$ and (1000). As we have seen, the former representation induces more adventurous choices than the latter.

A change of reference point alters the preference order for prospects. In particular, the present theory implies that a negative translation of a choice problem, such as arises from incomplete adaptation to recent losses, increases risk seeking in some situations. Specifically, if a risky prospect $(x, p; -y, 1-p)$ is just acceptable, then $(x-z, p; -y-z, 1-p)$ is preferred over $(-z)$ for $x, y, z > 0$, with $x > z$.

To prove this proposition, note that

$$V(x, p; y, 1-p) = 0 \quad \text{iff} \quad \pi(p)v(x) = -\pi(1-p)v(-y).$$

Furthermore,

$$
\begin{aligned}
V(x-z, p; &-y-z, 1-p) \\
&= \pi(p)v(x-z) + \pi(1-p)v(-y-z) \\
&> \pi(p)v(x) - \pi(p)v(z) + \pi(1-p)v(-y) \\
&\quad + \pi(1-p)v(-z) \quad \text{by the properties of } v. \\
&= -\pi(1-p)v(-y) - \pi(p)v(z) + \pi(1-p)v(-y) \\
&\quad + \pi(1-p)v(-z) \quad \text{by substitution,} \\
&= -\pi(p)v(z) + \pi(1-p)v(-z) \\
&> v(-z)[\pi(p) + \pi(1-p)] \quad \text{since } v(-z) < -v(z), \\
&> v(-z) \quad \text{by subcertainty.}
\end{aligned}
$$

This analysis suggests that a person who has not made peace with his losses is likely to accept gambles that would be unacceptable to him otherwise. The well known observation (McGlothlin, 1956) that the tendency to bet on long shots increases in the course of the betting day provides some support for the hypothesis that a failure to adapt to losses or to attain an expected gain induces risk seeking. For another example, consider an individual who expects to purchase insurance, perhaps because he has owned it in the past or because his friends do. This individual may code the decision to pay a premium y to protect against a loss x as a choice between $(-x+y, p; y, 1-p)$ and (0) rather than as a choice between $(-x, p)$ and $(-y)$. The preceding argument entails that insurance is likely to be more attractive in the former representation than in the latter.

Another important case of a shift of reference point arises when a person formulates his decision problem in terms of final assets, as advocated in decision analysis, rather than in terms of gains and losses, as people usually do. In this case, the reference point is set to zero on the scale of wealth and the value function is likely to be concave everywhere (Spetzler, 1968). According to the present analysis, this formulation essentially eliminates risk seeking, except for gambling with low probabilities. The explicit formulation of decision problems in terms of final assets is perhaps the most effective procedure for eliminating risk seeking in the domain of losses.

Many economic decisions involve transactions in which one pays money in exchange for a desirable prospect. Current decision theories analyze such problems as comparisons between the status quo and an alternative state which includes the acquired prospect minus its cost. For example, the decision whether to pay 10 for the gamble (1000, .01) is treated as a choice between (990, .01; −10, .99) and (0). In this analysis, readiness to purchase the positive prospect is equated to willingness to accept the corresponding mixed prospect.

The prevalent failure to integrate riskless and risky prospects, dramatized in the isolation effect, suggests that people are unlikely to perform the operation of subtracting the cost from the outcomes in deciding whether to buy a gamble. Instead, we suggest that people usually evaluate the gamble and its cost separately, and decide to purchase the gamble if the combined value is positive. Thus, the gamble (1000, .01) will be purchased for a price of 10 if $\pi(.01)v(1000) + v(-10) > 0$.

If this hypothesis is correct, the decision to pay 10 for (1000, .01), for example, is no longer equivalent to the decision to accept the gamble (990, .01; -10, .99). Furthermore, prospect theory implies that if one is indifferent between $(x(1-p), p; -px, 1-p)$ and (0) then one will not pay px to purchase the prospect (x, p). Thus, people are expected to exhibit more risk seeking in deciding whether to accept a fair gamble than in deciding whether to purchase a gamble for a fair price. The location of the reference point, and the manner in which choice problems are coded and edited emerge as critical factors in the analysis of decisions.

Extensions

In order to encompass a wider range of decision problems, prospect theory should be extended in several directions. Some generalizations are immediate; others require further development. The extension of equations (1) and (2) to prospects with any number of outcomes is straightforward. When the number of outcomes is large, however, additional editing operations may be invoked to simplify evaluation. The manner in which complex options, e.g., compound prospects, are reduced to simpler ones is yet to be investigated.

Although the present paper has been concerned mainly with monetary outcomes, the theory is readily applicable to choices involving other attributes, e.g., quality of life or the number of lives that could be lost or saved as a consequence of a policy decision. The main properties of the proposed value function for money should apply to other attributes as well. In particular, we expect outcomes to be coded as gains or losses relative to a neutral reference point, and losses to loom larger than gains.

The theory can also be extended to the typical situation of choice, where the probabilities of outcomes are not explicitly given. In such situations, decision weights must be attached to particular events rather than to stated probabilities, but they are expected to exhibit the essential properties that were ascribed to the weighting function. For example, if A and B are complementary events and neither is certain, $\pi(A) + \pi(B)$ should be less than utility – a natural analogue to subcertainty.

The decision weight associated with an event will depend primarily on the perceived likelihood of that event, which could be subject to major biases (Tversky & Kahneman, 1974). In addition, decision weights may be affected by other considerations, such as ambiguity or vagueness. Indeed, the work of Ellsberg (1961, Chapter 4, this volume) and Fellner (1965) implies that vagueness reduces decision weights. Consequently, subcertainty should be more pronounced for vague than for clear probabilities.

The present analysis of preference between risky options has developed two themes. The first theme concerns editing operations that determine how prospects are perceived. The second theme involves the judgmental principles that govern the evaluation of gains and losses and the weighting of uncertain outcomes. Although both themes should be developed further, they appear to provide a useful framework for the descriptive analysis of choice under risk.

Appendix

In this appendix we sketch an axiomatic analysis of prospect theory.[1] Since a complete self-contained treatment is long and tedious, we merely outline the essential steps and exhibit the key ordinal properties needed to establish the bilinear representation of equation (1). Similar methods could be extended to axiomatize equation (2).

Consider the set of all regular prospects of the form $(x, p; y, q)$ with $p + q < 1$. The extension to regular prospects with $p + q = 1$ is straightforward. Let $\gtrsim$ denote the relation of preference between prospects that is assumed to be connected, symmetric and transitive, and let $\simeq$ denote the associated relation of indifference. Naturally, $(x, p; y, q) \simeq (y, q; x, p)$. We also assume, as is implicit in our notation, that $(x, p; 0, q) \simeq (x, p; 0, r)$, and $(x, p; y, 0) \simeq (x, p; z, 0)$. That is, the null outcome and the impossible event have the property of a multiplicative zero.

Note that the desired representation [equation (1)] is additive in the probability-outcome pairs. Hence, the theory of additive conjoint measurement can be applied to obtain a scale V which preserves the preference order, and interval scales f and g in two arguments such that

$$V(x, p; y, q) = f(x, p) + g(y, q).$$

The key axioms used to derive this representation are:

Independence: $(x, p; y, q) \gtrsim (x, p; y', q')$ iff $(x', p'; y, q) \gtrsim (x', p'; y', q')$.

Cancellation: If $(x, p; y', q') \gtrsim (x', p'; y, q)$ and $(x', p'; y'', q'') \gtrsim (x'', p''; y', q')$, then $(x, p; y'', q'') \gtrsim (x'', p''; y, 'q)$.

Solvability: If $(x, p; y, q) \gtrsim (z, r) \gtrsim (x, p; y', q')$ for some outcome z and probability r, then there exist y'', q'' such that

$$(x, p; y'', q'') \gtrsim (z, r).$$

It has been shown that these conditions are sufficient to construct the desired additive representation, provided the preference order is Archimedean

---

[1] We are indebted to David H. Krantz for his help in the formulation of this section.

(Debreu, 1960, and Krantz et al., 1971). Furthermore, since $(x, p; y, q) \simeq (y, q; x, p)$, $f(x, p) + g(y, q) = f(y, q) + g(x, p)$, and letting $q = 0$ yields $f = g$.

Next, consider the set of all prospects of the form (x, p) with a single non-zero outcome. In this case, the bilinear model reduces to $V(x, p) = \pi(p)v(x)$. This is the multiplicative model, investigated in Roskies (1965) and Krantz et al. (1971). To construct the multiplicative representation we assume that the ordering of the probability-outcome pairs satisfies independence, cancellation, solvability, and the Archimedean axiom. In addition, we assume sign dependence (Krantz et al., 1971) to ensure the proper multiplication of signs. It should be noted that the solvability axiom used in Roskies (1965) and Krantz et al. (1971) must be weakened because the probability factor permits only bounded solvability.

Combining the additive and the multiplicative representations yields

$$V(x, p; y, q) = f[\pi(p)v(x)] + f[\pi(q)v(y)].$$

Finally, we impose a new distributivity axiom:

$$(x, p; y, p) \simeq (z, p) \quad \text{iff} \quad (x, q; y, q) \simeq (z, q).$$

Applying this axiom to the above representation, we obtain

$$f[\pi(p)v(x)] + f[\pi(p)v(y)] = f[\pi(p)v(z)]$$

implies

$$f[\pi(q)v(x)] + f[\pi(q)v(y)] = f[\pi(q)v(z)].$$

Assuming, with no loss of generality, that $\pi(q) < \pi(p)$, and letting $\alpha = \pi(p)v(x)$, $\beta = \pi(p)v(y)$, $\gamma = \pi(p)v(z)$, and $\theta = \pi(q)/\pi(p)$, yields $f(\alpha) + f(\beta) = f(\gamma)$ implies $f(\theta\alpha) + f(\theta\beta) = f(\theta\gamma)$ for all $0 < \theta < 1$.

Because f is strictly monotonic we can set $\gamma = f^{-1}[f(\alpha) + f(\beta)]$. Hence, $\theta\gamma = \theta f^{-1}[f(\alpha) + f(\beta)] = f^{-1}[f(\theta\alpha) + f(\theta\beta)]$.

The solution to this functional equation is $f(\alpha) = k\alpha^c$ (Aczél, 1966). Hence, $V(x, p; y, q) = k[\pi(p)v(x)]^c + k[\pi(q)v(y)]^c$, for some $k, c > 0$. The desired bilinear form is obtained by redefining the scales π, v, and V so as to absorb the constants k and c.

References

Aczél, J. *Lectures on Functional Equations and Their Applications,* Academic Press, New York, 1966.

Allais, M. "Le comportement de l'homme rationnel devant le risque: Critique des postulats et axioms de l'ecole americaine," *Econometrica, 21* (1953), 503–546.

Anderson, N. H., and Shanteau, J. C. "Information integration in risky decision making," *Journal of Experimental Psychology, 84* (1970), 441–451.

Arrow, K. J. *Essays in the Theory of Risk-Bearing,* Markham, Chicago, 1971.

Barnes, J. D., and Reinmuth, J. E. "Comparing imputed and actual utility functions in a competitive bidding setting," *Decision Sciences, 7* (1976), 801–812.

Coombs, C. H. "Portfolio theory and measurement of risk," in *Human Judgment and Decision Processes,* ed. by M. F. Kaplan and S. Schwartz, Academic Press, New York, 1975, 63–85.

Davidson, D., Suppes, P., and Siegel, S. *Decision-making: An Experimental Approach,* Stanford University Press, Stanford, 1957.

Debreu, G. "Topological methods in cardinal utility theory," in *Mathematical Methods in the Social Sciences,* ed. by K. J. Arrow, S. Karlin, and P. Suppes, Stanford University Press, Stanford, 1960, 16–26.

Edwards, W. "Subjective probabilities inferred from decisions," *Psychological Review, 69* (1962), 109–135.

Ellsberg, D. "Risk, ambiguity, and the Savage axioms," *Quarterly Journal of Economics, 75* (1961), 643–669. (Reprinted in this volume, as Chap. 4.)

Fellner, W. "Distortion of subjective probabilities as a reaction to uncertainty," *Quarterly Journal of Economics, 75* (1961), 670–689.

Probability and Profit – A Study of Economic Behavior Along the Bayesian Lines, R. D. Irwin, Homewood, Illinois, 1965.

Fishburn, P. C. "Mean-risk analysis with risk associated with below-target returns," *American Economic Review, 67* (1977), 116–126.

Fishburn, P. C., and Kochenberger, G. A. "Two-piece von Neumann-Morgenstern utility functions," *Decision Sciences, 10* (1979), 503–518.

Friedman, M., and Savage, L. J. "The utility analysis of choices involving risks," *Journal of Political Economy, 56* (1948), 279–304. Reprinted in *Reading in Price Theory,* ed. by G. Stigler and K. Boulding, Richard D. Irwin, Chicago, 1952.

Fuchs, V. R. "From Bismark to Woodcock: The 'irrational' pursuit of national health insurance," *Journal of Law and Economics, 19* (1976), 347–359.

Galanter, E., and Pliner, P. "Cross-modality matching of money against other continua," in *Sensation and Measurement,* ed. by H. R. Moskowitz, et al., Reidel, Dordrecht, 1974, 65–76.

Grayson, C. J. *Decisions under Uncertainty: Drilling Decisions by Oil and Gas Operators,* Graduate School of Business, Harvard University, Cambridge, Massachusetts, 1960.

Green, P. E. "Risk attitudes and chemical investment decisions," *Chemical Engineering Progress, 59* (1963), 35–40.

Grether, D. M., and Plott, C. R. "Economic theory of choice and the preference reversal phenomenon," *American Economic Review, 69* (1979), 623–638.

Halter, A. N., and Dean, G. W. *Decisions under Uncertainty,* South Western Publishing Co., Cincinnati, 1971.

Hansson, B. "The appropriateness of the expected utility model," *Erkenntnis, 9* (1975), 175–193.

Helson, H. *Adaptation-Level Theory,* Harper, New York, 1964.

Keeney, R. L., and Raiffa, H. *Decisions with Multiple Objectives: Preferences and Value Tradeoffs,* Wiley, New York, 1976.

Krantz, D. H., Luce, D. R., Suppes, P., and Tversky, A. *Foundations of Measurement,* Academic Press, New York, 1971.

Kunreuther, H., Ginsberg, R., Miller, L., Sagi, P., Slovic, P., Borkan, B., and Katz, N. *Disaster Insurance Protection: Public Policy Lessons,* Wiley, New York, 1978.

Lichtenstein, S., and Slovic, P. "Reversal of preference between bids and choices in gambling decisions," *Journal of Experimental Psychlogy, 89* (1971), 46–55.

MacCrimmon, K. R., and Larsson, S. "Utility theory: Axioms versus paradoxes," in *Expected Utility Hypotheses and the Allais Paradox,* ed. by M. Allais and O. Hagen, Reidel, Dordrecht, 1979, 333–409.

Markowitz, H. "The utility of wealth," *Journal of Political Economy, 60* (1952), 151–158.

Portfolio Selection, Wiley, New York, 1959.

McGlothlin, W. H. "Stability of choice among uncertain alternatives," *American Journal of Psychology, 69* (1956), 604–615.

Mosteller, F., and Nogee, P. "An experimental measurement of utility," *American Journal of Political Economy, 59* (1951), 371–404.

Pratt, J. W. "Risk aversion in the small and in the large," *Econometrica, 32* (1964), 122–136.

Raiffa, H. *Decision Analysis: Introductory Lectures on Choices Under Uncertainty,* Addison-Wesley, Reading, Mass., 1968.

Roskies, R. "A measurement axiomatization of essentially multiplicative representation of two factors," *Journal of Mathematical Psychology, 2* (1965), 266–276.

Savage, L. J. *The Foundations of Statistics,* John Wiley, New York, 1954; 2nd revised edition, Dover, New York, 1972.

Slovic, P., Fischhoff, B., Lichtenstein, S., Corrigan, B., and Coombs, B. "Preference for insuring against probable small losses: Insurance implications," *Journal of Risk and Insurance, 44* (1977), 237–258.

Slovic, P., and Tversky, A. "Who accepts Savage's axiom?," *Behavioral Science, 19* (1974), 368–373.

Spetzler, C. S. "The development of corporate risk policy for capital investment decisions," *IEEE Transactions on Systems Science and Cybernetics,* SSC-4 (1968), 279–300.

Swalm, R. O. "Utility theory – Insights into risk taking," *Review of Economic Studies, 44* (1966), 123–136.

Tversky, A. "Additivity, utility, and subjective probability," *Journal of Mathematical Psychology, 4* (1967), 175–201.

"Intransitivity of preferences," *Psychological Review, 76* (1969), 31–48.

"Elimination by aspects: A theory of choice," *Psychological Review, 79* (1972), 281–299.

Tversky, A., and Kahneman, D. "Judgment under uncertainty: Heuristics and biases," *Science, 185* (1974), 1124–1131. [Reprinted in Chapter 7.]

Tobin, J. "Liquidity preferences as behavior towards risk," *Review of Economic Studies, 26* (1958), 65–86.

von Neumann, J., and Morgenstern, O. *Theory of Games and Economic Behavior,* Princeton University Press, Princeton, 1944; 3d ed. John Wiley and Sons, 1953.

van Dam, C. "Another look at inconsistency in financial decision-making," presented at the Seminar on Recent Research in Finance and Monetary Economics, Cergy-Pontoise, March, 1975.

Williams, A. C. "Attitudes toward speculative risk as an indicator of attitudes toward pure risk," *Journal of Risk and Insurance, 33* (1966), 577–586.

7. Judgment under uncertainty: heuristics and biases

Amos Tversky and Daniel Kahneman

Many decisions are based on beliefs concerning the likelihood of uncertain events such as the outcome of an election, the guilt of a defendant, or the future value of the dollar. These beliefs are usually expressed in statements such as "I think that...," "chances are...," "it is unlikely that...," and so forth. Occasionally, beliefs concerning uncertain events are expressed in numerical form as odds or subjective probabilities. What determines such beliefs? How do people assess the probability of an uncertain event or the value of an uncertain quantity? This article shows that people rely on a limited number of heuristic principles which reduce the complex tasks of assessing probabilities and predicting values to simpler judgmental operations. In general, these heuristics are quite useful, but sometimes they lead to severe and systematic errors.

The subjective assessment of probability resembles the subjective assessment of physical quantities such as distance or size. These judgments are all based on data of limited validity, which are processed according to heuristic rules. For example, the apparent distance of an object is determined in part by its clarity. The more sharply the object is seen, the closer it appears to be. This rule has some validity, because in any given scene the more distant objects are seen less sharply than nearer objects. However, the reliance on this rule leads to systematic errors in the estimation of distance. Specifically, distances are often overestimated when visibility is poor because the contours of objects are blurred. On the other hand, distances are often underestimated when visibility is good because the objects are seen sharply. Thus, the reliance on clarity as an indication of distance leads to common biases. Such biases are also found in the intuitive judgment of probability. This article describes three heuristics that are employed to assess probabilities and to

Reprinted with permission from *Science* 185 (1974), 1124–31.

predict values. Biases to which these heuristics lead are enumerated, and the applied and theoretical implications of these observations are discussed.

1. Representativeness

Many of the probabilistic questions with which people are concerned belong to one of the following types: What is the probability that object A belongs to class B? What is the probability that event A originates from process B? What is the probability that process B will generate event A? In answering such questions, people typically rely on the representativeness heuristic, in which probabilities are evaluated by the degree to which A is representative of B, that is, by the degree to which A resembles B. For example, when A is highly representative of B, the probability that A originates from B is judged to be high. On the other hand, if A is not similar to B, the probability that A originates from B is judged to be low.

For an illustration of judgment by representativeness, consider an individual who has been described by a former neighbor as follows: "Steve is very shy and withdrawn, invariably helpful, but with little interest in people, or in the world of reality. A meek and tidy soul, he has a need for order and structure, and a passion for detail." How do people assess the probability that Steve is engaged in a particular occupation from a list of possibilities (for example, farmer, salesman, airline pilot, librarian, or physician)? How do people order these occupations from most to least likely? In the representativeness heuristic, the probability that Steve is a librarian, for example, is assessed by the degree to which he is representative of, or similar to, the stereotype of a librarian. Indeed, research with problems of this type has shown that people order the occupations by probability and by similarity in exactly the same way (Kahneman & Tversky, 1973, 4). This approach to the judgment of probability leads to serious errors, because similarity, or representativeness, is not influenced by several factors that should affect judgments of probability.

Insensitivity to prior probability of outcomes

One of the factors that has no effect on representativeness but should have a major effect on probability is the prior probability, or base-rate frequency, of the outcomes. In the case of Steve, for example, the fact that there are many more farmers than librarians in the population should enter into any reasonable estimate of the probability that Steve is a librarian rather than a farmer. Considerations of base-rate frequency, however, do not affect the similarity of Steve to the stereotypes of librarians and farmers. If people evaluate probability by representativeness, therefore, prior probabilities will be neglected. This hypothesis was tested in an experiment where prior probabilities were manipulated (Kahneman & Tversky, 1973, 4). Subjects were shown brief personality descriptions of several individuals, allegedly sampled at random from a group of 100 professionals – engineers and lawyers. The subjects were asked to assess, for each description, the probability that it belonged to an engineer rather than to a lawyer. In one experimental condition, subjects were told that the group from which the descriptions had been drawn consisted of 70 engineers and 30 lawyers. In another condition, subjects were told that the group consisted of 30 engineers and 70 lawyers. The odds that any particular description belongs to an engineer rather than to a lawyer should be higher in the first condition, where there is a majority of engineers, than in the second condition, where there is a majority of lawyers. Specifically, it can be shown by applying Bayes' rule that the ratio of these odds should be $(.7/.3)^2$, or 5.44, for each description. In a sharp violation of Bayes' rule, the subjects in the two conditions produced essentially the same probability judgments. Apparently, subjects evaluated the likelihood that a particular description belonged to an engineer rather than to a lawyer by the degree to which this description was representative of the two stereotypes, with little or no regard for the prior probabilities of the categories.

The subjects used prior probabilities correctly when they had no other information. In the absence of a personality sketch, they judged the probability that an unknown individual is an engineer to be .7 and .3, respectively, in the two base-rate conditions. However, prior probabilities were effectively ignored when a description was introduced, even when this description was totally uninformative. The responses to the following description illustrate this phenomenon:

Dick is a 30 year old man. He is married with no children. A man of high ability and high motivation, he promises to be quite successful in his field. He is well liked by his colleagues.

This description was intended to convey no information relevant to the question of whether Dick is an engineer or a lawyer. Consequently, the probability that Dick is an engineer should equal the proportion of engineers in the group, as if no description had been given. The subjects, however, judged the probability of Dick being an engineer to be .5 regardless of whether the stated proportion of engineers in the group was .7 or .3. Evidently, people respond differently when given no evidence and when given worthless evidence. When no specific evidence is given, prior probabilities are properly utilized; when worthless evidence is given, prior probabilities are ignored (Kahneman & Tversky, 1973, 4).

Insensitivity to sample size

To evaluate the probability of obtaining a particular result in a sample drawn from a specified population, people typically apply the representativeness heuristic. That is, they assess the likelihood of a sample result, for example, that the average height in a random sample of ten men will be 6 feet (180 centimeters), by the similarity of this result to the corresponding parameter (that is, to the average height in the population of men). The similarity of a sample statistic to a population parameter does not depend on the size of the sample. Consequently, if probabilities are assessed by representativeness, then the judged probability of a sample statistic will be essentially independent of sample size. Indeed, when subjects assessed the distributions of average height for samples of various sizes, they produced identical distributions. For example, the probability of obtaining an average height greater than 6 feet was assigned the same value for samples of 1000, 100, and 10 men (Kahneman & Tversky, 1972, 3). Moreover, subjects failed to appreciate the role of sample size even when it was emphasized in the formulation of the problem. Consider the following question:

A certain town is served by two hospitals. In the larger hospital about 45 babies are born each day, and in the smaller hospital about 15 babies are born each day. As you know, about 50 percent of all babies are boys. However, the exact percentage varies from day to day. Sometimes it may be higher than 50 percent, sometimes lower.

For a period of 1 year, each hospital recorded the days on which more than 60 percent of the babies born were boys. Which hospitals do you think recorded more such days?

        The larger hospital (21)
        The smaller hospital (21)
        About the same (that is, within 5 percent of each other) (53)

The values in parentheses are the number of undergraduate students who chose each answer.

Most subjects judged the probability of obtaining more than 60 percent boys to be the same in the small and in the large hospital, presumably because these events are described by the same statistic and are therefore equally representative of the general population. In contrast, sampling theory entails that the expected number of days on which more than 60 percent of the babies are boys is much greater in the small hospital than in the large one, because a large sample is less likely to stray from 50 percent. This fundamental notion of statistics is evidently not part of people's repertoire of intuitions.

A similar insensitivity to sample size has been reported in judgments of posterior probability, that is, of the probability that a sample has been drawn from one population rather than from another. Consider the following example:

Imagine an urn filled with balls, of which ⅔ are of one color and ⅓ of another. One individual has drawn 5 balls from the urn, and found that 4 were red and 1 was white. Another individual has drawn 20 balls and found that 12 were red and 8 were white. Which of the two individuals should feel more confident that the urn contains ⅔ red balls and ⅓ white balls, rather than the opposite? What odds should each individual give?

In this problem, the correct posterior odds are 8 to 1 for the 4:1 sample and 16 to 1 for the 12:8 sample, assuming equal prior probabilities. However, most people feel that the first sample provides much stronger evidence for the hypothesis that the urn is predominantly red, because the proportion of red balls is larger in the first than in the second sample. Here again, intuitive judgments are dominated by the sample proportion and are essentially unaffected by the size of the sample, which plays a crucial role in the determination of the actual posterior odds (Kahneman & Tversky, 1972). In addition, intuitive estimates of posterior odds are far less extreme than the correct values. The underestimation of the impact of evidence has been observed repeatedly in problems of this type (W. Edwards, 1968, **25**; Slovic & Lichtenstein, 1971). It has been labeled "conservatism."

Misconceptions of chance

People expect that a sequence of events generated by a random process will represent the essential characteristics of that process even when the sequence is short. In considering tosses of a coin for heads or tails, for example, people regard the sequence H-T-H-T-T-H to be more likely than the sequence H-H-H-T-T-T, which does not appear random, and also more likely than the sequence H-H-H-H-T-H, which does not represent the fairness of the coin (Kahneman & Tversky, 1972, **3**). Thus, people expect that the essential characteristics of the process will be represented, not only globally in the entire sequence, but also locally in each of its parts. A locally representative sequence, however, deviates systematically from chance expectation: it contains too many alternations and too few runs. Another consequence of the belief in local representativeness is the well-known gambler's fallacy. After observing a long run of red on the roulette wheel, for example, most people erroneously believe that black is now due, presumably because the occurrence of black will result in a more representative sequence than the occurrence of an additional red. Chance is commonly viewed as a self-correcting process in which a deviation in one direction induces a deviation in the opposite direction to restore the equilibrium. In fact, deviations are not "corrected" as a chance process unfolds, they are merely diluted.

Misconceptions of chance are not limited to naive subjects. A study of the statistical intuitions of experienced research psychologists (Tversky & Kahneman, 1971, **2**) revealed a lingering belief in what may be called the "law of small numbers," according to which even small samples are highly representative of the populations from which they are drawn. The responses of these investigators reflected the expectation that a valid hypothesis about a population will be represented by a statistically significant result in a sample – with little regard for its size. As a consequence, the researchers put too much faith in the results of small samples and grossly overestimated the replicability of such results. In the actual conduct of research, this bias leads to the selection of samples of inadequate size and to overinterpretation of findings.

Insensitivity to predictability

People are sometimes called upon to make such numerical predictions as the future value of a stock, the demand for a commodity, or the outcome of a football game. Such predictions are often made by representativeness. For example, suppose one is given a description of a company and is asked to predict its future profit. If the description of the company is very favorable, a very high profit will appear most representative of that description; if the description is mediocre, a mediocre performance will appear most representative. The degree to which the description is favorable is unaffected by the reliability of that description or by the degree to which it permits accurate prediction. Hence, if people predict solely in terms of the favorableness of the description, their predictions will be insensitive to the reliability of the evidence and to the expected accuracy of the prediction.

This mode of judgment violates the normative statistical theory in which the extremeness and the range of predictions are controlled by considerations of predictability. When predictability is nil, the same prediction should be made in all cases. For example, if the descriptions of companies provide no information relevant to profit, then the same value (such as average profit) should be predicted for all companies. If predictability is perfect, of course, the values predicted will match the actual values and the range of predictions will equal the range of outcomes. In general, the higher the predictability, the wider the range of predicted values.

Several studies of numerical prediction have demonstrated that intuitive predictions violate this rule, and that subjects show little or no regard for considerations of predictability (Kahneman & Tversky, 1973, **4**). In one of these studies, subjects were presented with several paragraphs, each describing the performance of a student teacher during a particular practice lesson. Some subjects were asked to *evaluate* the quality of the lesson described in the paragraph in percentile scores, relative to a specified population. Other subjects were asked to *predict*, also in percentile scores, the standing of each student teacher 5 years after the practice lesson. The judgments made under the two conditions were identical. That is, the prediction of a remote criterion (success of a teacher after 5 years) was identical to the evaluation of the information on which the prediction was based (the quality of the practice lesson). The students who made these predictions were undoubtedly aware of the limted predictabity of teaching competence on the basis of a single trial lesson 5 years earlier; nevertheless, their predictions were as extreme as their evaluations.

The illusion of validity

As we have seen, people often predict by selecting the outcome (for example, an occupation) that is most representative of the input (for example, the description of a person). The confidence they have in their prediction depends primarily on the degree of representativeness (that is, on the quality of the match between the selected outcome and the input) with little or no regard for the factors that limit predictive accuracy. Thus, people express great confidence in the prediction that a person is a librarian when given a description of his personality which matches the stereotype of librarians, even if the description is scanty, unreliable, or outdated. The unwarranted confidence which is produced by a good fit between the predicted outcome and the input information may be called the illusion of validity. This illusion persists even when the judge is aware of the factors that limit the accuracy of his predictions. It is a common observation that psychologists who conduct selection interviews often experience considerable confidence in their predictions, even when they know of the vast literature that shows selection interviews to be highly fallible. The continued reliance on the clinical interview for selection, despite repeated demonstrations of its inadequacy, amply attests to the strength of this effect.

The internal consistency of a pattern of inputs is a major determinant of one's confidence in predictions based on these inputs. For example, people express more confidence in predicting the final grade-point average of a student whose first-year record consists entirely of B's than in predicting the grade-point average of a student whose first-year record includes many A's and C's. Highly consistent patterns are most often observed when the input variables are highly redundant or correlated. Hence, people tend to have great confidence in predictions based on redundant input variables. However, an elementary result in the statistics of correlation asserts that, given input variables of stated validity, a prediction based on several such inputs can achieve higher accuracy when they are independent of each other than when they are redundant or correlated. Thus, redundancy among inputs decreases accuracy even as it increases confidence, and people are often confident in predictions that are quite likely to be off the mark (Kahneman & Tversky, 1973, 4).

Misconceptions of regression

Suppose a large group of children has been examined on two equivalent versions of an aptitude test. If one selects ten children from among those who did best on one of the two versions, he will usually find their performance on the second version to be somewhat disappointing. Conversely, if one selects ten children from among those who did worst on one version, they will be found, on the average, to do somewhat better on the other version. More generally, consider two variables X and Y which have the same distribution. If one selects individuals whose average X score deviates from the mean of X by k units, then the average of their Y scores will usually deviate from the mean of Y by less than k units. These observations illustrate a general phenomenon known as regression toward the mean, which was first documented by Galton more than 100 years ago.

In the normal course of life, one encounters many instances of regression toward the mean, in the comparison of the height of fathers and sons, of the intelligence of husbands and wives, or of the performance of individuals on consecutive examinations. Nevertheless, people do not develop correct intuitions about this phenomenon. First, they do not expect regression in many contexts where it is bound to occur. Second, when they recognize the occurrence of regression, they often invent spurious causal explanations for it (Kahneman & Tversky, 1973, 4). We suggest that the phenomenon of regression remains elusive because it is incompatible with the belief that the predicted outcome should be maximally representative of the input, and, hence, that the value of the outcome variable should be as extreme as the value of the input variable.

The failure to recognize the import of regression can have pernicious consequences, as illustrated by the following observation (Kahneman & Tversky, 1973, 4). In a discussion of flight training, experienced instructors noted that praise for an exceptionally smooth landing is typically followed by a poorer landing on the next try, while harsh criticism after a rough landing is usually followed by an improvement on the next try. The instructors concluded that verbal rewards are detrimental to learning, while verbal punishments are beneficial, contrary to accepted psychological doctrine. This conclusion is unwarranted because of the presence of regression toward the mean. As in other cases of repeated examination, an improvement will usually follow a poor performance and a deterioration will usually follow an outstanding performance, even if the instructor does not respond to the trainee's achievement on the first attempt. Because the instructors had praised their trainees after good landings and admonished them after poor ones, they reached the erroneous and potentially harmful conclusion that punishment is more effective than reward.

Thus, the failure to understand the effect of regression leads one to overestimate the effectiveness of punishment and to underestimate the effectiveness of reward. In social interaction, as well as in training, rewards are typically administered when performance is good, and punishments are typically administered when performance is poor. By regression alone, therefore, behavior is most likely to improve after punishment and most likely to deteriorate after reward. Consequently, the human condition is such that, by chance alone, one is most often rewarded for punishing others and most often punished for rewarding them. People are generally not aware of this contingency. In fact, the elusive role of regression in determining the apparent consequences of reward and punishment seems to have escaped the notice of students of this area.

2. Availability

There are situations in which people assess the frequency of a class or the probability of an event by the ease with which instances or occurrences can be brought to mind. For example, one may assess the risk of heart attack among middle-aged people by recalling such occurrences among one's acquaintances. Similarly, one may evaluate the probability that a given business venture will fail by imagining various difficulties it could encounter. This judgmental heuristic is called availability. Availability is a useful clue for assessing frequency or probability, because instances of large classes are usually reached better and faster than instances of less frequent classes. However, availability is affected by factors other than frequency and probability. Consequently, the reliance on availability leads to predictable biases, some of which are illustrated below.

Biases due to the retrievability of instances

When the size of a class is judged by the availability of its instances, a class whose instances are easily retrieved will appear more numerous than a class of equal frequency whose instances are less retrievable. In an elementary demonstration of this effect, subjects heard a list of well-known personalities of both sexes and were subsequently asked to judge whether the list contained more names of men than of women. Different lists were presented to different groups of subjects. In some of the lists the men were relatively more famous than the women, and in others the women were relatively more famous than the men. In each of the lists, the subjects erroneously judged that the class (sex) that had the more famous personalities was the more numerous (Tversky & Kahneman, 1973, **11**).

In addition to familiarity, there are other factors, such as salience, which affect the retrievability of instances. For example, the impact of seeing a house burning on the subjective probability of such accidents is probably greater than the impact of reading about a fire in the local paper. Furthermore, recent occurrences are likely to be relatively more available than earlier occurrences. It is a common experience that the subjective probability of traffic accidents rises temporarily when one sees a car overturned by the side of the road.

Biases due to the effectiveness of a search set

Suppose one samples a word (of three letters or more) at random from an English text. Is it more likely that the word starts with r or that r is the third letter? People approach this problem by recalling words that begin with r (road) and words that have r in the third position (car) and assess the relative frequency by the ease with which words of the two types come to mind. Because it is much easier to search for words by their first letter than by their third letter, most people judge words that begin with a given consonant to be more numerous than words in which the same consonant appears in the third position. They do so even for consonants, such as r or k, that are more frequent in the third position than in the first (Tversky & Kahneman, 1973, **11**).

Different tasks elicit different search sets. For example, suppose you are asked to rate the frequency with which abstract words (*thought, love*) and concrete words (*door, water*) appear in written English. A natural way to answer this question is to search for contexts in which the word could appear. It seems easier to think of contexts in which an abstract concept is mentioned (*love* in love stories) than to think of contexts in which a concrete word (such as *door*) is mentioned. If the frequency of words is judged by the availability of the contexts in which they appear, abstract words will be judged as relatively more numerous than concrete words. This bias has been observed in a recent study (Galbraith & Underwood, 1973) which showed that the judged frequency of occurrence of abstract words was much higher than that of concrete words, equated in objective frequency. Abstract words were also judged to appear in a much greater variety of contexts than concrete words.

Biases of imaginability

Sometimes one has to assess the frequency of a class whose instances are not stored in memory but can be generated according to a given rule. In such situations, one typically generates several instances and evaluates frequency or probability by the ease with which the relevant instances can be constructed. However, the ease of constructing instances does not always reflect their actual frequency, and this mode of evaluation is prone to biases. To illustrate, consider a group of 10 people who form committees of k members, $2 \le k \le 8$. How many different committees of k members can be formed? The correct answer to this problem is given by the binomial coefficient $\binom{10}{k}$ which reaches a maximum of 252 for $k = 5$. Clearly, the number of committees of k members equals the number of committees of $(10 - k)$ members, because any committee of k members defines a unique group of $(10 - k)$ nonmembers.

One way to answer this question without computation is to mentally construct committees of k members and to evaluate their number by the ease with which they come to mind. Committees of few members, say 2, are more available than committees of many members, say 8. The simplest scheme for the construction of committees is a partition of the group into disjoint sets. One readily sees that it is easy to construct five disjoint committees of 2 members, while it is impossible to generate even two disjoint committees of 8 members. Consequently, if frequency is assessed by imaginability, or by availability for construction, the small committees will appear more numerous than larger committees, in contrast to the correct bell-shaped function. Indeed, when naive subjects were asked to estimate the number of distinct committees of various sizes, their estimates were a decreasing monotonic function of committee size (Tversky & Kahneman, 1973, 11). For example, the median estimate of the number of committees of 2 members was 70, while the estimate for committees of 8 members was 20 (the correct answer is 45 in both cases).

Imaginability plays an important role in the evaluation of probabilities in real-life situations. The risk involved in an adventurous expedition, for example, is evaluated by imagining contingencies with which the expedition is not equipped to cope. If many such difficulties are vividly portrayed, the expedition can be made to appear exceedingly dangerous, although the ease with which disasters are imagined need not reflect their actual likelihood. Conversely, the risk involved in an undertaking may be grossly underestimated if some possible dangers are either difficult to conceive of, or simply do not come to mind.

Illusory correlation

Chapman and Chapman (1969) have described an interesting bias in the judgment of the frequency with which two events co-occur. They presented naive judges with information concerning several hypothetical mental patients. The data for each patient consisted of a clinical diagnosis and a drawing of a person made by the patient. Later the judges estimated the frequency with which each diagnosis (such as paranoia or suspiciousness) had been accompanied by various features of the drawing (such as peculiar eyes). The subjects markedly overestimated the frequency of co-occurrence of natural associates, such as suspiciousness and peculiar eyes. This effect was labeled illusory correlation. In their erroneous judgments of the data to which they had been exposed, naive subjects "rediscovered" much of the common, but unfounded, clinical lore concerning the interpretation of the draw-a-person test. The illusory correlation effect was extremely resistant to contradictory data. It persisted even when the correlation between symptom and diagnosis was actually negative, and it prevented the judges from detecting relationships that were in fact present.

Availability provides a natural account for the illusory-correlation effect. The judgment of how frequently two events co-occur should be based on the strength of the associative bond between them. When the association is strong, one is likely to conclude that the events have been frequently paired. Consequently, strong associates will be judged to have occurred together frequently. According to this view, the illusory correlation between suspiciousness and peculiar drawing of the eyes, for example, is due to the fact that suspiciousness is more readily associated with the eyes than with any other part of the body.

Lifelong experience has taught us that, in general, instances of large classes are recalled better and faster than instances of less frequent classes; that likely occurrences are easier to imagine than unlikely ones; and that the associative connections between events are strengthened when the events frequently co-occur. As a result, man has at his disposal a procedure (the availability heuristic) for estimating the numerosity of a class, the likelihood of an event, or the frequency of co-occurrences, by the ease with which the relevant mental operations of retrieval, construction, or association can be performed. However, as the preceding examples have demonstrated, this valuable estimation procedure results in systematic errors.

3. Adjustment and anchoring

In many situations, people make estimates by starting from an initial value that is adjusted to yield the final answer. The initial value, or starting point, may be suggested by the formulation of the problem, or it may be the result of a partial computation. In either case, adjustments are typically insufficient (Slovic & Lichtenstein, 1971). That is, different starting points yield different estimates, which are biased toward the initial values. We call this phenomenon anchoring.

Insufficient adjustment

In a demonstration of the anchoring effect, subjects were asked to estimate various quantities, stated in percentages (for example, the percentage of African countries in the United Nations). For each quantity, a number between 0 and 100 was determined by spinning a wheel of fortune in the subjects' presence. The subjects were instructed to indicate first whether that number was higher or lower than the value of the quantity, and then to estimate the value of the quantity by moving upward or downward from the given number. Different groups were given different numbers for each quantity, and these arbitrary numbers had a marked effect on estimates. For example, the median estimates of the percentage of African countries in the United Nations were 25 and 45 for groups that received 10 and 65, respectively, as starting points. Payoffs for accuracy did not reduce the anchoring effect.

Anchoring occurs not only when the starting point is given to the subject, but also when the subject bases his estimate on the result of some incomplete computation. A study of intuitive numerical estimation illustrates this effect. Two groups of high school students estimated, within 5 seconds, a numerical expression that was written on the blackboard. One group estimated the product

$$8 \times 7 \times 6 \times 5 \times 4 \times 3 \times 2 \times 1$$

while another group estimated the product

$$1 \times 2 \times 3 \times 4 \times 5 \times 6 \times 7 \times 8$$

To rapidly answer such questions, people may perform a few steps of computation and estimate the product by extrapolation or adjustment. Because adjustments are typically insufficient, this procedure should lead to underestimation. Furthermore, because the result of the first few steps of multiplication (performed from left to right) is higher in the descending sequence than in the ascending sequence, the former expression should be judged larger than the latter. Both predictions were confirmed. The median estimate for the ascending sequence was 512, while the median estimate for the descending sequence was 2,250. The correct answer is 40,320.

Biases in the evaluation of conjunctive and disjunctive events

In a recent study by Bar-Hillel (1973) subjects were given the opportunity to bet on one of two events. Three types of events were used: (i) simple events, such as drawing a red marble from a bag containing 50 percent red marbles and 50 percent white marbles; (ii) conjunctive events, such as drawing a red marble seven times in succession, with replacement, from a bag containing 90 percent red marbles and 10 percent white marbles; and (iii) disjunctive events, such as drawing a red marble at least once in seven successive tries, with replacement, from a bag containing 10 percent red marbles and 90 percent white marbles. In this problem, a significant majority of subjects preferred to bet on the conjunctive event (the probability of which is .48) rather than on the simple event (the probability of which is .50). Subjects also preferred to bet on the simple event rather than on the disjunctive event, which has a probability of .52. Thus, most subjects bet on the less likely event in both comparisons. This pattern of choices illustrates a general finding. Studies of choice among gambles and of judgments of probability indicate that people tend to overestimate the probability of conjunctive events (Cohen, Chesnick, & Haran, 1972, **24**) and to underestimate the probability of disjunctive events. These biases are readily explained as effects of anchoring. The stated probability of the elementary event (success at any one stage) provides a natural starting point for the estimation of the probabilities of both conjunctive and disjunctive events. Since adjustment from the starting point is typically insufficient, the final estimates remain too close to the probabilities of the elementary events in both cases. Note that the overall probability of a conjunctive event is lower than the probability of each elementary event, whereas the overall probability of a disjunctive event is higher than the probability of each elementary event. As a consequence of anchoring, the overall probability will be overestimated in conjunctive problems and underestimated in disjunctive problems.

Biases in the evaluation of compound events are particularly significant in the context of planning. The successful completion of an undertaking, such as the development of a new product, typically has a conjunctive character: for the undertaking to succeed, each of a series of events must occur. Even when each of these events is very likely, the overall probability of success can be quite low if the number of events is large. The general tendency to overestimate the probability of conjunctive events leads to unwarranted optimism in the evaluation of the likelihood that a plan will succeed or that a project will be completed on time. Conversely, disjunctive structures are typically encountered in the evaluation of risks. A complex system, such as a nuclear reactor or a human body, will malfunction if any of its essential components fails. Even when the likelihood of failure in each component is slight, the probability of an overall failure can be high if many components are involved. Because of anchoring, people will tend to underestimate the probabilities of failure in complex systems. Thus, the direction of the anchoring bias can sometimes be inferred from the structure of the event. The chain-like structure of conjunctions leads to overestimation, the funnel-like structure of disjunctions leads to underestimation.

Anchoring in the assessment of subjective probability distributions

In decision analysis, experts are often required to express their beliefs about a quantity, such as the value of the Dow-Jones average on a particular day, in the form of a probability distribution. Such a distribution is usually constructed by asking the person to select values of the quantity that correspond to specified percentiles of his subjective probability distribution. For example, the judge may be asked to select a number, X_{90}, such that his subjective probability that this number will be higher than the value of the Dow-Jones average is .90. That is, he should select the value X_{90} so that he is just willing to accept 9 to 1 odds that the Dow-Jones average will not exceed it. A subjective probability distribution for the value of the Dow-Jones average can be constructed from several such judgments corresponding to different percentiles.

By collecting subjective probability distributions for many different quantities, it is possible to test the judge for proper calibration. A judge is properly (or externally) calibrated in a set of problems if exactly Π percent of the true values of the assessed quantities falls below his stated values of X_{Π}. For example, the true values should fall below X_{01} for 1 percent of the quantities and above X_{99} for 1 percent of the quantities. Thus, the true values should fall in the confidence interval between X_{01} and X_{99} on 98 percent of the problems.

Several investigators (Alpert & Raiffa, 1969, **21**; Staël von Holstein, 1971; Winkler, 1967) have obtained probability distributions for many quantities from a large number of judges. These distributions indicated large and systematic departures from proper calibration. In most studies, the actual values of the assessed quantities are either smaller than X_{01} or greater than X_{99} for about 30 percent of the problems. That is, the subjects state overly narrow confidence intervals which reflect more certainty than is justified by their knowledge about the assessed quantities. This bias is common to naive and to sophisticated subjects, and it is not eliminated by introducing proper scoring rules, which provide incentives for external calibration. This effect is attributable, in part at least, to anchoring.

To select X_{90} for the value of the Dow-Jones average, for example, it is natural to begin by thinking about one's best estimate of the Dow-Jones and to adjust this value upward. If this adjustment – like most others – is insufficient, then X_{90} will not be sufficiently extreme. A similar anchoring effect will occur in the selection of X_{10}, which is presumably obtained by adjusting one's best estimate downward. Consequently, the confidence interval between X_{10} and X_{90} will be too narrow, and the assessed probability distribution will be too tight. In support of this interpretation it can be shown that subjective probabilities are systematically altered by a procedure in which one's best estimate does not serve as an anchor.

Subjective probability distributions for a given quantity (the Dow-Jones average) can be obtained in two different ways: (i) by asking the subject to select values of the Dow-Jones that correspond to specified percentiles of his probability distribution and (ii) by asking the subject to assess the probabilities that the true value of the Dow-Jones will exceed some specified values. The two procedures are formally equivalent and should yield identical distributions. However, they suggest different modes of adjustment from different anchors. In procedure (i), the natural starting point is one's best estimate of the quality. In procedure (ii), on the other hand, the subject may be anchored on the value stated in the question. Alternatively, he may be anchored on even odds, or 50–50 chances, which is a natural starting point in the estimation of likelihood. In either case, procedure (ii) should yield less extreme odds than procedure (i).

To contrast the two procedures, a set of 24 quantities (such as the air distance from New Delhi to Peking) was presented to a group of subjects who assessed either X_{10} or X_{90} for each problem. Another group of subjects received the median judgment of the first group for each of the 24 quantities. They were asked to assess the odds that each of the given values exceeded the true value of the relevant quantity. In the absence of any bias, the second group should retrieve the odds specified to the first group, that is, 9:1. However, if even odds or the stated value serve as anchors, the odds of the second group should be less extreme, that is, closer to 1:1. Indeed, the median odds stated by this group, across all problems, were 3:1. When the judgments of the two groups were tested for external calibration, it was found that subjects in the first group were too extreme, in accord with earlier studies. The events that they defined as having a probability of .10 actually obtained in 24 percent of the cases. In contrast, subjects in the second group were too conservative. Events to which they assigned an average probability of .34 actually obtained in 26 percent of the cases. These results illustrate the manner in which the degree of calibration depends on the procedure of elicitation.

4. Discussion

This article has been concerned with cognitive biases that stem from the reliance on judgmental heuristics. These biases are not attributable to motivational effects such as wishful thinking or the distortion of judgments by payoffs and penalties. Indeed, several of the severe errors of judgment reported earlier occurred despite the fact that subjects were encouraged to be accurate and were rewarded for the correct answers (Kahneman & Tversky, 1972, **3**; Tversky & Kahneman, 1973, **11**).

The reliance on heuristics and the prevalence of biases are not restricted to laymen. Experienced researchers are also prone to the same biases – when they think intuitively. For example, the tendency to predict the outcome that best represents the data, with insufficient regard for prior probability, has been observed in the intuitive judgments of individuals who have had extensive training in statistics (Kahneman & Tversky, 1973, **4**; Tversky & Kahneman, 1971, **2**). Although the statistically sophisticated avoid elementary errors, such as the gambler's fallacy, their intuitive judgments are liable to similar fallacies in more intricate and less transparent problems.

It is not surprising that useful heuristics such as representativeness and availability are retained, even though they occasionally lead to errors in prediction or estimation. What is perhaps surprising is the failure of people to infer from lifelong experience such fundamental statistical rules as regression toward the mean, or the effect of sample size on sampling variability. Although everyone is exposed, in the normal course of life, to numerous examples from which these rules could have been induced, very few people discover the principles of sampling and regression on their own. Statistical principles are not learned from everyday experience because the relevant instances are not coded appropriately. For example, people do not discover that successive lines in a text differ more in average word length than do successive pages, because they simply do not attend to the average word length of individual lines or pages. Thus, people do not learn the relation between sample size and sampling variability, although the data for such learning are abundant.

The lack of an appropriate code also explains why people usually do not detect the biases in their judgments of probability. A person could conceivably learn whether his judgments are externally calibrated by keeping a tally of the proportion of events that actually occur among those to which he assigns the same probability. However, it is not natural to group events by their judged probability. In the absence of such grouping it is impossible for an individual to discover, for example, that only 50 percent of the predictions to which he has assigned a probability of .9 or higher actually come true.

The empirical analysis of cognitive biases has implications for the theoretical and applied role of judged probabilities. Modern decision theory (de Finetti, 1968; Savage, 1954) regards subjective probability as the quantified opinion of an idealized person. Specifically, the subjective probability of a given event is defined by the set of bets about this event that such a person is willing to accept. An internally consistent, or coherent, subjective probability measure can be derived for an individual if his choices among bets satisfy certain principles, that is, the axioms of the theory. The derived probability is subjective in the sense that different individuals are allowed to have different probabilities for the same event. The major contribution of this approach is that it provides a rigorous subjective interpretation of probability that is applicable to unique events and is embedded in a general theory of rational decision.

It should perhaps be noted that, while subjective probabilities can sometimes be inferred from preferences among bets, they are normally not formed in this fashion. A person bets on team A rather than on team B because he believes that team A is more likely to win; he does not infer this belief from his betting preferences. Thus, in reality, subjective probabilities determine preferences among bets and are not derived from them, as in the axiomatic theory of rational decision (Savage, 1954).

The inherently subjective nature of probability has led many students to the belief that coherence, or internal consistency, is the only valid criterion by which judged probabilities should be evaluated. From the standpoint of the formal theory of subjective probability, any set of internally consistent probability judgments is as good as any other. This criterion is not entirely satisfactory, because an internally consistent set of subjective probabilities can be incompatible with other beliefs held by the individual. Consider a person whose subjective probabilities for all possible outcomes of a coin-tossing game reflect the gambler's fallacy. That is, his estimate of the probability of tails on a particular toss increases with the number of consecutive heads that preceded that toss. The judgments of such a person could be internally consistent and therefore acceptable as adequate subjective probabilities according to the criterion of the formal theory. These probabilities, however, are incompatible with the generally held belief that a coin has no memory and is therefore incapable of generating sequential dependencies. For judged probabilities to be considered adequate, or rational, internal consistency is not enough. The judgments must be compatible with the entire web of beliefs held by the individual. Unfortunately, there can be no simple formal procedure for assessing the compatibility of a set of probability judgments with the judge's total system of beliefs. The rational judge will nevertheless strive for compatibility, even though internal consistency is more easily achieved and assessed. In particular, he will attempt to make his probability judgments compatible with his knowledge about the subject matter, the laws of probability, and his own judgmental heuristics and biases.

5. Summary

This article described three heuristics that are employed in making judgments under uncertainty: (i) representativeness, which is usually employed when people are asked to judge the probability that an object or event A belongs to class or process B; (ii) availability of instances or scenarios, which is often employed when people are asked to assess the frequency of a class or the plausibility of a particular development; and (iii) adjustment from an anchor, which is usually employed in numerical prediction when a relevant value is available. These heuristics are highly economical and usually effective, but they lead to systematic and predictable errors. A better understanding of these heuristics and of the biases to which they lead could improve judgments and decisions in situations of uncertainty.

References

Alpert, W., & Raiffa, H. A progress report on the training of probability assessors. Unpublished manuscript, 1969.

Bar-Hillel, M. On the subjective probability of compound events. *Organizational Behavior and Human Performance,* 1973, *9,* 396–406.

Chapman, L. J., & Chapman, J. P. Illusory correlation as an obstacle to the use of valid psychodiagnostic signs. *Journal of Abnormal Psychology,* 1969, *74,* 271–280.

Cohen, J., Chesnick, E. I., & Haran, D. A confirmation of the inertial-ψ effect in sequential choice and decision. *British Journal of Psychology,* 1972, *63,* 41–46.

de Finetti, B. Probability: Interpretations. In D. E. Sills (Ed.), *International Encyclopedia of the Social Sciences* (Vol. 12). New York: Macmillan, 1968, Pp. 496–504.

Edwards, W. Conservatism in human information processing. In B. Kleinmuntz (Ed.), *Formal representation of human judgment.* New York: Wiley, 1968, 17–52.

Galbraith, R. C., & Underwood, B. J. Perceived frequency of concrete and abstract words. *Memory and Cognition,* 1973, *1,* 56–60.

Kahneman, D., & Tversky, A. Subjective probability: A judgment of representativeness. *Cognitive Psychology,* 1972, *3,* 430–454.

On the psychology of prediction. *Psychological Review,* 1973, *80,* 237–251.

Savage, L. J. *The foundations of statistics.* New York: Wiley, 1954.

Slovic, P., & Lichtenstein, S. Comparison of Bayesian and regression approaches to the study of information processing in judgment. *Organizational Behavior and Human Performance,* 1971, *6,* 649–744.

Staël von Holstein, C.-A. S. Two techniques for assessment of subjective probability distributions – An experimental study. *Acta Psychologica,* 1971, *35,* 478–494.

Tversky, A., & Kahneman, D. The belief in the "law of small numbers." *Psychological Bulletin,* 1971, *76,* 105–110.

Availability: A heuristic for judging frequency and probability. *Cognitive Psychology,* 1973, *5,* 207–232.

Winkler, R. L. The assessment of prior distributions in Bayesian analysis. *Journal of the American Statistical Association,* 1967, *62,* 776–800.

8. Alternative visions of rationality

Herbert A. Simon

One kind of optimism, or supposed optimism, argues that if we think hard enough, are rational enough, we can solve all our problems. The eighteenth century, the Age of Reason, was supposed to have been imbued with this kind of optimism. Whether it actually was or not I will leave to historians; certainly the hopes we hold out for reason in our world today are much more modest. . . .

In this [essay], I will focus initially on the very powerful formal models of rationality that have been constructed in this century and that must be counted among the jewels of intellectual accomplishment in our time. Since these models are well known, I will describe them only briefly, devoting most of my discussion to showing why, in application to real human affairs, they deliver somewhat less than they appear to promise. But my intent here is not mainly critical. The last half of this [essay] will develop a more realistic description of human bounded rationality, and will consider to what extent the limited capability for analysis that is provided by bounded rationality can meet the needs for reason in human affairs. . . .

In science one is supposed to deliver new truths. The most crushing verdict that can be pronounced on a scientific paper is the fabled referee's report, scribbled in the margin, "What's new here is not true, and what's true is not new." But these pages are not intended as reports of scientific discoveries and will not seek novelty. I will be satisfied if what I have to say is mainly true, even though it will not be at all new. As I shall argue in my discussion of human rationality, attention needs to be called periodically to important old truths.

Reprinted from *Reason in Human Affairs* by Herbert A. Simon with the permission of the publishers, Stanford University Press. © 1983 by the Board of Trustees of the Leland Stanford Junior University.

At the same time, I do not wish simply to repeat here things that I have said at length in my previous books, and especially in *Administrative Behavior* and *The Sciences of the Artificial,* both of which are deeply concerned with the concept of human rationality. In the former, I examined the implications of the limits of human rationality for organizational behavior. In the latter, I described properties that are common to all adaptive ("artificial") systems, giving us a basis for constructing a general theory of such systems. [Here] I have drawn on this previous work to the extent necessary to provide a framework for my discussion. But within this framework I have concentrated on topics that remain problematic or controversial and that are of critical importance for understanding the role of rationality in human affairs....

1. The limits of reason

Modern descendants of Archimedes are still looking for the fulcrum on which they can rest the lever that is to move the whole world. In the domain of reasoning, the difficulty in finding a fulcrum resides in the truism "no conclusions without premises." Reasoning processes take symbolic inputs and deliver symbolic outputs. The initial inputs are axioms, themselves not derived by logic but simply induced from empirical observations, or even more simply posited. Moreover, the processes that produce the transformations of inputs to outputs (rules of inference) are also introduced by fiat and are not the products of reason. Axioms and inference rules together constitute the fulcrum on which the lever of reasoning rests; but the particular structure of that fulcrum cannot be justified by the methods of reasoning. For an attempt at such a justification would involve us in an infinite regress of logics, each as arbitrary in its foundations as the preceding one.

This ineradicable element of arbitrariness – this Original Sin that corrupts the reasoning process, and therefore also its products – has two important consequences for our topic here. First, it puts forever beyond reach an unassailable principle of induction that would allow us to infer infallible general laws, without risk of error, from specific facts, even from myriads of them. No number of viewings of white swans can guarantee that a black one will not be seen next. Whether even a definite probability statement can be made about the color of the next swan is a matter of debate, with the negatives, I think, outnumbering the affirmatives.

Further, the foundations of these inductions – the facts – rest on a complex and sometimes unsteady base of observation, perception, and inference. Facts, especially in science, are usually gathered in with instruments that are themselves permeated with theoretical assumptions. No microscope without at least a primitive theory of light and optics; no human verbal protocols without a theory of short-term memory. Hence the fallibility of reasoning is guaranteed both by the impossibility of generating unassailable general propositions from particular facts, and by the tentative and theory-infected character of the facts themselves.

Second, the principle of "no conclusions without premises" puts for-ever beyond reach normative statements (statements containing an essen-tial *should*) whose derivation is independent of inputs that also contain *should*'s. None of the rules of inference that have gained acceptance are capable of generating normative outputs purely from descriptive inputs.[1] The corollary to "no conclusions without premises" is "no *ought*'s from *is*'s alone." Thus, whereas reason may provide powerful help in finding means to reach our ends, it has little to say about the ends themselves.

There is a final difficulty, first pointed out by Gödel, that rich systems of logic are never complete – there always exist true theorems that cannot be reached as outputs by applying the legal transformations to the inputs. Since the problem of logical incompleteness is much less important in the application of reason to human affairs than the difficulties that concern us here, I shall not discuss it further. Nor will I be concerned with whether the standard axioms of logic and the rules of inference themselves are to some extent arbitrary. For the purpose of this discussion, I shall regard them as unexceptionable.

Reason, then, goes to work only after it has been supplied with a suit-able set of inputs, or premises. If reason is to be applied to discovering and choosing courses of action, then those inputs include, at the least, a set of *should*'s, or values to be achieved, and a set of *is*'s, or facts about the world in which the action is to be taken. Any attempt to justify these *should*'s and *is*'s by logic will simply lead to a regress to new *should*'s and *is*'s that are similarly postulated.

2. Values

We see that reason is wholly instrumental. It cannot tell us where to go; at best it can tell us how to get there. It is a gun for hire that can be employed in the service of whatever goals we have, good or bad. It makes a great dif-ference in our view of the human condition whether we attribute our diffi-culties to evil or to ignorance and irrationality – to the baseness of goals or to our not knowing how to reach them.

Method in madness

A useful, if outrageous, exercise for sharpening one's thinking about the limited usefulness of reasoning, taken in isolation, is to attempt to read

---

[1] I will not undertake to make the argument here. It was stated well many years ago by Ayer, in *Language, Truth, and Logic,* rev. ed. (New York, 1946), chap. 6.

Hitler's *Mein Kampf* analytically – as though preparing for a debate. The exercise is likely to be painful, but is revealing about how facts, values, and emotions interact in our thinking about human affairs. I pick this particular example because the reader's critical faculties are unlikely, in this case, to be dulled by agreement with the views expressed.

Most of us would take exception to many of Hitler's "facts," especially his analysis of the causes of Europe's economic difficulties, and most of all his allegations that Jews and Marxists (whom he also mistakenly found indistinguishable) were at the root of them. However, if we were to suspend disbelief for a moment and accept his "facts" as true, much of the Nazi program would be quite consistent with goals of security for the German nation or even of welfare for the German people. Up to this point, the unacceptability of that program to us is not a matter of evil goals – no one would object to concern for the welfare of the German people – or of faulty reasoning from those goals, but rests on the unacceptability of the factual postulates that connect the goals to the program. From this viewpoint, we might decide that the remedy for Nazism was to combat its program by reason resting on better factual premises.

But somehow that calm response does not seem to match the outrage that *Mein Kampf* produces in us. There must be something more to our rejection of its argument, and obviously there is. Its stated goals are, to put it mildly, incomplete. Statements of human goals usually distinguish between a "we" for whom the goals are shaped and a "they" whose welfare is not "our" primary concern. Hitler's "we" was the German people – the definition of "we" being again based on some dubious "facts" about a genetic difference between Aryan and non-Aryan peoples. Leaving aside this fantasy of Nordic purity, most of us would still define "we" differently from Hitler. Our "we" might be Americans instead of Germans, or, if we had reached a twenty-first-century state of enlightenment, our "we" might even be the human species. In either case, we would be involved in a genuine value conflict with *Mein Kampf,* a conflict not resolvable in any obvious way by improvements in either facts or reasoning. Our postulation of a "we" – of the boundary of our concern for others – is a basic assumption about what is good and what is evil.

Probably the greatest sense of outrage that *Mein Kampf* generates stems from the sharpness of the boundary Hitler draws between "we" and "they." Not only does he give priority to "we," but he argues that any treatment of "they," however violent, is justifiable if it advances the goals of "we." Even if Hitler's general goals and "facts" were accepted, most of us would still object to the measures he proposes to inflict on "they" in order to nurture the welfare of "we." If, in our system of values, we do not regard "they" as being without rights, reason will disclose to us a conflict of values – a conflict between our value of helping "we" and our general goal of not inflicting harm on "they." And so it is not its reasoning for which we must fault *Mein Kampf,* but its alleged facts and its outrageous values.

There is another lesson to be learned from *Mein Kampf*. We cannot read many lines of it before detecting that Hitler's reasoning is not cold reasoning but hot reasoning. We have long since learned that when a position is declaimed with passion and invective, there is special need to examine carefully both its premises and its inferences. We have learned this, but we do not always practice it. Regrettably, it is precisely when the passion and invective resonate with our own inner feelings that we forget the warning and become uncritical readers or listeners.

Hitler was an effective rhetorician for Germans precisely because his passion and invectives resonated with beliefs and values already present in many German hearts. The heat of his rhetoric rendered his readers incapable of applying the rules of reason and evidence to his arguments. Nor was it only Germans who resonated to the facts and values he proclaimed. The latent anti-Semitism and overt anti-Communism of many Western statesmen made a number of his arguments plausible to them.

And so we learned, by bitter experience and against our first quick judgments, that we could not dismiss Hitler as a madman, for there was method in his madness. His prose met standards of reason neither higher nor lower than we are accustomed to encountering in writing designed to persuade. Reason was not, could not have been, our principle shield against Nazism. Our principal shield was contrary factual beliefs and values.

De gustibus est disputandum

Recognizing all these complications in the use of reason, hot or cold, and recognizing also that *ought*'s cannot be derived from *is*'s alone, we must still admit that it is possible to reason about conduct. For most of the *ought*'s we profess are not ultimate standards of conduct but only subgoals, adopted as means to other goals. For example, taken in isolation a goal like "live within your income" may sound unassailable. Yet a student might be well advised to go into debt in order to complete his or her education. A debt incurred as an investment in future productivity is different from a gambling debt.

Values can indeed be disputed (1) if satisfying them has consequences, present or future, for other values, (2) if they are acquired values, or (3) if they are instrumental to more final values. But although there has been widespread consensus about the rules of reasoning that apply to factual matters, it has proved far more difficult over the centuries to reach agreement about the rules that should govern reasoning about interrelated values. Several varieties of modal logic proposed for reasoning about imperative and deontic statements have gained little acceptance and even less application outside of philosophy.[2]

---

[2] I state the case against modal logics in Section 3 of my *Models of Discovery* (Dordrecht, 1977) and in "On Reasoning about Actions," chap. 8 of H. A. Simon and L. Siklóssy, eds., *Representation and Meaning* (Englewood Cliffs, N.J., 1972).

In the past half century, however, an impressive body of formal theory has been erected by mathematical statisticians and economists to help us reason about these matters – without introducing a new kind of logic. The basic idea of this theory is to load all values into a single function, the utility function, in this way finessing the question of how different values are to be compared. The comparison has in effect already been made when it is assumed that a utility has been assigned to each particular state of affairs.

This formal theory is called subjective expected utility (SEU) theory. Its construction is one of the impressive intellectual achievements of the first half of the twentieth century. It is an elegant machine for applying reason to problems of choice. Our next task is to examine it, and to make some judgments about its validity and limitations.

3. Subjective expected utility

Since a number of comprehensive and rigorous accounts of SEU theory are available in the literature,[3] I will give here only a brief heuristic survey of its main components.

The theory

First, the theory assumes that a decision maker has a well-defined *utility function,* and hence that he can assign a cardinal number as a measure of his liking of any particular scenario of events over the future. Second, it assumes that the decision maker is confronted with a well-defined *set of alternatives* to choose from. These alternatives need not be one-time choices, but may involve sequences of choices or strategies in which each subchoice will be made only at a specified time using the information available at that time. Third, it assumes that the decision maker can assign a consistent *joint probability distribution* to all future sets of events. Finally, it assumes that the decision maker will (or should) choose the alternative, or the strategy, that will *maximize the expected value,* in terms of his utility function, of the set of events consequent on the strategy. With each strategy, then, is associated a probability distribution of future scenarios that can be used to weight the utilities of those scenarios.

These are the four principal components of the SEU model: a cardinal utility function, an exhaustive set of alternative strategies, a probability distribution of scenarios for the future associated with each strategy, and a policy of maximizing expected utility.

Problems with the theory

Conceptually, the SEU model is a beautiful object deserving a prominent place in Plato's heaven of ideas. But vast difficulties make it impossible to

---

[3] For example, L. J. Savage's classic, *The Foundations of Statistics* (New York, 1954).

employ it in any literal way in making actual human decisions. I have said so much about these difficulties at other times and places (particularly in the pages of *Administrative Behavior*) that I will make only the briefest mention of them here.

The SEU model assumes that the decision maker contemplates, in one comprehensive view, everything that lies before him. He understands the range of alternative choices open to him, not only at the moment but over the whole panorama of the future. He understands the consequences of each of the available choice strategies, at least up to the point of being able to assign a joint probability distribution to future states of the world. He has reconciled or balanced all his conflicting partial values and synthesized them into a single utility function that orders, by his preference for them, all these future states of the world.

The SEU model finesses completely the origins of the values that enter into the utility function; they are simply there, already organized to express consistent preferences among all alternative futures that may be presented for choice. The SEU model finesses just as completely the processes for ascertaining the facts of the present and future states of the world. At best, the model tells us how to reason about fact and value premises; it says nothing about where they come from.

When these assumptions are stated explicitly, it becomes obvious that SEU theory has never been applied, and never can be applied – with or without the largest computers – in the real world. Yet one encounters many purported applications in mathematical economics, statistics, and management science. Examined more closely, these applications retain the formal structure of SEU theory, but substitute for the incredible decision problem postulated in that theory either a highly abstracted problem in a world simplified to a few equations and variables, with the utility function and the joint probability distributions of events assumed to be already provided, or a microproblem referring to some tiny, carefully defined and bounded situation carved out of a larger real-world reality.

SEU as an approximation

Since I have had occasion to use SEU theory in some of my own research in management science, let me throw the stone through my own window. Holt, Modigliani, Muth, and I constructed a procedure for making decisions about production levels, inventories, and work force in a factory under conditions of uncertainty.[4] The procedure fits the SEU model. The utility function is (the negative of) a cost function, comprising costs of production, costs of changing the level of production, putative costs of lost orders, and inventory holding costs. The utility function is assumed to be quadratic in

---

[4] C. C. Holt, F. Modigliani, J. R. Muth, and H. A. Simon, *Planning Production, Inventories and Work Force* (Englewood Cliffs, N.J., 1960).

the independent variables, an assumption made because it is absolutely essential if the mathematics and computation are to be manageable. Expected values for sales in each future period are assumed to be known. (The same assumption of the quadratic utility function fortunately makes knowledge of the complete probability distributions irrelevant.) The factory is assumed to have a single homogeneous product, or a set of products that can legitimately be represented by a single-dimensional aggregate.

It is clear that if this decision procedure is used to make decisions for a factory, that is very different from employing SEU theory to make decisions in the real world. All but one of the hard questions have been answered in advance by the assumption of a known, quadratic criterion function and known expected values of future sales. Moreover, this single set of production decisions has been carved out of the entire array of decisions that management has to make, and it has been assumed to be describable in a fashion that is completely independent of information about those other decisions or about any other aspect of the real world.

I have no urge to apologize for our decision procedure as a useful management science tool. It can be, and has been, applied to this practical decision task in a number of factory situations and seems to have operated satisfactorily. What I wish to emphasize is that it is applied to a highly simplified representation of a tiny fragment of the real-world situation, and that the goodness of the decisions it will produce depends much more on the adequacy of the approximating assumptions and the data supporting them than it does on the computation of a maximizing value according to the prescribed SEU decision rule. Hence, it would be perfectly conceivable for someone to contrive a quite different decision procedure, outside the framework of SEU theory, that would produce better decisions in these situations (measured by real-world consequences) than would be produced by our decision rule.

Exactly the same comments can be made about economic models formed within the SEU mold. Their veridicality and usefulness cannot be judged from the fact that they satisfy, formally, the SEU assumptions. In evaluating them, it is critical to know how close the postulated utilities and future events match those of the real world.

Once we accept the fact that, in any actual application, the SEU rule supplies only a crude approximation to an abstraction, an outcome that may or may not provide satisfactory solutions to the real-world problems, then we are free to ask what other decision procedures, unrelated to SEU, might also provide satisfactory outcomes. In particular, we are free to ask what procedures human beings actually use in their decision making and what relation those actual procedures bear to the SEU theory.

I hope I have persuaded you that, in typical real-world situations, decision makers, no matter how badly they want to do so, simply cannot apply the SEU model. If doubt still remains on this point, it can be dissipated by examining the results of laboratory experiments in which human subjects have been asked to make decisions involving risk and uncertainty in game-like situations [with] orders of magnitude simpler than the game of real life. The evidence, much of which has been assembled in several articles by Amos Tversky and his colleagues, leaves no doubt whatever that the human behavior in these choice situations – for whatever reasons – departs widely from the prescriptions of SEU theory.[5] Of course, I have already suggested what the principal reason is for this departure. It is that human beings have neither the facts nor the consistent structure of values nor the reasoning power at their disposal that would be required, even in these relatively simple situations, to apply SEU principles.

As our next task, we consider what they do instead.

4. The behavioral alternative

I will ask you to introspect a bit about how you actually make decisions, and I will make some assertions that you can check against your introspections. First, your decisions are not comprehensive choices over large areas of your life, but are generally concerned with rather specific matters, assumed, whether correctly or not, to be relatively independent of other, perhaps equally important, dimensions of life. At the moment you are buying a car, you are probably not also simultaneously choosing next week's dinner menu, or even deciding how to invest income you plan to save.

Second, when you make any particular decision, even an important one, you probably do not work out detailed scenarios of the future, complete with probability distributions, conditional on the alternative you choose. You have a general picture of your life-style and prospects, and perhaps of one or two major contemplated changes in the near future, and even of a couple of contingencies. When you are considering buying a car, you have a general notion of your use of automobiles, your income and the other demands on it, and whether you are thinking of getting a new job in another city. You are unlikely to envision large numbers of other possibilities that might affect what kind of car it makes sense to buy.

Third, the very fact that you are thinking about buying a car, and not a house, will probably focus your attention on some aspects of your life and some of your values to the relative neglect of others. The mere contemplation of buying a car may stimulate fond memories or dreams of travel, and divert your attention from the pleasures of listening to stereo or giving dinner parties for friends at home. Hence, it is unlikely that a single comprehensive utility function will watch over the whole range of decisions you make. On the contrary, particular decision domains will evoke particular values, and great inconsistencies in choice may result from fluctuating attention. We all know that if we want to diet, we should resist exposing ourselves to tempting

---

[5] See A. Tversky and D. Kahneman, "Judgment under Uncertainty: Heuristics and Biases," *Science* 185: 1124–31 (1974), and references cited there. [See Chapter 7.]

food. That would be neither necessary nor useful if our choices were actually guided by a single comprehensive and consistent utility function.

Fourth, a large part of whatever effort you devote to making your car-buying decision will be absorbed in gathering facts and evoking possibly relevant values. You may read *Consumer Reports* and consult friends; you may visit car dealers in order to learn more about the various alternatives, and to learn more about your own tastes as well. Once facts of this sort have been assembled, and preferences evoked, the actual choice may take very little time.

Bounded rationality

Choices made in the general way I have just been describing are sometimes characterized as instances of *bounded rationality*. Good reasons can be given for supposing that evolutionary processes might produce creatures capable of bounded rationality. Moreover, a great deal of psychological research supports the hunch to which our introspections have led us, namely that this is the way in which human decisions – even the most deliberate – are made. Let us call this model of human choice the behavioral model, to contrast it with the Olympian model of SEU theory.

Within the behavioral model of bounded rationality, one doesn't have to make choices that are infinitely deep in time, that encompass the whole range of human values, and in which each problem is interconnected with all the other problems in the world. In actual fact, the environment in which we live, in which all creatures live, is an environment that is nearly factorable into separate problems. Sometimes you're hungry, sometimes you're sleepy, sometimes you're cold. Fortunately, you're not often all three at the same time. Or if you are, all but one of these needs can be postponed until the most pressing is taken care of. You have lots of other needs, too, but these also do not all impinge on you at once.

We live in what might be called a nearly empty world – one in which there are millions of variables that in principle could affect each other but that most of the time don't. In gravitational theory everything is pulling at everything else, but some things pull harder than others, either because they're bigger or because they're closer. Perhaps there is actually a very dense network of interconnections in the world, but in most of the situations we face we can detect only a modest number of variables or considerations that dominate.

If this factorability is not wholly descriptive of the world we live in today – and I will express some reservations about that – it certainly describes the world in which human rationality evolved: the world of the cavemen's ancestors, and of the cavemen themselves. In that world, very little was happening most of the time, but periodically action had to be taken to deal with hunger, or to flee danger, or to secure protection against the coming winter.

Rationality could focus on dealing with one or a few problems at a time, with the expectation that when other problems arose there would be time to deal with those too.[6]

Mechanisms for bounded rationality

What characteristics does an organism need to enable it to exercise a sensible kind of bounded [rationality]? It needs some way of focusing attention – of avoiding distraction (or at least too much distraction) and focusing on the things that need attention at a given time. A very strong case can be made, and has been made by physiological psychologists, that focusing attention is one of the principal functions of the processes we call emotions. One thing an emotion can do for and to you is to distract you from your current focus of thought, and to call your attention to something else that presumably needs attention right now. Most of the time in our society we don't have to be out looking for food, but every so often we need to be reminded that food is necessary. So we possess some mechanisms that arouse periodically the feeling of hunger, to direct our attention to the need for food. A similar account can be given of other emotions.

Some of an organism's requirements call for continuous activity. People need to have air – access to it can be interrupted only for a short time – and their blood must circulate continually to all parts of their bodies. Of course, human physiology takes care of these and other short-term insistent needs in parallel with the long-term needs. We do not have to have our attention directed to a lack of oxygen in our bloodstream in order to take a breath, or for our heart to beat. But by and large, with respect to those needs that are intermittent, that aren't constantly with us, we operate very much as serial, one-at-a-time, animals. One such need is about as many as our minds can handle at one time. Our ability to get away with that limitation, and to survive in spite of our seriality, depends on the mechanisms, particularly emotional mechanisms, that assure new problems of high urgency a high priority on the agenda.

Second, we need a mechanism capable of generating alternatives. A large part of our problem solving consists in the search for good alternatives, or for improvements in alternatives that we already know. In the past 25 years, research in cognitive psychology and artificial intelligence has taught us a lot about how alternatives are generated. I have given a description of some of the mechanisms in Chapters 3 and 4 of *The Sciences of the Artificial*.[7]

Third, we need a capability for acquiring facts about the environment in which we find ourselves, and a modest capability for drawing inferences from these facts. Of course, this capability is used to help generate alternatives as

[6] A simple formal model of such rationality is provided by my "Rational Choice and the Structure of the Environment," *Psychological Review* 63: 129–38 (1956).

[7] Second ed. (Cambridge, Mass., 1981).

well as to assess their probable consequences, enabling the organism to maintain a very simple model of the part of the world that is relevant to its current decisions, and to do commonsense reasoning about the model.

What can we say for and about this behavioral version, this bounded rationality version, of human thinking and problem solving? The first thing we can say is that there is now a tremendous weight of evidence that this theory describes the way people, in fact, make decisions and solve problems. The theory has an increasingly firm empirical base as a description of human behavior. Second, it is a theory that accounts for the fact that creatures stay alive and even thrive, who – however smart they are or think they are – have modest computational abilities in comparison with the complexity of the entire world that surrounds them. It explains how such creatures have survived for at least the millions of years that our species has survived. In a world that is nearly empty, in which not everything is closely connected with everything else, in which problems can be decomposed into their components – in such a world, the kind of rationality I've been describing gets us by.

Consequences of bounded rationality

Rationality of the sort described by the behavioral model doesn't optimize, of course. Nor does it even guarantee that our decisions will be consistent. As a matter of fact, it is very easy to show that choices made by an organism having these characteristics will often depend on the order in which alternatives are presented. If A is presented before B, A may seem desirable or at least satisfactory; but if B is presented before A, B will seem desirable and will be chosen before A is even considered.

The behavioral model gives up many of the beautiful formal properties of the Olympian model, but in return for giving them up it provides a way of looking at rationality that explains how creatures with our mental capacities – or even, with our mental capacities supplemented with all the computers in Silicon Valley – get along in a world that is much too complicated to be understood from the Olympian viewpoint of SEU theory.

5. Intuitive rationality

A third model of human rationality has been much less discussed by social scientists than the two that I've considered so far, but is perhaps even more prominent in the popular imagination. I've referred to it as the intuitive model. The intuitive model postulates that a great deal of human thinking, and a great deal of the success of human beings in arriving at correct decisions, is due to the fact that they have good intuition or good judgment. The notions of intuition and judgment are particularly prominent in public discussion today because of the research of Roger Sperry and others, much supplemented by speculation, on the specialization of the left and right hemi-spheres of the human brain.

The two sides of the brain

In the minds and hands of some writers, the notion of hemisphere speciali-zation has been turned into a kind of romance. According to this romanti-cized account, there's the dull, pedestrian left side of the brain, which is very analytic. It either, depending on your beliefs, does the Olympian kind of reasoning that I described first, or – if it's just a poor man's left hemisphere – does the behavioral kind of thinking I described as the second model. In either case, it's a down-to-earth, pedestrian sort of hemisphere, capable per-haps of deep analysis but not of flights of fancy. Then there's the right hemi-sphere, in which is stored human imagination, creativity – all those good things that account for the abilities of human beings, if they would entrust themselves to this hemisphere, to solve problems in a creative way.

Before I try to characterize intuition and creativity (they are not always the same thing) in a positive way, I must comment on the romantic view I have just caricatured. When we look for the empirical evidence for it, we find that there is none. There is lots of evidence, of course, for specialization of the hemispheres, but none of that evidence really argues that any com-plex human mental function is performed by either of the hemispheres alone under normal circumstances. By and large, the evidence shows that any kind of complex thinking that involves taking in information, processing that information, and doing something with it employs both of our hemispheres in varying proportions and in various ways.

Of course, brain localization is not the important issue at stake. Regard-less of whether the same things or different things go on in the two hemi-spheres, the important question is whether there are two radically different forms of human thought – analytic thought and intuitive thought – and whether what we call creativity relies largely on the latter.

Intuition and recognition

What is intuition all about? It is an observable fact that people sometimes reach solutions to problems suddenly. They then have an "aha!" experience of varying degrees of intensity. There is no doubt of the genuineness of the phenomenon. Moreover, the problem solutions people reach when they have these experiences, when they make intuitive judgments, frequently are correct.

Good data are available on this point for chess masters. Show a chess position, from a mid-game situation in a reasonable game, to a master or grand master. After looking at it for only five or ten seconds, he will usually be able to propose a strong move – very often the move that is objectively best in the position. If he's playing the game against a strong opponent, he won't make that move immediately; he may sit for three minutes or half an hour in order to decide whether or not his first intuition is really correct. But perhaps 80 or 90 percent of the time, his first impulse will in fact show him the correct move.

The explanation for the chess master's sound intuitions is well known to psychologists, and is not really surprising.[8] It is no deeper than the explanation of your ability, in a matter of seconds, to recognize one of your friends whom you meet on the path tomorrow as you are going to class. Unless you are very deep in thought as you walk, the recognition will be immediate and reliable. Now in any field in which we have gained considerable experience, we have acquired a large number of "friends" – a large number of stimuli that we can recognize immediately. We can sort the stimulus in whatever sorting net performs this function in the brain (the physiology of it is not understood), and discriminate it from all the other stimuli we might encounter. We can do this not only with faces, but with words in our native language.

Almost every college-educated person can discriminate among, and recall the meanings of, fifty to a hundred thousand different words. Somehow, over the years, we have all spent many hundreds of hours looking at words, and we have made friends with fifty or a hundred thousand of them. Every professional entomologist has a comparable ability to discriminate among the insects he sees, and every botanist among the plants. In any field of expertise, possession of an elaborate discrimination net that permits recognition of any one of tens of thousands of different objects or situations is one of the basic tools of the expert and the principal source of his intuitions.

Counts have been made of the numbers of "friends" that chess masters have: the numbers of different configurations of pieces on a chessboard that are old familiar acquaintances to them. The estimates come out, as an order of magnitude, around fifty thousand, roughly comparable to vocabulary estimates for native speakers. Intuition is the ability to recognize a friend and to retrieve from memory all the things you've learned about the friend in the years that you've known him. And of course if you know a lot about the friend, you'll be able to make good judgments about him. Should you lend him money or not? Will you get it back if you do? If you know the friend well, you can say "yes" or "no" intuitively.

Acquiring intuitions and judgment

Why should we believe that the recognition mechanism explains most of the "aha!" experiences that have been reported in the literature of creativity?

---

[8] For a survey of the evidence, see my *Models of Thought* (New Haven, Conn., 1979), chaps. 6.2–6.5.

An important reason is that valid "aha!" experiences happen only to people who possess the appropriate knowledge. Poincaré rightly said that inspiration comes only to the prepared mind. Today we even have some data that indicate how long it takes to prepare a mind for world-class creative performance.

At first blush, it is not clear why it should take just as long in one field as in another to reach a world-class level of performance. However, human quality of performance is evaluated by comparing it with the performance of other human beings. Hence the length of human life is a controlling parameter in the competition; we can spend a substantial fraction of our lives, but no more, in increasing our proficiency. For this reason, the time required to prepare for world-class performance (by the people whose talents allow them to aspire to that level) should be roughly the same for different fields of activity.

Empirical data gathered by my colleague John R. Hayes for chess masters and composers, and somewhat less systematically for painters and mathematicians, indicate that ten years is the magic number. Almost no person in these disciplines has produced world-class performances without having first put in at least ten years of intensive learning and practice.

What about child prodigies? Mozart was composing world-class music perhaps by the time he was seventeen – certainly no earlier. (The standard Hayes used for music is five or more appearances of recordings of a piece of music in the Schwann catalog. Except for some Mozart juvenilia, which no one would bother to listen to if they hadn't been written by Mozart, there is no world-class Mozart before the age of seventeen.) Of course Mozart was already composing at the age of four, so that by age seventeen he had already been educating himself for thirteen years. Mozart is typical of the child prodigies whose biographies Hayes has examined. A *sine qua non* for outstanding work is diligent attention to the field over a decade or more.

Summary: the intuitive and behavioral models

There is no contradiction between the intuitive model of thinking and the behavioral model, nor do the two models represent alternative modes of thought residing in different cerebral hemispheres and competing for control over the mind. All serious thinking calls on both modes, both search-like processes and the sudden recognition of familiar patterns. Without recognition based on previous experience, search through complex spaces would proceed in snail-like fashion. Intuition exploits the knowledge we have gained through our past searches. Hence we would expect what in fact occurs, that the expert will often be able to proceed intuitively in attacking a problem that requires painful search for the novice. And we would expect also that in most problem situations combining aspects of novelty with familiar components, intuition and search will cooperate in reaching solutions.

6. Intuition and emotion

Thus far in our discussion of intuitive processes we have left aside one of the important characteristics these processes are said to possess: their frequent association with emotion. The searching, plodding stages of problem solving tend to be relatively free from intense emotion; they may be described as cold cognition. But sudden discovery, the "aha!" experience, tends to evoke emotion; it is hot cognition. Sometimes ideas come to people when they are excited about something.

Emotion and attention

Hence, in order to have anything like a complete theory of human rationality, we have to understand what role emotion plays in it. Most likely it serves several quite distinct functions. First of all, some kinds of emotion (e.g., pleasure) are consumption goods. They enter into the utility function of the Olympian theory, and must be counted among the goals we strive for in the behavioral model of rationality.

But for our purposes, emotion has particular importance because of its function of selecting particular things in our environments as the focus of our attention. Why was Rachel Carson's *Silent Spring* so influential? The problems she described were already known to ecologists and the other biologists at the time she described them. But she described them in a way that aroused emotion, that riveted our attention on the problem she raised. That emotion, once aroused, wouldn't let us go off and worry about other problems until something had been done about this one. At the very least, emotion kept the problem in the back of our minds as a nagging issue that wouldn't go away.

In the Olympian model, all problems are permanently and simultaneously on the agenda (until they are solved). In the behavioral model, by contrast, the choice of problems for the agenda is a matter of central importance, and emotion may play a large role in that choice.

Emotion does not always direct our attention to goals we regard as desirable. If I may go back to my example of *Mein Kampf,* we observed that the reasoning in that book is not cold reasoning but hot reasoning. It is reasoning that seeks deliberately to arouse strong emotions, often the emotion of hate, a powerful human emotion. And of course, the influence of *Mein Kampf,* like that of *Silent Spring* or Picasso's *Guernica,* was due in large part to the fact that it did have evocative power, the ability to arouse and fix the attention of its German readers on the particular goals it had in mind.

A behavioral theory of rationality, with its concern for the focus of attention as a major determinant of choice, does not dissociate emotion from human thought, nor does it in any respect underestimate the powerful effects of emotion in setting the agenda for human problem solving.

C. Newcomb's problem and causal decision theory

9.   Newcomb's problem and two principles of choice

Robert Nozick

Both it and its opposite must involve no mere artificial illusion such as at once vanishes upon detection, but a natural and unavoidable illusion, which even after it has ceased to beguile still continues to delude though not to deceive us, and which though thus capable of being rendered harmless can never be eradicated. (Immanuel Kant, *Critique of Pure Reason*, A422, B450)

1

Suppose a being in whose power to predict your choices you have enormous confidence. (One might tell a science-fiction story about a being from another planet, with an advanced technology and science, who you know to be friendly, etc.) You know that this being has often correctly predicted your choices in the past (and has never, so far as you know, made an incorrect prediction about your choices), and furthermore you know that this being has often correctly predicted the choices of other people, many of whom are similar to you, in the particular situation to be described below. One might tell a

It is not clear that I am entitled to present this paper. For the problem of choice which concerns me was constructed by someone else, and I am not satisfied with my attempts to work through the problem. But since I believe that the problem will interest and intrigue Peter Hempel and his many friends, and since its publication may call forth a solution which will enable me to stop returning, periodically, to it, here it is. It was constructed by a physicist, Dr. William Newcomb, of the Livermore Radiation Laboratories in California. I first heard the problem, in 1963, from my friend Professor Martin David Kruskal of the Princeton University Department of Astrophysical Sciences. I have benefitted from discussions, in 1963, with William Newcomb, Martin David Kruskal, and Paul Benacerraf. Since then, on and off, I have discussed the problem with many other friends whose attempts to grapple with it have encouraged me to publish my own. It is a beautiful problem. I wish it were mine.
Reprinted with permission from Nicholas Rescher, ed., *Essays in Honor of Carl G. Hempel* (Dordrecht: D. Reidel, 1970), 114–46.

longer story, but all this leads you to believe that almost certainly this being's prediction about your choice in the situation to be discussed will be correct.

There are two boxes, (B1) and (B2). (B1) contains $1000. (B2) contains either $1,000,000 ($M$), or nothing. What the content of (B2) depends upon will be described in a moment.

$$(B1) \; \{\$1000\} \qquad (B2) \left\{ \begin{array}{c} \$M \\ \text{or} \\ \$0 \end{array} \right\}$$

You have a choice between two actions:

(1)   taking what is in both boxes
(2)   taking only what is in the second box.

Furthermore, and you know this, the being knows that you know this, and so on:

(I)   If the being predicts you will take what is in both boxes, he does not put the M in the second box.
(II) If the being predicts you will take only what is in the second box, he does put the M in the second box.[1]

The situation is as follows. First the being makes its prediction. Then it puts the M in the second box, or does not, depending upon what it has predicted. Then you make your choice. What do you do?

There are two plausible looking and highly intuitive arguments which require different decisions. The problem is to explain why one of them is not legitimately applied to this choice situation. You might reason as follows:

First argument. If I take what is in both boxes, the being, almost certainly, will have predicted this and will not have put the M in the second box, and so I will, almost certainly, get only $1000. If I take only what is in the second box, the being, almost certainly, will have predicted this and will have put the M in the second box, and so I will, almost certainly, get M. Thus, if I take what is in both boxes, I, almost certainly, will get $1000. If I take only what is in the second box, I, almost certainly, will get M. Therefore I should take only what is in the second box.

Second argument. The being has already made his prediction, and has already either put the M in the second box, or has not. The M is either already sitting in the second box, or it is not, and which situation obtains is already fixed and determined. If the being has already put the M in the second box, and I take what is in both boxes I get $M + $1000, whereas if

---

[1] If the being predicts that you will consciously randomize your choice, e.g., flip a coin, or decide to do one of the actions if the next object you happen to see is blue, and otherwise do the other action, then he does not put the M in the second box.

I take only what is in the second box, I get only $M. If the being has not put the $M in the second box, and I take what is in both boxes I get $1000, whereas if I take only what is in the second box, I get no money. Therefore, whether the money is there or not, and which it is already fixed and determined, I get $1000 more by taking what is in both boxes rather than taking only what is in the second box. So I should take what is in both boxes.

Let me say a bit more to emphasize the pull of each of these arguments:

The first. You know that many persons like yourself, philosophy teachers and students, etc., have gone through this experiment. All those who took only what was in the second box, including those who knew of the second argument but did not follow it, ended up with $M. And you know that all the shrewdies, all those who followed the second argument and took what was in both boxes, ended up with only $1000. You have no reason to believe that you are any different, *vis-à-vis* predictability, than they are. Furthermore, since you know that I have all of the preceding information, you know that I would bet, giving high odds, and be rational in doing so, that if you were to take both boxes you would get only $1000. And if you were to irrevocably take both boxes, and there were some delay in the results being announced, would not it be rational for you to then bet with some third party, giving high odds, that you will get only $1000 from the previous transaction? Whereas if you were to take only what is in the second box, would not it be rational for you to make a side bet with some third party that you will get $M from the previous transaction? Knowing all this (though no one is actually available to bet with) do you really want to take what is in both boxes, acting against what you would rationally want to bet on?

The second. The being has already made his prediction, placed the $M in the second box or not, and then left. This happened one week ago; this happened one year ago. Box (B1) is transparent. You can see the $1000 sitting there. The $M is already either in the box (B2) or not (though you cannot see which). Are you going to take only what is in (B2)? To emphasize further, from your side, you cannot see through (B2), but from the other side it is transparent. I have been sitting on the other side of (B2), looking in and seeing what is there. Either I have already been looking at the $M for a week or I have already been looking at an empty box for a week. If the money is already there, it will stay there whatever you choose. It is not going to disappear. If it is not already there, if I am looking at an empty box, it is not going to suddenly appear if you choose only what is in the second box. Are you going to take only what is in the second box, passing up the additional $1000 which you can plainly see? Furthermore, I have been sitting there looking at the boxes, hoping that you will perform a particular action. Internally, I am giving you advice. And, of course, you already know which advice I am silently giving to you. In either case (whether or not I see the $M in the second box) I am hoping that you will take what is in both boxes. You know that the person sitting and watching it all hopes that you will take the contents of both boxes. Are you going to take only what is in the second box, passing up the additional $1000 which you can plainly see, and ignoring my internally given hope that you take both? Of course, my presence makes no difference. You are sitting there alone, but you know that if some friend having your interests at heart *were* observing from the other side, looking into both boxes, he *would* be hoping that you would take both. So will you take only what is in the second box, passing up the additional $1000 which you can plainly see?

I should add that I have put this problem to a large number of people, both friends and students in class. To almost everyone it is perfectly clear and obvious what should be done. The difficulty is that these people seem to divide almost evenly on the problem, with large numbers thinking that the opposing half is just being silly.[2]

Given two such compelling opposing arguments, it will not do to rest content with one's belief that one knows what to do. Nor will it do to just repeat one of the arguments, loudly and slowly. One must also disarm the opposing argument; explain away its force while showing it due respect.

Now for an unusual suggestion. It might be a good idea for the reader to stop reading this paper at the end of this section (but do, please, return and finish it), mull over the problem for a while (several hours, days) and then return. It is not that I claim to solve the problem, and do not want you to miss the joy of puzzling over an unsolved problem. It is that I want you to understand my thrashing about.

2

My strategy in attacking this problem is ostrich-like; that is, I shall begin by ignoring it completely (except in occasional notes) and proceed to discuss contemporary decision theory. Though the problem is not, at first, explicitly discussed, the course my discussion takes is influenced by my knowledge of the problem. Later in the paper, I shall remove my head from the sand, and face our problem directly, hopefully having advanced towards a solution, or at least having sharpened and isolated the problem.

Writers on decision theory state two principles to govern choices among alternative actions.

Expected Utility Principle. *Among those actions available to a person, he should perform an action with maximal expected utility.*

[2] Try it on your friends or students and see for yourself. Perhaps some psychologists will investigate whether responses to the problem are correlated with some other interesting psychological variable that they know of.

The expected utility of an action yielding the exclusive outcomes $O_1, \ldots, O_n$ with probabilities $p_1, \ldots, p_n$ respectively,

$$\left(\sum_{i=1}^{n} p_i = 1 \right) \text{ is } p_1 \times u(O_1) + p_2 \times u(O_2) + \cdots + p_n \times u(O_n),$$

$$\text{i.e., } \sum_{i=1}^{n} p_i \times u(O_i).$$

Dominance Principle. *If there is a partition of states of the world such that relative to it, action A weakly dominates action B, then A should be performed rather than B.*

Action A weakly dominates action B for person P iff, for each state of the world, P either prefers the consequence of A to the consequence of B, or is indifferent between the two consequences, and for some state of the world, P prefers the consequence of A to the consequence of B.

There are many interesting questions and problems about the framework used or assumed by these principles and the conditions governing preference, indifference, and probability which suffice to yield the utility measure, and the exact way the principles should be formulated.[3] The problem I want to begin with is raised by the fact that for some situations, one of the principles listed above requires that one choose one action whereas the other principle requires that one choose another action. Which should one follow?

Consider the following situation, where A and B are actions, S_1 and S_2 are states of the world, and the numerical entries give the utility of the consequences, results, effects, outcomes, upshots, events, states of affairs, etc., that obtain, happen, hold, etc., if the action is done and the state of the world obtains.

	S_1	S_2
A:	10	4
B:	8	3

According to the dominance principle, the person should do A rather than B. (In this situation A strongly dominates B, that is, for each state of nature the person prefers the consequence of A to the consequence of B.) But suppose the person believes it very likely that if he does A, S_2 will obtain, and if he does B, S_1 will obtain. Then he believes it very likely that if he does A he will get 4, and if he does B he will get 8. . . .

The expected utility of $A = \text{prob}(S_1/A)10 + \text{prob}(S_2/A)4$. The expected utility of $B = \text{prob}(S_1/B)8 + \text{prob}(S_2/B)3$. If, for example,

---

[3] If the questions and problems are handled as I believe they should be, then some of the ensuing discussion would have to be formulated differently. But there is no point to introducing detail extraneous to the central problem of this paper here.

$$\text{prob}(S_1/A) = .2$$
$$\text{prob}(S_2/A) = .8$$
$$\text{prob}(S_1/B) = .9$$
$$\text{prob}(S_2/B) = .1,$$

then the expected utility of $A = 5.2$, and the expected utility of $B = 7.5$. Thus the expected utility principle requires the person to do B rather than A.[4]

The dominance principle as presented here speaks of dominance relative to a partition of the states of the world. This relativization is normally not made explicit, which perhaps accounts for the fact that writers did not mention that it may be that relative to one partition of the states of the world, one action A dominates another, whereas relative to another partition of the states of the world, it does not.

It will be helpful to have before us two facts:

First. Suppose a matrix is given, with states $S_1, \ldots, S_n$, in which action A does not dominate action B. If there is some rearrangement of the utility entries in the row for action A which gives a new row which dominates the row for action B, then there are states $T_1, \ldots, T_n$ such that in the matrix with these states, action A dominates action B.

Proof: I shall describe how one can get the appropriate states $T_1, \ldots, T_n$ in one case. It is obvious how this procedure can be used generally. Suppose that $a_1, \ldots, a_n$ and $b_1, \ldots, b_n$ are utility numbers such that, for all i, $a_i \geq b_i$, and for some i, $a_i > b_i$. We may suppose that a_i is the entry in the A row for the ith column, that is, for state S_i. We might, for example, have the following matrix:

	S_1	S_2	S_3	....	S_n
A:	a_1	a_2	a_3	....	a_n
B:	b_{12}	b_3	b_{19}	....	b_6

Let

$$T_1 = A \ \& \ S_{12} \text{ or } B \ \& \ S_1{}^5$$
$$T_2 = A \ \& \ S_3 \ \text{ or } B \ \& \ S_2$$
$$T_3 = A \ \& \ S_{19} \text{ or } B \ \& \ S_3$$
$$\vdots$$
$$T_n = A \ \& \ S_6 \ \text{ or } B \ \& \ S_n.$$

Thus we get the matrix,

---

[4] This divergence between the dominance principle and the expected utility principle is pointed out in Robert Nozick, *The Normative Theory of Individual Choice,* unpublished doctoral dissertation, Princeton University, Princeton, 1963, and in Richard Jeffrey, *The Logic of Decision,* McGraw-Hill, New York, 1965.

[5] This is shorthand for: action A is done and state S_{12} obtains or action B is done and state S_1 obtains. The "or" is the exclusive or.

	T_1	T_2	T_3	....	T_n
A:	a_{12}	a_3	a_{19}	....	a_6
B:	b_{12}	b_3	b_{19}	....	b_6

In this matrix, action A dominates action B. Since the kind of procedure followed does not depend on any specific features of the example, the point is made.

Second. Suppose there is a matrix with states $S_1, \ldots, S_n$ such that action A dominates action B. If there is some rearrangement of the utility entries in the B row so that the rearranged row is not dominated by A, then there are states $T_1, \ldots, T_n$ such that if the matrix is set up with these states, B is not dominated by A.

Proof: Suppose that $a_i \geq b_i$, for all i; $a_i > b_i$ for some i; and that some B-row value is greater than some A-row value. (Given that there is some arrangement in which A dominates B, this last supposition follows from its being possible to rearrange the B row so that it is not dominated by the A row.) Suppose, without loss of generality that $b_{12} > a_2$. Thus we have the following matrix:

	S_1	S_2	S_3	....	S_n
A:	a_1	a_2	a_3	....	a_n
B:	b_1	b_2	b_3	....	b_n

Let

$T_1 = S_1$
$T_2 = A$ & S_2 or B & S_{12}
$T_3 = S_3$
$\vdots$
$T_{11} = S_{11}$
$T_{12} = A$ & S_{12} or B & S_2
$T_{13} = S_{13}$
$\vdots$
$T_n = S_n$.

Thus we get the following matrix:

	T_1	T_2	T_3	....	T_{12}	....	T_n
A:	a_1	a_2	a_3	....	a_{12}	....	a_n
B:	b_1	b_{12}	b_3	....	b_2	....	b_n

Since $b_{12} > a_2$, A does not dominate B.

It may seem that the states $T_1, \ldots, T_n$ defined in terms of the actions A and B, and the states $S_1, \ldots, S_n$ are contrived states, which some general condition could exclude. It should be noted that – since the states $S_1, \ldots, S_n$ can be defined in terms of the actions A and B and the states $T_1, \ldots, T_n$ (I will give some examples below) – attempts to show that $T_1, \ldots, T_n$ are contrived will

face many of the problems encountered in ruling out Goodman-style predi-
cates. Furthermore, as we shall see soon, there are cases where the S states
and the T states which are interdefinable in this way, both seem perfectly
natural and uncontrived.

The fact that whether one action dominates another or not may depend
upon which particular partition of the states of the world is used would
cause no difficulty if we were willing to apply the dominance principle to
any partition of the states of the world. Since we are not, this raises the
question of when the dominance principle is to be used. Let us look at some
examples.

Suppose that I am about to bet on the outcome of a horserace in which
only two horses, H_1 and H_2, are running. Let:

$S_1 = $ Horse H_1 wins the race.
$S_2 = $ Horse H_2 wins the race.
$A_1 = $ I bet on horse H_1.
$A_2 = $ I bet on horse H_2.

Suppose that I will definitely bet on one of the two horses, and can only bet
on one of the two horses, and that the following matrix describes the situation. (I might have been offered the opportunity to enter this situation by a
friend. Certainly no race track would offer it to me.)

	S_1	S_2
A_1:	I win $50	I lose $5
A_2:	I lose $6	I win $49

Suppose further that the personal probability for me that H_1 wins is .2, and
the personal probability for me that H_2 wins is .8. Thus the expected utility
of A_1 is $.2 \times u(/$ I win $50/) + .8 \times u(/$ I lose $5/)$. The expected utility of A_2
is $.2 \times u(/$ I lose $6/) + .8 \times u(/$ I win $49/)$. Given my utility assignment to
these outcomes, the expected utility of A_2 is greater than that of A_1. Hence
the expected utility principle would have me do A_2 rather than A_1.

However, we may set the matrix up differently. Let:

$S_3 = $ I am lucky in my bet.
$S_4 = $ I am unlucky in my bet.

(Given that I am betting on only one horse today, we could let $S_3 = $ The only
horse I bet on today wins. Similarly for S_4, with "loses" substituted for
"wins.") Thus we have the following matrix:

	S_3	S_4
A_1:	I win $50	I lose $5
A_2:	I win $49	I lose $6

But when set up in this way, A_1 dominates A_2. Therefore the dominance principle would have me do A_1 rather than A_2.[6]

In this example, the states are logically independent of which action I perform; from the fact that I perform A_1 (A_2) one cannot deduce which state obtains, and from the fact that S_1 (S_2, S_3, S_4) obtains one cannot deduce which action I perform. However one pair of states was not probabilistically independent of my doing the actions.[7] Assuming that S_1 and S_2 are each probabilistically independent of both A_1 and A_2, prob(S_3/I do A_1) = .2; prob(S_3/I do A_2) = .8; prob(S_4/I do A_1) = .8; prob(S_4/I do A_2) = .2. Thus neither of the states S_3 or S_4 is probabilistically independent of each of the actions A_1 and A_2.[8]

In this example, it is clear that one does not wish to follow the recommendation of the dominance principle. And the explanation seems to hinge

[6] Note that

$$S_1 = A_1 \ \& \ S_3 \ \text{or} \ A_2 \ \& \ S_4$$
$$S_2 = A_1 \ \& \ S_4 \ \text{or} \ A_2 \ \& \ S_3$$
$$S_3 = A_1 \ \& \ S_1 \ \text{or} \ A_2 \ \& \ S_2$$
$$S_4 = A_1 \ \& \ S_2 \ \text{or} \ A_2 \ \& \ S_1$$

Similarly, the above identities hold for Newcomb's example, with which I began, if one lets

S_1 = The money is in the second box.
S_2 = The money is not in the second box.
S_3 = The being predicts your choice correctly.
S_4 = The being incorrectly predicts your choice.
A_1 = You take only what is in the second box.
A_2 = You take what is in both boxes.

[7] State S is not probabilistically independent of actions A and B if prob(S obtains/A is done) $\neq$ prob(S obtains/B is done).

[8] In Newcomb's predictor example, assuming that "He predicts correctly" and "He predicts incorrectly" are each probabilistically independent of my actions, then it is not the case that "He puts the money in" and "He does not put the money in" are each probabilistically independent of my actions.

Usually it will be the case that if the members of the set of exhaustive and exclusive states are each probabilistically independent of the actions A_1 and A_2, then it will not be the case that the states equivalent to our contrived states are each probabilistically independent of both A_1 and A_2. For example, suppose prob(S_1/A_1) = prob(S_1/A_2) = prob(S_1); prob(S_2/A_2) = prob(S_2/A_1) = prob(S_2). Let:

$$S_3 = A_1 \ \& \ S_1 \ \text{or} \ A_2 \ \& \ S_2$$
$$S_4 = A_1 \ \& \ S_2 \ \text{or} \ A_2 \ \& \ S_1$$

If prob(S_1) $\neq$ prob(S_2), then S_3 and S_4 are not probabilistically independent of A_1 and A_2. For prob(S_3/A_1) = prob(S_1/A_1) = prob(S_1), and prob(S_3/A_2) = prob(S_2/A_2) = prob(S_2). Therefore if prob(S_1) $\neq$ prob(S_2), then prob(S_3/A_1) $\neq$ prob(S_3/A_2). If prob(S_1) = prob(S_2) = 1/2, then the possibility of describing the states as we have will not matter. For if, for example, A_1 can be shifted around so as to dominate A_2, then before the shifting it will have a higher expected utility than A_2. Generally, if the members of the set of exclusive and exhaustive states are probabilistically independent of both A_1 and A_2, then the members of the contrived set of states will be probabilistically independent of both A_1 and A_2 only if the probabilities of the original states which are components of the contrived states are identical. And in this case it will not matter which way one sets up the situation.

on the fact that the states are not probabilistically independent of the actions. Even though one can set up the situation so that one action dominates another, I believe that if I do A_1, the consequence will probably be the italicized consequence in its row, and I believe that if I do A_2, the consequence will probably be the italicized consequence in A_2's row. And given my assignment of utilities in this case, and the probabilities I assign (the conditional probabilities of the states given the actions) it is clear why I prefer to do A_2, despite the fact that A_1 dominates A_2.

	S_3	S_4
A_1:	I win \$50	*I lose \$5*
A_2:	*I win \$49*	I lose \$6

Let us consider another example: Suppose that I am playing roulette on a rigged wheel, and that the owner of the casino offers me a chance to choose between actions A_1 and A_2 so that the following matrix describes the situation (where S_1 = black comes up on the next spin; S_2 = red comes up on the next spin):

	S_1	S_2
A_1:	I win \$10	I win \$100
A_2:	I win \$5	I win \$90

Finally suppose that I know that the owner's employee, who is overseeing the wheel and who I am confident is completely loyal to the owner, has been instructed to make black come up on the next spin if I choose A_1 and to make red come up on the next spin if I choose A_2. Clearly even though A_1 dominates A_2, given my knowledge of the situation I should choose A_2. I take it that this needs no argument. It seems that the reason that I should not be guided by dominance considerations is that the states S_1 and S_2 are not probabilistically independent of my actions A_1 and A_2. We can set up the situation so that the states are probabilistically independent of the actions. But when set up in this way, I am led, given my utility assignment to the outcomes, to do A_2.

Let S_3 = the fellow running the roulette wheel follows his boss's instructions; S_4 = the fellow running the roulette wheel disobeys his boss's instructions. (Note that $S_3 = A_1$ & S_1 or A_2 & S_2; $S_4 = A_1$ & S_2 or A_2 & S_1.) We then have the following matrix:

	S_3	S_4
A_1:	I win \$10	I win \$100
A_2:	I win \$90	I win \$5

Even if I am not sure that S_3 is true, so long as the personal probability of S_3 for me is sufficiently high, I will be led to do A_2, given my utility assignment to the outcomes.

These examples suggest that one should not apply the dominance principle to a situation where the states are not probabilistically independent of the actions. One wishes instead to maximize the expected utility. However, the probabilities that are to be used in determining the expected utility of an action must now be the conditional probabilities of the states given that the action is done. (This is true generally. However when the states are probabilistically independent of the actions, the conditional probability of each state given that one of the actions is done will be equal to the probability of the state, so the latter may be used.) Thus in the roulette wheel example, we may still look at the first matrix given. However, one does not wish to apply the dominance principle but to find the expected utility of the actions, which in our example are:

$$\text{E.U.}(A_1) = \text{prob}(S_1/A_1) \times u(/\text{I win \$10}/)$$
$$+ \text{prob}(S_2/A_1) \times u(/\text{I win \$100}/)$$

$$\text{E.U.}(A_2) = \text{prob}(S_1/A_2) \times u(/\text{I win \$5}/)$$
$$+ \text{prob}(S_2/A_2) \times u(/\text{I win \$90}/).[9]$$

The following position appropriately handles the examples given thus far (ignoring Newcomb's example with which the paper opens) and has intuitive appeal.[10]

(1) It is legitimate to apply dominance principles if and only if the states are probabilistically independent of the actions.

(2) If the states are not probabilistically independent of the actions, then apply the expected utility principle, using as the probability-weights the conditional probabilities of the states given the actions.

Thus in the following matrix, where the entries in the matrix are utility numbers,

[9] Note that this procedure seems to work quite well for situations in which the states are not only not probabilistically independent of the actions, but are not logically independent either. Suppose that a person is asked whether he prefers doing A to doing B, where the outcome of A is $/p$ if S_1 and r if $S_2/$ and the outcome of B is $/q$ if S_2 and r if $S_1/$. And suppose that he prefers p to q to r, and that $S_1 = \text{I do } B$, and $S_2 = \text{I do } A$. The person realizes that if he does A, S_2 will be the case and the outcome will be r, and he realizes that if he does B, S_1 will be the case and the outcome will be r. Since the outcome will be r in any case, he is indifferent between doing A and doing B. So let us suppose he flips a coin in order to decide which to do. But given that the coin is fair, it is now the case that the probability of $S_1 = 1/2$ and the probability of $S_2 = 1/2$. If we mechanically started to compute the expected utility of A, and of B, we would find that A has a higher expected utility than does B. For mechanically computing the expected utilities, it would turn out that the expected utility of $A = 1/2 \times u(p) + 1/2 \times u(r)$, and the expected utility of $B = 1/2 \times u(q) + 1/2 \times u(r)$. If, however, we use the conditional probabilities, then the expected utility of $A = \text{prob}(S_1/A) \times u(p) + \text{prob}(S_2/A) \times u(r) = 0 \times u(p) + 1 \times u(r) = u(r)$. And the expected utility of $B = \text{prob}(S_2/B) \times u(q) + \text{prob}(S_1/B) \times u(r) = 0 \times u(q) + 1 \times u(r) = u(r)$. Thus the expected utilities of A and B are equal, as one would wish.

[10] This position was suggested, with some reservations due to Newcomb's example, in Robert Nozick, *The Normative Theory of Individual Choice, op. cit.* It was also suggested in Richard Jeffrey, *The Logic of Decision, op. cit.*

$$\begin{array}{llll} & S_1 & S_2 & \dots\dots\dots\dots\dots & S_n \\ A: & O_1 & O_2 & \dots\dots\dots\dots\dots & O_n \\ B: & U_1 & U_2 & \dots\dots\dots\dots\dots & U_n \end{array}$$

the expected utility of A is $\sum_{i=1}^{n} \text{prob}(S_i/A)O_i$, and the expected utility of B is $\sum_{i=1}^{n} \text{prob}(S_i/B)U_i$.

3

Is this position satisfactory? Consider the following example: P knows that S or T is his father, but he does not know which one is. S died of some terrible inherited disease, and T did not. It is known that this disease is genetically dominant, and that P's mother did not have it, and that S did not have the recessive gene. If S is his father, P will die of this disease; if T is his father, P will not die of this disease. Furthermore, there is a well-confirmed theory available, let us imagine, about the genetic transmission of the tendency to decide to do acts which form part of an intellectual life. This tendency is genetically dominant. S had this tendency (and did not have the recessive gene), T did not, and P's mother did not. P is now deciding whether (a) to go to graduate school and then teach, or (b) to become a professional baseball player. He prefers (though not enormously) the life of an academic to that of a professional athlete.

$$\begin{array}{lll} & S \text{ is } P\text{'s father} & T \text{ is } P\text{'s father} \\ A: & x & y \\ B: & z & w \end{array}$$

$x = P$ is an academic for a while, and then dies of the terrible disease; $z = P$ is a professional athlete for a while, and then dies of the terrible disease; $y = P$ is an academic and leads a normal academic life; $w = P$ is a professional athlete and leads the normal life of a professional athlete, though doing a bit more reading; and P prefers x to z, and y to w. However, the disease is so terrible that P greatly prefers w to x. The matrix might be as follows:

$$\begin{array}{lll} & S \text{ is } P\text{'s father} & T \text{ is } P\text{'s father} \\ A: & -20 & 100 \\ B: & -25 & 95 \end{array}$$

Suppose that our well-confirmed theory tells us, and P, that if P chooses the academic life, then it is likely that he has the tendency to choose it; if he does not choose the academic life, then it is likely that he does not have the tendency. Specifically

prob(P has the tendency/P decides to do A) = .9
prob(P does not have the tendency/P decides to do A) = .1
prob(P has the tendency/P decides to do B) = .1
prob(P does not have the tendency/P decides to do B) = .9.

Since P has the tendency iff S is P's father, we have

$$\text{prob}(S \text{ is } P\text{'s father}/P \text{ decides to do } A) = .9$$
$$\text{prob}(T \text{ is } P\text{'s father}/P \text{ decides to do } A) = .1$$
$$\text{prob}(S \text{ is } P\text{'s father}/P \text{ decides to do } B) = .1$$
$$\text{prob}(T \text{ is } P\text{'s father}/P \text{ decides to do } B) = .9.$$

The dominance principle tells P to do A rather than B. But according to the position we are now considering, in situations in which the states are not probabilistically independent of the actions, the dominance principle is not to be used, but rather one is to use the expected utility principle with the conditional probabilities as the weights. Using the above conditional probabilities and the above numerical assumptions about the utility values, we get:

The expected utility of $A = .9 \times -20 + .1 \times 100 = -8$
The expected utility of $B = .1 \times -25 + .9 \times 95 = 83.$

Since the expected utility of B is greater than that of A, the position we are considering would have P do B rather than A. But this recommendation is perfectly wild. Imagine P saying, "I am doing B because if I do it it is less likely that I will die of the dread disease." One wants to reply, "It is true that you have got the conditional probabilities correct. If you do A it is likely that S is your father, and hence likely that you will die of the disease, and if you do B it is likely that T is your father and hence unlikely that you will die of the disease. But which one of them is your father is already fixed and determined, and has been for a long time. The action you perform legitimately affects our estimate of the probabilities of the two states, but which state obtains does not depend on your action at all. By doing B you are not *making* it less likely that S is your father, and by doing B you are not making it less likely that you will die of the disease." I do not claim that this reply is without its problems.[11] Before considering another example, let us first state a principle not under attack:

The Dominance Principle is legitimately applicable to situations in which the states are probabilistically independent of the actions.[12]

[11] I should mention, what the reader has no doubt noticed, that the previous *example* is not fully satisfactory. For it seems that preferring the academic life to the athlete's life should be as strong evidence for the tendency as is choosing the academic life. And hence P's choosing the athlete's life, though he prefers the academic life, on expected utility grounds does not seem to make it likely that he does not have the tendency. What the example seems to require is an inherited tendency to decide to do A which is such that (1) The probability of its presence cannot be estimated on the basis of the person's preferences, but only on the basis of knowing the genetic make-up of his parents, or knowing his actual decisions; and (2) The theory about how the tendency operates yields the result that it is unlikely that it is present if the person decides not to do A in the example-situation, even though he makes this decision on the basis of the stated expected utility grounds. It is not clear how, for this example, the details are to be coherently worked out.

[12] That is, the Dominance Principle is legitimately applicable to situations in which $\sim(\exists S)(\exists A)(\exists B)[\text{prob}(S \text{ obtains}/A \text{ is done}) \neq \text{prob}(S \text{ obtains}/B \text{ is done})]$.

If the states are not probabilistically independent of the actions, it *seems* intuitive that the expected utility principle is appropriate, and that it is not legitimate to use the dominance principle if it yields a different result from the expected utility principle. However, in situations in which the states, though not probabilistically independent of the actions, are already fixed and determined, where the actions do not affect whether or not the states obtain, then it *seems* that it is legitimate to use the dominance principle, and illegitimate to follow the recommendation of the expected utility principle if it differs from that of the dominance principle.

For such situations – where the states are not probabilistically independent of the actions, though which one obtains is already fixed and determined – persons may differ over what principle to use.

Of the twelve sorts of situation in which it is not the case both that none of the states are already fixed and determined and none of the states are probabilistically independent of the actions, I shall discuss only one; namely, where each of the states is already fixed and determined, and none of the states are probabilistically independent of the alternative actions.[13]

The question before us is: In this sort of situation, in which all of the states are already fixed and determined, and none of the states are probabilistically independent of the acts, and the dominance principle requires that one do one action, whereas the expected utility principle requires that one do another, should one follow the recommendation of the dominance principle or of the expected utility principle?

The question is difficult. Some may think one should follow the recommendation of the dominance principle; others may think one should follow the recommendation of the expected utility principle in such situations.

Now for the example which introduces a bit of reflexivity which I hope will soon serve us in good stead. Suppose that there are two inherited tendencies ('tendencies' because there is some small probability that it would not be followed in a specific situation):

---

[13] The other eleven possibilities about the states are:

	Already fixed and determined		Not already fixed and determined	
	probabilistically independent of the actions	not probabilistically independent of the actions	prob. ind. of the actions	not prob. ind. of the actions
(1)	some	some	some	some
(2)	some	some	some	none
(3)	some	some	none	some
(4)	some	some	none	none
(5)	some	none	some	some
(6)	some	none	some	none
(7)	some	none	none	some
(8)	all	none	none	none
(9)	none	some	some	some
(10)	none	some	some	none
(11)	none	some	none	some

(1)   an inherited tendency to think that the expected utility principle should be used in such situations. (If P has this tendency, he is in state S_1.)

(2)   an inherited tendency to think that the dominance principle should be used in such situations. (If P has this tendency, he is in state S_2.)

It is known on the basis of *post mortem* genetic examinations that

(a) P's mother had two neutral genes. (A gene for either tendency genetically dominates a neutral gene. We need not here worry about the progeny who has a gene for each tendency.)

(b)   One of the men who may be P's father had two genes for the first tendency.

(c)   The other man who may be P's father had two genes for the second tendency.

So it is known that P has one of the tendencies, but it is not known which one he has. P is faced with the following choice:

	S_1	S_2
A:	10	4
B:	8	3

The choice matrix might have arisen as follows. A deadly disease is going around, and there are two effective vaccines against it. (If both are given, the person dies.) For each person, the side effects of vaccine B are worse than that of vaccine A, and each vaccine has worse side effects on persons in S_2 than either does on persons in S_1.

Now suppose that the theory about the inherited tendencies to choice, tells us, and P knows this, that from a person's choice in *this* situation the probabilities of his having the two tendencies, given that he has one of the two, can be estimated, and in particular

$$\text{prob}(S_1/A) = .1$$
$$\text{prob}(S_2/A) = .9$$
$$\text{prob}(S_1/B) = .9$$
$$\text{prob}(S_2/B) = .1.$$

What should P do? What would you do in this situation?

P may reason as follows: if I do A, then very probably S_2 obtains, and I will get 4. If I do B, then very probably S_1 holds, and I will get 8. So I will do B rather than A.

One wants to reply: whether S_1 or S_2 obtains is already fixed and determined. What you decide to do would not bring about one or the other of them. To emphasize this, let us use the past tense. For you are in S_1 iff you were in S_1 yesterday; you are in S_2 iff you were in S_2 yesterday. But to reason "If I do A then very probably I was in S_2 yesterday, and I will get 4. If I do B, then very probably, I was in S_1 yesterday, and I will get 8. So I will now do B rather than A" is absurd. What you decide to do does not affect which state you were in yesterday. For either state, over which you have no control, you are better off doing A rather than B. To do B for reasons such as the above is no less absurd than someone who has already taken vaccine B yesterday doing some other act C today because the prob(He was in S_1 yesterday/He does C today) is very high, and he wants the (delayed) side effects of the vaccine he has already taken to be less severe.

If an explanation runs from x to y, a correct explanatory theory will speak of the conditional probability prob(y/x). Thus the correct explanatory theory of P's choice in this situation will speak of

prob(P does A/P is in S_1)
prob(P does A/P is in S_2)
prob(P does B/P is in S_1)
prob(P does B/P is in S_2).

From these, the theory may enable us to determine

prob(P is in S_1/P does A)
prob(P is in S_2/P does A)
prob(P is in S_1/P does B)
prob(P is in S_2/P does B)

but these would not be the basic explanatory probabilities. Supposing that probabilistic explanation is legitimate, we could explain why P does A by having among our antecedent conditions the statement that P is in S_2, but we cannot *explain* why P is in S_2 by having among our antecedent conditions the statement that P does A (though P's doing A may be our reason for believing he is in S_2). Given that when the explanatory line runs from x to y (x is part of the explanation of y) and not from y to x, the theory will speak of and somehow distinguish the conditional probabilities prob(y/x), then the probability prob(x/y) will be a *likelihood* (as, I think, this term is used in the statistical literature). Looking at the likelihoods of the states given the actions may perhaps give one the illusion of control over the states. But I suggest that when the states are already fixed and determined, and the explanatory theory has the influence running from the states to the actions, so that the conditional probabilities of the states on the actions are likelihoods, then if the dominance principle applies, it should be applied.

If a state is part of the explanation of deciding to do an action (if the decision is made) and this state is already fixed and determined, then the decision, which has not yet been made, cannot be part of the explanation of the state's obtaining. So we need not consider the case where prob(state/action) is in the basic explanatory theory, for an already fixed state.[14] What other

[14] Unless it is possible that there be causality or influence backwards in time. I shall not here consider this possibility, though it may be that only on its basis can one defend, for some choice situations, the refusal to use the dominance principle. I try to explain later why, for some situations, even if one grants that there is no influence back in time, one may not escape the feeling that, somehow, there is.

possibilities are there for already fixed and determined states? One possibility would be a situation in which the states are not part of the explanation of the decision, and the decision is not part of the explanation of which state obtains, but some third thing is part of the explanation of the states obtaining, and the decision's being made. Hence neither prob(state of the matrix obtaining/P does a specific action) nor prob(P does a specific action/state of the matrix obtains) would be part of the basic explanatory theory (which has conditional probabilities from antecedent to consequent going in the direction of explanation).

Let us consider a case like this, whose matrix exemplifies the structure of the prisoners' dilemma situation, much discussed by game theorists.[15] There are two people, (I) and (II) and the following matrix describes their situation (where the first entry in each box represents the payoff to person (I) and the second entry represents the payoff to person (II)). The situation arises just once, and the persons cannot get together to agree upon a joint plan of action.

		(II)	
		C	D
(I)	A:	10.3	4.4
	B:	8.8	3.10

Notice that for person (I), action A dominates action B, and for person (II), action D dominates action C. Hence if each performs his dominant action, each ends up with 4. But if each performs the non-dominant action, each ends up with 8. So, in this situation, both persons' following the dominance principle leaves each worse off than if both did not follow the dominance principle.

People may differ over what should be done in this situation. Let us, once again, suppose that there are two inherited tendencies, one to perform the dominant action in this situation, and one to perform the other action. Either tendency is genetically dominant over a possible third inherited trait. Persons (I) and (II) are identical twins, who care only about their own payoffs as represented in this matrix, and know that their mother had the neutral gene, one of their two possible fathers had only the gene to perform the dominant action, and the other had only the gene not to perform the dominant action. Neither knows which man was their father, nor which of the genes they have. Each knows, given the genetic theory, that it is almost certain that if he performs the dominant (dominated) action his brother will also. We must also suppose that the theory tells us and them that given all this information upon which they base their choice, the correlation between their actions holds as almost certain, and also given *this* additional information, it holds as almost certain, etc.

I do not wish here to discuss whether one should or should not perform the dominant action in Prisoners' Dilemma situations. I wish merely to consider

[15] Cf. R. Duncan Luce and Howard Raiffa, *Games and Decisions,* John Wiley & Sons, New York, 1957, pp. 94–102.

the following argument for not performing the dominant action in the situation I have just described. Suppose brother I argues: "If I perform the dominant action then it is almost certain$_1$ that I have that gene, and therefore that my brother does also, and so it is almost certain$_2$[16] that he will also perform the dominant action and so it is almost certain$_2$ that I will get 4. Whereas if I perform the dominated action, for similar reasons, it is almost certain that my brother will also, and hence it is almost certain that I will get 8. So I should perform the dominated action."

Here one surely wishes to reply that *this* argument is not a good argument for performing the dominated action. For what this brother does will not affect what the other brother does. (To emphasize this, suppose that brother II has already acted, though brother I does not yet know what he has done.) Perhaps in prisoners' dilemma situations one should perform the dominated action, but *this* argument does not show that one should in this situation.

The examples thus far considered lead me to believe that if the actions or decisions to do the actions do not affect, help bring about, influence, etc., *which* state obtains, then whatever the conditional probabilities (so long as they do not indicate an influence), one should perform the dominant action.

If the considerations thus far adduced are convincing, then it is clear that one should also choose the dominant act in the following situations, having the same structure (matrix) as Newcomb's, and differing only in that:

(1)   The being makes his prediction and sets the process going whereby the \$M gets placed in the second box, or not. You then make your choice, and *after* you do, the (long) process terminates and the \$M gets in the box, or not. So while you are deciding, the \$M is not already there, though at this time he has already decided whether it will be or not.

(2)   The being gathers his data on the basis of which he makes his prediction. You make your choice (e.g., press one of two buttons which will open one or both boxes later by delayed action), and he then makes his prediction, on the basis of the data previously gathered, and puts the \$M in, or not.

This suggests that the crucial fact is *not* whether the states are already fixed and determined but whether the actions *influence* or *affect* which state obtains.

Setting up a simple matrix,[17] we have the following possibilities (with the matrix entries being recommended decision policies for the situation).

[16] Almost certainty$_1$ > almost certainty$_2$, since almost certainty$_2$ is some function of the probability that brother I has the dominant action gene given that he performs the dominant action (= almost certainty$_1$), and of the probability that brother II does the dominant action given that he has the dominant action gene.

[17] In choosing the headings for the rows, I have ignored more complicated possibilities, which must be investigated for a fuller theory, e.g., some actions influence which state obtains and others do not.

	A dominant action is available	No dominant action is available
The actions influence which state obtains. The conditional probabilities differ.	(I) Maximize Expected Utility	(II) Maximize Expected Utility
No influence of actions on states. However conditional probabilities differ.	(III)	(IV)
No influence of actions on states. The conditional probabilities are all the same.	(V) Do dominant action (or, equivalently, Maximize Expected Utility)	(VI) Maximize Expected Utility

The standard theories make the recommendations in (V) and (VI). They do not consider (I) and (II), but (ignoring other difficulties there might be with the policy) Maximizing Expected Utility seems reasonable here. The difficulties come in the middle row. (III) is the situation exemplified by Newcomb's situation and the other examples we have listed from the person choosing whether to lead the academic life, onwards. I have argued that in these situations, one should choose the dominant action and ignore the conditional probabilities which do not indicate an influence. What then should one do in situation (IV), where which action is done does not influence which state obtains, where the conditional probabilities of the states given the actions differ, and where *no* dominant action is available? If the lesson of case (III) is that one should ignore conditional probabilities which do not indicate an influence, must not one ignore them completely in case (IV) as well?

Not exactly. What one should do, in a choice between two actions A and B, is the following.[18] Let $p_1, \ldots, p_n$ be the conditional probability distribution of action A over the n states; let $q_1, \ldots, q_n$ be the conditional probability distribution of action B over the n states. A probability distribution $r_1, \ldots, r_n$, summing to 1, is between $p_1, \ldots, p_n$ and $q_1, \ldots, q_n$ iff for each i, r_i is in the closed interval $[p_i, q_i]$ or $[q_i, p_i]$. (Note that according to this account, $p_1, \ldots, p_n$, and $q_1, \ldots, q_n$ are each between $p_1, \ldots, p_n$ and $q_1, \ldots, q_n$.) Now for a recommendation: If relative to each probability distribution between $p_1, \ldots, p_n$ and $q_1, \ldots, q_n$, action A has a higher expected utility than action B, then do action A. The expected utility of A and B is computed with respect to the same probability distribution. It will not, of course, be the case that relative to every possible probability distribution A has a higher expected utility than B. For, by hypothesis, A does not dominate B. However it may be

---

[18] I here consider only the case of two actions. Obvious and messy problems for the kind of policy about to be proposed are raised by the situation in which more than two actions are available (e.g., under what conditions do pairwise comparisons lead to a linear order), whose consideration is best postponed for another occasion.

that relative to each probability distribution between $p_1, ..., p_n$ and $q_1, ..., q_n$, A has a higher expected utility than B. If, on the other hand, it is not the case that relative to each probability distribution between $p_1, ..., p_n$, and $q_1, ..., q_n$, A has a higher expected utility than B (and it is not the case that relative to each, B has a higher expected utility than A), then we are faced with a problem of decision under constrained uncertainty (the constraints being the end probability distributions), on which kind of problem there is not, so far as I know, agreement in the literature.[19] Since consideration of the issues raised by such problems would take us far afield, we thankfully leave them.

To talk more objectively than some would like, though more intuitively than we otherwise could, since the actions do not affect or influence which state obtains, there is some one probability distribution, which we do not know, relative to which we would like to compare the action A and B. Since we do not know the distribution, we cannot proceed as in cases (V) and (VI). But since there is *one* unknown correct distribution "out there," unaffected by what we do, we must, in the procedure we use, compare each action with respect to the *same* distribution. Thus it is, at this point, an irrelevant fact that one action's expected utility computed with respect to one probability distribution is higher than another action's expected utility computed with respect to *another* probability distribution. It may seem strange that for case (IV) we bring in the probabilities in some way (even though they do not indicate an influence) whereas in case (III) we do not. This difference is only apparent, since we could bring in the probabilities in case (III) in exactly the same way. The reason why we need not do this, and need only note that A dominates B, is that if A dominates B, then relative to each probability distribution (and therefore for each one between the conditional ones established by the two actions) A has a higher expected utility than B.[20]

---

[19] See R. Duncan Luce and Howard Raiffa, *op. cit.*, pp. 275–298 and the references therein; Daniel Ellsberg, "Risk, Ambiguity, and the Savage Axioms," *Quarterly Journal of Economics* **75** (1961), 643–669, and the articles by his fellow symposiasts Howard Raiffa and William Feller.

[20] If the distinctions I have drawn are correct, then some of the existing literature is in need of revision. Many of the writers might be willing to just draw the distinctions we have adumbrated. But for the specific theories offered by some personal probability theorists, it is not clear how this is to be done. For example, L. J. Savage in *The Foundations of Statistics*, John Wiley & Sons, New York, 1954, recommends unrestricted use of dominance principles (his postulate $P2$), which would not do in case (I). And Savage seems explicitly to wish to deny himself the means of distinguishing case (I) from the others. (For further discussion, some of which must be revised in the light of this paper, of Savage's important and ingenious work, see Robert Nozick, *op. cit.*, Chapter V.) And Richard Jeffrey, *The Logic of Decision*, *op. cit.*, recommends universal use of maximizing expected utility relative to the conditional probabilities of the states given the actions (see footnote 10 above). This will not do, I have argued, in cases (III) and (IV). But Jeffrey also sees it as a special virtue of this theory that it does not utilize certain notions, and these notions look like they might well be required to draw the distinctions between the different kinds of cases.

While on the subject of how to distinguish the cases, let me (be the first to) say that I have used without explanation, and in this paper often interchangeably, the notions of influency,

Now, at last, to return to Newcomb's example of the predictor. If one believes, for this case, that there is backwards causality, that your choice causes the money to be there or not, that it causes him to have made the prediction that he made, then there is no problem. One takes only what is in the second box. Or if one believes that the way the predictor works is by looking into the future; he, in some sense, sees what you are doing, and hence is no more likely to be wrong about what you do than someone else who is standing there at the time and watching you, and would normally see you, say, open only one box, then there is no problem. You take only what is in the second box. But suppose we establish or take as given that there is no backwards causality, that what you actually decide to do does not affect what he did in the past, that what you actually decide to do is not part of the explanation of why he made the prediction he made. So let us agree that the predictor works as follows: He observes you sometime before you are faced with the choice, examines you with complicated apparatus, etc., and then uses his theory to predict on the basis of this state you were in, what choice you would make later when faced with the choice. Your deciding to do as you do is not part of the explanation of why he makes the prediction he does, though your being in a certain state earlier, is part of the explanation of why he makes the prediction he does, and why you decide as you do.

I believe that one should take what is in both boxes. I fear that the considerations I have adduced thus far will not convince those proponents of taking only what is in the second box. Furthermore I suspect that an adequate solution to this problem will go much deeper than I have yet gone or shall go in this paper. So I want to pose one question. I assume that it is clear that in the vaccine example, the person should not be convinced by the probability argument, and should choose the dominant action. I assume also that it is clear that in the case of the two brothers, the brother should not be convinced by the probability argument offered. The question I should like to put to proponents of taking only what is in the second box in Newcomb's example (and hence not performing the dominant action) is: what is the difference between Newcomb's example and the other two examples which make the difference between not following the dominance principle, and following it?

If no such difference is produced one should not rush to conclude that one should perform the dominant action in Newcomb's example. For it must be granted that, at the very least, it is not *as clear* that one should perform the

affecting, etc. I have felt free to use them without paying them much attention because even such unreflective use serves to open a whole area of concern. A detailed consideration of the different possible cases with many actions, some influencing, and in different degrees, some not influencing, combined with an attempt to state detailed principles using precise "influence" notions undoubtedly would bring forth many intricate and difficult problems. These would show, I think, that my quick general statements about influence and what distinguishes the cases, are not, strictly speaking, correct. But going into these details would necessitate going into these details. So I will not.

dominant action in Newcomb's example, as in the other two examples. And one should be wary of attempting to force a decision in an unclear case by producing a similar case where the decision is clear, and challenging one to find a difference between the cases which makes a difference to the decision. For suppose the undecided person, or the proponent of another decision, cannot find such a difference. Does not the forcer, now, have to find a difference between the cases which explains why one is clear, and the other is not? And might not *this* difference then be produced by the other person as that which perhaps should yield different decisions in the two cases? Sometimes this will be implausible: e.g., if the difference is that one case is relatively simple, and the other has much additional detail, individually irrelevant, which prevent the other case from being taken in as a whole. But it does seem that someone arguing as I do about a case must not only (a) describe a similar case which is clear, and challenge the other to state a difference between them which should make a difference to how they are handled, but must also (b) describe a difference between the cases which explains why though one case is clear, the other is not, or one is tempted to handle the other case differently. And, assuming that all accept the difference stated in (b) as explaining what it is supposed to explain,

(I)   The simplest situation is that in which all agree that the difference mentioned in (b) is not a reason for different decisions in the two cases.

(II) However, if the forcer says it is not a reason for different decisions in the two cases, and the other person says it is or may be, difficult questions arise about upon whom, if anyone, the burden of further argument falls.

What then is the difference that makes some cases clear and Newcomb's example unclear, yet does not make a difference to how the cases should be decided? Given my account of what the crucial factors are (influence, etc.) my answer to this question will have to claim that the clear cases are clear cases of no influence (or, to recall the cases which we considered at the beginning, of influence), and that in Newcomb's example there is the *illusion* of influence. The task is to explain in a sufficiently forceful way what gives rise to this illusion so that, even as we experience it, we will not be deceived by it.

I have said that if the action is referred to in an explanation of the state's obtaining, so that the doing of the action affects or influences which state obtains, then the Dominance Principle should not be applied. And if the explanation of the states' obtaining does not make reference to the action, the action does not influence which state obtains, does not (partly) bring it about that a state obtains, then the Dominance Principle should be applied to such situations where a dominant action is available. But if this is so, where is there room for unclarity about a case? What other possibility is there? Either the action is referred to in the explanation of the state's obtaining, or it is not. How does the temptation to take only what is in the second box arise in the Newcomb example, and why does it linger?

The possibility to which I wish to call attention can be described differently, depending upon other views which one holds. (I describe the possibility specifically with Newcomb's example in mind.) (1) The action *is* referred to in the explanation of the state's obtaining, but the term which refers to the action occurs in the explanation, in a nonextensional belief context. Thus it does not follow from the fact that the action is referred to, in this way, in the explanation of the state's obtaining, that the doing of the action affects which state obtains. (2) The action is not referred to in the explanation of the state's obtaining. What is brought in by the explanation of the state's obtaining is some being's well-founded beliefs about the person's doing the action. Since the person's doing the action is not part of the explanation of the state's obtaining, it does not affect or influence which state obtains.

In Newcomb's example, the predictor makes his prediction on the basis of determining what state the person is in, and what his theory tells him about what such a person will do in the choice situation. Believing his theory accurate, he puts the money in or not, according to his belief about the person's future actions, where this belief depends upon his finding out what initial state the person is in, and what his theory tells him about a person in such an initial state. Thus, if the predictor puts the M in the second box, part of the explanation of this is his belief that the person will take only what is in the second box. If he does not put the M in the second box, part of the explanation of this is his belief that the person will take what is in both boxes. Thus the explanation of the money's being in the second box (or not) refers to the person's action only in a nonextensional belief context (or does not refer to it at all but only to the predictor's beliefs about it).

It is apparently a persistent temptation for people to believe, when an explanation of something x brings in terms referring to y in a nonextensional belief context (or brings in beliefs about y), that y, in some way, influences or affects x. Thus one finds writers on teleological explanation having to state that in the simple case where someone goes to the refrigerator to get an apple, it is not the apple's being there when he gets there which caused him to go, or which (partly) explains his actions, but rather his beliefs about an apple's being there. But this cannot be the whole story about Newcomb's example. For there are many persons not at all tempted to say that the apple's being there when he gets there influenced his action of going there, who do want to or are tempted to take only what is in the second box.

Let us return to the writers on teleology. To show that the apple's being there does not influence the person's actions, but rather it is his beliefs about the apple's being there that do, they usually argue that even if the apple were not there, so long as the person had the beliefs, he would act in the same way. The relevant feature of nonextensional belief contexts here is that from

P believes that ... x ..., it does not follow that x exists, from P believes that p, it does not follow that p is true. So, the argument runs, he *could* have his beliefs without there being an apple there, and this shows that the apple does not influence his actions in this case. And surely the explanation of his action should be the same, in the case where the apple is in the refrigerator, as in the case where it is not though he believes it is. The parallel argument for Newcomb's example would run: The predictor could believe that you will take only the second even if you do not. This shows that your action does not influence whether or not the money is there, but rather the predictor's beliefs about your action has this influence. But by the conditions of the problem, the predictor is almost certain to predict correctly, so that it is not clear that the predictor could believe that you will take only the second even if you do not. Thus, the condition of the problem which has the predictor's predictions almost certainly being correct tends to get us to treat the predictor's beliefs as though they do not have these nonextensional features. For if his predictions are almost certainly correct, then almost certainly: if he believes you will do A then you will do A.

One further thing should be mentioned. It is a reasonably intuitive principle that if R brings it about that p, and if p if and only if q (for some "iff" stronger than the material biconditional), then R brings it about that q. Or, if it is up to R whether p, and p iff q (for some strong "iff"), then it is up to R whether q. Thus one finds writers arguing that if there are necessary and sufficient causal conditions for our actions, which conditions go back to a time before we were born, then what we do is not up to us. For, so the argument runs, those conditions obtaining before we were born clearly were not up to us, and so what they are necessary and sufficient for is not up to us either. I do not wish here to discuss whether this principle is correct. All that is required for my purposes is that the principle have intuitive appeal, and be a hard one to escape.

This would also reinforce the feeling that as choosers in Newcomb's example, we can, somehow, influence what the predictor did. For, one might argue, Newcomb's problem is a problem for the chooser only if what he does is up to him. And if one assumes this, and the principle is operating, then it will be difficult to escape the feeling that what the predictor did is up to you, the chooser.

I do not claim that this last principle alone creates the problem. For the problem does not arise in, e.g., the vaccine case.[21] But it does, I believe, contribute to it.

Thus I wish to claim that Newcomb's example is less clear than the others because

    (a)   in it the explanation of the state's obtaining refers to the action (though this reference occurs in a nonextensional belief-context)

---

[21] Though perhaps it explains why I *momentarily* felt I had succeeded too well in constructing the vaccine case, and that perhaps one *should* perform the non-dominant action there.

and

(b) the conditions of the problem prevent one obvious way of refuting the teleologist's view, in this case, which view depends upon the truth that generally if y is part of the explanation of x, then y influences x.

This leads to the feeling that, somehow, you as chooser can influence what the predictor did, and this feeling is perhaps reinforced by the operation of the intuitive principle. All this leads to the lurking feeling that one can now choose to take only what is in the second box, and so make oneself the sort of person who does so, and so, somehow, influence what the predictor did. I hope you find this explanation of why some cases are clear and Newcomb's is not, acceptable, and that it is clear that this difference between the cases should not make a difference to how they are decided.[22]

At this point one perhaps wants to say, "If you produce a case having the features you say distinguish Newcomb's example from the others, where it is clear that the dominant action should be performed, then I will be convinced that the dominant action should be performed in Newcomb's example. But not until." If I am right about the role of similar examples, then this cannot be done; an answer to Newcomb's example cannot be forced in this way. Or rather, if it can be done, then it will show that I have not picked out the right difference. For if one case that fits my description is clear, and another which fits it is not clear, then we still have to produce features to explain why one is clear and the other is not. And perhaps *those* features should make a difference between the decisions in the two cases. At some point, given an acceptable explanation of why one case is clear and another is not, one just has to see that the explanatory features do not make a difference to what should be decided in the two cases. Or, at any rate, the point that the explanatory features do not make a difference to what should be decided can itself be forced by a clear case only at the cost of the claim that those very features explain why some cases are clear and others are not.

In closing this paper, I must muddy up the waters a bit (more?).

(1) Though Newcomb's example suggests much about when to apply the dominance principle, and when to apply the expected utility principle (and hence is relevant to formal decision theory), it is not the expected utility principle which leads some people to choose only what is in the second box. For suppose the probability of the being's predicting correctly was just .6.

---

[22] But it also seems relevant that in Newcomb's example not only is the action referred to in the explanation of which state obtains (though in a nonextensional belief context), but also there is another explanatory tie between the action and the state; namely, that both the state's obtaining, and your actually performing the action are both partly explained in terms of some third thing (your being in a certain initial state earlier). A fuller investigation would have to pursue yet more complicated examples which incorporated this.

Then the expected utility of taking what is in both boxes = prob(he predicts correctly/I take both) × u(I receive $1000) + prob(he predicts correctly/I take only second) × u(I receive $1,001,000) = .6 × u($1000) + .4 × u($1,001,000).

The expected utility of taking only what is in the second box is equal to .6 × u($1000000) + .4 × u($0).

And given the utility I assume each of my readers assigns to obtaining these various monetary amounts, the expected utility of taking only what is in the second box is greater than the expected utility of taking what is in both boxes. Yet, I presume, if the probability of the beings predicting correctly were only .6, each of us would choose to take what is in both boxes.

So it is not (just) the expected utility argument that operates here to create the problem in Newcomb's example. It is crucial that the predictor is almost certain to be correct. I refrain from asking a proponent of taking only what is in the second box in Newcomb's example: if .6 is not a high enough probability to lead you to take only what is in the second box, and almost certainty of correct predictions leads you to take only the second, what is the minimum probability of correct prediction which leads you to take only what is in the second box? I refrain from asking this question because I am very unsure about the force of drawing-the-line arguments, and also because the person who wishes to take what is in both boxes may also face a problem of drawing the line, as we shall see in a moment.

(2) If the fact that it is almost certain that the predictor will be correct is crucial to Newcomb's example, this suggests that we consider the case where it *is* certain, where you know the prediction is correct (though you do not know what the prediction is). Here one naturally argues: I know that if I take both, I will get $1000. I know that if I take only what is in the second, I get M. So, of course, I will take only what is in the second. And does a proponent of taking what is in both boxes in Newcomb's example, (e.g., me) really wish to argue that it is the probability, however minute, of the predictor's being mistaken which makes the difference? Does he really wish to argue that if he knows the prediction will be correct, he will take only the second, but that if he knows someone using the predictor's theory will be wrong once in every 20 billion cases, he will take what is in both boxes? Could the difference between one in n, and none in n, for arbitrarily large finite n, make this difference? And how exactly does the fact that the predictor is certain to have been correct dissolve the force of the dominance argument?

To get the mind to really boggle, consider the following.

	S_1	S_2
A:	10	4
B:	8	3

Suppose that you know that either S_1 or S_2 already obtains, but you do not know which, and you know that S_1 will cause you to do B, and S_2 will cause you to do A. Now choose! ("Choose?")

To connect up again with a causalized version of Newcomb's example, suppose you know that there are two boxes, (B1) and (B2). (B1) contains $1000. (B2) contains either a valuable diamond or nothing. You have to choose between taking what is in both boxes, and taking only what is in the second. You know that there are two states: S_1 and S_2. You do not know which obtains, but you know that whichever does, it has obtained for the past week. If S_2 obtains, it causes you to take only what is in the second, and it has already caused a diamond to be produced in box (B2). If S_1 obtains, it causes you to take what is in both boxes, and does not cause a diamond to be produced in the second box. You know all this. What do you choose to do?

While we are at it, consider the following case where what you decide (and why) either (1) does affect which future state will obtain, upon which consequences depend, or (though this would not be the same problem for the view I have proposed, it might be for yours) (2) even if it does not affect which state obtains, the conditional probabilities of the states, given what you do and why, differ.

$$
\begin{array}{ccc}
 & S_1 & S_2 \\
A: & \text{live} & \text{die} \\
B: & \text{die} & \text{live}
\end{array}
$$

(1) Apart from your decisions (if you do not know of this matrix, or know of it and cannot reach a decision), prob $S_1 >$ prob S_2

(2) prob(S_1/do A with (1) as reason) $<$ prob(S_2/do A with (1) as reason)

(3) prob(S_1/do B with (2) as reason) $>$ prob(S_2/do B with (2) as reason)

⋮

even (n) prob(S_1/do A with $n-1$ as reason) $<$ prob(S_2/do A with $n-1$ as reason)

odd (n) prob(S_1/do B with $n-1$ as reason) $>$ prob(S_2/do B with $n-1$ as reason)

⋮

Also: prob(S_1/you do what you do because indifferent between A and B) $>$ prob(S_2/you do what you do because indifferent between A and B)

prob(S_1/doing A with all of the above as reason) $<$
prob(S_2/doing A with all of the above as reason)
and
prob(S_1/doing B with all of the above as reason) $>$
prob(S_2/doing B with all of the above as reason).

Finally, where "all this" refers to all of what is above this place, and
   reflexively, to the next two, in which it appears:

prob(S_1/doing A with all this as reason) <

prob(S_2/doing A with all this as reason)

and

prob(S_1/doing B with all this as reason) >

prob(S_2/doing B with all this as reason).

What do you do?

10. Causal decision theory

David Lewis

1. Introduction

Decision theory in its best-known form[1] manages to steer clear of the thought that what's best to do is what the agent believes will most tend to cause good results. Causal relations and the like go unmentioned. The theory is simple, elegant, powerful, and conceptually economical. Unfortunately it is not quite right. In a class of somewhat peculiar cases, called Newcomb problems, this noncausal decision theory gives the wrong answer. It commends an irrational policy of managing the news so as to get good news about matters which you have no control over.

I am one of those who have concluded that we need an improved decision theory, more sensitive to causal distinctions. Noncausal decision theory will do when the causal relations are right for it, as they very often are, but even then the full story is causal. Several versions of causal decision theory are on the market in the works of Gibbard and Harper, Skyrms, and Sobel,[2]

This paper is based on a talk given at a conference on Conditional Expected Utility at the University of Pittsburgh in November 1978. It has benefited from discussions and correspondence with Nancy Cartwright, Allan Gibbard, William Harper, Daniel Hunter, Frank Jackson, Richard Jeffrey, Gregory Kavka, Reed Richter, Brian Skyrms, J. Howard Sobel, and Robert Stalnaker.

Reprinted with permission from *Australasian Journal of Philosophy* 59 (1981), 5–30, as reprinted in Lewis, *Philosophical Papers,* vol. 2 (New York: Oxford University Press, 1986).

[1] As presented, for instance, in Richard C. Jeffrey, *The Logic of Decision* (New York: McGraw-Hill, 1965).

[2] Allan Gibbard and William Harper, "Counterfactuals and Two Kinds of Expected Utility," in C. A. Hooker, J. J. Leach, and E. F. McClennen, eds., *Foundations and Applications of Decision Theory,* Volume 1 (Dordrecht, Holland: D. Reidel, 1978); Brian Skyrms, "The Role of Causal Factors in Rational Decision," in his *Causal Necessity* (New Haven: Yale University Press, 1980); and Jordan Howard Sobel, *Probability, Chance and Choice: A Theory of Rational Agency* (unpublished; presented in part at a workshop on Pragmatics and Conditionals at the University of Western Ontario in May 1978).

and I shall put forward a version of my own. But also I shall suggest that we causal decision theorists share one common idea, and differ mainly on matters of emphasis and formulation. The situation is not the chaos of disparate approaches that it may seem.

Of course there are many philosophers who understand the issues very well, and yet disagree with me about which choice in a Newcomb problem is rational. This paper is about a topic that does not arise for them. Noncausal decision theory meets their needs and they want no replacement. I will not enter into debate with them, since that debate is hopelessly deadlocked and I have nothing new to add to it. Rather, I address myself to those who join me in presupposing that Newcomb problems show the need for some sort of causal decision theory, and in asking what form that theory should take.

2. Preliminaries: credence, value, options

Let us assume that a (more or less) rational agent has, at any moment, a *credence* function and a *value* function. These are defined in the first instance over single possible worlds. Each world W has a credence $C(W)$, which measures the agent's degree of belief that W is the actual world. These credences fall on a scale from zero to one, and they sum to one. Also each world W has a value $V(W)$, which measures how satisfactory it seems to the agent for W to be the actual world. These values fall on a linear scale with arbitrary zero and unit.

We may go on to define credence also for sets of worlds. We call such sets *propositions,* and we say that a proposition *holds* at just those worlds which are its members. I shall not distinguish in notation between a world W and a proposition whose sole member is W, so all that is said of propositions shall apply also to single worlds. We sum credences: for any proposition X,

$$C(X) \stackrel{\text{df}}{=} \Sigma_{W \in X} C(W).$$

We define conditional credences as quotients of credences, defined if the denominator is positive:

$$C(X/Y) \stackrel{\text{df}}{=} C(XY)/C(Y),$$

where XY is the conjunction (intersection) of the propositions X and Y. If $C(Y)$ is positive, then $C(-/Y)$, the function that assigns to any world W or proposition X the value $C(W/Y)$ or $C(X/Y)$, is itself a credence function. We say that it *comes from* C *by conditionalising on* Y. Conditionalising on one's total evidence is a rational way to learn from experience. I shall proceed on the assumption that it is the only way for a fully rational agent to learn from experience; however, nothing very important will depend on that disputed premise.

We also define (expected) value for propositions. We take credence-weighted averages of values of worlds: for any proposition X,

$$V(X) \stackrel{df}{=} \Sigma_W C(W/X) V(W) = \Sigma_{W \in X} C(W) V(W)/C(X).$$

A *partition* (or a *partition of X*) is a set of propositions of which exactly one holds at any world (or at any *X*-world). Let the variable *Z* range over any partition (in which case the *XZ*'s, for fixed *X* and varying *Z*, are a partition of *X*). Our definitions yield the following *Rules of Additivity* for credence, and for the product of credence and expected value:

$$C(X) = \Sigma_Z C(XZ),$$
$$C(X) V(X) = \Sigma_Z C(XZ) V(XZ). \tag{1}$$

This *Rule of Averaging* for expected values follows:

$$V(X) = \Sigma_Z C(Z/X) V(XZ). \tag{2}$$

Thence we can get an alternative definition of expected value. For any number v, let $[V = v]$ be the proposition that holds at just those worlds *W* for which $V(W)$ equals v. Call $[V = v]$ a *value-level proposition*. Since the value-level propositions are a partition,

$$V(X) = \Sigma_v C([V = v]/X) v. \tag{3}$$

I have idealised and oversimplified in three ways, but I think the dodged complications make no difference to whether, and how, decision theory ought to be causal. First, it seems most unlikely that any real person could store and process anything so rich in information as the C and V functions envisaged. We must perforce make do with summaries. But it is plausible that someone who really did have these functions to guide him would not be so very different from us in his conduct, apart from his supernatural prowess at logic and mathematics and *a priori* knowledge generally. Second, my formulation makes straightforward sense only under the fiction that the number of possible worlds is finite. There are two remedies. We could reformulate everything in the language of standard measure theory, or we could transfer our simpler formulations to the infinite case by invoking nonstandard summations of infinitesimal credences. Either way the technicalities would distract us, and I see little risk that the fiction of finitude will mislead us. Third, a credence function over possible worlds allows for partial beliefs about the way the world is, but not for partial beliefs about who and where and when in the world one is. Beliefs of the second sort are distinct from those of the first sort; it is important that we have them; however, they are seldom very partial. To make them partial we need either an agent strangely lacking in self-knowledge, or else one who gives credence to strange worlds in which he has close duplicates. I here ignore the decision problems of such strange agents.[3]

---

[3] I consider them in "Attitudes *De Dicto* and *De Se*," *The Philosophical Review,* 88 (1979): pp. 513–543, especially p. 534. There, however, I ignore the causal aspects of decision theory. I trust there are no further problems that would arise from merging the two topics.

Let us next consider the agent's options. Suppose we have a partition of propositions that distinguish worlds where the agent acts differently (he or his counterpart, as the case may be). Further, he can act at will so as to make any one of these propositions hold, but he cannot act at will so as to make any proposition hold that implies but is not implied by (is properly included in) a proposition in the partition. The partition gives the most detailed specifications of his present action over which he has control. Then this is the partition of the agents' alternative *options*.[4] (Henceforth I reserve the variable A to range over these options.) Say that the agent *realises* an option iff he acts in such a way as to make it hold. Then the business of decision theory is to say which of the agent's alternative options it would be rational for him to realise.

All this is neutral ground. Credence, value, and options figure both in noncausal and in causal decision theory, though of course they are put to somewhat different uses.

3. Noncausal decision theory

Noncausal decision theory needs no further apparatus. It prescribes the rule of V-maximising, according to which a rational choice is one that has the greatest expected value. An option A is V-*maximal* iff $V(A)$ is not exceeded by any $V(A')$, where A' is another option. The theory says that to act rationally is to realise some V-maximal option.

Here is the guiding intuition. How would you like to find out that A holds? Your estimate of the value of the actual world would then be $V(A)$, if you learn by conditionalising on the news that A. So you would like best to find out that the V-maximal one of the A's holds (or one of the V-maximal ones, in case of a tie). But it's in your power to find out that whichever one you like holds, by realising it. So go ahead – find out whichever you'd like best to find out! You make the news, so make the news you like best.

This seeking of good news may not seem so sensible, however, if it turns out to get in the way of seeking good results. And it does.

4. Newcomb problems

Suppose you are offered some small good, take it or leave it. Also you may suffer some great evil, but you are convinced that whether you suffer it or not is entirely outside your control. In no way does it depend causally on what you do now. No other significant payoffs are at stake. Is it rational to take the small good? Of course, say I.

---

[4] They are his narrowest options. Any proposition implied by one of them might be called an option for him in a broader sense, since he could act at will so as to make it hold. But when I speak of options, I shall always mean the narrowest options.

I think enough has been said already to settle that question, but there is some more to say. Suppose further that you think that some prior state, which may or may not obtain and which also is entirely outside your control, would be conducive both to your deciding to take the good and to your suffering the evil. So if you take the good, that will be evidence that the prior state does obtain and hence that you stand more chance than you might have hoped of suffering the evil. Bad news! But is that any reason not to take the good? I say not, since if the prior state obtains, there's nothing you can do about it now. In particular, you cannot make it go away by declining the good, thus acting as you would have been more likely to act if the prior state had been absent. All you accomplish is to shield yourself from the bad news. That is useless. (*Ex hypothesi,* dismay caused by the bad news is not a significant extra payoff in its own right. Neither is the exhilaration or merit of boldly facing the worst.) To decline the good lest taking it bring bad news is to play the ostrich.

The trouble with noncausal decision theory is that it commends the ostrich as rational. Let G and $-G$ respectively be the propositions that you take the small good and that you decline it; suppose for simplicity that just these are your options. Let E and $-E$ respectively be the propositions that you suffer the evil and that you do not. Let the good contribute g to the value of a world and let the evil contribute $-e$; suppose the two to be additive, and set an arbitrary zero where both are absent. Then by Averaging,

$$V(-G) = C(E/-G)V(E-G) + C(-E/-G)V(-E-G) = -eC(E/-G)$$
$$V(G) = C(E/G)V(EG) + C(-E/G)V(-EG) = -eC(E/G) + g \tag{4}$$

That means that $-G$, declining the good, is the V-maximal option iff the difference $(C(E/G) - C(E/-G))$, which may serve as a measure of the extent to which taking the good brings bad news, exceeds the fraction g/e. And that may well be so under the circumstances considered. If it is, noncausal decision theory endorses the ostrich's useless policy of managing the news. It tells you to decline the good, though doing so does not at all tend to prevent the evil. If a theory tells you that, it stands refuted.

In Newcomb's original problem,[5] verisimilitude was sacrificed for extremity. $C(E/G)$ was close to one and $C(E/-G)$ was close to zero, so that declining the good turned out to be V-maximal by an overwhelming margin. To make it so, we have to imagine someone with the mind-boggling power to detect the entire vast combination of causal factors at some earlier time that would cause you to decline the good, in order to inflict the evil if any such combination is present. Some philosophers have refused to learn anything from such a tall story.

5 Presented in Robert Nozick, "Newcomb's Problem and Two Principles of Choice," in N. Rescher *et al.,* eds., *Essays in Honor of Carl G. Hempel* (Dordrecht, Holland: D. Reidel, 1970). [See Chapter 9.]

If our aim is to show the need for causal decision theory, however, a more moderate version of Newcomb's problem will serve as well. Even if the difference of $C(E/G)$ and $C(E/-G)$ is quite small, provided that it exceeds g/e, we have a counterexample. More moderate versions can also be more down-to-earth, as witness the medical Newcomb problems.[6] Suppose you like eating eggs, or smoking, or loafing when you might go out and run. You are convinced, contrary to popular belief, that these pleasures will do you no harm at all. (Whether you are right about this is irrelevant.) But also you think you might have some dread medical condition: a lesion of an artery, or nascent cancer, or a weak heart. If you have it, there's nothing you can do about it now and it will probably do you a lot of harm eventually. In its earlier stages, this condition is hard to detect. But you are convinced that it has some tendency, perhaps slight, to cause you to eat eggs, smoke, or loaf. So if you find yourself indulging, that is at least some evidence that you have the condition and are in for big trouble. But is that any reason not to indulge in harmless pleasures? The V-maximising rule says yes, if the numbers are right. I say no.

So far, I have considered pure Newcomb problems. There are also mixed problems. You may think that taking the good has some tendency to produce (or prevent) the evil, but also is a manifestation of some prior state which tends to produce the evil. Or you may be uncertain whether your situation is a Newcomb problem or not, dividing your credence between alternative hypotheses about the causal relations that prevail. These mixed cases are still more realistic, yet even they can refute noncausal decision theory.

However, no Newcomb problem, pure or mixed, can refute anything if it is not possible. The Tickle Defence of noncausal decision theory[7] questions whether Newcomb problems really can arise. It runs as follows: "Supposedly the prior state that tends to cause the evil also tends to cause you to take the good. The dangerous lesion causes you to choose to eat eggs, or whatever. How can it do that? If you are fully rational your choices are governed entirely by your beliefs and desires so nothing can influence your choices except by influencing your beliefs and desires. But if you are fully rational, you

[6] Discussed in Skyrms, and Nozick, *opera cit.*; in Richard C. Jeffrey, "Choice, Chance, and Credence," in G. H. von Wright and G. Fløistad, eds., *Philosophy of Logic* (Dordrecht, Holland: M. Nijhoff, 1980); and in Richard C. Jeffrey, "How Is it Reasonable to Base Preferences on Estimates of Chance?" in D. H. Mellor, ed., *Science, Belief and Behaviour: Essays in Honour of R. B. Braithwaite* (Cambridge: Cambridge University Press, 1980). I discuss another sort of moderate and down-to-earth Newcomb problem in "Prisoners' Dilemma is a Newcomb Problem," *Philosophy and Public Affairs,* 8 (1979): pp. 235–240.

[7] Discussed in Skyrms, *op. cit.*; and most fully presented in Ellery Eells, "Causality, Utility and Decision," *Synthese,* 48 (1981): 295–329. Eells argues that Newcomb problems are stopped by assumptions of rationality and self-knowledge somewhat weaker than those of the simple Tickle Defence considered here, but even those weaker assumptions seem to me unduly restrictive.

know your own mind. If the lesion produces beliefs and desires favourable to eating eggs, you will be aware of those beliefs and desires at the outset of deliberation. So you won't have to wait until you find yourself eating eggs to get the bad news. You will have it already when you feel that tickle in the tastebuds – or whatever introspectible state it might be – that manifests your desire for eggs. Your consequent choice tells you nothing more. By the time you decide whether to eat eggs, your credence function already has been modified by the evidence of the tickle. Then $C(E/G)$ does not exceed $C(E/-G)$, their difference is zero and so does not exceed g/e, $-G$ is not V-maximal, and noncausal decision theory does not make the mistake of telling you not to eat the eggs."

I reply that the Tickle Defence does establish that a Newcomb problem cannot arise for a fully rational agent, but that decision theory should not be limited to apply only to the fully rational agent.[8] Not so, at least, if rationality is taken to include self-knowledge. May we not ask what choice would be rational for the partly rational agent, and whether or not his partly rational methods of decision will steer him correctly? A partly rational agent may very well be in a moderate Newcomb problem, either because his choices are influenced by something besides his beliefs and desires or because he cannot quite tell the strengths of his beliefs and desires before he acts. ("How can I tell what I think till I see what I say?" – E. M. Forster.) For the dithery and the self-deceptive, no amount of *Gedankenexperimente* in decision can provide as much self-knowledge as the real thing. So even if the Tickle Defence shows that noncausal decision theory gives the right answer under powerful assumptions of rationality (whether or not for the right reasons), Newcomb problems still show that a general decision theory must be causal.

5. Utility and dependency hypotheses

Suppose someone knows all there is to know about how the things he cares about do and do not depend causally on his present actions. If something is beyond his control, so that it will obtain – or have a certain chance of obtaining – no matter what he does, then he knows that for certain. And if something is within his control, he knows that for certain; further, he knows the extent of his influence over it and he knows what he must do to influence it one way or another. Then there can be Newcomb problems for

---

[8] In fact, it may not apply to the fully rational agent. It is hard to see how such an agent can be uncertain what he is going to choose, hence hard to see how he can be in a position to deliberate. See Richard C. Jeffrey, "A Note on the Kinematics of Preference," *Erkenntnis*, 11 (1977): 135–141. Further, the "fully rational agent" required by the Tickle Defence is, in one way, not so very rational after all. Self-knowledge is an aspect of rationality, but so is willingness to learn from experience. If the agent's introspective data make him absolutely certain of his own credences and values, as they must if the Defence is to work, then no amount of evidence that those data are untrustworthy will ever persuade him not to trust them.

him. Whatever news his actions may bring, they cannot change his mind about the likely outcomes of his alternative actions. He knew it all before.

Let us call the sort of proposition that this agent knows – a maximally specific proposition about how the things he cares about do and do not depend causally on his present actions – a *dependency hypothesis* (for that agent at that time). Since there must be some truth or other on the subject, and since the dependency hypotheses are maximally specific and cannot differ without conflicting, they comprise a partition. Exactly one of them holds at any world, and it specifies the relevant relations of causal dependence that prevail there.

It would make no difference if our know-it-all didn't really know. If he concentrates all his credence on a single dependency hypothesis, whether rightly or wrongly, then there can be no Newcomb problems for him. His actions cannot bring him news about which dependency hypothesis holds if he already is quite certain which one it is.

Within a single dependency hypothesis, so to speak, V-maximising is right. It is rational to seek good news by doing that which, according to the dependency hypothesis you believe, most tends to produce good results. That is the same as seeking good results. Failures of V-maximising appear only if, first, you are sensible enough to spread your credence over several dependency hypotheses, and second, your actions might be evidence for some dependency hypotheses and against others. That is what may enable the agent to seek good news not in the proper way, by seeking good results, but rather by doing what would be evidence for a good dependency hypothesis. That is the recipe for Newcomb problems.

What should you do if you spread your credence over several dependency hypotheses? You should consider the expected value of your options under the several hypotheses; you should weight these by the credences you attach to the hypotheses; and you should maximise the weighted average. Henceforth I reserve the variable K to range over dependency hypotheses (or over members of partitions that play a parallel role in other versions of causal decision theory). Let us define the (*expected*) *utility* of an option A by:

$$U(A) \overset{\mathrm{df}}{=} \Sigma_K C(K) V(AK).$$

My version of causal decision theory prescribes the rule of U-*maximising* according to which a rational choice is one that has the greatest expected utility. Option A is U-maximal iff $U(A)$ is not exceeded by any $U(A')$, and to act rationally is to realise some U-maximal option.

In putting this forward as the rule of rational decision, of course I speak for myself; but I hope I have found a neutral formulation which fits not only my version of causal decision theory but also the versions proposed by Gibbard and Harper, Skyrms, and Sobel. There are certainly differences about the nature of dependency hypotheses; but if I am right, these are small matters compared to our common advocacy of utility maximising as just defined.

In distinguishing as I have between V and U – value and utility – I have followed the notation of Gibbard and Harper. But also I think I have followed the lead of ordinary language, in which "utility" means much the same as "usefulness." Certainly the latter term is causal. Which would you call the useful action: the one that tends to produce good results? Or the one that does no good at all (or even a little harm) and yet is equally welcome because it is a sign of something else that does produce good results? (Assume again that the news is not valued for its own sake.) Surely the first – and that is the one with greater utility in my terminology, though both may have equal value.

It is essential to define utility as we did using the unconditional credences $C(K)$ of dependency hypotheses, not their conditional credences $C(K/A)$. If the two differ, any difference expresses exactly that news-bearing aspect of the options that we meant to suppress. Had we used the conditional credences, we would have arrived at nothing different from V. For the Rule of Averaging applies to any partition; and hence to the partition of dependency hypotheses, giving

$$V(A) = \Sigma_K C(K/A) V(AK). \tag{5}$$

Let us give noncausal decision theory its due before we take leave of it. It works whenever the dependency hypotheses are probabilistically independent of the options, so that all the $C(K/A)$'s equal the corresponding $C(K)$'s. Then by (5) and the definition of U, the corresponding $V(A)$'s and $U(A)$'s also are equal. V-maximising gives the same right answers as U-maximising. The Tickle Defence seems to show that the K's must be independent of the A's for any fully rational agent. Even for partly rational agents, it seems plausible that they are at least close to independent in most realistic cases. Then indeed V-maximising works. But it works because the agent's beliefs about causal dependence are such as to make it work. It does not work for reasons which leave causal relations out of the story.

I am suggesting that we ought to undo a seeming advance in the development of decision theory. Everyone agrees that it would be ridiculous to maximise the "expected utility" defined by

$$\Sigma_Z C(Z) V(AZ)$$

where Z ranges over just any old partition. It would lead to different answers for different partitions. For the partition of value-level propositions, for instance, it would tell us fatalistically that all options are equally good! What to do? Savage suggested, in effect, that we make the calculation with unconditional credences, but make sure to use only the right sort of partition.[9] But what sort is that? Jeffrey responded that we would do better to make the

---

[9] Leonard J. Savage, *The Foundations of Statistics* (New York: Wiley, 1954): p. 15. The suggestion is discussed by Richard C. Jeffrey in "Savage's Omelet," in F. Suppe and P. D. Asquith, eds., *PSA 1976*, Volume 2 (East Lansing, Michigan: Philosophy of Science Association, 1977).

calculation with conditional credences, as in the right hand side of (2). Then we need not be selective about partitions, since we get the same answer, namely V(A), for all of them. In a way, Jeffrey himself was making decision theory causal. But he did it by using probabilistic dependence as a mark of causal dependence, and unfortunately the two need not always go together. So I have thought it better to return to unconditional credences and say what sort of partition is right.

As I have formulated it, causal decision theory is causal in two different ways. The dependency hypotheses are causal in their content: they class worlds together on the basis of likenesses of causal dependence. But also the dependency hypotheses themselves are causally independent of the agent's actions. They specify his influence over other things, but over them he has no influence. (Suppose he did. Consider the dependency hypothesis which we get by taking account of the ways the agent can manipulate dependency hypotheses to enhance his control over other things. This hypothesis seems to be right no matter what he does. Then he has no influence over whether this hypothesis or another is right, contrary to our supposition that the dependency hypotheses are within his influence.) Dependency hypotheses are "act-independent states" in a causal sense, though not necessarily in the probabilistic sense. If we say that the right sort of partition for calculating expected utility is a causally act-independent one, then the partition of dependency hypotheses qualifies. But I think it is better to say just that the right partition is the partition of dependency hypotheses, in which case the emphasis is on their causal content rather than their act-independence.

If any of the credences C(AK) is zero, the rule of U-maximising falls silent. For in that case V(AK) becomes an undefined sum of quotients with denominator zero, so U(A) in turn is undefined and A cannot be compared in utility with the other options. Should that silence worry us? I think not, for the case ought never to arise. It may seem that it arises in the most extreme sort of Newcomb problem: suppose that taking the good is thought to make it absolutely certain that the prior state obtains and the evil will follow. Then if A is the option of taking the good and K says that the agent stands a chance of escaping the evil, C(AK) is indeed zero and U(A) is indeed undefined. What should you do in such an extreme Newcomb problem? V-maximise after all?

No; what you should do is not be in that problem in the first place. Nothing should ever be held as certain as all that, with the possible exception of the testimony of the senses. Absolute certainty is tantamount to firm resolve never to change your mind no matter what, and that is objectionable. However much reason you may get to think that option A will not be realised if K holds, you will not if you are rational lower C(AK) quite to zero. Let it by all means get very, very small; but very, very small denominators do not make utilities go undefined.

What of the partly rational agent, whom I have no wish to ignore? Might he not rashly lower some credence C(AK) all the way to zero? I am inclined to think not. What makes it so that someone has a certain credence is that its ascription to him is part of a systematic pattern of ascriptions, both to him and to others like him, both as they are and as they would have been had events gone a bit differently, that does the best job overall of rationalising behaviour.[10] I find it hard to see how the ascription of rash zeros could be part of such a best pattern. It seems that a pattern that ascribes very small positive values instead always could do just a bit better, rationalising the same behaviour without gratuitously ascribing the objectionable zeros. If I am right about this, rash zeros are one sort of irrationality that is downright impossible.[11]

6. Reformulations

The causal decision theory proposed above can be reformulated in various equivalent ways. These will give us some further understanding of the theory, and will help us in comparing it with other proposed versions of causal decision theory.

Expansions

We can apply the Rule of Averaging to expand the $V(AK)$'s that appear in our definition of expected utility. Let Z range over any partition. Then we have

$$U(A) = \Sigma_K \Sigma_Z C(K) C(Z/AK) V(AKZ). \tag{6}$$

(If any $C(AKZ)$ is zero we may take the term for K and Z as zero, despite the fact that $V(AKZ)$ is undefined.) This seems only to make a simple thing complicated; but if the partition is well chosen, (6) may serve to express the utility of an option in terms of quantities that we find it comparatively easy to judge.

Let us call a partition *rich* iff, for every member S of that partition and for every option A and dependency hypothesis K, $V(AKS)$ equals $V(AS)$. That means that the AS's describe outcomes of options so fully that the addition of a dependency hypothesis tells us no more about the features of the outcomes that matter to the agent. Henceforth I reserve the variable S to range over rich partitions. Given richness of the partition, we can factor the value terms in (6) part way out, to obtain

---

[10] See my "Radical Interpretation," *Synthese,* 23 (1974): pp. 331–344. I now think that discussion is too individualistic, however, in that it neglects the possibility that one might have a belief or desire entirely because the ascription of it to him is part of a systematic pattern that best rationalises the behaviour of *other* people. On this point, see my discussion of the madman in "Mad Pain and Martian Pain," in Ned Block, ed., *Readings in Philosophy of Psychology,* Volume 1 (Cambridge, Massachusetts: Harvard University Press, 1980).

[11] Those who think that credences can easily fall to zero often seem to have in mind credences conditional on some background theory of the world which is accepted, albeit tentatively, in an all-or-nothing fashion. While I don't object to this notion, it is not what I mean by credence. As I understand the term, what is open to reconsideration does not have a credence of zero or one; these extremes are not to be embraced lightly.

$$U(A) = \Sigma_S(\Sigma_K C(K) C(S/AK)) V(AS). \tag{7}$$

Equation (7) for expected utility resembles equation (2) for expected value, except that the inner sum in (7) replaces the conditional credence $C(S/A)$ in the corresponding instance of (2). As we shall see, the analogy can be pushed further. Two examples of rich partitions to which (7) applies are the partition of possible worlds and the partition of value-level propositions $[V = v]$.

Imaging

Suppose we have a function that selects, for any pair of a world W and a suitable proposition X, a probability distribution W_X. Suppose further that W_X assigns probability only to X-worlds, so that $W_X(X)$ equals one. (Hence at least the empty proposition must not be "suitable.") Call the function an *imaging function,* and call W_X the *image of W on X.* The image might be sharp, if W_X puts all its probability on a single world; or it might be blurred, with the probability spread over more than one world.

Given an imaging function, we can apply it to form images also of probability distributions. We sum the superimposed images of all the worlds, weighting the images by the original probabilities of their source worlds. For any pair of a probability distribution C and a suitable proposition X, we define C_X, the *image of C on X,* as follows. First, for any world W',

$$C_X(W') \stackrel{\mathrm{df}}{=} \Sigma_W C(W) W_X(W');$$

think of $C(W) W_X(W')$ as the amount of probability that is moved from W to W' in making the image. We sum as usual: for any proposition Y,

$$C_X(Y) \stackrel{\mathrm{df}}{=} \Sigma_{W \in Y} C_X(W).$$

It is easy to check that C_X also is a probability distribution; and that it assigns probability only to X-worlds, so that $C_X(X)$ equals one. Imaging is one way – conditionalising is another – to revise a given probability distribution so that all the probability is concentrated on a given proposition.[12]

For our present purposes, what we want are images of the agent's credence function on his various options. The needed imaging function can be defined in terms of the partition of dependency hypotheses: let

---

[12] Sharp imaging by means of a Stalnaker selection function is discussed in my "Probabilities of Conditionals and Conditional Probabilities," *The Philosophical Review,* 85 (1976): pp. 297–315, especially pp. 309–311. . . . This generalisation to cover blurred imaging as well is due to Peter Gärdenfors, "Imaging and Conditionalization," *Journal of Philosophy,* 79 (1982): 747–760; a similar treatment appears in Donald Nute, *Topics in Conditional Logic* (Dordrecht, Holland: D. Reidel, 1980), Chapter 6. What is technically the same idea, otherwise motivated and under other names, appears in my "Counterfactuals and Comparative Possibility," *Journal of Philosophical Logic,* 2 (1973): pp. 418–446, Section 8; in John L. Pollock, *Subjunctive Reasoning* (Dordrecht, Holland: D. Reidel, 1976): pp. 219–236; and in Sobel, *op. cit.* The possibility of deriving an imaging function from a partition was suggested by Brian Skyrms in discussion of a paper by Robert Stalnaker at the 1979 annual meeting of the American Philosophical Association, Eastern Division.

$$W_A(W') \stackrel{\mathrm{df}}{=} C(W'/AK_W)$$

for any option A and worlds W and W', where K_W is the dependency hypothesis that holds at W. In words: move the credence of world W over to the A-worlds in the same dependency hypothesis, and distribute it among those worlds in proportion to their original credence. (Here again we would be in trouble if any of the $C(AK)$'s were zero, but I think we needn't worry.) It follows from the several definitions just given that for any option A and proposition Y,

$$C_A(Y) = \Sigma_K C(K) C(Y/AK). \tag{8}$$

The inner sum in (7) therefore turns out to be the credence, imaged on A, of S. So by (7) and (8) together,

$$U(A) = \Sigma_S C_A(S) V(AS). \tag{9}$$

Now we have something like the Rule of Averaging for expected value, except that the partition must be rich and we must image rather than conditionalising. For the rich partition of possible worlds we have

$$U(A) = \Sigma_W C_A(W) V(W), \tag{10}$$

which resembles the definition of expected value. For the rich partition of value-level propositions we have something resembling (3):

$$U(A) = \Sigma_v C_A([V = v]) v. \tag{11}$$

7. Primitive imaging: Sobel

To reformulate causal decision theory in terms of imaging, I proceeded in two steps. I began with the dependency hypotheses and used them to define an imaging function; then I redefined the expected utility of an option in terms of imaging. We could omit the first step and leave the dependency hypotheses out of it. We could take the imaging function as primitive, and go on as I did to define expected utility by means of it. That is the decision theory of J. Howard Sobel, *op. cit.*

Sobel starts with the images of worlds, which he calls *world-tendencies*. (He considers images on all propositions possible relative to the given world, but for purposes of decision theory we can confine our attention to images on the agent's options.) Just as we defined C_A in terms of the W_A's, so Sobel goes on to define images of the agent's credence function. He uses these in turn to define expected utility in the manner of (10), and he advocates maximising the utility so defined rather than expected value.

Sobel unites his decision theory with a treatment of counterfactual conditionals in terms of closest antecedent-worlds.[13] If $W_A(W')$ is positive, then

---

[13] As in my *Counterfactuals* (Oxford: Blackwell, 1973), without the complications raised by possible infinite sequences of closer and closer antecedent-worlds.

we think of W' as one of the A-worlds that is in some sense closest to the world W. What might be the case if it were the case that A, from the standpoint of W, is what holds at some such closest A-world; what would be the case if A, from the standpoint of W, is what holds at all of them. Sobel's apparatus gives us quantitative counterfactuals intermediate between the mights and the woulds. We can say that if it were that A, it would be with probability p that X; meaning that $W_A(X)$ equals p, or in Sobel's terminology that X holds on a subset of the closest A-worlds whose tendencies, at W and on the supposition A, sum to p.

Though Sobel leaves the dependency hypotheses out of his decision theory, we can perhaps bring them back in. Let us say that worlds *image alike* (on the agent's options) iff, for each option, their images on that option are exactly the same. Imaging alike is an equivalence relation, so we have the partition of its equivalence classes. If we start with the dependency hypotheses and define the imaging function as I did, it is immediate that worlds image alike iff they are worlds where the same dependency hypothesis holds; so the equivalence classes turn out to be just the dependency hypotheses.

The question is whether dependency hypotheses could be brought into Sobel's theory by defining them as equivalence classes under the relation of imaging alike. Each equivalence class could be described, in Sobel's terminology, as a maximally specific proposition about the tendencies of the world on all alternative suppositions about which option the agent realises. That sounds like a dependency hypothesis to me. Sobel tells me (personal communication, 1980) that he is inclined to agree, and does regard his decision theory as causal; though it is hard to tell that from his written presentation, in which causal language very seldom appears.

If the proposal is to succeed technically, we need the following thesis: if K_W is the equivalence class of W under the relation of imaging alike (of having the same tendencies on each option) then, for any option A and world W', $W_A(W')$ equals $C(W'/AK_W)$. If so, it follows that if we start as Sobel does with the imaging function, defining the dependency hypotheses as equivalence classes, and thence defining an imaging function as I did, we will get back the same imaging function that we started with. It further follows, by our results in Section 6, that expected utility calculated in my way from the defined dependency hypotheses is the same as expected utility calculated in Sobel's way from the imaging function. They must be the same, if the defined dependency hypotheses introduced into Sobel's theory are to play their proper role.

Unfortunately, the required thesis is not a part of Sobel's theory; it would be an extra constraint on the imaging function. It does seem a very plausible constraint, at least in ordinary cases. Sobel suspends judgement about imposing a weaker version of the thesis (Connection Thesis 1, discussed in his Section 6.7). But his reservations, which would carry over to our version, entirely concern the extraordinary case of an agent who thinks he may somehow have foreknowledge of the outcomes of chance processes. Sobel gives no reason, and I know of none, to doubt either version of the thesis except in extraordinary cases of that sort. Then if we assume the thesis, it seems that we are only setting aside some very special cases – cases about which I, at least, have no firm views. (I think them much more problematic for decision theory than the Newcomb problems.) So far as the remaining cases are concerned, it is satisfactory to introduce defined dependency hypotheses into Sobel's theory and thereby render it equivalent to mine.

8. Factors outside our influence: Skyrms

Moving on to the version of causal decision theory proposed by Brian Skyrms, *op. cit.,* we find a theory that is formally just like mine. Skyrms' definition of *K-expectation* – his name for the sort of expected utility that should be maximised – is our equation (6). From that, with a trivial partition of Z's, we can immediately recover my first definition of expected utility. Skyrms introduces a partition of hypotheses – the K's which give K-expectation its name – that play just the same role in his calculation of expected utility that the dependency hypotheses play in mine. (Thus I have followed Skyrms in notation.) So the only difference, if it is a difference, is in how the K's are characterised.

Skyrms describes them at the outset as maximally specific specifications of the factors outside the agent's influence (at the time of decision) which are causally relevant to the outcome of the agent's action. He gives another characterisation later, but let us take the first one first.

I ask what Skyrms means to count as a "factor." Under a sufficiently broad construal, I have no objection to Skyrms' theory and I think it no different from mine. On a narrower and more literal construal, I do not think Skyrms' theory is adequate as a general theory of rational decision, though I think that in practice it will often serve. Insofar as Skyrms is serving up a general theory rather than practical rules of thumb, I think it is indeed the broad construal that he intends.

(I also ask what Skyrms means by "relevant to the outcome." I can't see how any factor, broadly or narrowly construed, could fail to be relevant to some aspect of the outcome. If the outcome is that I win a million dollars tomorrow, one aspect of this outcome may be that it takes place just one thousand years after some peasant felled an oak with ninety strokes of his axe. So I suppose Skyrms' intent was to include only factors relevant to those features of the outcome that the agent cares about, as opposed to those that are matters of indifference to him. That would parallel a like exclusion of matters of indifference in my definition of dependency hypotheses. In neither case is the exclusion important. Richer hypotheses, cluttered with matters of indifference, ought to give the same answers.)

On the broad construal, a "factor" need not be the sort of localised particular occurrence that we commonly think of as causing or being caused. It might be any matter of contingent fact whatever. It might indeed be some particular occurrence. It might be a vast dispersed pattern of occurrences throughout the universe. It might be a law of nature. It might be a dependency hypothesis. On the broad construal, Skyrms is saying only that the K's are maximally specific propositions about matters outside the agent's influence and relevant to features of the outcome that the agent cares about.

A dependency hypothesis is outside the agent's influence. It is relevant to features of the outcome that he cares about. (*Causally* relevant? – Not clear, but if we're construing "factor" broadly, we can let that by as well.) Any specification of something outside the agent's influence is included in a dependency hypothesis – recall that they cover what doesn't depend on the agent's actions as well as what does – unless it concerns something the agent doesn't care about. I conclude that on the broad construal, Skyrms' K's are nothing else than the dependency hypotheses. In that case his theory is the same as mine.

On the narrow construal, a "factor" must be the sort of localised occurrence – event, state, omission, etc. – that we normally think of as a cause. In the medical Newcomb problems, for instance, the lesion or the nascent cancer or the weak heart is a causal factor narrowly and literally. In motivating his theory, it is factors like these that Skyrms considers.

Our topic is rational decision according to the agent's beliefs, be they right or wrong. So it seems that we should take not the factors which really are outside his influence, but rather those he thinks are outside his influence. But what if he divides his credence between several hypotheses as to which factors are outside his influence, as well he might? Skyrms responds to this challenge by redescribing his partition of hypotheses. On his new description, each hypothesis consists of two parts: (i) a preliminary hypothesis specifying which of the relevant causal factors are outside the agent's influence, and (ii) a full specification of those factors that are outside his influence according to part (i).

That is a welcome amendment, but I think it does not go far enough. Influence is a matter of degree, so shouldn't the hypotheses say not just that the agent has some influence over a factor or none, but also how much? And if the hypothesis says that the agent has influence over a factor, shouldn't it also say which way the influence goes? Given that I can influence the temperature, do I make it cooler by turning the knob clockwise or counterclockwise? Make Skyrms' amendment and the other needed amendments, and you will have the dependency hypotheses back again.

To illustrate my point, consider an agent with eccentric beliefs. He thinks the influence of his actions ramifies but also fades, so that everything in the far future is within his influence but only a little bit. Perhaps he thinks that his actions raise and lower the chances of future occurrences, but only very slightly. Also he thinks that time is circular, so that the far future includes the present and the immediate past and indeed all of history. Then he gives all his credence to a single one of Skyrms' two-part hypotheses: the one saying that no occurrence whatever – no factor, on the narrow construal – is entirely outside his influence. That means that on Skyrms' calculation his $U(A)$'s reduce to the corresponding $V(A)$'s, so V-maximising is right for him. That's wrong. Since he thinks he has very little influence over whether he has the dread lesion, his decision problem about eating eggs is very little different from that of someone who thinks the lesion is entirely outside his influence. V-maximising should come out wrong for very much the same reason in both cases.

No such difficulty threatens Skyrms' proposal broadly construed. The agent may well wonder which of the causal factors narrowly construed are within his influence, but he cannot rationally doubt that the dependency hypotheses are entirely outside it. On the broad construal, Skyrms' second description of the partition of hypotheses is a gloss on the first, not an amendment. The hypotheses already specify which of the (narrow) factors are outside the agent's influence, for that is itself a (broad) factor outside his influence. Skyrms notes this, and that is why I think it must be the broad construal that he intends. Likewise the degrees and directions of influence over (narrow) factors are themselves (broad) factors outside the agent's influence, hence already specified according to the broad construal of Skyrms' first description.

Often, to be sure, the difference between the broad and narrow construals will not matter. There may well be a correlation, holding throughout the worlds which enjoy significant credence, between dependency hypotheses and combinations of (narrow) factors outside the agent's influence. The difference between good and bad dependency hypotheses may in practice amount to the difference between absence and presence of a lesion. However, I find it rash to assume that there must always be some handy correlation to erase the difference between the broad and narrow construals. Dependency hypotheses do indeed hold in virtue of lesions and the like, but they hold also in virtue of the laws of nature. It would seem that uncertainty about dependency hypotheses might come at least partly from uncertainty about the laws.

Skyrms is sympathetic, as am I,[14] to the neo-Humean thesis that every contingent truth about a world – law, dependency hypothesis, or what you will – holds somehow in virtue of that world's total history of manifest matters of particular fact. Same history, same everything. But that falls short of implying that dependency hypotheses hold just in virtue of casual factors, narrowly construed; they might hold partly in virtue of dispersed patterns of particular fact throughout history, including the future and the distant present. Further, even if we are inclined to accept the neo-Humean thesis,

[14] Although sympathetic, I have some doubts; see my "A Subjectivist's Guide to Objective Chance," in R. C. Jeffrey, ed., *Studies in Inductive Logic and Probability,* Volume 2 (Berkeley and Los Angeles: University of California Press, 1980): pp. 290–292. . . .

it still seems safer not to make it a presupposition of our decision theory. Whatever we think of the neo-Humean thesis, I conclude that Skyrms' decision theory is best taken under the broad construal of "factor" under which his K's are the dependency hypotheses and his calculation of utility is the same as mine.[15]

9. Counterfactual dependence: Gibbard and Harper

If we want to express a dependency hypothesis in ordinary language, it is hard to avoid the use of counterfactual conditionals saying what would happen if the agent were to realise his various alternative options. Suppose that on a certain occasion I'm interested in getting Bruce to purr. I could try brushing, stroking, or leaving alone; pretend that these are my narrowest options. Bruce might purr loudly, softly, or not at all; pretend that these alternatives are a rich partition. (Those simplifying pretences are of course very far from the truth.) Much of my credence goes to the dependency hypothesis given by these three counterfactuals:

> I brush Bruce $\Box\!\!\rightarrow$ he purrs loudly;
> I stroke Bruce $\Box\!\!\rightarrow$ he purrs softly;
> I leave Bruce alone $\Box\!\!\rightarrow$ he doesn't purr.

($\Box\!\!\rightarrow$ is used here as a sentential connective, read "if it were that . . . it would be that . . . ." I use it also as an operator which applies to two propositions to make a proposition; context will distinguish the uses.) This hypothesis says that loud and soft purring are within my influence – they depend on what I do. It specifies the extent of my influence, namely full control. And it specifies the direction of influence, what I must do to get what. This is one dependency hypothesis. I give some of my credence to others, for instance this (rather less satisfactory) one:

> I brush Bruce $\Box\!\!\rightarrow$ he doesn't purr;
> I stroke Bruce $\Box\!\!\rightarrow$ he doesn't purr;
> I leave Bruce alone $\Box\!\!\rightarrow$ he doesn't purr.

That dependency hypothesis says that the lack of purring is outside my influence, it is causally independent of what I do. Altogether there are twenty-

---

[15] The decision theory of Nancy Cartwright, "Causal Laws and Effective Strategies," *Noûs,* 13 (1979): pp. 419–437, is, as she remarks, "structurally identical" to Skyrms' theory for the case where value is a matter of reaching some all-or-nothing goal. However, hers is not a theory of subjectively rational decision in the single case, like Skyrms' theory and the others considered in this paper, but instead is a theory of objectively effective generic strategies. Since the subject matters are different, the structural identity is misleading. Cartwright's theory might somehow imply a single-case theory having more than structure in common with Skyrms' theory, but that would take principles she does not provide; *inter alia,* principles relating generic causal conduciveness to influence in the single case. So it is not clear that Cartwright's decision theory, causal though it is, falls under my claim that "we causal decision theorists share one common idea."

seven dependency hypotheses expressible in this way, though some of them get very little credence.

Note that it is the pattern of counterfactuals, not any single one of them, that expresses causal dependence or independence. As we have seen, the same counterfactual

I leave Bruce alone $\square\!\!\rightarrow$ he doesn't purr

figures in the first hypothesis as part of a pattern of dependence and in the second as part of a pattern of independence.

It is clear that not just any counterfactual could be part of a pattern expressing causal dependence or independence. The antecedent and consequent must specify occurrences capable of causing and being caused, and the occurrences must be entirely distinct. Further, we must exclude "back-tracking counterfactuals" based on reasoning from different supposed effects back to different causes and forward again to differences in other effects. Suppose I am convinced that stroking has no influence over purring, but that I wouldn't stroke Bruce unless I were in a mood that gets him to purr softly by emotional telepathy. Then I give credence to

I stroke Bruce $\square\!\!\rightarrow$ he purrs softly

taken in a back-tracking sense, but not taken in the sense that it must have if it is to be part of a pattern of causal dependence or independence.

Let us define *causal counterfactuals* as those that can belong to patterns of causal dependence or independence. Some will doubt that causal counterfactuals can be distinguished from others except in causal terms; I disagree, and think it possible to delimit the causal counterfactuals in other terms and thus provide noncircular counterfactual analyses of causal dependence and causation itself. But that is a question for other papers.[16] For present purposes, it is enough that dependency hypotheses can be expressed (sometimes, at least) by patterns of causal counterfactuals. I hope that much is adequately confirmed by examples like the one just considered. And that much can be true regardless of whether the pattern of counterfactuals provides a noncircular analysis.

Turning from language to propositions, what we want are causal counterfactuals $A \square\!\!\rightarrow S$, where A is one of the agent's options and S belongs to some rich partition. The rich partition must be one whose members specify combinations of occurrences wholly distinct from the actions specified by the agent's options. It seems a safe assumption that some such rich partition exists. Suppose some definite one to be chosen (it should make no difference which one). Define a *full pattern* as a set consisting of exactly one such counterfactual proposition for each option. I claim that the conjunction of the counterfactuals in any full pattern is a dependency hypothesis.

---

[16] In particular, my "Causation," *Journal of Philosophy,* 70 (1973): pp. 556–567; and "Counterfactual Dependence and Time's Arrow," *Noûs,* 13 (1979): pp. 455–476.

Conjunctions of different full patterns are contraries, as any two dependency hypotheses should be. For if S and S' are contraries, and A is possible (which any option is), then also $A \mathbin{\square\!\!\rightarrow} S$ and $A \mathbin{\square\!\!\rightarrow} S'$ are contraries;[17] and any two full patterns must differ by at least one such contrary pair.

What is not so clear is that some full pattern or other holds at any world, leaving no room for any other dependency hypotheses besides the conjunctions of full patterns. We shall consider this question soon. But for now, let us answer it by fiat. Assume that there is a full pattern for every world, so that the dependency hypotheses are all and only the conjunctions of full patterns.

That assumption yields the causal decision theory proposed by Allan Gibbard and William Harper, *op. cit.,* following a suggestion of Robert Stalnaker. My statement of it amounts to their Savage-style formulation with conjunctions of full patterns of counterfactuals as act-independent states; and their discussion of consequences in their Section 6 shows that they join me in regarding these conjunctions as expressing causal dependence or independence. Although they do not explicitly distinguish causal counterfactuals from others, their Section 2 sketches a theory of counterfactuals which plainly is built to exclude back-trackers in any ordinary situation. This is essential to their purpose. A theory which used counterfactuals in formally the same way, but which freely admitted back-trackers, would not be a causal decision theory. Its conjunctions of full patterns including back-trackers would not be causal dependency hypotheses, and it would give just those wrong answers about Newcomb problems that we causal decision theorists are trying to avoid.[18]

Consider some particular A and S. If a dependency hypothesis K is the conjunction of a full pattern that includes $A \mathbin{\square\!\!\rightarrow} S$, then AK implies S and $C(S/AK)$ equals one. If K is the conjunction of a full pattern that includes not $A \mathbin{\square\!\!\rightarrow} S$ but some contrary $A \mathbin{\square\!\!\rightarrow} S'$, then AK contradicts S and $C(S/AK)$ equals zero. *Ex hypothesi,* every dependency hypothesis K is of one kind or the other. Then the K's for which $C(S/AK)$ equals one comprise a partition of $A \mathbin{\square\!\!\rightarrow} S$, while $C(S/AK)$ equals zero for all other K's. It follows by the Rule of Additivity for credence that

$$C(A \mathbin{\square\!\!\rightarrow} S) = \Sigma_K C(K)C(S/AK). \tag{12}$$

(Comparing (12) with (8), we find that our present assumptions equate $C(A \mathbin{\square\!\!\rightarrow} S)$ with $C_A(S)$, the credence of S imaged on the option A.) Substituting (12) into (7) we have

$$U(A) = \Sigma_S C(A \mathbin{\square\!\!\rightarrow} S)V(AS), \tag{13}$$

---

[17] Here and henceforth, I make free use of some fairly uncontroversial logical principles for counterfactuals: namely, those given by the system $CK + ID - MP$ of Brian F. Chellas, "Basic Conditional Logic," *Journal of Philosophical Logic,* 4 (1975): pp. 133–153.

[18] Such a theory is defended in Terence Horgan, "Counterfactuals and Newcomb's Problem," *Journal of Philosophy,* 78 (1981): 331–356.

which amounts to Gibbard and Harper's defining formula for the "genuine expected utility" they deem it rational to maximise.[19]

We have come the long way around to (13), which is not only simple but also intuitive in its own right. But (13) by itself does not display the causal character of Gibbard and Harper's theory, and that is what makes it worthwhile to come at it by way of dependency hypotheses. No single $C(A \; \square \!\!\rightarrow S)$ reveals the agent's causal views, since it sums the credences of hypotheses which set $A \; \square \!\!\rightarrow S$ in a pattern of dependence and others which set $A \; \square \!\!\rightarrow S$ in a pattern of independence. Consequently the roundabout approach helps us to appreciate what the theory of Gibbard and Harper has in common with that of someone like Skyrms who is reluctant to use counterfactuals in expressing dependency hypotheses.

10. Counterfactual dependence with chancy outcomes

The assumption that there is a full pattern for each world is a consequence of Stalnaker's principle of Conditional Excluded Middle,[20] which says that either $X \; \square \!\!\rightarrow Y$ or $X \; \square \!\!\rightarrow -Y$ holds at any world (where $-Y$ is the negation of Y). It follows that if $Y, Y', \ldots$ are a partition and X is possible, then $X \; \square \!\!\rightarrow Y$, $X \; \square \!\!\rightarrow Y', \ldots$ also are a partition. The conjunctions of full patterns are then a partition because, for any option A, the counterfactuals $A \; \square \!\!\rightarrow S, A \; \square \!\!\rightarrow S', \ldots$ are a partition.

Conditional Excluded Middle is open to objection on two counts, one more serious than the other. Hence so is the decision theory of Gibbard and Harper, insofar as it relies on Conditional Excluded Middle to support the assumption that there is a full pattern for each world. Gibbard and Harper themselves are not to be faulted, for they tell us that their "reason for casting the rough theory in a form which gives these principles is that circumstances where these can fail involve complications which it would be best to ignore in preliminary work." (*Op. cit.*: 128) Fair enough; still, we have unfinished business on the agenda.

The first objection to Conditional Excluded Middle is that it makes arbitrary choices. It says that the way things would be on a false but possible supposition X is no less specific than the way things actually are. Some single, fully specific possible world is the one that would be actualised if it were that X. Since the worlds $W, W', \ldots$ are a partition, so are the counterfactuals $X \; \square \!\!\rightarrow W, X \; \square \!\!\rightarrow W', \ldots$ saying exactly how things would be if X. But surely some questions about how things would be if X have no nonarbitrary answers: if you had a sister, would she like blintzes?

---

[19] To get exactly their formula, take their "outcomes" as conjunctions AS with "desirability" given by V(AS); and bear in mind (i) that $A \; \square \!\!\rightarrow AS$ is the same as $A \; \square \!\!\rightarrow S$, and (ii) that if A and A' are contraries, $A \; \square \!\!\rightarrow A'S$ is the empty proposition with credence zero.

[20] Robert C. Stalnaker, "A Theory of Conditionals," in N. Rescher, ed., *Studies in Logical Theory* (Oxford: Blackwell, 1968), gives a semantic analysis in which Conditional Excluded Middle follows from ordinary Excluded Middle applied to the selected antecedent-world.

The less specific the supposition, the less it settles; the more far-fetched it is, the less can be settled by what carries over from actuality; and the less is settled otherwise, the more must be settled arbitrarily or not at all. But the supposition that an agent realises one of his narrowest options is neither unspecific nor far-fetched. So the Arbitrariness Objection may be formidable against the general principle of Conditional Excluded Middle, yet not formidable against the special case of it that gives us a full pattern for each world.

Further, Bas van Fraassen has taught us a general method for tolerating arbitrariness.[21] When forced to concede that certain choices would be arbitrary, we leave those choices unmade and we ask what happens on all the alternative ways of making them. What is constant over all the ways of making them is determinate, what varies is indeterminate. If the provision of full patterns for certain worlds is partly arbitrary, so be it. Then indeed some arbitrary variation may infect the $C(K)$'s, $C(S/AK)$'s, $C(A \Box\!\!\rightarrow S)$'s, and even the $U(A)$'s. It might even infect the set of U-maximal options. Then indeed it would be (wholly or partly) indeterminate which options the Gibbard–Harper theory commends as rational. All of that might happen, but it needn't. The arbitrary variation might vanish part way through the calculation, leaving the rest determinate. The less arbitrary variation there is at the start, of course, the less risk that there will be any at the end.

I conclude that the Arbitrariness Objection by itself is no great threat to Gibbard and Harper's version of causal decision theory. We can well afford to admit that the theory might fail occasionally to give a determinate answer. Indeed, I admit that already, for any version, on other grounds. I think there is sometimes an arbitrary element in the assignment of C and V functions to partly rational agents. No worries, so long as we can reasonably hope that the answers are mostly determinate.

Unfortunately there is a second, and worse, objection against Conditional Excluded Middle and the Gibbard–Harper theory. In part it is an independent objection; in part an argument that van Fraassen's method of tolerating arbitrariness would be severely overloaded if we insisted on providing full patterns all around (and *a fortiori* if we insisted on saving Conditional Excluded Middle generally), and we could not reasonably hope that the answers are mostly determinate. Suppose the agent thinks – as he should if he is well-educated – that the actual world may very well be an indeterminate one, where many things he cares about are settled by chance processes. Then he may give little of his credence to worlds where full patterns hold. In fact he may well give little credence to any of the $A \Box\!\!\rightarrow S$ counterfactuals that make up these patterns.

Consider again my problem of getting Bruce to purr. I think that Bruce works by firing of neurons, I think neurons work by chemical reactions, and

[21] See Bas van Fraassen, "Singular Terms, Truth-Value Gaps and Free Logic," *Journal of Philosophy,* 63 (1966): pp. 481–495. Use of van Fraassen's method to concede and tolerate arbitrariness in counterfactuals was suggested to me by Stalnaker in 1968 (personal communication) and is discussed in my *Counterfactuals*: pp. 81–83.

I think the making or breaking of a chemical bond is a chance event in the same way that the radioactive decay of a nucleus is. Maybe I still give some small credence to the twenty-seven full patterns considered in Section 9 – after all, I might be wrong to think that Bruce is chancy. But mostly I give my credence to the denials of all the counterfactuals that appear in those patterns, and to such counterfactuals as

> I brush Bruce □→ a chance process goes on in him which has certain probabilities of eventuating in his purring loudly, softly, or not at all;

and likewise for the options of stroking and leaving alone. A diehard supporter of the Gibbard–Harper theory (not Gibbard or Harper, I should think) might claim that I give my credence mostly to worlds where it is arbitrary which one of the twenty-seven full patterns holds, but determinate that some one of them holds. If he is right, even this easy little decision problem comes out totally indeterminate, for the arbitrary variation he posits is surely enough to swing the answer any way at all. Nor would it help if I believe that whichever I did, all the probabilities of Bruce's purring loudly, softly, or not at all would be close to zero or one. Nor would a more realistic decision problem fare any better: unless the agent is a fairly convinced determinist, the answers we want vanish into indeterminacy. The diehard destroys the theory in order to save it.

Anyway, the diehard is just wrong. If the world is the chancy way I mostly think it is, there's nothing at all arbitrary or indeterminate about the counterfactuals in the full patterns. They are flatly, determinately false. So is their disjunction; the diehard agrees that it is determinate in truth value, but the trouble is that he thinks it is determinately true.

Unlike the Arbitrariness Objection, the Chance Objection seems to me decisive both against Conditional Excluded Middle generally and against the assumption that there is a full pattern for each world. Our conception of dependency hypotheses as conjunctions of full patterns is too narrow. Fortunately, the needed correction is not far to seek.

I shall have to assume that anyone who gives credence to indeterministic worlds without full patterns is someone who – implicitly and in practice, if not according to his official philosophy – distributes his credence over contingent propositions about single-case, objective chances. Chance is a kind of probability that is neither frequency nor credence, though related to both. I have no analysis to offer, but I am convinced that we do have this concept and we don't have any substitute for it.[22]

Suppose some rich partition to be chosen which meets the requirement of distinct occurrences laid down in Section 9. Let the variable p range over candidate probability distributions for this rich partition: functions assigning to each S in the partition a number $p(S)$ in the interval from zero to one,

---

[22] For a fuller discussion of chance and its relations to frequency and credence, see "A Subjectivist's Guide to Objective Chance."

such that the $p(S)$'s sum to one. Let $[P = p]$ be the proposition that holds at just those worlds where the chances of the S's, as of the time when the agent realises his chosen option, are correctly given by the function p. Call $[P = p]$ a *chance proposition,* and note that the chance propositions are a partition. Now consider the causal counterfactuals $A \,\square\!\!\rightarrow [P = p]$ from the agent's options to the chance propositions. Define a *probabilistic full pattern* as a set containing exactly one such counterfactual for each option. I claim that the conjunction of the counterfactuals in any probabilistic full pattern is a causal dependency hypothesis. It specifies plain causal dependence or independence of the chances of the S's on the A's, and thereby it specifies a probabilistic kind of causal dependence of the S's themselves on the A's.

Here, for example, are verbal expressions of three chance propositions.

$[P = p_1]$ The chance that Bruce purrs loudly is 50%; the chance that he purrs softly is 40%; and the chance that he purrs not at all is 10%.

$[P = p_2]$ (similar, but with 30%, 50%, 20%).

$[P = p_3]$ (similar, but with 10%, 10%, 80%).

(The chance is to be at the time of my realising an option; the purring or not is to be at a certain time shortly after.) And here is a dependency hypothesis that might get as much of my credence as any:

I brush Bruce $\square\!\!\rightarrow [P = p_1]$ holds;
I stroke Bruce $\square\!\!\rightarrow [P = p_2]$ holds;
I leave Bruce alone $\square\!\!\rightarrow [P = p_3]$ holds.

Observe that this hypothesis addresses itself not only to the question of whether loud and soft purring are within my influence, but also to the question of the extent and the direction of my influence.

If a chance proposition says that one of the S's has a chance of one, it must say that the others all have chances of zero. Call such a chance proposition *extreme.* I shall not distinguish between an extreme proposition and the S that it favours. If they differ, it is only on worlds where something with zero chance nevertheless happens. I am inclined to think that they do not differ at all, since there are no worlds where anything with zero chance happens; the contrary opinion comes of mistaking infinitesimals for zero. But even if there is a difference between extreme chance propositions and their favoured S's, it will not matter to calculations of utility so let us neglect it. Then our previous dependency hypotheses, the conjunctions of full patterns, are subsumed under the conjunctions of probabilistic full patterns. So are the conjunctions of mixed full patterns that consist partly of $A \,\square\!\!\rightarrow S$'s and partly of $A \,\square\!\!\rightarrow [P = p]$'s.

Dare we assume that there is a probabilistic full pattern for every world, so that on this second try we have succeeded in capturing all the dependency hypotheses by means of counterfactuals? I shall assume it, not without misgivings. That means accepting a special case of Conditional Excluded Middle, but (i) the Chance Objection will not arise again,[23] (ii) there should not be too much need for arbitrary choice on other grounds, since the options are quite specific suppositions and not far-fetched, and (iii) limited arbitrary choice results in nothing worse than a limited risk of the answers going indeterminate.

So my own causal decision theory consists of two theses. My main thesis is that we should maximise expected utility calculated by means of dependency hypotheses. It is this main thesis that I claim is implicitly accepted also by Gibbard and Harper, Skyrms, and Sobel. My subsidiary thesis, which I put forward much more tentatively and which I won't try to foist on my allies, is that the dependency hypotheses are exactly the conjunctions of probabilistic full patterns.

(The change I have made in the Gibbard–Harper version has been simply to replace the rich partition of S's by the partition of chance propositions [P = p] pertaining to these S's. One might think that perhaps that was no change at all: perhaps the S's already were the chance propositions for some other rich partition. However, I think it at least doubtful that the chance propositions can be said to "specify combinations of occurrences" as the S's were required to do. This question would lead us back to the neo-Humean thesis discussed in Section 8.)

Consider some particular A and S. If a dependency hypothesis K is the conjunction of a probabilistic full pattern, then for some p, K implies $A \square\!\!\rightarrow [P = p]$. Then AK implies [P = p]; and $C(S/AK)$ equals $p(S)$, at least in any ordinary case.[24] For any p, the K's that are conjunctions of probabilistic full patterns including $A \square\!\!\rightarrow [P = p]$ are a partition of $A \square\!\!\rightarrow [P = p]$. So we have

$$\Sigma_P C(A \square\!\!\rightarrow [P = p]) p(S) = \Sigma_K C(K) C(S/AK). \tag{14}$$

Substituting (14) into (7) gives us a formula defining expected utility in terms of counterfactuals with chance propositions as consequents.

$$U(A) = \Sigma_S \Sigma_p C(A \square\!\!\rightarrow [P = p]) p(S) V(AS). \tag{15}$$

For any S and any number q from zero to one, let $[P(S) = q]$ be the proposition that holds at just those worlds where the chance of S, at the time when the agent realises his option, is q. It is the disjunction of those [P = p]'s for which $p(S)$ equals q. We can lump together counterfactuals in (14) and

---

23 Chances aren't chancy: if [P = p] pertains to a certain time, its own chance at that time of holding must be zero or one, by the argument of "A Subjectivist's Guide to Objective Chance": pp. 276–277. . . .

24 That follows by what I call the Principal Principle connecting chance and credence, on the assumption that: (i) AK holds or fails to hold at any world entirely in virtue of the history of that world up to action time together with the complete theory of chance for that world, and (ii) the agent gives no credence to worlds where the usual asymmetries of time break down. Part (ii) fails in the case which we have already noted in Section 7 as troublesome, in which the agent thinks he may have foreknowledge of the outcomes of chance processes. See "A Subjectivist's Guide to Objective Chance": pp. 266–276. . . .

(15) to obtain reformulations in which the consequents concern chances of single S's:

$$\Sigma_q C(A \mathbin{\square\!\!\rightarrow} [P(S) = \mathrm{q}])\mathrm{q} = \Sigma_K C(K)C(S/AK), \tag{16}$$

$$U(A) = \Sigma_S \Sigma_q C(A \mathbin{\square\!\!\rightarrow} [P(S) = \mathrm{q}])\mathrm{q}V(AS). \tag{17}$$

There are various ways to mix probabilities and counterfactuals. I have argued that when things are chancy, it isn't good enough to take credences of plain $A \mathbin{\square\!\!\rightarrow} S$ counterfactuals. The counterfactuals themselves must be made probabilistic. I have made them so by giving them chance propositions as consequents. Sobel makes them so in a different way: as we noted in Section 7, he puts the probability in the connective. Under our present assumptions (and setting aside extraordinary worlds where the common asymmetries of time break down), the two approaches are equivalent. Sobel's quantitative counterfactual with a plain consequent

If it were that A, it would be with probability q that S

holds at W iff $W_A(S)$ equals q. Given my derivation of the imaging function from the dependency hypotheses, that is so iff $C(S/AK_W)$ equals q. That is so (setting aside the extraordinary worlds) iff K_W implies $A \mathbin{\square\!\!\rightarrow} [P(S) = \mathrm{q}]$. Given that there is a probabilistic full pattern for each world, that is so iff $A \mathbin{\square\!\!\rightarrow} [P(S) = \mathrm{q}]$ holds at W. Hence the Sobel quantitative counterfactual with a plain consequent is the same proposition as the corresponding plain counterfactual with a chance consequent. If ever we must retract the assumption that there is a probabilistic full pattern for each world (or if we want to take the extraordinary worlds into account), the two approaches will separate and we may need to choose; but let us cross that bridge if we come to it.

11. The Hunter–Richter problem

That concludes an exposition and survey of causal decision theory. In this final section, I wish to defend it against an objection raised by Daniel Hunter and Reed Richter.[25] Their target is the Gibbard–Harper version; but it depends on nothing that is special to that version, so I shall restate it as an objection against causal decision theory generally.

Suppose you are one player in a two-person game. Each player can play red, play white, play blue, or not play. If both play the same colour, each gets a thousand dollars; if they play different colours, each loses a thousand dollars; if one or both don't play, the game is off and no money changes hands. Value goes by money; the game is played only once; there is no communication or prearrangement between the players; and there is nothing to

[25] "Counterfactuals and Newcomb's Paradox," *Synthese,* 39 (1978): pp. 249–261, especially pp. 257–259.

give a hint in favour of one colour or another – no "Whites rule OK!" sign placed where both can see that both can see it, or the like. So far, this game seems not worthwhile. But you have been persuaded that you and the other player are very much alike psychologically and hence very likely to choose alike, so that you are much more likely to play and win than to play and lose. Is it rational for you to play?

Yes. So say I, so say Hunter and Richter, and so (for what it is worth) says noncausal decision theory. But causal decision theory seems to say that it is not rational to play. If it says that, it is wrong and stands refuted. It seems that you have four dependency hypotheses to consider, corresponding to the four ways your partner might play:

K_1 Whatever you do, he would play red;
K_2 Whatever you do, he would play white;
K_3 Whatever you do, he would play blue;
K_4 Whatever you do, he would not play.

By the symmetry of the situation, K_1 and K_2 and K_3 should get equal credence. Then the expected utility of not playing is zero, whereas the expected utilities of playing the three colours are equal and negative. So we seem to reach the unwelcome conclusion that not playing is your U-maximal option.

I reply that Hunter and Richter have gone wrong by misrepresenting your partition of options. Imagine that you have a servant. You can play red, white, or blue; you can not play; or you can tell your servant to play for you. The fifth option, delegating the choice, might be the one that beats not playing and makes it rational to play. Given the servant, each of our previous dependency hypotheses splits in three. For instance K_1 splits into:

$K_{1,1}$ Whatever you do, your partner would play red, and your
             servant would play red if you delegated the choice;
$K_{1,2}$ Whatever you do, your partner would play red, and your
             servant would play white if you delegated the choice;
$K_{1,3}$ Whatever you do, your partner would play red, and your
             servant would play blue if you delegated the choice.

(If you and your partner are much alike, he too has a servant, so we can split further by dividing the case in which he plays red, for instance, into the case in which he plays red for himself and the case in which he delegates his choice and his servant plays red for him. However, that difference doesn't matter to you and is outside your influence, so let us disregard it.) The information that you and your partner (and your respective servants) are much alike might persuade you to give little credence to the dependency hypotheses $K_{1,2}$ and $K_{1,3}$ but to give more to $K_{1,1}$; and likewise for the subdivisions of K_2 and K_3. Then you give your credence mostly to dependency hypotheses according to which you would either win or break even by delegating your choice. Then causal decision theory does not tell you, wrongly, that it is rational not to play. Playing by delegating your choice is your U-maximal option.

But you don't have a servant. What of it? You must have a tie-breaking procedure. There must be something or other that you do after deliberation that ends in a tie. Delegating your choice to your tie-breaking procedure is a fifth option for you, just as delegating it to your servant would be if you had one. If you are persuaded that you will probably win if you play because you and your partner are alike psychologically, it must be because you are persuaded that your tie-breaking procedures are alike. You could scarcely think that the two of you are likely to coordinate *without* resorting to your tie-breaking procedures, since *ex hypothesi* the situation plainly *is* a tie! So you have a fifth option, and as the story is told, it has greater expected utility than not playing. This is not the option of playing red, or white, or blue, straightway at the end of deliberation, although if you choose it you will indeed end up playing red or white or blue. What makes it a different option is that it interposes something extra – something other than deliberation – after you are done deliberating and before you play.

Postscript to "Causal decision theory"

Reply to Rabinowicz

In a recent article, Włodzimierz Rabinowicz carries the comparison between my theory and Sobel's farther than I had done.[26] He also advances two criticisms against my discussion. One uncovers a clear mistake on my part, but the other rests on a misunderstanding.

First the mistake. Suppose we start, as Sobel does, with the imaging function – in Sobel's terminology, the tendencies of worlds – and we take equivalence classes under the relation of imaging alike. Call these classes *tendency propositions*. I suggested that these should turn out to be the same as my dependency hypotheses. Rabinowicz rightly objects (p. 311). *Distinguo:* let a *practical* dependency hypothesis be a maximally specific proposition about how the things the agent cares about do and do not depend causally on his present actions; let a *full* dependency hypothesis be a maximally specific proposition about how all things whatever do and do not depend causally on the agent's present actions. By my definition, a "dependency hypothesis" is a practical dependency hypothesis; whereas a tendency proposition is, if anything, not a practical but a full dependency hypothesis. Luckily my mistake does not damage my discussion, since it would have made no difference if I had worked in terms of full rather than practical dependency hypotheses throughout.

---

[26] "Two Causal Decision Theories: Lewis vs. Sobel," in Tom Pauli et al., eds., *320311: Philosophical Essays Dedicated to Lennart Åqvist on his Fiftieth Birthday* (Uppsala: Filosofiska Studier, 1982).

Next the misunderstanding. I had presupposed (1) that any option would be compatible with any dependency hypothesis; I had also supposed (2) that at least sometimes, an image of a world on a proposition would be "blurred," dividing its probability over several worlds. My discussion of counterfactuals elsewhere indicated that I also accept (3) an assumption of "centering." But Rabinowicz shows that (1), (2), and (3) are inconsistent (Theorem 1, p. 313). This looks like trouble for me. Not so – *distinguo* again:

(3A) *Centering of the imaging function* is the thesis that whenever a proposition A holds at a world W, the image of W on A is the distribution that puts all its probability on world W.

(3B) *Centering of counterfactuals* is the thesis that whenever a proposition A holds at a world W, a "would" counterfactual with antecedent A holds at W iff its consequent does.

What Rabinowicz shows is that (1), (2) and (3A) are inconsistent. What my discussion of counterfactuals indicates is that I accept (3B). I do indeed. But I reject (3A); therefore, Rabinowicz's difficulties for decision theory with a centered imaging function are no threat to me.

Sobel discusses counterfactuals and decision theory together, using the same apparatus of imaging (or "tendency") functions. His theory of counterfactuals says that a "would" counterfactual with antecedent A holds at a world W iff its consequent holds at every world to which the image of W on A assigns positive probability. That means that for Sobel, centering of the imaging function and of counterfactuals are equivalent. Not so for me. I might have done well to warn the reader that I disagree with Sobel on this point, though strictly speaking a disagreement about counterfactuals is irrelevant to the comparison of our decision theories.

Example. A coin is about to be tossed (proposition A). The coin will be tossed fairly, with equal chance of heads and tails. It will in fact fall heads. Then I say that the image of our world on A is blurred, not centered: it distributes probability equally between heads-worlds (among them ours) and tails-worlds. But I also say, by centering of counterfactuals, that if it were that A – as is in fact the case – then the coin would fall heads. *Contra* Sobel's theory, this counterfactual holds although its consequent does not hold at all worlds to which the image assigns positive probability.

(I don't deny that if it were that A, then there would be some chance that the coin would fall tails. For this too follows from centering of counterfactuals. There would be some chance of it; but it would not happen. I say that the counterfactuals about outcomes and the counterfactuals about chances are compatible. . . .)

Part II

Game theory and group decision making

This part of the book consists of two main sections: A. Games, Cooperation, and the Prisoner's Dilemma, and B. Impossibility Theorems for Social Choice. In various ways the essays in these two sections go beyond the basic issues about individual decision theory represented in Part I.

A. Games, cooperation, and the prisoner's dilemma

This section consists of three essays that raise important questions about the significance of competition and cooperation in rational decision making. In "Advances in Understanding Rational Behavior," John Harsanyi explains how economic theory, decision theory, and recent game theory can improve our understanding of the notion of rational action. He begins with the commonsense notion of rationality as choosing the best means available to a given goal, and explains how limitations on this notion lead to decision-theoretic notions of rational action. He also explains how game theory is needed to accommodate situations involving two or more decision makers who have different interests. Harsanyi clarifies the distinction between cooperative and noncooperative games, in terms of whether the relevant decision makers can make fully binding agreements. He uses a prisoner's dilemma to illustrate a two-person noncooperative game. (See my general introduction to this volume for a general characterization of the prisoner's dilemma.) Harsanyi explains how we can solve noncooperative games in terms of the decision makers' expectations converging to a certain "equilibrium point" as the solution of the game.

In "The Emergence of Cooperation among Egoists," Robert Axelrod aims to identify conditions under which cooperation will emerge in a world of egoists without a central authority. Specifically, he aims to identify a mechanism that can move a population from noncooperative to cooperative equilibrium. Axelrod's paradigm case of a noncooperative game is the prisoner's dilemma (again, see the general introduction). He claims that if two egoists play this game a known finite number of times, they will have no incentive to cooperate, but that if this game is played an indefinite (unknown) number of times, cooperation can emerge. Axelrod explores the conditions required for such cooperation to occur. He explains how "cooperation can emerge from small clusters of individuals, as long as these individuals have even a small proportion of their interactions with each other."

In "Maximization Constrained: The Rationality of Cooperation," David Gauthier aims to challenge "Hobbes's Foole," who claims that one should agree to a cooperative venture only if one expects this agreement to pay, and that one should adhere to the agreement only if one expects this adherence to pay. The Foole is, in effect, advising one to adhere only if this is utility-maximizing; in this view reason interferes with cooperation. Gauthier aims to explain the rational basis for entering and adhering to cooperative ventures. He characterizes a *straightforward maximizer* as a person who aims to maximize his or her utility given the strategies of those with whom the person interacts. And he characterizes a *constrained maximizer* as a person who seeks in some situations to maximize his or her utility, given not the strategies but the utilities of those with whom the person interacts. A constrained maximizer is willing to cooperate in ways that, when followed by all concerned, would produce outcomes he or she considers beneficial to all and unfair to none. Basically, Gauthier's thesis is that one's being disposed to constrained maximizing is the more rational of the two strategies because straightforward maximizers will eventually be recognized as such and excluded from cooperative ventures. Straightforward maximizers will lose the opportunity to gain benefits from their exploiting joint strategies. This assumes, of course, that straightforward maximizers can be recognized as such by others, that they are transparent. But people can deceive. Gauthier thus pursues the issue of how translucent people must be in order for a disposition toward constrained maximizing to be rational. One of Gauthier's main conclusions is that "when we correctly understand how utility-maximization is identified with practical rationality, we see that morality is an essential part of maximization."

B. Impossibility theorems for social choice

This section contains three essays on social choice theory; they focus on impossibility theorems for social choice. In "Values and Collective Decision-Making," Kenneth Arrow describes the main problem of social choice as "the aggregation of the multiplicity of individual preference scales about alternative social actions." He characterizes a *welfare judgment* as a second-order judgment about evaluations of social actions in terms of their consequences. The formation of welfare judgments is, on Arrow's view, a *constitution,* that is, a rule for selecting a preferred action out of every set of mutually exclusive actions. Arrow proposes that any constitution must meet four conditions:

1. Collective rationality: The social choice function is derivable from a preference ordering.
2. Pareto principle: If alternative X is preferred to alternative Y by every individual according to his or her ordering, then the social ordering also ranks X above Y.
3. The independence of irrelevant alternatives: A social choice in an environment depends only on the orderings of individuals regarding alternatives in that environment.
4. Non-dictatorship: No individual has preferences that are automatically society's preferences independent of the preferences of all other members of society.

Arrow's impossibility theorem is that there can be no constitution that simultaneously satisfies these four conditions. Given this theorem, Arrow considers dispensing with the condition of the independence of irrelevant alternatives. He proposes a principle that allows us to consider unavailable alternatives in social choice, and suggests that this principle is basic to many of our welfare judgments.

In "The Impossibility of a Paretian Liberal," Amartya Sen aims to show that certain liberal values, even mild liberal values, are inconsistent with the Pareto principle if a certain condition of unrestricted domain holds. Sen's theorem depends on three conditions:

1. Unrestricted domain: Every logically possible set of individual orderings is included in the domain of the collective choice rule.
2. Pareto principle: If every individual prefers any alternative X to another alternative Y, then society must prefer X to Y.
3. Minimal liberalism: There are at least two individuals such that for each of them there is at least one pair of alternatives over which he is decisive (i.e., his preference of X over Y entails that society should prefer X to Y).

Sen's theorem is that there is no social choice function that can simultaneously satisfy these conditions. The moral, according to Sen, is that liberal values conflict with the Pareto principle. If we accept the Pareto principle and an unrestricted domain, we cannot permit even minimal liberalism.

In "Liberty and Social Choice," Amartya Sen elaborates on the argument of "The Impossibility of a Paretian Liberal." Sen has three main objectives: (i) to clarify the relevance of his impossibility theorem to some issues in ethics and welfare economics, (ii) to distinguish three different interpretations of social preference, and (iii) to clarify the notion of liberty in social choice theory. Sen focuses on the following three interpretations of his impossibility theorem:

1. Outcome-evaluation impossibility: For some configuration of individual preferences, there can be no consistent and complete evaluation of social states satisfying the Pareto principle and minimal liberalism (as defined above);
2. Normative-choice impossibility: There is no good way of organizing social decision making so that, regardless of the individual preferences, some state gets chosen from any nonempty set of states, when the goodness of the decision making satisfies the Pareto principle and minimal liberalism;
3. Descriptive-choice impossibility: Any actual social decision-system that can choose some state from any nonempty set of states will be unable to satisfy the Pareto principle and minimal liberalism.

Sen clarifies the conditions for liberalism in social choice theory by distinguishing between liberalism as a value judgment about *procedures* for an individual and liberalism as a view about right *outcomes* under the control of the individual. Sen argues that an adequate view of liberalism must account not only for direct control, but also for what a person *would have chosen if he had control*. Sen also argues that the possibility of Pareto-improving contracts does not undercut his impossibility theorem.

A. Games, cooperation, and the prisoner's dilemma

11. Advances in understanding rational behavior

John C. Harsanyi

Abstract. It will be argued that economic theory, decision theory, and some recent work in game theory, make important contributions to a deeper understanding of the concept of rational behavior. The paper starts with a discussion of the common-sense notion of rational behavior. Then, the rationality concepts of classical economics and of Bayesian decision theory are described. Finally, some (mostly fairly recent) advances in game theory are discussed, such as probabilistic models for games with incomplete information; the role of equilibrium points in non-cooperative games, and the standard game-theoretical approach to the prisoner's dilemma problem; the concept of perfect equilibrium points; the use of non-cooperative bargaining models in analyzing cooperative games; and the Harsanyi-Selten solution concept for non-cooperative games.

1. Introduction[1]

The concept of rational behavior (or of practical rationality) is of considerable philosophical interest. It plays an important role in moral and political philosophy, while the related concept of theoretical rationality is connected with many deep problems in logic, epistemology, and the philosophy of science. Both practical and theoretical rationality are important concepts in

Reprinted with permission from R. E. Butts and J. Hintikka, eds., *Foundational Problems in the Special Sciences* (Dordrecht: D. Reidel, 1977), 315–43.
[1] The author wishes to express his thanks to the National Science Foundation for supporting this research by Grant GS-3222 to the Center for Research in Management Science, University of California, Berkeley.

psychology and in the study of artificial intelligence. Furthermore, rational-behavior models are widely used in economics and, to an increasing extent, also in other social sciences. This fact is all the more remarkable since rationality is a normative concept and, therefore, it has been claimed (incorrectly, as I shall argue) that it is out of place in non-normative, empirically oriented studies of social behavior.

Given the important role that the concept of rationality plays in philosophy and in a number of other disciplines, I have thought it may be of some interest to this interdisciplinary audience if I report on some work in decision theory and in game theory that holds out the prospect of replacing our common-sense notion of rational behavior by a much more general, much more precise, and conceptually very much richer notion of rationality. I feel that successful development of an analytically clear, informative, and intuitively satisfactory concept of rationality would have significant philosophical implications.

I shall first discuss the common-sense notion of rational behavior. Then, I shall briefly describe the rationality concepts of classical economic theory and of Bayesian decision theory. Finally, I shall report on some, mostly very recent, results in game theory, which, I believe, are practically unknown to non-specialists. Of course, within the space available, I cannot do more than draw a sketchy and very incomplete picture of the relevant work – a picture no doubt strongly colored by my own theoretical views.

2. The means–ends concept of rational behavior

In everyday life, when we speak of "rational behavior," in most cases we are thinking of behavior involving a choice of the best *means* available for achieving a given *end*. This implies that, already at a common-sense level, rationality is a *normative* concept: it points to what we *should* do in order to attain a given end or objective. But, even at a common-sense level, this concept of rationality does have important *positive* (non-normative) applications: it is used for *explanation,* for *prediction,* and even for mere *description,* of human behavior.

Indeed, the assumption that a given person has acted or will act rationally, often has very considerable explanatory and predictive power, because it may imply that we can explain or predict a large number of possibly very complicated facts about his behavior in terms of a small number of rather simple hypotheses about his goals or objectives.

For example, suppose a given historian comes to the conclusion that Napoleon acted fairly rationally in a certain period. This will have the implication that Napoleon's actions admit of explanation in terms of his political and military objectives – possibly in terms of a rather limited number of objectives – and that other, often less easily accessible, psychological variables need not be used to any major extent to account for his behavior. On the other hand, if our historian finds that Napoleon's behavior was not very rational, then this will imply that no set of reasonably well-defined policy objectives could be found that would explain Napoleon's behavior, and that any explanation of it must make use of some "deeper" motivational factors and, ultimately, of some much more specific assumptions about the psychological mechanisms underlying human behavior.

Yet, we do make use of the notion of rationality also in cases where we are not interested in an explanation or prediction of human behavior, but are merely interested in providing an adequate *description* of it. For instance, any historical narrative of Napoleon's political and military decisions will be seriously incomplete, even at a descriptive level, if it contains no discussion of the rationality or irrationality of these decisions. Thus, it will not be enough to report that, in a particular battle, Napoleon attacked the enemy's right wing. Rather, we also want to know whether, under the existing conditions, this attack was a sensible (or perhaps even a brilliant) tactical move or not.

Philosophers, and social scientists outside the economics profession, have often expressed puzzlement about the successful use of the normative concept of rational behavior in positive economics – and, more recently, also in other social sciences[2] – for explanation and prediction, and even for mere description, of human behavior. But there is really nothing surprising about this. All it means is that human behavior is mostly *goal-directed,* often in a fairly consistent manner, in many important classes of social situations. For example, suppose that people are *mainly* after money in business life (even if they do also have a number of other objectives), or are mainly after election or re-election to public office in democratic politics, or are mainly after social status in many social activities, or are mainly after national self-interest in international affairs – at least that these statements are true as a matter of reasonable first approximation. Then, of course, it is in no way surprising if we can explain and sometimes even predict, and can also meaningfully describe, their behavior in terms of the assumption that they are after money, or after public office, or after social status, or after national self-interest.

Even if the subject matter of our investigation were not human behavior, but rather the behavior of goal-pursuing robots, a model of "rational" (i.e. goal-pursuing) robot behavior would be a very valuable analytical tool. Of course, just as in the case of human beings, such a rationalistic model would only work with highly "rational" (i.e. with very well-functioning) robots. To explain the behavior of a robot with a faulty steering mechanism, we would need a more complicated model, based on fairly detailed assumptions about the robot's internal structure and operation.

To be sure, while we could at least conceive of a perfectly well-constructed goal-pursuing robot, completely consistent and completely single-minded in working for his pre-established goal, human beings are seldom that consistent.

[2] For references, see Harsanyi (1969, p. 517, footnote 9).

In some situations, they will be deflected from their objectives by Freudian-type emotional factors, while in others they will fail to pursue any well-defined objectives altogether. Moreover, even if they do aim at well-defined objectives, their limitations in computing (information-processing) ability may prevent them from discovering the most effective strategies (or any reasonably effective strategies) for achieving these objectives. (Of course, any robot of less than infinite structural complexity will be subject to similar computational limitations. But he may not be subject to anything resembling emotional problems.)

Obviously, this means that in *some* situations models of rational behavior will not be very useful in analyzing human behavior – except perhaps after substantial modification (e.g. along the lines suggested by Simon's (1960) theory of limited rationality). Clearly, it is an empirical question what types of social situations lend themselves, and to what extent, to analysis in terms of rational-behavior models. But recent work in political science, in international relations, and in sociology, has shown that a much wider range of social situations seems to admit of rationalistic analysis than most observers would have thought even ten years ago.[3]

3. The rational-behavior model of economic theory

Even at a common-sense level, the means-ends model is not the only model of rational behavior we use. Another, though perhaps less important, model envisages rational behavior as choosing an object (or a person) satisfying certain stipulated formal (possibly non-causal) *criteria*. For instance, if my aim is to climb the highest mountain in California, then it will be rational for me to climb Mount Whitney, and it will be irrational for me to climb any other mountain. But we would not normally say that climbing Mount Whitney is a *means* to climbing the highest mountain in California, because my climbing of Mount Whitney does not causally *lead* to a climbing of the highest mountain. Rather, it already *is* a climbing of the highest mountain. It is a rational action in the sense of being an action (and, indeed, the only action) satisfying the stipulated criterion.[4]

Thus, it would be rather artificial to subsume criterion-satisfying behavior under the means-ends model of rationality. It is more natural to do the converse, and argue that looking for a means to a given end is a special case of looking for an object satisfying a particular criterion, viz. the criterion of being causally effective in attaining a given end.

This implies that the means-ends concept of rational behavior is too narrow because it fails to cover criterion-satisfying behavior. An even more

---

[3] See footnote 2.

[4] The concept of criterion-satisfying behavior is probably not very important in everyday life. But it is very important in ethics (see Harsanyi, 1958).

important limitation of this concept lies in the fact that it restricts rational behavior to a choice among alternative *means* to a given end, and fails to include a rational choice among alternative *ends*. Therefore, it cannot explain why a given person may shift from one end to another.

To overcome this limitation, already 19th and early 20th century economists introduced a broader concept of rationality which defines rational behavior as a choice among alternative ends, on the basis of a given set of *preferences* and a given set of *opportunities* (i.e. a given set of available alternatives). If I am choosing a given end (or a given set of mutually compatible ends, which can be described as a unique composite end), then typically I have to give up many alternative ends. Giving up these alternative ends is the *opportunity cost* of pursuing this particular end. Thus, under this model, rational behavior consists in choosing one specific end, after careful consideration and in full awareness of the opportunity costs of this choice.

This model will often enable us to explain why a given individual has changed over from pursuing one objective to pursuing another, even if his basic preferences have remained the same. The explanation will lie in the fact that the opportunity costs of various possible objectives (i.e. the advantages and the disadvantages associated with them) have changed, or at least the information he has about these opportunity costs has done so.

For example, a given person may seek admission to a particular university, but then may change his mind and fail to attend. He may do so because the tuition fees or other monetary costs have increased; or because the studies he would have to undertake have turned out to be harder or less interesting than he thought they would be; or because he has received unfavorable information about the hoped-for economic advantages of a university degree, etc. All these explanations are compatible with the assumption that, during the whole period, his basic preferences remained the same, and that only the situation (i.e. his opportunity costs), or his information about the situation, have changed.[5]

It is easy to verify that the preferences-opportunities model includes both the means-ends model and the criterion-satisfaction model as special cases.

An important result of economic theory has been to show that, if a given person's preferences satisfy certain consistency and continuity axioms, then these preferences will admit of representation by a well-defined (and, indeed, continuous) utility function. (For proof, see Debreu, 1959, pp. 55–59.) Accordingly, for such a person, rational behavior – as defined by the preferences-opportunities model – will be equivalent to *utility-maximization* (utility-maximization theorem).

---

[5] Of course, in many cases, when a person has changed his goals, the most natural explanation will be that his preferences themselves have changed. In such cases, the model of rational behavior will be inapplicable, or at least will have to be supplemented by other explanatory theories, e.g. by learning theory, etc.

4. Bayesian decision theory

Classical economic theory was largely restricted to analyzing human behavior under *certainty*, i.e. under conditions where the decision maker can uniquely predict the outcome of any action he may take (or where one can assume this to be the case at least as a matter of first approximation). It has been left to modern decision theory to extend this analysis to human behavior under risk and uncertainty.

Both risk and uncertainty refer to situations where the decision maker cannot always uniquely predict the outcomes of his action. But, in the case of *risk,* he will know at least the objective probabilities associated with all possible outcomes. In contrast, in the case of *uncertainty,* even some or all of these objective probabilities will be unknown to him (or may even be undefined altogether).

The utility-maximization model provides a satisfactory characterization of rational behavior under certainty, but fails to do so under risk and under uncertainty. This is so because it is not sufficient to assume that any given lottery (whether it is a "risky" lottery involving known probabilities, or is an "uncertain" lottery involving unknown probabilities) will have a well-defined numerical utility to the decision maker. Rather, we need a theory specifying *what value* this utility will have, and how it will depend on the utilities associated with the various prizes. This is exactly what decision theory is trying to specify.

The main conclusion of decision theory is this. If the decision maker's behavior satisfies certain consistency and continuity axioms (a larger number of axioms than we needed to establish the utility-maximization theorem in the case of certainty), then his behavior will be equivalent to *maximizing his expected utility,* i.e. to maximizing the mathematical expectation of his cardinal utility function. In the case of *risk,* this expected utility can be defined in terms of the relevant objective probabilities (which, by assumption, will be known to the decision maker). On the other hand, in the case of *uncertainty,* this expected utility must be defined in terms of the decision maker's own subjective probabilities whenever the relevant objective probabilities are unknown to him (expected-utility maximization theorem).[6]

This result leads to the *Bayesian* approach to decision theory, which proposes to define rational behavior under risk and under certainty as expected-utility maximization.[7]

---

[6] A very simple proof of this theorem for *risk* is given by Luce and Raiffa (1957, pp. 23–31). But note that their Assumptions 1 and 5 could be easily stated as one axiom, whereas Assumption 6 could be omitted because it follows from the other axioms. (Of course, the use of extra axioms was intentional and made it possible for the authors to simplify their statement of the proof.) Note also that their substitutability axiom (Assumption 4) could be replaced by a form of the sure-thing principle (see below). A simple proof of the theorem for *uncertainty* is found in Anscombe and Aumann (1963).

[7] The term "Bayesian approach" is often restricted to the proposal of using expected-utility

Besides the axioms used already in the case of certainty, we need one additional consistency axiom to establish the expected-utility maximization theorem in the cases of risk and of uncertainty. This axiom is the *sure-thing principle,* which can be stated as follows. "Let X be a bet[8] that would yield a given prize x to the decision maker if a specified event E took place (e.g. if a particular horse won the next race). Let Y be a bet that would yield him another prize y, which he *prefers* over x, if this event E took place. There are no other differences between the two bets. Then, the decision maker will consider bet Y to be *at least as desirable* as bet X." (Actually, unless he assigns zero probability to event E, he will no doubt positively *prefer* bet Y, which would yield the more attractive prize y, if event E took place. But we do not need this slightly stronger assumption.)

In my opinion, it is hard to envisage any rational decision maker who would knowingly violate the sure-thing principle (or who would violate the – somewhat more technical – continuity axiom we need to prove the expected-utility maximization theorem). This fact is, of course, a strong argument in favor of the Bayesian definition of rational behavior. Another important argument lies in the fact that all alternative definitions of rational behavior (and, in particular, all definitions based on the once fashionable maximin principle and on various other related principles) can be shown to lead to highly irrational decisions in many practically important situations. (See Radner and Marschak, 1954; also Harsanyi, 1975a.)

In the case of risk, acceptance of Bayesian theory is now virtually unanimous. In the case of uncertainty, the Bayesian approach is still somewhat controversial, though the last two decades have produced a clear trend toward its growing acceptance by expert opinion. Admittedly, support for Bayesian theory is weaker among scholars working in other fields than it is among decision theorists and game theorists. (I must add that some of the criticism directed against the Bayesian approach has been rather uninformed, and has shown a clear lack of familiarity with the relevant literature.)

5. A general theory of rational behavior

Whatever the merits of the rationality concept of Bayesian decision theory may be, it is still in need of further generalization, because it does not adequately cover rational behavior in *game situations,* i.e. in situations where the outcome depends on the behavior of two or more rational individuals who may have partly or wholly divergent interests. Game situations may be considered to represent a special case of uncertainty, since in general none of the players will be able to predict the outcome, or even the probabilities associated with different possible outcomes. This is so because he will not be

---

maximization as a definition of rational behavior in the case of *uncertainty,* where expected utility must be computed in terms of *subjective* probabilities.

[8] The terms "bet" and "lottery" will be used interchangeably.

able to predict the strategies of the other players, or even the probabilities associated with their various possible strategies. (To be sure, as we shall argue, at least in principle, game-theoretical analysis does enable each player to discover the solution of the game and, therefore, to predict the strategies of the other players, provided that the latter will act in a rational manner. But the point is that, prior to such a game-theoretical analysis, he will be unable to make such predictions.)

Game theory defines rational behavior in game situations by defining solution concepts for various classes of games.

Since the term "decision theory" is usually restricted to the theory of rational behavior under risk and uncertainty, I shall use the term *utility theory* to describe the broader theory which includes both decision theory and the theory of rational behavior under certainty (as established by classical economic theory).

Besides utility theory and game theory, I propose to consider *ethics,* also, as a branch of the general theory of rational behavior, since ethical theory can be based on axioms which represent specializations of some of the axioms used in decision theory (Harsanyi, 1955).

Thus, under the approach here proposed, the *general theory of rational behavior* consists of three branches:

(1)   *Utility theory,* which is the theory of *individual* rational behavior under certainty, under risk, and under uncertainty. Its main result is that, in these three cases, rational behavior consists in *utility maximization* or *expected-utility maximization.*

(2)   *Game theory,* which is the theory of rational behavior by *two or more* interacting rational individuals, each of them determined to maximize his own interests, whether selfish or unselfish, as specified by his own utility function (payoff function). (Though some or all players may very well assign high utilities to clearly altruistic objectives, this need not prevent a conflict of interest between them since they may possibly assign high utilities to quite *different,* and perhaps strongly conflicting, altruistic objectives.)

(3)   *Ethics,* which is the theory of rational moral value judgments, i.e. of rational judgments of preference based on impartial and impersonal criteria. I have tried to show that rational moral value judgments will involve *maximizing* the *average utility level* of all individuals in society. (See Harsanyi, 1953, 1955, 1958, 1975a, and 1975b.)

Whereas game theory is a theory of possibly conflicting (but not necessarily selfish) *individual* interests, ethics can be regarded as a theory of the *common* interests (or of the general welfare) of society as a whole.

6. Games with incomplete information

We speak of a game with *complete information* if the players have full information about all *parameters* defining the game, i.e. about all variables fully determined *before* the beginning of the game. These variables include the players' payoff functions (utility functions), the strategical possibilities available to each player, and the amount of information each player has about all of these variables. We speak of a game with *incomplete information* if some or all of the players have less than full information about these parameters defining the game.

This distinction must not be confused with another, somewhat similar distinction. We speak of a game with *perfect information* if the players always have full information about the *moves* already made in the game, including the *personal moves* made by the individual players and the *chance moves* decided by chance. Thus, perfect information means full information about all game events that took part *after* the beginning of the game. We speak of a game with *imperfect information* if some or all players have less than full information about the moves already made in the game.

It was a major limitation of classical game theory that it could not handle games with *incomplete* information (though it did deal both with games involving perfect and imperfect information). For, many of the most important real-life game situations are games with incomplete information: the players may have only limited knowledge of each other's payoff functions (i.e. of each other's real objectives within the game), and may also know very little about the strategies as well as the information available to the other players.

In the last few years we have discovered how to overcome this limitation. How this is done can be best shown in an example. Suppose we want to analyze arms control negotiations between the United States and the Soviet Union. The difficulty is that neither side really knows the other side's true intentions and technological capabilities. (They may have reasonably good intelligence estimates about each other's weapon systems in actual use, but may know very little about any new military inventions not yet used in actual weapon production.) Now we can employ the following model. The American player, called A, and the Russian player, called R, both can occur in the form of a number of different "types." For instance, the Russian player could be really R_1, a fellow with very peaceful intentions but with access to very formidable new weapon technologies; and with the expectation that the American player will also have peaceful intentions, yet a ready access to important new technologies. Or, the Russian player could be R_2, who is exactly like R_1, except that he expects the American player to have rather aggressive intentions. Or, the Russian player could be R_3, who shows still another possible combination of all these variables, etc.

Likewise, the American player could be of type A_1 or A_2 or A_3, etc., each of them having a different combination of policy objectives, of access to new technologies, and of expectations about Russian policy objectives and about Russian access to new technologies. (We could, of course, easily add still further variables to this list.)

The game is played as follows. At the beginning of the game, nature conducts a lottery to decide which particular types of the American player and of the Russian player (one type of each) will actually participate in the game. Each possible combination (A_i, R_j) of an American player type and of a Russian player type has a pre-assigned probability p_{ij} of being selected. When a particular pair (A_i, R_j) has been chosen, they will actually play the game. Each player will know his own type but will be ignorant of his opponent's actual type. But, for any given type of his opponent, he will be able to assign a numerical probability to the possibility that his opponent is of this particular type, because each player will know the probability matrix $P = (p_{ij})$.

What this model does is to reduce the original game with *incomplete* information, G, to an artificially constructed game with *complete* information, G^*. The *incomplete* information the players had in G about the basic parameters of the game is represented in the new game G^* as *imperfect* information about a certain chance move at the beginning of the game (viz. the one which determines the types of the players). As the resulting new game G^* is a game with complete (even if with imperfect) information, it is fully accessible to the usual methods of game-theoretical analysis.

The model just described is not the most general model we use in the analysis of games with incomplete information. It makes the assumption that all players' expectations about each other's basic characteristics (or, technically speaking, all players' subjective probability distributions over all possible types of all other players) are sufficiently consistent to be expressible in terms of one basic probability matrix $P = (p_{ij})$. We call this the assumption of *mutually consistent expectations*. In many applications, this is a natural assumption to make and, whenever this is the case, it greatly simplifies the analysis of the game. (See Harsanyi, 1967–68.)

There are, however, cases where this assumption seems to be inappropriate. As Reinhard Selten has pointed out (in private communication – cf. Harsanyi, 1967–68, pp. 496–497), even in such cases, the game will admit of analysis in terms of an appropriate probabilistic model, though a more complicated one than would be needed on the assumption of consistent expectations.

7. Non-cooperative games and equilibrium points: the prisoner's dilemma problem

We have to distinguish between *cooperative* games, where the players can make fully binding and enforceable commitments (fully binding promises, agreements, and threats, which absolutely *have* to be implemented if the stipulated conditions arise), and *non-cooperative* games, where this is not the case. In real life, what makes commitments fully binding is usually a law-enforcing authority. But in some cases prestige considerations (a fear of losing face) may have similar effects.

Nash (1950 and 1951), who first proposed this distinction, defined cooperative games as games with enforceable commitments *and* with free communication between the players. He defined non-cooperative games as games without enforceable commitments and without communication. These were somewhat misleading definitions. Presence or absence of free communication is only of secondary importance. The crucial issue is the possibility or impossibility of binding and enforceable agreements. (For example, in the prisoner's dilemma case, as I shall argue below, the cooperative solution will be unavailable to the players if no enforceable agreements can be made. This will be true regardless of whether the players can talk to each other or not.)

In a cooperative game, the players can agree on any possible combination of strategies since they can be sure that any such agreement would be kept. In contrast, in a non-cooperative game, only self-enforcing agreements are worth making because only self-enforcing agreements have any real chance of implementation.

A self-enforcing agreement is called an equilibrium point. A more exact definition can be stated as follows. A given strategy of a certain player is called a *best reply* to the other players' strategies if it maximizes this player's payoff so long as the other players' strategies are kept constant. A given combination of strategies (containing exactly one strategy for each player) is called an *equilibrium point* if every player's strategy is a best reply to all other players' strategies. The concept of an equilibrium point, also, is due to Nash (1950, 1951).

For example, suppose that the following two-person game is played as a non-cooperative game, so that no enforceable agreements can be made:

	B_1	B_2
A_1	2, 2	0, 3
A_2	3, 0	1, 1

This type of game is called a prisoner's dilemma. (For an explanation of this name, see Luce and Raiffa, 1957, pp. 94–95.)

In this game, the strategy pair (A_2, B_2) is an equilibrium point, because player 1's best reply to B_2 is A_2, whereas player 2's best reply to A_2 is B_2. Indeed, the game has no other equilibrium point. If the two players use their equilibrium strategies A_2 and B_2, then they will obtain the payoffs (1, 1).

Obviously, both players would be better off if they could use the strategies A_1 and B_1, which would yield them the payoffs (2, 2). But these two strategies do not form an equilibrium point. Even if the two players explicitly *agreed* to use A_1 and B_1, they would not do so, and would *know* they would not do so. Even if we assumed for a moment that the two players did expect the strategy pair (A_1, B_1) to be the outcome of the game, *this very expectation would make them use another strategy pair* (A_2, B_2) instead. For instance, if player 1 expected player 2 to use strategy B_1, he himself would not use A_1 but would rather use A_2, since A_2 would be his best reply to player 2's expected strategy B_1. Likewise, if player 2 expected player 1 to use A_1, he himself would not use B_1 but would rather use B_2, since B_2 would be his best reply to player 1's expected strategy A_1.

Of course, if the game were played as a cooperative game, then agreements would be fully enforceable, and the two players would have no difficulty in agreeing to use strategies A_1 and B_1 so as to obtain the higher payoffs $(2, 2)$. Once they agreed on this, they could be absolutely sure that this agreement would be fully observed.

Thus, we must conclude that, if the game is played as a non-cooperative game, then the outcome will be the equilibrium point (A_2, B_2), which is often called the *non-cooperative solution*. On the other hand, if the game is played as a cooperative game, then the outcome will be the non-equilibrium point strategy pair (A_1, B_1), which is called the *cooperative solution*.

More generally, the solution of a non-cooperative game must always be an equilibrium point. In other words, each player's solution strategy must be a best reply to the other players' solution strategies. This is so because the solution, by definition, must be a strategy combination that the players can rationally *use,* and that they can also rationally *expect* one another to use. But, if any given player's solution strategy were *not* his best reply to the other players' solution strategies, then the very expectation that the other players would use their solution strategies would make it rational for this player *not* to use his solution strategy (but rather to use a strategy that was a best reply to the solution strategies he expected the other players to use). Hence, the alleged "solution" would not satisfy our definition of a solution.

This argument does not apply to a cooperative game, where each player can irrevocably commit himself to using a given strategy even if the latter is *not* a best reply to the other players' strategies. But it does apply to any non-cooperative game, where such a commitment would have no force.

This conclusion is accepted by almost all game theorists. It is, however, rejected by some distinguished scholars from other disciplines, because it seems to justify certain forms of socially undesirable non-cooperative behavior in real-life conflict situations. Their sentiments underlying this theoretical position are easy to understand and deserve our respect, but I cannot say the same thing about their logic. I find it rather hard to comprehend how anybody can deny that there is a fundamental difference between social situations where agreements are strictly enforceable and social situations where this is not the case; or how anybody can deny that, in situations where agreements are wholly unenforceable, the participants may often have every reason to distrust each other's willingness (and sometimes even to distrust each other's very ability) to keep agreements, in particular if there are strong incentives to violate these agreements.

To be sure, it is quite possible that, in a situation that *looks like* a prisoner's dilemma game, the players will be able to achieve the cooperative solution. Usually this will happen because the players are decent persons and therefore attach considerable disutility to using a non-cooperative strategy like A_2 or B_2 when the other player uses a cooperative strategy like A_1 or B_1. Of course, if the players take this attitude, then this will change the payoff matrix of the game. For instance, suppose that both players assign a disutility of 2 units to such an outcome. This will reduce the utility payoff that player 1 associates with the outcome (A_2, B_1) to $3 - 2 = 1$. Likewise, it will also reduce the utility payoff that player 2 associates with the outcome (A_1, B_2) to $3 - 2 = 1$. (If the players assigned a special disutility to violating an agreement, and then actually agreed to use the strategy pair (A_1, B_1), this would have similar effects on the payoff matrix of the game.) Consequently, the game will now have the following payoff matrix:

	B_1	B_2
A_1	2, 2	0, 1
A_2	1, 0	1, 1

This new game, of course, is no longer a prisoner's dilemma since now *both* (A_1, B_1) *and* (A_2, B_2) are equilibrium points. Hence, even if the game remains formally a non-cooperative game without enforceable agreements, the players will now have no difficulty in reaching the outcome (A_1, B_1), which we used to call the cooperative solution, so as to obtain the payoffs $(2, 2)$. This conclusion, of course, is fully consistent with our theory because now (A_1, B_1) *is* an equilibrium point.

This example shows that we must clearly distinguish between two different problems. One is the problem of whether a game that *looks like* a prisoner's dilemma *is* in fact a prisoner's dilemma: does the proposed payoff matrix of the game (which would make the game a prisoner's dilemma) correctly express the players' true payoff functions, in accordance with their real preferences and their real strategy objectives within the game? This is *not* a game-theoretical question, because game theory regards the players' payoff functions as *given*. It is, rather, an empirical question about the players' psychological makeup. The other question *is* a game-theoretical question: it is the question of how to define the solution of the game, once the payoff matrix has been correctly specified. A good deal of confusion can be avoided if these two questions are kept strictly apart.

As a practical matter, social situations not permitting enforceable agreements often have a socially very undesirable incentive structure, and may give rise to many very painful human problems. But these problems cannot be solved by arguing that people should not act as if agreements were

enforceable, even though they are not; or that people should trust each other, even though they have very good reasons to withhold this trust. The solution, if there is one, can only lie in actually providing effective incentives
to keep agreements (or in persuading people to assign high utility to keeping agreements, even in the absence of external incentives). What we have
to do, if it can be done, is to *change* non-cooperative games into cooperative
games by making agreements enforceable, rather than pretend that we live
in a make-believe world, where we can take non-cooperative games as they
are, and then analyze them simply as if they were cooperative games, if we
so desire.

   I have discussed at some length the principle that the solution of a non-
cooperative game must be an equilibrium point, because this principle will
play an important role in the game-theoretical investigations I am going to
report on.

8. Perfect equilibrium points

After Nash's discovery of the concept of equilibrium points in 1950, for many
years game theorists were convinced that the only rationality requirement in
a non-cooperative game was that the players' strategies should form an equilibrium point. But in 1965 Richard Selten proposed counterexamples to show
that even equilibrium points might involve irrational behavior (Selten, 1965).
He has suggested that only a special class of equilibrium points, which he
called *perfect* equilibrium points, represent truly rational behavior in a non-
cooperative game.

   Since the difference between perfect and imperfect equilibrium points is
obscured in the normal-form representation,[9] let us consider the following
two-person non-cooperative game, given in extensive form (game-tree form):

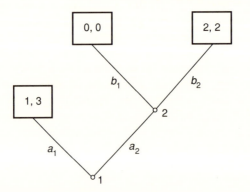

In this game, the first move belongs to player 1. He can choose between
moves a_1 and a_2. If he chooses a_1, then the game will end with the payoffs

---

[9] For a non-technical explanation of the terms "normal form" and "extensive form," see Luce
  and Raiffa (1957, Chapter 3).

(1, 3) to the two players, without player 2 having any move at all. On the other hand, if player 1 chooses move a_2, then player 2 has a choice between moves b_1 and b_2. If he chooses the former, then the game will end with the payoffs (0, 0); while if he chooses the latter, then the game will end with the payoffs (2, 2). The normal form of this game is as follows:

	B_1	B_2
A_1	1, 3	1, 3
A_2	0, 0	2, 2

The players' strategies have the following interpretation. Strategy A_1 (or A_2) means that player 1 will choose move a_1 (or a_2) at the beginning of the game. On the other hand, strategy B_1 (or B_2) means that player 2 will choose move b_1 (or b_2) *if player* 1 *chooses move* a_2 (while if player 1 chooses move a_1, then player 2 will do nothing). Player 2's strategies can be described only in terms of these *conditional* statements since he will have a move only if player 1 chooses move a_2.

A look at the normal form will reveal that the game has two pure-strategy equilibrium points, viz. $E_1 = (A_1, B_1)$ and $E_2 = (A_2, B_2)$. E_2 is a perfectly reasonable equilibrium point. But, as I propose to show, E_1 is not: it involves irrational behavior, and irrational expectations by the players about each other's behavior.

In fact, player 1 will use strategy A_1 (as E_1 requires him to do) only if he expects player 2 to use strategy B_1. (For if player 2 used B_2, then player 1 would be better off by using A_2.) But it is *irrational* for player 1 to expect player 2 to use strategy B_1, i.e. to expect player 2 to make move b_1 should player 1 himself make move a_2. This is so because move b_1 will yield player 2 only the payoff 0, whereas move b_2 would yield him the payoff 2.

To put it differently, player 2 will obviously prefer the outcome (A_1, B_1), yielding him 3 units of utility, over the outcome (A_2, B_2), yielding him only 2 units. Therefore, player 2 may very well try to induce player 1 to use strategy A_1, i.e. to make move a_1: for instance, he may threaten to use strategy B_1, i.e. to punish player 1 by making move b_1, should player 1 counter his wishes by making move a_2. But the point is that this would *not* be a credible threat because, by making move b_1, player 2 would not only punish player 1 but rather would just as much punish himself. This is so because move b_1 would reduce *both* of their payoffs to 0 (while the alternative move b_2 would give both of them payoffs of 2 units).

To be sure, if player 2 could irrevocably *commit* himself to punish player 1 in this way, and could do this *before* player 1 had made his move, then it would be rational for player 2 to make such a commitment in order to deter player 1 from making move a_2. But, in actual fact, player 2 cannot make such a commitment because this is a non-cooperative game. On the other hand, if player 2 is *not* compelled by such a prior commitment to punish player 1, then he will have no incentive to do so since, once player 1 has made his move, player 2 cannot gain anything by punishing him at the cost of reducing his own payoff at the same time.

To conclude, $E_1 = (A_1, B_1)$ is an irrational equilibrium point because it is based on the unreasonable assumption that player 2 would punish player 1 if the latter made move a_2 – even though this punishing move would reduce not only player 1's payoff but also player 2's own payoff. Following Selten's proposal, we shall call such unreasonable equilibrium points *imperfect* equilibrium points. In contrast, equilibrium points like $E_2 = (A_2, B_2)$, which are not open to such objections, will be called *perfect* equilibrium points.

The question naturally arises how it is possible that an equilibrium point should use a highly irrational strategy like B_1 as an equilibrium strategy at all. The answer lies in the fact that, as long as the two players follow their equilibrium strategies A_1 and B_1, player 2 will never come in a position *where he would have to make the irrational move b_1* prescribed by strategy B_1. For, strategy B_1 would require him to make move b_1 only if player 1 made move a_2. But this contingency will never arise because player 1 follows strategy A_1 (which requires him to make move a_1 rather than a_2).[10]

In other words, strategy B_1 would require player 2 to make move b_1 only if the game reached the point marked by 2 on our game tree[11] (since this is the point where he had to choose between moves b_1 and b_2). But, so long as the players follow the strategies A_1 and B_1, this point will never be reached by the game.

This fact suggests a mathematical procedure for eliminating imperfect equilibrium points from the game. All we have to do is to assume that, whenever any player tries to make a specific move, he will have a very small but positive probability ϵ of making a "mistake," which will divert him into making another move than he wanted to make, so that *every* possible move will occur with some positive probability. The resulting game will be called a *perturbed game*. As a result of the players' assumed "mistakes," in a perturbed game every point of the game tree will always be reached with a positive probability whenever the game is played. It can be shown that, if the game is perturbed in this way, only the perfect equilibrium points of the original game will remain equilibrium points in the perturbed game, whereas the imperfect equilibrium points will lose the status of equilibrium points. (More exactly, we can find the perfect equilibrium points of the original game if we

---

[10] From a logical point of view, strategy B_1 does satisfy the formal criteria for an equilibrium strategy because, in applying these criteria, the conditional statement defining strategy B_1 ("player 2 would make move b_1 if player 1 made move a_2") is interpreted as *material implication*. In contrast, B_1 fails to satisfy our informal criteria for a "rational" strategy because, in applying these latter criteria, the same conditional statement is automatically interpreted as a *subjunctive conditional*.

[11] We say that a given point of the game tree is *reached* by the game if it either represents the starting position in the game or is reached by a branch representing an actual move by a player or by chance. Thus, in our example, the point marked by 1 is always reached whereas the point marked by 2 is reached only if player 1 chooses to make move a_2 (rather than move a_1).

take the equilibrium points of the perturbed game, and then let the mistake probabilities ϵ go to zero.)

Thus, in our example, suppose that, if player 1 tries to use strategy A_1, then he will be able to implement the intended move a_1 only with probability $(1-\epsilon)$, and will be forced to make the unintended move a_2 with the remaining small probability ϵ. Consequently, it will not be costless any more for player 2 to use strategy B_1 when player 1 uses A_1. This is so because now player 1 will make move a_2 with a positive probability and, therefore, player 2 will have to counter this by making the costly move b_1, likewise with a positive probability. As a result, strategy B_1 will no longer be a best reply to A_1, and (A_1, B_1) will no longer be an equilibrium point.

The difference between perfect and imperfect equilibrium points can be easily recognized in the extensive form of a game but is often hidden in the normal form. This implies that, contrary to a view that used to be the commonly accepted view by game theorists, the normal form of the game in general fails to provide all the information we need for an adequate game-theoretical analysis of the game, and we may have to go back to the extensive form to recover some of the missing information.

On the other hand, if the normal form often contains too little information, the extensive form usually contains far too much, including many unnecessary details about the chance moves and about the time sequence in which individual moves have to be made. For this reason, Reinhard Selten and I have defined an intermediate game form, called the *agent normal form,* which omits the unnecessary details but retains the essential information about the game. (We obtain the agent normal form if we replace each player by as many "agents" as the number of his information sets in the game, and then construct a normal form with these agents as the players.) For a more extensive and more rigorous discussion of perfect equilibrium points and of the agent normal form, see Selten (1975).

9. Non-cooperative bargaining models for cooperative games

Ever since 1944 (the year when von Neumann and Morgenstern first published the *Theory of Games and Economic Behavior*), most research in game theory has been devoted either to a study of the mathematical properties of saddle points in *two-person zero-sum* games, or to a construction and study of solution concepts for *cooperative* games. Many very interesting cooperative solution concepts were proposed. But this work on cooperative games showed little theoretical unity: taken as a group, the different solution concepts that were suggested shared few common theoretical assumptions and no clear criteria emerged to decide under what conditions one particular solution concept was to be used and under what conditions another.

Part of the problem is that the authors of the different solution concepts have seldom made it sufficiently clear what institutional arrangements (negotiation rules) each particular solution concept is meant to assume about the bargaining process among the players, through which these players are supposed to reach an agreement about the final outcome of the game. Yet, it is well known that the very same cooperative game may have quite different outcomes, depending on the actual negotiation rules governing this bargaining process in any particular case. The nature of the agreements likely to arise will be often quite sensitive to such factors as who can talk to whom and, in particular, who can talk to whom *first,* ahead of other people; the degree to which negotiations are kept public, or can be conducted in private by smaller groups if the participants so desire; the conditions that decide whether any agreement remains open to repeal and to possible re-negotiation, or is made final and irrevocable; the possibility or impossibility of unilaterally making binding promises and/or threats, etc.

As a simple example, consider the following three-person cooperative game (called a three-person majority game). Each player, acting alone, can only achieve a zero payoff. Any coalition of two players can obtain a joint payoff of $100. The three-person coalition of all three players can likewise obtain a joint payoff of $100. Obviously, in this game, if pairs of players can meet separately, then the two players who manage to meet first are very likely to form a two-person coalition, and to divide the $100 in a ratio 50:50 between them. In contrast, if the negotiation rules disallow pairwise meetings, and if the negotiation time permitted is too short for forming any two-person coalition during the three-person negotiating session, then the likely outcome is a three-person coalition, with payoffs $33\frac{1}{3} : 33\frac{1}{3} : 33\frac{1}{3}$. Finally, under most other negotiation rules, both two-person and three-person coalitions will arise from time to time, and the probability of either outcome will depend on the extent to which these rules tend to help or hinder two-person agreements.

Another limitation of most cooperative solution concepts is this. Their application is basically restricted to fully cooperative games, and does not extend to that very wide range of real-life game situations which have a status intermediate between fully cooperative games and fully non-cooperative games – such as social situations where some kinds of agreements are enforceable while others are not, or where different agreements may be enforceable to different extents and with different probabilities; or where enforceable agreements are possible among some particular players but are impossible among other players; or where enforceable agreements cannot be concluded at some stages of the game but can be concluded at other stages, etc. In many contexts, it is particularly regrettable that most of these cooperative solution concepts are inapplicable to games possessing a strongly sequential structure, making the emergence of agreements a very gradual process, later agreements being built on earlier agreements and extending the former in various ways.

Yet, John Nash, when he introduced the very concepts of cooperative and of non-cooperative games, also suggested what, in my opinion, is a possible remedy to these deficiencies in the theory of cooperative games (Nash, 1951, p. 295). He suggested that an analysis of any cooperative game should start with constructing a precisely defined formal bargaining model (bargaining game) to represent the bargaining process among the players. Of course, this bargaining model must provide a mathematical representation, in the abstract language appropriate to such models, for the negotiation rules we want to assume, whether on empirical or on theoretical grounds, to govern this bargaining process. Then, according to Nash's proposal, this bargaining model should be analyzed as a *non-cooperative* game, by a careful study of its equilibrium points.

Nash's suggestion is based on the assumption that close cooperation among the players in a cooperative game usually requires a prior agreement about the payoffs, which, in most cases, can be achieved only by bargaining among the players. But this bargaining itself must have the nature of a non-cooperative game, unless we want to assume that the players will agree in an even earlier subsidiary bargaining game on how they will act in the main bargaining game – which would be not only a rather implausible assumption but would also lead to an infinite regress.

Nash's proposal, if it can be successfully implemented, will enable us to unify the whole theory of cooperative games, because it provides a uniform method of analysis for all cooperative games. Of course, even under Nash's proposal, it will remain true that any given cooperative game may have a number of different solutions, depending on the details of the bargaining process assumed to occur among the players. But, as we have argued, this is how it should be, since in real life different bargaining methods do lead to different outcomes. Yet, the game-theoretical analysis of this bargaining process can be based on the same theoretical principles in all cases.[12]

Indeed, Nash's approach will result in a unification of *both* the theory of cooperative games *and* of the theory of non-cooperative games, because it essentially reduces the problem of solving a cooperative game to the problem of solving a non-cooperative bargaining game. Moreover, it can be easily extended to games which have any kind of intermediate status between fully cooperative games and fully non-cooperative games (including games of a sequential nature, mentioned before).

10. A Bayesian solution concept for non-cooperative games

Nash's proposal, however, runs into a very basic difficulty – the same difficulty, which, up to very recently, also prevented the emergence of any really

---

[12] While Nash's proposal has many advantages, it certainly does not provide an easy routine method for solving cooperative games because, except in the very simplest cases, finding a suitable formal bargaining model for any given game – just as a modeling of any other complicated dynamic process – may be a very difficult task, requiring a good deal of insight and ingenuity, and subject to no mechanical rules.

useful theory of non-cooperative games. This difficulty lies in the fact that almost any interesting non-cooperative game – including almost any interesting non-cooperative bargaining game – will have a great many, and often infinitely many, very different equilibrium points. (This remains true even if we restrict ourselves to perfect equilibrium points.) This means that, if all we can say is that the outcome of the game will be an equilibrium point (or even that it will be a perfect equilibrium point), then we are saying little more than that almost anything can happen in the game.

For instance, consider the very simplest kind of two-person bargaining game, in which the two players have to divide $100. If they cannot agree on how to divide it, then both of them will receive zero payoffs. This game can be analyzed by means of the following formal bargaining model. Both players name a number between 0 and 100. Let the numbers named by players 1 and 2 be x_1 and x_2. (Intuitively, these numbers represent the two players' payoff demands.) If $x_1 + x_2 \leq 100$, then player 1 will obtain x_1 and player 2 will obtain x_2. On the other hand, if $x_1 + x_2 > 100$, then both players will get $0.

If we assume that money can be divided in any possible fractional amount, then this game has infinitely many equilibrium points, since any pair (x_1, x_2) of payoff demands is an equilibrium point so long as $x_1 + x_2 \leq 100$. (Of course, by the rules we have assumed for the game, we must also have $0 \leq x_i \leq 100$ for $i = 1, 2$.) But even if we assumed that money can be divided only in amounts corresponding to whole numbers of dollars, the game will still have 101 equilibrium points. (Of these, 99 equilibrium points will even be perfect equilibrium points. Only the two "extreme" equilibrium points giving one player $100 and giving the other player $0 turn out to be imperfect.) The situation will be even worse if we study more interesting, and therefore inevitably more complicated, bargaining games.

In view of these facts, several years ago Reinhard Selten and I decided to look into the possibility of defining a new solution concept for non-cooperative games, which will always select *one* particular equilibrium point as the solution for the game. This research project proved to be much more difficult than we had anticipated. But in 1974 we did find such a solution concept which seems to satisfy all intuitive and mathematical requirements. Conceptually, it amounts to an extension of the Bayesian approach, so successful in the analysis of one-person decision situations, to an analysis of non-cooperative games. The definition of this solution concept is based on the disturbed agent normal form of the game (see Section 8 above).

Let me introduce the following notation. We shall assume that a given player i ($i = 1, 2, \ldots, n$) has K_i different pure strategies. Therefore, a mixed strategy s_i of player i will be a probability vector of the form $s_i = (s_i^1, s_i^2, \ldots, s_i^{K_i})$, where s_i^k ($k = 1, 2, \ldots, K_i$) is the probability that this mixed strategy s_i assigns to the kth pure strategy of player i.

A strategy combination of all n players will be denoted as $s = (s_1, s_2, \ldots, s_n)$. Let $\bar{s}_i$ denote the strategy combination we obtain if we omit player i's strategy s_i from the strategy combination s. Thus, $\bar{s}_i$ is a strategy combination of the $(n-1)$ players *other* than player i. We can write $\bar{s}_i = (s_1, ..., s_{i-1}, s_{i+1}, ..., s_n)$.

Our solution is defined in two steps. As a first step, we construct a *prior probability distribution* p_i, over the pure strategies of each player i ($i = 1, 2, ..., n$). The second step involves a mathematical procedure which selects one specific equilibrium point $s^* = (s_1^*, s_2^*, ..., s_n^*)$ as the solution of the game, on the basis of these n prior probability distributions $p_1, p_2, ..., p_n$.

Each prior probability distribution p_i over the pure strategies of a given player i has the form of a probability vector $p_i = (p_i^1, p_i^2, ..., p_i^{K_i})$, where each component p_i^k ($k = 1, 2, ..., K_i$) is the initial *subjective* probability that every other player j ($j \neq i$) is assumed to assign to the possibility that player i will use his kth pure strategy in the game. Consequently, the prior probability distribution p_i is a probability vector of the same mathematical form as is any mixed strategy s_i of player i. But, of course, p_i has a very different game-theoretical interpretation. Whereas a mixed strategy s_i expresses the *objective* probabilities s_i^k that player i *himself* chooses to associate with his various pure strategies as a matter of his own strategical decision, the prior probability distribution p_i expresses the *subjective* probabilities p_i^k that the *other* players are assumed to associate with player i's various pure strategies, simply because they do not know in advance which particular strategy player i is going to use.

The numerical prior probability p_i^k our theory assigns to a given pure strategy of each player i is meant to express the theoretical probability that a rational individual, placed in player i's position, will actually use this particular pure strategy in the game. More specifically, p_i^k is meant to express the theoretical probability that player i will find himself in a situation where his best reply is to use this particular pure strategy. (This theoretical probability p_i^k, of course, is not directly given, but can only be obtained from a suitable probabilistic model about the players' behavior in the game.)

For convenience, I shall write the n-vector consisting of the n prior probability distributions as $p = (p_1, p_2, ..., p_n)$. I shall write the $(n-1)$-vector consisting of the $(n-1)$ prior probability distributions associated with the $(n-1)$ players other than player i as $\bar{p}_i = (p_1, ..., p_{i-1}, p_{i+1}, ..., p_n)$. Thus, $\bar{p}_i$ is the $(n-1)$-vector we obtain if we omit the ith component p_i from the n-vector p.

The second step in defining our solution involves a mathematical procedure, based on Bayesian ideas, for selecting one particular equilibrium point s^* as solution, when the vector p of all prior probability distributions is given. The simplest Bayesian model would be to assume that each player i would use a strategy s_i that was his best reply to the prior probability distribution vector $\bar{p}_i$ he would associate with the other $(n-1)$ players' pure strategies, and then to define the solution as the strategy combination $s = (s_1, s_2, ..., s_n)$. But this simple-minded approach is unworkable because in general this best-reply strategy combination s will not be an equilibrium point of the game.

Accordingly, our theory uses a mathematical procedure, called the *tracing procedure,* which takes the best-reply strategy combination s as a starting point, but then systematically modifies this strategy combination in a continuous manner, until it is finally transformed into an equilibrium point s^*, which will serve as the solution of the game.

This mathematical procedure is meant to model the psychological process, to be called the *solution process,* by which the players' expectations converge to a specific equilibrium point as the solution of the game. At the beginning, the players' initial expectations about the other players' strategies will correspond to the subjective probability distributions (prior distributions) p_i, and their initial reaction to these expectations will be an inclination to use their best-reply strategies s_i. Then, they will gradually modify their expectations and their tentative strategy choices until in the end *both* their expectations and their strategy choices will converge to the equilibrium strategies s_i^* corresponding to the solution s^*. (See Harsanyi, 1975.)

Of course, within the confines of this paper, I could do no more than sketch the barest outlines of our solution concept for non-cooperative games and, more generally, could draw only a very incomplete picture of some recent work in game theory. But I feel my paper has achieved its purpose if it has induced a few people from other disciplines to take some interest in the results of Bayesian decision theory and in some recent developments in game theory, and in the implications both of these may have for a deeper understanding of the nature of rational behavior.

References

Anscombe, F. J. and Aumann, R. J.: 1963, "A Definition of Subjective Probability," *Annals of Mathematical Statistics* **34**, 199–205.

Debreu, G.: 1959, *Theory of Value,* John Wiley & Sons, New York.

Harsanyi, J. C.: 1953, "Cardinal Utility in Welfare Economics and in the Theory of Risk-taking," *Journal of Political Economy* **61**, 434–435.

1955, "Cardinal Welfare, Individualistic Ethics, and Interpersonal Comparisons of Utility," *Journal of Political Economy* **63**, 309–321.

1958, "Ethics in Terms of Hypothetical Imperatives," *Mind* **47**, 305–316.

1967-68, "Games with Incomplete Information Played by 'Bayesian' Players," *Management Science* **14**, 159–182, 320–334, and 486–502.

1969, "Rational-Choice Models of Political Behavior vs. Functionalist and Conformist Theories," *World Politics* **21**, 513–538.

1975, "The Tracing Procedure: A Bayesian Approach to Defining a Solution for *n*-Person Non-cooperative Games," *International Journal of Game Theory* **4**, 61–94.

1975a, "Can the Maximin Principle Serve as a Basis for Morality? A Critique of John Rawls's Theory," *American Political Science Review* **59**, 594–606.

1975b, "Nonlinear Social Welfare Functions," *Theory and Decision* **7**, 61–82.

Luce, R. D. and Raiffa, H.: 1957, *Games and Decisions.* John Wiley & Sons, New York.

Nash, J. F.: 1950, "Equilibrium Points in *n*-Person Games," *Proceedings of the National Academy of Sciences, U.S.A.* **36**, 48–49.

1951, "Non-cooperative Games," *Annals of Mathematics* **54**, 286–295.

Radner, R. and Marschak, J.: 1954, "Note on Some Proposed Decision Criteria," in R. M. Thrall *et al., Decision Processes,* John Wiley & Sons, New York, 1954, pp. 61–68.

Selten, R.: 1965, "Spieltheoretische Behandlung eines Oligopolmodells mit Nachfrageträgheit," *Zeitschrift für die gesamte Staatswissenschaft* **121**, 301–324 and 667–689.

1975, "Reexamination of the Perfectness Concept for Equilibrium Points in Extensive Games," *International Journal of Game Theory* **4**, 25–55.

Simon, H. A.: 1960, *The New Science of Management Decision,* Harper & Brothers, New York.

von Neumann, J. and Morgenstern, O.: 1944, *Theory of Games and Economic Behavior,* Princeton University Press, Princeton, N.J.

12. The emergence of cooperation among egoists

Robert Axelrod

Under what conditions will cooperation emerge in a world of egoists without central authority? This question has played an important role in a variety of domains including political philosophy, international politics, and economic and social exchange. This article provides new results which show more completely than was previously possible the conditions under which cooperation will emerge. The results are more complete in two ways. First, *all* possible strategies are taken into account, not simply some arbitrarily selected subset. Second, not only are equilibrium conditions established, but also a mechanism is specified which can move a population from noncooperative to cooperative equilibrium.

The situation to be analyzed is the one in which narrow self-maximization behavior by each person leads to a poor outcome for all. This is the famous Prisoner's Dilemma game. Two individuals can each either cooperate or defect. No matter what the other does, defection yields a higher payoff than cooperation. But if both defect, both do worse than if both cooperated. Figure 1 shows the payoff matrix with sample utility numbers attached to the payoffs. If the other player cooperates, there is a choice between cooperation which yields R (the reward for mutual cooperation) or defection which yields T (the temptation to defect). By assumption, $T > R$, so it pays to defect if the other player cooperates. On the other hand, if the other player defects, there is a choice between cooperation which yields S (the sucker's payoff), or defection which yields P (the punishment for mutual defection). By assumption, $P > S$, so it pays to defect if the other player defects. Thus no matter what the other player does, it pays to defect. But if both defect,

I would like to thank John Chamberlin, Michael Cohen, Bernard Grofman, William Hamilton, John Kingdon, Larry Mohr, John Padgett and Reinhard Selten for their help, and the Institute of Public Policy Studies for its financial support.
Reprinted with permission from *American Political Science Review* 75 (1981), 306-18.

	Cooperate	Defect
Cooperate	$R=3, R=3$	$S=0, T=5$
Defect	$T=5, S=0$	$P=1, P=1$

$$T > R > P > S$$
$$R > (S+T)/2$$

Note: The payoffs to the row choosers are listed first.

Figure 1

both get P rather than the R they could both have got if both had cooperated. But R is assumed to be greater than P. Hence the dilemma. Individual rationality leads to a worse outcome for both than is possible.

To insure that an even chance of exploitation or being exploited is not as good an outcome as mutual cooperation, a final inequality is added in the standard definition of the Prisoner's Dilemma. This is just $R > (T+S)/2$.

Thus two egoists playing the game once will both choose their dominant choice, defection, and get a payoff, P, which is worse for both than the R they could have got if they had both cooperated. If the game is played a known finite number of times, the players still have no incentive to cooperate. This is certainly true on the last move since there is no future to influence. On the next-to-last move they will also have no incentive to cooperate since they can anticipate mutual defection on the last move. This line of reasoning implies that the game will unravel all the way back to mutual defection on the first move of any sequence of plays which is of known finite length (Luce and Raiffa, 1957, pp. 94–102). This reasoning does not apply if the players will interact an indefinite number of times. With an indefinite number of interactions, cooperation can emerge. This article will explore the precise conditions necessary for this to happen.

The importance of this problem is indicated by a brief explanation of the role it has played in a variety of fields.

1. *Political philosophy.* Hobbes regarded the state of nature as equivalent to what we now call a two-person Prisoner's Dilemma, and he built his justification for the state upon the purported impossibility of sustained cooperation in such a situation (Taylor, 1976, pp. 98–116). A demonstration that mutual cooperation could emerge among rational egoists playing the iterated Prisoner's Dilemma would provide a powerful argument that the role of the state should not be as universal as some have argued.

2. *International politics.* Today nations interact without central control, and therefore the conclusions about the requirements for the emergence of cooperation have empirical relevance to many central issues of international politics. Examples include many varieties of

the security dilemma (Jervis, 1978) such as arms competition and its obverse, disarmament (Rapoport, 1960); alliance competition (Snyder, 1971); and communal conflict in Cyprus (Lumsden, 1973). The selection of the American response to the Soviet invasion of Afghanistan in 1979 illustrates the problem of choosing an effective strategy in the context of a continuing relationship. Had the United States been perceived as continuing business as usual, the Soviet Union might have been encouraged to try other forms of non-cooperative behavior later. On the other hand, any substantial lessening of U.S. cooperation risked some form of retaliation which could then set off counter-retaliation, setting up a pattern of mutual defection that could be difficult to get out of. Much of the domestic debate over foreign policy is over problems of just this type.

3. *Economic and social exchange.* Our everyday lives contain many exchanges whose terms are not enforced by any central authority. Even in economic changes, business ethics are maintained by the knowledge that future interactions are likely to be affected by the outcome of the current exchange.

4. *International political economy.* Multinational corporations can play off host governments to lessen their tax burdens in the absence of coordinated fiscal policies between the affected governments. Thus the commodity exporting country and the commodity importing country are in an iterated Prisoner's Dilemma with each other, whether they fully appreciate it or not (Laver, 1977).

In the literatures of these areas, there has been a convergence on the nature of the problem to be analyzed. All agree that the two-person Prisoner's Dilemma captures an important part of the strategic interaction. All agree that what makes the emergence of cooperation possible is the possibility that interaction will continue. The tools of the analysis have been surprisingly similar, with game theory serving to structure the enterprise.

As a paradigm case of the emergence of cooperation, consider the development of the norms of a legislative body, such as the United States Senate. Each senator has an incentive to appear effective for his or her constituents even at the expense of conflicting with other senators who are trying to appear effective for *their* constituents. But this is hardly a zero-sum game since there are many opportunities for mutually rewarding activities between two senators. One of the consequences is that an elaborate set of norms, or folkways, have emerged in the Senate. Among the most important of these is the norm of reciprocity, a folkway which involves helping out a colleague and getting repaid in kind. It includes vote trading, but it extends to so many types of mutually rewarding behavior that "it is not an exaggeration to say that reciprocity is a way of life in the Senate" (Matthews, 1960, p. 100; see also Mayhew, 1975).

Washington was not always like this. Early observers saw the members of the Washington community as quite unscrupulous, unreliable, and characterized by "falsehood, deceit, treachery" (Smith, 1906, p. 190). But by now the practice of reciprocity is well established. Even the significant changes in the Senate over the last two decades toward more decentralization, more openness, and more equal distribution of power have come without abating the folkway of reciprocity (Ornstein, Peabody and Rhode, 1977). I will show that we do *not* need to assume that senators are more honest, more generous, or more public-spirited than in earlier years to explain how cooperation based on reciprocity has emerged and proven stable. The emergence of cooperation can be explained as a consequence of senators pursuing their own interests.

The approach taken here is to investigate how individuals pursuing their own interests will act, and then see what effects this will have for the system as a whole. Put another way, the approach is to make some assumptions about micro-motives, and then deduce consequences for macro-behavior (Schelling, 1978). Thinking about the paradigm case of a legislature is a convenience, but the same style of reasoning can apply to the emergence of cooperation between individuals in many other political settings, or even to relations between nations. While investigating the conditions which foster the emergence of cooperation, one should bear in mind that cooperation is not always socially desirable. There are times when public policy is best served by the prevention of cooperation – as in the need for regulatory action to prevent collusion between oligopolistic business enterprises.

The basic situation I will analyze involves pairwise interactions.[1] I assume that the player can recognize another player and remember how the two of them have interacted so far. This allows the history of the particular interaction to be taken into account by a player's strategy.

A variety of ways to resolve the dilemma of the Prisoner's Dilemma have been developed. Each involves allowing some additional activity which alters the strategic interaction in such a way as to fundamentally change the nature of the problem. The original problem remains, however, because there are many situations in which these remedies are not available. I wish to consider the problem in its fundamental form.

1.   There is no mechanism available to the players to make enforceable threats or commitments (Schelling, 1960). Since the players cannot

---

[1] A single player may be interacting with many others, but the player is interacting with them one at a time. The situations which involve more than pairwise interaction can be modeled with the more complex *n*-person Prisoner's Dilemma (Olson, 1965; G. Hardin, 1968; R. Hardin, 1971; Schelling, 1973). The principal application is to the provision of collective goods. It is possible that the results from pairwise interactions will help suggest how to undertake a deeper analysis of the *n*-person case as well, but that must wait. For a parallel treatment of the two-person and *n*-person cases, see Taylor (1976, pp. 29–62).

make commitments, they must take into account all possible strategies which might be used by the other player, and they have all
possible strategies available to themselves.

2.   There is no way to be sure what the other player will do on a given
move. This eliminates the possibility of metagame analysis (Howard, 1971) which allows such options as "make the same choice as
the other player is about to make." It also eliminates the possibility
of reliable reputations such as might be based on watching the other
player interact with third parties.

3.   There is no way to change the other player's utilities. The utilities
already include whatever consideration each player has for the interests of the other (Taylor, 1976, pp. 69–83).

Under these conditions, words not backed by actions are so cheap as to be
meaningless. The players can communicate with each other only through the
sequence of their own behavior. This is the problem of the iterated Prisoner's Dilemma in its fundamental form.

Two things remain to be specified: how the payoff of a particular move
relates to the payoff in a whole sequence, and the precise meaning of a strategy. A natural way to aggregate payoffs over time is to assume that later
payoffs are worth less than the earlier ones, and that this relationship is
expressed as a constant discount per move (Shubik, 1959, 1970). Thus the
next payoff is worth only a fraction, w, of the same payoff this move. A
whole string of mutual defections would then have a "present value" of
$P + wP + w^2P + w^3P... = P/(1-w)$. The discount parameter, w, can be given
either of two interpretations. The standard economic interpretation is that
later consumption is not valued as much as earlier consumption. An alternative interpretation is that future moves may not actually occur, since the
interaction between a pair of players has only a certain probability of continuing for another move. In either interpretation, or a combination of the
two, w is strictly between zero and one. The smaller w is, the less important
later moves are relative to earlier ones.

For a concrete example, suppose one player is following the policy of always
defecting, and the other player is following the policy of TIT FOR TAT.
TIT FOR TAT is the policy of cooperating on the first move and then doing
whatever the other player did on the previous move. This means that TIT
FOR TAT will defect once for each defection by the other player. When the
other player is using TIT FOR TAT, a player who always defects will get T
on the first move, and P on all the subsequent moves. The payoff to someone using ALL D when playing with someone using TIT FOR TAT is thus:

$$V(ALL\,D\,|\,TFT) = T + wP + w^2P + w^3P...$$
$$= T + wP(1 + w + w^2...)$$
$$= T + wP/(1-w).$$

Both *ALL D* and *TIT FOR TAT* are strategies. In general, a *strategy* (or decision rule) is a function from the history of the game so far into a probability of cooperation on the next move. Strategies can be stochastic, as in the example of a rule which is entirely random with equal probabilities of cooperation and defection on each move. A strategy can also be quite sophisticated in its use of the pattern of outcomes in the game so far to determine what to do next. It may, for example, use Bayesian techniques to estimate the parameters of some model it might have of the other player's rule. Or it may be some complex combination of other strategies. But a strategy must rely solely on the information available through this one sequence of interactions with the particular player.

The first question one is tempted to ask is, "What is the best strategy?" This is a good question, but unfortunately there is no best rule independent of the environment which it might have to face. The reason is that what works best when the other player is unconditionally cooperative will not in general work well when the other player is conditionally cooperative, and vice versa. To prove this, I will introduce the concept of a *nice strategy*, namely, one which will never be the first to defect.

Theorem 1. *If the discount parameter, w, is sufficiently high, there is no best strategy independent of the strategy used by the other player.*

Proof: Suppose A is a strategy which is best regardless of the strategy used by the other player. This means that for any strategies A' and B, $V(A|B) \geq (A'|B)$. Consider separately the cases where A is nice and A is not nice. If A is nice, let $A' = ALL\ D$, and let $B = ALL\ C$. Then $V(A|B) = R/(1-w)$ which is less than $V(A'|B) = T/(1-w)$. On the other hand, if A is not nice, let $A' = ALL\ C$, and let B be the strategy of cooperating until the other player defects and then always defects. Eventually A will be the first to defect, say, on move n. The value of n is irrelevant for the comparison to follow, so assume that $n = 1$. To give A the maximum advantage, assume that A always defects after its first defection. Then $V(A|B) = T + wP/(1-w)$. But $V(A'|B) = R/(1-w) = R + wR/(1-w)$. Thus $V(A|B) < V(A'|B)$ whenever $w > (T-R)/(T-P)$. Thus the immediate advantage gained by the defection of A will eventually be more than compensated for by the long-term disadvantage of B's unending defection, assuming that w is sufficiently large. Thus, if w is sufficiently large, there is no one best strategy.

In the paradigm case of a legislature, this theorem says that if there is a large enough chance that a member of Congress will interact *again* with another member of Congress, then there is no one best strategy to use independently of the strategy being used by the other person. It would be best to be cooperative with someone who will reciprocate that cooperation in the future, but not with someone whose future behavior will not be very much affected by this interaction (see, for example, Hinckley, 1972). The very possibility of achieving stable mutual cooperation depends upon there being a good chance of a continuing interaction, as measured by the magnitude of w. Empirically, the chance of two members of Congress having a continuing interaction has increased dramatically as the biennial turnover rates in Congress have fallen from about 40 per cent in the first 40 years of the Republic to about 20 per cent or less in recent years (Young, 1966, pp. 87–90; Jones, 1977, p. 254; Patterson, 1978, pp. 143–44). That the increasing institutionalization of Congress has had its effects on the development of congressional norms has been widely accepted (Polsby, 1968, esp. n. 68). We now see how the diminished turnover rate (which is one aspect of institutionalization) can allow the development of reciprocity (which is one important part of congressional folkways).

But saying that a continuing chance of interaction is necessary for the development of cooperation is not the same as saying that it is sufficient. The demonstration that there is not a single best strategy still leaves open the question of what patterns of behavior can be expected to emerge when there actually is a sufficiently high probability of continuing interaction between two people.

1. The tournament approach

Just because there is no single best decision rule does not mean analysis is hopeless. For example, progress can be made on the question of which strategy does best in an environment of players who are using strategies designed to do well. To explore this question, I conducted a tournament of strategies submitted by game theorists in economics, psychology, sociology, political science and mathematics (Axelrod, 1980a). Announcing the payoff matrix shown in Figure 1, and a game length of two hundred moves, I ran the fourteen entries and *RANDOM* against each other in a round robin tournament. The result was that the highest average score was attained by the simplest of all the strategies submitted, *TIT FOR TAT*.

I then circulated the report of the results and solicited entries for a second round. This time I received sixty-two entries from six countries.[2] Most of the contestants were computer hobbyists, but there were also professors of evolutionary biology, physics, and computer science, as well as the five disciplines represented in the first round. *TIT FOR TAT* was again submitted by the winner of the first round, Anatol Rapoport of the Institute for Advanced Study (Vienna). And it won again. An analysis of the three million choices which were made in the second round shows that *TIT FOR TAT* was a very robust rule because it was nice, provocable into a retaliation by

---

[2] In the second round, the length of the games was uncertain, with an expected median length of two hundred moves. This was achieved by setting the probability that a given move would not be the last one at $w = .99654$. As in the first round, each pair was matched in five games. See Axelrod (1980b) for a complete description.

a defection of the other, and yet forgiving after it took its one retaliation (Axelrod, 1980b).

2. The ecological approach

To see if *TIT FOR TAT* would do well in a whole series of simulated tournaments, I calculated what would happen if each of the strategies in the second round were submitted to a hypothetical next round in proportion to its success in the previous round. This process was then repeated to generate the time path of the distribution of strategies. The results showed that as the less-successful rules were displaced, *TIT FOR TAT* continued to do well with the rules which initially scored near the top. In the long run, *TIT FOR TAT* displaced all the other rules and went to what biologists call fixation (Axelrod, 1980b).

This is an ecological approach because it takes as given the varieties which are present and investigates how they do over time when interacting with each other. It provides further evidence of the robust nature of the success of *TIT FOR TAT*.

3. The evolutionary approach

A much more general approach would be to allow all possible decision rules to be considered, and to ask what are the characteristics of the decision rules which are stable in the long run. An evolutionary approach recently introduced by biologists offers a key concept which makes such an analysis tractable (Maynard Smith, 1974, 1978). This approach imagines the existence of a whole population of individuals employing a certain strategy, B, and a single mutant individual employing another strategy, A. Strategy A is said to *invade* strategy B if $V(A|B) > V(B|B)$ where $V(A|B)$ is the expected payoff an A gets when playing a B, and $V(B|B)$ is the expected payoff a B gets when playing another B. Since the B's are interacting virtually entirely with other B's, the concept of invasion is equivalent to the single mutant individual being able to do better than the population average. This leads directly to the key concept of the evolutionary approach. A strategy is *collectively stable* if no strategy can invade it.[3]

---

[3] Those familiar with the concepts of game theory will recognize this as a strategy being in Nash equilibrium with itself. My definitions of invasion and collective stability are slightly different from Maynard Smith's (1974) definitions of invasion and evolutionary stability. His definition of invasion allows $V(A|B) = V(B|B)$ provided that $V(B|A) > V(A|A)$. I have used the new definitions to simplify the proofs and to highlight the difference between the effect of a single mutant and the effects of a small number of mutants. Any rule which is evolutionarily stable is also collectively stable. For a nice rule, the definitions are equivalent. All theorems in the text remain true if "evolutionary stability" is substituted for "collective stability" with the exception of Theorem 3, where the characterization is necessary but no longer sufficient.

The biological motivation for this approach is based on the interpretation of the payoffs in terms of fitness (survival and fecundity). All mutations are possible, and if any could invade a given population it would have had the chance to do so. Thus only a collectively stable strategy is expected to be able to maintain itself in the long-run equilibrium as the strategy used by all.[4] Collectively stable strategies are important because they are the only ones which an entire population can maintain in the long run if mutations are introduced one at a time.

The political motivation for this approach is based on the assumption that all strategies are possible, and that if there were a strategy which would benefit an individual, someone is sure to try it. Thus only a collectively stable strategy can maintain itself as the strategy used by all – provided that the individuals who are trying out novel strategies do not interact too much with one another.[5] As we shall see later, if they do interact in clusters, then new and very important developments become possible.

A difficulty in the use of this concept of collective stability is that it can be very hard actually to determine which strategies have it and which do not. In most biological applications, including both the Prisoner's Dilemma and other types of interactions, this difficulty has been dealt with in one of two ways. One method has been to restrict the analysis to situations where the strategies take some particularly simple form such as in one-parameter models of sex-ratios (Hamilton, 1967). The other method has been to restrict the strategies themselves to a relatively narrow set so that some illustrative results could be attained (Maynard Smith and Price, 1973; Maynard Smith, 1978).

The difficulty of dealing with all possible strategies was also faced by Michael Taylor (1976), a political scientist who sought a deeper understanding of the issues raised by Hobbes and Hume concerning whether people in a state of nature would be expected to cooperate with each other. He too employed the method of using a narrow set of strategies to attain some illustrative results. Taylor restricted himself to the investigation of four particular strategies (including *ALL D, ALL C, TIT FOR TAT,* and the rule "cooperate until the other defects, and then always defect"), and one set of strategies which retaliates in progressively increasing numbers of defections for each defection by the other. He successfully developed the equilibrium conditions when these are the only rules which are possible.[6]

---

[4] For the application of the results of this article to biological contexts, see Axelrod and Hamilton (1981). For the development in biology of the concepts of reciprocity and stable strategy, see Hamilton (1964), Trivers (1971), Maynard Smith (1974), and Dawkins (1976).

[5] Collective stability can also be interpreted in terms of a commitment by one player, rather than the stability of a whole population. Suppose player Y is committed to using strategy B. Then player X can do no better than use this same strategy B if and only if strategy B is collectively stable.

[6] For the comparable equilibrium conditions when all possible strategies are allowed, see below, Theorems 2 through 6. For related results on the potential stability of cooperative behavior, see Luce and Raiffa (1957, p. 102), Kurz (1977) and Hirshleifer (1978).

Before running the computer tournament, I believed that it was impossible to make very much progress if all possible strategies were permitted to enter the analysis. However, once I had attained sufficient experience with a wide variety of specific decision rules, and with the analysis of what happened when these rules interacted, I was able to formulate and answer some important questions about what would happen if all possible strategies were taken into account.

The remainder of this article will be devoted to answering the following specific questions about the emergence of cooperation in the iterated Prisoner's Dilemma:

(1) Under what conditions is *TIT FOR TAT* collectively stable?
(2) What are the necessary and sufficient conditions for any strategy to be collectively stable?
(3) If virtually everyone is following a strategy of unconditional defection, when can cooperation emerge from a small cluster of newcomers who introduce cooperation based on reciprocity?

4. *TIT FOR TAT* as a collectively stable strategy

TIT FOR TAT cooperates on the first move, and then does whatever the other player did on the previous move. This means that any rule which starts off with a defection will get T, the highest possible payoff, on the first move when playing *TIT FOR TAT*. Consequently, *TIT FOR TAT* can only avoid being invadable by such a rule if the game is likely to last long enough for the retaliation to counteract the temptation to defect. In fact, no rule can invade *TIT FOR TAT* if the discount parameter, w, is sufficiently large. This is the heart of the formal result contained in the following theorem. Readers who wish to skip the proofs can do so without loss of continuity.

Theorem 2. *TIT FOR TAT is a collectively stable strategy if and only if $w \geq \max((T-R)/(T-P), (T-R)/(R-S))$. An alternative formulation of the same result is that TIT FOR TAT is a collectively stable strategy if and only if it is invadable neither by ALL D nor the strategy which alternates defection and cooperation.*

Proof: First we prove that the two formulations of the theorem are equivalent, and then we prove both implications of the second formulation. To say that *ALL D* cannot invade *TIT FOR TAT* means that $V(ALL\,D\,|\,TFT) \leq V(TFT\,|\,TFT)$. As shown earlier, $V(ALL\,D\,|\,TFT) = T + wp/(1-w)$. Since *TFT* always cooperates with its twin, $V(TFT\,|\,TFT) = R + wR + w^2R... = R/(1-w)$. Thus *ALL D* cannot invade *TIT FOR TAT* when $T + wP/(1-w) \leq R/(1-w)$, or $T(1-w) + wP \leq R$, or $T - R \leq w(T-P)$ or $w \geq ((T-R)/(T-P))$. Similarly, to say that alternation of D and C cannot invade *TIT FOR TAT* means that $(T+wS)/(1-w^2) \leq R/(1-w)$, or $((T-R)/(R-S)) \leq w$. Thus $w \geq ((T-R)/(T-P))$ and $w \geq ((T-R)/(R-S))$

is equivalent to saying that *TIT FOR TAT* is invadable by neither *ALL D* nor the strategy which alternates defection and cooperation. This shows that the two formulations are equivalent.

Now we prove both of the implications of the second formulation. One implication is established by the simple observation that if *TIT FOR TAT* is a collectively stable strategy, then no rule can invade, and hence neither can the two specified rules. The other implication to be proved is that if neither *ALL D* nor Alternation of *D* and *C* can invade *TIT FOR TAT,* then no strategy can.

TIT FOR TAT has only two states, depending on what the other player did the previous move (on the first move it assumes, in effect, that the other player has just cooperated). Thus if *A* is interacting with *TIT FOR TAT*, the best which any strategy, *A*, can do after choosing *C* is to choose *C* or *D*. Similarly, the best *A* can do after choosing *D* is to choose *C* or *D*. This leaves four possibilities for the best *A* can do with *TIT FOR TAT:* repeated sequences of *CC, CD, DC,* or *DD*. The first does the same as *TIT FOR TAT* with another *TIT FOR TAT*. The second cannot do better than both the first and the third. This implies if the third and fourth possibilities cannot invade *TIT FOR TAT,* than no strategy can. These two are equivalent, respectively, to Alternation of *D* and *C*, and *ALL D*. Thus if neither of these two can invade *TIT FOR TAT,* no rule can, and *TIT FOR TAT* is a collectively stable strategy.

The significance of this theorem is that it demonstrates that if everyone in a population is cooperating with everyone else because each is using the *TIT FOR TAT* strategy, no one can do better using any other strategy *provided* the discount parameter is high enough. For example, using the numerical values of the payoff parameters given in Figure 1, *TIT FOR TAT* is uninvadable when the discount parameter, w, is greater than 2/3. If w falls below this critical value, and everyone else is using *TIT FOR TAT,* it will pay to defect on alternative moves. For w less than 1/2, *ALL D* can also invade.

One specific implication is that if the other player is unlikely to be around much longer because of apparent weakness, then the perceived value of w falls and the reciprocity of *TIT FOR TAT* is no longer stable. We have Caesar's explanation of why Pompey's allies stopped cooperating with him. "They regarded his [Pompey's] prospects as hopeless and acted according to the common rule by which a man's friends become his enemies in adversity" (trans. by Warner, 1960, p. 328). Another example is the business institution of the factor who buys a client's accounts receivable. This is done at a very substantial discount when the firm is in trouble because

once a manufacturer begins to go under, even his best customers begin refusing payment for merchandise, claiming defects in quality, failure to meet specifications, tardy delivery, or what-have-you. The great enforcer of morality in commerce is the continuing relationship, the belief that one will have to do business again with this customer, or this supplier, and when a failing company loses this automatic enforcer, not even a strong-arm factor is likely to find a substitute (Mayer, 1974, p. 280).

Similarly, any member of Congress who is perceived as likely to be defeated in the next election may have some difficulty doing legislative business with colleagues on the usual basis of trust and good credit.[7]

There are many other examples of the importance of long-term interaction for the stability of cooperation in the iterated Prisoner's Dilemma. It is easy to maintain the norms of reciprocity in a stable small town or ethnic neighborhood. Conversely, a visiting professor is likely to receive poor treatment by other faculty members compared to the way these same people treat their regular colleagues.

Another consequence of the previous theorem is that if one wants to prevent rather than promote cooperation, one should keep the same individuals from interacting too regularly with each other. Consider the practice of the government selecting two aerospace companies for competitive development contracts. Since firms specialize to some degree in either air force or in navy planes, there is a tendency for firms with the same specialties to be frequently paired in the final competition (Art, 1968). To make tacit collusion between companies more difficult, the government should seek methods of compensating for the specialization. Pairs of companies which shared a specialization would then expect to interact less often in the final competitions. This would cause the later interactions between them to be worth relatively less than before, reducing the value of w. If w is sufficiently low, reciprocal cooperation in the form of tacit collusion ceases to be a stable policy.

Knowing when *TIT FOR TAT* cannot be invaded is valuable, but it is only a part of the story. Other strategies may be, and in fact are, also collectively stable. This suggests the question of what a strategy has to do to be collectively stable. In other words, what policies, if adopted by everyone, will prevent any one individual from benefiting by a departure from the common strategy?

5. The characterization of collectively stable strategies

The characterization of all collectively stable strategies is based on the idea that invasion can be prevented if the rule can make the potential invader worse off than if it had just followed the common strategy. Rule B can prevent invasion by rule A if B can be sure that no matter what A does later, B will hold A's total score low enough. This leads to the following useful definition: B has a *secure position* over A on move n if no matter what A does from move n onwards, $V(A|B) \leq V(B|B)$, assuming that B defects from move n onwards. Let $V_n(A|B)$ represent A's discounted cumulative score in the moves before move n. Then another way of saying that B has a secure position over A on move n is that

---

[7] A countervailing consideration is that a legislator in electoral trouble may receive help from friendly colleagues who wish to increase the chances of reelection of someone who has proven in the past to be cooperative, trustworthy, and effective. Two current examples are Morris Udall and Thomas Foley. (I wish to thank an anonymous reviewer for this point.)

$$V_n(A|B) + w^{n-1}P/(1-w) \leq V(B|B),$$

since the best A can do from move n onwards if B defects is get P each time. Moving the second term to the right side of the inequality gives the helpful result that B has a secure position over A on move n if $V_n(A|B)$ is small enough, namely if

$$V_n(A|B) \leq V(B|B) - w^{n-1}P/(1-w). \tag{1}$$

The theorem which follows embodies the advice that if you want to employ a collectively stable strategy, you should only cooperate when you can afford an exploitation by the other side and still retain your secure position.

Theorem 3. *The Characterization Theorem. B is a collectively stable strategy if and only if B defects on move n whenever the other player's cumulative score so far is too great, specifically when $V_n(A|B) > V(B|B) - w^{n-1}(T + wP/(1-w))$.*

Proof: First it will be shown that a strategy B which defects as required will always have a secure position over any A, and therefore will have $V(A|B) \leq V(B|B)$ which in turn makes B a collectively stable strategy. The proof works by induction. For B to have a secure position on move 1 means that $V(A|ALL\ D) \leq V(ALL\ D|ALL\ D)$ according to the definition of secure position applied to $n = 1$. Since this is true for all A, B has a secure position on move 1. If B has a secure position over A on move n, it has a secure position on move $n+1$. This is shown in two parts.

First, if B defects on move n, A gets at most P, so

$$V_{n+1}(A|B) \leq V_n(A|B) + w^{n-1}P.$$

Using Equation (1) gives:

$$V_{n+1}(A|B) \leq V(B|B) - w^{n-1}P/(1-w) + w^{n-1}P$$

$$V_{n+1}(A|B) \leq V(B|B) - w^nP|(1-w).$$

Second, B will only cooperate on move n when

$$V_n(A|B) \leq V(B|B) - w^{n-1}(T + wP/(1-w)).$$

Since A can get at most T on move n, we have

$$V_{n+1}(A|B) \leq V(B|B) - w^{n-1}(T + wP/(1-w)) + w^{n-1}T$$

$$V_{n+1}(A|B) \leq V(B|B) - w^nP/(1-w).$$

Therefore, B always has a secure position over A, and consequently B is a collectively stable strategy.

The second part of the proof operates by contradiction. Suppose that B is a collectively stable strategy and there is an A and an n such that B does not defect on move n when

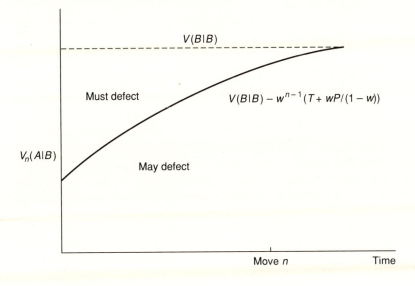

Figure 2

$$V_n(A \mid B) > V(B \mid B) - w^{n-1}(T + wP/(1 - w)),$$

that is, when

$$V_n(A \mid B) + w^{n-1}(T + wP/(1 - w)) > V(B \mid B). \tag{2}$$

Define A' as the same as A on the first $n-1$ moves, and D thereafter. A' gets T on move n (since B cooperated then), and at least P thereafter. So,

$$V(A' \mid B) \geq V_n(A \mid B) + w^{n-1}(T + wP/(1 - w)).$$

Combined with (2) this gives $V(A' \mid B) > V(B \mid B)$. Hence A' invades B, contrary to the assumption that B is a collectively stable strategy. Therefore, if B is a collectively stable strategy, it must defect when required.

Figure 2 illustrates the use of this theorem. The dotted line shows the value which must not be exceeded by any A if B is to be a collectively stable strategy. This value is just $V(B \mid B)$, the expected payoff attained by a player using B when virtually all the other players are using B as well. The solid curve represents the critical value of A's cumulative payoff so far. The theorem simply says that B is a collectively stable strategy if and only if it defects whenever the other player's cumulative value so far in the game is above this line. By doing so, B is able to prevent the other player from eventually getting a total expected value of more than rule B gets when playing another rule B.

The characterization theorem is "policy-relevant" in the abstract sense that it specifies what a strategy, B, has to do at any point in time as a function of the previous history of the interaction in order for B to be a collectively stable strategy.[8] It is a complete characterization because this requirement is both a necessary and a sufficient condition for strategy B to be collectively stable.

Two additional consequences about collectively stable strategies can be seen from Figure 2. First, as long as the other player has not accumulated too great a score, a strategy has the flexibility to either cooperate or defect and still be collectively stable. This flexibility explains why there are typically many strategies which are collectively stable. The second consequence is that a nice rule (one which will never defect first) has the most flexibility since it has the highest possible score when playing an identical rule. Put another way, nice rules can afford to be more generous than other rules with potential invaders because nice rules do so well with each other.

The flexibility of a nice rule is not unlimited, however, as shown by the following theorem. In fact, a nice rule must be *provoked* by the very first defection of the other player, that is, on some later move the rule must have a finite chance of retaliating with a defection of its own.

Theorem 4. *For a nice strategy to be collectively stable, it must be provoked by the first defection of the other player.*

Proof: If a nice strategy were not provoked by a defection on move n, then it would not be collectively stable because it could be invaded by a rule which defected only on move n.

Besides provocability, there is another requirement for a nice rule to be collectively stable. This requirement is that the discount parameter w, be sufficiently large. This is a generalization of the second theorem, which showed that for *TIT FOR TAT* to be collectively stable, w has to be large enough. The idea extends beyond just nice rules to any rule which might be the first to cooperate.

Theorem 5. *Any rule, B, which may be the first to cooperate is collectively stable only when w is sufficiently large.*

Proof: If B cooperates on the first move, $V(ALL\,D\,|\,B) \geq T + wP(1-w)$. But for any B, $R/(1-w) \geq V(B\,|\,B)$ since R is the best B can do with another B by the assumptions that $R > P$ and $R > (S+T)/2$. Therefore $V(ALL\,D\,|\,B) > V(B\,|\,B)$ is so whenever $T + wP/(1-w) > R/(1-w)$. This implies that $ALL\,D$ invades a B which cooperates on the first move whenever $w < ((T-R)/(T-P))$. If B has a positive chance of cooperating on the

---

[8] To be precise, $V(B\,|\,B)$ must also be specified in advance. For example, if B is never the first to defect, $V(B\,|\,B) = R(1-w)$.

first move, then the gain of $V(ALL\,D\,|\,B)$ over $V_1(B\,|\,B)$ can only be nullified if w is sufficiently large. Likewise, if B will not be the first to cooperate until move n, $V_n(ALL\,D\,|\,B) = V_n(B\,|\,B)$ and the gain of $V_{n+1}(ALL\,D\,|\,B)$ over $V_{n+1}(B\,|\,B)$ can only be nullified if w is sufficiently large.

There is one strategy which is *always* collectively stable, that is regardless of the value of w or the payoff parameters T, R, P, and S. This is *ALL D,* the rule which defects no matter what.

Theorem 6. *ALL D is always collectively stable.*

Proof: ALL D is always collectively stable because it always defects and hence it defects whenever required by the condition of the characterization theorem.

This is an important theorem because of its implications for the evolution of cooperation. If we imagine a system starting with individuals who cannot be enticed to cooperate, the collective stability of *ALL D* implies that no single individual can hope to do any better than just to go along and be uncooperative as well. A world of "meanies" can resist invasion by anyone using any other strategy – provided that the newcomers arrive one at a time.

The problem, of course, is that a single newcomer in such a mean world has no one who will reciprocate any cooperation. If the newcomers arrive in small clusters, however, they will have a chance to thrive. The next section shows how this can happen.

6. The implications of clustering

To consider arrival in clusters rather than singly, we need to broaden the idea of "invasion" to invasion by a cluster.[9] As before, we will suppose that strategy B is being used by virtually everyone. But now suppose that a small group of individuals using strategy A arrives and interacts with both the other A's and the native B's. To be specific, suppose that the proportion of the interactions by someone using strategy A with another individual using strategy A is p. Assuming that the A's are rare relative to the B's, virtually all the interactions of B's are with other B's. Then the average score of someone using A is $pV(A\,|\,A) + (1-p)V(A\,|\,B)$ and the average score of someone using B is $V(B\,|\,B)$. Therefore, a *p-cluster of A invades B* if $pV(A\,|\,A) + (1-p)V(A\,|\,B) > V(B\,|\,B)$, where p is the proportion of the interactions by a player using strategy A with another such player. Solving for p, this means that invasion is possible if the newcomers interact enough with each other, namely when

---

[9] For related concepts from biology, see Wilson (1979) and Axelrod and Hamilton (1981).

$$p > \frac{V(B|B) - V(A|B)}{V(A|A) - V(A|B)}. \tag{3}$$

Notice that this assumes that pairing in the interactions is not random. With random pairing, an A would rarely meet another A. Instead, the clustering concept treats the case in which the A's are a trivial part of the environment of the B's, but a nontrivial part of the environment of the other A's.

The striking thing is just how easy invasion of $ALL\ D$ by clusters can be. Specifically, the value of p which is required for invasion by $TIT\ FOR\ TAT$ of a world of $ALL\ D$'s is surprisingly low. For example, suppose the payoff values are those of Figure 1, and that $w = .9$, which corresponds to a 10 per cent chance two interacting players will never meet again. Let A be $TIT\ FOR\ TAT$ and B be $ALL\ D$. Then $V(B|B) = P/(1-w) = 10$; $V(A|B) = S + wP/(1-w) = 9$; and $V(A|A) = R/(1-w) = 30$. Plugging these numbers into Equation (3) shows that a p-cluster of $TIT\ FOR\ TAT$ invades $ALL\ D$ when $p > 1/21$. Thus if the newcomers using $TIT\ FOR\ TAT$ have any more than about 5 per cent of their interactions with others using $TIT\ FOR\ TAT$, they can thrive in a world in which everyone else refuses ever to cooperate.

In this way, a world of meanies can be invaded by a cluster of $TIT\ FOR\ TAT$ – and rather easily at that. To illustrate this point, suppose a business school teacher taught a class to give cooperative behavior a chance, and to reciprocate cooperation from other firms. If the students did, and if they did not disperse too widely (so that a sufficient proportion of their interactions were with others from the same class), then the students would find that their lessons paid off.

When the interactions are expected to be of longer duration (or the time discount factor is not as great), then even less clustering is necessary. For example, if the median game length is two hundred moves (corresponding to $w = .99654$) and the payoff parameters are as given in Figure 1, even one interaction out of a thousand with a like-minded follower of $TIT\ FOR\ TAT$ is enough for the strategy to invade a world of $ALL\ D$'s. Even when the median game length is only two moves ($w = .5$), anything over a fifth of the interactions by the $TIT\ FOR\ TAT$ players with like-minded types is sufficient for invasion to succeed and cooperation to emerge.

The next result shows which strategies are the most efficient at invading $ALL\ D$ with the least amount of clustering. These are the strategies which are best able to discriminate between themselves and $ALL\ D$. A strategy is *maximally discriminating* if it will eventually cooperate even if the other has never cooperated yet, and once it cooperates it will never cooperate again with $ALL\ D$ but will always cooperate with another player using the same strategy.

Theorem 7. *The strategies which can invade ALL D in a cluster with the smallest value of p are those which are maximally discriminating, such as TIT FOR TAT.*

Proof: To be able to invade *ALL D,* a rule must have a positive chance of cooperating first. Stochastic cooperation is not as good as deterministic cooperation with another player using the same rule since stochastic cooperation yields equal probability of S and T, and $(S+T)/2 < R$ in the Prisoner's Dilemma. Therefore, a strategy which can invade with the smallest p must cooperate first on some move, n, even if the other player has never cooperated yet. Employing Equation (3) shows that the rules which invade $B = ALL\ D$ with the lowest value of p are those which have the lowest value of p^*, where $p^* = (V(B|B) - V(A|B))/(V(A|A) - V(A|B))$. The value of p^* is minimized when $V(A|A)$ and $V(A|B)$ are maximized (subject to the constraint that A cooperates for the first time on move n) since $V(A|A) > V(B|B) > V(A|B)$. $V(A|A)$ and $V(A|B)$ are maximized subject to this constraint if, and only if, A is a maximally discriminating rule. (Incidentally, it does not matter for the minimal value of p just when A starts to cooperate.) *TIT FOR TAT* is such a strategy because it always cooperates for $n = 1$, it cooperates only once with *ALL D,* and it always cooperates with another *TIT FOR TAT.*

The final theorem demonstrates that nice rules (those which never defect first) are actually better able than other rules to protect themselves from invasion by a cluster.

Theorem 8. *If a nice strategy cannot be invaded by a single individual, it cannot be invaded by any cluster of individuals either.*

Proof: For a cluster of rule A to invade a population of rule B, there must be a $p \leq 1$ such that $pV(A|A) + (1-p)V(A|B) > V(B|B)$. But if B is nice, then $V(A|A) \leq V(B|B)$. This is so because $V(B|B) = R/(1-w)$ which is the largest value attainable when the other player is using the same strategy. It is the largest value since $R > (S+T)/2$. Since $V(A|A) \leq V(B|B)$, A can invade as a cluster only if $V(A|B) > V(B|B)$. But that is equivalent to A invading as an individual.

This shows that nice rules do not have the structural weakness displayed in *ALL D. ALL D* can withstand invasion by any strategy, as long as the players using other strategies come one at a time. But if they come in clusters (even in rather small clusters), *ALL D* can be invaded. With nice rules, the situation is different. If a nice rule can resist invasion by other rules coming one at a time, then it can resist invasion by clusters, no matter how large. So nice rules can protect themselves in a way that *ALL D* cannot.[10]

In the illustrative case of the Senate, Theorem 8 demonstrates that once cooperation based on reciprocity has become established, it can remain stable even if a cluster of newcomers does not respect this senatorial folkway. And

---

[10] This property is possessed by population mixes of nice rules as well. If no single individual can invade a population of nice rules, no cluster can either.

Theorem 6 has shown that without clustering (or some comparable mechanism) the original pattern of mutual "treachery" could not have been overcome. Perhaps these critical early clusters were based on the boardinghouse arrangements in the capital during the Jeffersonian era (Young, 1966). Or perhaps the state delegations and state party delegations were more critical (Bogue and Marlaire, 1975). But now that the pattern of reciprocity is established, Theorems 2 and 5 show that it is collectively stable, as long as the biennial turnover rate is not too great.

Thus cooperation can emerge even in a world of unconditional defection. The development cannot take place if it is tried only by scattered individuals who have no chance to interact with each other. But cooperation can emerge from small clusters of individuals, as long as these individuals have even a small proportion of their interactions with each other. Moreover, if nice strategies (those which are never the first to defect) eventually come to be adopted by virtually everyone, then those individuals can afford to be generous in dealing with any others. The population of nice rules can also protect themselves against clusters of individuals using any other strategy just as well as they can protect themselves against single individuals. But for a nice strategy to be stable in the collective sense, it must be provocable. So mutual cooperation can emerge in a world of egoists without central control, by starting with a cluster of individuals who rely on reciprocity.

For a fuller treatment of these themes see Robert Axelrod, *The Evolution of Cooperation* (1984).

References

Art, R. J. (1968). *The TFX Decision: McNamara and the Military.* Boston: Little, Brown.

Axelrod, R. (1980a). "Effective Choice in the Prisoner's Dilemma." *Journal of Conflict Resolution* 24: 3–25.

(1980b). "More Effective Choice in the Prisoner's Dilemma." *Journal of Conflict Resolution* 24: 379–403.

(1984). *The Evolution of Cooperation.* New York: Basic Books.

Axelrod, R., and W. D. Hamilton (1981). "The Evolution of Cooperation." *Science* 211: 1390–96.

Bogue, A. G., and M. P. Marlaire (1975). "Of Mess and Men: The Boardinghouse and Congressional Voting, 1821–1842." *American Journal of Political Science* 19: 207–30.

Dawkins, R. (1976). *The Selfish Gene.* New York: Oxford University Press.

Hamilton, W. D. (1964). "The Genetical Theory of Social Behavior (I and II)." *Journal of Theoretical Biology* 7: 1–16, 17–32.

(1967). "Extraordinary Sex Ratios." *Science* 156: 477–88.

Hardin, G. (1968). "The Tragedy of the Commons." *Science* 162: 1243–48.

Hardin, R. (1971). "Collective Action as an Agreeable *n*-Prisoner's Dilemma." *Behavioral Science* 16: 472–81.

Hinckley, B. (1972). "Coalitions in Congress: Size and Ideological Distance." *Midwest Journal of Political Science* 26: 197–207.

Hirshleifer, J. (1978). "Natural Economy versus Political Economy." *Journal of Social and Biological Structures* 1: 319–37.

Howard, N. (1971). *Paradoxes of Rationality: Theory of Metagames and Political Behavior.* Cambridge, MA: MIT Press.

Jervis, R. (1978). "Cooperation under the Security Dilemma." *World Politics* 30: 167–214.

Jones, C. O. (1977). "Will Reform Change Congress?" In Lawrence C. Dodd and Bruce I. Oppenheimer, eds., *Congress Reconsidered.* New York: Praeger.

Kurz, M. (1977). "Altruistic Equilibrium." In B. Balassa and R. Nelson eds., *Economic Progress, Private Values, and Public Policy.* Amsterdam: North Holland.

Laver, M. (1977). "Intergovernmental Policy on Multinational Corporations, A Simple Model of Tax Bargaining." *European Journal of Political Research* 5: 363–80.

Luce, R. D., and H. Raiffa (1957). *Games and Decisions.* New York: Wiley.

Lumsden, M. (1973). "The Cyprus Conflict as a Prisoner's Dilemma." *Journal of Conflict Resolution* 17: 7–32.

Matthews, D. R. (1960). *U.S. Senators and Their World.* Chapel Hill: University of North Carolina Press.

Mayer, M. (1974). *The Bankers.* New York: Ballantine.

Mayhew, D. R. (1975). *Congress: The Electoral Connection.* New Haven, CT: Yale University Press.

Maynard Smith, J., and R. Price (1973). "The Logic of Animal Conflict," *Nature* 246: 15–18.

    (1974). "The Theory of Games and the Evolution of Animal Conflict." *Journal of Theoretical Biology* 47: 209–21.

    (1978). "The Evolution of Behavior." *Scientific American* 239: 176–92.

Olson, M., Jr. (1965). *The Logic of Collective Action.* Cambridge, MA: Harvard University Press.

Ornstein, N., R. L. Peabody, and D. W. Rhode (1977). "The Changing Senate: From the 1950s to the 1970s." In L. C. Dodd and B. I. Oppenheimer, eds., *Congress Reconsidered.* New York: Praeger.

Patterson, S. (1978). "The Semi-Sovereign Congress." In A. King (ed.), *The New American Political System.* Washington, DC: American Enterprise Institute.

Polsby, N. (1968). "The Institutionalization of the U.S. House of Representatives." *American Political Science Review* 62: 144–68.

Rapoport, A. (1960). *Fights, Games, and Debates.* Ann Arbor: University of Michigan.

Schelling, T. C. (1960). *The Strategy of Conflict.* Cambridge, MA: Harvard University Press.

    (1973). "Hockey Helmets, Concealed Weapons, and Daylight Savings: A Study of Binary Choices with Externalities." *Journal of Conflict Resolution* 17: 381–428.

    (1978). "Micromotives and Macrobehavior." In T. Schelling, ed., *Micromotives and Microbehavior.* New York: Norton, pp. 9–43.

Shubik, M. (1959). *Strategy and Market Structure: Competition, Oligopoly, and the Theory of Games.* New York: Wiley.

Smith, M. B. (1906). *The First Forty Years of Washington Society.* New York: Scribner's.

Snyder, G. H. (1971). "'Prisoner's Dilemma' and 'Chicken' Models in International Politics." *International Studies Quarterly* 15: 66–103.

Taylor, M. (1976). *Anarchy and Cooperation.* New York: Wiley.

Trivers, R. L. (1971). "The Evolution of Reciprocal Altruism." *Quarterly Review of Biology* 46: 35–57.

Warner, R., (trans.) (1960). *War Commentaries of Caesar.* New York: New American Library.

Wilson, D. S. (1979). *Natural Selection of Populations and Communities.* Menlo Park, CA: Benjamin/Cummings.

Young, J. S. (1966). *The Washington Community, 1800–1828.* New York: Harcourt, Brace & World.

13. Maximization constrained: the rationality of cooperation

David Gauthier

1

What follows these introductory remarks is part of chapter six of my book, *Morals by Agreement*.[1] In the first section of the chapter, not included here, I discuss the problem posed by Hobbes's Foole, who "hath sayd in his heart, there is no such thing as Justice... seriously alleaging, that every mans conservation, and contentment, being committed to his own care, there could be no reason, why every man might not do what he thought conduced thereunto: and therefore also to make, or not make; keep, or not keep Covenants, was not against Reason, when it conduced to one's benefit."[2]

Think of the state of nature as a condition in which each person seeks straightforwardly to maximize her individual utility. In interaction with her fellows, then, each chooses what she believes to be a utility-maximizing response to the choices she expects the others to make. Is it always possible for each person to be successful – that is, for each to act in a way that is utility-maximizing given the actions of the others? No – not if we take "action" in its ordinary sense. If you and I must choose between going to Toronto and going to Pittsburgh, and I want to go where you go, and you want to go where I do not go, then one of us will act in a way that is not utility-maximizing, given what the other does. But if we replace "action" by "strategy," where a strategy is a probability distribution over possible actions, then it is always possible for each person to be successful – for each person's strategy to be utility-maximizing given the others' strategies.[3] (There are

© David Gauthier 1986. Reprinted from *Morals by Agreement* by David Gauthier (1986) by permission of Oxford University Press.
[1] Published by Oxford University Press, 1986.
[2] Hobbes (1651), ch. 15.
[3] This is proved by John F. Nash (1951).

some qualifications here; there must be only finitely many persons each with only finitely many actions. But they are not important.)

Suppose then that everyone is successful. We say that the outcome is in equilibrium – no one could do better for herself, given what the others do. No one could benefit from a unilateral change of strategy. But all may not be well. For although each is doing her best for herself, given what the others do, it may be possible for all to do better. The outcome may not be optimal (in the Pareto sense); some alternative might afford some persons greater utility and no person lesser utility.

In every (finite) situation, there is at least one outcome in equilibrium and at least one optimal outcome, but in some situations, no outcome is both in equilibrium and optimal. The Prisoner's Dilemma is the most familiar example of a situation with a unique equilibrium (mutual confession) which is not optimal (since mutual non-confession is better for both prisoners). If each person maximizes her utility given the strategies of others, then at least some person receives less utility than she might given each other person's utility. And if each person receives as much utility as she can, given each other person's utility, then at least some person does not maximize her utility given the strategies of others.

In the state of nature, each seeks to maximize her own utility. And so in some situations the outcome is not optimal. This provides a basis for society, considered (in Rawlsian terms) as "a cooperative venture for mutual advantage."[4] Think of a cooperative venture as implementing a joint choice, without requiring each person's strategy to be utility-maximizing given the others. And think of mutual advantage as affording each person greater utility than she would expect otherwise – greater, then, than she would expect were each to maximize her utility given the others' choices.

The Foole then says, "Agree to a cooperative venture, but only if you expect agreement to pay." This is sound advice. But the Foole goes on to say, "And adhere to a cooperative venture, but only if you expect adherence to pay." This is not sound advice. In effect, the Foole advises you to adhere only if it proves utility-maximizing. But then no one does better than if each were to maximize her utility given the others' choices. The venture does not improve on the state of nature.

On the Foole's view, reason stands in the way of cooperation. What follows seeks to refute the Foole – to exhibit the rational basis, not merely for entering, but for adhering to, cooperative ventures.

In my discussion I refer to the preceding chapter five of the book, in which I argue that rational cooperation satisfies the principle of minimax relative concession. When straightforwardly maximizing behavior yields a sub-optimal outcome, there may be many different possible joint choices or cooperative ventures, each of which would afford mutual advantage. Not

[4] Rawls (1971), p. 4.

every such venture will be rationally acceptable to all concerned. Think of persons bargaining over possible cooperative ventures.[5] Each considers her share of the benefits from cooperation, as compared with others' shares. Each begins by claiming as large a share as possible – the greatest utility for herself compatible with no one doing worse than in the absence of cooperation. To reach agreement on a particular venture from these claims, each must concede a part of her claim, but no one can be rationally expected to concede more, proportionately, than she recognizes some person must concede to reach agreement. Thus rational bargainers agree on that cooperative venture for which the maximum proportionate or relative concession made by any person is a minimum.

I refer also to condition A' for strategic rationality. The underlying condition A is that each person's choice must be a rational response to the choices he expects the others to make. The usual interpretation of this treats a rational response as a utility-maximizing response. But this leaves everyone in the state of nature. Condition A' states that each person's choice must be a fair optimizing response (where fairness is captured by the requirements of minimax concession) to the choices he expects the others to make, provided such a response is available to him; otherwise, his choice must be a utility-maximizing response. I defend condition A'.

2.1

The Foole, and those who share his conception of practical reason, must suppose that there are potentialities for cooperation to which each person would rationally agree, were he to expect the agreement to be carried out, but that remain unactualized, since each rationally expects that someone, perhaps himself, perhaps another, would not adhere to the agreement. In chapter five we argued that cooperation is rational if each cooperator may expect a utility nearly equal to what he would be assigned by the principle of minimax relative concession. The Foole does not dispute the necessity of this condition but denies its sufficiency. He insists that for it to be rational to comply with an agreement to cooperate, the utility an individual may expect from cooperation must also be no less than what he would expect were he to violate his agreement. And he then argues that for it to be rational to agree to cooperate, then, although one need not consider it rational to comply oneself, one must believe it rational for the others to comply. Given that everyone is rational, fully informed, and correct in his expectations, the Foole supposes that cooperation is actualized only if each person expects a utility from cooperation no less than his non-compliance utility. The benefits that could be realized through cooperative arrangements that do not

---

[5] The account of bargaining sketched here is developed in several of my papers, beginning with (1974) and culminating in (1985c).

afford each person at least his non-compliance utility remain forever beyond the reach of rational human beings – forever denied us because our very rationality would lead us to violate the agreements necessary to realize these benefits. Such agreements will not be made.

The Foole rejects what would seem to be the ordinary view that given neither unforeseen circumstances nor misrepresentation of terms, it is rational to comply with an agreement if it is rational to make it. He insists that holders of this view have failed to think out the full implications of the maximizing conception of practical rationality. In choosing, one takes one's stand in the present and looks to the expected utility that will result from each possible action. What has happened may affect this utility; that one has agreed may affect the utility one expects from doing, or not doing, what would keep the agreement. But what has happened provides in itself no reason for choice. That one had reason for making agreement can give one reason for keeping it only by affecting the utility of compliance. To think otherwise is to reject utility-maximization.

Let us begin our answer to the Foole with the distinction between an individual strategy and a joint strategy.[6] An individual strategy is a lottery over the possible actions of a single actor. A joint strategy is a lottery over possible outcomes. Cooperators have joint strategies available to them.

We may think of participation in a cooperation activity, such as a hunt, in which each huntsman has his particular role coordinated with that of the others, as the implementation of a single joint strategy. We may also extend the notion to include participation in a practice, such as the making and keeping of promises, where each person's behavior is predicated on the conformity of others to the practice.

An individual is not able to ensure that he acts on a joint strategy since whether he does depends, not only on what he intends, but on what those with whom he interacts intend. But we may say that an individual bases his action on a joint strategy insofar as he intentionally chooses what the strategy requires of him. Normally, of course, one bases one's action on a joint strategy only if one expects those with whom one interacts to do so as well, so that one expects actually to act on that strategy. But we need not import such an expectation into the conception of basing one's action on a joint strategy.

A person cooperates with his fellows only if he bases his actions on a joint strategy; to agree to cooperate is to agree to employ a joint rather than an individual strategy. The Foole insists that it is rational to cooperate only if the utility one expects from acting on the cooperative joint strategy is at least equal to the utility one would expect were one to act instead on one's best individual strategy. This defeats the end of cooperation, which is in

6 This answer to the Foole supersedes my discussion in (1975).

effect to substitute a joint strategy for individual strategies in situations in which this substitution is to everyone's benefit.

A joint strategy is fully rational only if it yields an optimal outcome or, in other words, only if it affords each person who acts on it the maximum utility compatible in the situation with the utility afforded each other person who acts on the strategy. Thus we may say that a person acting on a rational joint strategy maximizes his utility, subject to the constraint set by the utilities it affords to every other person. An individual strategy is rational if, and only if, it maximizes one's utility given the *strategies* adopted by the other persons; a joint strategy is rational only if (but not if, and only if) it maximizes one's utility given the *utilities* afforded to the other persons.

Let us say that a *straightforward* maximizer is a person who seeks to maximize his utility given the strategies of those with whom he interacts. A *constrained* maximizer, on the other hand, is a person who seeks in some situations to maximize her utility, given not the strategies but the utilities of those with whom she interacts. The Foole accepts the rationality of straightforward maximization. We, in defending condition A' for strategic rationality, accept the rationality of constrained maximization.

A constrained maximizer has a conditional disposition to base her actions on a joint strategy, without considering whether some individual strategy would yield her greater expected utility. But not all constraint could be rational; we must specify the characteristics of the conditional disposition. We shall therefore identify a constrained maximizer as someone (i) who is conditionally disposed to base her actions on a joint strategy or practice should the utility she expects were everyone so to base his action (a) be no less than what she would expect were everyone to employ individual strategies, and (b) approach what she would expect from the cooperative outcome determined by minimax relative concession, and (ii) who actually acts on this conditional disposition should her expected utility be greater than what she would expect were everyone to employ individual strategies. Or, in other words, a constrained maximizer is ready to cooperate in ways that, if followed by all, would yield outcomes that she would find beneficial and not unfair, and she does cooperate should she expect an actual practice or activity to be beneficial. In determining the latter, she must take into account the possibility that some persons will fail, or refuse, to act cooperatively. Henceforth, unless we specifically state otherwise, we shall understand by a constrained maximizer one with this particular disposition.

There are three points in our characterization of constrained maximization that should be noted. The first is that a constrained maximizer is conditionally disposed to act not only on the unique joint strategy that would be prescribed by a rational bargain, but on any joint strategy that affords her a utility approaching what she would expect from fully rational cooperation. The range of acceptable joint strategies is, and must be left, unspecified. The idea is that in real interaction it is reasonable to accept cooperative arrangements that fall short of the ideal of full rationality and fairness provided they do not fall too far short. At some point, of course, one decides to ignore a joint strategy, even if acting on it would afford one an expected utility greater than one would expect were everyone to employ an individual strategy, because one hopes thereby to obtain agreement on, or acquiescence in, another joint strategy which in being fairer is also more favorable to oneself. At precisely what point one decides this we make no attempt to say. We simply defend a conception of constrained maximization that does not require that all acceptable joint strategies be ideal.

The second point is that a constrained maximizer does not base her actions on a joint strategy whenever a nearly fair and optimal outcome would result were everyone to do likewise. Her disposition to cooperate is conditional on her expectation that she will benefit in comparison with the utility she could expect were no one to cooperate. Thus she must estimate the likelihood that others involved in the prospective practice or interaction will act cooperatively and calculate not the utility she would expect were all to cooperate, but the utility she would expect if she cooperates, given her estimate of the degree to which others will cooperate. Only if this exceeds what she would expect from universal non-cooperation does her conditional disposition to constraint actually manifest itself in a decision to base her actions on the cooperative joint strategy.

Thus, faced with persons whom she believes to be straightforward maximizers, a constrained maximizer does not play into their hands by basing her actions on the joint strategy she would like everyone to accept, but rather, to avoid being exploited, she behaves as a straightforward maximizer, acting on that individual strategy that maximizes her utility given the strategies she expects the others to employ. A constrained maximizer makes reasonably certain that she is among like-disposed persons before she actually constrains her direct pursuit of maximum utility.

But note that a constrained maximizer may find herself required to act in such a way that she would have been better off had she not entered into cooperation. She may be engaged in a cooperative activity that, given the willingness of her fellows to do their part, she expects to be fair and beneficial, but that, should chance so befall, requires her to act so that she incurs some loss greater than had she never engaged herself in the endeavor. Here she would still be disposed to comply, acting in a way that results in real disadvantage to herself, because given her *ex ante* beliefs about the dispositions of her fellows and the prospects of benefit, participation in the activity affords her greater expected utility than non-participation.

And this brings us to the third point, that constrained maximization is not straightforward maximization in its most effective disguise. The constrained maximizer is not merely the person who, taking a larger view than her fellows, serves her overall interest by sacrificing the immediate benefits of ignoring joint strategies and violating cooperative arrangements in order to obtain the long-term benefits of being trusted by others.[7] Such a person exhibits no real constraint. The constrained maximizer does not reason more effectively about how to maximize her utility, but reasons in a different way. We may see this most clearly by considering how each faces the decision whether to base her action on a joint strategy. The constrained maximizer considers (i) whether the outcome, should everyone do so, be nearly fair and optimal, and (ii) whether the outcome she realistically expects should she do so affords her greater utility than universal non-cooperation. If both of these conditions are satisfied, she bases her action on the joint strategy. The straightforward maximizer considers simply whether the outcome he realistically expects, should he base his action on the joint strategy, affords him greater utility than the outcome he would expect were he to act on any alternative strategy – taking into account, of course, long-term as well as short-term effects. Only if this condition is satisfied, does he base his action on the joint strategy.

Consider a purely isolated interaction in which both parties know that how each chooses will have no bearing on how each fares in other interactions. Suppose that the situation has the familiar Prisoner's Dilemma structure; each benefits from mutual cooperation but each benefits from non-cooperation whatever the other does. In such a situation, a straightforward maximizer chooses not to cooperate. A constrained maximizer chooses to cooperate if, given her estimate of whether or not her partner will choose to cooperate, her own expected utility is greater than the utility she would expect from the non-cooperative outcome.

Constrained maximizers can thus obtain cooperative benefits that are unavailable to straightforward maximizers, however farsighted the latter may be. But straightforward maximizers can, on occasion, exploit unwary constrained maximizers. Each supposes her disposition to be rational. But who is right?

2.2

To demonstrate the rationality of suitably constrained maximization we solve a problem of rational choice. We consider what a rational individual would choose, given the alternatives of adopting straightforward maximization and of adopting constrained maximization, as his disposition for strategic behavior. Although this choice is about interaction, to make it is not to engage in interaction. Taking others' dispositions as fixed, the individual

---

[7] Thus constrained maximization is not parallel to such strategies as "Tit-for-Tat" that have been advocated for so-called iterated Prisoner's Dilemmas. Constrained maximizers may cooperate even if neither expects her choice to affect future situations. There is no appeal to the kind of reciprocity needed by Robert Axelrod's account. [See Chapter 12.]

reasons parametrically to his own best disposition. Thus he compares the expected utility of disposing himself to maximize utility given others' expected strategy choices with the utility of disposing himself to cooperate with others in bringing about nearly fair and optimal outcomes.

To choose between these dispositions, a person needs to consider only those situations in which they would yield different behavior. If both would be expressed in a maximizing individual strategy or if both would lead one to base action on the joint strategy one expects from others, then their utility expectations are identical. But if the disposition to constraint would be expressed in basing action on a joint strategy whereas the disposition to maximize straightforwardly would be expressed in defecting from the joint strategy, then their utility expectations differ. Only situations giving rise to such differences need be considered. These situations must satisfy two conditions. First, they must afford the prospect of mutually beneficial and fair cooperation, since otherwise constraint would be pointless. And second, they must afford some prospect for individually beneficial detection, since otherwise no constraint would be needed to realize the mutual benefits.

We suppose, then, an individual, considering what disposition to adopt, for situations in which his expected utility is u should each person act on an individual strategy, u' should all act on a cooperative joint strategy, and u'' should he act on an individual strategy and the others base their actions on a cooperative joint strategy, and u is less than u' (so that he benefits from cooperation as required by the first condition) and u' in turn is less than u'' (so that he benefits from defection as required by the second condition).

Consider these two arguments which this person might put to himself:

Argument (1). Suppose I adopt straightforward maximization. Then if I expect the others to base their actions on a joint strategy, I defect to my best individual strategy and expect a utility, u''. If I expect the others to act on individual strategies, then so do I, and expect a utility, u. If the probability that others will base their actions on a joint strategy is p, then my overall expected utility is $(pu'' + (1-p)u)$.

Suppose I adopt constrained maximization. Then if I expect the others to base their actions on a joint strategy, so do I, and expect a utility u'. If I expect the others to act on individual strategies, then so do I, and expect a utility, u. Thus my overall expected utility is $(pu' + (1-p)u)$.

Since u'' is greater than u', $(pu'' + (1-p)u)$ is greater than $(pu' + (1-p)u)$, for any value of p other than 0 (and for $p = 0$, the two are equal). Therefore, to maximize my overall expectation of utility, I should adopt straightforward maximization.

Argument (2). Suppose I adopt straightforward maximization. Then I must expect the others to employ maximizing individual strategies in interacting with me; so do I, and expect a utility, u.

Suppose I adopt constrained maximization. Then if the others are conditionally disposed to constrained maximization, I may expect them to base their actions on a cooperative joint strategy in interacting with me; so do I, and expect a utility u'. If they are not so disposed, I employ a maximizing strategy and expect u as before. If the probability that others are disposed to constrained maximization is p, then my overall expected utility is $(pu' + (1-p)u)$.

Since u' is greater than u, $(pu' + (1-p)u)$ is greater than u for any value of p other than 0 (and for $p = 0$, the two are equal). Therefore, to maximize my overall expectation of utility, I should adopt constrained maximization.

Since these arguments yield opposed conclusions, they cannot both be sound. The first has the form of a dominance argument. In any situation in which others act non-cooperatively, one may expect the same utility whether one is disposed to straightforward or to constrained maximization. In any situation in which others act cooperatively, one may expect a greater utility if one is disposed to straightforward maximization. Therefore, one should adopt straightforward maximization. But this argument would be valid only if the probability of others acting cooperatively were, as the argument assumes, independent of one's own disposition. And this is not the case. Since persons disposed to cooperation only act cooperatively with those whom they suppose to be similarly disposed, a straightforward maximizer does not have the opportunities to benefit which present themselves to the constrained maximizer. Thus argument (1) fails.

Argument (2) takes into account what argument (1) ignores – the difference between the way in which constrained maximizers interact with those similarly disposed and the way in which they interact with straightforward maximizers. Only those disposed to keep their agreements are rationally acceptable as parties to agreements. Constrained maximizers are able to make beneficial agreements with their fellows that the straightforward cannot, not because the latter would be unwilling to agree, but because they would not be admitted as parties to agreement given their disposition to violation. Straightforward maximizers are disposed to take advantage of their fellows should the opportunity arise; knowing this, their fellows would prevent such opportunity arising. With the same opportunities, straightforward maximizers would necessarily obtain greater benefits. A dominance argument establishes this. But because they differ in their dispositions, straightforward and constrained maximizers differ also in their opportunities, to the benefit of the latter.

But argument (2) unfortunately contains an undefended assumption. A person's expectations about how others will interact with him depend strictly on his own choice of disposition only if that choice is known by the others. What we have shown is that if the straightforward maximizer and the constrained maximizer appear in their true colors, then the constrained maximizer must do better. But need each so appear? The Foole may agree, under the pressure of our argument and its parallel in the second argument we ascribed to Hobbes, that the question to be asked is not whether it is or is not rational to keep (particular) covenants, but whether it is or is not rational to be (generally) disposed to the keeping of covenants, and he may recognize that he cannot win by pleading the cause of straightforward maximization in a direct way. But may he not win by linking straightforward maximization to the appearance of constraint? Is not the Foole's ultimate argument that the truly prudent person, the fully rational utility-maximizer, must seek to appear trustworthy, an upholder of his agreements? For then he will not be excluded from the cooperative arrangements of his fellows, but will be welcomed as a partner, while he awaits opportunities to benefit at their expense – and, preferably, without their knowledge, so that he may retain the guise of constraint and trustworthiness.

There is a short way to defeat this maneuver. Since our argument is to be applied to ideally rational persons, we may simply add another idealizing assumption and take our persons to be *transparent*.[8] Each is directly aware of the dispositions of his fellows and so aware whether he is interacting with straightforward or constrained maximizers. Deception is impossible; the Foole must appear as he is.

But to assume transparency may seem to rob our argument of much of its interest. We want to relate our idealizing assumptions to the real world. If constrained maximization defeats straightforward maximization only if all persons are transparent, then we shall have failed to show that under actual, or realistically possible, conditions, moral constraints are rational. We shall have refuted the Foole but at the price of robbing our refutation of all practical import.

However, transparency proves to be a stronger assumption than our argument requires. We may appeal instead to a more realistic *translucency,* supposing that persons are neither transparent nor opaque, so that their disposition to cooperate or not may be ascertained by others, not with certainty, but as more than mere guesswork. Opaque beings would be condemned to seek political solutions for those problems of natural interaction that could not be met by the market. But we shall show that for beings as translucent as we may reasonably consider ourselves to be, moral solutions are rationally available.

2.3

If persons are translucent, then constrained maximizers (CMs) will sometimes fail to recognize each other and will then interact non-cooperatively even if cooperation would have been mutually beneficial. CMs will sometimes

[8] That the discussion in my (1975) assumes transparency was pointed out to me by Derek Parfit. See his discussion of "the self-interest theory" in Parfit (1984). See also the discussion of my (1975) in Darwall (1983), especially pp. 197–98.

fail to identify straightforward maximizers (SMs) and will then act cooperatively; if the SMs correctly identify the CMs, they will be able to take advantage of them. Translucent CMs must expect to do less well in interaction
than would transparent CMs; translucent SMs must expect to do better than
would transparent SMs. Although it would be rational to choose to be a CM
were one transparent, it need not be rational if one is only translucent. Let
us examine the conditions under which the decision to dispose oneself to
constrained maximization is rational for translucent persons and ask if these
are (or may be) the conditions in which we find ourselves.

As in the preceding subsection, we need consider only situations in which
CMs and SMs may fare differently. These are situations that afford both the
prospect of mutually beneficial cooperation (in relation to non-cooperation)
and individually beneficial defection (in relation to cooperation). Let us simplify by supposing that the non-cooperative outcome results unless (1) those
interacting are CMs who achieve mutual recognition, in which case the cooperative outcome results, or (2) those interacting include CMs who fail to
recognize SMs but are themselves recognized, in which case the outcome
affords the SMs the benefits of individual defection and the CMs the costs
of having advantage taken of mistakenly basing their actions on a cooperative strategy. We ignore the inadvertent taking of advantage when CMs mistake their fellows for SMs.

There are then four possible payoffs: non-cooperation, cooperation, defection, and exploitation (as we may call the outcome for the person whose
supposed partner defects from the joint strategy on which he bases his action). For the typical situation, we assign defection the value one, cooperation u'' (less than one), non-cooperation u' (less than u''), and exploitation
zero (less than u'). We now introduce three probabilities. The first, p, is the
probability that CMs will achieve mutual recognition and so successfully
cooperate. The second, q, is the probability that CMs will fail to recognize
SMs but will themselves be recognized, so that defection and exploitation
will result. The third, r, is the probability that a randomly selected member
of the population is a CM. (We assume that everyone is a CM or a SM,
so the probability that a randomly selected person is a SM is $(1-r)$.) The
values of p, q, and r must, of course, fall between zero and one.

Let us now calculate expected utilities for CMs and SMs in situations affording both the prospect of mutually beneficial cooperation and individually beneficial defection. A CM expects the utility u' unless (1) she succeeds
in cooperating with other CMs or (2) she is exploited by a SM. The probability of (1) is the combined probability that she interacts with a CM, r,
and that they achieve mutual recognition, p, or rp. In this case, she gains
$(u''-u')$ over her non-cooperative expectation u'. Thus the effect of (1) is to
increase her utility expectation by a value $(rp(u''-u'))$. The probability of
(2) is the combined probability that she interacts with a SM, $1-r$, and that
she fails to recognize him but is recognized, q, or $(1-r)q$. In this case she

received zero, so she loses her non-cooperative expectation u'. Thus the effect of (2) is to reduce her utility expectation by a value $((1-r)qu')$. Taking both (1) and (2) into account, a CM expects the utility $(u'+(rp(u''-u')))-(1-r)qu')$.

A SM expects the utility u' unless he exploits a CM. The probability of this is the combined probability that he interacts with a CM, r, and that he recognizes her but is not recognized by her, q, or rq. In this case he gains $(1-u')$ over his non-cooperative expectation u'. Thus the effect is to increase his utility expectation by a value $(rq(1-u'))$. A SM thus expects the utility $(u'+(rq(1-u')))$.

It is rational to dispose oneself to constrained maximization if, and only if, the utility expected by a CM is greater than the utility expected by a SM, which obtains if, and only if, p/q is greater than $((1-u')/(u''-u')+((1-r)u')/(r(u''-u')))$.

The first term of this expression, $((1-u')/(u''-u'))$, relates the gain from defection to the gain through cooperation. The value of defection is of course greater than that of cooperation, so this term is greater than one. The second term, $(((1-r)u')/(r(u''-u')))$, depends for its value on r. If $r=0$ (that is, if there are no CMs in the population), then its value is infinite. As r increases, the value of the expression decreases, until if $r=1$ (that is, if there are only CMs in the population) its value is zero.

We may now draw two important conclusions. First, it is rational to dispose oneself to constrained maximization only if the ratio of p to q, that is, the ratio between the probability that an interaction involving CMs will result in cooperation and the probability that an interaction involving CMs and SMs will involve exploitation and defection, is greater than the ratio between the gain from defection and the gain through cooperation. If everyone in the population is a CM, then we may replace 'only if' by 'if, and only, if' in this statement, but in general it is only a necessary condition of the rationality of the disposition to constrained maximization.

Second, as the proportion of CMs in the population increases (so that the value of r increases), the value of the ratio of p to q that is required for it to be rational to dispose oneself to constrained maximization decreases. The more constrained maximizers there are, the greater the risks a constrained maximizer may rationally accept of failing to achieve mutual recognition for cooperation with other CMs and failing to recognize SMs and so being exploited by them. However, these risks, and particularly the latter, must remain relatively small.

We may illustrate these conclusions by introducing typical numerical values for cooperation and non-cooperation and then considering different values for r. One may suppose that, on the whole, there is no reason that the typical gain from defection over cooperation would be either greater or smaller than the typical gain from cooperation over non-cooperation and, in turn, no reason that the latter gain would be greater or smaller that the typical loss from non-cooperation to exploitation. And so, since defection has the value one and exploitation zero, let us assign cooperation the value two-thirds and non-cooperation one-third.

The gain from defection, $(1-u')$, thus is two-thirds; the gain through cooperation, $(u''-u')$, is one-third. Since p/q must exceed $((1-u')/(u''-u') + ((1-r)u')/(r(u''-u')))$ for constrained maximization to be rational, in our typical case the probability p that CMs successfully cooperate must be more than twice the probability q that CMs are exploited by SMs, however great the probability r that a randomly selected person is a CM. In general, p/q must be greater than $(2+(1-r)/r)$ or, equivalently, greater than $(r+1)/r$. If three persons out of four are CMs, so that $r = 3/4$, then p/q must be greater than 7/3; if one person out of two is a CM, then p/q must be greater than three; if one person in four is a CM, then p/q must be greater than five.

Suppose a population evenly divided between constrained and straightforward maximizers. If the constrained maximizers are able to cooperate successfully in two-thirds of their encounters and to avoid being exploited by straightforward maximizers in four-fifths of their encounters, then constrained maximizers may expect to do better than their fellows. Of course, the even distribution will not be stable; it will be rational for the straightforward maximizers to change their disposition. These persons are sufficiently translucent for them to find morality rational.

2.4

A constrained maximizer is conditionally disposed to cooperate in ways that, followed by all, would yield nearly optimal and fair outcomes and does cooperate in such ways when she may actually expect to benefit. In the two preceding subsections, we have argued that one is rationally so disposed if persons are transparent or persons are sufficiently translucent and enough are like-minded. But our argument has not appealed explicitly to the particular requirement that cooperative practices and activities be nearly optimal and fair. We have insisted that the cooperative outcome afford one a utility greater than non-cooperation, but this is much weaker than the insistence that it approach the outcome required by minimax relative concession.

But note that the larger the gain from cooperation, $(u''-u')$, the smaller the minimum value of p/q that makes the disposition to constrained maximization rational. We may take p/q to be a measure of translucency; the more translucent constrained maximizers are, the better they are at achieving cooperation among themselves (increasing p) and avoiding exploitation by straightforward maximizers (decreasing q). Thus, as practices and activities fall short of optimality, the expected value of cooperation, u'', decreases, and so the degree of translucency required to make cooperation rational increases. And as practices and activities fall short of fairness, the expected value of cooperation for those with less than fair shares decreases, and so the degree of translucency required to make cooperation rational for them increases. Thus our argument does appeal implicitly to the requirement that cooperation yield nearly fair and optimal outcomes.

But there is a further argument in support of our insistence that the conditional disposition to cooperate be restricted to practices and activities yielding nearly optimal and fair outcomes. And this argument turns, as does our general argument for constraint, on how one's dispositions affect the characteristics of the situations in which one may reasonably expect to find oneself. Let us call a person who is disposed to cooperate in ways that, followed by all, yield nearly optimal and fair outcomes, *narrowly compliant*. And let us call a person who is disposed to cooperate in ways that, followed by all, merely yield her some benefit in relation to universal non-cooperation, *broadly compliant*. We need not deny that a broadly compliant person would expect to benefit in some situations in which a narrowly compliant person would not. But in many other situations a broadly compliant person must expect to lose by her disposition. For insofar as she is known to be broadly compliant, others will have every reason to maximize their utilities at her expense, by offering "cooperation" on terms that offer her but little more than she could expect from non-cooperation. Since a broadly compliant person is disposed to seize whatever benefit a joint strategy may afford her, she finds herself with opportunities for but little benefit.

Since the narrowly compliant person is always prepared to accept cooperative arrangements based on the principle of minimax relative concession, she is prepared to cooperate whenever cooperation can be mutually beneficial on terms equally rational and fair to all. In refusing other terms, she does not diminish her prospects for cooperation with other rational persons, and she ensures that those not disposed to fair cooperation do not enjoy the benefits of any cooperation, thus making their unfairness costly to themselves, and so irrational.

2.5

We should not suppose it is rational to dispose oneself to constrained maximization if one does not also dispose oneself to exclude straightforward maximizers from the benefits realizable by cooperation. Hobbes notes that those who think they may with reason violate their covenants may not be received into society except by the error of their fellows. If their fellows fall into that error, then they will soon find that it pays no one to keep covenants. Failing to exclude straightforward maximizers from the benefits of cooperative arrangements does not, and cannot, enable them to share in the long-run benefits of cooperation; instead, it ensures that the arrangements will prove ineffective, so that there are no benefits to share. And then there is nothing to be gained by constrained maximization; one might as well join the straightforward maximizers in their descent to the natural condition of humankind.

Nor should we suppose it rational to dispose oneself to constrained maximization if one does not cultivate the ability to detect the dispositions of others. Consider once again the probabilities p and q, the probability that CMs will achieve mutual recognition and cooperate, and the probability that CMs will fail to recognize SMs but will be recognized by them and so be exploited. It is obvious that CMs benefit from increasing p and decreasing q. And this is reflected in our calculation of expected utility for CMs; the value of $(u' + (rp(u'' - u')) - (1 - r)qu')$ increases as p increases and as q decreases.

What determines the values of p and q? p depends on the ability of CMs to detect the sincerity of other CMs and to reveal their own sincerity to them. q depends on the ability of CMs to detect the insincerity of SMs and to conceal their own sincerity from them and the ability of SMs to detect the sincerity of CMs and conceal their own insincerity from them. Since any increase in the ability to reveal one's sincerity to other CMs is apt to be offset by a decrease in the ability to conceal one's sincerity from SMs, a CM is likely to rely primarily on her ability to detect the dispositions of others, rather than on her ability to reveal or conceal her own.

The ability to detect the dispositions of others must be well developed in a rational CM. Failure to develop this ability, or neglect of its exercise, will preclude one from benefitting from constrained maximization. And it can then appear that constraint is irrational. But what is actually irrational is the failure to cultivate or exercise the ability to detect others' sincerity or insincerity.

Both CMs and SMs must expect to benefit from increasing their ability to detect the disposition of others. But if both endeavor to maximize their abilities (or the expected utility, net of costs, of so doing), then CMs may expect to improve their position in relation to SMs. The benefits gained by SMs, by being better able to detect their potential victims, must be on the whole offset by the losses they suffer as the CMs become better able to detect them as potential exploiters. On the other hand, although the CMs may not enjoy any net gain in their interactions with SMs, the benefits they gain by being better able to detect other CMs as potential cooperators are not offset by corresponding losses, but rather increased as other CMs become better able to detect them in return.

Thus, as persons rationally improve their ability to detect the dispositions of those with whom they interact, the value of p may be expected to increase, while the value of q remains relatively constant. But then p/q increases, and the greater it is, the less favorable need be other circumstances for it to be rational to dispose oneself to constrained maximization. . . .

3.1

In defending constrained maximization we have implicitly reinterpreted the utility-maximizing conception of practical rationality. The received interpretation, commonly accepted by economists and elaborated in Bayesian decision theory and the Von Neumann–Morgenstern theory of games, identifies rationality with utility maximization at the level of particular choices. A choice is rational if, and only if, it maximizes the actor's expected utility. We identify rationality with utility maximization at the level of dispositions to choose. A disposition is rational if, and only if, an actor holding it can expect his choices to yield no less utility than the choices he would make were he to hold any alternative disposition. We shall consider whether particular choices are rational if, and only if, they express a rational disposition to choose.

It might seem that a maximizing disposition to choose would express itself in maximizing choices. But we have shown that this is not so. The essential point in our argument is that one's disposition to choose affects the situations in which one may expect to find oneself. A straightforward maximizer, who is disposed to make maximizing choices, must expect to be excluded from cooperative arrangements which he would find advantageous. A constrained maximizer may expect to be included in such arrangements. She benefits from her disposition, not in the choices she makes, but in her opportunities to choose.

We have defended the rationality of constrained maximization as a disposition to choose by showing that it would be rationally chosen. Now this argument is not circular; constrained maximization is a disposition for strategic choice that would be parametrically chosen. But the idea of a choice among dispositions to choose is a heuristic device to express the underlying requirement that a rational disposition to choose be utility-maximizing. In parametric contexts, the disposition to make straightforwardly maximizing choices is uncontroversially utility-maximizing. We may therefore employ the device of a parametric choice among dispositions to choose to show that in strategic contexts, the disposition to make constrained choices, rather than straightforwardly maximizing choices, is utility-maximizing. We must however emphasize that it is not the choice itself, but the maximizing character of the disposition in virtue of which it is choiceworthy, that is the key to our argument.

But there is a further significance in our appeal to a choice among dispositions to choose for we suppose that the capacity to make such choices is itself an essential part of human rationality. We could imagine beings so wired that only straightforward maximization would be a psychologically possible mode of choice in strategic contexts. Hobbes may have thought that human beings were so wired, that we were straightforwardly maximizing machines. But if he thought this, then he was surely mistaken. At the core of our rational capacity is the ability to engage in self-critical reflection. The fully rational being is able to reflect on his standard of deliberation and to change that standard in the light of reflection. Thus we suppose it possible for persons who may initially assume that it is rational to extend straight-forward maximization from parametric to strategic contexts to reflect on the implications of this extension and to reject it in favor of constrained maximization. Such persons would be making the very choice, of a disposition to choose, that we have been discussing.

And in making that choice, they would be expressing their nature not only as rational beings, but also as moral beings. If the disposition to make straightforwardly maximizing choices were wired into us, we could not constrain our actions in the way required for morality. Moral philosophers have rightly been unwilling to accept the received interpretation of the relation between practical rationality and utility-maximization because they have recognized that it left no place for a rational constraint on directly utility-maximizing behavior, and so no place for morality as ordinarily understood. But they have then turned to a neo-Kantian account of rationality which has led them to dismiss the idea that those considerations that constitute a person's reasons for acting must bear some particular relationship to the person.[9] They have failed to relate our nature as moral beings to our everyday concern with the fulfilment of our individual preferences. But we have shown how morality issues from that concern. When we correctly understand how utility-maximization is identified with practical rationality, we see that morality is an essential part of maximization.

3.2

An objector might grant that it may be rational to dispose oneself to constrained maximizations but deny that the choices one is then disposed to make are rational.[10] The objector claims that we have merely exhibited another instance of the rationality of not behaving rationally. And before we can accuse the objector of paradox, he brings further instances before us.

Consider, he says, the costs of decision-making. Maximizing may be the most reliable procedure, but it need not be the most cost-effective. In many circumstances, the rational person will not maximize but satisfice – set a threshold level of fulfillment and choose the first course of action of those coming to mind that one expects to meet this level. Indeed, our objector may suggest, human beings, like other higher animals, are natural satisficers. What distinguishes us is that we are not hard-wired, so that we can choose

[9] See, for example, Nagel (1970), pp. 90–124.
[10] The objector might be Derek Parfit; see Parfit (1984), pp. 19–23.

differently, but the costs are such that it is not generally advantageous to exercise our option, even though we know that most of our choices are not maximizing.

Consider also, he says, the tendency to wishful thinking. If we set ourselves to calculate the best or maximizing course of action, we are likely to confuse true expectations with hopes. Knowing this, we protect ourselves by choosing on the basis of fixed principles, and we adhere to these principles even when it appears to us that we could do better to ignore them for we know that in such matters appearances often deceive. Indeed, our objector may suggest, much of morality may be understood not as constraints on maximization to ensure fair mutual benefit, but as constraints on wish-fulfilling behavior to ensure a closer approximation to maximization.

Consider again, he says, the benefits of threat behavior. I may induce you to perform an action advantageous to me if I can convince you that, should you not do so, I shall then perform an action very costly to you, even though it would not be my utility-maximizing choice. Hijackers seize airplanes and threaten the destruction of everyone aboard, themselves included, if they are not transported to Havana. Nations threaten nuclear retaliation should their enemies attack them. Although carrying out a threat would be costly, if it works, the cost need not be borne and the benefit, not otherwise obtainable, is forthcoming.

But, our objector continues, a threat can be effective only if credible. It may be that to maximize one's credibility and one's prospect of advantage, one must dispose oneself to carry out one's threats if one's demands are not met. And so it may be rational to dispose oneself to threat enforcement. But then, by parity of reasoning with our claims about constrained maximization, we must suppose it to be rational actually to carry out one's threats. Surely we should suppose instead that, although it is clearly irrational to carry out a failed threat, yet it may be rational to dispose oneself to just this sort of irrationality. And so, similarly, we should suppose that although it is clearly irrational to constrain one's maximizing behavior, yet it may be rational to dispose oneself to this irrationality.

We are unmoved. We agree that an actor who is subject to certain weaknesses or imperfections may find it rational to dispose himself to make choices that are not themselves rational. Such dispositions may be the most effective way of compensating for the weakness or imperfection. They constitute a second-best rationality, as it were. But although it may be rational for us to satisfice, it would not be rational for us to perform the action so chosen if, cost-free, the maximizing action were to be revealed to us. And although it may be rational for us to adhere to principles as a guard against wish-fulfillment, it would not be rational for us to do so if, beyond all doubt, the maximizing action were to be revealed to us.

Contrast these with constrained maximization. The rationale for disposing oneself to constraint does not appeal to any weakness or imperfection in the reasoning of the actor; indeed, the rationale is most evident for perfect reasoners who cannot be deceived. The disposition to constrained maximization overcomes externalities; it is directed to the core problem arising from the structure of interaction. And the entire point of disposing oneself to constraint is to adhere to it in the face of one's knowledge that one is not choosing the maximizing action.

Imperfect actors find it rational to dispose themselves to make less than rational choices. No lesson can be drawn from this about the dispositions and choices of the perfect actor. If her dispositions to choose are rational, then surely her choices are also rational.

But what of the threat enforcer? Here we disagree with our objector; it may be rational for a perfect actor to dispose herself to threat enforcement, and if it is, then it is rational for her to carry out a failed threat. Equally, it may be rational for a perfect actor to dispose herself to threat resistance, and if it is, then it is rational for her to resist despite the cost to herself. Deterrence, we have argued elsewhere, may be a rational policy, and non-maximizing deterrent choices are then rational.[11]

In a community of rational persons, however, threat behavior will be proscribed. Unlike cooperation, threat behavior does not promote mutual advantage. A successful threat simply redistributes benefits in favor of the threatener; successful threat resistance maintains the *status quo*. Unsuccessful threat behavior, resulting in costly acts of enforcement or resistance, is necessarily non-optimal; its very *raison d'être* is to make everyone worse off. Any person who is not exceptionally placed must then have the *ex ante* expectation that threat behavior will be disadvantageous overall. Its proscription must be part of a fair and optimal agreement among rational persons; one of the constraints imposed by minimax relative concession is abstinence from the making of threats. Our argument thus shows threat behavior to be both irrational and immoral.

Constrained maximizers will not dispose themselves to enforce or to resist threats among themselves. But there are circumstances, beyond the moral pale, in which a constrained maximizer might find it rational to dispose herself to threat enforcement. If she found herself fallen among straightforward maximizers, and especially if they were too stupid to become threat resisters, disposing herself to threat enforcement might be the best thing she could do. And, for her, carrying out failed threats would be rational, though not utility-maximizing.

Our objector has not made good his case. The dispositions of a fully rational actor issue in rational choices. Our argument identifies practical rationality with utility maximization at the level of dispositions to choose and carries through the implications of that identification in assessing the rationality of particular choices.

[11] See my (1984), appearing also in MacLean (1984).

References

Axelrod, R. (1981). "The Emergence of Cooperation Among Egoists." *American Political Science Review* 75: 306–18.

Darwall, S. L. (1983). *Impartial Reason*. Ithaca, NY: Cornell University Press.

Gauthier, D. (1974). "Rational Cooperation." *Noûs* 8: 53–65.

(1975). "Reason and Maximization." *Canadian Journal of Philosophy* 4: 411–33.

(1984). "Deterrence, Maximization, and Rationality." *Ethics* 94: 474–95.

(1985a). *Morals by Agreement*. Oxford: Clarendon Press.

(1985b). "Maximization Constrained: The Rationality of Cooperation."

(1985c). "Bargaining and Justice." *Social Philosophy and Policy* 2.

Hobbes, Thomas. (1651). *Leviathan*.

Hume, David. (1751). *An Enquiry Concerning the Principles of Morals*.

MacLean, D., ed. (1984). *The Security Gamble: Deterrence Dilemmas in the Nuclear Age*. Totowa, NJ: Rowman and Allanheld.

Nagel, T. (1970). *The Possibility of Altruism*. Oxford: Oxford University Press.

Nash, J. F. (1951). "Non-cooperative Games." *Annals of Mathematics* 54: 286–95.

Parfit, D. (1984). "The Self-Interest Theory." In *Reasons and Persons*. Oxford: Clarendon Press.

Rawls, J. (1971). *A Theory of Justice*. Cambridge, MA: Harvard University Press.

B. *Impossibility theorems for social choice*

14. Values and collective decision making

Kenneth J. Arrow

1. Values of a single individual

As an exercise in clarifying terminology, let us consider what can be said about the values of an imaginary, completely isolated individual. His personal skills and qualities and the physical world available to him jointly delimit a range of *actions* possible to him. To be precise, I shall so define the concept of action that alternative actions are mutually exclusive. An action, then, means a complete description of all the activities that an individual carries on, and two alternative actions are any two descriptions which differ in any relevant way. For example, an individual may describe his activities by indicating the amount of time he spends on each of the alternative modalities of performance available to him; thus, three hours at farming, three hours at hunting, four hours of violin playing, etc. A change in any one of these time allocations would represent a change in action. This particular definition is truly a formal choice of language, and does not by itself change the nature of the problem. It simply brings out formally that the basic question of the individual is a choice of actions.

1.1. Values, tastes, and hypothetical imperatives

To an economist, and I suppose to most philosophers, a value system would, in these terms, be simply the rule an individual uses to choose which of the mutually exclusive actions he will undertake. If an individual is facing a

This paper is a slightly revised version of "Public and Private Values," presented at a symposium on *Human Values and Economic Policy* at the New York University Institute of Philosophy in 1966.
Reprinted with permission from P. Laslett and W. G. Runciman, eds., *Philosophy, Politics, and Society* (Oxford: Basil Blackwell, 1967).

given set of alternative actions, he will choose one, and there seems to be little interesting to talk about. However, the problem, at least to the economist, is put in slightly different form. Consider an individual who does not yet know which actions will be available and which will not. Let us term the set of available actions the *environment*. One might ask him what action he *would choose* if offered some particular environment. By repeating this question for many alternative environments we have obtained a description of his value system in the sense of a rule giving his hypothetical choice for many or all possible environments.[1]

One might want to reserve the term "values" for a specially elevated or noble set of choices. Perhaps choices in general might be referred to as "tastes." We do not ordinarily think of the preference for additional bread over additional beer as being a value worthy of philosophic inquiry. I believe, though, that the distinction cannot be made logically, and certainly not in dealing with a single isolated individual. If there is any distinction between values and tastes it must lie in the realm of interpersonal relations.

1.2. The assumptions of ordering

The description of a value system as a correlation between possible environments and the hypothetical choices to be made from them is not by itself a very informative procedure. Economists have been accustomed to adding considerable strength (empirical restrictiveness) by specifying that the value system shall have a particular structure – namely, being derivable from an *ordering*. To define this concept let us first consider environments consisting of just two alternative actions. For such two-member environments we can find the one chosen, in accordance with the individual's value system, and we will speak of it as having been *preferred* to the other action in the environment. We may have to admit that the individual is equally willing to choose neither of the two actions, in which case we speak of the two actions as being *indifferent*. The assumption of an ordering means that certain consistency assumptions are postulated about the relations of preference and indifference, and it is further assumed that choices from any environment can be described in terms of the ordering, which relates to choices in two-member environments.

The first assumption is that of *connexity* (or connectedness, or completeness, or comparability). It is assumed that for each pair of alternatives, either one is preferred to the other or the two are indifferent. The second assumption is that of *transitivity*. Consider three alternatives, to be designated by

---

[1] For technical mathematical reasons one must admit that sometimes more than one action should be regarded as chosen in a given environment, by which is meant the individual does not care which of the chosen actions is in fact adopted in a particular set of circumstances. We must allow for the fact that there may be no chosen action; for an example of the latter, consider an individual with a normal desire for money who can choose any amount of gold less than (but not equal to) one ounce.

x, y, and z. Then if x is preferred to y, and y is preferred to z, we assume that x is preferred to z. We can and must also include in the definition cases where some of the choices are indifferent; for example, if x is indifferent to y, and y is indifferent to z, then x is indifferent to z.

For later use we introduce some symbolic notation to express these ordering relations. Specifically, we denote alternatives by x, y, ... Then

> xPy means "x is preferred to y,"
> xIy means "x is indifferent to y,"
> xRy means "x is preferred or indifferent to y."

If we start with the relation R (that is, only knowing for which ordered pairs of alternatives x, y, the statement xRy holds), then we can define the relations P and I in terms of R:

> xIy is defined to be xRy and yRx;
> xPy is defined to be xRy and not yRx.

The assumption of connexity can be stated:

> For all x and y, xRy or yRx.

(Here, and below, "or" does not exclude "and.") The assumption of transitivity can be stated:

> For all x, y, and z, if xRy and yRz, then xRz.

Finally, and perhaps most important, it is assumed that the choice from any environment is determined by the ordering in the sense that if there is an alternative which is preferred to every other alternative in the environment, then it is the chosen element. This is an additional assumption not logically implied by the existence of an ordering itself.

In symbols, let S be any environment (set of alternatives), C(S) the alternative (or alternatives) chosen from S. Then

> C(S) is the set of alternatives x in S for which xRy for all y in S.

It is easy to see that if x^1 and x^2 are both in C(S) (both chosen alternatives in S), then $x^1 I x^2$.

Obviously, the assumption of ordering is by no means unreasonable. The notion of connexity carries the idea that choices have to be made whether we will or no. The idea of transitivity clearly corresponds to some strong feeling of the meaning of consistency in our choice. Economists have typically identified the concept of rationality with the notion of choices derivable from an ordering.

It may be worth while dwelling on the meaning of these two assumptions a little more, in view of their importance. It is not at all uncommon to find denials of the connexity assumption. Sufficiently remote alternatives are held to be incomparable. But I must say I do not find this line of argument at all convincing. If a choice has to be made, it has to be made. In most practical choice situations there is some *null* alternative, which will be chosen in the absence of what might be termed a positive decision. Thus, if there is dispute about the nature of new legislation, the pre-existing legislation remains in force. But this does not mean that no choice is made; it means rather that the system produces as its choice the null alternative. I think what those who emphasize incomparability have in mind is rather that if one is forced to make a choice between alternatives which are difficult to compare, then the choice is not apt to satisfy the assumption of transitivity.

The possibility of regarding inaction as an always available alternative is part of the broader question of whether social choices should be historically conditioned. It is here that the importance of transitivity becomes clear. Transitivity implies that the final choice made from any given environment is independent of the path by which it has been derived. From any environment there will be a given chosen alternative, and in the absence of a deadlock no place for the historically given alternatives to be chosen by default.

1.3. Independence of irrelevant alternatives

Since the chosen element from any environment is completely defined by knowledge of the preferences as between it and any other alternative in the environment, it follows that the choice depends only on the ordering of the elements of that environment. In particular, the choice made does not depend on preferences as between alternatives which are not in fact available in the given environment, nor – and this is probably more important – on preferences as between elements in the environment and those not in the environment. It is never necessary to compare available alternatives with those which are not available at a given moment in order to arrive at a decision. It is this point which is being made when it is argued that only ordinal measures of utility or preference are relevant to decisions. Any cardinal measure, any attempt to give a numerical representation of utility, depends basically on comparisons involving alternative actions which are not, or at least may not be, available, given the environment prevailing at the moment.

1.4. Omitted considerations

For the sake of economy of discussion we pass by many interesting issues. Most important, probably, is the relation between hypothetical choices and real ones. It is implied in the above discussion and below that a preference will in fact be translated into a choice if the opportunity ever comes. But the question may be raised how we can possibly know about hypothetical choices if they are not actually made. This is not merely a problem of finding out about somebody else's values; we may not know our own values until put to the crucial test.

Even the actual preferences may not be regarded as in some sense true values. An observer looking from the outside on our isolated individual may say that his decision was wrong either in the sense that there is some other standard of values to which it does not conform or in the sense that it was made on the grounds of insufficient information or improper calculation. The latter possibility is a real and important one, but I will simply state that I am abstracting from it in the course of the present discussion. The former interpretation I am rejecting here. For the single isolated individual there can be no other standard than his own values. He might indeed wish to change them under criticism, but this, I take it, means basically that he hasn't fully thought through or calculated the consequences of his actions and upon more consideration wishes to modify them.

2. Public values

2.1. Interpersonal nature of social action

The fundamental fact which causes the need for discussing public values at all is that all significant actions involve joint participation of many individuals. Even the apparently simplest act of individual decision involves the participation of a whole society.

It is important to note that this observation tells us all non-trivial actions are essentially the property of society as a whole, not of individuals. It is quite customary to think of each individual as being able to undertake actions on his own (e.g., decisions of consumption, production, and exchange, moving from place to place, forming and dissolving families). Formally, a social action is then taken to be the resultant of all individual actions. In other words, any social action is thought of as being factored into a sequence of individual actions.

I certainly do not wish to deny that such factoring takes place, but I do wish to emphasize that the partition of a social action into individual components, and the corresponding assignment of individual responsibility, is *not* a datum. Rather, the particular factoring in any given context is itself the result of a social policy and therefore already the outcome of earlier and logically more primitive social values.

In economic transactions the point is clearest when we consider what we call property. Property is clearly a creation of society through its legal structure. The actions of buying and selling through offers of property are only at a superficial level the actions of an individual. They reflect a whole series of social institutions, and with different institutions different people would be having control over any given piece of property. Furthermore, the very notion of control over one's "own" property, as is apparent upon the most casual inspection, itself acquires its meaning through the regulations of society.

These are no idle or excessively nice distinctions. When it comes to racial discrimination, notions of liability and responsibility for injury to others, or the whole concept of a corporation and its special and complex relations to the world as a whole, economic and social, we know that social values have altered considerably the terms on which property can be used in the marketplace or transmitted to others. Needless to say, the taxation system constitutes one of the strongest examples in which the state, as one aspect of society, makes clear the relative nature of ownership. Nor, in this context, should it be forgotten that the claims of society, as modifying the concept of ownership, are by no means confined to the state. Our particular culture has tended to minimize non-coercive obligations relative to the predominant role they have played elsewhere, but they are far from absent even today. There is certainly a whole complex of obligations implied in the concept of a "good neighbor." The use of one's real property is limited by more than legal conditions. As everyone knows – sometimes painfully – there are obligations of generosity and organized giving appropriate to an individual's income status and social position. In short, we argue that the facts of social life show clearly that there is no universally acceptable division of actions with regard to property into mine and thine.

To be sure, there is another category of actions, those which involve the person himself as opposed to his property. We have a stronger feeling here that there is a natural meaning to speaking of one's own actions as opposed to others. Presumably there is a meaningful sense in which we say that I am writing this paper – not anyone else. But of course even here the action is full of social interconnections. I am here in a conference arranged by others, using words which are a common part of the culture, expressing ideas which draw upon a wide range of concepts of others, and which embody my education.

To be sure, I am using my own capacities at some point in this process. But how logically do we distinguish between the capacities which somehow define the person, and those which are the result of external actions of a society? I may see well because my vision is intrinsically good or because I have glasses. Is the vision more peculiarly *mine* in one case than in the other? One may concede that there is more of an intrinsic idea of property here in certain personal actions, but I think this whole matter needs deeper exploration than it has received thus far. In any case, there are obviously very strong social obligations on personal behavior and the use of one's personal capacities, just as there are on the use of property.

To conclude, then, we must in a general theory take as our unit a social action, that is, an action involving a large proportion or the entire domain of society. At the most basic axiomatic level, individual actions play little role. The need for a system of public values then becomes evident; actions being collective or interpersonal in nature, so must the choice among them. A public or social value system is essentially a logical necessity.

The point is obvious enough in the contexts that we tend to regard as specifically political. The individuals in a country cannot have separate foreign policies or separate legal systems. Among economists the matter has been somewhat confused because economic analysis has supplied us with a model of factorization of social actions, that achieved through the price system. The system itself is certainly one of the most remarkable of social institutions and the analysis of its working is, in my judgment, one of the more significant intellectual achievements of mankind. But the factorization implied is a particular one made in a particular way. It is one that has turned out to be highly convenient, particularly from the point of view of economizing on the flow of information in the economic system. But at the fundamental level of discourse we are now engaged in we cannot regard the price system as a datum. On the contrary, it is to be thought of as one of the instrumentalities, possibly the major one, by which whatever social value system there may be is realized.

2.2. Individual preferences for social actions

The individual plays a central role in social choice as the judge of alternative social actions according to his own standards. We presume that each individual has some way of ranking social actions according to his preferences for their consequences. These preferences constitute his value system. They are assumed to reflect already in full measure altruistic or egoistic motivations, as the case may be.

Following the discussion in Part 1, we assume that the values are expressed in the form of an ordering. Thus, in effect, individuals are taken to be rational in their attitudes toward social actions.

In symbols, we now let $x, y, \ldots$, represent alternative social actions. Then the ith individual has an ordering among these actions which, as in 1.2, can be represented by a relation, to be denoted by R_i:

$x R_i y$ means "x is preferred or indifferent to y in the view of individual i."

As before, we can define P_i (preference in the view of individual i) and I_i (indifference in the view of individual i) in terms of R_i:

$x P_i y$ is defined to be $x R_i y$ and not $y R_i x$;
$x I_i y$ is defined to be $x R_i y$ and $y R_i x$.

We are face to face with an extremely difficult point. A standard liberal point of view in political philosophy, which also has dominated formal welfare economics, asserts that an individual's preferences are or ought to be (a distinction not usually made clear) concerned only with the effects of social actions on him. But there is no logical way to distinguish a particular class of consequences which pertain to a given individual. If I feel that my satisfaction is reduced by somebody else's poverty (or, for that matter, by somebody else's wealth), then I am injured in precisely the same sense as if my purchasing power were reduced. To parallel the observations of the preceding section, I am in effect arguing here that just as we cannot factor social actions so as to make each component pertain to a given individual, so we cannot factor the consequences of social actions in any meaningful way into separable consequences to individual members of the society. That is, let me make it clear, we cannot do it as a matter of fact. The interdependence of mankind is after all not a novel ethical doctrine. The man who questioned whether he was his brother's keeper was, according to an ancient source, not highly approved of. The general conclusion here is not one that I find myself entirely comfortable with. I do share the general liberal view that every individual should have the opportunity to find his own way to personal development and satisfaction. The question of interference with the actions of others has been raised most acutely in recent years in legal rather than economic contexts, specifically in the English discussion on laws regulating deviant sexual behavior. Homosexual behaviour between consenting adults is probably a classic example of an action affecting no one else, and therefore should be exempt from social control. Yet many find themselves shocked and outraged. They would strongly prefer, let us say, the situation to be different. Similarly, I may be disturbed that the Negro is discriminated against and judge accordingly social actions which lead to this result.

One could of course say that the general principle of restraint in judging the affairs of others is an empirical assumption that people in fact do not care about (or strictly have no preferences concerning) matters which would in the usual terminology be regarded as none of their business. But of course empirically we know that this is quite false. The very fact that restrictive legislation is passed or even proposed shows clearly that people are willing to sacrifice effort and time because of the satisfactions to be received from seeing others' patterns of life altered.

The only rational defence of what may be termed a liberal position, or perhaps more precisely a principle of limited social preference, is that it is itself a value judgment. In other words, an individual may have as part of his value structure precisely that he does not think it proper to influence consequences outside a limited realm. This is a perfectly coherent position, but I find it difficult to insist that this judgment is of such overriding importance that it outweighs all other considerations. Personally, my values are such that I am willing to go very far indeed in the direction of respect for the means by which others choose to derive their satisfactions.

At this stage I want to emphasize that value judgments in favour of limited social preference, just as other value judgments emphasizing social solidarity, must be counted as part of the value systems which individuals use in the judgment of alternative social actions.

3. Welfare judgments and the aggregation of preferences

The problem of social choice is the aggregation of the multiplicity of individual preference scales about alternative social actions.

3.1. Welfare judgments and constitutions

Classical utilitarianism specifies that alternative social actions be judged in terms of their consequences for people. In the present terminology I take this to mean that they are to be judged in terms of the individual preference scales. This by itself does not supply a sufficient basis for action in view of the multiplicity and divergence of individual preference scales. It is therefore at least implicit in classical utilitarianism that there is a second level at which the individual judgments are themselves evaluated, and this point has been given explicit recognition in a classic paper of Abram Bergson.[2] Let us call this second-order evaluation a *welfare judgment;* it is an evaluation of the consequences to all individuals based on their evaluations. If in each individual evaluation two social actions are indifferent, then the welfare judgment as between the two must also be one of indifference.

The process of formation of welfare judgments is logically equivalent to a social decision process or *constitution*. Specifically, a constitution is a rule which associates to each possible set of individual orderings a social choice function, i.e., a rule for selecting a preferred action out of every possible environment. That a welfare judgment is a constitution indeed follows immediately from the assumption that a welfare judgment can be formed given any set of individual preference systems for social actions. The classification of welfare judgments as constitutions is at this stage a tautology, but what makes it more than that is a specification of reasonable conditions to be imposed on constitutions, and it is here that any dispute must lie.

3.2. Social decision processes and the notion of social welfare

While I have just argued that a welfare judgment is necessarily a constitution or process of social decision, the converse need not be true, at least not without further clarification of the meaning of "welfare judgment." A welfare judgment requires that some one person is judge; a rule for arriving at social decisions may be agreed upon for reasons of convenience and necessity without its outcomes being treated as evaluations by anyone in particular.[3] Indeed, I would go further and argue that the appropriate standpoint

[2] "A Reformulation of Certain Aspects of Welfare Economics," *Quarterly Journal of Economics,* 52 (1938), 310–34; reprinted in A. Bergson, *Essays in Normative Economics* (Cambridge, Mass.: Harvard University Press, 1966), 1–49.

[3] This point has been well stressed by I. M. D. Little, "Social Choice and Individual Values," *Journal of Political Economy,* 60 (1952), 422–32.

for analysing social decision processes is precisely that they not be welfare judgments of any particular individuals. This seems contrary to Bergson's point of view.[4] In my view, the location of welfare judgments in any individual, while logically possible, does not appear to be very interesting. "Social welfare" is related to social policy in any sensible interpretation; the welfare judgments of any single individual are unconnected with action and therefore sterile. In a more recent paper Bergson has recognized that there may be this alternative interpretation of the concept of social welfare; I quote the passage at length since it displays the issue so well:

I have been assuming that the concern of welfare economics is to counsel individual citizens generally. If a public official is counselled, it is on the same basis as any other citizen. In every instance reference is made to some ethical values which are appropriate for the counselling of the individual in question. In all this I believe I am only expressing the intent of welfare writings generally; or if this is not the intent, I think it should be. But some may be inclined nevertheless to a different conception, which allows still another interpretation of Arrow's theorem. *According to this view, the problem is to counsel not citizens generally but public officials.* [Emphasis added.] Furthermore, the values to be taken as data are not those which would guide the official if he were a private citizen. The official is envisaged instead as more or less neutral ethically. His one aim in life is to implement the values of other citizens as given by some rule of collective decision making.[5]

My interpretation of the social choice problem agrees fully with that given by Bergson beginning with the italicized statement, though, as can be seen, this is not the view that he himself endorses.

4. Some conditions for a social decision process and the impossibility theorem

The fundamental problem of public value formation, then, is the construction of constitutions. In general, of course, there is no difficulty in constructing a rule if one is content with arbitrary ones. The problem becomes meaningful if reasonable conditions are suggested, which every constitution should obey.[6]

4.1. Some conditions on constitutions

I suggest here four conditions which seem very reasonable to impose on any constitution. More can undoubtedly be suggested but unfortunately, as we shall see in Section 4.2 below, these four more than suffice.

---

[4] A. Bergson, "On the Concept of Social Welfare," *Quarterly Journal of Economics*, 68 (1954), 233–52, reprinted in *Essays in Normative Economics, op. cit.*, 27–49, esp. pp. 35–6.

[5] A. Bergson, "On the Concept of Social Welfare," *op. cit.*, p. 242; *Essays, op. cit.*, pp. 37–8.

[6] The analysis that follows is based on my book *Social Choice and Individual Values* (New York, London, and Sydney: Wiley: 1st ed. 1951; 2nd ed. 1963).

Recall that a constitution is a rule which assigns to any set of individual preference orderings a rule for making society's choices among alternative social actions in any possible environment. Thus, for a given set of individual orderings the result of the process is a particular value system in the sense of Part 1; that is, a rule for making selections out of all possible environments. The first condition may be termed that of

Collective Rationality: For any given set of orderings, the social choice function is derivable from an ordering.

In other words, the social choice system has the same structure as that which we have already assumed for individual value systems. The next condition is one that has been little disputed and is advanced by almost every writer in the economic literature:

Pareto Principle: If alternative x is preferred to alternative y by every single individual according to his ordering, then the social ordering also ranks x above y.

Notice that we can use the term "social ordering" in view of the previous condition of Collective Rationality. The next condition is perhaps the most important as well as the most controversial. For my own part, I am less tempted to regard it as ultimately satisfactory than I formerly did, but it has strong pragmatic justification:

Independence of Irrelevant Alternatives: The social choice made from any environment depends only on the orderings of individuals with respect to the alternatives in that environment.

To take an extreme case, suppose that individuals are informed that there are a certain number of social actions available. They are not even aware that there are other conceivable social actions. They develop their own preference systems for the alternatives contained in this particular environment, and then the constitution generates a choice. Later they are told that in fact there were alternatives which were logically possible but were not in fact available. For example, a city is taking a poll of individual preferences on alternative methods of transportation (rapid transit, automobile, bus, etc.). Someone suggests that in evaluating these preferences they also ought to ask individual preferences for instantaneous transportation by dissolving the individual into molecules in a ray gun and reforming him elsewhere in the city as desired. There is no pretence that this method is in any way an available alternative. The assumption of Independence of Irrelevant Alternatives is that such preferences have no bearing on the choice to be made.

It is of course obvious that ordinary political decision-making methods satisfy this condition. When choosing among candidates for an elected office, all that is asked are the preferences among the actual candidates, not also preferences among other individuals who are not candidates and who are not available for office.

Finally, we enunciate probably the least controversial of all the conditions,

Non-Dictatorship: There is no individual whose preferences are automatically society's preferences independent of the preferences of all other individuals.

There is a difference between the first two conditions and the last two which is worth noting. The assumptions of Collective Rationality and the Pareto Principle are statements which apply to any fixed set of individual orderings. They do not involve comparisons between social orderings based on different sets of individual orderings. On the contrary, the condition of Independence of Irrelevant Alternatives and of Non-Dictatorship are assertions about the responsiveness of the social ordering to variations in individual orderings.

4.2. Impossibility theorem

The conditions of Collective Rationality and of the Independence of Irrelevant Alternatives taken together imply that in a generalized sense all methods of social choice are of the type of voting. If we consider environments composed of two alternatives alone, then the condition of Independence of Irrelevant Alternatives tells us that the choice is determined solely by the preferences of the members of the community as between those two alternatives, and no other preferences are involved. Define a set of individuals to be *decisive* for alternative x over alternative y if the constitution prescribes that x is chosen over y whenever all individuals in the set prefer x to y and all others prefer y to x. Then the rule for choosing from any two-member environment has the form of specifying which sets of individuals are decisive for x over y and which for y over x. The majority voting principle, for example, states simply that any set containing a majority of the voters is decisive for any alternative over any other.

Then, if the social value system is generated by a social ordering, all social preferences are determined by the choices made for two-member environments, and hence by pairwise votes (thus systems like plurality voting are excluded).

Now it has been known for a long time that the system of majority voting can give rise to paradoxical consequences. Consider the following example. There are three alternatives, x, y, and z, among which choice is to be made. One-third of the voters prefer x to y and y to z, one-third prefer y to z and z to x, and one-third prefer z to x and x to y. Then x will be preferred to y by a majority, y to z by a majority, and z to x by a majority.[7]

---

[7] This paradox seems to have been first observed by the Marquis de Condorcet, *Essai sur l'application de l'analyse à la probabilité des décisions rendues à la pluralité des voix* (Paris, 1785). That a rational voting scheme requires knowledge of all preferences among the candidates and not only the first choice was already argued even earlier by Jean-Charles de Borda,

One might be tempted to suppose that the paradox of voting is an imperfection in the particular system of majority voting, and more ingenious methods could avoid it. But unfortunately this is not so. The following general theorem may be stated:

There can be no constitution simultaneously satisfying the conditions of Collective Rationality, the Pareto Principle, the Independence of Irrelevant Alternatives, and Non-Dictatorship.

The proof is given in the following Section 4.3.

This conclusion is quite embarrassing, and it forces us to examine the conditions which have been stated as reasonable. It's hard to imagine anyone quarrelling either with the Pareto Principle or the condition of Non-Dictatorship. The principle of Collective Rationality may indeed be questioned. One might be prepared to allow that the choice from a given environment be dependent on the history of previous choices made in earlier environments, but I think many would find that situation unsatisfactory. There remains, therefore, only the Independence of Irrelevant Alternatives, which will be examined in greater detail in Section 4.4 below.

4.3. Proof of the impossibility theorem

We assume the existence of a social choice mechanism satisfying the conditions of Collective Rationality, the Pareto Principle, the Independence of Irrelevant Alternatives, and Non-Dictatorship, and show that the assumption leads to a contradiction. Since the condition of Collective Rationality requires that social choice be derivable from an ordering, we can speak of social preference and social indifference. In particular, as defined in the last section, a set of individuals V is *decisive* for x against y if x is socially preferred to y whenever all individuals in V prefer x to y and all others prefer y to x.[8]

The proof falls into two parts. It is first shown that if an individual is decisive for some pair of alternatives, then he is a dictator, contrary to the condition of Non-Dictatorship. Hence, no individual is decisive for any pair of alternatives, and the Impossibility Theorem itself then follows easily with the aid of the Pareto Principle.

We first distinguish one individual, called I, and introduce the following notations for statements about the constitution:

"Mémoire sur les élections au scrutin," *Mémoires de l'Académie Royale des Sciences,* 1781, 657–65. For a modern analysis of Condorcet's work on voting, see G.-G. Granger, *La Mathématique Social du Marquis de Condorcet* (Paris: Presses Universitaries de France, 1956, esp. pp. 94–129). For an English translation of Borda's work see A. de Grazia, "Mathematical Derivation of an Election System," *Isis,* 44 (1953), 42–51. For a general history of the theory of social choice, see D. Black, *The Theory of Committees and Elections* (Cambridge, U.K.: Cambridge University Press, 1958), Part II.

[8] The following proof is quoted, with minor alterations, from Arrow, *op. cit.,* pp. 98–100.

$x\bar{D}y$ means that x is socially preferred to y whenever
individual I prefers x to y, regardless of the orderings
of other individuals; (1)

xDy means that x is socially preferred to y if individual I
prefers x to y and all other individuals prefer y to x. (2)

Notice that this notation is legitimate only because of the assumption of Independence of Irrelevant Alternatives. Note too that the statement, $x\bar{D}y$, implies xDy and that xDy is the same as the assertion that I is a decisive set for x against y.

Suppose then that xDy holds for some x and y. We will first suppose that there are only three alternatives altogether. Let the third alternative be z. Suppose I orders the alternatives, x, y, z, in descending order, whereas all other individuals prefer y to both x and z, but may have any preferences as between the last two. Then I prefers x to y, whereas all others prefer y to x; from (2) this means that xPy. All individuals prefer y to z; by the Pareto Principle, yPz. Then by transitivity, xPz; but then this holds whenever xP_iz, regardless of the orderings of other individuals as between x and z. In symbols,

$$xDy \text{ implies } x\bar{D}z. \tag{3}$$

Again suppose xDy, but now suppose that I orders the alternatives, z, x, y, whereas all other individuals prefer both z and y to x. By a similar argument, xPy and zPx, so that zPy.

$$xDy \text{ implies } z\bar{D}y. \tag{4}$$

Interchanging y and z in (4) yields

$$xDz \text{ implies } y\bar{D}z. \tag{5}$$

Replacing x by y, y by z, and z by x in (3) yields

$$yDz \text{ implies } y\bar{D}x. \tag{6}$$

Since $x\bar{D}z$ implies xDz, and $y\bar{D}z$ implies yDz, we can, by chaining the implications (3), (5), and (6), deduce

$$xDy \text{ implies } y\bar{D}x. \tag{7}$$

If we interchange x and y in (3), (4), and (7), we arrive at the respective implications

$$yDx \text{ implies } y\bar{D}z,$$
$$yDx \text{ implies } z\bar{D}x,$$
$$yDx \text{ implies } x\bar{D}y,$$

and these can each be chained with the implication (7) to yield

$$xDy \text{ implies } y\bar{D}z, z\bar{D}x, \text{ and } x\bar{D}y. \tag{8}$$

Implications (3), (4), (7), and (8) together can be summarized as saying

> If xDy, then $u\bar{D}v$ are for every ordered pair u, v from the three alternatives x, y, and z;   (9)

i.e., individual I is a dictator for the three alternatives.

We can extend this result to any number of alternatives by an argument due to Blau.[9] Suppose aDb holds, and let x and y be any pair of alternatives. If x and y are the same as a and b, either in the same or in the reverse order, we add a third alternative c to a and b; then we can apply (9) to the triple a, b, c and deduce $x\bar{D}y$ by letting u = x, v = y. If exactly one of x and y is distinct from a and b, add it to a and b to form a triple to which again (9) is applicable. Finally, if both x and y are distinct from a and b, two steps are needed. First, add x to a and b, and deduce from (9) that $a\bar{D}x$ and therefore aDx. Then, again applying (9) to the triple a, x, y, we find that $x\bar{D}y$. Thus, aDb for some a and b implies that $x\bar{D}y$ for all x and y, i.e., individual I is a dictator. From the Condition of Non-Dictatorship it can be concluded that

> xDy cannot hold for any individual I and any pair x, y.   (10)

The remainder of the proof is now an appropriate adaptation of the paradox of voting. By the Pareto Principle, there is at least one decisive set for any ordered pair, x, y, namely, the set of all individuals. Among all sets of individuals which are decisive for some pairwise choice, pick one such that no other is smaller; by (10) it must contain at least two individuals. Let V be the chosen set, and let the ordered pair for which it is decisive be x, y. Divide V into two parts, V_1, which contains only a single individual, and V_2, which contains all the rest. Let V_3 be the set of individuals not in V.

Consider now the case where the preference order of V_1 is x, y, z, that of all members of V_2 is z, x, y, and that of all members of V_3 is y, z, x. Since V is decisive for x against y, all members of V prefer x to y while all others have the opposite preference xPy. On the other hand, it is impossible that society prefers z to y since that would require that V_2 be decisive on this issue; this is impossible since V_2 has fewer members than V, which, by construction, has as few members as a decisive set can have. Hence, yRz, and, since xPy, society must prefer x to z. But then the single member of V_1 would be decisive, and we have shown that to be impossible.

Thus the contradiction is established.

4.4. The Independence of Irrelevant Alternatives and interpersonal comparisons of intensity

Modern economic theory has insisted on the ordinal concept of utility; that is, only orderings can be observed, and therefore no measurement of utility

---

[9] J. H. Blau, "The Existence of Social Welfare Functions," *Econometrica,* 25 (1957), 310.

independent of these orderings has any significance. In the field of consumer's demand theory the ordinalist position turned out to create no problems; cardinal utility had no explanatory power above and beyond ordinal. Leibniz's Principle of the Identity of Indiscernibles demanded then the excision of cardinal utility from our thought patterns. Bergson's formulation of the social welfare function carried out the same principle in the analysis of social welfare. Social choices were to depend only on individual orderings; hence, welfare judgments were based only on interpersonally observable behaviour.

The condition of Independence of Irrelevant Alternatives extends the requirement of observability one step farther. Given the set of alternatives available for society to choose among, it could be expected that ideally one could observe all preferences among the available alternatives, but there would be no way to observe preferences among alternatives not feasible for society.

I now feel, however, that the austerity imposed by this condition is stricter than desirable. In many situations we do have information on preferences for non-feasible alternatives. It can certainly be argued that when available this information should be used in social choice. Unfortunately, it is clear, as I have already suggested, that social decision processes which are independent of irrelevant alternatives have strong practical advantages, and it remains to be seen whether a satisfactory social decision procedure can really be based on other information.

The potential usefulness of irrelevant alternatives is that they may permit empirically meaningful interpersonal comparisons. The information which might enable us to assert that one individual prefers alternative x to alternative y more strongly than a second individual prefers y to x must be based on comparisons by the two individuals of the two alternatives, not only with respect to each other but also to other alternatives.

Let me conclude by suggesting one type of use of irrelevant alternatives, which may be termed "extended sympathy." We do seem prepared to make comparisons of the form: Action x is better (or worse) for me than action y is for you. This is probably in fact the standard way in which people make judgments about appropriate income distributions; if I am richer than you, I may find it easy to make the judgment that it is better for you to have the marginal dollar than for me.

How is this consistent with our general point of view that all value judgments are at least hypothetical choices among alternative actions? Interpersonal comparisons of the extended sympathy type can be put in operational form. The judgment takes the form: It is better (in my judgment) to be myself under action x than to be you under action y.

In this form the characteristics that define an individual are included in the comparison. In effect, these characteristics are put on a par with the items usually regarded as constituting an individual's wealth. The possession of tools is ordinarily regarded as part of the social state which is being evaluated; why not the possession of the skills to use those tools, and the intelligence which lies behind those skills? Individuals, in appraising each other's states of well-being, not only consider material possessions but also find themselves "desiring this man's scope and that man's art."[10] The principle of extended sympathy as a basis for interpersonal comparisons seems basic to many of the welfare judgments made in ordinary practice. It remains to be seen whether an adequate theory of social choice can be derived from this and other acceptable principles.

[10] The moral implications of the position that many attributes of the individual are similar in nature to external possessions have been discussed by V. C. Walsh, *Scarcity and Evil* (Englewood Cliffs, N.J.: Prentice-Hall, 1961).

15. The impossibility of a Paretian liberal

Amartya Sen

1. Introduction

The purpose of this paper is to present an impossibility result that seems to have some disturbing consequences for principles of social choice. A common objection to the method of majority decision is that it is illiberal. The argument takes the following form: Given other things in the society, if you prefer to have pink walls rather than white, then society should permit you to have this, even if a majority of the community would like to see your walls white. Similarly, whether you should sleep on your back or on your belly is a matter in which the society should permit you absolute freedom, even if a majority of the community is nosey enough to feel that you must sleep on your back. We formalize this concept of individual liberty in an extremely weak form and examine its consequences.

2. The theorem

Let R_i be the ordering of the ith individual over the set X of all possible social states, each social state being a complete description of society including every individual's position in it. There are n individuals. Let R be the social preference relation that is to be determined.

Definition 1: A collective choice rule is a functional relationship that specifies one and only one social preference relation R for any set of n individual orderings (one ordering for each individual).

A special case of a collective choice rule is one that Arrow (1951) calls a social welfare function, namely, a rule such that R must be an ordering.

For comments and criticisms I am grateful to Kenneth Arrow, Peter Diamond, Milton Friedman, Tapas Majumdar, Stephen Marglin, and Thomas Schelling.
Reprinted with permission from *Journal of Political Economy* 78 (1970), 152–7.

Definition 2: A social welfare function is a collective choice rule, the range of which is restricted to orderings.

A weaker requirement is that each R should generate a "choice function," that is, in every subset of alternatives there must be a "best" alternative, or, in other words, there must be some (but not necessarily only one) alternative that is at least as good as all the other alternatives in that subset. This may be called a "social decision function."

Definition 3: A social decision function is a collective choice rule, the range of which is restricted to social preference relations that generate a choice function.

It was shown in Sen (1969) that the conditions that were proven to be inconsistent by Arrow (1951, 1963) in his justly famous "impossibility theorem" in the context of a social welfare function are in fact perfectly consistent if imposed on a social decision function. The impossibility theorem to be presented here holds, however, for social decision functions as well.

Arrow's condition of collective rationality (Condition 1') can be seen to be merely a requirement that the domain of the collective choice rule should not be arbitrarily restricted.

Condition U (Unrestricted Domain): Every logically possible set of individual orderings is included in the domain of the collective choice rule.

Arrow used a weak version of the Pareto principle.

Condition P: If every individual prefers any alternative x to another alternative y, then society must prefer x to y.

Finally, we introduce the condition of individual liberty in a very weak form.

Condition L (Liberalism): For each individual i, there is at least one pair of alternatives, say (x, y), such that if this individual prefers x to y, then society should prefer x to y, and if this individual prefers y to x, then society should prefer y to x.[1]

The intention is to permit each individual the freedom to determine at least one social choice, for example, having his own walls pink rather than white, other things remaining the same for him and the rest of the society.[2]

---

[1] The term "liberalism" is elusive and is open to alternative interpretations. Some uses of the term may not embrace the condition defined here, while many uses will. I do not wish to engage in a debate on the right use of the term. What is relevant is that Condition L represents a value involving individual liberty that many people would subscribe to. Whether such people are best described as liberals is a question that is not crucial to the point of this paper.

[2] Even this informal statement, which sounds mild, is much more demanding than Condition L. If the individual's preference over a personal choice (like choosing the colour of his wall) is to be accepted by the society, other things remaining the same, then this gives the individual rights not only over one pair, which is all that is required by Condition L, but over many pairs (possibly an infinite number of pairs) varying with the "other things." If it is socially all right

The following impossibility theorem holds.

Theorem I. *There is no social decision function that can simultaneously satisfy Conditions U, P, and L.*

In fact, we can weaken the condition of liberalism further. Such freedom may not be given at all, but to a proper subset of individuals. However, to make sense the subset must have more than one member, since if it includes only one then we might have a dictatorship. Hence, we demand such freedom for at least two individuals.

Condition L* (Minimal Liberalism): There are at least two individuals such that for each of them there is at least one pair of alternatives over which he is decisive, that is, there is a pair of x, y, such that if he prefers x (respectively y) to y (respectively x), then society should prefer x (respectively y) to y (respectively x).

The following theorem is stronger than Theorem I and subsumes it.

Theorem II. *There is no social decision function that can simultaneously satisfy Conditions U, P, and L*.*

Proof: Let the two individuals referred to in Condition L^* be 1 and 2, respectively, and the two pairs of alternatives referred to be (x, y) and (z, w), respectively. If (x, y) and (z, w) are the same pair of alternatives, then there is a contradiction. They have, therefore, at most one alternative in common, say $x = z$. Assume now that person 1 prefers x to y, and person 2 prefers w to $z(=x)$. And let everyone in the community including 1 and 2 prefer y to w. There is in this no inconsistency for anyone, not even for 1 and 2, and their respective orderings are: 1 prefers x to y and y to w, while 2 prefers y to w and w to x. By Condition U this should be in the domain of the social decision mechanism. But by Condition L^*, x must be preferred to y, and w must be preferred to $x(=z)$, while by the Pareto principle, y must be preferred to w. Thus, there is no best element in the set $(x = z, y, w)$ in terms of social preference, and every alternative is worse than some other. A choice function for the society does not therefore exist.

Next, let x, y, z, and w be all distinct. Let 1 prefer x to y, and 2 prefer z to w. And let everyone in the community including 1 and 2 prefer w to x and y to z. There is no contradiction for 1 or 2, for 1 simply prefers w to x, x to y, and y to z, while 2 prefers y to z, z to w, and w to x. By Condition U this configuration of individual preferences must yield a social choice function. But by Condition L^* society should prefer x to y and z to w, while by the Pareto principle society must prefer w to x, and y to z. This means that there

---

for me to have my walls either pink or white as I like in a social state where you smoke cigars, it should be socially all right for me to do the same where you indulge yourself in ways other than smoking cigars. Even this is not required by Condition L, which seems to demand very little.

is no best alternative for this set, and a choice function does not exist for any set that includes these four alternatives. Thus, there is no social decision function satisfying Conditions U, P, and L^*, and the proof is complete.[3]

3. An example

We give now a simple example of the type of impossibility that is involved in Theorem II by taking a special case of two individuals and three alternatives. There is one copy of a certain book, say *Lady Chatterley's Lover,* which is viewed differently by 1 and 2. The three alternatives are: that individual 1 reads it (x), that individual 2 reads it (y), and that no one reads it (z). Person 1, who is a prude, prefers most that no one reads it, but given the choice between either of the two reading it, he would prefer that he read it himself rather than exposing gullible Mr. 2 to the influences of Lawrence. (Prudes, I am told, tend to prefer to be censors rather than being censored.) In decreasing order of preference, his ranking is z, x, y. Person 2, however, prefers that either of them should read it rather than neither. Furthermore, he takes delight in the thought that prudish Mr. 1 may have to read Lawrence, and his first preference is that person 1 should read it, next best that he himself should read it, and worst that neither should. His ranking is, therefore, x, y, z.

Now if the choice is precisely between the pair (x, z), i.e., between person 1 reading the book and no one reading it, someone with liberal values may argue that it is person 1's preference that should count; since the prude would not like to read it, he should not be forced to. Thus, the society should prefer z to x. Similarly, in the choice exactly between person 2 reading the book (y) and no one reading it (z), liberal values require that person 2's preference should be decisive, and since he is clearly anxious to read the book he should be permitted to do this. Hence y should be judged socially better than z. Thus, in terms of liberal values it is better that no one reads it rather than person 1 being forced to read it, and it is still better that person 2 is permitted to read the book rather than no one reading it. That is, the society should prefer y to z, and z to x. This discourse could end happily with the book being handed over to person 2 but for the fact that it is a Pareto inferior alternative, being worse than person 1 reading it, in the view of both persons, i.e., x is Pareto superior to y.

Every solution that we can think of is bettered by some other solution, given the Pareto principle and the principle of liberalism, and we seem to have an inconsistency of choice. This is an example of the type of problem that is involved in Theorems I and II.

---

[3] We can strengthen this theorem further by weakening Condition L^* by demanding only that 1 be decisive for x against y, but not vice versa, and 2 be decisive for z against w, but not vice versa, and require that $x \neq z$, and $y \neq w$. This condition, too, can be shown to be inconsistent with Condition U and P, but the logical gain involved in this extension does not, alas, seem to be associated with any significant increase of relevance that I can think of.

4. Relevance

The dilemma posed here may appear to be somewhat disturbing. It is, of course, not necessarily disturbing for every conceivable society, since the conflict arises with only particular configurations of individual preferences. The ultimate guarantee for individual liberty may rest not on rules for social choice but on developing individual values that respect each other's personal choices. The conflict posed here is concerned with societies where such a condition does not hold and where pairwise choice based on liberal values may conflict with those based on the Pareto principle. Like Arrow's "General Possibility Theorem," here also the Condition of Unrestricted Domain is used.

However, unlike in the theorem of Arrow, we have not required transitivity of social preference. We have required neither transitivity of strict preference, nor transitivity of social preference. We have required neither transitivity of strict preference, nor transitivity of indifference, but merely the existence of a best alternative in each choice situation.[4] Suppose society prefers x to y, and y to z, and is indifferent between z and x. Arrow would rule this out, since there is an intransitivity; but we do not, for here alternative x is "best" in the sense of being at least as good as both the other alternatives. Our requirements are, in this respect, very mild, and we still have an impossibility.

Second, we have not imposed Arrow's much debated condition of "the independence of irrelevant alternatives."[5] Many people find the relaxation of this condition to be an appealing way of escaping the Arrow dilemma.

---

[4] It may appear that one way of solving this dilemma is to dispense with the social choice function based on a binary relation, that is, to relax not merely transitivity but also *acyclicity*. A choice function that need not correspond to any binary relation has undoubtedly a wider scope. But then Condition P and Condition L would have to be redefined, for example, (1) x should not be chosen when y is available, if everyone prefers y to x, and (2) for each individual there is a pair (x_i, y_i) such that if he prefers x_i (respectively y_i) to y_i (respectively x_i), then y_i (respectively x_i) should not be chosen if x_i (respectively y_i) is available. Thus redefined, the choice set for the set of alternatives may be rendered empty even without bringing in acyclicity, and the contradiction will reappear. This and other possible "ways out" are discussed more fully in my book (Sen, 1970, chap. 6).

[5] Using the condition of the independence of irrelevant alternatives, A. Gibbard, in an unpublished paper, has recently proved the following important theorem: Any social decision function that must generate social preferences that are all transitive in the strict relation (quasi-transitive) and which must satisfy Conditions U, P, non-dictatorship, and the independence of irrelevant alternatives, must be an oligarchy in the sense that there is a unique group of individuals each of whom, by preferring x to y, can make the society regard x to be at least as good as y, and by all preferring x to y can make the society prefer x to y, irrespective of the preferences of those who are not in this group. Gibbard's Theorem is disturbing, for the conditions look appealing but the resultant oligarchy seems revolting, and it is a major extension of the problem posed by Arrow (1951, 1963). Gibbard argues against the simultaneous insistence on a binary relation of social preference generating a choice function and on the condition of the independence of irrelevant alternatives. We have not imposed the latter.

This way out is not open here, for the theorem holds without imposing this condition.

The Pareto principle is used here in a very weak version, as in Arrow. We do not necessarily require that if someone prefers x to y and everyone regards x to be at least as good as y, then x is socially better. We permit the possibility of having collective choice rules that will violate this provided everyone strictly preferring x to y must make x socially better than y.

Nevertheless it turns out that a principle reflecting liberal values even in a very mild form cannot possibly be combined with the weak Pareto principle, given an unrestricted domain. If we do believe in these other conditions, then the society cannot permit even minimal liberalism. Society cannot then let more than one individual be free to read what they like, sleep the way they prefer, dress as they care, etc., *irrespective* of the preferences of others in the community.

What is the moral? It is that in a very basic sense liberal values conflict with the Pareto principle. If someone takes the Pareto principle seriously, as economists seem to do, then he has to face problems of consistency in cherishing liberal values, even very mild ones.[6] Or, to look at it in another way, if someone does have certain liberal values, then he may have to eschew his adherence to Pareto optimality. While the Pareto criterion has been thought to be an expression of individual liberty, it appears that in choices involving more than two alternatives it can have consequences that are, in fact, deeply illiberal.

References

Arrow, K. J., *Individual Values and Social Choice* (New York: Wiley, 1951; 2nd edn., 1963).

Sen, A. K., "Quasi-transitivity, Rational Choice and Collective Decisions." Discussion paper no. 45, Harvard Institute of Economic Research, 1968. *Rev. Econ. Studies,* 36, no. 3 (July 1969): 381–93.

  Collective Choice and Social Welfare (San Francisco: Holden-Day; and Edinburgh: Oliver & Boyd, 1970).

[6] The difficulties of *achieving* Pareto optimality in the presence of externalities are well known. What is at issue here is the *acceptability* of Pareto optimality as an objective in the context of liberal values, given certain types of externalities.

16. Liberty and social choice

Amartya Sen

Does individual liberty conflict with the Pareto principle – that cornerstone of welfare economics which insists that unanimous individual preference rankings must be reflected in social decisions? A result in social choice theory – the so-called "impossibility of the Paretian liberal" – has indicated that there can indeed be such a conflict,[1] and this result has been followed by a great many other results – some extending the conflict and others proposing ways of avoiding it (see section 4 below). However, the rather special format of social choice theory makes it a little difficult to be sure of the *relevance* of this class of results to ethics, welfare economics, or social and political philosophy. This paper is concerned with discussing that issue.

There are two further objectives. First, the formal conditions used in social choice theory can be given more than one interpretation, and the practical import of the results clearly does depend on the interpretations chosen. This applies not merely to the impossibility of the Paretian liberal, but also to other results in the field, including the deeper impossibility result presented by Kenneth Arrow.[2] One particular source of variation is the content of "social preference," and in this paper three different interpretations are distinguished and discussed.

Second, the formulation of liberty (more accurately, that of some minimal implications of respecting liberty) in social choice theory has been deeply

For helpful comments, I am grateful to Peter Hammond, Susan Hurley, Isaac Levi, Jim Mirrlees, Robert Sugden, John Vickers, and Bernard Williams.

Reprinted with permission from *The Journal of Philosophy* 80, no. 1 (January 1983), 5–28.

[1] See my "The Impossibility of a Paretian Liberal," *Journal of Political Economy,* 78 (1970): 152–157, and *Collective Choice and Social Welfare* (San Francisco: Holden-Day, 1970).

[2] *Social Choice and Individual Values* (New York: Wiley, 2nd ed., 1963); parenthetical page references to Arrow will be to this book. The interpretational question, specifically in the context of the Arrow theorem, is discussed in my "Social Choice Theory: A Re-examination," *Econometrica,* 45 (1977): 53–89, and "Personal Utilities and Public Judgments, or What's Wrong with Welfare Economics?" *Economic Journal,* 89 (1979): 537–558.

questioned,[3] and indeed that formulation is at variance with at least some of the more traditional characterizations of liberty, seeing liberty in terms of procedures rather than outcomes. An attempt is made in this paper to go into this broader question of how liberty should be seen, and in this context a critique of purely procedural formulations of liberty is offered.

1. Social preference

The typical social-choice-theoretic format is that of transforming a set (in fact, an n-tuple) of individual preference orderings into a social preference relation or a social choice function. Arrow required the social preference relation to be a complete weak ordering (reflexive, complete, and transitive) and the social choice function to specify the best elements (the choice set) with respect to that social preference relation for each nonempty set of social states (the feasible set, or the "menu"). Others have demanded less exacting properties of the social preference relation (permitting intransitivity or incompleteness), or less limiting types of social choice function (permitting nonbinary choice), and various possibility and impossibility results have been presented.

Though various interpretations of social preference are possible, here I shall confine myself to only three interpretations of "x is socially preferred to y":

(1) *outcome evaluation:* "x is judged to be a better state of affairs for the society than y";
(2) *normative choice:* "decision making in the society should be so organized that y must not be chosen when x is available";
(3) *descriptive choice:* "social decision systems are so organized that y will not be chosen when x is available."

I should emphasize that although the latter two interpretations link preference to choice, neither of them requires that the choice function – normative

---

[3] See especially Robert Nozick, "Distributive Justice," *Philosophy and Public Affairs,* 3, 1 (Fall 1973): 45–126, and *Anarchy, State and Utopia* (Oxford: Blackwell, 1974), pp. 149–182; Peter Bernholz, "Is a Paretian Liberal Really Impossible?" *Public Choice,* 19 (1974): 99–107; C. K. Rowley and A. T. Peacock, *Welfare Economics: A Liberal Restatement* (London: Martin Robertson, 1975); James Buchanan, "An Ambiguity in Sen's Alleged Proof of the Impossibility of the Paretian Liberal," mimeographed, Virginia Polytechnic, 1976; Kevin Roberts, "Liberalism and Welfare Economics: A Note," mimeographed, St. Catherine's College, Oxford, 1976; Peter Gärdenfors, "Rights, Games and Social Choice," *Noûs,* 15, 3 (September 1981): 341–356; Robert Sugden, *The Political Economy of Public Choice* (Oxford: Martin Robertson, 1981; parenthetical page references to Sugden will be to this book); Brian Barry, "Lady Chatterley's Lover and Doctor Fischer's Bomb Party: Liberalism, Pareto Optimality, and the Problem of Objectionable Preferences,"...in J. Elster and A. Hylland, eds., *Foundations of Social Choice Theory,* Cambridge University Press; Bruce Chapman, "Rights as Constraints: Nozick versus Sen," mimeographed, Westminster Institute for Ethics and Human Values, 1981.

or descriptive – be "binary" in character, in the sense of being representable by a binary relation.[4] Each just imposes a condition that the choice functions – respectively – should *or* will satisfy; whether or not the totality of social choices can be captured by a binary relation is left open.

Within these three broad interpretations, there are, of course, further distinctions, based on the context of the statements. For example, the outcome-evaluation statement can reflect a *particular person's* moral judgment, or the result of the application of some *evaluation procedure* (e.g., yielded by a particular "objective function" used in planning or policy making).

2. The impossibility of the Paretian liberal

The Pareto principle, in its weak form, demands that, if every individual prefers a social state x to a social state y, then x must be socially preferred to y. Individual liberty can be seen to require – among other things – that each individual should have a *recognized personal sphere* in which his preference and his alone would count in determining the social preference. For example, consider a person who would like to read a particular novel, other things given, and assume that for some given configuration of other things that choice is in his recognized personal sphere; then the social preference must put his reading the novel above not reading it, given the other things. The condition of *minimal liberty* (ML, for short) is, in fact, a weaker requirement than this, demanding that there be such a nonempty recognized personal sphere for *at least two* persons (not necessarily for all – which would do, but isn't required).[5]

A *social decision function* determines a complete and consistent (free from cycles) social preference defined over the set of alternative social states for any set (in fact, n-tuple) of individual preference orderings (one ordering per person). A social decision function has an *unrestricted domain* if it works

---

[4] On the issue of binariness of choice functions, see Bengt Hansson, "Choice Structures and Preference Relations," *Synthese,* 18, 4 (October 1968): 443–458; Amartya Sen, "Choice Functions and Revealed Preference," *Review of Economic Studies,* 37 (1971): 307–317; Hans Herzberger, "Ordinal Preference and Rational Choice," *Econometrica,* 41 (1973): 187–237; Peter Fishburn, *The Theory of Social Choice* (Princeton, N.J.: University Press, 1973); Thomas Schwartz, "Choice Functions, 'Rationality' Conditions, and Variations on the Weak Axiom of Revealed Preference," *Journal of Economic Theory,* 12 (1976): 414–427; Charles Plott, "Axiomatic Social Choice Theory: An Overview and Interpretation," *American Journal of Political Science,* 20 (1976): 511–596.

[5] This condition was originally christened "minimal liberalism," with a warning about possible misunderstanding: "The term 'liberalism' is elusive and open to alternative interpretations. Some uses of the term may not embrace the condition defined here. What is relevant is that Condition L represents a value involving individual liberty that many people would subscribe to" ("The Impossibility of a Paretian Liberal," p. 153). In a later paper the condition was called "minimal libertarianism." Neither term is very satisfactory, and the term used here – "minimal liberty" – has the advantage of concentrating on the concept of liberty itself rather than on its advocacy through one approach or another.

for any logically possible *n*-tuple of individual preference orderings. The impossibility of the Paretian liberal is the theorem establishing that there cannot exist a social decision function satisfying unrestricted domain, the Pareto principle (even in its weak form), and minimal liberty ML.

The traditional interpretation of preference has been in terms of desires,[6] and I shall stick to that usage. An alternative approach, developed under the theory of "revealed preference," defines preference as the binary relation underlying choice. This rather unnatural usage of preference empties the term of much of its normal meaning, and – more importantly – the implied identification of two distinct notions leaves us short of one important concept. Further, not all choice functions have binary representation.

Though it is not sensible to identify preference and choice definitionally, it is traditional in social choice theory to make the empirical assumption that individual choices will, in fact, be entirely based on individual preference. Arrow has outlined the characteristics of such a model of individual behavior (ch. II, pp. 9–21), and I shall call this the assumption of *universal preference-based choice*. A much weaker version of this assumption is adequate for the social-choice characterization of liberty, to wit, that, in choices over an individual's *recognized personal sphere,* the individual will be guided entirely by his preference. If (x, y) is a pair of states such that it belongs to i's recognized personal sphere and he strictly prefers x to y, then he will not choose y when x is available to him to choose.[7] I shall call this the assumption of *minimal preference-based choice,* of which *universal* preference-based choice is a special case.

Consider now any configuration of recognized personal spheres over which the respective individuals are acknowledged – under rules satisfying ML – to have a special authority; the exact content of that authority is specified by the chosen interpretation of social preference. Let (x, y) belong to i's recognized personal sphere, and let him strictly prefer x to y. Not only does he desire to have x rather than y, but also – under the assumption of limited preference-based choice (and *a fortiori* under universal preference-based

---

[6] This is true in traditional economic theory as well; see for example John Hicks, *Value and Capital* (Oxford: Clarendon Press, 1939). Also in moral discussions; see, for example, Richard Hare, *The Language of Morals* (Oxford: Clarendon Press, 1952).

[7] The issue here concerns what the person would choose *if x* and *y* are both, in fact, *available* to him for choosing (possibly along with other alternatives). This question of preference-choice correspondence should not be confused with the different – but important – issue discussed by Allan Gibbard ["A Pareto-consistent Libertarian Claim," *Journal of Economic Theory,* 7 (1974): 388–410; parenthetical page references to Gibbard will be to this article] of what an individual should choose if his preferred alternative (x, in this case) is *not actually available* because of the exercise of other people's rights or the application of the Pareto principle. It is, of course, an *implication* of the theorem of the impossibility of the Paretian liberal that both the alternatives in a pair in each individual's personal sphere cannot actually be made available to him for choosing in the way specified by minimal liberty ML, if the Pareto-inferior alternatives must also be rejected.

choice) – he will choose x if he has to choose one of the two alternatives. He will, in fact, never choose y if he is actually given the choice over a set that contains x. Under the outcome-evaluation interpretation of social preference, the condition of liberty incorporating ML requires that, given the circumstances specified, x be judged to be a better state of affairs for the society than y [see (1) in the last section].

Under the normative-choice interpretation, it is required that decision making in the society should be so organized that, in the circumstances specified, y must not be chosen when x is available [see (2)]. This is, it should be noticed, a less demanding requirement than the condition that the choice between x and y (with or without the presence of other alternatives) be left to individual i himself, so that he can dislodge an about-to-be-chosen y and get his preferred x selected instead. If it were left to him, he would of course not choose y. Such an assumption of "individual control" is adequate for ML, but not necessary, since ML needs only that, no matter how social decisions are made, y does not end up being chosen. As the theorem under discussion is an *impossibility* result, a weaker requirement cannot be objected to, since the impossibility must remain unaffected by any strengthening of the condition – by requiring that i be given "individual control" in the choice or non-choice of y when x is also available.

Under the descriptive-choice interpretation, it is postulated that the social decision systems are so organized that y is not chosen when x is a feasible choice [see (3)].

Similar interpretational variations are applied to the weak Pareto principle, using the different interpretations of social preference given by (1), (2), and (3), respectively.

It is now straightforward to see the contents of the impossibility of the Paretian liberal under three different interpretations, respectively:

(I)   *Outcome-evaluation impossibility:* For some configuration of individual preferences, there can be no consistent and complete evaluation of social states satisfying the weak Pareto principle and minimal liberty, interpreted as in (1).

(II)   *Normative-choice impossibility:* There is no good way of organizing decision making in the society so that – no matter what the individual preferences happen to be – some state gets chosen from any nonempty set of states, when the goodness of the decision making requires satisfying the weak Pareto principle and minimal liberty, interpreted as in (2).

(III) *Descriptive-choice impossibility:* Any actual social decision system that is able to choose – no matter what the individual preferences are – some state from any nonempty set of states, will be unable to satisfy the weak Pareto principle and minimal liberty, interpreted as in (3).

3. An illustration

Various illustrations of the Pareto-liberty conflict have been presented in the literature.[8] The example involving the reading or not of *Lady Chatterley's Lover*[9] has probably had more attention than it deserves, and I shall use here a less tired example, viz., the so-called "work-choice case."[10]

Persons 1 and 2 both prefer having a full-time job (1) to a half-time job (½) and a half-time job to being unemployed (0), given the job situation of the other. But, spoiled as they are by the competitive society in which they live, each prefers that the other be jobless (that is, 0 to ½ to 1, for the other). Indeed, each is green-eyed enough to get more fulfillment out of the joblessness of the other than from his own job. Given the nature of the jobs involved, there happen to be four possible alternative states for these two persons, represented here by four pairs, with the first number of each pair describing person 1's job situation and the second number person 2's. The two persons' preferences are the following, in descending order:

Person 1	*Person 2*
(½, 0)	(0, ½)
(1, ½)	(½, 1)
(0, ½)	(½, 0)
(½, 1)	(1, ½)

Let persons 1 and 2 each have a recognized personal sphere with the properties specified by minimal liberty ML. Individual 1's personal sphere covers the choice over the pair (1, ½) and (0, ½); he should be free to work if he so prefers, given the job situation (½) of the other. Similarly individual 2's personal sphere covers the choice over (½, 1) and (½, 0), and person 2 also should be free to work if he so prefers, given the job situation (½) of person 1.

Now consider the three different interpretations of social preference. With the outcome-evaluation interpretation, the exercise is one of ranking the four alternative states in terms of how good they are for the society of these two people. One particular context may be that of a person's "social welfare judgment," discussed earlier. The judge could be an outsider *or* indeed either of these two persons themselves making a *moral* judgment. On grounds of

---

[8] For different types of example, see my *Collective Choice and Social Welfare,* ch. 6; Gibbard, *op. cit.;* Jonathan Barnes, "Freedom, Rationality and Paradox," *Canadian Journal of Philosophy,* 10, 4 (December 1980): 545–565; J. Fountain, "Bowley's Analysis of Bilateral Monopoly and Sen's Liberal Paradox in Collective Choice Theory: A Note," *Quarterly Journal of Economics,* 95 (1980): 809–812; E. T. Green, "Libertarian Aggregation of Preferences: What the 'Coase Theorem' Might Have Said," *Social Science Working Paper* No. 315, California Institute of Technology, 1980.

[9] Presented in my *Collective Choice and Social Welfare,* p. 80.

[10] Presented in my "Liberty, Unanimity and Rights," *Economica,* 43 (1976): 217–245, pp. 222/3.

minimal liberty, the judge puts $(1, \frac{1}{2})$ over $(0, \frac{1}{2})$, since person 1 actually prefers $(1, \frac{1}{2})$, person 2 isn't directly involved in this decision about 1's job, and in fact the pair is in 1's personal sphere. On similar grounds, $(\frac{1}{2}, 1)$ is put above $(\frac{1}{2}, 0)$, in line with 2's preference, noting that 1 is not directly involved in this particular choice and that in fact the pair is in 2's personal sphere. But if the judge also adheres to the Pareto principle, then he must put $(\frac{1}{2}, 0)$ over $(1, \frac{1}{2})$, since both prefer the former, and on exactly similar grounds place $(0, \frac{1}{2})$ over $(\frac{1}{2}, 1)$. And this combination involves a cycle of social preference: $(1, \frac{1}{2})$ is better than $(0, \frac{1}{2})$, which is better than $(\frac{1}{2}, 1)$, which is better than $(\frac{1}{2}, 0)$, which is better than $(1, \frac{1}{2})$. Every state is worse than some other state.

Consider next the *descriptive*-choice interpretation. Perhaps the simplest case is that of direct control over one's personal sphere. If $(0, \frac{1}{2})$ is about to be chosen, person 1 is given the power to get $(1, \frac{1}{2})$ chosen instead. Similarly, if $(\frac{1}{2}, 0)$ is about to be chosen, then person 2 has the power to make $(\frac{1}{2}, 1)$ be chosen instead. So the actual choice will be confined to $(1, \frac{1}{2})$ and $(\frac{1}{2}, 1)$. But *both* happen to be Pareto inefficient.

Under the *normative*-choice interpretation, ML requires that a good system of making social decisions not lead to $(\frac{1}{2}, 0)$ or $(0, \frac{1}{2})$ being chosen, and the weak Pareto principle requires that a good system not lead to the choice of $(1, \frac{1}{2})$ or $(\frac{1}{2}, 1)$. So nothing can be chosen, and there is no good system of choice in the required sense.

4. Restrictions, extentions and reformulations

The impossibility of the Paretian liberal is based on the inconsistency of three conditions, viz., unrestricted domain, the weak Pareto principle, and the condition of minimal liberty. To avoid the inconsistency, at least one of the conditions has to be dropped or weakened in some substantial way. In the literature on the subject, each of these three avenues has been extensively explored.

Weakening unrestricted domain amounts to ruling out certain configurations – "profiles" – of individual preferences, so that with the remaining profiles the conflict cannot occur. Examples of this line of reconciliation include assuming that the actual preferences show "tolerance" in the sense of the individual's being *indifferent* over pairs belonging to other people's recognized personal spheres,[11] or "empathy" in the sense of the individual's *mirroring* other people's preferences over their respective private spheres,[12] or being "nonmeddlesome" or "liberal" in the sense of the individual's attaching greater importance to ranking the alternatives over his own personal sphere

---

[11] See C. Seidl, "On Liberal Values," *Zeitschrift für Nationalökonomie,* 35 (1975): 257–292.

[12] See F. Breyer and G. A. Gigliotti, "Empathy and the Respect for the Right of Others," *Zeitschrift für Nationalökonomie,* 40 (1980), 59–64.

vis-à-vis ranking the alternatives in other people's personal spheres,[13] or satisfying some other adequate restrictions.[14] These explorations throw light on the nature of the underlying conflict and are possibly relevant for thinking about education and value formation.

Restricting the domain does not, however, amount to an adequate way out of the conflict, since it does not tell us what social judgments would be made (or what states should be chosen, or how decision mechanisms should be organized) in dealing with profiles that violate the required restrictions, when such profiles actually happen to occur. Nevertheless, corresponding to any domain restriction, ruling out some preference profiles, there exist related solutions that take the form of negating *either* the weak Pareto principle *or* the condition of minimal liberty *for each profile that does not belong to the permissible domain.* Meddlesome individuals could be "penalized" by the denial of their special authority over their *own* personal spheres,[15] or their preferences could be either ignored or "amended" in dealing with the weak Pareto judgment.[16] These modifications amount to weakening the minimal-liberty condition or the weak Pareto principle, respectively. Other ways of restricting these conditions have also been investigated – some of them helping to avoid the conflict and others leaving it unaffected.[17]

[13] J. H. Blau, "Liberal Values and Independence," *Review of Economic Studies,* 42 (1975): 395–402; Breyer, "The Liberal Paradox, Decisiveness over Issues, and Domain Restrictions," *Zeitschrift für Nationalökonomie,* 37, 4 (1977): 45–60, and *Das Liberal Paradox* (Meisenheim am Glan, 1978).

[14] Benevolence toward each other can do the trick, as discussed by Ted Bergstrom, "A 'Scandinavian Consensus' Solution for Efficient Income Distribution among Nonmalevolent Consumers," *Journal of Economic Theory,* 2 (1970): 383–398. So could – possibly more surprisingly – systematic malevolence, if one individual directs it against the preferences of all others. These and other related conditions are explored in a planned joint paper by Eric Maskin, Barry Nalebuff, and myself.

[15] See Gibbard, *op. cit.;* Blau, *op. cit.;* D. E. Campbell, "Democratic Preference Functions," *Journal of Economic Theory,* 12 (1976): 259–272; J. A. Ferejohn, "The Distribution of Rights in Society," in H. W. Gottinger and W. Leinfellner, eds., *Decision Theory and Social Ethics: Issues in Social Choice* (Dordrecht: Reidel, 1978); W. Gaertner and L. Krüger, "Self-supporting Preferences and Individual Rights: The Possibility of Paretian Libertarianism," *Economica,* 47 (1981): 241–252.

[16] See M. J. Farrell, "Liberalism in the Theory of Social Choice," *Review of Economic Studies,* 43 (1976): 3–10; Sen, "Liberty, Unanimity and Rights"; K. Suzumura, "On the Consistency of Libertarian Claims," *Review of Economic Studies,* 45 (1978): 329–342; P. J. Hammond, "Liberalism, Independent Rights and the Pareto Principle," forthcoming in the *Proceedings of the 6th International Congress of Logic, Methodology and Philosophy of Science;* D. Austen-Smith, "Restricted Pareto and Rights," forthcoming in *Journal of Economic Theory;* P. Coughlin and A. K. Sen, unpublished notes, Institute of Economics and Statistics, Oxford, 1981.

[17] See J. S. Kelly, "The Impossibility of a Just Liberal," *Economica,* 43 (1976): 67–76; J. Aldrich, "The Dilemma of a Paretian Liberal: Some Consequences of Sen's Theorem," *Public Choice,* 30 (1977): 1–21; D. C. Mueller, *Public Choice* (Cambridge: University Press, 1979); F. Breyer and R. Gardner, "Liberal Paradox, Game Equilibrium, and Gibbard Optimum," *Public Choice,* 35 (1980): 469–481; Gardner, "The Strategic Inconsistency of Paretian Liberal," *Public Choice,* 35 (1980): 241–252; Suzumura, "Equity, Efficiency and Rights in Social

While methods of resolving the conflict have received much of the attention in the literature on the subject, there has also been interesting work in extending and generalizing the conflict. Allan Gibbard (388–397) has shown that individual liberties can even turn out to be internally inconsistent if the condition of minimal liberty is strengthened, permitting the individual to fix one "feature" of the social state, no matter what others choose and no matter how the individual chooses his "feature." If I am decisive on my wall color given everything else (including your wall color) and you are decisive on yours given everything else (including my wall color), then we can have a cycle if, for example, I want to *match* your wall color, but you want to *differentiate* from mine.

To avoid this problem – the "Gibbard paradox" – either the assignment of rights has to be more restrictive (making them – to use Suzumura's expression – "coherent," e.g., as with ML), or rights have to be conditional on individual preferences satisfying a condition of "separability."[18] Separability requires that my ranking of my "personal" features (e.g., the color of my walls) be independent of the choice of other people over their respective personal features. These restrictions which avoid the Gibbard paradox, may in fact be quite justifiable within the rationale of giving people rights over personal choices. If I am trying to paint my walls in a color different from yours, my ambition is not quite a "personal" or "self-regarding" one, and it is not unreasonable to desist from insisting that the fulfillment of such contingent preferences be a necessary part of my personal liberty. Even when the Gibbard paradox is avoided (through having "coherent" rights *or* separable preferences), the impossibility of the Paretian liberal continues to hold,[19] and some further restriction is called for to avoid that conflict.[20]

In another important departure, introduced by R. N. Batra and P. K. Pattanaik,[21] the impossibility of the Paretian liberal has been extended to show that the Pareto principle conflicts not only with individual liberty but also with *group rights* (e.g., rights given by "federalism" or "pluralism"), and for much the same analytical reasons.[22]

Choice," *Discussion Paper* No. 155, revised June 1981; J. L. Wriglesworth, "Solution to the Gibbard and Sen Paradoxes Using Information Available from Interpersonal Comparisons," mimeographed, Lincoln College, Oxford.

[18] Gibbard, *op cit.;* Farrell, *op. cit.;* Kelly, *Arrow Impossibility Theorems* (New York: Academic Press, 1978); Hammond, *op. cit.*

[19] Gibbard, *op. cit.* pp. 394–397; Suzumura, "On the Consistency of Libertarian Claims"; Hammond, *op. cit.*

[20] Gibbard's own solution, referred to earlier, takes the form of "waiving" some individual rights.

[21] "On Some Suggestions for Having Non-binary Social Choice Functions," *Theory and Decision,* 3, 1 (October 1972): 1–11. See also D. N. Stevens and J. E. Foster, "The Possibility of Democratic Pluralism," *Economica,* 45 (1978): 391–400; Wriglesworth, "The Possibility of Democratic Pluralism: A Comment," *Economica,* 49 (1982).

[22] For extensions in a different direction, see Albert Weale, "The Impossibility of Liberal Egalitarianism," *Analysis,* 60.1, 185 (January 1980): 13–9; Iain McLean, "Liberty, Equality and the Pareto Principle: A Comment on Weale," *ibid.,* 60.4, 188 (October 1980): 212/3.

The ways of avoiding the conflict and those of extending it, discussed above, operate within the general format of social choice theory. The legitimacy of that perspective on liberty has been disputed, and it has been forcefully argued that the very characterization of liberty in social choice theory is fundamentally misconceived. I turn now to that general question and also examine some alternative formulations of liberty.

5. Liberty, control and social choice

Robert Nozick raised a question of importance when – discussing the impossibility of the Paretian liberal – he criticized "treating an individual's rights to choose among alternatives as the right to determine the relative ordering of these alternatives within a social ordering."[23] Instead, Nozick characterizes rights in terms of giving the individual *control* over certain decisions, and "each person may exercise his right as he chooses." "The exercise of these rights fixes some features of the world. Within the constraints of these fixed features, a choice may be made by a social choice mechanism based upon a social ordering; if there are any choices left to make!" (166).

A similar criticism has been made by several other authors,[24] and the point has been put thus by Robert Sugden, commenting on the impossibility of the Paretian liberal:

The flaw in this ingenious argument lies, I suggest, in Sen's formulation of the principle of liberty. Although he claims (Sen, 1976 ["Liberty, Unanimity and Rights"], p. 218) that he is appealing to the same ideas of liberty as Mill did, there is a crucial difference between what Mill meant by liberty and what Sen means. Mill would have agreed that "there are certain personal matters in which each person should be free to decide what should happen"; but would he have agreed that "in choices over these things whatever he or she thinks is better must be taken to be better for society as a whole"? The first of these two propositions is a value judgment about procedures: it says that certain issues ought to be delegated to, or reserved for, individual decision-making. The second proposition is a value judgment about end states: it says, in effect, that the procedure of reserving these issues for individual decision-making invariably leads to the selection of the best feasible end states. But why should a liberal have to claim this? ... So far as specifically liberal values are concerned, there is nothing inherently dignified or undignified about the act of reading *Lady Chatterley's Lover* (196/7).

The point is cogently argued, but it is based on taking an unduly narrow view of the possible content of "social preference" – of being regarded as

---

[23] Nozick, *Anarchy, State and Utopia,* p. 165.

[24] See fn 3 above. However, see also Peter Hammond, "Liberalism, Independent Rights and the Pareto Principle," and "Utilitarianism, Uncertainty and Information," in A. Sen and B. Williams, eds., *Utilitarianism and Beyond* (Cambridge: University Press, 1982); C. R. Perelli-Minetti, "Nozick on Sen: A Misunderstanding," *Theory and Decision,* 8, 4 (October 1977): 387–393; Paul Grout, "On Minimal Liberalism in Economics," mimeographed, Birmingham University, 1980.

"better for society." In fact, a social-preference statement may well reflect nothing more than a condition on the choice function, as was explained in section 1. But even if the outcome-evaluation interpretation is considered, that need not be a judgment about the "inherent" goodness or badness of the states. In the context of the procedural judgment that Sugden attributes to Mill, social preference can be seen as reflecting the ranking – not necessarily complete – of alternatives in terms of consistency with the right procedures. There is nothing unusual about procedure-based judgments of the relative merits of different outcomes; there are plenty of such judgments made by Mill himself.[25] A judgment about anything need not be a function only of the inherent qualities of that thing. To take an analogy from a different field, contrast the following statements about the goodness of Mitterand as a spokesman for France:

(A)   Mitterand is the best person to speak for France, since he won the Presidential election.

(B)   Mitterand is the best person to speak for France, since no one else has his ability to interpret the soul of France.

Procedure-based judgments of the goodness of states are comparable to (A) rather than to (B).

When the outcome-evaluation interpretation of social preference is considered in the context of a purely procedure-based view of liberty, an outcome that is regarded as "better for society" from the point of view of liberty is so regarded precisely because that is what would be chosen by the person in question. Even "a value judgment about procedures" implies – given the behavioral parameters – judgments about what states *should* emerge, viz., the consequences of the use of the right procedures. Social preference can be made to reflect that judgment.[26] So, even if it were the case that procedural judgments are adequate for fully characterizing liberty in social decisions (a view that I will presently dispute in section 6), even then the condition of minimal liberty can be correspondingly interpreted, and justified, within that framework. If a social state can emerge only through the violation of the

[25] It should, however, be mentioned that although Mill did endorse procedural judgment of the kind referred to by Sugden, he did not, in fact, take a *purely* procedural view of liberty.

[26] In terms of Isaac Levi's distinction between "social value" and "social welfare" ("Liberty and Welfare," in Sen and Williams, eds. *op cit.*), this interpretation of the condition of minimal liberty relates to "social value" rather than to "social welfare." Levi himself confines his discussion to the interpretation that minimal liberty is a condition on "social welfare" (presumably associated with individual welfares rather than with any procedural condition of choice). The term "social welfare" in social choice theory does have this "welfarist" ring, but it *need not* have the "welfarist" *content* (see my *Collective Choice and Social Welfare*, pp. 33/4), and can well be seen in the same way that Levi sees "social value": "some standard of social value which evaluates social states with respect to whether they are better or worse" (p. 240). As Levi rightly points out, even "rugged libertarianism" has implications for social value, requiring "modification of the standard of social value when its fit with libertarian choice mechanisms turns out to be poor" (p. 242).

right procedure, then an indictment of that state in that context is implicit in the procedure-based value system itself. And the impossibility of the Paretian liberal – under the outcome-evaluation interpretation combined with a purely procedural concept of liberty – is concerned with the inconsistency of the ranking based on such indictment (reflected in the corresponding interpretation of "minimal liberty") and the Pareto quasi-ordering.

If instead of the outcome-evaluation interpretation of social preference, the normative-choice interpretation is considered, then it is even more straightforward to see the condition of minimal liberty in terms of the perspective of liberty as control. It insists that the outcomes to emerge must not be different from what would be chosen if certain issues are delegated to, or reserved for, individual decision making. If that condition were violated, then of course there would be a violation *also* of the principle – as described by Sugden – "that certain issues ought to be delegated to, or reserved for, individual decision-making." The impossibility of the Paretian liberal under the normative-choice interpretation asserts – *inter alia* – that such a principle of choice procedure cannot be combined – for an unrestricted domain – with insistence on the Pareto optimality of outcomes.

These misunderstandings about the content of the social choice propositions are partly the fault of social choice theory itself. The language of social choice theory – though precisely formulated – has tended to be rather remote from the standard language of social and political philosophy, and the skill of the social choice theorist in obtaining technical results has not been quite matched by the inclination to discuss issues of interpretation. In particular, there is need to clarify the different substantive contents of a given result corresponding to the different interpretations of such concepts as social preference, and also to relate these different contents to the traditional issues of social and political philosophy.

It is also worth emphasizing that the conditions of liberty – such as Condition L and Condition ML – used in social choice theory do not attempt to present a comprehensive view of liberty; rather, only of some of its implications. This is adequate for the impossibility results, since the inconsistency of the Pareto principle with liberty can be shown by demonstrating its inconsistency with some *implications* of liberty, without having to characterize liberty fully.

For example, someone could insist that liberty requires *not merely* that the individual get what he *would* choose *but also* that he get it *through* choosing it himself. In this case there is an asymmetry in judging the liberty aspect of (i) his getting and (ii) his not getting, what he would choose. If we know that he has *not* got what he would choose, we know that his liberty has been violated, and that kind of deduction is all that is required for the impossibility of the Paretian liberal. On the other hand, even if we know that he *has* got what he would choose, the quoted view of liberty will not yet permit us to be sure of the fulfillment of his liberty, since his liberty *would have been* violated if – say – somebody else had chosen for him what he would him-self choose. The quoted view is thus not denied – nor of course asserted – in deriving the impossibility of the Paretian liberal.

6. Control and indirect liberty

I now take up the postponed question of whether liberty is concerned just with actual control. It certainly *is* concerned with control – that is not in dis-pute – but is it *just* control that it is concerned with?

First consider the case of a person – Ed – who has been injured in a car accident, but is fully conscious. The doctor tells him that she can treat him in one of two ways, *A* and *B*, and though both would be effective, she is cer-tain that *A* would be very much better for him in terms of side effects. Ed says that he understands the options and accepts that *A* would indeed serve his welfare better, but he has some moral objection to treatment *A* (its de-velopment involved cruelty to animals) and would therefore prefer to have treatment *B*. It is easy to argue here that Ed's liberty is better served by the doctor giving him treatment *B*, even though his welfare would have been better served by *A*. I shall describe this as a case in which Ed's *direct* liberty is better served by *B*.

Now consider the case in which Ed is unconscious after the car accident, but his companion knows about Ed's moral beliefs and the strength of his convictions. The same choice arises with the doctor making the same assess-ment. The companion says that she is completely convinced that Ed *would have chosen* treatment *B* despite accepting that *A* would serve his welfare better. It seems reasonable to argue that, in this case too, Ed's liberty would be better served by the doctor's giving him treatment *B*, even though Ed himself is not exercising any direct control over the particular choice. I shall describe this as a case of Ed's *indirect* liberty's being better served by *B*.

It is, of course, tempting to think that, in the second case, what is involved in the choice made by the doctor and Ed's companion is Ed's welfare. But the example was so specified that the presumption is not easy to entertain, since neither the doctor, nor Ed's companion, nor indeed Ed, can be taken to as-sume that *B* would serve Ed's welfare better. Quite the contrary. The argu-ment for treatment *B* rather than *A* is precisely that Ed *would have chosen* it, and that is clearly a liberty-type consideration rather than a welfare-type consideration. What Isaiah Berlin calls "the extent of a man's, or a people's, liberty to choose to live as they desire"[27] does seem to require counterfactual exercises of this kind. To see liberty exclusively in terms of who is exercising control is inadequate.

The relevance of *indirect* liberty seems quite substantial in modern society. Police action in preventing crime in the streets may serve my liberty well –

---

[27] *Four Essays on Liberty* (New York: Oxford, 1969), p. 70.

since I don't want to be mugged or roughed up – but the control here is exercised not by me, but by the police. (The fact that it may also serve my *welfare* well is, of course, a different consideration.) What is relevant for my indirect liberty in this case is the understanding that *if* I had control over the crime *specifically directed against me,* I would have exercised my choice to stop it. Of course, it is *conceivable* that a person would have chosen to be mugged or roughed up or hit by a car going the wrong way on a one-way street, but the presumption on which the consideration of *indirect* liberty is based is that he would not have so chosen.

There is a danger that in crudely identifying liberty with direct control – overlooking the counterfactual exercises involved in indirect liberty – a lot that is important might be lost. Society cannot typically be organized in such a way that each person himself controls all the levers related to his personal sphere.[28] But it would be a mistake to assume that considerations of liberty of a person are irrelevant in a particular choice if he himself is not making the choice. Giving the unconscious Ed treatment *A* – though acknowledged by all to be better for his welfare – is a violation of Ed's liberty in a manner that giving him treatment *B* is not. What a person *would have chosen if* he had control is an important consideration in judging the person's liberty.

The social-choice characterization of liberty compares what emerges with what a person *would have chosen,* whether or not he actually does the choosing. This leaves out something that may be important to liberty, to wit, whether what he gets was actually *chosen by him* and not merely what he *would have chosen* (though not necessarily chosen by him). This is a gap, and although this gap does not affect the impossibility of the Paretian liberal in any way (as discussed in the last section), it can be important for a more general treatment of liberty (as opposed to that of just some of its implications). The gap can be closed only by enriching the description of social states in such a way that the agency of choice is incorporated in it. This involves a departure from the existing format of social choice theory, in which people choose between social states without the description of the choice being incorporated in the description of the states themselves, and I shall not pursue the problem further here.[29]

On the other hand, the characterization of liberty just in terms of "who actually controls what" is also inadequate. Although the impossibility of the Paretian liberal – appropriately interpreted – holds also for that perspective on liberty (as was discussed earlier), the social-choice framework permits analysis of *indirect* liberty, but the actual-control framework does not.

---

[28] The question involves what Christian Seidl has called "the technological factors of liberalism" ("On Liberal Values," p. 260).

[29] See, however, my "Rights and Agency," *Philosophy and Public Affairs,* 11, 1 (Winter 1982): 3–39, and "Evaluator Relativity and Consequential Evaluation,"...in vol. 12 of the same journal (1983).

7. Preference, choice, and personal spheres

As was discussed in section 2, the link between preference and choice over an individual's recognized personal sphere plays a rather crucial role in the social-choice characterization of liberty. This assumption of "minimal preference-based choice" is much less demanding than the more common assumption of "universal preference-based choice" (as used by Arrow and others), but even the "minimal" assumption may well be questioned.

The force of preferring as a ground for choosing is altogether more powerful in decisions about one's personal life, which do not directly affect others, than in decisions of other kinds. One's desire is a good reason for choosing in one's own personal sphere, but less compelling for choosing in other people's personal spheres or even in public spheres.

To illustrate the contrast, take an example – the old decision problem of the person who prefers peaches to apples and encounters the fruitbasket going round the table after dinner.[30] There happens to be only one peach but many apples in the basket. The choice is not a purely personal choice for him, since his taking the peach would leave some with no choice at all. It is, of course, quite possible that our man at the dinner table will grab the peach with a sigh of relief that the basket got to him in the nick of time. But suppose he does not, and nobly chooses an apple. It is not clear yet that in this choice he is actually acting against his own preference or desire, since, despite his general preference for peaches over apples, he might in this case prefer to have an apple rather than the solitary peach, taking everything into account (morals, embarrassment, etc.). However, it is also quite possible that on balance he does, in fact, prefer or desire having that lovely peach. If under these circumstances he decides that he must not choose the peach despite his desire and thus acts against his own preference (defined in terms of desire rather than choice), then we would indeed see a violation of the assumption of "universal" preference-based choice. But not – and this is the important point here – of "minimal" preference-based choice; for his choice of fruit *in this case* cannot be seen to be in his personal sphere since it *directly* affects others, and that is crucial to his decision. The case is quite different from one in which there are enough fruits of each type for all.

The assumption of minimal preference-based choice demands only that individual choices be guided by the respective individual preferences over the *recognized* personal spheres given by the chosen condition of liberty. A recognized personal sphere of an individual will be just a *part* of his or her "personal sphere" in the more general sense, viz., where others are not directly affected. Indeed it could be minute for two people and empty for others under the condition of "minimal liberty."

[30] See P. H. Nowell-Smith, *Ethics* (Harmondsworth: Penguin, 1954), pp. 102/3.

8. The Prisoner's Dilemma: comparison and contrast

The individual preferences underlying the impossibility of the Paretian liberal have been compared with those in the "Prisoner's Dilemma."[31] Though this is instructive to note, and the similarity is clear enough in the example involving *Lady Chatterley's Lover,* the analogy can be misleading in at least three respects. First, in the usual analysis of the Prisoner's Dilemma, no question is raised about the status of individual preference in determining the goodness of the outcome, and Pareto optimality is taken to be the obvious goal. But that is precisely a central issue in the analysis of the impossibility of the Paretian liberal.

Second, in the Prisoner's Dilemma each person has a list of strategies to choose from (to confess or not to confess, say), and each person's strategy availabilities are independent of the actions of the other. This is similar to the "feature" or "issue" formulation of the liberty conditions, where each person fixes some feature of the social state (e.g., person i fixes whether he reads *Lady Chatterley's Lover* or not).[32] But in the real world, such fully "independent" choice of individual features might not be "technologically feasible," even for those issues which are regarded as matters for personal decision *to the extent* to which independent choice is possible.[33] For example, in the work-choice case, the over-all employment opportunities are such that the feasible combinations are confined to four alternatives only, and this does not permit either individual to freely choose his own employment independently of the other. On the other hand, to the extent that such a choice does exist – as it does for precisely one pair for each (each person has the option of working full-time or not at all *if* the other person happens to work half-time) – the consideration of liberty is taken to require that each person's options should be resolved by the person himself. This case illustrates the impossibility of the Paretian liberal, but it does not have the form of the Prisoner's Dilemma game.

Third, even when each individual can choose his personal "feature" or "issue" independently of the choice of others, the impossibility of the Paretian liberal can hold without the game's being a variant of the Prisoner's Dilemma.[34] Consider, for example, a variant of the work-choice case, with each

---

[31] See Ben Fine, "Individual Liberalism in a Paretian Society," *Journal of Political Economy,* 83 (1975): 1277–1282. Thomas Schelling has commented in 1969 on the similarity in his response (pre-publication) to my "Impossibility of a Paretian Liberal."

[32] See Gibbard, *op. cit.;* Bernholz, *op. cit.;* Nozick, *Anarchy, State and Utopia;* Gärdenfors, *op. cit.;* and Levi, *op. cit.*

[33] The problem relates to what Christian Seidl (*op. cit.*) calls a "technologically compound" situation. A similar "compound" situation arises in the interesting example considered by Jonathan Barnes, *op. cit.*

[34] The former has a wider domain than the latter. In fact, Kevin Roberts (*op. cit.*) has established and analyzed an impossibility result that works on a domain that is wider than that of Prisoner's Dilemma but narrower than that of the impossibility of the Paretian liberal.

person having the choice of working (1) or not (0), and being free to choose his employment as he likes. Person 1, whom I shall call the "envious worker," has the preference ordering: (1, 0), (0, 0), (1, 1), (0, 1), in decreasing order, and person 2 – the "egalitarian shirker" – has the ordering: (0, 0), (1, 1), (1, 0), (0, 1), in decreasing order. Compared with no one working, i.e., (0, 0), person 1 prefers (1, 0), and, given that choice, would freely choose to work. Compared with (1, 0), person 2 prefers (1, 1), and he too – given that choice – would freely choose to work. Though each has made a prudent choice, given the choice of the other, and the outcome (1, 1) is a "Nash equilibrium," it is Pareto-inferior to (0, 0), which completes a Pareto-liberty cycle. It is, in this case, impossible to combine the Paretian judgment with equilibrium of individual preference-based choice over the respective personal spheres.[35] But the game is not a Prisoner's Dilemma – indeed person 2 has no dominant strategy.

9. Solution by collusion?

Irrespective of whether or not the game form coincides with the Prisoner's Dilemma, given the Pareto-inefficient result of individual exercise of rights, neither person can bring about a Pareto improvement based on his own action. But potentially the individuals *together* can, of course, bring about a Pareto improvement through collusive action, thereby resolving the Pareto inefficiency of the libertarian outcome. In order to permit such collusive action, the characterization of individual rights has to permit "marketing" of rights. For example, in the work-choice case, each person may make a commitment not to use his right to accept more employment, in exchange for the other's making a similar commitment.

Some authors (e.g., Buchanan, Gärdenfors, Barry) have seen in this possibility a "solution" to the impossibility of the Paretian liberal. I believe this is not a solution, but the possibility of such collusive action to move away from Pareto-inefficient "liberal" outcomes must be considered. In fact, the possibility of such a move away was already noted in the original presentation of the impossibility result, where it was pointed out that the so-called "liberal" solution is "not merely not Pareto-optimal, it is also a point of disequilibrium" and that quite possibly "the market will not achieve the Pareto-inoptimal 'liberal' solution either" (*Collective Choice and Social Welfare*, p. 84).

---

[35] In such cases as well as in cases corresponding to the Prisoner's Dilemma, the equilibrium property of the Pareto-inefficient outcome is based on each person taking the other's strategy as *given*. Neither has indeed any incentive to change his strategy given that of the other. Isaac Levi ("Liberty and Welfare") has considered the case in which the individuals do not know what the other has chosen. With that assumption and the further assumption that each person's belief about the other person's strategy is a function of his own strategy, Levi shows that the Pareto inefficiency of the outcome of individual choice can be avoided, provided the beliefs are of the right sort.

Why does this line of reasoning not provide a solution to the impossibility of the Paretian liberal? There are several distinct barriers to this "solution," and here I shall present only a brief discussion of the main issues involved.[36] There are four distinct questions to deal with:

(1) *The legitimacy issue:* Will the scope of individual rights admit such marketlike contracts?

(2) *The Pareto-end issue:* Will the individuals actually try to get away from the results of individual exercises of rights, to a Pareto-superior state?

(3) *The contract-means issue:* If the only way of getting to such a Pareto-superior state is through a binding contract, will the individuals still try to get there?

(4) *The instability issue:* If the individuals do try to move to such a Pareto-superior state through a binding contract, will they be able to sustain the contractual outcome?

Questions can indeed be raised about the legitimacy of a contract that requires both parties to renounce their freedom to choose within their personal spheres (e.g., to accept employment), and such questioning may even get some support from John Stuart Mill's argument that "the principle of freedom cannot require that the person be free not to be free" and that "it is not freedom to be allowed to alienate his freedom."[37] But Mill was dealing with the rather extreme case of slavery in making these remarks, and the argument clearly does not readily apply to, say, mutual employment-denying contracts.

There is, however, the somewhat different issue whether such contracts should be publicly enforceable, even if there is nothing illegitimate in making such a contract. The distinction – as Rawls has argued – can be important. The role of an enforcer checking whether you have broken your contract not to accept employment (or ascertaining whether the prude has broken his agreement to read *Lady Chatterley's Lover* every morning) is morally problematic, aside from being deeply chilling.

The Pareto-end issue raises a question of a different type. The fact that a Pareto-superior state is higher in everyone's preference scale is certainly *an* argument for trying to get to such a state. On the other hand, the status of preference – either in the form of desire or of satisfaction – is by no means above moral questioning. John Broome has argued that preferences do need rational assessment,[38] and it is of course quite possible that some types of envy-based preferences – such as those against the other person's employment in the work-choice case – may fail to pass such assessment. Questions

---

[36] See also my "Liberty as Control: An Appraisal," *Midwest Studies in Philosophy,* 7 (1982).

[37] *On Liberty;* reprinted in M. Lerner, ed., *Essential Works of John Stuart Mill* (New York: Bantam Books, 1965), p. 348.

[38] "Choice and Value in Economics," *Oxford Economic Papers,* 30 (1978).

can be raised about "nosey" preferences too, e.g., being more concerned with other peoples' reading habits than with one's own. Though a preference may be seen to be "irrational" even by the person holding it, it does not by any means follow that his preference will actually change – immediately or ever – and cease to have that quality. In such a situation it would not be unreasonable for a person to decide that he must be guided not by his actual preferences only, but also by his "metarankings" reflecting what he would like his preference to be.[39]

There is a further question here. Even if the person is perfectly at peace with his preferences and finds them by no means irrational, he might still wish to discriminate between different parts of his preferences. He could agree with Mill that "there is no parity between the feeling of a person for his opinion, and the feeling of another who is offended at his holding it," and that "a person's taste is as much his own peculiar concern as his opinion or his purse" (*On Liberty,* p. 331). There is nothing inconsistent, or even peculiar, in being sure about the rightness of one's preference and at the same time not wanting it to "count"[40] when it happens to deal with other people's personal lives (e.g., "I would have preferred if you were not to do this, but it is *your* life, not mine, and I would ask you to ignore my preference").

My point here is not that it will be wrong for a person to seek a Pareto-improvement of the kind under discussion if he considers such a move to be good, but that he may well not consider such a move to be good. The person's *decisions* in such fields involving other people's personal lives should not be taken for granted even when there is no uncertainty as to what his *preferences* are.

Turning now to the contract-means issue, even when each person would like the other person's life to be run differently from what that person wants, neither person might nevertheless want to achieve that result *through* an enforced contract. This is a traditional problem in matters of love and friendship, but it can arise in other types of situations as well, and the worth – and indeed the nature – of an outcome might well be taken to be sensitive to how it is brought about. I don't know how important this type of means-based consideration might be – it obviously would vary from case to case – but it is an issue that has to be faced in seeking solution by collusion.

---

[39] On the relevance of preferences over preferences for a person's moral decisions, see my "Choice, Orderings and Morality," in Stefan Körner, ed., *Practical Reason* (Oxford: Blackwell, 1974). See also Kurt Baier, "Rationality and Morality," *Erkenntnis,* 11, 2 (August 1977): 197–232; R. Harrison, ed., *Rational Action* (New York: Cambridge, 1979), including the papers by M. Hollis and A. Sen; R. J. van der Veen, "Meta-rankings and Collective Optimality," *Social Science Information,* 20 (1981); A. Hirschman, *Shifting Involvements* (Princeton, N.J.: University Press, 1982), ch. 4.

[40] For a formal use of the notion of "counting" in social choice theory, see my "Liberty, Unanimity and Rights," pp. 235–237, 243/4.

Finally, ignoring all these difficulties, consider the case in which all the parties do try to have a Pareto-improving contract and it is agreed that such a contract is perfectly legitimate for them to have. Would this solve the problem? Indeed not, since the incentive to break the contract *remains*. The important point about the possibility of the Pareto-improving contract is that it disequilibrates the Pareto-inefficient outcome resulting from the individual exercise of rights,[41] but it need not make the contracted arrangement itself an equilibrium. Indeed, in a situation exemplifying the conflict between the Pareto principle and individual liberty, there might exist no equilibrium at all – with some states being rejected by the Pareto-improving contract and the others being rejected by individual decisions over their own personal spheres. The difficulty of enforcing contractual behavior in personal lives is daunting, and doubts about the moral legitimacy of enforcing such contracts – noted earlier – do not make the problem any easier.

The impossibility of the Paretian liberal – interpreted in terms of descriptive choice – leads to a game with an empty "core." The instability problem can be shown to be deeply ingrained in the nature of the conflict,[42] and there seems to be a general confluence of the possibilty of Pareto-improving contracts on the one hand, and the existence of cyclical or intransitive group decisions, on the other.[43]

The Pareto-improving contract is not so much a "solution" of the impossibility of the Paretian liberal as a part of the "problem" itself. Consider first the *descriptive-choice* version. *Without* such contracts, the stable outcomes may well be Pareto inefficient, and *with* them there may well be no stable outcomes at all! It is, of course quite possible that in some particular cases of the conflict, such contracts will be sought, made, and successfully enforced, and the outcomes will happen to be stable. But such a contingent occurrence – dependent on the variety of circumstances discussed above – can scarcely count as a general solution of the impossibility of the Paretian liberal.

With the *normative-choice* interpretation, these difficulties do, of course, remain. But further questions are raised about the normative relevance of such exchanges and their enforcement, even when they do take place and produce a stable outcome. It is important to note that the normative problems –

[41] This was the point of the statement in *Collective Choice and Social Welfare* (p. 84) quoted earlier.

[42] See J. Aldrich, "The Dilemma of a Paretian Liberal: Some Consequences of Sen's Theorem," and "Liberal Games: Further Comments on Social Choice and Social Theory," *Public Choice,* 30 (1976): 29–34; M. Miller, "Social Preference and Game Theory: A Comment on 'The Dilemma of a Paretian Liberal,'" *Public Choice,* 30 (1976): 23–28; Gardner, *op. cit.;* and Green, *op. cit.*

[43] See Bernholz, "Liberalism, Logrolling, and Cyclical Group Preferences," *Kyklos,* 29 (1976): 26–37, and "A General Social Dilemma: Profitable Exchange and Intransitive Group Preferences," *Zeitschrift für Nationalökonomie,* 40 (1980): 1–23; Schwartz, "Collective Choice, Separation of Issues, and Vote Trading," *American Political Science Review,* 72 (1977).

both of *choice* and of *outcome-evaluation* – may be viewed not merely from the position of outsiders, but also from the position of the involved individuals themselves. In that context, the individual's choice behavior cannot – obviously – be taken as given. The question that has to be faced then is: "Should I seek such a contract?" and not whether others have any reason to object if I were to seek such a contract. To try to "solve" this problem by invoking one's preference as the great arbitrator is surely to beg an important moral question.

Indeed, the status of preference is one of the central issues involved in the impossibility of the Paretian liberal.[44] It can be seen as showing the impossibility of giving priority to preferences over personal spheres while accepting the priority of unanimous preference rankings. In the context of the morality of personal choice, this conflict has to be faced. The possibility of a Pareto-improving contract does nothing to resolve it.

10. Concluding remarks

I have argued that there are several distinct interpretations of "social preference" in social choice theory, and, correspondingly, of "liberty" in that framework. The impossibility of the Paretian liberal holds under each of these interpretations, but has correspondingly different – though related – contents. Outcome evaluation, normative choice, and descriptive choice are examples of alternative interpretations.

Second, I have also argued that the formulation of liberty in terms of the individual's having actual *control,* independent of the nature of the *outcomes,* is fundamentally inadequate. What has been called here "indirect liberty" is systematically ignored by the "control view" of liberty.

Third, the conflict between the Pareto principle and individual liberty holds also under the "control" interpretation, and the issue of the inadequacy of that interpretation does not, therefore, have a decisive bearing on this *particular* conflict.

Fourth, the possibility of Pareto-improving contracts does not – contrary to some claims – eliminate (or "resolve") the impossibility problem under any of the alternative interpretations.

Finally, there is nothing much to "resolve" anyway. The impossibility of the Paretian liberal just brings out a conflict of principles – a conflict which might not have been immediately apparent. There are, of course, many such conflicts. The really interesting issues relate to the implications of the conflict.[45] There are implications both for evaluation of outcomes and for choice of decision procedures. I have tried to discuss some of these implications.

[44] See my "Utilitarianism and Welfarism," *Journal of Philosophy,* 76 (1979), pp. 479–487.
[45] See the literature cited in sections 4 and 5.

Part III

Reasons, desires, and irrationality

This part of the book consists of two main sections: A. Reasons, Desires, and Values, and B. Irrationality. The essays in these sections are more straightforwardly philosophical than the essays in Parts I and II. In fact, the following essays can be read apart from Parts I and II.

A. Reasons, desires, and values

This section includes three essays that deal with the roles of desires and values in rational action. In "Internal and External Reasons," Bernard Williams distinguishes two senses of "Person S has a reason to perform act A." On the "internal" interpretation, the sentence implies that S has some motive that will be advanced by S's A-ing. On the "external" interpretation, in contrast, the reason-ascribing sentence will not be falsified by S's not having a motive that would be advanced by his A-ing. Williams proposes that if something can be a reason for action, then that thing must be able to figure in an explanation of someone's acting. Further, on his view, since something that explains an agent's actions must be something that motivates the agent to act, an external reason cannot provide an explanation of the agent's actions. Williams argues that, given their neglect of considerations of motivation in a person having a reason, external reason statements are false, incoherent, or something else misleadingly expressed.

In "The Concept of Rational Action," Richard Brandt proposes that the phrase "it would be rational to perform act A" functions to guide action by both recommending action and making a claim that evaluates the available action in terms of a standard. Brandt pursues the issue of what sort of strategy of using information to select actions will enable a person to achieve his or her objectives as effectively as any other known strategy. Brandt identifies a number of constraints that a person's preferences must meet if they are to determine the objectives of a strategy for rational decisions. Brandt's distinctive constraint is that a rational decision maker's preferences must be able to survive upon being subjected to "repeated vivid reflection on relevant facts." In conclusion, Brandt compares his notion of rational action with the notion of rational action found in many decision-theoretic accounts.

In "Rationality and Valuation," Robert Audi begins with an assessment of the instrumentalist notion of rational action according to which what is essential to rational action is an action's success as a means to realizing some of the agent's aims. Audi focuses here on accounts that propose maximization of expected utility. His main objection is that such accounts require the formation of beliefs about precise probabilities that rational agents typically seem to lack. Audi also critically assesses the approaches to rational action developed by Carl Hempel and Richard Brandt. Audi's constructive account takes rationality to be "well-groundedness," thus exploiting an analogy between the theory of knowledge and the theory of rational action. His account focuses on the conditions for the rationality of motivational factors such as valuations. Valuations, on this view, can be well grounded by virtue of being grounded either in an experience of the relevant kind of state of affairs (e.g., viewing a painting), or in a well-grounded belief of a certain sort (e.g., a grounded belief that something is pleasant). Audi contrasts his account with coherentist accounts of rational action and with the account of Richard Brandt. (For Brandt's account, see Chapter 18).

B. Irrationality

This section contains two essays that deal with conditions for irrationality. In "Paradoxes of Irrationality," Donald Davidson claims that the existence of reason explanations is a built-in aspect of intentional actions; such explanations enable us to see the actions as reasonable from the agent's viewpoint. But this raises the question of how we can explain, or even allow as possible, irrational actions. Davidson claims that any satisfactory explanation of irrationality must rely on some of Freud's most important theses. Davidson defines *the Plato Principle* as the view that no intentional action can be internally irrational, and *the Medea Principle* as the view that a person can act against his or her better judgment, but only when an alien force overwhelms his or her will. Davidson examines these principles in connection with cases of weakness of will. What needs explanation in such cases is the action of an agent who, having judged that the preponderance of reasons favors doing one thing rather than another, acts against this judgment. An account of rational action must explain why the agent did not act otherwise, given his or her judgment that all things considered it would be better. Davidson proposes that many examples of irrationality can be explained by the fact that there is a mental cause of belief or intention that is not a reason for the belief or intention. This explanation relies on the Freudian view that parts of the mind are independent to some degree, where one "department" of the mind can find a certain action to be best all things considered, whereas another part of the mind prompts another course of action.

In "Rational Dilemmas and Rational Supererogation," Michael Slote examines the case for the possibility of rational dilemmas and of supererogatory degrees of practical rationality. A rational dilemma is a situation in which an agent, through no fault of his or her own, finds it impossible to act rationally. The key issue is whether principles of practical rationality can conflict for an agent in such a way that in a particular situation there is no way for the agent to act rationally. Since Slote is concerned with the possibility of rational dilemmas independent of moral dilemmas, he asks about the impossibility of a person acting rationally with regard to self-regarding aims. Slote formulates a purely hypothetical case that is an instance of rational dilemma, and then asks whether the dilemma arises from reliance on an optimizing/maximizing model of rational choice. Slote notes that most philosophers have taken it for granted that it is irrational to do one thing when, from a rational standpoint, it would be better for the agent to do something else. But he suggests that if we allow for rational supererogation (i.e., a gap between rationality and ideal rationality), we may be able to preclude rational dilemmas. Slote gives reasons for acknowledging rational supererogation, and explains how this acknowledgment enables us to avoid his case of rational dilemma.

A. *Reasons, desires, and values*

17. Internal and external reasons

Bernard Williams

Sentences of the forms "A has a reason to ϕ" or "There is a reason for A to ϕ" (where "ϕ" stands in for some verb of action) seem on the face of it to have two different sorts of interpretation. On the first, the truth of the sentence implies, very roughly, that A has some motive which will be served or furthered by his ϕ-ing, and if this turns out not to be so the sentence is false: there is a condition relating to the agent's aims, and if this is not satisfied it is not true to say, on this interpretation, that he has a reason to ϕ. On the second interpretation, there is no such condition, and the reason-sentence will not be falsified by the absence of an appropriate motive. I shall call the first the "internal," the second the "external," interpretation. (Given two such interpretations, and the two forms of sentence quoted, it is reasonable to suppose that the first sentence more naturally collects the internal interpretation, and the second the external, but it would be wrong to suggest that either form of words admits only one of the interpretations.)

I shall also for convenience refer sometimes to "internal reasons" and "external reasons," as I do in the title, but this is to be taken only as a convenience. It is a matter for investigation whether there are two sorts of reasons for action, as opposed to two sorts of statements about people's reasons for action; indeed, as we shall eventually see, even the interpretation in one of the cases is problematical.

I shall consider first the internal interpretation, and how far it can be taken. I shall then consider, more sceptically, what might be involved in an external interpretation. I shall end with some brief remarks connecting all this with the issue of public goods and free-riders....

The simplest model for the internal interpretation would be this: A has a reason to ϕ iff A has some desire the satisfaction of which will be served

Reprinted with permission from R. Harrison, ed., *Rational Action* (Cambridge: Cambridge University Press, 1979), 17–28.

by his ϕ-ing. Alternatively, we might say...some desire, the satisfaction of which A believes will be served by his ϕ-ing; this difference will concern us later. Such a model is sometimes ascribed to Hume, but since in fact Hume's own views are more complex than this, we might call it *the sub-Humean model*. The sub-Humean model is certainly too simple. My aim will be, by addition and revision, to work it up into something more adequate: in the course of trying to do this, I shall assemble four propositions which seem to me to be true of internal reason statements.

Basically, and by definition, any model for the internal interpretation must display a relativity of the reason statement to the agent's *subjective motivational set,* which I shall call the agent's *S.* The contents of *S* we shall come to, but we can say:

(i)   An internal reason statement is falsified by the absence of some appropriate element from *S.*

The simplest sub-Humean model claims that any element in *S* gives rise to an internal reason. But there are grounds for denying this, not because of regrettable, imprudent, or deviant elements in *S* – they raise different sorts of issues – but because of elements in *S* based on false belief.

The agent believes that this stuff is gin, when it is in fact petrol. He wants a gin and tonic. Has he reason, or a reason, to mix this stuff with tonic and drink it? There are two ways here (as suggested already by the two alternatives for formulating the sub-Humean model). On the one hand, it is just very odd to say that he has a reason to drink this stuff, and natural to say that he has no reason to drink it, although he thinks that he has. On the other hand, if he does drink it, we not only have an explanation of his doing so (a reason why he did it), but we have such an explanation which is of the reason-for-action form. This explanatory dimension is very important, and we shall come back to it more than once; if there are reasons for action, it must be that people sometimes act for those reasons, and if they do, their reasons must figure in some correct explanation of their action (it does not follow that they must figure in all correct explanations of their action). The difference between false and true beliefs on the agent's part cannot alter the *form* of the explanation which will be appropriate to his action. This consideration might move us to ignore the intuition which we noticed before, and lead us just to legislate that in the case of the agent who wants gin, he has a reason to drink this stuff which is petrol.

I do not think, however, that we should do this. It looks in the wrong direction, by implying in effect that the internal reason conception is only concerned with explanation, and not at all with the agent's rationality; and this may help to motivate a search for other sorts of reason which are connected with his rationality. But it is concerned with his rationality: what we can correctly ascribe to him in a third-personal internal reason statement is also what he can ascribe to himself as a result of deliberation, as we shall see. So I think that we should rather say:

(ii)   A member of S, D, will not give A a reason for ϕ-ing if either the existence of D is dependent on false belief, or A's belief in the relevance of ϕ-ing to the satisfaction of D is false.

(This double formulation can be illustrated from the gin/petrol case: D can be taken in the first way as the desire to drink what is in the bottle, and in the second way as the desire to drink gin.) It will, all the same, be true that if he does ϕ in these circumstances, there was not only a reason why he ϕ-ed, but also that that displays him as, relative to his false belief, acting rationally.

We can note the epistemic consequence:

(iii)   (a) A may falsely believe an internal reason statement about himself,

and we can add

(b) A may not know some true internal reason statement about himself.

(b) comes from two different sources. One is that A may be ignorant of some fact such that if he did know it he would, in virtue of some element in S, be disposed to ϕ: we can say that he has a reason to ϕ, though he does not know it. For it to be the case that he actually has such a reason, however, it seems that the relevance of the unknown fact to his actions has to be fairly close and immediate; otherwise one merely says that A would have a reason to ϕ if he knew the fact. I shall not pursue the question of the conditions for saying the one thing or the other, but it must be closely connected with the question of when the ignorance forms part of the explanation of what A actually does.

The second source of (iii) is that A may be ignorant of some element in S. But we should notice that an unknown element in S, D, will provide a reason for A to ϕ only if ϕ-ing is rationally related to D; that is to say, roughly, a project to ϕ could be the answer to a deliberative question formed in part by D. If D is unknown to A because it is in the unconscious, it may well not satisfy this condition, although of course it may provide the reason why he ϕ's, that is, may explain or help to explain his ϕ-ing. In such cases, the ϕ-ing may be related to D only symbolically.

I have already said that

(iv)   internal reason statements can be discovered in deliberative reasoning.

It is worth remarking the point, already implicit, that an internal reason statement does not apply only to that action which is the uniquely preferred result of the deliberation. "A has reason to ϕ" does not mean "the action which A has overall, all-in, reason to do is ϕ-ing." He can have reason to do a lot of things which he has other and stronger reasons not to do.

The sub-Humean model supposes that ϕ-ing has to be related to some element in S as causal means to end (unless, perhaps, it is straightforwardly the carrying out of a desire which is itself that element in S). But this is only one case: indeed, the mere discovery that some course of action is the causal means to an end is not in itself a piece of practical reasoning.[1] A clear example of practical reasoning is that leading to the conclusion that one has reason to ϕ because ϕ-ing would be the most convenient, economical, pleasant etc. way of satisfying some element in S; and this of course is controlled by other elements in S, if not necessarily in a very clear or determinate way. But there are much wider possibilities for deliberation, such as: thinking how the satisfaction of elements in S can be combined, e.g. by time-ordering; where there is some irresoluble conflict among the elements of S, considering which one attaches most weight to (which, importantly, does not imply that there is some one commodity of which they provide varying amounts); or, again, finding constitutive solutions, such as deciding what would make for an entertaining evening, granted that one wants entertainment.

As a result of such processes an agent can come to see that he has reason to do something which he did not see he had reason to do at all. In this way, the deliberative process can add new actions for which there are internal reasons, just as it can also add new internal reasons for given actions. The deliberative process can also subtract elements from S. Reflection may lead the agent to see that some belief is false, and hence to realise that he has in fact no reason to do something he thought he had reason to do. More subtly, he may think he has reason to promote some development because he has not exercised his imagination enough about what it would be like if it came about. In his unaided deliberative reason, or encouraged by the persuasions of others, he may come to have some more concrete sense of what would be involved, and lose his desire for it; just as, positively, the imagination can create new possibilities and new desires. (These are important possibilities for politics as well as for individual action.)

We should not, then, think of S as statically given; the processes of deliberation can have all sorts of effect on S, and this is a fact which a theory of internal reasons should be very happy to accommodate. So also it should be more liberal than some theorists have been about the possible elements in S. I have discussed S primarily in terms of desires, and this term can be used, formally, for all elements in S. But this terminology may make one forget that S can contain such things as dispositions of evaluation, patterns of emotional reaction, personal loyalties, and various projects, as they may be abstractly called, embodying commitments of the agent. Above all, there is of course no supposition that the desires or projects of an agent have to be egoistic; he will, one hopes, have non-egoistic projects of various kinds, and these equally can provide internal reasons for action.

There is a further question, however, about the contents of S: whether it should be taken, consistently with the general idea of internal reasons, as

---

[1] A point made by Aurel Kolnai: see his "Deliberation is of Ends," in *Ethics, Value and Reality* (London and Indianapolis, 1978). See also David Wiggins, "Deliberation and Practical Reason," *PAS,* 76 (1975–6); reprinted in part in *Practical Reasoning,* ed. J. Raz (Oxford, 1978).

containing *needs*. It is certainly quite natural to say that A has a reason to pursue X, just on the ground that he needs X; but will this naturally follow in a theory of internal reasons? There is a special problem about this only if the agent's needs are not taken up into his desires or motivations: if it is possible for the agent to be unmotivated to pursue what he needs. I shall not try to discuss here the nature of needs, but I take it that insofar as there are determinately recognisable needs, this is a possibility, and there can be an agent who lacks an interest in getting what he indeed needs. I take it, further, that the lack of interest can remain after deliberation; and that it would be wrong to say that such a lack of interest must always rest on false belief. (Insofar as it does rest on false belief, then we can accommodate it under (ii), in the way already discussed.)

If an agent really is uninterested in pursuing what he needs; and this is not the product of false belief; and he could not reach any such motive from motives he has by the kind of deliberative processes we have discussed; then I think we do have to say that in the internal sense he indeed has no reason to pursue these things. In saying this, however, we have to bear in mind how strong these assumptions are, and how seldom we are likely to think that we know them to be true. When we say that a person has reason to take medicine which he needs, although he consistently and persuasively denies any interest in preserving his health, we may well still be speaking in the internal sense, with the thought that really at some level he *must* want to be well.

However, if we become clear that we have no such thought, and persist in saying that the person has this reason, then we must be speaking in another sense, and this is the external sense. People do say things that ask to be taken in the external interpretation. In James' story of Owen Wingrave, from which Britten made an opera, Owen's father urges on him the necessity and importance of his joining the army, since all his male ancestors were soldiers, and family pride requires him to do the same. Owen Wingrave has no motivation to join the army at all, and all his desires lead in another direction: he hates everything about military life and what it means. His father might have expressed himself by saying that *there was a reason for Owen to join the army*. Knowing that there was nothing in Owen's S which would lead, through deliberative reasoning, to his doing this would not make him withdraw the claim or admit that he made it under a misapprehension. He means it in an external sense. What is that sense?

A preliminary point is that this is not the same question as that of the status of a supposed categorical imperative, in the Kantian sense of an "ought" which applies to an agent independently of what the agent happens to want: or rather, it is not undoubtedly the same question. First, a categorical imperative has often been taken, as by Kant, to be necessarily an imperative of morality, but external reason statements do not necessarily relate to morality. Second, it remains an obscure issue what the relation is between "there is a reason for A to . . ." and "A ought to . . ." Some philosophers take them to be equivalent, and under that view the question of external reasons of course comes much closer to the question of a categorical imperative. However, I shall not make any assumption about such an equivalence, and shall not further discuss "ought."

In considering what an external reason statement might mean, we have to remember again the dimension of possible explanation, a consideration which applies to any reason for action: if something can be a reason for action, then it could be someone's reason for acting on a particular occasion, and it would then figure in an explanation of that action. Now no external reason statement could *by itself* offer an explanation of anyone's action. Even if it were true (whatever that might turn out to mean) that there was a reason for Owen to join the army, that fact by itself would never explain anything that Owen did, not even his joining the army. For if it was true at all, it was true when Owen was not motivated to join the army. The whole point of external reason statements is that they can be true independently of the agent's motivations. But nothing can explain an agent's (intentional) actions except something that motivates him so to act. So something else is needed besides the truth of the external reason statement to explain action, some psychological link; and that psychological link would seem to be belief. *A*'s believing an external reason statement about himself may help to explain his action.

External reason statements have been introduced merely in the general form "there is a reason for A to...."; but we now need to go beyond that form, to specific statements of reasons. No doubt there are some cases of an agent's ϕ-ing because he believes that there is a reason for him to ϕ, while he does not have any belief about what that reason is. They would be cases of his relying on some authority whom he trusts, or, again, of his recalling that he did know of some reason for his ϕ-ing, but his not being able to remember what it was. In these respects, reasons for action are like reasons for belief. But, as with reasons for belief, they are evidently secondary cases: the basic case must be that in which A ϕ's, not because he believes only that there is some reason or other for him to ϕ, but because he believes of some determinate consideration that it constitutes a reason for him to ϕ. Thus Owen Wingrave might come to join the army because (now) he believes that it is a reason for him to do so that his family has a tradition of military honour.

Does believing that a particular consideration is a reason to act in a particular way provide, or indeed constitute, a motivation to act? If it does not, then we are no further on. Let us grant that it does. This claim indeed seems plausible, so long at least as the connexion between such beliefs and the disposition to act is not tightened to that unnecessary degree which excludes *akrasia*. The claim is in fact *so* plausible, that this agent, with this belief, appears to be one about whom, now, an *internal* reason statement could truly be made: he is one with an appropriate motivation in his S. A man who does believe that considerations of family honour constitute reasons for action is a man with a certain disposition to action, and also dispositions of approval, sentiment, emotional reaction, and so forth.

Now it does not follow from this that there is nothing in external reason statements. What does follow is that their content is not going to be revealed by considering merely the state of one who believes such a statement, and how that state explains action, for that state is merely the state with regard to which an internal reason statement could truly be made. Rather, the content of the external type of statement will have to be revealed by considering what it is to *come to believe* such a statement – it is there, if at all, that their peculiarity will have to emerge.

We will take the case (we have implicitly been doing so already) in which an external reason statement is made about someone who, like Owen Wingrave, is not already motivated in the required way, and so is someone about whom an internal statement could not also be truly made. (Since the difference between external and internal statements turns on the implications accepted by the speaker, external statements can of course be made about agents who are already motivated; but that is not the interesting case.) The agent does not presently believe the external statement. If he comes to believe it, he will be motivated to act; so coming to believe it must, essentially, involve acquiring a new motivation. How can that be?

This is closely related to an old question, of how "reason can give rise to a motivation," a question which has famously received from Hume a negative answer. But in that form, the question is itself unclear, and is unclearly related to the argument – for of course reason, that is to say, rational processes, can give rise to new motivations, as we have seen in the account of deliberation. Moreover, the traditional way of putting the issue also (I shall suggest) picks up an onus of proof about what is to count as a "purely rational process" which not only should it not pick up, but which properly belongs with the critic who wants to oppose Hume's general conclusion and to make a lot out of external reason statements – someone I shall call "the external reasons theorist."

The basic step lies in recognising that the external reasons theorist must conceive in a special way the connexion between acquiring a motivation and coming to believe the reason statement. For of course there are various means by which the agent could come to have the motivation and also to believe the reason statement, but which are the wrong kind of means to interest the external reasons theorist. Owen might be so persuaded by his father's moving rhetoric that he acquired both the motivation and the belief. But this excludes an element which the external reasons theorist essentially wants: that the agent should acquire the motivation *because* he comes to believe the reason statement, and that he should do the latter, moreover, because, in some way, he is considering the matter aright. If the theorist is to hold on to these conditions, he will, I think, have to make the condition under which the agent appropriately comes to have the motivation something like this, that he should deliberate correctly; and the external reasons statement itself might be taken as roughly equivalent to, or at least as entailing, the claim that if the agent rationally deliberated, then, whatever motivations he originally had, he would come to be motivated to ϕ.

But if this is correct, there does indeed seem great force in Hume's basic point, and it is very plausible to suppose that all external reason statements are false. For, *ex hypothesi*, there is no motivation for the agent to deliberate *from*, to reach this new motivation. Given the agent's earlier existing motivations, and this new motivation, what has to hold for external reason statements to be true, on this line of interpretation, is that the new motivation could be in some way rationally arrived at, granted the earlier motivations, yet at the same time that it should not bear to the earlier motivations the kind of rational relation which we considered in the earlier discussion of deliberation – for in that case an internal reason statement would have been true in the first place. I see no reason to suppose that these conditions could possibly be met.

It might be said that the force of an external reason statement can be explained in the following way. Such a statement implies that a rational agent would be motivated to act appropriately; and it can carry this implication, because a rational agent is precisely one who has a general disposition in his S to do what (he believes) there is reason for him to do. So when he comes to believe that there is reason for him to ϕ, he is motivated to ϕ, even though, before, he neither had a motive to ϕ, nor any motive related to ϕ-ing in one of the ways considered in the account of deliberation.

But this reply merely puts off the problem. It reapplies the desire and belief model (roughly speaking) of explanation to the actions in question, but using a desire and a belief the content of which are in question. *What* is it that one comes to believe when he comes to believe that there is reason for him to ϕ, if it is not the proposition, or something that entails the proposition, that if he deliberated rationally, he would be motivated to act appropriately? We were asking how any true proposition could have that content; it cannot help, in answering that, to appeal to a supposed desire which is activated by a belief which has that very content.

These arguments about what it is to accept an external reason statement involve some idea of what is possible under the account of deliberation already given, and what is excluded by that account. But here it may be objected that the account of deliberation is very vague, and has for instance allowed the use of the imagination to extend or restrict the contents of the agent's S. But if that is so, then it is unclear what the limits are to what an agent might arrive at by rational deliberation from his existing S.

It is certainly a feature of the present account of deliberative reasoning (or rather, promissory sketch of such an account) both that it is vague, and that it is more permissive than would have been allowed by the sub-Humean. I do not think that these features could be or should be eliminated in a fuller account. There is an essential indeterminacy in what can be counted a rational deliberative process: it is a heuristic process, and an imaginative one, and there are no fixed boundaries on the continuum from rational thought to inspiration and conversion. Now to someone who thinks that reasons for action are basically to be understood in terms of the internal reasons model, this is not a difficulty. There is indeed a vagueness about "A has reason to ϕ," in the internal sense, insofar as the deliberative processes which could lead from A's present S to his being motivated to ϕ may be more or less ambitiously conceived. But this is no embarrassment to those who take as basic the internal conception of reasons for action: it merely shows that there is a wider range of states, and a less determinate one, than one might have supposed, which can be counted as A's having a reason to ϕ.

It is rather the external reasons theorist who faces the problem at this point. There are of course many things that a speaker may say to one who is not disposed to ϕ when the speaker thinks that he should be: as that he is inconsiderate, or cruel, or selfish, or imprudent; or that things, and he, would be a lot nicer if he were so motivated. Any of these can be sensible things to say. But one who makes a great deal out of putting the criticism in the form of the external reason statement seems concerned to say that what is particularly wrong with the agent is that he is *irrational*. It is this theorist who particularly needs to make this charge precise: in particular, because he wants any rational agent, as such, to acknowledge the requirement to do the thing in question.

Owen Wingrave's father indeed expressed himself in terms other than "a reason." But as we imagined, he could have used the external reasons formulation; and this fact itself provides some difficulty for the external reasons theorist. This theorist, who sees the truth of an external reason statement as potentially grounding a charge of irrationality against the agent who ignores it, might well want to say that if Wingrave *père* put his complaints against Owen in this form, he would very probably be claiming something which, in this particular case, was false. But what the theorist would have a harder time showing would be that the words *meant* something different as used by Wingrave from what they mean when they are, as he supposes, truly uttered. But what they mean when uttered by Wingrave is almost certainly *not* that rational deliberation would get Owen to be motivated to join the army – which is (very roughly) the meaning or implication we have found for them, if they are to bear the kind of weight such theorists wish to give them.

The sort of considerations which, I fear loosely and sketchily, have been offered here strongly suggest to me that external reason statements, when definitely isolated as such, are false, incoherent, or really something else misleadingly expressed. It is in fact harder to isolate them in people's speech than the introduction of them at the beginning of this paper suggested: those who use these words often seem, rather, to be entertaining an optimistic internal reason claim. But sometimes the statement is indeed offered as standing definitely outside the agent's S and what he might derive from it in rational deliberation, and then there is, I suggest, a great unclarity about what is meant. Sometimes it is little more than that things would be better if the agent so acted. But the formulation in terms of reasons does have an effect, particularly in its suggestion that the agent is being irrational, and this suggestion, once the basis of an internal reason claim has been clearly laid aside, is bluff.

If this is so, the only real claims about reasons for action will be internal claims.... [I]t may be helpful...if I end by merely setting out a set of questions, together with the answers that would be given to them by one who thinks (to put it cursorily) that the only rationality of action is the rationality of internal reasons.

1. Can we define notions of rationality which are not purely egoistic?
   Yes.

2. Can we define notions of rationality which are not pure means–end?
   Yes.

3. Can we define a notion of rationality where the action rational for A is in no way relative to A's existing motivations?
   No.

4. Can we show that a man who only has egoistic motivations is irrational in not pursuing non-egoistic ends?
   Not necessarily, though we may be able to in special cases. (The trouble with the egoistic man is not characteristically irrationality.)

Let there be some good, G, and a set of persons, P, such that each member of P has egoistic reason to want G provided, but delivering G requires action C, which involves costs, by each of some proper sub-set of P; and let A be a member of P: then

5. Has A egoistic reason to do C if he is reasonably sure either that too few members of P will do C for G to be provided, or that enough other members of P will do C, so that G will be provided?
   No.

6. Are there any circumstances of this kind in which A can have egoistic reason to do C?
   Yes, but in those cases...in which reaching the critical number of those doing C is sensitive to his doing C, or he has reason to think this.

7. Are there any motivations which would make it rational for A to do C, even though not in the situation just referred to?
   Yes, if he is not purely egoistic: many. For instance, there are expressive motivations – these may be rather inappropriate in [some]

case, but not e.g. in the celebrated voting case.[2] There are also motivations which derive from the sense of fairness. This can precisely transcend the dilemma of "either useless or unnecessary," by the form of argument "somebody, but no reason to omit any particular body, so everybody."

8. Is it irrational for an agent to have such motivations?

In any sense in which the question is intelligible, no.

9. Is it rational for society to bring people up with these sorts of motivations?

In so far as the question is intelligible, yes. And certainly we have reason to encourage people to have these dispositions – e.g. in virtue of possessing them ourselves.

I confess that I cannot see any other major questions which, at this level of generality, bear on these issues. All these questions have clear answers which are entirely compatible with a conception of practical rationality in terms of internal reasons for action, and are also, it seems to me, entirely reasonable answers.

[2] A well-known treatment is by M. Olson Jr., *The Logic of Collective Action* (Cambridge, Mass., 1965). On expressive motivations in this connexion, see S. I. Benn, "Rationality and Political Behaviour," in S. I. Benn and G. W. Mortimore, eds., *Rationality and the Social Sciences* (London, 1976). On the point about fairness, which follows in the text, there is of course a very great deal more to be said: for instance, about how members of a group can, compatibly with fairness, converge on strategies more efficient than everyone's doing *C* (such as people taking turns).

18. The concept of rational action

Richard B. Brandt

There are long-standing disagreements about what it is rational to do, or
want – at least there are, if different philosophers have had the same concept
of "rationality" in mind. Take: "Is it rational to act morally if it conflicts
with self-interest?" (Somewhat similar: "Is it rational to place your daughter's interests ahead of your self-interest?") Or, "Is it rational to pursue fame
(or happiness, or perfection) for its own sake?" (Sidgwick would say, No,
about fame, but a popular view since Hume has been that ultimate ends are
not subject to rational appraisal at all.) More recently, many social scientists
have thought that, given an agent has beliefs about the probabilities of consequences of an act, he acts rationally if and only if he acts so as to maximize
his expected utility; but there have been disagreements about this, and much
more about what it is rational to do in the absence of beliefs about probable
consequences, whether to act so as to maximize possible gain, minimize possible loss, minimize regret, and so on.

Needless to say, these disagreements persist in part because participants
do not mean the same thing by "is a rational action," and partly because they
do not or may not mean anything definite at all. Sometimes, "it is rational
for X to" seems to be identified with "X ought to," and the concept is thought
too simple for further explanation. Some have used the term in quite a different way: R. M. Hare, for instance, stipulates that "rational choice" be
understood simply as one made in full awareness of what concrete difference
it would make were that choice made, in contrast with others open to the

This paper is a descendant of a John Dewey lecture presented at the University of Vermont,
Dec. 5, 1980. Versions of the paper have been read to groups at the University of Michigan, the
University of Maryland, the Florida State University, the University of California at Irvine and
to the Georgia State Philosophy Club and the Washington Philosophy Club. Members of all
these groups made helpful suggestions. I am especially indebted to Professors Arthur Kuflik,
Stephen Stich, Steven Kuhn, Allan Gibbard and most of all Mark Overvold.
Reprinted with permission from *Social Theory and Practice* 9 (1983), 143–64.

agent.[1] Again, it is sometimes or often not clear whether economists who regard rational action as expectable-utility-maximizing action view their claim as an analytic statement given the ordinary meaning of their own stipulated meaning for "rational," or as a synthetic statement supportable by evidence, or just a recommendation.

Obviously it would help resolve controversies if parties explained their meanings. But does it make any difference which sense writers adopt so long as they explain it? We may say, No, on the ground that it can hardly be important which words we choose to use, so long as our meaning is clear and understood. Professor Rawls has recently remarked that there is no one best interpretation of "rationality."[2] Possibly any zeal for defending one definition of "is a rational act" in preference to another is misdirected.

In what follows I propose to pursue a less tolerant line. I shall hold that "it would be rational to," in its ordinary use in connection with actions yet to be performed, functions to guide action by both recommending and making a claim which in effect evaluates the prospective action in terms of a certain standard. (In uses in connection with actions already performed, or the evaluation of the rationality of an agent in acting, we shall see that "was a rational action" performs very much, but not quite, the same evaluative function.) The claim made and the standard used are not precise in ordinary speech, although we shall see that some fairly definite things can be said of the ordinary use of the phrase. I shall then go on to argue that, given what we know about the psychology of action and motivation, a certain construction, explication, or understanding of the term, compatible with the just-mentioned features of its ordinary use, would facilitate its special recommending role by clarifying how reason/cognition can properly direct decision making. If we assume that such a whole package deserves to be called *the* proper analysis or definition of the term, as I think it does, then our reflections will have led us (with some qualifications) to an exclusively correct account of the proper use of the term. (The reflections that lead us to accept a particular conception of "rational," incidentally, are quite similar to the reflections that justify adopting a particular construction of moral language.)[3] We shall then be in a position to assess the status of the view of some economists that rationality is "conscious and logical adaptation of means to coherent ends."[4]

[1] R. M. Hare, "What Makes Choices Rational," *Review of Metaphysics* 32 (1979): 623–37.
[2] John Rawls, "Kantian Constructivism in Moral Theory," *Journal of Philosophy* 77 (1980): 529.
[3] See my "The Explanation of Moral Language," forthcoming. The present essay is not intended as a defense of the conception of "rational" put forward in *A Theory of the Good and the Right* (Oxford: Clarendon Press, 1979). In fact, the careful reader will notice some ambivalence on this matter not only as between the foregoing essay and the book, but also in the book itself, and as between this essay and "Two Concepts of Utility," in *The Limits of Utilitarianism,* ed. Harlan B. Miller and William H. Williams (University of Minnesota Press, Minneapolis 1982): 169–85.
[4] J. Baudin, "Irrationality in Economics," *Quarterly Journal of Economics* 68 (1954): 487.

1. The core meaning of "rational action"

I have suggested that "rational to do" is used in both of two contexts: that of advice-giving (perhaps to one's self) when the action is prospective ("It would be rational for you to take an umbrella to the game, in view of a 70 percent forecast of rain"), and that of act- or agent-appraisal when the action is past ("It's your own fault: you were irrational not to take your umbrella in view of the forecast of rain"). Let us identify some features of the standard ordinary use of our term, beginning with the prospective use.

(1) The predicate "would be rational" contrasts with "would be the best thing" to do. You might be sure that taking an umbrella is the rational thing to do in the circumstances, but not want to commit yourself to saying it would be the *best* thing, since the advisee might be lucky and enjoy a dry afternoon without the burden of an umbrella. Another example: you might say that the rational thing for a given person to do, in view of all the medical data, is to give up smoking, but concede that he might be a lucky person who combines smoking all his life with no lung cancer and no heart attack. The difference seems to be that "the best thing" makes an objective forecast that could be right irrespective of the indications now, while "the rational thing" goes with the *evidence*.

(2) But *whose* evidence, and how is the action supposed to be related to the evidence in order for it to be rational?

A natural answer to the first question is to say "the agent's." And it is clearly true that if only the university's meteorologist knows that there is a 70 percent chance of rain, we shall not criticize a fan for going to the game without his umbrella – nor should we say it is irrational to do so.

There is a problem here, however, which introduces some complications. For it does seem that I might naturally say to my physician, "Is it rational for a man of my age to take up jogging?" (One might deny we ever raise this question as distinct from "Would it be harmful or dangerous for a man my age...?" But I suggest we do.) This question is surely not an invitation to my physician to give advice based on *my* information. The proper answer of the physician, however, puts the question in the right perspective. I think the proper answer is this: "You had three options: to jog, not to jog, and to get more information before deciding. Given your (past) information, it was rational to adopt the third, and ask me as a way of getting more information. Let me now divulge the fact you need to know – that the evidence is a bit divided: jogging is good for the cardiovascular system, but a bit harmful to the knees and feet. I would say that, considering all these risks, and the importance in your value system of keeping your cardiovascular system in good order, it is now rational for you to jog." The physician's answer functions to make an addition to my information. So, whereas formerly, as he suggests, the rational thing to do was to delay and get more information, now, with the new information, the rational thing is to work out a jogging program good for my cardiovascular system, perhaps with some deference to the condition of my knees and feet! These reflections, of course, are consistent with holding that the evidence relevant to judgments of rational action is the agent's.

If an advisor wants to speak from the point of view of his *own* information, what he can say is: "Given my information, *probably* the *best* thing for you to do is...."

So far, of course, I have said nothing about how an action is supposed to be related to an agent's evidence, in order for it to be the rational thing for him to do.

(3) But what positively is being done by a "it is rational for X to" statement in an advice-giving context? If one person is giving advice to another it is clear that the expression serves to encourage or recommend the action said to be rational, whereas if one says a proposed action would be irrational he is discouraging or discommending it. (If I am speaking to myself, "it is rational to" functions as self-encouragement.) But, in saying an action would be rational, one is not saying (to another) merely, "I hereby express my favoring of your performing it." Quite the contrary, sometimes. I can say to a chess opponent that a certain move of his would be rational, when I am much *against* his making the move, which will result in my being checkmated. So, if the rationality-predication is construed to commend or express a favoring attitude, it must express favor from a certain point of view: from that of the goals (or better, as we shall see, utility in a broad sense, to be explained) of the *agent,* and also his information. (The possible contrast between the actual goals and the "utility" of the agent permits a speaker to criticize a projected action as irrational because he thinks the actual goals of the agent are crazy, although normally no such disparity will exist – for example, in the normal case when the physician assumes the patient's goals include longevity and good health.) So the speaker can be adopting a favoring attitude toward an action because he thinks it good strategy from the point of view of the agent's goals (utility) and his information: we can *approve* what we don't personally *want*. So, as a first approximation, we might translate "It is rational for X to do A" as "I hereby recommend that X do A (or I hereby express myself as favoring X doing A), while taking as my sole objective maximizing X's goal realization (utility-maximization), and as having his information."[5]

But this is not enough. It does not make clear that, or how, the recommendation is related to, or required by, the speaker's objectives and information, leaving open the possibility that it is arbitrary or impulsive. Whereas it seems that to say an action would be rational is to claim some logical or factual or coercive support for it, by the objective of maximizing goal (utility) maximization and the information available to the agent. Indeed, we

---

[5] This paragraph is indebted to conversations with Allan Gibbard (who does or did defend a noncognitive view of rationality) and William Frankena (who is or was inclined toward a combined noncognitive-naturalist view of rationality, parallel to his view about the analysis of "morally right").

might say that this claim is the important thing, and that the recommendation derives from this claim.

So much seems to be affirmed by "would be a rational action" (for advice-giving contexts) according to my own linguistic intuitions. But this is vague. I doubt we can be less vague without going beyond our linguistic intuitions. It may be helpful if I propose an explication that would be somewhat more satisfactory, from the point of view of clarity and definiteness, just to give an idea of a possible reconstruction. "It would be rational for X to do A" might, then, be construed as "I hereby express my favoring/recommending that X do A while taking as my sole objective maximizing X's goal realization (or utility maximization), and having his information, for the reason that doing A will exemplify a strategy of utilizing information to select actions that we can know is a strategy that in the long run will enable anyone to achieve his objectives (utility) as effectively as any other strategy can be known to do." We could omit all the part about voicing the recommendation, so that the statement contextually implies that the speaker is recommending, but without voicing this fact. We could construe an agent's self-assuring comment along this line.

(4) Let us now turn to the retrospective appraisal sense of "rational action." Suppose our fan does take his umbrella to the game when there was a forecast of a 70 percent chance of rain. He has then done what it was rational to do in the advice-giving sense (let us suppose). But that is not a *sufficient* condition of his having acted rationally in the retrospective sense. He cannot claim his action *was* rational unless he took the umbrella in part *because* he believed there was a good chance of rain and wanted not to get wet. His act of taking it would not qualify as rational if he absentmindedly picked up his umbrella, from habit, on his way out the door – and the same if he took his briefcase with him and later, to his surprise, found it contained a folding umbrella. To sustain a claim to have acted rationally, let us say as a first approximation, an agent must show that he acted as he did because of an internal program that reliably leads to rational acts in the prospective sense. (There is a somewhat similar contrast in the case of beliefs, as Professor Firth has pointed out: a belief of mine may be justified by my evidence, but I am not justified *in* believing it if I do not believe it *on account* of the evidence.) This is not to say he must deliberate, much less at length. It is enough if there is a program – perhaps largely unconscious – which ties his action to information and goals.

We should note that if "is rational" in the retrospective sense implies or asserts an internal program of a certain sort in the agent, then the charge of acting irrationally is somewhat similar to the charge of having acted in a morally blameworthy fashion. Both charges imply a defect in the agent. A charge of blameworthiness implies a defect of *character* – for example, lack of sympathy, honesty, fidelity, and so forth – a matter in which society takes an interest. What kind of defect is implied by a charge of irrationality? Possibly certain intellectual defects: say, failure to understand or implement or see the reason for a general strategy for decision making. Not if the defect is just a poor memory or inability to add, but clearly some writers would call a decision irrational if it manifested confusion in the theory of permutations, combinations, or probability. But irrationality of action may also manifest nonintellectual defects. It is hard work to think of options, consequences, and so forth, and a person may be too lazy to do it. It is also painful, sometimes, to close off one's options and do something; a procrastinator may be one who cannot face this pain. Are these traits of *character?* Perhaps not, since they are insufficiently important to society to engage its concern. They are, however, defects in a person, from the point of view of his long-range welfare. A person with these traits does *not* have an internal program that tends to lead from his information and objectives to action rational in the prospective sense. Perhaps we should say that irrationality in the retrospective sense has *degrees;* the more fundamental the departure from an intelligent internal program leading from goals and information to action, the higher the degree of irrationality.

So far I have said only that being rational in the prospective sense is not a sufficient condition of being rational in the retrospective sense. But is it a *necessary* condition? (Remember that an action may be objectively right morally without escaping the charge of blameworthiness, but it may also be objectively wrong and not be morally blameworthy.) It would seem not. It is true that if a person employs an optimal decision procedure, given (corrected?) goals and information, in a letter-perfect way, he will do the prospectively rational thing. But there are defects of execution, such as errors of calculation, or failure to recall at the time of decision some fact he knows perfectly well, which may prevent him from doing the prospectively rational thing. We do not charge a person with a defect of irrationality in decision making unless there is a non-trivial shortcoming in his decision procedure. To know this, we need a picture of the optimal procedure; if we have that, we may be able to estimate how importantly defective an agent's actual internal program is, as manifest in a given action. When we can estimate this, we can estimate the degree of retrospective irrationality of a given action.

It appears, then, that in order to spell out a reconstruction for "rational action" in either the prospective or the retrospective sense, we need to develop more fully *what kind of strategy* of utilizing information to select actions will enable a person to achieve his objectives (utility) as effectively as any other strategy can be known to do. I turn to this issue from here on. At the end I shall reformulate the proposal for a reconstruction of "rational action" in the prospective sense, but shall say no more about "rational action" in the retrospective sense.

We shall concede that there is not a sharp distinction between prospective (advice-giving) and retrospective uses of our term, in actual practice. Sometimes, for instance, we say that a *past* action was irrational in the sense that it is not one we would have *advised* on the basis of the agent's information, had we been asked *before* the action was taken.

2. The theory of action: a basis for the explication of "rational"

I shall now provide a thumbnail sketch of the theory of action I take to be espoused by contemporary empirical psychology. This will provide some clues to a possible way of contrasting rational with irrational action, and at the same time rule out some ways. Some philosophers may think this empirical theory purely speculation, and to be ignored; I disagree, while conceding that it is not the most solid part of empirical science, or even of psychology.

Roughly the general idea of the theory is that what a person *does* is a function of several variable features of himself at the time of action, as follows: (1) His representation of his location in the world – not just as a piece of physical geography, but also as a socio-cultural map that places him in respect of this salary, social position, and so forth. (2) His representation of the options for action open to him, of which there will almost always be at least two, one of which may be just doing nothing, staying where he is. (3) His representation at least vaguely of some possible consequences of each course of action of interest to him at the moment, along with some conception of how much more likely these will be made by a given action – perhaps with the conviction that the added likelihood of some consequences cannot be estimated objectively on his evidence. (Notice that a householder, while making a purchase, may have in mind only one or two of the to him well-known features of an item he is considering, which ones perhaps depending on the identity of his company, whether a child, etc.)[6] (4) The degree of vividness of all these representations. (This may vary from the very faint to vividness as intense as sense perception. Vividness is not the same as a judgment of probability; I may be certain I shall have to take an examination a year from now, but the representation of this may be very faint today.) (5) The attractiveness or aversiveness of each of the represented consequences (count an act itself as one of its consequences) at the time of decision. (How attractive or aversive may vary swiftly, for example, if the agent becomes angry or lonely.)

The main postulate or assertion of the theory, then, is this: An agent will perform that envisaged act, the represented consequences of which are, on balance, most attractive to him at the moment, the attractiveness/repulsiveness of each consequence being diminished somewhat according to its estimated improbability if the action is performed, and according as the consequence is represented faintly rather than vividly.[7]

This postulate is obviously incomplete, or an approximation. For instance, not much is known about the sum-total impact of the attractiveness/aver-

---

[6] R. E. Quandt, "A Probabilistic Theory of Consumer Behavior," *Quarterly Journal of Economics* 70 (1956): 507–36.

[7] See Brandt, *Theory of the Good*, chaps. 2 and 3 for a description of the theory and references to the psychological literature.

siveness of several consequences, all conceived more or less likely if a given action is taken. It is also only part of the story: a theory is needed to explain and predict why a given agent represents to himself what he does at a given time, and also to explain why he wants what he wants as much as he does at the time (for example, he wants water partly because dehydrated).

This theory is not very restrictive: it allows for stupid behavior as well as thoughtful deliberated behavior. The agent may think of only one action at a given moment; he may think of only one possible consequence of it; some one feature of it may be attractive to him and he will straightaway act. Action within such an intellectually constricted framework is what we call "impulsive" action. Action may also be aprudential, in the sense that the agent considers only the most immediate consequences of an action, and gives no thought to the morrow. Consequences may attract or repel him, or not, in a way that shows he is out of touch with reality, failing to appreciate what any thoughtful person would appreciate, or contrariwise setting store by qualities of a consequence that an experienced thoughtful person would set no store by. The theory also accommodates action more deliberated but with the consequences poorly thought out, perhaps because there is an emotional or crisis situation. Historians sometimes frame their reconstructions of crucial actions of important figures by reliance on this kind of framework. For instance, an admiral gives an order execution of which inevitably leads to a collision course of his ships and his own death. Why? Presumably he did not want the ships to collide or to die himself, but he failed to see that execution of his order would lead precisely to this effect.[8]

If we suppose that the main postulate of the above theory is true of *all* actions, then it clearly accommodates both actions we should want to call rational and ones we should want to call irrational. So if we want to find features of an action that distinguish the rational from the irrational, it seems we must look to those variables of which action is a function, and consider how they may take on mistaken or misleading values. For instance, an action may be nonoptimal from the point of view of the agent's goals (utility), because of his misrepresentation or his failure to represent, or the degree of vividness with which he represents something. Or, it could be there is something unfortunate about the person's wants or aversions.

One might ask: Is it possible that actions can be made more rational by the agent, if the main lawlike postulate of the theory is true? One answer is that an agent can always represent to himself, as one of the possible courses of action, that of delay and deliberation, when the issue is important and does not require immediate response. Of course, that may not occur to him; but the thought is surely not beyond his powers – one always knows how to do this, whether one does it or not.

---

[8] See J. W. N. Watkins, "Imperfect Rationality," in *Explanation in the Behavioral Sciences,* ed. Robert Borger and Frank Cioffi (Cambridge: Cambridge University Press, 1970), esp. pp. 208–16.

3. A more precise concept, coherent with what we know

Some philosophers have suggested that a *belief* is rational, if it occurs in a person whose beliefs are fixed by a good or effective strategy for reaching truth. A parallel possibility worth exploring is the idea that a rational *action* is one a person would perform if his actions were selected by a good or effective strategy for bringing about the good. The parallel will turn out to be far from exact, but is worthwhile bearing in mind partly in order to see where the parallel lapses. (For one thing, it is not clear that the goal of rational action is to bring about "the good.")

It will be useful to begin our quest for a more precise concept of rational action, coherent with what we know and particularly psychology, by quoting from a letter written by Benjamin Franklin in 1772, to a friend who was having trouble making a decision. Franklin is talking about how to make good decisions, and is thereby speaking to our concern of identifying a good strategy for decision making. Franklin wrote:

I cannot, for want of sufficient premises, counsel you *what* to determine; but if you please, I will tell you *how*. When these difficult cases occur, they are difficult chiefly because, while we have them under consideration, all the reasons *pro* and *con* are not present to the mind at the same time; but sometimes one set present themselves; and at other times another, the first being out of sight. Hence the various purposes or inclinations that alternatively prevail, and the uncertainty that perplexes us. To get over this, my way is, to divide half a sheet of paper by a line into two columns: writing over the one *pro* and over the other *con;* then during three or four days' consideration, I put down under the different heads, short hints of the different motives that at different times occur to me, *for* or *against* the measure. When I have thus got them all together in one view, I endeavor to estimate their respective weights, and where I find two, (one to each side) that seem equal, I strike them both out. If I find a reason *pro* equal to some *two* reasons *con,* I strike out the *three*...and thus proceeding, I find at length where the *balance* lies; and if after a day or two of farther consideration, nothing new that is of importance comes on either side, I come to a determination accordingly. And though the weight of the reasons cannot be taken with the precision of algebraic quantities, yet, when each is considered separately and comparatively, and the whole lies before me, I think I can judge better, and am less liable to make a rash step; and in fact I have found great advantage from this kind of equation, in what may be called moral or prudential algebra.[9]

What is Franklin proposing as good strategy for decision making? Essentially two things. First, he is proposing to take steps so that there is a maximally full picture in mind of the consequences of an action that might be of interest to an agent either pro or con. He is certainly rejecting the idea that it is rational to act on the basis of just the consequences which first occur to one. Furthermore, Franklin is aware of the difficulty of getting a sensitive synoptic response of a person's preference-system to a complex set of

[9] Benjamin Franklin, *Private Correspondence* (no date), I, pp. 17–18.

anticipated consequences. When we know all the pros and cons of a given Mustang and a given Omni, there is still the hard question which one we want altogether. Franklin's idea is to proceed so that each of one's relevant desires/aversions is induced to play its part in the decision in accordance with its strength. Hence his proposal to pair single pro and con considerations of equal motivational weight, strike such pairs from the deliberation, and form a synoptic preference between the remaining, greatly winnowed and hence more manageable, sets of consequences associated with the prospective actions.

I have already adverted in effect to the fact that the possibility of Franklin's procedure raises interesting questions about the psychology of practical reflection. For it presupposes that people can be trained to delay action by the prospect of more optimal results, be motivated by this same prospect to rehearse probable outcomes of different actions, and to determine when one is indifferent between various probable outcomes and strike such pairs from consideration. Evidently people can do the things Franklin suggests they should; an adequate cognitive and motivational psychology will explain how.

It is clear that Franklin's suggestion should be absorbed into an optimal conception of decision making, with some reservations. Franklin's view takes into account the obvious fact that an agent has mental resources useful for making plans for realizing the various objectives (utility) that appeal to him as a person existing through a period of time, the attractiveness of which may not be obvious or moving at any particular moment. Given time, he can think of options that do not occur to him at once. Given time, he can think of likely outcomes of a given action that are attractive or repulsive to him, which do not occur to him at once. Given time, he can simplify his choice problem, without prejudice to many desires or aversions to which a mere insensitive synoptic response could not do justice, by pairing off equally weighty pro and con considerations and eliminating them from further reflection. If we look back at the list of variables of which action is a function, listed in the preceding section, we can see that Franklin is essentially proposing that the agent tap his mental resources to expand the representations considered as (2) and (3) to the full, and take steps to make sure that the act that is "most attractive" at the time of decision is one responding to a simplified situation devised so that the several desires/aversions are taken fully into account, with their appropriate intensity. The procedure essentially permits the whole person – all his reasonably justified beliefs, all his reflections about options, all his desires/aversions – to be fully represented in the decision. Obviously decision making of this sort implements a sound strategy for enabling a person to realize his long-range objectives (utility), and hence is properly incorporated into a reconstruction of "rational action."

There is a serious omission in Franklin's account. This is his failure to notice that an agent often does not *know* what the consequences of an action will be, but at most can make a rough estimate of the probabilities. To take an example suggested earlier, a person deliberating whether to take an umbrella to a game can at most learn that it is 70 percent probable that he will get wet if he fails to take an umbrella. Therefore, in making the comparisons Franklin describes as helpful in simplifying the problem (or making the final decision), one is not able to compare simply the irksomeness of lugging an umbrella with the experience of getting wet, but only with a *70 percent chance* of getting wet. Some writers are justifiably (I think) puzzled about what might be going on when one considers whether one is indifferent between the bother of taking an umbrella and a 70 percent chance of getting wet. However, it does seem that such probability-information is often (always?) the best we can get, and that we do sometimes find ourselves preferring one such entity to another, or being indifferent between them. Incidentally, puzzlement about such comparisons cannot be resolved by assigning cardinal utility numbers to outcomes, so that it would be possible to assess a prospect by taking the product of this number and the probability of the outcome: for the assignment of such utility numbers has to be made (for example, using the methods essentially of von Neumann and Morgenstern) in a way that presupposes indifference between gambles, which is the very thing about which we are puzzling.

There is another omission in Franklin's proposal for a strategy of decision. He talks freely about considerations pro and con, and we have just seen he should have talked of the "probable" features/consequences of an action pro and con. But should he not have said something about distinguishing between what the agent *thinks* are the features/consequences pro and con, even probable ones, and what he is *justified by his evidence* in thinking? If a native of Vermont believes in the reliability of water-divining, should he base his decision whether to employ the services of a diviner on the basis of his *beliefs* about reliability? If we are devising and advocating a *strategy* for good decision making, it would seem proper to be demanding, and require that an agent rely only on beliefs about consequences that would be formed by applying the principles of sound logic (inductive and deductive) to his evidence – where his "evidence" is construed to refer ultimately to what is in his memory bank about particular observed events in the past.

The reason for introducing this restriction of the beliefs about options, consequences and the likelihood of consequences of an action is that a strategy of decision making, so restricted, will, in the long run, enable a person to achieve his objective (utility) more effectively than any other known strategy. This could be questioned. There is first the old question whether extrapolating past frequencies to future frequencies is justified; but the more serious question is whether assignment of probabilities to single events, on the basis of relevant past statistics, is a responsible guide for action, in view of the fact that an agent is interested in what actually *will* happen, not in what may be expected to happen with a certain frequency in a long run of cases. To this question the correct answer seems to be that each decision is one among a large number of decisions over a lifetime; thus, whereas it may be true that reliance on statistically based probability estimates will often go wrong, the policy of reliance on such estimates over a lifetime is presumably a policy which will work out best. Hence making decisions on the basis of probability-estimates of outcomes of alternative actions (or of options open), by applying principles of inductive logic to one's evidence about past events, appears the most promising strategy available, certainly better than known different strategies.

There is a further requirement that should be added, which Franklin does not notice. This arises from the consideration of the fourth among the variables listed as those on which action depends. It is that, in the course of decision making, the consequence sets on the basis of which the choice is made be represented with *equal* vividness (and the same for the probabilities assigned to each member of these). There seems good evidence that a person can in some sense believe an act of his will have a certain consequence but not be moved by it because the representation of it is dim – a fact apparently recognized by Aristotle in his discussion of *akrasia*. It is clear that a "fair" evaluation of a pair of consequence-sets, one permitting each relevant desire/aversion to be represented in accordance with its strength, requires each of them to be represented with an equal degree of vividness.

Franklin ignores altogether another, and very important, way in which decision-strategy might be improved. This way is judicious criticism of an agent's objectives. I have throughout attempted to leave open the question whether it is the agent's actual objectives, or his *utility in the sense of criticized or corrected objectives,* that a rational act would be geared to maximize. ("Utility" is usually defined by economists in terms of the agent's *actual* preference-ordering.) When an advisor assures an agent that a prospective action would be "rational," and claims there is "coercive intellectual support" or "logical and factual support" for it, he may intend that some support of this sort can be given for goals, as well as for means adopted to realize the goals. Would such a claim be coherent with what we know? Or does what we know lay some restrictions on an agent's goals?

Writers on decision theory normally assume that the preference-ordering of a rational person must be transitive. Why is this stipulated? Possibly the stipulation derives partly from the thought that if a person wants a certain kind of thing, he must want it with a certain intensity, either more than, or less than, or to the same degree as, he wants something else, and if this is true, transitivity follows as a fact. But in realistic situations it seems that intransitivity is a fact, and not obviously irrational: say, if a person prefers a certain type of Chevette to a certain type of Mustang to a certain type of Omni, but prefers the Omni to the Chevette, when they are presented to him pairwise, for a preference judgment. (If persons with such preference problems had followed Franklin's procedure of elimination of equally liked features, and based their final decision only on those left over, this might not occur.) If the agent acts on his intransitive preferences (for example, bets accordingly), an unscrupulous adversary can quickly drain his resources – he can become a "money-pump." This fact is a serious pragmatic reason for the requirement that intransitive preferences be avoided. Indeed, if preferences are not transitive, the ideal of maximizing desire-satisfaction becomes an elusive target, although intransitivities in a preference-system as a whole are not incompatible with the rationality of particular actions. There seems no good reason, however, for quarrelling with the tradition on the matter, and we may therefore assume that a good strategy for decision making will require the agent to avoid intransitive systems of preferences.

There is another feature of a system of preferences that can lead to mistakes of action. It derives from the fact that agents want some states of affairs for themselves, and other states of affairs only because they are means to states of affairs with the former status. Call desires for things for themselves "ultimate." These two types must be distinguished, else duplications are liable to infect appraisals of actions. Consider a student who wants an "A" in a course only because his parents have promised to fund a summer in Europe if he gets it. His desire for an "A," then, is manifestly nonultimate. But suppose he is deciding whether to study, on a given evening, or to attend a movie. It is obvious that he should not count *both* the prospect of the vacation *and* the prospect of an "A" in the course, in deciding what to do. That would be to count the same utility twice. One might propose to avoid this by allowing only ultimate objectives in decision making. Such a demand would be unrealistic, since people seldom have their desires so neatly divided. But we can insist that double-counting in weighing the desirability of alternate actions not be permitted. This is, then, a second restriction on goals to be included in our concept of rational decision.

If a person has identified his ultimate objectives and is allowing only these, somehow, to influence his decision making, and if his ultimate preferences are transitive, need we lay further restrictions on his desires or objectives, in order to have a strategy for decision making implementation which permits us to say that an agent's act satisfies the conditions of "coercive intellectual support"? It seems there are some further requirements. Suppose a person makes a decision when he is angry, say when he wants to injure someone who has insulted him. Or suppose a person is deliberating on a day when he feels lonely, depressed, or incompetent as compared with others, with correspondingly stronger desires for company, admiration, or success. Or consider a longer-term fluctuation of interest: a person acquires an interest in the ability to speak French, has it for six months, then loses it altogether and regrets the time spent. All of these persons may have perfectly transitive preference-orderings at the time. One might object, saying that ultimate desires do not fluctuate, and that there is only one ultimate desire, for personal happiness or satisfaction; this would fit a suggestion which has been made, that a desire now for something be counted only to the extent it is reasonable to think the desired state of affairs will be liked when it arrives. The one-desire theory, however, is implausible, and no reason is given why a person's wanting something at one particular time should be decisive, for example, as compared with later regrets. I shall not attempt to say what program for counting or weighing desires is an optimal strategy, but simply observe that it seems that *some* well-thought-out program should be adopted so that actions are not assessed just by their promise of satisfying actual desires at the time. Much the same may be said of another puzzle, that people often desire that they do not have the desires they have; for instance, a strictly brought-up young man might wish that he had no lusts of the flesh.

Thus far nothing has been said to suggest that a person's consistent ultimate desires – at least, the unemotional long-term ones – should meet any further requirement if they are to fix the objective of a strategy for decisions. What has been said does permit, however, appraisal of an *action to change* one's desires, say by seeking aversive conditioning or psychosurgery. As an action, this action is subject to rational appraisal like any other; a strategy of maximizing goal-satisfaction could call for removal of some desire, for example, for drugs such as alcohol and morphine. Indeed, it is possible that a strategy promising to maximize goal-satisfaction would call for medical intervention so as to reduce the influence of one's sympathetic responses.

Philosophers have thought that actual ultimate desires are often defective, and if they have supporting reasons for this view the conclusion cannot well be ignored by any strategy for decision making implementation of which might reasonably claim to have "coercive intellectual support." Aristotle, for instance, thought that various aspirations are unsuitable because their objectives would not be fully satisfying by themselves, or as means to further desired goals.[10] His reasoning is not convincing. Sidgwick thought that a rational person would not seek fame, and indeed that the only goals that might attract a rational person are happiness and human perfection.[11] Various others (for example, Ramsey, Sen, Sidgwick)[12] have thought that time-preferences are irrational, for example, a preference for some state of affairs now to the same state of affairs later (the satisfactoriness expected to be equal), to some extent because such preferences take no account of symmetries. Harsanyi views preferences based on factual errors as irrational,[13] although such preferences perhaps do not qualify as "ultimate." Some philosophers have thought that preference for a good for one's self over an

[10] See Nicholas White, "Goodness and Human Aims in Aristotle's Ethics," in *Studies in Aristotle,* ed. Domonic J. O'Meara (Washington, D.C.: Catholic University of America Press, 1981).

[11] Henry Sidgwick, *The Methods of Ethics* (London: Macmillan & Co., 1922): 9.

[12] F. P. Ramsey, "A Mathematical Theory of Saving," *Economic Journal* 38 (1928): 543–59; A. K. Sen, "On Optimising the Rate of Saving," *Economic Journal* 71 (1961): 479–96; Sidgwick, *Methods of Ethics,* p. 381.

[13] John Harsanyi, "Rationality, Reasons, Hypothetical Imperatives, and Morality," *Working Papers in Management Science* (Berkeley: University of California, May 1978): 12.

equal good for someone else is irrational; others (sometimes the same philosophers in a different mood) have thought the absence of such a preference is irrational.

The arguments of these philosophers, even the more convincing of them, do not share a common form, but their use manifests divergence from the popular view that facts and logic cannot show whether something should or should not be wanted for itself, as distinct from showing that, in view of causal relations, something should be done or wanted if something else is already wanted. The popular view, however, does appear to be a dogma which itself has not been proved. It thus seems that various arguments in appraisal of the status of various goals must be examined on their individual merits. I have myself argued[14] that some persons harbor the aspirations they do because of some sheer cognitive mistake – for instance, an "ultimate" desire for achievement because of believing falsely, for a long period of time, that achievement buys affection. I have argued that if we understood ourselves and our desires (including their genesis) better, or became clearer about other facts relevant to the objects desired, and reminded ourselves of such matters over a period of time, many desires would be extinguished. A fully informed person, in that sense of "fully informed," would be without them. I have also argued that a person who knew that certain ones of his desires *would* extinguish if he were fully informed in that sense would wish to be without them, would not regret their not being satisfied, and at least normally would not wish to take them into account in decision making. So we might conclude that a strategy for selecting actions that could claim "coercive intellectual support" would hardly include desires that had such questionable status, among those it is aimed to satisfy. I should not want to count satisfaction of these desires as enhancing an agent's "utility," and thus a utility-maximizing strategy would not aim to include satisfaction of them. Incidentally, there is no clear reason why desires acceptable in this sense may not include altruistic ones, or "external" ones in the sense of desires for something different from some preferred state of the agent.

Many or most of the arguments offered by philosophers in criticism of ultimate desires may be unconvincing. Still, it is also unconvincing to propose that a person's actual desires, or preference-ordering, just as they stand at the time, can be viewed as the sole goal in terms of which a strategy for decision making should be evaluated. So, if we are to define "rational action" in terms of a good strategy for decision making, we must leave some space for, and acknowledge some requirement of, evaluation of goals which is itself value-free.

4. An expanded explication and its status

I have suggested that there are some features of decision making that are fixed by human nature, the ones about which the empirical psychology of

[14] Brandt, *Theory of the Good,* chaps. 6 and 8.

action tells us: that any act performed is the one among envisaged options, the total consequences of which are most attractive at the time, the normal attractiveness of each having been reduced by the believed unlikelihood of the consequence if the action is performed, and the relative faintness of the representation. So much about decision making is fixed, and appraisals of it as rational or not are not to any purpose. What can be modified, and hence will be considered in an optimal decision making strategy, are such matters as what options are before the mind at the time, whether a given option is justifiably believed to be an option, what consequences are before the mind at the time, whether the probability of a given consequence if a given option is taken is correctly assessed, and how vividly the whole situation is represented. The agent can do something about these matters. Moreover, although there is a decided limitation on how much of all this he can have before his mind at the moment of decision, there is a strategy he can use to get the effect of a synoptic reaction to a complex whole, without having an impossibly complex whole before his mind. Moreover, there are things an agent can do to sort out his desires, so that only ultimate, or transitive, desires are salient at the moment of decision – at least to a large extent. Over a longer time-span, he can remove some objectionable desires altogether, so that they play no role in decision making. He can limit the influence of some desires, say mood-dependent ones, by confining attention to aspects of a situation to which they are not relevant. It is not so easy to see how an agent can altogether rid himself of the effects of desires he has concluded he ought not to have, or get the benefit of desires he has concluded he ought to have but doesn't, but the second-order desires to have (not have) desires of certain sorts will be of some assistance. At any rate, it seems fair to conclude that while psychology rules out the possibility of a decision-strategy changing some aspects of decision making, it leaves the agent room to make important changes by adopting a proper strategy. It is in this area that appraisals of decision making as rational have an important role.

Obviously a person will want to employ the best strategy for realizing his goals, for maximizing satisfaction of his desires – at least his criticized goals and desires. The function of rationality appraisals is to point out whether a person has employed the best, or at least an acceptable level of, strategy in utilizing his materials – his information and goals as they stand – for this purpose. How then may we helpfully construe the meaning of "it is rational to . . ."? Here, assuming the basic framework of a recommendation from the point of view of the agent's desires (utility) and information, a judgment-decision is necessary about the most helpful items that can be included in a compact expression.

My proposal for an explication of the prospective use of "would be rational for X to do A" is as follows, although clearly it is only a second approximation and needs more refinement: "I hereby recommend that X do A, while taking as my objective maximizing satisfaction of the transitive mood-independent ultimate desires of X, as they would be if they had been subjected to repeated vivid reflection on relevant facts, and having as my beliefs about options for actions and consequences those which are justified on X's evidence – a recommendation made because A is that one among the options justifiably believed to be open, choice of which exemplifies a strategy for decision making which we know will in the long run satisfy the (as above) corrected desires of X as effectively as any other strategy can be known to do."

This proposal is complex, and obviously not an account of what most people would recognize as what they mean when they say an action is rational. The reader can strike parts of it. If he is unimpressed by the reasons for talking of "corrected" desires and thinks that when judging the rationality of an act we must simply accept the agent's preferences as they are, he can strike the restrictions on the desires of X. Or, he may wish to remove the requirement that the beliefs are to be justified by the evidence, and leave them just as they are, or perhaps subject to some milder restriction. Various writers[15] have suggested that we must recognize different degrees of rationality, and we might construe this to mean meeting more or less restrictive conceptions of rationality. The definition could also be expanded, say by filling in principles of inductive logic, or probability theory, or principles connecting a person's justified beliefs with the content of his memory.

One might object to the foregoing proposal on the ground that it obviously demands more of an agent, in order to act rationally, than "it is rational" actually does. True: but such demands are made by the optimal strategy for decision making. And in any case we are asking the agent to do what may be difficult for him, the moment we ask him to avoid impulsive action – not to go on the beliefs before his mind at the moment, or, say, the angry desires of the moment. The agent himself might repudiate even this modest demand, if he is impulsive or aprudential.

But if the function of "it would be rational to..." statements is to identify the act which exemplifies an optimal strategy for decision making and in that sense has intellectually coercive support, then an understanding of the expression in the way explained would facilitate discharge of its function.

Some modification of the above explication is required for "was a rational act" in the retrospective sense, so as to imply some defect in the agent if his act was not rational. I do not attempt to formulate such an explication here.

It may be worthwhile to comment briefly on the similarity between the above conception and one popular among many social scientists and decision theorists for situations of "risk" – where the agent either has objective information about probabilities or at least is prepared to make probability judgments about outcomes, were a certain act performed. The basic conception of rationality, according to this view, is that a "rational" agent has a complete and transitive set of preferences/indifferences among all possible gambles involving outcomes of actions, however complex – there being

---

[15] See, for instance, Robert Nozick, *The Normative Theory of Individual Choice,* microfilm of Ph.D. dissertation at Princeton University, 1963, p. 330.

indifference between gambles and gambles over gambles, of equal value. Furthermore, it is part of the definition of a "rational" agent that for every outcome A, B, C, preference-ranked in this order, there will be for him some probability p, such that he is indifferent between B for certain and a gamble of A with probability p or else C with a probability $(1-p)$. It follows that if arbitrary numbers are assigned to two outcomes (the larger number to the preferred one), numbers can then be assigned to all other outcomes, corresponding to their status in the preference-order, unique up to a linear transformation. Then, if we construe an "act" as expressive of a preference among gambles, it is an analytic truth that an act of a "rational" person always maximizes expected utility (a maximal sum of the products of the probabilities of the outcomes and their utility numbers). This manner of defining "rational action" is useful for the analysis of many problems. We should note, however, that if an agent aspires to be rational in the sense of this theory, he finds considerable demands made on him: identification of transitive preferences/indifferences among not only all outcomes but all possible gambles involving outcomes. In other respects the proposal seems not complex enough. It ignores the epistemic situation of the agent: it has nothing to say about what the probability judgments of the agent must be in their relation to his evidence, if action based on them is to be rational. It assumes a static set of preferences: it ignores the fact that preferences at a time may be mood-based (perhaps *always* are), and that preferences change over time. It also ignores the possibility that some preferences may be subject to criticism. It proposes no strategy by which an agent may try to deal with these realistic situations. Unlike Franklin, it does not contemplate any help to an agent trying to make up his mind between complex prospects (for example, via elimination of equally liked pros and cons); if there is any problem about how to arrive at a rational preference ordering, the theory ignores it. It appears, then, that this theory is addressed only to special types of problems. If it is intended to be an explication of "rational," it is far from clear what are the ground-rules on the basis of which the explication is adopted. Which conception of "rationality" is more useful the reader can decide.

19. Rationality and valuation

Robert Audi

A major problem in the philosophy of action is what constitutes a rational action on the part of an individual person. This problem is also important in the social sciences, particularly insofar as their tasks may be conceived as conceptual or critical, and in ethics, which has traditionally viewed the relation between rational action and moral action as one of its major problems. Rational action will be a central concern of this paper; but since the rationality of an action is apparently dependent on that of the agent's motivation and cognition, we must also explore what constitutes the rationality of motivational and cognitive elements, and how it bears on that of actions based on them. Thus, beliefs and wants, which may be plausibly conceived as the basic cognitive and motivational elements, will be one of our major concerns. The rationality of values will also be explored. This is in part because there has been so much controversy over whether our basic values can be rational and in part because, if they can be, that is important for understanding rational action.

Section 1 will assess a highly influential conception of rational action – instrumentalism – and critically compare it with broader views. Section 2 will consider developments and refinements in instrumentalism, particularly by Carl Hempel. Section 3 will briefly consider a contextualist approach to ra-

This paper was written for the Berlin Symposium on Analytical and Sociological Theory of Action. I benefited much from discussing the paper at the Symposium, as well as at the Universities of Nebraska and Oklahoma. I particularly want to thank my commentators at the Berlin Symposium, Rainer Döbert and Wilhelm Vossenkuhl, for their helpful critical assessments. I have also benefited from discussing the penultimate version with members of the National Endowment for the Humanities Seminar that I directed in 1983. I also thank William Alston, Richard Brandt, Albert Casullo, John King-Farlow, Eric Kraemer, Don Locke, Alfred Mele, Mark Overvold, Louis Pojman, and Allison Nespor.
Reprinted with permission from G. Seebass and R. Tuomela, eds., *Social Action* (Dordrecht: D. Reidel, 1985), 243–77.

tional action and will address the controversy between Hempel and William Dray. In Section 4, an important contemporary account of rational action, Richard Brandt's, will be explored. Against this background, Section 5 will introduce a largely new conception of rational action. This conception is inspired by the analogy between the theory of action and the theory of knowledge. Section 6 will develop this conception and indicate some directions for further research. The concluding section will point out some of the ways in which the rationality of actions is related to that of persons and will suggest how our results bear on theoretical work in the social sciences.

1. The instrumentalist conception of rational action

A natural way to approach the question of what constitutes a rational action is to consider what it is to go about realizing one's aims in a rational way. For the question whether an action is rational very commonly arises when it is not clear that the action well serves some aim(s) the agent has in performing it. It usually does not arise when an action can be seen to be a satisfactory way to realize what appear to be the agent's aims in the circumstances. One might think, then, that the crucial mark of a rational action is its appropriateness to the aim(s) of the agent at the time of action. This approach is reinforced by the view, held or suggested by many philosophers, that an action is rational only if it arises from practical reasoning.[1] For it is then natural to construe the rationality of the action in terms of how good a means it is, judged on the assumption of the truth of the premises of the reasoning, to realize the aim expressed in the major premise. To be sure, a proponent of this view might still want to take account of whether the aim and belief(s) expressed in the premises are themselves rational; but as we shall see, an instrumentalist may argue that this question is not strictly relevant to the rationality of the action. If what is really crucial to rational action is its success as a means to realizing one or more of the agent's aims, then the character of these aims should be irrelevant, except insofar as realizing one may be at odds with realizing another or with maximum realization of the overall set.

On an instrumentalist approach to rational action, one will be especially interested in cases in which the agent (S) has not only one or more aims, but also quite specific beliefs about what constitute his alternatives and their possible outcomes. It is an empirical question how common such cases are, but they have seemed common enough to most instrumentalists and many

---

[1] This view is not frequently stated, but there are some philosophers who conceive all intentional actions as arising from practical reasoning, and clearly at least the most important kinds of rational actions are intentional. See, e.g., Davidson, Donald: "How is Weakness of the Will Possible?," in Feinberg, Joel (ed.), *Moral Concepts,* London and New York 1969, p. 110; and Harman, Gilbert, "Practical Reasoning," *Review of Metaphysics* 29 (1976), 451 (cp. p. 442). I have assessed both views in "A Theory of Practical Reasoning," *American Philosophical Quarterly* 19 (1982).

others to give great interest to the conception of rational actions as, para-digmatically, those that maximize expectable utility. Roughly, S's A-ing max-imizes his expectable utility if, and only if, it has at least as much expected utility as any alternative he supposes he has.[2]

The expected utility of an action, on this view, is computed as follows: one determines (a) the courses of action S supposes he has, (b) what he be-lieves are their possible outcomes, and (c) the subjective value for S (using arbitrarily chosen numbers from negative to positive) of each outcome; one then multiplies the subjective value of each outcome by the subjective prob-ability of that outcome, and adds these products for each alternative action. A rational action for S in such a situation is one with a score at least as high as that of any of S's alternatives. Consider Sue, a surgeon who supposes she has two options: surgery and non-intervention. (The patient, let us assume, has asked Sue to make the final decision.) Sue might regard surgery as hav-ing a probability of .60 of curing the patient, an outcome she values at 100; and a probability of .40 of resulting in death, an outcome she values at −75. She might regard non-intervention as having a probability of .50 of result-ing in cure, one of .20 of resulting in death, and one of .20 of yielding long-term partial remission, which she values at 30. We thus have, for surgery, $(.60 \times 100) + (.40 \times -75)$, i.e., 30; and, for non-intervention, $(.50 \times 100) + (.20 \times -75) + (.30 \times 30)$, i.e., 44. Thus, the rational action, on this model, is non-intervention.

There are various ways of interpreting subjective probability and subjec-tive utility. For our purposes nothing is lost if we interpret the former in terms of beliefs and the latter in terms of wants. Let us assume, then, that to say that the subjective probability, for S, of an outcome's occurring, is n, is to say that S believes the likelihood of its occurring to be n. This belief may of course be dispositional. Hence S need not have the corresponding thought, at the time of action or any other time. Similarly, to say that the subjective utility of an outcome is n is to say that n is the degree to which S wants it, or, in the case of negative utility, wants to avoid it.[3] In both cases, it appears that one need presuppose only ordinal scales; but this weak presupposition appears appropriate, since the notion of a rational action need not be conceived as quantitative in any sense implying the possibility

[2] One could restrict this characterization to *actual* alternatives, but one would then have a highly problematic conception of rationality. For one thing, if S had an alternative which he did not *believe* he had, he would presumably lack the required probability beliefs regarding its outcomes. One would need a number of stipulations to work the view out, and I believe that the result would still be a less plausible conception of rational action. For further discus-sion of both the maximization of expected utility conception of rational action and Hempel's treatment of it (which will be discussed shortly), see Davidson, Donald: "Hempel on Ex-plaining Action," in: Davidson's *Essays on Actions and Events,* Oxford and New York 1980.

[3] That *wanting* is a suitably broad concept for this purpose is strongly suggested by my argu-ments for its breadth, as a general motivational notion, in "Intending," *Journal of Philoso-phy* 70 (1973). I have explicated this broad notion of wanting in "The Concept of Wanting," *Philosophical Studies* 21 (1973).

of interval or ratio measurement of the rationality in question. What is crucial is that we be able to rank actions, not determine precisely how rational
they are.

It has been widely recognized that the particular instrumentalist conception of rational action just sketched applies only in special cases. But there
seems to have been a tendency, in some quarters, to exaggerate the frequency
of such cases in ordinary behavior, including problem-solving behavior generally considered *prima facie* rational. A main reason for this tendency may
be the assumption that if, on considering the question of how probable a
possible outcome of his *A*-ing is, *S would* assign a probability, then he believes, at least dispositionally, that its occurrence has that probability. But
as I have elsewhere argued, this assumption assimilates dispositionally believing to a disposition to believe.[4] To illustrate, one may be cognitively so
constituted that if someone asked whether there was a brass band playing
in one's backyard, one would immediately dissent. It does not follow that,
prior to entertaining this proposition, one believed it false. A machine analogue may help here: the difference is like that between a computer's being
so designed that, immediately upon being "asked" the distance between London and Berlin, it calculates this from its cartographic tables and displays
the figure, and, on the other hand, this figure's *already* being in its memory bank.

It is quite similar with probability beliefs. We are often so disposed that
on contemplating a possible event we form a probability belief about its occurrence; but it does not follow that we already had such a belief. This point
applies especially to assignments of probability *S* would make to alternative
possible outcomes of his action *after* he has acted and realized one. For the
experience of realizing the outcome often evokes beliefs about how likely it
was given the means taken to produce it. Moreover, a reasonably cautious
person may be very reluctant to make such probability assignments and is
often forced to hypothesize instead a *range* of values, such as between .50
and .75. Recall our surgeon. Even if she has statistics on the incidence of
death from the kind of surgery in question, each patient is different, and
she might well form only the cautious belief that the chance of death from
the surgery is better than even. Somewhat paradoxically, the better one understands probability and the complex field of future possibilities, the less
often one's behavior satisfies the maximization of expected utility conception of rational action (other things being equal). For one becomes increasingly cautious about forming beliefs regarding the precise probabilities of
the relevant outcomes. This is emphatically not to suggest that rational agents
do not take account of probabilities or often form beliefs about ranges of
probabilities. But my point is only that the maximization of expected utility
conception seems to presuppose the formation of beliefs a rational agent
would often be unlikely to have.

---

[4] In my "Believing and Affirming," *Mind* 91 (1982).

A natural reply here would be that while it may be important to see that the applicability of this conception is severely limited, I have still shown no deficiency in it for those cases to which it does apply. Indeed, I have not. But there surely are deficiencies. To see some of them, let us consider the resources of a sophisticated elaboration of this conception, by Hempel.

2. A modified instrumentalist conception of rational action

Hempel's most general statement of his position on the nature of rational actions is perhaps this:

To qualify a given action as rational is to put forward an *empirical hypothesis* and a *critical appraisal*. The hypothesis is to the effect that the action was done for certain reasons, that it can be explained as having been motivated by them. The reasons will include the ends that the agent presumably sought to attain, and the beliefs he presumably entertained concerning the availability, propriety, and probable effectiveness of alternative means of attaining those ends. The critical appraisal is to the effect that, judged in the light of the agent's beliefs, the action he decided upon constituted a *reasonable* or *appropriate* choice of means for achieving his end.[5]

Clearly Hempel is adding at least one important element to the instrumentalist conception set forth above, namely, the requirement that a rational action be explainable in terms of relevant beliefs and wants (I take wants to represent the ends of which Hempel speaks). He is quite aware, however, that his characterization does not apply to actions under uncertainty, i.e., those such that while S has definite beliefs about what his alternatives are and what are their possible outcomes, he does not (or cannot) assign probabilities to the latter. Hempel discusses some possible strategies for characterizing rationality in these cases, including the maximin and maximax rules. But he not only does not endorse these; he even warns against the "assumption that the idea of rationality, or of the best way to act in a given situation, is reasonably clear."[6]

Our later discussion will bear on how clear a conception of rationality we should expect to be able to sustain. But a prior task is to examine Hempel's defense of his instrumentalist conception of rational action where the conception does apply. This section will simply consider his case for ignoring the rationality or irrationality of the beliefs and wants that determine S's (subjective) probabilities and utilities. The next section will take up Hempel's requirement that (in my terminology) these beliefs and wants must explain the relevant action.

After Hempel raises the question whether, if S's A-ing is rational, the belief(s) on the basis of which S A's must be supported by evidence, he says that

if we wish to construct a concept of rational action that might later prove useful in explaining certain types of human behavior, then it seems preferable not to impose

---

[5] Hempel, Carl G., *Aspects of Scientific Explanation,* New York 1965, p. 463.
[6] *Ibid.,* p. 469.

on it a requirement of evidential support; for in order to explain an action in terms of the agent's reasons, we need to know what the agent believed, but not necessarily on what grounds.[7]

Similarly, he says that he "will not impose the requirement that there must be 'good reasons' for adopting the given ends and norms: rationality of an action will be understood in a strictly relative sense, as its suitability, judged by the given information, for achieving the specified objective."[8]

These remarks call for several comments. First, although Hempel defends his rejection of an evidence requirement by appeal to the aim of constructing an explanatory concept of rational action, he begins his paper on rational action with the suggestion that he is explicating an antecedently available concept (and in one of the statements I have quoted seems to identify acting rationally with "the best way to act" in the relevant situation). If *that* is a main part of his aim, he needs a direct argument to the effect that the relevant concept implies no evidence requirement. For surely there is no familiar concept of rational action for which it is clear that no evidence requirement applies, particularly a weak and merely negative one to the effect that the belief(s) responsible for a rational action are not held in blatant disregard of what S sees is significant counter-evidence. Such a requirement is especially plausible if one thinks of rational actions as the best thing, or even a good thing, for the agent to do. Second, and more important, surely a concept of rational action which does embody an evidence requirement can be explanatory, in what seems the relevant case: that its application to an action implies that the action is explainable in terms of certain sorts of reasons, namely, by appeal to the sorts of wants and beliefs we have described. Beliefs based on evidence, and wants based on reasons, can explain actions at least as well as beliefs and wants with no rational basis.

Granted, without any evidence requirement the concept of rational action will doubtless apply to more actions, and more of them will thus qualify as explainable by appeal to the sorts of beliefs and wants which Hempel takes to underlie rational action. Thus, the *explanatory scope* of the concept of rational action would be greater. But the *explanatory power* of the concept, where it does apply, would be no greater. Hempel does not explicitly distinguish these two aspects of explanatory usefulness, and there is no good reason to consider the former more important, particularly given that the action-explaining relevance of both concepts of rational action is derivative in the same way from that of wants and beliefs. In both cases what is explanatorily crucial is that calling an action rational implies that there was something S wanted, to which, in some way, he believed the action would contribute (e.g., be a good means).

In any event, whether or not considerations of explanatory power favor omitting an evidence requirement from an instrumentalist conception of ra-

[7] *Ibid.,* p. 463.
[8] *Ibid.,* p. 463. On this point and others it is interesting to compare the views of R. M. Hare; see esp. his "What Makes Choices Rational?," *Review of Metaphysics* 32 (1979), esp. p. 635.

tional action, there may be good instrumentalist reasons for imposing *some* requirement on the rationality, or at least the nature, of the relevant want(s) and belief(s). For even a thoroughgoing instrumentalist need not suppose, as Hempel in some places seems to, that the rationality of our actions should be subordinate to just any beliefs and wants of the sorts that figure in calculations of expected utility. Let us consider wants and beliefs in turn.

It is presumably our intrinsic wanting – roughly, wanting something for its own sake – that is the crucial source of subjective utilities, even for a thoroughgoing instrumentalist. Suppose, e.g., that by virtue of a psychological abnormality S could want to jog for the sake of strengthening his legs yet not want, for its own sake, either to strengthen his legs or to achieve anything to which he takes it to be connected as a means. This might occur where S somehow has an ungrounded chain of wants, say where (a) through motivational inertia, his instrumental wants fail to disappear when the intrinsic want(s) to which they are subordinate do, or (b) where – if this is possible – S has an infinite or circular chain of wants connected by instrumental beliefs (wanting x as a means to y, y as a means to z, etc.). In case (a), S would want to strengthen his legs, but not in virtue of properties he takes to be intrinsic to doing so, nor on the basis of any instrumental properties he takes doing so to have. We would thus have a want that is neither extrinsic nor properly intrinsic. In case (b), we would have a want not connected by instrumental beliefs to any intrinsic want.

Supposing that either (a) or (b) is possible, should an instrumentalist say that S's jogging would be rational provided S believed it would strengthen his legs and jogged for precisely that reason? An instrumentalist certainly *need* not say this. For one thing, the action is at least psychologically abnormal. Moreover, since it is not, given S's beliefs, a contribution to fulfilling any of his basic ends, i.e. (roughly), those he would want to realize even if (other things being equal) he did not believe their fulfillment to be a means of realizing any other ends of his, there is nothing he has, as an unconditional (even if revisable) end, to provide an adequate answer to the question why the jogging is worth while for him. The point is not that an instrumentalist must posit a set of final ends which all rational agents must seek; it is that even on an instrumentalist view the rationality of an action is plausibly relativized to *some* end wanted for its own sake *in the context*.

An instrumentalist may plausibly go further and maintain that the sorts of ungrounded wants we have considered are neither rational nor capable of rendering rational any action performed in order to realize them. Even supposing instrumentalists do not take this last step, however, they should certainly grant that an action may fail to be rational because of the irrationality of an *instrumental* want on which it is based. S may, e.g., have an instrumental want on the basis of which he unwittingly acts to the detriment of an intrinsic want, merely for the sake of an instrumental one. Suppose he wants to save money, purely as a means to furthering his daughter's education, which he intrinsically wants to further. He might discover that he can save money by not buying her certain books which are available at a library, and then, in order to save money, and with no thought of his ultimate reason for wanting to do so, decline to buy the books. By doing so, he might act rationally in a narrow instrumentalist sense, namely that, relative to the wants and beliefs of which he is aware and on the basis of which he assigns utilities and probabilities, he maximized expected utility. If, however, the damage to her education from not owning the books obviously outweighs – and should have been seen by him to outweigh – the benefits to her of the saving, the action is not rational from the broad instrumentalist point of view of maximizing S's basic aims.

An appropriate instrumentalist reply here is that S simply ignored a relevant outcome, the negative effect on his child's education. Granted, but this move raises the problem of how one decides the relevance of outcomes, given that many of our actions have significant consequences for basic wants of ours to which we would not readily see their connection. Here I want to bypass that troublesome problem. My point is that if – following what is suggested by the formulation quoted from Hempel we consider only the aim by which S is actuated in the circumstances, then we should have to call S's declining to buy the books rational, since relative to *that* aim (saving money) it is optimal. Moreover, presumably even instrumentalists may say that in the circumstances S's want to save money on the books is not rational, since it should be obvious to S that realizing it will detract from realizing the want on which it is ultimately based. The sense of "rational" here is perhaps purely instrumentalist; but my point is simply that even on an instrumentalist view the nonrationality of an actuating want is relevant to the rationality of the action it explains.

It is also worth stressing that the point is not simply a matter of want strength. For if we imagine that somehow S's instrumental want to save money became, at the time, stronger than his want to further the child's education, it does not follow that either the former want or the action it produces is instrumentally rational. The action would still be, one wants to say, a means to the wrong end. Thus, even on an instrumentalist view, the rationality of an action is not simply a matter of its producing the greatest amount of want satisfaction possible on the agent's beliefs at the time. Intrinsic wants are, in a limited context, privileged and can serve as a basis for judging the rationality of extrinsic wants and of actions based on the latter. This is why, e.g., an instrumentalist cannot allow giving something wanted merely as a means a positive utility *in addition* to the utility it has by virtue of its probability of realizing an intrinsic want. If S wants to go to the drug store only to get medicine, and wants medicine only to get well (which he intrinsically wants), going to the drug store may not be given a utility both for its contribution to getting medicine and its contribution to getting him well.

Now consider the role of beliefs in determining rationality. Suppose that *S* irrationally believes that jogging will strengthen his legs, against the evidence both of experience and expert testimony, though he does have a rational want to strengthen his legs. Must an instrumentalist say that the action is rational? It would seem not: *S* ought to see that in so acting he is not advancing his basic ends, or indeed any end of his. *S*'s jogging, in this case, may be excusable, but it is by no means clearly rational.

I am not suggesting that an instrumentalist must adopt the requirement that there really be (objective) evidence *for* the relevant belief(s), or good grounds for wanting the relevant states of affairs. That might be appropriate to a conception (on which I shall comment later) of the objectively rational thing to do, but it is not appropriate here. The point is rather that when *S* – whether he has positive evidence or not – believes something *against* which he has enough evidence to dissuade a rational person in his position, and then acts on that belief, the rationality of his action can be undermined even from an instrumentalist point of view. The same applies, as I have argued, to acting on an extrinsic want whose realization would be obviously undesirable from the point of view of the intrinsic want(s) to which it is subordinate. Hempel's conception of rational action, then, represents a quite restricted option even for an instrumentalist. So far, however, we have said nothing about his requirement that the factors in terms of which an action is rational must bear an explanatory relation to it. This requirement is controversial and has been attacked, at least as Hempel conceives it, by contextualists, most notably William Dray. Let us explore the issue in some detail.

3. Causalist versus contextualist conceptions of rational action

On Hempel's conception of rational choice, the reasons in virtue of which an action is rational must be sufficient to explain why the agent so acted. The central idea, I think, is that an action is rational only if the belief(s) and want(s) from which it derives its rationality also play an explanatory part, either as initiating or as sustaining factors (presumably in a broadly causal way). Hempel takes this sort of view to be challenged by Dray. According to Dray, the goal of rational explanation, which he conceives as the sort that displays the rationale of the action in question, "is to show that what was done was the thing to have done for the reasons given, rather than merely the thing that is done on such occasions, perhaps in accordance with certain laws."[9] On Dray's view, it appears that the sense in which reasons must explain the action whose rationale they indicate is non-causal. What the relevant sort of explanation requires is neither causal nor nomic connections,

---

[9] See Dray, William, *Laws and Explanation in History,* Oxford 1957, p. 124. Dray's views are developed by him in later work, e.g. "'Explaining What' in History," in Gardiner, Patrick (ed.), *Theories in History,* Glencoe, Illinois 1959. For another contextualist perspective see Scriven, Michael: "Truisms as Grounds for Historical Explanations," also in Gardiner.

but, apparently, a placement of the action in a context of reasons such that, in the light of them, it is the reasonable thing to do.[10]

Hempel resolutely rejects this as a conception of explanation *why* something is the case:

For any adequate answer to the question why a certain event occurred will surely have to provide us with information which, if accepted as true, would afford good grounds for believing that the event did indeed occur – even if there were no other evidence for its occurrence.[11]

This proposed necessary condition on explanations of why something is so has been challenged by philosophers of science as well as action theorists, and the issues it raises cannot be discussed here.[12] Fortunately, we can narrow the problem to the specific question whether the belief(s) and want(s) in virtue of which an action is rational must play *some* role in bringing about or sustaining it even if their occurrence is not taken to be sufficient to provide, by itself, good reason to expect the agent to do the thing in question. It seems to me that this is the minimal thesis which should be held by theorists taking a covering-law approach to explanation and to rational action. For it seems the weakest plausible thesis that (apparently) requires a covering law linking the agent's reasons to the action that is rational on the basis of them. Even this weak view is controversial, and Dray seems to deny it as well as its stronger cousins.

I cannot assess this view in detail here; but I believe that if we observe an important distinction not brought to bear by either Hempel or Dray (and often overlooked in the literature), we can reasonably judge the view. Consider Tom, who is (irrationally) afraid of heights. Suppose that as a result of his fear he impulsively takes an ugly route to visit a friend, thereby avoiding a safe but mountainous road. Assume further that whereas on the mountain route he would not *see* the land below in a way that frightens him, on the ugly route he will have to negotiate many dangerous curves. If he knows this, yet, fearing just being high up, takes the ugly route against his better judgment, his doing so would be irrational. For the motivating fear is irrational, and in addition he chooses, against his better judgment, the route he knows is significantly dangerous. It might be, however, that he knows that the ugly route is somewhat shorter, though this factor is, for him, too insignificant to affect his actual motivation to take the ugly, shorter route.

---

[10] See, e.g., Dray, *op. cit.,* pp. 124–126 and 132. Cf. G. E. M. Anscombe's remark that "To give a motive [. . .] is to say something like 'See the action in this light.' To explain one's own actions by an account indicating a motive is to put them in a certain light." See *Intention,* Oxford 1957, p. 21.

[11] Hempel, *op. cit.,* pp. 470–471.

[12] I have discussed them in detail and considered other positions concerning them, in "Wants and Intentions in the Explanation of Action," *Journal for the Theory of Social Behavior* 9 (1980); and "Inductive-Nomological Explanations and Psychological Laws," *Theory and Decision* 13 (1981).

It is thus no part of the reason why he in fact takes the shorter route. For all that, it is easy to imagine his answering "Why did you take the ugly road?" with "It is shorter."

This reply would be a clear case of *rationalization:* he has rationalized his action, not explained why he performed it. May we conclude, then, that while Hempel is roughly right about explanation, Dray and other contextualists are right about rational action? That would be premature. For there is an immense difference between the action-*type,* taking the shorter route, being a rational thing to do, and the action-token, Tom's taking the shorter route at *t,* being rational.[13] The distinction can be seen by recalling something forcefully maintained by Kant: one can do the right thing for the wrong reasons; and when one does, one is not acting morally. I suggest that Tom's case is similar. He does a rational (type of) thing for the wrong reasons, and his doing it (the token) is thus not rational. It is one thing for one's doing a particular thing, *A,* to be rational; it is quite another for *A*-ing to be a rational kind of thing to do and something one in fact does. Doing a rational kind of thing does not entail that one's doing of it is rational. I doubt the converse entailment as well. One could, for good reasons – such as credible testimony from generally reliable people – rationally do something (say, try to swim in a rapids) that is in fact not a rational kind of thing to do, discovering only afterwards that one was cleverly deceived.

What, then, is the connection between rationalization and rationality? What does a rationalization of one's action – if it cites a good reason one had for the action – show to be rational? On my view, it is at best the relevant action-type, not the token, that such rationalizations show to be rational. Taking the ugly, shorter route might be shown to be the rational thing to do by what Tom says, but what he says does not show that *his* taking it is rational: he does it on the basis of irrational fear and against his better judgment. Unfortunately, it is easy to conflate the rationality of types with that of tokens because, for one thing, we have so many locutions that apply to both. We speak of rational action, acting rationally, a rational thing to do, rational choice, approaching a problem rationally, and so on. Any of these phrases can refer either to the type of thing *S* has done or to his particular doing of something of that type.

Once we steadfastly distinguish these two kinds of things, we can see that much (though not all) of what Dray says about rational action applies to types, whereas Hempel's points against him apply mainly to tokens. Now there may be a kind of explanation which reasons that rationalize a type of action provide: they yield understanding of why one might do something of that type. Max Weber may have been suggesting something similar to

---

[13] As used here, the type-token distinction does not prejudge the ontological question whether individual actions at a given time are "concrete" particulars or something quite different, to be individuated non-extensionally. One could instead speak of the kind of thing *S* does, as opposed to his doing something of precisely that kind on a particular occasion. But this has no clear ontological advantage and is less convenient.

explanation of this sort in some of his famous discussions of ideal types.[14] But even if there are reasons, in a given context, in virtue of which A-ing is the (or a) rational (type of) thing for S to do, and even if S has these reasons for A-ing – since he knows of them and of their bearing on A-ing – if they play no initiating or sustaining role in his A-ing, then they do not render that particular action rational. He may rationalize, but not explain, his A-ing by appeal to them; but he is no more rational in his particular A-ing than a person who, purely for selfish reasons, does what morality requires, is acting morally in doing the particular thing in question. The difference is very much like the Kantian distinction between, on the one hand, acting out of a sense of duty, and thereby following a moral rule, and on the other hand merely acting in accordance with duty or with a moral rule.

My conclusion in this section, then, is that if we are to distinguish rational actions from *rationalizable* ones, a particular action should be considered rational in virtue of a set of beliefs and wants expressing reasons for it, only if these wants and beliefs play a role in generating or sustaining it. This does not, however, give us the makings of a sufficient condition for rational action. For one thing, even if S A's because of a rational want which conflicts with no other wants of his, and because of a rational belief that his A-ing is necessary to realize this want, his A-ing may still fail to be rational owing to a wayward causal chain supplanting the normal connection between these motivational elements and the actions they produce. These elements might, e.g., cause another agent with control of S's behavior to make S A in such a way that S's A-ing is neither voluntary nor rational.[15] It is no easy matter to explicate such chains, but there is a locution we can use to imply their absence. If S A's (wholly) *for the reason*(s) expressed in the explaining want(s) and belief(s), they do not waywardly cause it. One sufficient (but not necessary) condition for acting rationally, then, might be acting (wholly) for a good reason. How this might be interpreted will be considered in Section 5. Our conclusion in this section is simply the necessary condition thesis that if a reason in virtue of which S A's renders his A-ing rational, then he A's at least in part *for* that reason.[16]

4. The information-responsiveness conception of rationality

So far, we have seen reason to doubt that purely instrumentalist conceptions of rational action, particularly a narrowly instrumentalist maximization of expected utility conception, can be adequate to the concept of rational action

---

[14] Weber, Max: *Wirtschaft und Gesellschaft,* 4th edn., Tübingen 1956, first published in 1922. Relevant parts are translated in Runciman, W. G. and Matthews, E. (eds.), *Max Weber,* Cambridge 1978.

[15] This problem has been widely discussed. See, e.g., Goldman, Alvin I.: *A Theory of Human Action,* Englewood Cliffs 1970, and Tuomela, Raimo: *Human Action and Its Explanation,* Dordrecht and Boston 1977.

[16] The causal sustaining requirement implicit in this condition is argued for in my "Rationalization and Rationality," *Synthese* 65 (1985), 159–84.

implicit in our common-sense reflective criticism and description of action. This is an important conclusion. I take it to be at least in the spirit of a number of philosophers, including Aristotle, Kant, and Mill, and to be suggested by Max Weber, when, e.g., he distinguished between a kind of instrumental rationality and a kind involving intrinsic evaluation: whereas "A person acts rationally in the 'means-end' sense when his action is guided by considerations of ends, means and secondary consequences [...]. When, on the other hand, he has to choose between competing and conflicting ends and consequences, his decision may be rational in the sense of being based on his conception of absolute values."[17] But how can we determine when a person's valuing (or wanting) something intrinsically[18] is rational? Determining this will be crucial for understanding rational action if the rationality of an action is in part a matter of the rationality of some intrinsic value (or want) to which it can be traced.

This problem has been addressed in great detail by Richard Brandt, who has developed a powerful action-guiding conception of rational action. His strategy is to propose what he calls reforming (as opposed to lexical) definitions. First, he characterizes a broadly instrumentalist conception of rational action; then, using this conception, he defines stronger conceptions:

I shall call a person's action "rational" in the sense of being rational to a first approximation, if and only if it is what he would have done if all the mechanisms determining action except for his desires and aversions (which are taken as they are) – that is, the *cognitive* inputs influencing decision/action – had been optimal as far as possible [...] Second, I shall call a desire or aversion "rational" if and only if it is what it would have been had the person undergone *cognitive psycho-therapy*. [...] Finally, I shall say that an action is "rational" in the sense of fully rational if and only if the desires and aversions which are involved in the action are rational, and if the condition is met for rationality to a first approximation.[19]

Methodologically, this procedure is attractive. Brandt starts with a plausible strengthening of the maximization of expected utility view, and then argues that if a fully rational action is to represent the best thing one can do (or at least something to which no alternative is preferable), then even actions rational by the strengthened criterion are not fully rational. To be fully rational an action must be based not only on minimally adequate cognitive inputs, but on minimally adequate desires or aversions. Minimal adequacy occurs when the cognitive inputs (e.g., beliefs) and the agent's desires and aversions would survive were "every item of *relevant available* information

---

[17] Weber, *op. cit.,* p. 29 in the Runciman and Matthews edition. Note the *prima facie* causal phrases here: "guided by" and "based on."

[18] Very roughly, *S* values *x* (purely) intrinsically if and only if he values it for its own sake, i.e., for properties intrinsic to it and in such a way that he does not value it on the basis of valuing anything to which he believes its realization would (or might) lead.

[19] Brandt, Richard: *A Theory of the Good and the Right,* Oxford 1979, p. 11. Presumably the sense in which Brandt takes the relevant wants and beliefs to be "involved in the action" is causal.

[...] present to awareness, vividly, at the focus of attention, or with an equal share of attention."[20] Now

A piece of information is relevant if its presence to awareness would make a difference to the person's tendency to perform a certain act, or to the attractiveness of some prospective outcome to him. Hence it is an essentially causal notion. [...] Second [...] I prefer to define "all available information" as the propositions accepted by the science of the agent's day, plus factual propositions justified by publicly accessible evidence (including testimony of others about themselves) and the principles of logic.[21]

These ideas are developed at length by Brandt, and I cannot do him justice here. My aim is simply to bring out some central features of his approach by examining three topics: available information, relevant information, and unextinguishability as a sufficient condition for rational desire.

Given Brandt's rather inclusive notion of available information, even his conception of action rational to a first approximation is quite strong. For there are surely many things we do that are well planned, and even quite efficient in accomplishing reasonable goals, which we would not have done if we had all the information relevant in his sense. Often, e.g., there is an even more efficient procedure which we do not know of, though more experienced people do. But if the difference between the alternatives is not highly significant, the action still seems, in a common and important sense, rational. Brandt is doubtless aware of this, and my point is not that his proposed definition is somehow mistaken, but simply that it sets a high – perhaps idealized – standard of rational action. Doubtless this is appropriate *if* we think of a rational action as the *best* thing to do in the circumstances.

Brandt's notion of relevance is harder to assess. One would expect the relevance of information to a belief or desire to be at least mainly a matter of a semantic or epistemic relation to its content. Why does he characterize the relation causally? There seem to be at least three reasons: relevance is extremely hard to explicate semantically or epistemically; a causal criterion is naturalistic and thus avoids evaluative notions of the kind he wishes to explicate by using his definition of "rational"; and if information is not relevant in Brandt's causal sense, an agent can hardly be faulted for not taking account of it, and hence may still be said to have done the *best he could*. If these are not among Brandt's reasons for using a causal criterion of relevance, they are at least plausible reasons.

Let us start with a *prima facie* counterexample. Suppose that S's brain has been manipulated by a diabolical neurosurgeon in such a way that S is no longer moved by coming to believe certain propositions which seem clearly relevant to some intrinsic desire of his. To take a consideration which Brandt himself views as highly relevant to the rationality of an intrinsic desire, suppose S's brain is altered so that his realization that an intrinsic desire of his

[20] *Ibid.,* p. 11.
[21] *Ibid.,* pp. 12–13.

is artificial has no tendency to extinguish the desire, where intrinsic wants or aversions are artificial if they "could not have been brought about by experience with actual situations which the desires are for and the aversions are against [...] for instance, a non-prestige occupation like garbage collection or marriage to a person of another race, religion, or nationality."[22] I agree with Brandt that if S realizes that, say, his intrinsic desire to avoid marrying someone of another nationality could not have arisen from the relevant kind of experience, this should tend to extinguish the want and is relevant to its rationality. But would it be any less relevant if S could not react appropriately to it? That seems doubtful, at least if "rational" is commendatory. One would think that a desire should never be commendable simply because the person cannot alter it.

The problem arises because unextinguishability implies rationality, but artificiality, which the unextinguishable desire in question exhibits, implies, for Brandt, irrationality. Such a desire is possible, I think, because the criterion of relevance is too narrow. Even apart from that, however, it appears that a person could have a non-rational (even irrational) desire that would survive cognitive psychotherapy. Brandt must call it rational. He might reply that since the imagined surgery is surely not unalterable in a sense making it nomically impossible for S to react appropriately, it is not impossible for S's desire to extinguish through cognitive psychotherapy. But even if it is not nomically impossible for S to react appropriately under *some* conditions, it could be nomically impossible for cognitive psychotherapy to produce the desired results. Moreover, we may still ask about the (presumably) logically possible case in which S nomically cannot react appropriately. There, too, the information would still appear relevant. S's inability to respond to a relevant criticism surely does not make it irrelevant. S's prejudice may be "wired in" and thereby evoke our sympathy, but it still seems an irrational attitude.

In any event, I believe that Brandt's way of dealing with this problem does not depend on moves of this sort. He says at one point:

If a desire will not extinguish, then it is not irrational. This result is consistent with the general view that a desire (etc.) is rational if it has been influenced by facts and logic as much as possible. Unextinguishable desires meet this condition.[23]

The central ideal here seems to be that rationality results when facts and logic have done all they possibly (nomically?) can. Thus, to say that an unextinguishable want can be irrational is to demand more than is possible for S on the basis of his using logic and grasping facts. If S cannot be moved to cease intrinsically wanting x by any amount of exposure to logic and facts, surely we should conclude that *for him* the want is rational. The point can be supported by appeal to the distinction, stressed above, between the

[22] *Ibid.*, p. 117.
[23] *Ibid.*, p. 113.

rationality of tokens and that of types: we can say that while this particular want is rational, it does not follow that the type it represents is, in the sense that by and large wants of that type are rational.

This position is certainly defensible, but let me offer an alternative. Just as we can distinguish acting rationally from acting merely excusably, we can distinguish having a rational desire from having an excusable one. Now clearly an unextinguishable desire is (for S) excusable, since there is nothing he can do (using logic and facts) to uproot it. But why must we then use the commendatory, action-guiding term "rational"? For Brandt, the reasoning might run, in part, as follows: since "rational" is taken to mean "not irrational,"[24] and what is irrational in S is presumably such that he is criticizable for it, whereas one is presumably not criticizable for what is excusable, unextinguishable desires are not irrational, and hence are rational.

This raises the question whether "rational" and "irrational" should be regarded as contradictories. I think not. For one thing, one is commendatory, the other condemnatory, yet the things – such as actions, values, and wants – to which they apply vary, in the relevant respects, along a continuum. There are more good reasons, for instance, for some of the things we do, and want, than for others; and both our actions and our wants are *influenced* by reasons to different degrees. There should thus be cases to which neither term appropriately applies. This does not entail that Brandt is unjustified in using "rational" and "irrational" as contradictories; but if he does, we must at least conclude that in some possible cases, such as that of the diabolical surgery, "rational" is not commendatory. The victim ought to try to resist the influence of the artificial desire, even though he cannot extinguish it. If we must say, with Brandt, that the desire is (fully) rational, we are at least hard pressed to explain why he ought to try to resist acting on it and, toward that end, to strengthen competing wants.[25]

These points should not be allowed to obscure my substantial agreement with Brandt in many things he says. Indeed, I believe he has made a major advance beyond instrumentalist views. Moreover, his book provides a convincing case against viewing uncritically, as some instrumentalists may have, Aristotle's point that we do not deliberate about ends,[26] and against Hume's narrow view of the senses in which desires can be called unreasonable.[27] A

24 *Ibid.,* p. 112. Brandt's position here is not merely terminological. He seems to conceive rationality as occurring where one has not made (and would not make, upon appropriate reflection) certain mistakes. It then becomes natural to treat "rational" as equivalent to "not irrational," since the latter suggests mistakes or similar deficiencies.

25 Brandt is aware of this problem and speaks to it on p. 122 in relation to intrinsic desires for money, caused by its perceived usefulness in realizing intrinsic wants. He seems to think that if a want is either wired in or is causally inevitable on the basis of a rational want (such as an extrinsic want for money), it is rational. "This is simply what I'm like," S might say to a critic of the intrinsic want. But would such inescapability imply rationality?

26 See, e.g., *Nicomachean Ethics* 1112b.

27 See, e.g., the *Treatise,* Bk. II, Part III, Sec. 2. Weber is not committed to a Humean position, but his position on this issue does not seem fully worked out.

number of Brandt's points will be reflected in the alternative views about rationality which I shall develop in the next section.

5. Rationality as well-groundedness

Central to Brandt's conception of rationality are at least two notions: that of responsiveness to relevant available information, and that of optimality: roughly, being as responsive to available relevant information as possible. The first notion is used to specify the sort of thing required for rationality, namely, information-responsiveness; the second specifies the appropriate degree of information-responsiveness. A quite different way to conceive rationality, however, is on analogy with the (epistemic) justification of belief. It appears that "rational belief" has a use in which it is equivalent to "justified belief," and the two phrases are commendatory in very similar ways. To be sure, justified belief may be no easier to understand than rationality; but there is at least a rich epistemological literature to draw on, and even apart from that it is surely desirable to unify our theories of rational action and rational motivation with our theory of rational belief. This is a task for which I now want to lay some groundwork.

The epistemological analogy

To begin with, I shall assume that we may explicate justified belief using the notion of *well-groundedness*. In outline, the idea is this. Some beliefs on the part of a person, S, such as certain introspective, perceptual, and *a priori* beliefs, may be conceived as directly justified by virtue of being well-grounded in something – such as an appropriate experience or a certain sort of apprehension or the self-evidence of the proposition believed – not in need of justification, or even amenable to it. Any other justified beliefs of S's may be conceived as indirectly justified (and indirectly grounded) in relation to the former, the directly justified beliefs. On one plausible view, indirectly justified beliefs need not derive all their justification from the directly justified ones, but will derive enough of it from them so that even if the indirectly justified beliefs ceased to have whatever justification they derive from other sources, they would remain justified, in the sense that they would still be epistemically reasonable, i.e., S's retaining them would be more reasonable then his withholding belief from the relevant propositions. This allows that some degree of justification arise from coherence; it simply rules out coherence being an independently necessary condition for justification.

   The view is a version of modest foundationalism, and because it is modest it does not imply that directly justified beliefs are, say, infallible or indubitable, nor that only through deductive inferences can they transmit justification to superstructure beliefs based on them. The view is controversial;

but I have elaborated and defended it elsewhere,[28] as have others, and my purpose here is simply to suggest how it may illuminate rational action and the rationality of valuations, wants, and other propositional attitudes that motivate action.

Clearly, a fully developed foundationalist theory of justified belief must provide accounts of direct justification and of the transmission of justification from foundational beliefs to superstructure beliefs, i.e., beliefs that are appropriately based on the former. In both cases, there are many possibilities. For our purposes, just two sorts of account need be mentioned in each case. First, regarding the justification of foundational beliefs, one might hold that they are justified by virtue of being produced by a reliable process, such as the process by which the ring of one's telephone normally causes one to believe that one's telephone is ringing.[29] Another possibility is to conceive direct justification as accruing to certain beliefs by virtue of their content, e.g., by virtue of their being a certain kind of belief about one's immediate experience.[30] Concerning the transmission of justification, a foundationalist might require that for a foundational belief, say, that p, to justify a superstructure belief, say, that q, the propositional object of the former must entail that of the latter (e.g., p would have to entail q). A weaker view would countenance transmission of justification without such entailment, e.g., with a nomic relation or a suitably strong probabilistic relation between p and q. Since modest foundationalists hold the weaker view regarding transmission, that is the one we shall consider. It will be necessary, however, to consider both of the above conceptions of direct justification.

The notion of a well-grounded action seems to presuppose that of well-grounded motivational elements. Wants, conceived broadly, are the most common cases of such elements, but there are other cases, including valuation, i.e., roughly, a person's valuing of something. The next section will take up the rationality of motivational elements, with valuations – which are of special interest because of their connections with problems in ethics – as the central case.

28 In, e.g., my "Psychological Foundationalism," *The Monist* 62 (1978), and "Axiological Foundationalism," *Canadian Journal of Philosophy* 12 (1982). See also Pastin, Mark: "Modest Foundationalism and Self-Warrant," *American Philosophical Quarterly Monograph Series* 9 (1975); and Alston, William P.: "Two Types of Foundationalism," *The Journal of Philosophy* 73 (1976).

29 For representative reliability theories of (empirical) knowledge and of justified belief, see Dretske, Fred I.: "Conclusive Reasons," *Australasian Journal of Philosophy* 49 (1971) and *Knowledge and the Flow of Information,* Cambridge: Bradford Books and MIT Press, 1981, esp. Chs. 4 and 5; and Goldman, Alvin I.: "What is Justified Belief?," in Pappas, George S. (ed.), *Justification and Knowledge,* Dordrecht and Boston: D. Reidel, 1980.

30 This characterization seems applicable to Descartes, and a highly qualified form of the view is illustrated by Chisholm, R. M., in "A Version of Foundationalism," in his *The Foundations of Knowing,* Minneapolis: University of Minnesota Press, 1982. It is not necessary, however, for a proponent of the view to be a Cartesian.

Rational intrinsic valuations

It seems obvious that valuations, like wants, may be appropriately assessed as rational or not rational. I shall also assume (more controversially) that the objects of valuations and wants are states of affairs, but nothing significant for our main purposes will turn on this. Valuations, wants, and beliefs are the only propositional attitudes I shall consider, but much of what is said should apply to at least many other propositional attitudes. For instance, if we can use the notion of well-groundedness to explicate rational valuations and wants, quite parallel points will apply, I think, to rational intentions and to other propositional attitudes.[31]

How might a valuation be well-grounded? If we begin with intrinsic valuations – valuations of something for its own sake – and draw on the analogy with directly justified beliefs, we should find that some intrinsic valuations are directly grounded, and well grounded, in the experience (or apprehension) of the relevant kind of state of affairs, say, one's viewing a painting. This leaves open what it is for an intrinsic valuation to be well grounded. To begin to solve that problem we need to distinguish two cases.

First, there are cases in which S justifiably believes something appropriate about the valued state of affairs, such as his viewing (certain sorts of) paintings. S might believe that it is worth while, enriching, pleasant, or a beautiful experience. We might call such properties *desirability* characteristics, since (in the present scheme) they are conceived as the sorts of properties in virtue of which a state of affairs really is valuable (or desirable). S's belief might also be *de re;* e.g., he might justifiably believe, of the viewing of a certain painting and the property of being pleasant, that the former has the latter, in which case S (who may be a small child) need not conceptualize either paintings or pleasantness in the (presumably richer) way required for *de dicto* belief. Thus, a quite wide range of beliefs may serve here (depending on what restrictions are needed to enable the belief to ground the rationality of the relevant intrinsic valuation). In either case, we may speak of *cognitive grounding,* since the relevant beliefs are the basis of the rationality of the valuation.

There seems to be at least one other kind of grounding through which an intrinsic valuation can be rational. Suppose that S simply enjoys viewing paintings in virtue of experiencing the desirability characteristics of such viewing, e.g., the perception of balance, the sense of color contrasts, etc. Could this not render S's intrinsic valuing of viewing paintings rational, even if he forms no belief to the effect that his viewing them has these qualities? It would seem so. Indeed, it may be that this second kind of grounding – *experiential grounding,* we might call it – is more basic than the first. Perhaps if one could not intrinsically value viewing paintings simply for the desirable

---

[31] Some of the relevant points are made in my "Axiological Foundationalism," cited in note 28.

qualities of such viewing, one's intrinsic valuation of viewing them could not be rational because one believes one's viewing them to have those qualities.

How might an epistemic conception of the rationality of an intrinsic valuation account for its rationality? One possibility is to give well-groundedness for intrinsic valuations a reliabilist interpretation analogous to a reliabilist interpretation of what justifies direct, i.e. (roughly), non-inferential, empirical beliefs. Consider cognitive grounding first. Just as a belief, such as that there is paper before me, can apparently be justified by virtue of being causally generated, in a reliable way, by an experience of the paper which the belief is about and in virtue of whose presence it is true, so a belief that viewing a certain painting is a beautiful experience might be reliably produced by an experience of the design, contrasts, colors, and other relevant properties of the painting in question, and can, in turn, reliably produce an intrinsic valuation of viewing the painting *for* those qualities.

The idea is roughly that just as the belief that there is paper before me is justified because it is produced, by that very paper, through a reliable process and is hence *likely to be true,* the valuation is rational because it is produced, via the justified belief about the desirability characteristics of the experience, by a process reliable in the sense that valuations generated, by something valuable, through that process, are likely to be *correct,* i.e., to be directed toward what actually *is* valuable. (Similarly, wants, including desires, that are generated, by something desirable, through such a process, are likely to be, as I suggest we might put it, *sound,* i.e., to correspond to (to be wants or desires for) what actually is desirable.)

For extrinsic valuations whose rationality depends on that of at least one instrumental belief, the suggested account must be complicated. (Some of the required criteria will be indicated shortly.) In neither case, however, am I suggesting an *analysis* of justified belief or rational valuation. I am simply sketching a partial theory, available to an epistemic account of rationality, of what constitutes their rationality, at least for direct (empirical) beliefs and cognitively grounded intrinsic valuations.

Experiential grounding also (and perhaps more readily) admits of a reliabilist interpretation. It appears that an intrinsic valuation might be reliably produced by the relevant qualities of one's viewing a painting without the mediation of a belief that it has these qualities. Such a valuation would be a closer analogue of a directly justified perceptual belief than would be cognitively grounded intrinsic valuation. Rather as the belief arises from perceptual experience, the valuation arises, on this conception, in a similarly direct way, from aesthetic experience. When it is reliably produced by properties of the experience in virtue of which the experience is valuable, the intrinsic valuation of the experience is likely to be correct and is rational. Neither its rationality nor its correctness, however, implies an analogue of incorrigibility: on the view suggested, even the rationality of intrinsic valuations is defeasible under special conditions.

In both the cognitive and experiential cases, this epistemic conception of rational intrinsic valuations anchors them "to the world." They are grounded in the world either directly, via experience of something, or indirectly, via a belief that is itself justified by virtue of being grounded in the world. Despite appearances, this conception of rational intrinsic valuations does not entail a naturalistic conception of either rationality or value or desirability, though it does entail realist, as opposed, e.g., to emotivist, notions of value and desirability, since if nothing really is valuable or desirable, intrinsic valuations (and wants) can hardly be rational through being reliably produced by properties in virtue of which the thing in question is valuable or desirable. Naturalism is not entailed, however, because value and desirability can be real properties even if they supervene on natural properties but are not themselves natural properties.[32] (These points presuppose, of course, that there is a distinction between natural and non-natural – e.g., normative – properties. I am inclined to believe that there is, but cannot try to show that here.)

If value and desirability are not natural properties, however, then there is a problem for the reliabilist interpretation. For it is not obvious that non-natural properties can enter into causal relations, hence not clear that they can reliably produce an intrinsic valuation of something for such properties. We do speak of being moved by the beauty of a painting, and perhaps such locutions can be taken to imply recognition of direct causal connections. But it may be that what actually moves us is the relevant combination of design, color, contrast, etc., and that is apparently a set of natural physical properties. Let us suppose this for the sake of argument. It is crucial to see that these are just the sorts of natural properties on which the beauty of paintings supervenes, and that all the reliabilist needs here is the thesis that these properties appropriately produce our intrinsic valuing of viewing the painting. For one thing, if a painting is beautiful in virtue of them, then its having them is clearly a reliable indication of that beauty. Notice also that even in certain perceptual cases there is an analogue of this point. When one perceptually believes, through sight, that there is a person before one, it is presumably not personhood, but some of the visual properties in virtue of which (in part) the individual one sees is a person, that produce one's belief. Thus, whatever the (admittedly substantial) difficulties in explicating the relevant kind of reliability, we need not conclude that reliabilism is simply inapplicable to relations between non-natural properties and intrinsic valuation.

This is a good place to reiterate that the justification of foundational beliefs *need* not be construed along reliabilist lines. Thus, the valuational (and cognitive) analogy can also be detached from reliabilism. Perhaps, for example, it is simply a constitutive principle of reason that it is rational to value (and want) intrinsically (say) pleasurable experiences. Could a rational

---

[32] For defense of a realist conception of value properties see Butchvarov, Panayot: "That Simple, Indefinable, Nonnatural Property *Good*," *Review of Metaphysics* 36 (1982); and for an account of supervenience relevant to our discussion here see Kim, Jaegwon: "Psychophysical Supervenience as a Mind-Body Theory," *Cognition and Brain Theory* 5 (1982).

person *not* value such experiences to *some* degree? And if someone does not value (or want) something he believes is pleasurable, do we not expect an explanation, say in terms of its bad effects, or perhaps other special qualities? Normally we do not allow for the possibility that such experiences are not intrinsically valued *qua* pleasurable.

To be sure, the rationality of intrinsically valuing pleasurable experiences is not quite self-evident. But it is at least quite plausible to take such valuations as rational. The same holds for intrinsic valuations of (and wants for) one's own happiness, as Aristotle apparently believed. Note, for instance, that we normally take the fact that S enjoys something both to explain why he values it intrinsically and to exhibit the valuation as natural for him in a sense implying that it is at least *prima facie* rational. We may wonder *why* S enjoys whatever it is, or think he *ought* not to enjoy it. But if he does, it seems *prima facie* rational for him to value it intrinsically. Similarly, it might be held to be an *a priori* truth that if viewing a beautiful painting really is intrinsically valuable – say because it is a beautiful experience – then intrinsically valuing viewing it on the basis of the properties in virtue of which it is a beautiful experience, is *prima facie* rational.

There are other possible views a realist about value and desirability might take to preserve the epistemological analogy, but there is no need to outline them here. We should, however, ask whether the analogy can be made out on a non-cognitivist interpretation of sentences of the form of "S's intrinsic valuation of x is rational," where "rational" is treated like "morally good." Let us proceed to this question.

The main problem here is that for the non-cognitivist there is no property of (intrinsic) value or desirability and thus no analogue of truth. If the non-cognitivist thinks of the relevant sentences as, say, expressing attitudes, it will still be possible to distinguish between good and bad grounds for having (or expressing) these attitudes. Presumably beliefs could be crucial to these grounds. A kind of cognitive grounding would thus be possible. One might, e.g., say that if S justifiably believes that viewing a painting gives him pleasure, he is *prima facie* rational in holding, on that ground, the positive attitude he would express by, e.g., "My intrinsic valuing of viewing it is rational." We would have, then, a structural but not a substantive epistemological analogy. This would be significant and would help to undermine the irrationalist interpretation sometimes given to non-cognitivism. But however that may be, I shall not pursue non-cognitivism further. If the epistemological analogy I am developing is plausible, we shall have less reason to give a non-cognitivist interpretation to terms like "rational" in the first place.

The rationality of extrinsic valuations

We must now ask how the rationality of extrinsic, i.e., instrumental, valuations is to be understood on the well-groundedness conception. The basic idea is that their rationality (or at least enough of it to render them reasonable) is transmitted from well-grounded intrinsic valuations. Consider a simple case in which S has only one relevant intrinsic valuation, namely one of playing the piano well, and extrinsically values playing scales (as a means to playing well). A paradigm of transmission of rationality from the former to the latter valuation would occur where (a) the latter is wholly based on the former (e.g., because playing scales is valued *only* as a *means* to playing the piano well) and (b) S *justifiably* believes that playing scales will lead to playing the piano well. Parallel points hold for intrinsic and extrinsic wants, and it should be noted that a rational extrinsic valuation can be grounded in a suitable intrinsic *want* as well as in an intrinsic valuation. (I take it that valuations embody wants in any case, though they do not seem reducible to wants.)

This transmission of rationality from foundational (hence intrinsic) valuations to superstructure valuations is of course analogous to the inferential justification of a belief, and as in that case there are many varieties and many subtleties. All I can add here is that the transmission of rationality from well-grounded intrinsic valuations may pass through many elements. We then have a *valuational chain*. The length of such chains is theoretically unlimited, but in practice they often seem quite short. It is important to see, however, that only the first valuation after the foundational one need be directly based on it, i.e., such that S values the relevant object on the basis of what he believes to be its contribution to realizing the intrinsic valuation, e.g., to producing the intrinsically valued experience. The valuational basis relation is non-transitive: each element, except the foundational one, must be directly based on its predecessor; but none need be directly based on any other besides it predecessor. S could conceivably value playing the piano well wholly on the basis of valuing one's playing good music, and value playing dull exercises wholly on the basis of valuing playing well, yet never form any belief to the effect that playing the exercises will contribute to one's playing good music. S's valuation of playing the exercises would thus not be (directly) based on his valuation of playing good music.

To be sure, S may have two well-grounded intrinsic valuations such that, given his rational beliefs, incompatible extrinsic valuations would be at least *prima facie* rational (where incompatible valuations are valuations that cannot be jointly satisfied, e.g., valuations of talking (now) exclusively with Jane and talking (now) exclusively with John). Similarly, one might rationally want to practice one's tennis now as a means to playing well, and rationally want to weed one's garden now as a means to eating well. These possibilities should not be surprising; analogues apply in the domain of belief, e.g., in certain cases where S has evidence for incompatible propositions each of which is *prima facie* justified for him. There are many ways of deciding which extrinsic valuation (or want), if either, is more rational. Other things equal, the one grounded in the stronger intrinsic valuation is more rational and, in action, should (and will tend to) prevail; e.g., if S values eating well more than playing tennis well, we would expect, and approve of, his weeding the garden rather than playing tennis if we expect either. But other things need not be equal; one of the intrinsic valuations may be more rational, or more important to S's overall system of values, than the other. The problems raised here are complicated; but they or their counterparts beset any plausible theory of rational valuation (or wanting), and there is no need to try to solve them here.

Rational valuations, then, may be plausibly conceived as well-grounded valuations understood along the lines suggested. The same points hold, *mutatis mutandis,* for wants. There is much to be said to clarify this conception, but at least the core of the idea is now before us. Rather than go into a detailed discussion of rational valuations and wants, I want now to extend the suggested conception to actions.

Rational action

This section will concern only intentional actions. Some non-intentional actions, such as those knowingly performed *in* doing something intentionally – the sort Bentham called obliquely intentional – may also be rational; but they may presumably be accounted for on the basis of an adequate conception of rationality for intentional actions. In outlining a conception of rationality for intentional actions, I shall simply assume that they are explainable in terms of the agent's wants and beliefs, and that the rationality of wants can be understood along the lines just indicated. If so, then perhaps actions can be conceived as rational in relation to intrinsic wants rather as extrinsic valuations and wants are rational in relation to intrinsic valuations and wants (beliefs play a crucial part in all three cases). A rational action, then, might be conceived as a well-grounded one. I refer, of course, to tokens, not types. Our subject is the rationality of particular actions, not that of a type for a person.

Let us explore the suggested conception of rational action. Suppose first that the foundational rational wants are those that are directly grounded, and well-grounded, either in certain justified beliefs or in appropriate experiences. Some actions may be directly based on these, i.e., performed in order to realize them. If S believes, with respect to an action he is considering and a basic rational want of his, that the former is certain to realize the latter, and on this basis performs the action, the action is *prima facie* well-grounded. In this way, regularly practicing the piano could be well-grounded for S relative to his rational intrinsic want to play well. Again, we have an analogue of inferential justification. Indeed, some writers have held that there is always a practical inference mediating between motivational wants (or other motivational elements) and the actions they explain.[33]

---

[33] See the references in note 1. While I believe that this view is too strong, I accept the underlying idea that practical arguments represent the *structure* of the relation between intentional actions and the wants and beliefs on which they are based.

It may be, of course, that an action is only indirectly and distantly based on a foundational want. We then have a *purposive chain,* analogous to a valuational chain: S A's in order to realize x, wants to realize x in order to realize y, and so on, until we reach something S wants intrinsically. As in the case of the valuational basis relation, this in-order-to relation, which I shall call the *purposive connecting relation,* is non-transitive. S can jog in order to maintain his health, and maintain his health in order to enhance his chances of a good life, yet not – if he does not "make the connection" between the first and third elements – jog in order to enhance his chances of a good life. But in both cases the terminal element is well-grounded only if rationality is adequately transmitted from the foundational element(s), and this presumably requires that every *connecting belief,* such as the belief that jogging will help maintain one's health, is justified. A single action may, of course, be grounded in *more* than one rational intrinsic want, say a want to enhance one's chances of a good life and a want to complete marathons. It may thus be rational in virtue of coterminous purposive chains. Coherence criteria may also play a role; take, e.g., the overall appropriateness of the action to S's total system of motivation and cognition. The conception being developed simply makes well-groundedness central; it need not be the only source of rationality.

It should also be stressed that, as in the case of rational extrinsic desires, an epistemic conception of rational action may employ varying sorts of transmission principles. An approach modeled on modest foundationalism is unlikely to allow any action to be indefeasibly rational, i.e. (roughly), rational in such a way that the agent could not have had a set of wants and beliefs in the light of which it would not have been rational. Certainly there should be room for an action to fail to be rational because, although it is grounded, by a purposive chain, in a rational intrinsic want, w, a condition like one of the following occurs: (1) an alternative action would have been preferable for S because it would have been, and he could have readily seen that it would be, grounded in a stronger competing intrinsic want, w', or (2) S has a belief, which he has temporarily forgotten, that an alternative would more readily satisfy w.

Alternatives (1) and (2) can each be further specified, and there are other defeasibility conditions that simply cannot be discussed here. But something must be said about cases in which S mistakenly but justifiably believes that his A-ing is rational in the relevant sense. It seems natural to call such an action *subjectively rational.* Beliefs may be subjectively rational (or subjectively justified) in a parallel sense. But just as such beliefs, if true, do not represent knowledge, subjectively rational actions lack something: they might be said not to be, from the overall point of view of rationality, the right thing for S to do. Here, too, there are distinctions we cannot develop. Two common ways in which the rationality of an action is defeated are these: S might A on the basis of a *non*-rational want which he justifiably believes his

A-ing will realize, or on the basis of a rational want which he *un*justifiably believes his *A*-ing will realize. In these cases he may or may not believe his *A*-ing is rational, but we might still want to speak of a kind of subjectively rational action. An adequate epistemic account of rational action, then, will have to be complicated. I believe, however, that other plausible accounts of rational action, such as Brandt's, are on balance at least equally complicated.

6. Well-groundedness versus other conceptions of rationality

The epistemic approach to rationality provides an interesting basis for comparing different conceptions of rationality. From an epistemic perspective, e.g., one might say that on the sort of maximization of expected utility conception of rational action discussed in Sections 1 and 2, the only appropriate criteria of assessment in the rationality dimension are *coherence criteria*. It does not matter what is the content of the agent's wants, nor whether they or his beliefs are rational; the rationality of an action is entirely relative to the agent's wants and his instrumental beliefs. An action may, for instance, be irrational because it shortchanges the agent on the criterion of intrinsic want satisfaction, but not because of any defect in an intrinsic want which it efficiently satisfies, or even because the relevant probability beliefs are not rational.

The epistemic perspective also puts us in a good position to see how the view that well-groundedness is what is central to the rationality of intrinsic wants differs from the Brandtian account of their rationality. First, Brandt does not require any close analogue of grounding. For him, rational intrinsic wants need not have any particular kind of content or type of origin in experience, e.g., being based on appropriate beliefs or appropriate experiences. They are rational if they would pass a certain test. Undoubtedly, Brandt would suppose that in fact few if any intrinsic wants (and valuations) are rational unless they *do* rest on such beliefs or experiences. My point is simply that his view contains no positive conceptual requirement corresponding to well-groundedness. Second, the notion of well-groundedness admits of degree; so, on the well-groundedness conception, a rational intrinsic desire need not be optimally grounded. Third, the well-groundedness conception is neutral with respect to naturalism, whereas Brandt's view, properly understood, is naturalistic.

Speaking from an epistemic perspective, then, we may say that unlike the maximization of expected utility view, Brandt's is not happily conceived as purely coherentist. For his criteria of rational wants and rational belief are by no means purely coherence criteria, and he also strongly restricts the sorts of wants and beliefs in virtue of which *S*'s *A*-ing may be rational: roughly, *S*'s wants must be capable of surviving cognitive psychotherapy, and his beliefs must reflect adequate information. But if Brandt's view is foundationalist, it is, at least as regards wants, a *procedural foundationalism:* rational intrinsic wants, the foundational motivating elements, need not have any particular content or type of content; they must simply be capable of surviving exposure to appropriate information. This in turn leaves open the sort of action that may be rational (even if Brandt's view of justified belief should be a version of foundationalism – a matter on which I offer no interpretation of him). The question of what wants will survive such exposure is empirical. In principle, they might be egoistic or altruistic, hedonistic or puritanical, democratic or oligarchical.

By contrast, while I have attributed to the epistemic conception of rationality no theses about the sorts of wants and beliefs that are rational, even a modest foundationalist conception of rationality will presuppose that some particular wants, e.g., intrinsic wants for one's own happiness, and some specific beliefs, e.g., those about certain aspects of one's current immediate experience, are, under appropriate conditions, rational. Different theories will give different accounts of such foundational rationality and will differ as to what is foundationally rational. But a fully worked out epistemic theory of rationality will try to reflect certain plausible intuitions as to what sorts of elements are rational and which among these are properly taken to be foundational.[34] In any case, let us apply to some examples a few of the contrasts between Brandt's view and the epistemic view outlined in this paper.

Take first the question of what determines the relevance of a consideration to the rationality of intrinsic desires. Returning to our victim of diabolical surgery, regardless of whether his intrinsic desire concerning marriage will extinguish, it need not be well-grounded. He neither has a justified belief, nor any appropriate experience, in virtue of which the desire is rational. This can explain why it is not rational, whereas, if cognitive psychotherapy will not extinguish it, Brandt's view must, implausibly, I think, take it to be rational. The well-groundedness view can also explain why obviously contradictory states of affairs cannot be rationally wanted intrinsically: S cannot have experienced them, nor (presumably) can he justifiably believe them to have desirability characteristics. Suppose, on the other hand, that S researches pianos and buys a good one at a good price, yet overlooks information available to him which would have led to his getting a slightly better price. On the well-groundedness view, one could explain why S did not act

---

[34] In *A Theory of Justice,* Cambridge: Harvard University Press 1971, John Rawls conceives certain goods, e.g., freedom of the person, imagination, and vigor, as *primary goods,* and he maintains that a rational person wants these whatever else he wants. See, e.g., p. 62 and Chapter 3, Section 25. Rawls certainly represents these goods as valuable as means, but this is consistent with holding – what seems plausible at least for certain natural primary goods, such as self-respect, and health – that they are also intrinsically desirable. It is an interesting question (which unfortunately I cannot pursue here) to what extent Rawls might regard some things as intrinsically desirable (or intrinsically valuable) and might conceive certain wants or valuations regarding them as capable of playing a foundational role, such as I have outlined, in the motivational system of a rational person. I am grateful to Dagfinn Føllesdal for suggesting that Rawls might possibly be interpreted as holding a modest foundationalist view somewhat of the sort I have been exploring.

optimally, yet still conceive his action as well-grounded to a high degree and thus as rational. On Brandt's scheme, the action must be called irrational (though it should be pointed out that some irrational actions are not far from rational). No doubt there are other cases of intrinsic wants, and of actions, whose rationality or lack of it would be differently characterized on the well-groundedness conception than on Brandt's theory, though extensionally I would expect the two views to be close. This is not to imply that we can establish precise, uncontroversial criteria of well-groundedness for all intrinsic wants (or valuations). But for at least a great many we can give some account of their rationality, or lack of it, by appeal to cognitive or experiential grounding conceived in the ways suggested in this paper.

Moreover, while on a realist conception of value and desirability a want or valuation may be in some objective sense unsound, a realist epistemic conception of rationality may grant that two people may have well-grounded intrinsic wants for mutually incompatible states of affairs, e.g., one for a predominance of classical music on the radio, one for a predominance of popular music on the radio. Some proponents of the conception might argue that these wants cannot both be *maximally* well-grounded, but that view is not essential to the position, any more than the claim that a maximally justified belief must be true is essential to a realist conception of epistemic justification. The position certainly allows for the joint possibility that Jane, e.g., has a fully rational intrinsic desire to listen (herself) to classical music, while Tom has a fully rational intrinsic desire to listen (himself) to popular music. They may, e.g., have different response patterns and different capacities. Thus, a kind of relativity is compatible with the well-groundedness view. For Brandt, on the other hand, there is a stronger relativity: if the two incompatible wants imagined (regarding radio broadcasting) do not change under appropriate exposure to information – as it seems right they might not – there is no room for the view that one may be better grounded and in a sense more rational.

From much of what has been said it will be apparent that the main variables determining rationality on the well-groundedness conception admit of degree. The belief that a kind of experience has a certain desirability characteristic may be more or less justified. How much one wants a kind of experience may result from differing intensities of one's experience of, or differing degrees of apprehension of, its desirability characteristics. Connecting beliefs, such as that A-ing will realize a want, may be more or less justified. They may also be an inadequate basis for action even if justified: if S justifiably believes A-ing will realize his want, but should see that B-ing instead would realize it much more efficiently, he is overlooking a preferable and incompatible alternative, and his A-ing would be at best *prima facie* well-grounded. Thus, not only does well-groundedness admit of degrees; a want, valuation, or action may be sufficiently well-grounded to be rational, yet nowhere near maximally rational.

7. Conclusion

Much work must be done to develop the well-groundedness conception of rationality as a critical and descriptive tool in the theory of action and, particularly, in the social sciences. That project is impossible here, but I can point out some implications of the conception which suggest that the project is quite worth doing.

First, the well-groundedness conception of rationality is psychologically realistic and connects the rationality of actions, values, and other elements, with psychological properties of persons – such as their beliefs and wants – that are important for understanding human behavior in general, individual and social. The conception is realistic because it does not make rationality something few if any persons can often achieve, nor does it require that all rational actions, rational valuations, or rational wants be backed by *actual* reasoning processes, such as episodes of practical reasoning, or even that all rational propositional attitudes be conscious. Often rational elements do emerge from such processes; and they may derive rationality from the relevant premises and other factors. But often rational actions are "automatic," and frequently rational valuations are spontaneous. The well-groundedness conception makes this easy to understand. For neither valuational nor purposive chains need be constituted by explicitly inferential links, nor is self-consciousness or deliberation required for transmission of rationality from foundational to superstructure elements. It may, e.g., be rational for S to do exercises because he believes exercising is appropriately connected with his leading a certain kind of life, one which S intrinsically and rationally values, even if he has not connected the former to the latter by a series of inferences, or self-consciously evaluated either exercising or the kind of life to which (however indirectly) the exercising is connected by his instrumental beliefs.

Given this view of the transmission of rationality – which accords with, but does not entail, a reliabilist conception of its transmission – the well-groundedness conception of rationality may differ from many traditional ones. But it is important to realize that in other respects the conception may be taken to be a plausible extension of Aristotle's foundationalist notion of rational desire and, implicitly, rational valuation, as I have elsewhere argued.[35] Much the same may be said about Mill, who seems to be quite Aristotelian on this point,[36] and there are surely other historically influential figures whose conception of rationality can be explained, or at least reconstructed, along the lines I have indicated.

If the well-groundedness conception of rationality has the psychological connections I have stressed, one might think that, as Hempel maintains,

---

[35] I have spelled out the case for this, referring to the *Nicomachean Ethics* 1097a15–1097b20, in "Axiological Foundationalism," cited in note 28.

[36] I have developed this idea in "The Structure of Motivation," *Pacific Philosophical Quarterly* 61 (1980), with reference to *Utilitarianism,* esp. Ch. IV.

rationality is an explanatory concept. There is an ambiguity here. If an explanatory concept of rationality is one such that we can explain why certain events or states occur by saying that they are rational, then Hempel's contention is not quite correct. What one may claim, both for Hempel's notion of rational action and for the much broader concept of rationality I have sketched, is that they are *obliquely explanatory,* in the sense that their application to an action or propositional attitude entails that it *can* be explained in a certain way. For instance, if an action is rational, then there is a want-belief (intentionalistic) explanation for it; and if a valuation is rational, it is explainable, at least in part, either in terms of a valuation (or want) prior to it in a valuational chain or (when it is intrinsic) in terms of a well-grounded belief or an appropriate experience.

Rationality, then, for all the rational elements we have discussed, entails that they are embedded in an explanatory framework. Does this also apply to the rationality of persons, or to that of social actions on the part of institutions or groups of people? I should think so. For surely the rationality of a person is at least mainly determined by the rationality of his actions, action tendencies, and propositional attitudes; and presumably the rationality of group or institutional action (tokens) is at least mainly determined by that of individual action (tokens).

These points might be thought to imply that human actions, individual and social, admit of causal explanation. They do not imply that. The nature of the relevant explanations is left open by the well-groundedness conception of rationality. I do believe, however, that the relevant explanatory framework is *nomic*[37] and that everyday want-belief explanations of action may be conceived as tacitly appealing to laws. But at least some of these laws are special. For one thing, they employ dispositional rather than event properties to explain events, most notably actions. For another, the kind of dispositions that figure in them, propositional attitudes, have special properties, such as intentionality. In part for these reasons, we need not conceive the relevant explanations as causal, nor collapse the distinction between reasons and causes. Thus, on the overall conception of rationality I propose, the social sciences may be regarded not only as appropriately studying rational human actions rather than mere human behavior, but as studying action, with the goal of discovering a nomic – even if non-causal, non-mechanistic – theoretical framework for its interpretation.

I have argued that a purely instrumentalist conception of rationality is too narrow and that the contextualist account cuts rational actions off from the systems of propositional attitudes from which, by virtue of an explanatory connection, they derive their rationality. Brandt's full-information, optimality conception of rationality is far superior to either approach, and it

---

[37] This idea is developed in "Wants and Intentions in the Explanation of Action," cited in note 12. Cf. Goldman, *op. cit.;* Tuomela, *op. cit.;* and Thalberg, Irving: *Perception, Emotion and Action,* Oxford 1977, esp. Chapter 3, "Are Reasons We Act on Causally or Logically Connected with Our Deeds?"

embodies a number of ideas that any plausible view of rationality should incorporate. But I have argued that his causal criterion of relevant information is inadequate and that we seem well advised not to take "rational" as an absolute term with such strong necessary conditions. The contrasting proposal I have been exploring conceives rationality as a kind of well-groundedness. The resulting theory enables us to unify our concept of rational action with our concept of rational belief and indeed of rational propositional attitudes in general; and for all of these cases it provides a way to distinguish rationality from rationalizability, and to articulate a range of variables in terms of which we can develop a reasonably clear comparative concept of rationality. The view also enables us to conceive rationality in an explanatory framework that seems essential in the social sciences, whether we conceive it as nomic or in some other way. And it enables us to anchor the rationality of actions, values, wants, and persons themselves, to our experiences in a shared world.

B. *Irrationality*

20. Paradoxes of irrationality

Donald Davidson

The idea of an irrational action, belief, intention, inference or emotion is paradoxical. For the irrational is not merely the nonrational, which lies outside the ambit of the rational; irrationality is a failure within the house of reason. When Hobbes says only man has "the privilege of absurdity" he suggests that only a rational creature can be irrational. Irrationality is a mental process or state – a rational process or state – gone wrong. How can this be?

The paradox of irrationality is not as simple as the seeming paradox in the concept of an unsuccessful joke, or of a bad piece of art. The paradox of irrationality springs from what is involved in our most basic ways of describing, understanding, and explaining psychological states and events. Sophia is pleased that she can tie a bowline. Then her pleasure must be due to her belief that she can tie a bowline and her positive assessment of that accomplishment. Further, and doubtless more searching, explanations may be available, but they cannot displace this one, since this one flows from what it is to be pleased that something is the case. Or take Roger, who intends to pass an examination by memorizing the Koran. This intention must be explained by his desire to pass the examination and his belief that by memorizing the Koran he will enhance his chances of passing the examination. The existence of reason explanations of this sort is a built-in aspect of intentions, intentional actions, and many other attitudes and emotions. Such explanations explain by rationalizing: they enable us to see the events

A precursor of this paper was delivered as the Ernest Jones lecture before the British Psychoanalytical Association on 26 April 1978. Dr Edna O'Shaughnessy commented and I have profited from her informative remarks. I am also indebted for further useful suggestions to Dagfinn Føllesdal, Sue Larson and Richard Wollheim.
Reprinted with permission from R. Wollheim and J. Hopkins, eds., *Philosophical Essays on Freud* (Cambridge: Cambridge University Press, 1982), 289–305.

or attitudes as reasonable from a point of view of the agent. An aura of rationality, of fitting into a rational pattern, is thus inseparable from these phenomena, at least as long as they are described in psychological terms. How then can we explain, or even tolerate as possible, irrational thoughts, actions or emotions?

Psychoanalytic theory as developed by Freud claims to provide a conceptual framework within which to describe and understand irrationality. But many philosophers think there are fundamental errors or confusions in Freud's thought. So I consider here some elements in that thought that have often come under attack, elements that consist of a few very general doctrines central to all stages of Freud's mature writings. After analysing the underlying problem of explaining irrationality, I conclude that any satisfactory view must embrace some of Freud's most important theses, and when these theses are stated in a sufficiently broad way, they are free from conceptual confusion. It perhaps needs to be emphasized that my "defence" of Freud is directed to some only of Freud's ideas, and these are ideas at the conceptual, in contrast to the empirical, end of that vague spectrum.

Much that is called irrational does not make for paradox. Many might hold that it is irrational, given the dangers, discomforts, and meagre rewards to be expected on success, for any person to attempt to climb Mt. Everest without oxygen (or even with it). But there is no puzzle in explaining the attempt if it is undertaken by someone who has assembled all the facts he can, given full consideration to all his desires, ambitions and attitudes, and has acted in the light of his knowledge and values. Perhaps it is in some sense irrational to believe in astrology, flying saucers, or witches, but such beliefs may have standard explanations if they are based on what their holders take to be the evidence. It is sensible to try to square the circle if you don't know it can't be done. The sort of irrationality that makes conceptual trouble is not the failure of someone else to believe or feel or do what we deem reasonable, but rather the failure, within a single person, of coherence or consistency in the pattern of beliefs, attitudes, emotions, intentions and actions. Examples are wishful thinking, acting contrary to one's own best judgment, self-deception, believing something that one holds to be discredited by the weight of the evidence.

In attempting to explain such phenomena (along with much more, of course), Freudians have made the following claims:

First, the mind contains a number of semi-independent structures, these structures being characterized by mental attributes like thoughts, desires, and memories.

Second, parts of the mind are in important respects like people, not only in having (or consisting of) beliefs, wants and other psychological traits, but in that these factors can combine, as in intentional action, to cause further events in the mind or outside it.

Third, some of the dispositions, attitudes, and events that characterize the various substructures in the mind must be viewed on the model of physical dispositions and forces when they affect, or are affected by, other substructures in the mind.

A further doctrine about which I shall say only a little is that some mental phenomena that we normally assume to be conscious, or at least available to consciousness, are not conscious, and can become accessible only with difficulty, if at all. In most functional respects, these unconscious mental states and events are like conscious beliefs, memories, desires, wishes and fears.

I hope it will be agreed that these doctrines are all to be found in Freud, and that they are central to his theories. They are, as I have said, far less strong and detailed than Freud's views. Yet even in reduced form, they require more defence than is possible, in the view of many philosophers. The criticisms I shall be attempting to meet are related in various ways, but they are essentially of two sorts.

First, the idea that the mind can be partitioned at all has often been held to be unintelligible, since it seems to require that thoughts and desires and even actions be attributed to something less than, and therefore distinct from, the whole person. But can we make sense of acts and attitudes that are not those of an agent? Also, as Sartre suggests, the notion of responsibility would lose its essential point if acts and intentions were pried loose from people and attached instead to semi-autonomous parts of the mind. The parts would then stand proxy for the person: each part would become a little woman, man or child. What was once a single mind is turned into a battlefield where opposed forces contend, deceive one another, conceal information, devise strategies. As Irving Thalberg and others point out, sometimes it even happens that one segment protects itself from its own forces (thoughts). The prime agent may appear as a sort of chairman of the board, arbiter or dictator. It is not surprising that doubts have arisen as to whether these metaphors can be traded for a consistent theory.

A second, though related, set of worries concerns the underlying explanatory methodology. On the one hand, psychoanalytic theory extends the reach of teleological or reason explanation by discovering motives, wishes and intentions that were not recognized before. In this respect, as has often been noted, Freud greatly increased the number and variety of phenomena that can be viewed as rational: it turns out that we have reasons for our forgettings, slips of the tongue, and exaggerated fears. But on the other side, Freud wants his explanations to yield what explanations in natural science often promise: causal accounts that permit control. In this vein, he applies to mental events and states terms drawn from hydraulics, electromagnetism, neurology and mechanics. Toulmin, Flew, MacIntyre and Peters among philosophers have at one time or another suggested that psychoanalytic theories attempt the impossible by trying to bring psychological phenomena (which require explanations in terms of reasons) under causal laws: they think this accounts for, but does not justify, Freud's constant use, when talking of the mind, of metaphors drawn from other sciences.[1]

It seems then, that there are two irreconcilable tendencies in Freud's methodology. On the one hand he wanted to extend the range of phenomena subject to reason explanations, and on the other to treat these same phenomena as forces and states are treated in the natural sciences. But in the natural sciences, reasons and propositional attitudes are out of place, and blind causality rules.

In order to evaluate these charges against psychoanalytic theory, I want first to rehearse part of what I think is a correct analysis of normal intentional action. Then we can consider irrationality.

A man walking in a park stumbles on a branch in the path. Thinking the branch may endanger others, he picks it up and throws it in a hedge beside the path. On his way home it occurs to him that the branch may be projecting from the hedge and so still be a threat to unwary walkers. He gets off the tram he is on, returns to the park, and restores the branch to its original position. Here everything the agent does (except stumble on the branch) is done for a reason, a reason in the light of which the corresponding action was reasonable. Given that the man believed the stick was a danger if left on the path, and a desire to eliminate the danger, it was reasonable to remove the stick. Given that, on second thought, he believed the stick was a danger in the hedge, it was reasonable to extract the stick from the hedge and replace it on the path. Given that the man wanted to take the stick from the hedge, it was reasonable to dismount from the tram and return to the park. In each case the reasons for the action tell us what the agent saw in his action, they give the intention with which he acted, and they thereby give an explanation of the action. Such an explanation, as I have said, must exist if something a person does is to count as an action at all.

The pattern of reason explanations has been noted by many philosophers. Hume puts it pithily: "Ask a man why he uses exercise: he will answer, because he desires to keep his health. If you then enquire why he desires health, he will readily reply, because sickness is painful."[2] The pattern is so familiar that we may miss its subtlety. What is to be explained is the action, say taking exercise. At the minimum, the explanation calls on two factors: a value, goal, want or attitude of the agent, and a belief that by acting in the way to

---

[1] See, for examples, Antony Flew, "Motives and the unconscious" in *Minnesota Studies in the Philosophy of Science,* vol. 1, eds. H. Feigl and M. Scriven (University of Minnesota Press, Minneapolis, 1956); Alasdair MacIntyre, *The Unconscious* (Routledge, London, 1958); R. S. Peters, *The Concept of Motivation* (Routledge, London, 1958); Charles Taylor, *The Explanation of Behaviour* (Routledge, London, 1965).

[2] David Hume, *An Inquiry Concerning the Principles of Morals,* ed. L. A. Selby-Bigge (The Clarendon Press, Oxford, 1957), Appendix 1, p. 293.

be explained he can promote the relevant value or goal, or will be acting in accord with his attitude. The action on the one hand, and the belief–desire pair which give the reason on the other, must be related in two very different ways to yield an explanation. First, there must be a logical relation. Beliefs and desires have a content, and these contents must be such as to imply that there is something valuable or desirable about the action. Thus a man who finds something desirable in health, and believes that exercise will make him healthy can conclude that there is something desirable in exercise, which may explain why he takes exercise. Second, the reasons an agent has for acting must, if they are to explain the action, be the reasons on which he acted; the reasons must have played a *causal* role in the occurrence of the action. These two conditions on reason explanations are both necessary, but they are not sufficient, since some causal relations between belief–desire pairs and actions do not give reason explanations. (This complication will not concern us here, though there are no doubt irrational actions that hinge on the complication.)

This much of the analysis of action makes clear why all intentional actions, whether or not they are in some further sense irrational, have a rational element at the core; it is this that makes for one of the paradoxes of irrationality. But we also see that Freud can be defended on one important point: there is no inherent conflict between reason explanations and causal explanations. Since beliefs and desires are causes of the actions for which they are reasons, reason explanations include an essential causal element.

What can be said of intentional action can be extended to many other psychological phenomena. If a person intends to steal some Brussels sprouts, then whether or not he executes his intention, the intention itself must be caused by a desire to possess some Brussels sprouts and a belief that by stealing them he will come into possession of them. (Once again, the logical, or rational, aspect of the intention is obvious.) Similarly, most of our wishes, hopes, desires, emotions, beliefs and fears depend upon a simple inference (usually, no doubt, unnoticed) from other beliefs and attitudes. We fear poverty because we believe it will bring what we hold to be evils; we hope it will rain because we believe rain will help the crops, and we want the crops to prosper; we believe rain will help the crops on the basis of induction or hearsay or reading; and so on. In each of these cases, there is the logical connection between the contents of various attitudes and beliefs, and what they cause.

The conclusion up to this point is that merely to label a psychological state or event as being or entailing what is loosely called a propositional attitude is to guarantee the relevance of a reason explanation, and hence an element of rationality. But of course if such states and events can be irrational, the element of rationality cannot prevent their being at the same time less than rational. Consider the case of an action where the agent acts counter to what he believes, everything considered, is better. (Aristotle called such behaviour a case of akrasia; other terms are "incontinence" or "weakness of the will." It is easy to imagine that the man who returned to the park to restore the branch to its original position in the path realizes that his action is not sensible. He has a motive for moving the stick, namely, that it may endanger a passer-by. But he also has a motive for not returning, which is the time and trouble it costs. In his own judgment, the latter consideration outweighs the former; yet he acts on the former. In short, he goes against his own best judgment.

The problem of explaining such behaviour has puzzled philosophers and moralists at least since Plato. According to Plato, Socrates argued that since no one willingly acts counter to what he knows to be best, only ignorance can explain foolish or evil acts. This is often called a paradox, but Socrates' view is paradoxical only because it denies what we all believe, that there are akratic acts. If Socrates is right – if such actions are ruled out by the logic of the concepts – then there is nothing puzzling about the facts to be explained. Nevertheless, Socrates (or Plato) has brought our problem to a head: there is a conflict between the standard way of explaining intentional action and the idea that such an action can be irrational. Since the view that no intentional action can be internally irrational stands at one extreme in the continuum of possible views, let me give it a name: the *Plato Principle*. It is the doctrine of pure rationality.

At an opposite extreme is the *Medea Principle*. According to this doctrine, a person can act against his better judgment, but only when an alien force overwhelms his or her will. This is what happens when Medea begs her own hand not to murder her children. Her hand, or the passion of revenge behind it, overcomes her will. Some such treatment of weakness of the will is popular.[3] And given the thesis, the term is suitable, for the will of the agent is weaker than the alien passion. Moralists particularly have been attracted to this view, since it suggests that no more is needed to overcome temptation than greater resolve to do the right. Just the same, it is a strange doctrine, since it implies that akratic acts are not intentional, and so not in themselves actions for which the agent can be held responsible. If the agent is to blame, it is not for what he did, but because he did not resist with enough vigour. What the agent found himself doing had a reason – the passion or impulse that overcame his better judgment – but the reason was not *his*. From the agent's point of view, what he did was the effect of a cause that came from outside, as if another person had moved him.

Aristotle suggested that weakness of the will is due to a kind of forgetting. The akrates has two desires; in our example, he wants to save his time and effort, and also wants to move the branch. He can't act on both desires, but Aristotle will not let him get so far as to appreciate his problem, for

---

[3] For further discussion of these issues, and references, see my "How is weakness of the will possible?" in Donald Davidson, *Essays on Actions and Events* (Oxford University Press, London, 1980).

according to Aristotle the agent loses active touch with his knowledge that by not returning to the park he can save time and effort. It is not quite a case of a conscious and an unconscious desire in conflict; rather there is a conscious and an unconscious piece of knowledge, where action depends on which piece of knowledge is conscious.

There are situations in which Aristotle's analysis is appropriate, and other situations ruled by the Medea Principle. But such situations are not the only ones, and they are not the defining cases of akrasia, where the agent acts intentionally while aware that everything considered a better course of action is open to him. For when the Medea Principle is at work, intention is not present; and in Aristotle's analysis, the agent is not aware of an alternative.

On reflection it is obvious that neither the Medea Principle nor Aristotle's analysis allows for straightforward cases of conflict, cases in which an agent has good reasons both for doing, and for refraining from, a course of action; or, what comes to the same thing, good reasons for doing each of two mutually exclusive things. Such situations are too familiar to require special explanation: we are not normally paralysed when competing claims are laid on us, nor do we usually suppress part of the relevant information, or drive one of our desires underground. Usually we can face situations where a decision must be made, and we decide best when we manage to keep all the considerations, the pros and the cons, before us.

What requires explaining is the action of an agent who, having weighed up the reasons on both sides, and having judged that the preponderance of reasons is on one side, then acts against this judgment. We should not say he has no reason for his action, since he has reasons both for and against. It is because he has a reason for what he does that we can give the intention with which he acted. And like all intentional actions, his action can be explained, by referring to the beliefs and desires that caused it and gave it a point.

But although the agent has a reason for doing what he did, he had better reasons, by his own reckoning, for acting otherwise. What needs explaining is not why the agent acted as he did, but why he *didn't* act otherwise, given his judgment that all things considered it would be better.

A person who appreciates the fact that he has good reasons both for and against an action should not be thought to be entertaining a contradiction. It follows that moral principles, or the judgments that correspond to desires, cannot be expressed by sentences like "It is wrong to lie" or "It is good to give pleasure." Not, that is, if these sentences are taken in the natural way to express universal statements like "All lies are wrong" or "All acts that give pleasure are good." For one and the same act may be a lie and an act that gives pleasure, and so be both wrong and good. On many moral theories, this is a contradiction. Or to take an even simpler case, if it is right to keep promises and wrong to break them, then someone who through no fault of his own has made incompatible promises will do something wrong if he does something right.

The solution to this puzzle about the logic of practical reasoning is to recognize that evaluative principles are not correctly stated in the form "It is wrong to lie." For not all lies are wrong; there are cases when one ought to lie for the sake of some more important consideration. The fact that an action is a lie, or the breaking of a promise, or a consumer of time is a count against the action, to be weighed along with other reasons for the action. Every action we perform, or consider performing, has something to be said for it and something against; but we speak of conflict only when the pros and cons are weighty and close to being in balance. Simple deduction can tell me that if I wish to keep promise *A* I must be in Addis Ababa on a certain date, and if I wish to keep promise *B* I must be in Bora Bora at that same time; but logic cannot tell me which to do.

Since logic cannot tell me which to do, it is unclear in what respect either action would be irrational. Nor is the irrationality evident if we add that I judge that all things considered I ought to keep promise *A*, and yet I keep promise *B*. For the first judgment is merely conditional: in the light of all my evidence, I ought to do *A*; and this cannot contradict the unconditional judgment that I ought to do *B*. Pure internal inconsistency enters only if I also hold – as in fact I do – that I ought to act on my own best judgment, what I judge best or obligatory, everything considered.

A purely formal description of what is irrational in an akratic act is, then, that the agent goes against his own second-order principle that he ought to act on what he holds to be best, everything considered. It is only when we can describe his action in just this way that there is a puzzle about explaining it. If the agent does not have the principle that he ought to act on what he holds to be best, everything considered, then though his action may be irrational from *our* point of view, it need not be irrational from his point of view – at least not in a way that poses a problem for explanation. For to explain his behaviour we need only say that his desire to do what he held to be best, all things considered, was not as strong as his desire to do something else.

But someone who knowingly and intentionally acts contrary to his own principle; how can we explain that? The explanation must, it is evident, contain some feature that goes beyond the Plato Principle; otherwise the action is perfectly rational. On the other hand, the explanation must retain the core of the Plato Principle; otherwise the action is not intentional. An account like this seems to satisfy both requirements: there is, we have agreed, a normal reason explanation for an akratic action. Thus the man who returns to the park to replace the branch has a reason: to remove a danger. But in doing this he ignores his principle of acting on what he thinks is best, all things considered. And there is no denying that he has a motive for ignoring his principle, namely that he wants, perhaps very strongly, to return the branch to its original position. Let us say this motive does explain the fact that he fails to act on his principle. This is the point at which irrationality enters. For the desire to replace the branch has entered into the decision to do it twice over. First it was a consideration in favour of replacing the branch, a consideration that, in the agent's opinion, was less important than the reasons against returning to the park. The agent then held that everything considered he ought not to return to the park. Given his principle that one ought to act on such a conclusion, the rational thing for him to do was, of course, not to return to the park. Irrationality entered when his desire to return made him ignore or override his principle. For though his motive for ignoring his principle was a reason for ignoring the principle, it was not a reason against the principle itself, and so when it entered in this second way, it was irrelevant as a reason, to the principle and to the action. The irrationality depends on the distinction between a reason for having, or acting on, a principle, and a reason for the principle.

Another, and simpler, example will make the point clear. Suppose a young man very much wishes he had a well-turned calf and this leads him to believe he has a well-turned calf. He has a normal reason for wanting to have this belief – it gives him pleasure. But if the entire explanation of his holding the belief is that he wanted to believe it, then his holding the belief is irrational. For the wish to have a belief is not evidence for the truth of the belief, nor does it give it rational support in any other way. What his wish to have this belief makes rational is that this proposition should be true: He believes that he has a well-turned calf. This does not rationalize his believing: I have a well-turned calf. This is a case of wishful thinking which is a model for the simplest kind of irrationality. Simple as it is, however, the model has a complexity which is obscured by the ambiguity of the phrase "reason for believing."

In some cases of irrationality it is unlikely, and perhaps impossible, for the agent to be fully aware of all that is going on in his mind. If someone "forgets" that today is Thursday because he does not want to keep a disagreeable social commitment, it is perhaps ruled out that he should be aware of this. But in many cases there is no logical difficulty in supposing the agent knows what is going on. The young man may know he believes he has a well-turned calf only because he wants to believe it, just as the man who returns to the park to replace the branch may realize both the absurdity and the explanation of his action.

In standard reason explanations, as we have seen, not only do the propositional contents of various beliefs and desires bear appropriate logical relations to one another and to the contents of the belief, attitude or intention they help explain; the actual states of belief and desire cause the explained state or event. In the case of irrationality, the causal relation remains, while the logical relation is missing or distorted. In the cases of irrationality we have been discussing, there is a mental cause that is not a reason for what it causes. So in wishful thinking, a desire causes a belief. But the judgment that a state of affairs is, or would be, desirable, is not a reason to believe that it exists.

It is clear that the cause must be mental in this sense: it is a state or event with a propositional content. If a bird flying by causes a belief that a bird is flying by (or that an airplane is flying by) the issue of rationality does not arise; these are causes that are not reasons for what they cause, but the cause has no logical properties, and so cannot of itself explain or engender irrationality (of the kind I have described). Can there be other forms of irrationality? The issue is not clear, and I make no claims concerning it. So far my thesis is only that many common examples of irrationality may be characterized by the fact that there is a mental cause that is not a reason. This characterization points the way to one kind of explanation of irrationality.

Irrationality of this kind may turn up wherever rationality operates. Just as incontinent actions are irrational, there can be irrational intentions to act, whether or not they are acted out. Beliefs may be irrational, as may courses of reasoning. Many desires and emotions are shown to be irrational if they are explained by mental causes that are not reasons for them. The general concept applies also to unchanges. A person is irrational if he is not open to reason – if, on accepting a belief or attitude on the basis of which he ought to make accommodating changes in his other beliefs, desires or intentions, he fails to make those changes. He has a reason which does not cause what it is a sufficient reason for.

We now see how it is possible to reconcile an explanation that shows an action, belief, or emotion to be irrational with the element of rationality inherent in the description and explanation of all such phenomena. Thus we have dealt, at least in a preliminary way, with one paradox of irrationality. But now a second source of paradox emerges which cannot be so easily dissipated.

If events are related as cause and effect, they remain so no matter in what vocabulary we choose to describe them. Mental or psychological events are such only under a manner of description, for these very events surely are at the same time neurophysiological, and ultimately physical, events, though recognizable and identifiable within these realms only when given neurophysiological or physical descriptions. As we have seen, there is no difficulty in general in explaining mental events by appeal to neurophysiological or physical causes; this is central to the analysis of perception or memory, for example. But when the cause is described in non-mental terms, we necessarily lose touch with what is needed to explain the element of irrationality. For irrationality appears only when rationality is evidently appropriate: where both cause and effect have contents that have the sort of logical relations that make for reason or its failure. Events conceived solely in terms of their physical or physiological properties cannot be judged as reasons, or as in conflict, or as concerned with a subject matter. So we face the following dilemma: if we think of the cause in a neutral mode, disregarding its mental status as a belief or other attitude – if we think of it merely as a force that works on the mind without being identified as part of it – then we fail to explain, or even describe, irrationality. Blind forces are in the category of the non-rational, not the irrational. So, we introduce a mental description of the cause, which thus makes it a candidate for being a reason. But we still remain outside the only clear pattern of explanation that applies to the mental, for that pattern demands that the cause be more than a candidate for being a reason; it must *be* a reason, which in the present case it cannot be. For an explanation of a mental effect we need a mental cause that is also a reason for this effect, but, if we have it, the effect cannot be a case of irrationality. Or so it seems.

There is however, a way one mental event can cause another mental event without being a reason for it, and where there is no puzzle and not necessarily any irrationality. This can happen when cause and effect occur in different minds. For example, wishing to have you enter my garden, I grow a beautiful flower there. You crave a look at my flower and enter my garden. My desire caused your craving and action, but my desire was not a reason for your craving, nor a reason on which you acted. (Perhaps you did not even know about my wish.) Mental phenomena may cause other mental phenomena without being reasons for them, then, and still keep their character as mental, provided cause and effect are adequately segregated. The obvious and clear cases are those of social interaction. But I suggest that the idea can be applied to a single mind and person. Indeed, if we are going to explain irrationality at all, it seems we must assume that the mind can be partitioned into quasi-independent structures that interact in ways the Plato Principle cannot accept or explain.

To constitute a structure of the required sort, a part of the mind must show a larger degree of consistency or rationality than is attributed to the whole.[4] Unless this is the case, the point of the analogy with social interaction is destroyed. The idea is that if parts of the mind are to some degree independent, we can understand how they are able to harbour inconsistencies, and to interact on a causal level. Recall the analysis of akrasia. There I mentioned no partitioning of the mind because the analysis was at that point more descriptive than explanatory. But the way could be cleared for explanation if we were to suppose two semi-autonomous departments of the mind, one that finds a certain course of action to be, all things considered, best, and another that prompts another course of action. On each side, the side of sober judgment and the side of incontinent intent and action, there is a supporting structure of reasons, of interlocking beliefs, expectations, assumptions, attitudes and desires. To set the scene in this way still leaves

---

4 Here as elsewhere my highly abstract account of the partitioning of the mind deviates from Freud's. In particular, I have nothing to say about the number or nature of divisions of the mind, their permanence or aetiology. I am solely concerned to defend the idea of mental compartmentalization, and to argue that it is necessary if we are to explain a common form of irrationality. I should perhaps emphasize that phrases like "partition of the mind," "part of the mind," "segment" etc. are misleading if they suggest that what belongs to one division of the mind cannot belong to another. The picture I want is of overlapping territories.

much unexplained, for we want to know why this double structure developed, how it accounts for the action taken and also, no doubt, its psychic consequences and cure. What I stress here is that the partitioned mind leaves the field open to such further explanations, and helps resolve the conceptual tension between the Plato Principle and the problem of accounting for irrationality.

The partitioning I propose does not correspond in nature or function to the ancient metaphor of a battle between Virtue and Temptation or Reason and Passion. For the competing desires or values which akrasia demands do not, on my account, in themselves suggest irrationality. Indeed, a judgment that, all things considered, one ought to act in a certain way presupposes that the competing factors have been brought within the same division of the mind. Nor is it a matter of the bald intervention of a fey and alien emotion, as in the Medea Principle. What is called for is organized elements, within each of which there is a fair degree of consistency, and where one element can operate on another in the modality of non-rational causality.

Allowing a degree of autonomy to provinces of the mind dissipates to a degree the problems we have discussed, but it generates others. For to the extent that the Plato Principle fails to explain the workings of the mind, mere causal relations replace it, and these explain best, or make most progress toward science, as they can be summarized in laws. But there is a question how far the workings of the mind can be reduced to strict, deterministic laws as long as the phenomena are identified in mental terms. For one thing, the realm of the mental cannot form a closed system; much that happens in it is perforce caused by events with no mental description. And for another, once we contemplate causal relations between mental events in partial disregard of the logical relations between the descriptions of those events, we enter a realm without a unified and coherent set of constitutive principles: the concepts employed must be treated as mixed, owing allegiance partly to their connections with the world of non-mental forces, and partly to their character as mental and directed to a propositional content. These matters bear directly on the important question what kind of laws or generalizations will be found to hold in this area, and therefore on the question how scientific a science of the mental can be: that is, however, a subject I have put to one side.

There is one other problem that springs from recognizing semi-independent departments within the same mind. We attribute beliefs, purposes, motives and desires to people in an endeavour to organize, explain and predict their behaviour, verbal and otherwise. We describe their intentions, their actions and their feelings in the light of the most unified and intelligible scheme we can contrive. Speech yields no more direct access into this scheme than any other behaviour, since speech itself must be interpreted; indeed speech requires at least two levels of interpretation, there being both the question what the speaker's words mean, and the question what the speaker means in speaking them. Not that an agent knows directly what he believes, wants and intends in some way that reduces observers to mere detectives. For though he can often say what is on his mind, an agent's words have meaning in the public domain; what his words mean is up to the interpreter as well as to him. How he is to be understood is a problem for him as it is for others.

What makes interpretation difficult is the multiplicity of mental factors that produce behaviour and speech. To take an instance, if we know that in speaking certain words a man meant to assert that the price of plutonium is rising, then generally we must know a great deal more about his intentions, his beliefs, and the meaning of his words. If we imagine ourselves starting out from scratch to construct a theory that would unify and explain what we observe – a theory of the man's thoughts and emotions and language – we should be overwhelmed by the difficulty. There are too many unknowns for the number of equations. We necessarily cope with this problem by a strategy that is simple to state, though vastly complex in application: the strategy is to assume that the person to be understood is much like ourselves. That is perforce the opening strategy, from which we deviate as the evidence piles up. We start out assuming that others have, in the basic and largest matters, beliefs and values similar to ours. We are bound to suppose someone we want to understand inhabits our world of macroscopic, more or less enduring, physical objects with familiar causal dispositions; that his world, like ours, contains people with minds and motives; and that he shares with us the desire to find warmth, love, security, and success, and the desire to avoid pain and distress. As we get to matters of detail, or to matters in one way or another less central to our thinking, we can more and more easily allow for differences between ourselves and others. But unless we can interpret others as sharing a vast amount of what makes up our common sense we will not be able to identify any of their beliefs and desires and intentions, any of their propositional attitudes.

The reason is the holistic character of the mental. The meaning of a sentence, the content of a belief or desire, is not an item that can be attached to it in isolation from its fellows. We cannot intelligibly attribute the thought that a piece of ice is melting to someone who does not have many true beliefs about the nature of ice, its physical properties connected with water, cold, solidity, and so forth. The one attribution rests on the supposition of many more – endlessly more. And among the beliefs we suppose a man to have, many must be true (in our view) if any are to be understood by us. The clarity and cogency of our attributions of attitude, motive and belief are proportionate, then, to the extent to which we find others consistent and correct. We often, and justifiably, find others irrational and wrong; but such judgments are most firmly based when there is the most agreement. We understand someone best when we hold him to be rational and sage, and this understanding is what gives our disputes with him a keen edge.

There is no question but that the precept of unavoidable charity in inter-pretation is opposed to the partitioning of the mind. For the point of parti-tioning was to allow inconsistent or conflicting beliefs and desires and feelings to exist in the same mind, while the basic methodology of all interpretation tells us that inconsistency breeds unintelligibility.

It is a matter of degree. We have no trouble understanding small pertur-bations against a background with which we are largely in sympathy, but large deviations from reality or consistency begin to undermine our ability to describe and explain what is going on in mental terms. What sets a limit to the amount of irrationality we can make psychological sense of is a purely conceptual or theoretical matter – the fact that mental states and events are constituted the states and events they are by their location in a logical space. On the other hand, what constrains the amount and kind of consistency and correspondence with reality we find in our fellow men and women is the frailty of human nature: the failure of imagination or sympathy on the part of the interpreter, and the stubborn imperfection of the interpreted. The underlying paradox of irrationality, from which no theory can entirely es-cape, is this: if we explain it too well, we turn it into a concealed form of rationality; while if we assign incoherence too glibly, we merely compromise our ability to diagnose irrationality by withdrawing the background of ra-tionality needed to justify any diagnosis at all.

What I have tried to show, then, is that the very general features of psy-choanalytic theory that I listed as having puzzled philosophers and others are, if I am right, features that will be found in any theory that sets itself to explain irrationality.

The first feature was that the mind is to be regarded as having two or more semi-autonomous structures. This feature we found to be necessary to account for mental causes that are not reasons for the mental states they cause. Only by partitioning the mind does it seem possible to explain how a thought or impulse can cause another to which it bears no rational relation.

The second feature assigned a particular kind of structure to one or more subdivisions of the mind: a structure similar to that needed to explain ordi-nary actions. This calls for a constellation of beliefs, purposes and affects of the sort that, through the application of the Plato Principle, allow us to characterize certain events as having a goal or intention. The analogy does not have to be carried so far as to demand that we speak of parts of the mind as independent agents. What is essential is that certain thoughts and feelings of the person be conceived as interacting to produce consequences on the principles of intentional actions, these consequences then serving as causes, but not reasons, for further mental events. The breakdown of reason-relations defines the boundary of a subdivision. Though I talk here, with Freud, of parts and agencies, there does not seem to be anything that demands a metaphor. The parts are defined in terms of function; ultimately, in terms of the concepts of reason and of cause. The idea of a quasi-autonomous division is not one that demands a little agent in the division; again, the operative concepts are those of cause and reason.

The third feature on which we remarked was that certain mental events take on the character of mere causes relative to some other mental events in the same mind. This feature also we found to be required by any account of irrationality. It is a feature that can be accommodated, I argued, but in order to accommodate it we must allow a degree of autonomy to parts of the mind.

The three elements of psychoanalytic theory on which I have concentrated, the partitioning of the mind, the existence of a considerable structure in each quasi-autonomous part, and non-logical causal relations between the parts; these elements combine to provide the basis for a coherent way of describing and explaining important kinds of irrationality. They also account for, and justify, Freud's mixture of standard reason explanations with causal interactions more like those of the natural sciences, interactions in which reason does not play its usual normative and rationalizing role.

Finally, I must mention the claim that many mental phenomena which normally are accessible to consciousness are sometimes neither conscious nor easily accessible to consciousness. The reason I have said nothing about this claim is that I think the relevant objections to unconscious mental states and events are answered by showing that the theory is acceptable without them. It is striking, for example, that nothing in the description of akrasia requires that any thought or motive be unconscious – indeed, I criticized Aristotle for introducing something like an unconscious piece of knowledge when this was not necessary. The standard case of akrasia is one in which the agent knows what he is doing, and why, and knows that it is not for the best, and knows why. He acknowledges his own irrationality. If all this is possible, then the description cannot be made untenable by supposing that sometimes some of the thoughts or desires involved are unconscious.

If to an otherwise unobjectionable theory we add the assumption of unconscious elements, the theory can only be made more acceptable, that is, capable of explaining more. For suppose we are led to realize by a genius like Freud that if we posit certain mental states and events we can explain much behaviour that otherwise goes unexplained; but we also discover that the associated verbal behaviour does not fit the normal pattern. The agent denies he has the attitudes and feelings we would attribute to him. We can reconcile observation and theory by stipulating the existence of unconscious events and states that, aside from awareness, are like conscious beliefs, desires and emotions. There are, to be sure, further puzzles lurking here. But these seem to be puzzles that result from other problems; unconscious mental events do not add to the other problems but are natural companions of them.

I have urged that a certain scheme of analysis applies to important cases of irrationality. Possibly some version of this scheme will be found in every case of "internal" inconsistency or irrationality. But does the scheme give a sufficient condition for irrationality? It would seem not. For simple cases of association do not count as irrational. If I manage to remember a name by humming a certain tune, there is a mental cause of something for which it is not a reason; and similarly for a host of further cases. But far more interesting, and more important, is a form of self-criticism and reform that we tend to hold in high esteem, and that has even been thought to be the very essence of rationality and the source of freedom. Yet it is clearly a case of mental causality that transcends reason (in the somewhat technical sense in which I have been using the concept).

What I have in mind is a special kind of second-order desire or value, and the actions it can touch off. This happens when a person forms a positive or negative judgment of some of his own desires, and he acts to change these desires. From the point of view of the changed desire, there is no reason for the change – the reason comes from an independent source, and is based on further, and partly contrary, considerations. The agent has reasons for changing his own habits and character, but those reasons come from a domain of values necessarily extrinsic to the contents of the views or values to undergo change. The cause of the change, if it comes, can therefore not be a reason for what it causes. A theory that could not explain irrationality would be one that also could not explain our salutary efforts, and occasional successes, at self-criticism and self-improvement.

21. Rational dilemmas and rational supererogation

Michael Slote

The recent literature of philosophy contains many discussions of moral dilemmas. The idea that there may be situations where (through no prior fault or guilt of one's own) one finds it impossible to avoid guilt, to avoid wrongdoing, has been defended, criticized, and mined for its implications: with increasing frequency, the idea of moral dilemmas has become a focus of ethical discussion. In this essay, I would like to consider a related issue which may be useful in casting light on the merits of the case for moral dilemmas, but which is of considerable independent interest. We are by now familiar with the ways in which issues concerning morality and concerning practical rationality can run parallel, and although I would not want to suggest that rationality and morality are in every way analogous, it seems to me we have devoted insufficient attention to a possible major parallel: the case for the possibility of rational dilemmas has yet to be explicitly made. In what follows I would like to consider how that case might be made and to what extent it differs from what may be said in favor of the existence of moral dilemmas. In the course of doing so, we shall find ourselves having to consider the unsettling possibility that, in parallel with what is frequently said about morality, there may be such a thing as rational supererogation, i.e., supererogatory degrees of practical rationality. But the latter topic is perhaps best left alone till our unfolding discussion of rational dilemmas forces us to consider it.

What would count as a rational dilemma? Presumably, and there is no reason to question this, a situation in which through no practical fault of her own, an agent found it impossible to act rationally, to make a rational choice among two or more alternatives. Let us see whether we can model

Reprinted with permission from *Philosophical Topics* 14 (1986), 59–76.

such a situation on considerations in the area of practical rationality that parallel the factors that are said, by defenders of moral dilemmas, to give rise to moral dilemmas.

In the most frequently-discussed putative case of moral dilemmas, Agamemnon has to choose between violating his duty as a parent and violating his duty as the leader of a military expedition, and defenders of the view that his situation is truly (morally) tragic have held that each of these duties applies with undiminished force despite the existence and applicability of the other.[1] That is, neither duty overrides the other so as to make it right not to fulfill the other; rather both have their full force as duties, all things considered, and for that reason Agamemnon must incur guilt (not just an obligation to make amends) whatever he decides to do.

Those advocating the existence of a moral dilemma in such a case as this hold that each of the conflicting obligations or duties has moral force of its own, and that it is a superiority of common-sense morality over consequentialism that it allows for such varying sources of moral obligation and thus can accommodate the complexity of the moral life. The existence of dilemmas is but one illustration, according to this view, of the richness, subtlety and difficulty of the moral life. Now whether consequentialism or utilitarianism is really banned from the enjoyment of this intellectual bounty is a question to which we shall return a little later. For the moment let us consider whether any structure similar to what arguably exists in Agamemnon's situation of tragic choice can be found in any case of rational decision making. Can precepts or principles of practical rationality conflict for a given agent in a given situation in such way that there is no way for the agent to act rationally, no action which it would be rational for the agent to choose?

We can see what such a situation would have to be like in order to represent a convincing analogue of Agamemnon-type moral dilemmas. There are precepts like "one ought to give weight to one's future interests" and "one ought not take unnecessary chances with one's own life" which can readily be seen as common-sensical *prima facie* principles of rationality. A Rossian-type view of such precepts would treat them as mutually adjustable and balanceable in such a way that whenever they conflict, one or another (or some group) of them always takes precedence over, overrides, or outweighs, those in conflict with it, with the result that there is at least one rational or rationally justified thing for one to do. But one could question this view by claiming, in parallel with what has been said about Agamemnon's tragic situation, that there is no guarantee that amid the welter of conflicting rational principles there will always be a decision, choice, or action which is rationally justified or rational. The accumulating effect of the rational principles in force in a given situation may be to prescribe *a* without qualification

---

[1] See, for example, Bernard Williams, "Ethical Consistency," *Problems of the Self,* Cambridge University Press, 1973, Ch. 11.

and prescribe *b* without qualification, even though they cannot both be performed, thus leaving the aware intelligent agent with the sense that he cannot act in a rational or justified way in the situation he is in.

This, then, is what a defense of rational dilemmas analogous to what has been said of the Agamemnon example would have to look like. But that still leaves us without a plausible example of such a dilemma. And we have to ask ourselves whether we can plausibly give life to the structure of a rational dilemma based on the Agamemnon choice paradigm of a moral dilemma. Can we suggest any plausible or vivid example where, say, two precepts of rationality conflict and where an agent finds it impossible to fulfill the requirements of rationality, to act rationally? And can we do so without relying precisely on the moral examples that are used to support the idea of moral dilemma? For, of course, the idea that moral precepts or requirements are rational requirements, reasons for action, might allow us to turn examples of moral dilemma into examples of rational dilemma.[2] If Agamemnon is wrong whatever he does, then it is natural (in the light of our own belief in the rationality of acting morally) to characterize his plight as one where whatever choice he made would have been unjustified, where nothing could count as a reasonable practical answer.

But when we began by speculating about the possibility of rational dilemmas, we were looking for a form of dilemma arising outside the usual area of morality and having to do with the impossibility of acting rationally, or justifiably. A practical dilemma based in a moral dilemma was not what we had in mind. What would really interest us would be a case where it was impossible for an individual to act rationally with regard to her purely egoistic or self-regarding aims, a case of individualistic rational dilemma. And the Agamemnon example is not of this sort.

Foot mentions a non-moral prudential case where "pressing business has given one overriding reason to go to town" but "one nevertheless *ought* to be at home nursing a cold."[3] But it seems appropriate to treat such a case (Foot herself seems to treat the case) as understandable in fundamentally Rossian terms, as a case where one rational precept or imperative overrides another, and where, therefore, there is at least one thing it is rational for one to do.

In order to have an example of a rational dilemma, we need to describe a situation where, all things considered, every practical solution is fatally flawed and rationally unacceptable. And I have been unable to come up with a plausible example of a rational dilemma in this strong sense that possesses anything like the structure of the Agamemnon example, and not just what we find in Rossian examples of moral or other overriding. But it would be a major, though it might be a natural, mistake at this point to

[2] See P. R. Foot, "Moral Realism and Moral Dilemma," *Journal of Philosophy* 80, 1983, pp. 394f.
[3] *Op. cit.*, p. 383.

give up on the idea of rational dilemma until some rational parallel to the Agamemnon example could be unearthed. The Agamemnon example involved conflicting principles or precepts, the injunction: protect your daughter, and the injunction: as commander do what is necessary to ensure the success of your enterprise.

But as Ruth Marcus has pointed out, a conflict of obligations can arise from a single principle, like the obligation to keep promises, when it turns out that through no fault of one's own one cannot keep all the promises one has made; the promises may be of sufficient weight so that guilt is appropriate whatever one one breaks.[4] Here wrongdoing is inevitable and there is a conflict of obligations, but a single moral principle is behind the conflict: particular obligations derived from application of a single principle cannot both be fulfilled. So not every conceivable or putative example of moral dilemma is based on conflicting general principles.

Marcus goes on to argue that although there can be moral dilemmas based on a single principle like that enjoining promise-keeping, act-utilitarian and act-consequentialist moral theories advocating a single principle of right or obligatory action cannot yield dilemmas because such theories base the moral characterization of actions solely on their consequences. For a dilemma to occur, according to Marcus, at least one moral principle that bases the moral assessment of actions on their intrinsic character must be in play, and this of course is ruled out by strict consequentialism.

I have elsewhere argued that this is a mistake.[5] There are single-principle versions of utilitarian act-consequentialism which allow for dilemmas, for situations in which, in the light of the principle, one cannot avoid wrongdoing. Thus consider the principle of utility as put forward in the 1789 original edition of Bentham's *An Introduction to the Principles of Morals and Legislation* (and retained in the 1823 version though implicitly qualified – or contradicted? – in footnote, by a different and to us more familiar version of the principle). Bentham says that the rightness or wrongness of an act depends on whether it contributes (overall) to human happiness or to human unhappiness. This principle allows for dilemmas, because it seems in no way impossible for a person to be in a situation where whatever she does (including doing nothing) will (in one way or another) be harmful to overall human happiness. (Some examples of historically possible situations where an agent faces this sort of dilemma are mentioned in my article.)

I believe that it is from utilitarian moral dilemmas that we can best learn how to construct a plausible example of (non-moral) rational dilemma. The natural self-regarding rational analogue of the above example of moral dilemma would be one based on the single principle that an act is (self-regardingly) rational if and only if it contributes to the well-being or happiness, increases

---

[4] In "Moral Dilemmas and Consistency," *Journal of Philosophy* 77, 1980, pp. 124f.
[5] In "Utilitarianism, Moral Dilemmas, and Moral Cost," *American Philosophical Quarterly* 22, 1985, pp. 161–68.

the well-being or happiness, of the agent. Such a principle would allow for rational dilemma if true, because where an agent cannot help but make his situation worse whatever he does, nothing he does will count as rational according to the principle, even if he chooses the least self-damaging option available to him. But the principle is not plausible and neither, as a form of utilitarianism, is the original Bentham principle that allows for dilemmas. Nevertheless the principle does allow us to see that intrinsic non-consequentialistic characterizations need not figure in every set of principles that permits dilemmas. And having seen as much, perhaps we can find a more plausible act-consequentialist utilitarian principle that allows for dilemmas – perhaps, even the usually accepted present version(s) of the principle of utility have unsuspected capacity for dilemma. And this in fact turns out to be the case. At least in principle, there can be situations in which it is impossible to optimize utility, to perform an act with consequences at least as good as those of any other available act. And on contemporary versions of act-utilitarianism or act-consequentialism such a situation would constitute a moral dilemma.

But how is such a thing even in principle possible? Will there not always be some act with consequences better than or at least as good as those of all the other acts available to the agent? Not if the agent is capable of doing any of an infinite number of acts and no one of them is first or tied-first in the goodness of its consequences. Consider the following logically coherent science-fiction scenario (it may be possible to think of more mundane cases illustrating the same point but I have not been able to think of any). If, for any n, one can stand $1/n^{th}$ of an inch from a given wall and God will create n happy people (or add n happy days to the life of already existent people) if one stands $1/n^{th}$ of an inch away from that wall at a given time, then under various simplifying assumptions, any act one performs will have less good consequences than some other act one could have performed; no act one can perform at the time in question will be either best or tied-best and by the usual act-utilitarian criterion one will inevitably act wrongly.

So even under plausible contemporary interpretations of the principle of utility, moral dilemma is coherently imaginable, and this result may encourage us to look for analogous cases in which self-regarding rational dilemma is unavoidable. After all, egoistic, individualistic, extramoral practical rationality is often, is paradigmatically, understood in terms of an optimizing, maximizing model. The rational individual (in a situation where only her own well-being or satisfactions are at stake) seeks to maximize her satisfactions, does what she believes will have the best, most satisfying, consequences for herself. And if situations are imaginable in which no action one can perform has better overall consequences than any other action one can perform, is it not likewise possible to conceive a case where no action a given individual can perform has optimal consequences for that very individual, a situation where there is no way for the agent to achieve what is best for herself, because, for any given act she performs, there is available to her some alternative action with better consequences for herself?

This possibility does exist and it can be illustrated along the lines of our just-mentioned example of utilitarian/consequentialist moral dilemma. The examples of rational dilemma to be mentioned are purely hypothetical: they all involve unrealistic, or science-fictional, assumptions about human powers and opportunities. But they are nonetheless relevant to the issue of principle we are considering. If rational dilemmas are distinctly conceivable that will have important conceptual and philosophical implications for the way we understand practical rationality.

Imagine a science-fictionalized fountain of youth with some very special properties. This fountain emits life-and-happiness-giving rays and can work for a given person only once and at a certain precise moment. Depending on how far from the fountain one is at the exact time when its rays bombard one, one will be given additional days of life and happiness. Assume further that one is capable of standing as close as one pleases to the fountain. For any n, one is capable of standing $1/n^{th}$ of an inch away from the fountain, and if one stays a $1/n^{th}$ of an inch away one will receive n extra days of happiness (if one touches the fountain all bets are off). In such a case, any proximity one chooses will be less than some other proximity one could have chosen, and so however many happy days one adds to one's life, one could have added many – equally many, twice as many, etc. – more. Assuming that one has reason to prefer more to fewer happy days, one inevitably performs some act of standing at a certain distance from the fountain such that there was a better act to perform: for example, one stands at $1/n^{th}$ of an inch from the machine, and it would have been better if one had stood $1/2n^{th}$ of an inch from the machine. One has more reason on balance to stand $1/2n^{th}$ inches away than to stand $1/n^{th}$ inches away and so for any action one performs there is some alternative in one's power which one had more reason to perform. If it is irrational to do one thing, when one has more reason to perform some alternative, when it would have been better for one to have performed some definitely available alternative, then one has, inevitably, acted irrationally in the circumstances just mentioned. We have described a rational dilemma.

But just as the idea of moral dilemma invariably evokes a great deal of opposition, there is something inherently, or at least initially, repugnant in the idea of a rational dilemma.[6] It is usually held, and it is natural to hold, that an intelligent person always has it within her power to figure out at least

---

[6] The possibility of undeserved tragic moral dilemma entails the possibility of one kind of moral luck, and, of course, the idea of moral luck is offensive to (one side of) common moral opinion. But act-utilitarianism treats luck as essential to moral evaluation, through its exclusive emphasis on (foreseen and unforeseen) consequences, so perhaps act-utilitarianism has *less* reason to recoil from the moral dilemmas it treats as possible than common-sense morality has with regard to the Agamemnon example and others like it.

one rational course of action in any given situation, or at least that within
any given practical context there is always at least one rational, reasonable
course of action which it is in principle possible for a rational agent to dis-
cern.[7] But the above examples, together with some seemingly innocuous assumptions and inferences about rationality, have led to the denial of what
we usually take for granted, and, as so often occurs with putative examples
of moral dilemma, it may be suspected at this point that some subtle fault
in our assumptions about rationality may have led us astray.

Perhaps our problems arise, for example, from relying on an optimizing/
maximizing model of rational choice and action, on the assumption that a
rational agent must (in appropriate self-regarding contexts) choose what is
best for herself. The recent literature of economics suggests the possibility
that in some situations where one cannot figure out what course of action is
best, it may be rationally acceptable to satisfice, choose some good enough
course of action, rather than attempting to optimize. And even where what
is better or worse is known to the agent, it may not be irrational to choose
one course of action even when there is some other available action that one
knows would allow one to do better for oneself. There is a clear conceptual
distinction between an act with best results for oneself (or for all concerned)
and a best act, and we learn this distinction from moral theories that make
room for rational altruism (or for the rational non-optimific honoring of
certain deontological restrictions). But even in purely self-regarding or individualistic contexts where the results of every alternative are known we can
distinguish between what it is best (most rational) for an agent to do and
what would allow an agent to do best for herself. I have elsewhere argued
at some length that our ordinary conception of moderation allows it to be
rational, or not irrational, for an individual modest or moderate in his desires
deliberately to choose a given course of action while knowing that he could
do better for himself by another.[8] A person may turn down a second cup of
tea or an afternoon snack which he thinks he would enjoy, which he thinks
of as a good thing, because he considers himself well enough off as he is;
and in the fairy-tale situation where one is offered as much wealth as one
wishes, and one chooses to be moderately well-off, the moderate individual
may choose as he does, not because he fears asking for more or because he
thinks himself constitutionally incapable of benefiting from greater wealth,
but because such great wealth represents much more than he thinks he needs
(much more than he cares about). Reasons like "I'm fine as I am" or "That's

---

[7] One reason for the qualification: Joel Feinberg's well-known example of an agent prevented
from making a decision by a coughing fit: perhaps such an agent never had it in his power to
act rationally in that particular situation. See Feinberg's "Problematic Responsibility in Law
and Morals," in *Doing and Deserving,* Princeton Univ. Press, 1970.

[8] See "Moderation, Rationality, and Virtue," in *The Tanner Lectures on Human Values,* 7,
1986; also, more briefly, *Commonsense Morality and Consequentialism,* Boston and London,
Routledge and Kegan Paul, 1985, pp. 38–44.

much more than I need" are, for certain moderate individuals,[9] reasons for not choosing what (admittedly) would be best for themselves (their own greatest well-being). But to that extent, such individuals need not be considered to act irrationally. Although they sometimes choose what is less than best for themselves, on such occasions, according to their lights, the balance of reasons favors making such a choice; so they can hold it is better for them to do what is less good for themselves, a distinction already familiar from moral contexts.

There is thus, even in individualistic contexts, a distinction to be made between best actions (choices) and actions (choices) that are best for (have the best results for) oneself.[10] And if we find this distinction at all convincing, then we must be careful not to fudge it in attempting to show the possibility of rational dilemma. In the putative example of rational dilemma mentioned above, a rational individual must inevitably make a choice which is less good for himself than certain definitely available alternatives. But it may not automatically follow that he makes a less good choice than he might. And if that further inference requires us to assume an optimizing model of rationality that rules out rational moderation as described above, then I think we have at best a doubtful argument for the possibility of rational dilemmas.

However, although I have strong doubts about whether individualistic rational choice (under certainty) universally requires optimization and would like to leave room for the possibility of rational moderation as described briefly above, I think the example of adding happy days to one's life naturally invites the optimizing model of rationality.[11] Satisfaction with less than immortality, or with a shorter rather than a longer life, is not part of our

---

[9] These individuals are not moderate as a means to an overall greater balance of happiness or well-being, in the manner recommended by the Epicureans; but neither are they ascetics: they are not seeking to avoid satisfactions whenever possible. On these points, see "Moderation, Rationality, and Virtue."

[10] Although one who performs best actions can in some sense be said to optimize, that is not the usual sense of the term nor the sense I am making use of here.

[11] Indeed, it was chosen for that very reason. Somewhat similar examples occurring in the recent philosophic literature raise somewhat similar problems about the nature of rationality. (See, for example, John Pollock, "How Do You Maximize Expectation Value?," *Noûs* 17, 1984, pp. 409–21; my *Common-sense Morality and Consequentialism*, pp. 44, 144f.; and "Utilitarianism, Moral Dilemmas, and Moral Cost," p. 168n.) But the previous examples were not used to support the possibility of rational dilemma (indeed Pollock explicitly denies the possibility of dilemma); and in fact those examples may yield dilemmas only if we assume the universal applicability of the optimizing model of rationality, thus denying the rationality (non-irrationality) of non-instrumental moderation. For some of the examples seem to involve choosing among an infinite number of better and worse results where it doesn't seem to make much difference whether one chooses the better or less good results and where a rational but moderate individual might not care about, be influenced by, such differences in utility. The examples I have used and will be using here are not naturally thought of in terms of "diminishing returns," and as we shall see, they allow no ready foothold for the idea of non-optimizing moderation.

ordinary conception of moderation, or modesty of desire: the moderate individual may be indifferent (at a certain point) to more happiness in the sense of greater or more intense happiness, but there seems to be no element of moderation in a willingness to allow one's life to end sooner rather than later.[12] (Perhaps it is irrational for us humans not to *accept* our unavoidable mortality, but it hardly follows that we would have reasons of moderation, or of any other kind, to reject immortality if it were ever on offer.) And so in the fountain-of-youth example it is very difficult to block the move from "choice with better results for oneself" to "better choice." It would appear that for any distance one chooses to stand from the fountain, there are other closer positions which he had more reason to choose. And since it seems self-evidently irrational to make a given choice when a better, more rationally supported choice is clearly available, we appear to have a rational dilemma.

Of course, we could easily evade the dilemma if, with Bernard Williams,[13] we held that immortality was not a good thing and attempted to infer that there was some (vaguely specifiable) finite length of life beyond which it is worth no one's while to live. But such a way out would be as paradoxical as the idea of rational dilemma itself, and it seems that the latter fairly forces itself upon us in our attempt to describe the example we have been focusing on. If one is really pleased at the prospect of n additional happy days of life, one will have reason to prefer $2n$ additional days, and it seems undeniable not only that the person who stands $1/n$ inch away and gets n extra happy days would have been better off if she had chosen to stand $1/2n$ inches away, but that she would have done better to stand $1/2n$ inches away. She was capable of standing at the latter distance and there was reason for her to stand at that distance rather than at the distance she actually chose (she has no reason of moderation to be reluctant or indifferent about choosing to stand closer and have the longer life). So whatever she chooses to do, it would, on the balance of reasons have been better for her to choose otherwise.

Moreover, even if, in this case, the existence of dilemma depends on an assumption about the goodness of indefinitely long pleasurable existence, it is possible to construct a rather similar example requiring no such assumption. Imagine that God has condemned some wine connoisseur to an infinite life with only as finitely much of his favorite wine, Château Effete, as he asks for on a certain occasion. How many bottles of Château Effete should he ask for as a consolation for the unpleasant tedium of his largely wineless immortality? Since no finite amount is an immoderate quantity when consumed over infinite time, the man will have reason to specify as large a finite

---

[12] About an additional pleasure or increment of wealth one may say "who needs it?," but this is not the response one would expect to an offer of happy longer life. And "I'm fine as I am" may be a reason for turning down an additional enjoyment, but is irrelevant, of course, to the offer of a longer life.

[13] See "The Makropulos Case: Reflections on the Tedium of Immortality," in *Problems of the Self*.

amount as possible; and whatever amount he actually specifies, there will be (more) reason for him to choose some larger amount.

Practical rational dilemma thus seems inevitable in the case of our wine connoisseur, and given some rather plausible assumptions about the desirability of indefinitely long (happy) life, in the fountain-of-youth case as well. Even if we may wish to hold that it can be self-regardingly rational to choose less than the best (results) for oneself, it seems self-evidently irrational to make a given choice when, as in our examples, a better, a more rationally supported, choice is clearly available.

But there is another possibility. Even granting that whatever a given person chooses, there will be some other better choice, we may still hold that there are degrees of rationality in the cases we have described. Clearly, it would be irrational in our first example for someone to stand only a quarter of an inch from the "fountain of youth" (or, in our second example, for the connoisseur to ask for only five bottles of Château Effete). To stand one billionth of an inch away from the fountain would be a much better thing to do, and perhaps there are degrees of proximity that it would be rational (not irrational) to choose, even though it would have been better, more rational, to have chosen some even greater degree of proximity. In other words, it may be possible for an act (choice) not to count as irrational or bad, even if it is less than ideally rational, less than the best available.

But such a way out of rational dilemma involves one in denying an assumption that, as far as I am aware, has been always accepted as obvious by philosophers discussing practical rationality, the assumption (roughly) that it is irrational to act one way when one believes there is some alternative action which one has, on balance, more reason to perform, which it would be better (and the sense of "better" here is in no way limited to moral considerations) to perform. One finds this assumption in recent works by such philosophers as Donald Davidson and David Pears, but it is taken for granted, as far as I can tell, by everyone who has dealt with practical reason and practical rationality.[14]

Taking it for granted amounts to a denial of the possibility of rational supererogation. The morally supererogatory exists, we know, if there are some moral or non-immoral acts that are morally less good than some of their alternatives. For an act is morally supererogatory if it is morally better than some alternative that would not have been wrong. However, even if common-sense morality seems to make abundant room for supererogation, there are moral theories which rule it out. Act-consequentialists and Act-utilitarians, for example, rank acts according to their consequences and nowadays typically hold that right actions must have optimal consequences relative to their alternatives, and thus be better than (or as good as) any of their alternatives. So for such a utilitarian no act can be right unless there is no

---

[14] Davidson, "How is Weakness of the Will Possible?," in J. Feinberg, ed., *Moral Concepts,* Oxford Univ. Press, 1969; Pears, *Motivated Irrationality,* Oxford Univ. Press, 1984.

alternative open to the agent which is morally better than it. But this is not in general true of moral views, and common sense allows for the moral acceptability of behavior to which there are morally superior, e.g., heroic and saintly, alternatives.

However, on the topic of rational supererogation there has been no such division of opinion, or perhaps we should say that there has simply never been such a topic as rational supererogation, because everyone has taken it for granted that it is irrational to do one thing when from a rational standpoint it would be better for one to do something else. But perhaps we have motive and reason to question this assumption, once we realize that only by doing so can we avoid another assumption that philosophers would tend to question and reject out of hand, the assumption that through no rational fault of one's own, one may end up in a position where one cannot avoid acting irrationally. If we allow for rational supererogation, if we allow that an act may be rational (non-irrational) or be a good (or not a bad) act to perform, even though there is more reason and it would be better to perform some alternative, then we may be able to avoid the initially and perhaps persistently repugnant idea that there can be rational dilemmas.[15] Further, once we have been given a motive for questioning the assumption that rationality requires doing what is rationally best (or what is rationally not less than the best),[16] we may begin to notice reasons for questioning that assumption that are quite independent of any felt need to rule out rational dilemmas.

What I have in mind is perhaps best introduced via recent discussion of akrasia. Unlike most discussions of akrasia, Donald Davidson's "How is Weakness of the Will Possible?" makes it abundantly clear that more than two alternatives can be at issue in cases of akrasia. According to Davidson, if act b is believed better than act a and the agent chooses b, she is not off the akratic hook if there is some further action c which she thinks is better than b. And I think we can produce some good reasons to doubt whether this must always be the case. In certain complex cases of what must on standard accounts be regarded as akrasia, it is not unnatural or strained to speak of degrees of rationality, to regard less than ideal or maximum rationality as rational enough, as not simply irrational.

Let us consider two examples. A man and his wife have quarreled and in a fit of pique the wife has gone back to her mother's, threatening to stay there indefinitely. The man is disconcerted, hurt, angry; he feels greater and greater frustration as the situation drags on, but he believes his wife will come back to him and hopes to be able to help bring this about. However, right now, his wife being still away, he is at a party and one of the female

---

[15] Later on, we shall see that certain non-optimizing forms of act-consequentialism allow one to avoid the utilitarian moral dilemma described above.

[16] The qualification in parentheses rationally permits one to choose between tied-best actions and between incommensurable actions, but still rules out the less-than-best actions described in the text.

guests begins to flirt with him, indeed suggests her sexual availability, and the man is tempted. But he believes it would be wrong and a (prudential) mistake for him to get physically involved with her in any way. He also believes that it would be possible, though very difficult, for him entirely to resist her advances. In his state of frustration and anxiety he gives in to the blandishments to a certain extent, engages in what used to be called "heavy necking." Somehow the lesser physical intimacy takes the edge off his frustration and actually helps him resist greater intimacy. But he may know, and we may assume, that most men in his position would have completely succumbed to the blandishments, and, in particular, that most men who had gone as far as he has would have gone all the way. So although he has not done what he deems best, has fallen short of what his own conception of ideal rationality dictates in the circumstances, his feelings after the fact may be more those of relief and even pride, than of shame or regret. He may feel that although going as far as he did was not the best available action, it was not, in the circumstances, a bad thing for him to do.[17] What he did was not ideally rational, but neither, he may feel, was what he did simply irrational: although it demonstrated some weakness of will, it demstrated considerable strength of will as well. If he exerted more rational control than we can reasonably expect of most people, then perhaps his act of going-as-far-as-he-did-but-no-farther is rational enough so that it would be a mistake simply to call it irrational.

Take another example. A man is angry at his boss and believes (for good reasons we needn't enter into) that it would be in his own interest and on the whole a good thing to tell the boss off when they next meet. He believes it would be best to do so in a loud enough voice so that everyone in the office will know what is happening. But both he and his fellow employees have long been intimidated by the boss, and the employee knows it will be difficult to stand up to the boss and tell him what he thinks, and even more difficult (though not impossible) to do so in the loud and angry tones he thinks most appropriate. When the time comes to confront the boss, he manages with considerable effort to speak his mind, but allows himself to be intimidated to the extent of not daring to do so loudly and angrily; and indeed from a rational standpoint and relative to the man's own values, it would have been better for him to speak angrily to the boss than to express his opinion in conversational tones. But the latter may have been difficult enough so that on the whole the man is more proud than ashamed at his performance. Even though his performance may be less than the best that lay within his power, it may be good enough for him and for us not to regard it as simply irrational. So again we seem to have a rational analogue of what common-sense morality requires for supererogation. Moral supererogation is possible if

[17] I cannot think of any other area where "good (not bad) f" entails "best (available) f." Wouldn't it in fact be odd if this entailment held with respect to good choice and action, but nowhere else?

there can be (extended) action which from a moral standpoint is less than ideal, less good than it could be, but which is nonetheless good enough from a moral standpoint not to count as immoral or wrong. And our above examples seem, analogously, to involve less than ideally rational choice and action that need not be regarded as irrational *simpliciter*.

We have two sorts of reasons, then, for admitting the notions of rational supererogation and of less-than-ideal practical rationality (non-irrationality): the linguistic and phenomenological *naturalness* of conceiving certain examples in those terms and the desire to avoid rational dilemmas. And we must now consider how the idea of supererogation can help us to evade dilemma in the fountain-of-youth case (or the case of accumulating Château Effete).

It seems outright irrational for someone with the powers we have assumed to stand at certain distances, e.g., ¼ of an inch, away from the science-fiction fountain of youth,[18] but how much closer does one have to choose to stand in order for one's choice no longer to count as irrational? In the supererogation-friendly examples of yielding partially to sexual temptation and of failure to speak loudly to the boss, the agent accomplishes most, the most important part, of what ideal rationality requires, but it would be difficult to apply this notion to the fountain-of-youth case, where one inevitably gains only an (infinitesimally) small fraction of the number of extra happy days one had reason, and the power, to obtain. In order to treat such examples as dilemma-free, we must borrow another feature of our "natural" paradigms of rational supererogation.

The performance of the man who does everything but speak loudly need not be regarded as simply irrational, because of the great difficulty of doing (rationally) better than he has done. (It may be unreasonable, for example, to expect others to do as well as he has done.) And we can similarly imagine in the fountain-of-youth case that, even though one can stand at any finite close distance, still the closer the distance the more difficult it would be to summon the concentration and the intelligence required to stand at that distance. The difficulty of standing at closer and closer distances thus approaches the limits of the agent's power and skill. In that case, an agent who through great effort and concentration chose to stand at a distance so near that it would have been very difficult (for him or for anyone else) to choose

---

[18] Optimizing assumptions about rationality lead to problems in the cases Pollock mentions, but in the light of those problems, Pollock goes to the opposite extreme of holding that in the problem cases, anything one does (chooses) is rationally permissible, non-irrational. For reasons already mentioned, this seems an implausible solution for the sorts of cases mentioned here (and indeed it seems implausible for Pollock's examples as well, though that implausibility is less obvious if, like Pollock, one doesn't consider questions of degree, what it would be *more* or *less* rational to do). What I have sought to do is take a middle path between the view that everything is rationally permissible in our problem cases and the view that they should be treated as dilemmas where no rational choice is possible. This makes them more like what under ordinary assumptions the moral life is like, with impermissible, non-supererogatory permissible, and supererogatory courses of action all available to one.

to stand any nearer, may count as having chosen rationally, or at least not irrationally.[19] And we can see how to avoid the admission of rational dilemmas by allowing for rational supererogation, for a gap between rationality and ideal rationality.[20]

On the other hand, someone – even someone who finds the idea of rational dilemma initially objectionable – may regard our "natural" examples of rational supererogation as more convincing than the above attempt to avoid dilemmas, and so end up accepting both rational supererogation and rational dilemmas. But the issues widen at this point, because what one wants to say about rational dilemmas and supererogation is understandably influenced by what one wants to say about moral dilemmas and supererogation. There is a long ethical tradition of drawing analogies between rationality and morality, and this tendency, and the fact that the usual direction of influence has been from conceptions of rationality to moral views or theories, may serve to explain some features of recent and traditional moral theory and suggest some possibilities for the future.

Act-utilitarianism is often seen as basing morality on a rational extension of the principle of egoistic rational choice. Self-regarding rationality involves maximizing the agent's well-being or satisfactions, and in its most familiar form, the principle of utility requires agents to maximize the satisfactions or well-being of all mankind or of all sentient beings. Although many other features of rationality have served as bases for moral theorizing (and although many disanalogies between rationality and morality have also been asserted and defended),[21] one particular aspect of rationality that has influenced moral theory is of particular concern to us. The most popular forms of act-utilitarianism and of act-consequentialism more generally bear the imprint of another feature commonly ascribed to practical rationality, the absence of supererogation. As I mentioned earlier, the principle of utility requires agents always to perform the morally best act they are capable of performing at a given time.[22] But of course the analogous feature is familiar in the case of practical rationality and as far as I know, no one has doubted that for an act/choice to count as rational there can be no known better alternatives: that much has always seemed self-evident to the extent that philosophers have even considered the issue.

[19] For the interesting application of similar notions to the problem of free will, see Patricia Greenspan's "Unfreedom and Responsibility," forthcoming in a collection of essays on moral responsibility edited by F. Schoeman. Note that in the fountain-of-youth case it is quite natural to assume that the personal costs of greater efforts are less than the benefits to be gained through greater efforts.

[20] The idea of dilemma for such an example could then be resuscitated only if one could make coherent sense of the supposition that (in other possible cases) standing nearer and nearer (without touching) the fountain need not get, or tend to get, more and more difficult.

[21] Cf. Derek Parfit's *Reasons and Persons,* Oxford, 1984.

[22] For utilitarians, the question what kind of person is morally best is not rigidly tied to the question which actions are morally best.

Ordinary act-utilitarianism and act-consequentialism thus seem to model their notion of what is morally good enough to be morally acceptable on the accepted view of what is rationally good enough to be rationally acceptable. Sometimes this analogy has been based on the assumption that morality (moral obligation) is nothing more than what is rational (what one must choose on pain of being irrational) or that all moral distinctions can be reduced to (supervene upon) distinctions about what one has more or less reason to do. But whatever its sources or inspiration, it has led act-consequentialists to regard the supererogation that ordinary morality allows for as some sort of illusion.

Even those who have defended (common-sense) moral supererogation would not have been willing to defend rational supererogation. But although this difference of view concerning morality and rationality will seem suspect to those who think morality ought as much as possible to be understood on the model of rationality, defenders, e.g., of common-sense morality will certainly be able to reply that significant differences ought not to be glossed over or denied in the name of an illusory ideal of theoretical simplicity. If there are no supererogations of practical reason, that fact, they may say, ought not to be allowed to attenuate the strong and obvious intuition that in morality at least it is possible to avoid wrongdoing without doing the morally best act available.

For the most part, then, (implicit) total views of rationality-cum-morality have come in two forms. Either they have accepted moral supererogation, but implicitly denied the possibility of rational supererogation, or (out of a desire to model morality as closely as possible on rationality) they have not allowed either rational or moral supererogation. Almost all act-utilitarians have been in the latter group, and defenders of deontology or common sense have been in the former. But it is possible to advocate a form of act-utilitarianism or act-consequentialism that falls or lets one fall into the first group. Bentham's original version of the principle of utility considers an act right if it produces more happiness than unhappiness on balance, and this principle and various other (and as I have argued elsewhere, more plausible) versions of act-utilitarianism allow for supererogation.[23] Familiar optimizing utilitarianism is often considered too demanding precisely because it always requires an agent to do what is morally best. And even if one believes that objectively good consequences are the only thing relevant to the moral assessment of actions, one may also feel that room needs to be made for moral supererogation and that an act with good enough consequences may be morally acceptable even when better consequences (a better act) could have been produced. And that feeling, as with defenders of common-sense morality, may be strong enough so that one wants to allow for moral supererogation even while denying the possibility of rational supererogation. (If one allows

[23] See *Common-sense Morality and Consequentialism*, Ch. 3.

for moral supererogation one may be able to avoid utilitarian moral dilemmas of the kind described earlier; this is one motive for holding a supererogation-allowing non-optimizing form of utilitarianism that is quite independent of one's views about rational supererogation or one's knowledge of the possibility of rational dilemmas.)

But once we see the possibility of rational dilemmas and the various examples mentioned in the text above are brought into view, a third and unaccustomed position on rationality-cum-morality begins to emerge, one which allows for rational supererogation and moral supererogation both. Its advocacy permits one to retain the hope of basing morality in practical rationality without falling into the typical utilitarian's anti-common-sensical denial of moral supererogation.[24] And the utilitarian who allows for moral and rational supererogation may also be able to evade both the utilitarian moral dilemmas discussed earlier and the rational dilemmas we have focused on. But any such view is, for all these possible advantages, both unexpected and unprecedented, and it will take a good deal more careful examination and exploration before anyone can be confident that this third way of construing rationality-cum-morality really does represent a viable alternative to traditional views.[25]

[24] From the standpoint of this emerging position, a fundamental mistake of supererogation-denying utilitarianism may lie not in its attempt to model morality on rationality, but in the way it understands the structure of rationality itself. I am indebted for this way of putting things to Gregory Trianosky.

[25] For interesting exploration of the idea of less-than-ideal *epistemic* rationality see, e.g., Earl Conee's "Utilitarianism and Rationality," *Analysis* 42, 1982, pp. 55–59; Frederick Kroon, "Rationality and Paradox," *Analysis* 43, 1983, pp. 156–60; Christopher Cherniak, *Minimal Rationality,* Bradford Books, 1986. My greatest debt, in the present paper, is to the work of Herbert Simon. I would also like to thank Jonathan Adler, Earl Conee, Carl Cranor, Patricia Greenspan, and Gregory Trianosky for their helpful suggestions.

Bibliography on rational action

General

Agassi, Joseph, and Ian Jarvie, eds. *Rationality: The Critical View.* Dordrecht: Nijhoff, 1987.

Audi, Robert. *Practical Reasoning.* London: Routledge, 1989.

Audi, Robert, ed. *Action, Decision, and Intention: Studies in the Foundations of Action Theory as an Approach to Understanding Rationality and Decision.* Dordrecht: Reidel, 1986.

Aune, Bruce. *Reason and Action.* Dordrecht: Reidel, 1977.

Baron, Jonathon. *Rationality and Intelligence.* Cambridge: Cambridge University Press, 1985.

Becker, Gary. *The Economic Approach to Human Behavior.* Chicago: University of Chicago Press, 1976.

Benn, S. I., and G. W. Mortimore, eds. *Rationality and the Social Sciences: Contributions to the Philosophy and Methodology of the Social Sciences.* London: Routledge and Kegan Paul, 1976.

Binkley, Robert, Richard Bronaugh, and Ausonio Marras, eds. *Agent, Action, and Reason.* Toronto: University of Toronto Press, 1971.

Black, Max. *The Prevalence of Humbug, and Other Essays.* Ithaca, NY: Cornell University Press, 1983.

Bond, E. J. *Reason and Value.* Cambridge: Cambridge University Press, 1983.

Bradie, Michael, and Kenneth Sayre, eds. *Reason and Decision.* Bowling Green, OH: Bowling Green State University, 1982.

Brandt, Richard. *A Theory of the Good and the Right.* Oxford: Clarendon Press, 1979.

Bratman, Michael. *Intention, Plans, and Practical Reason.* Cambridge, MA: Harvard University Press, 1987.

Brubaker, Rogers. *The Limits of Rationality: An Essay on the Social and Moral Thought of Max Weber.* London: Allen and Unwin, 1984.

Darwall, Stephen. *Impartial Reason.* Ithaca, NY: Cornell University Press, 1983.

Dearden, R. F., P. H. Hirst, and R. S. Peters, eds. *Reason*. London: Routledge and Kegan Paul, 1972.

Elster, Jon. *Ulysses and the Sirens: Studies in Rationality and Irrationality*. Cambridge: Cambridge University Press, 1979.

  Sour Grapes: Studies in the Subversion of Rationality. Cambridge: Cambridge University Press, 1983.

  Solomonic Judgments: Studies in the Limitation of Rationality. Cambridge: Cambridge University Press, 1989.

Garver, Newton, and Peter H. Hare, eds. *Naturalism and Rationality*. Buffalo, NY: Prometheus Books, 1986.

Gauthier, David. *Morals By Agreement*. Oxford: Clarendon Press, 1986.

Gottlieb, Gidon. *The Logic of Choice: An Investigation of the Concepts of Rule and Rationality*. New York: Macmillan, 1968.

Grandy, Richard E., and Richard Warner, eds. *Philosophical Grounds of Rationality: Intentions, Categories, Ends*. Oxford: Clarendon Press, 1986.

Griffin, James. *Well-Being*. Oxford: Clarendon Press, 1986.

Hahn, Frank, and Martin Hollis, eds. *Philosophy and Economic Theory*. New York: Oxford University Press, 1979.

Harris, Anthony R., ed. *Rationality and Collective Belief*. Norwood, NJ: Ablex, 1986.

Harrison, Ross, ed. *Rational Action*. Cambridge: Cambridge University Press, 1979.

Hogarth, Robin M., and Melvin W. Reder, eds. *Rational Choice: The Contrast between Economics and Psychology*. Chicago: University of Chicago Press, 1987.

Hollis, Martin. *The Cunning of Reason*. Cambridge: Cambridge University Press, 1987.

Hollis, Martin, and Steven Lukes, eds. *Rationality and Relativism*. Oxford: Blackwell, 1982.

Hook, Sidney, ed. *Human Values and Economic Policy*. New York: New York University Press, 1967.

Jarvie, Ian. *Rationality and Relativism: In Search of a Philosophy and History of Anthropology*. London: Routledge and Kegan Paul, 1984.

Levi, Isaac. *The Enterprise of Knowledge: An Essay on Knowledge, Credal Probability, and Chance*. Cambridge, MA: MIT Press, 1980.

  Decisions and Revisions. Cambridge: Cambridge University Press, 1984.

Michalos, Alex. *Foundations of Decision-Making*. Ottawa: Canadian Library of Philosophy, 1978.

Nathanson, Stephen. *The Ideal of Rationality*. Atlantic Highlands, NJ: Humanities Press, 1985.

Norman, Richard J. *Reasons for Actions: A Critique of Utilitarian Rationality*. New York: Barnes and Noble, 1971.

Parfit, Derek. *Reasons and Persons*. Oxford: Clarendon Press, 1984.

Raz, Joseph, ed. *Practical Reasoning*. Oxford: Oxford University Press, 1978.

Rescher, Nicholas. *Rationality: A Philosophical Inquiry into the Nature and the Rationale of Reason*. Oxford: Clarendon Press, 1988.

Rescher, Nicholas, ed. *The Logic of Decision and Action*. Pittsburgh: University of Pittsburgh Press, 1967.

Richards, D. A. J. *A Theory of Reasons for Action*. Oxford: Clarendon Press, 1971.

Schelling, Thomas. *Choice and Consequence.* Cambridge, MA: Harvard University Press, 1984.

Schick, Frederick. *Having Reasons: An Essay on Rationality and Sociality.* Princeton, NJ: Princeton University Press, 1984.

Sen, Amartya. *Choice, Welfare, and Measurement.* Cambridge, MA: MIT Press, 1982.

On Ethics and Economics. Oxford: Basil Blackwell, 1987.

Sidgwick, Henry. *The Methods of Ethics.* 7th ed. London: Macmillan, 1907.

Simon, Herbert. *Administrative Behavior.* 2d ed. New York: Free Press, 1965.

Models of Bounded Rationality. Cambridge, MA: MIT Press, 1982.

Reason in Human Affairs. Stanford: Stanford University Press, 1983.

Slote, Michael. *Beyond Optimizing: A Study of Rational Choice.* Cambridge, MA: Harvard University Press, 1988.

Tamny, Martin, and K. D. Irani, eds. *Rationality in Thought and Action.* New York: Greenwood Press, 1986.

Walkerdine, Valerie. *The Mastery of Reason: Cognitive Development and the Production of Rationality.* London: Routledge, 1988.

Wilson, Bryan R., ed. *Rationality.* New York: Harper and Row, 1970.

Individual decision theory

Allais, Maurice, and Ole Hagen, eds. *Expected Utility Hypotheses and the Allais Paradox: Contemporary Discussions of Decisions Under Uncertainty with Allais' Rejoinder.* Dordrecht: Reidel, 1979.

Arrow, Kenneth. *Individual Choice under Certainty and Uncertainty.* Cambridge, MA: Harvard University Press, 1984.

Boyer, Marcel, and Richard E. Kihlstrom, eds. *Bayesian Models in Economic Theory.* Amsterdam: North-Holland, 1984.

Campbell, Richmond, and Lanning Sowden, eds. *Paradoxes of Rationality and Cooperation: Prisoner's Dilemma and Newcomb's Problem.* Vancouver: University of British Columbia Press, 1985.

Carlsson, C., and Y. Kochetkov, eds. *Theory and Practice of Multiple Criteria Decision Making.* Amsterdam: North-Holland, 1983.

Chankong, Vira, and Yacov Y. Haimes. *Multiobjective Decision Making: Theory and Methodology.* Amsterdam: North-Holland, 1983.

Chernoff, Herman, and Lincoln Moses. *Elementary Decision Theory.* New York: Wiley, 1959.

Chipman, John, Leonid Hurwicz, Marcel Richter, and Hugo Sonnenschein, eds. *Preferences, Utility, and Demand.* New York: Harcourt, Brace, and Jovanovich, 1971. (Includes extensive bibliography on decision theory.)

Davidson, Donald, Patrick Suppes, and Sidney Siegel. *Decision Making: An Experimental Approach.* Stanford: Stanford University Press, 1957.

Edwards, Ward, and Amos Tversky, eds. *Decision Making.* Baltimore: Penguin Books, 1967.

Eells, Ellery. *Rational Decision and Causality.* Cambridge: Cambridge University Press, 1982.

Elster, Jon, ed. *Rational Choice.* New York: New York University Press, 1986.

Fishburn, Peter C. *Decision and Value Theory.* New York: Wiley, 1964.
   Utility Theory for Decision Making. New York: Wiley, 1970.
   Mathematics of Decision Theory. The Hague: Mouton, 1973.
French, Simon. *Decision Theory: An Introduction to the Mathematics of Rationality.* New York: Halsted Press, 1986.
Gärdenfors, Peter, and Nils-Eric Sahlin, eds. *Decision, Probability, and Utility: Selected Readings.* Cambridge: Cambridge University Press, 1988.
Good, Irving J. *Probability and the Weighing of Evidence.* London: Charles Griffin, 1950.
   Good Thinking. Minneapolis: University of Minnesota Press, 1983.
Hacking, Ian. *The Emergence of Probability.* Cambridge: Cambridge University Press, 1975.
Hindess, Barry. *Choice, Rationality, and Social Theory.* London: Unwin, 1988.
Hogarth, Robin. *Judgement and Choice.* 2d ed. New York: Wiley, 1987.
Hooker, C. A., J. J. Leach, and E. F. McClennen, eds. *Foundations and Applications of Decision Theory.* Dordrecht: Reidel, 1978.
Jeffrey, Richard C. *The Logic of Decision.* 2d ed. Chicago: University of Chicago Press, 1983.
Kahneman, Daniel, Paul Slovic, and Amos Tversky, eds., *Judgment Under Uncertainty: Heuristics and Biases.* Cambridge: Cambridge University Press, 1982.
Levi, Isaac. *Hard Choices: Decision Making Under Unresolved Conflict.* Cambridge: Cambridge University Press, 1986.
Luce, R. D. *Individual Choice Behavior.* New York: Wiley, 1959.
McClennen, Edward. *Rationality and Dynamic Choice.* Cambridge: Cambridge University Press, 1990.
Raiffa, Howard. *Applied Statistical Decision Theory.* Boston: Graduate School of Business Administration, Harvard University, 1961.
   Decision Analysis. Reading, MA: Addison Wesley, 1968.
Rapoport, Anatol, and A. M. Chammah. *Prisoner's Dilemma: A Study in Conflict and Cooperation.* Ann Arbor: University of Michigan Press, 1965.
Resnick, Michael D. *Choices: An Introduction to Decision Theory.* Minneapolis: University of Minnesota Press, 1987.
Savage, Leonard. *The Foundations of Statistics.* 2d ed. New York: Dover, 1972.
Thrall, R. M., C. H. Coombs, and R. L. Davis, eds. *Decision Processes.* New York: Wiley, 1954.
Watson, Stephen, and Dennis Buede. *Decision Synthesis.* Cambridge: Cambridge University Press, 1987.

Game theory

Blackwell, David, and M. A. Girschick. *Theory of Games and Statistical Decisions.* New York: Dover, 1979.
Brams, Steven J. *Game Theory and Politics.* New York: Free Press, 1975.
   Rational Politics: Decisions, Games, and Strategy. Washington, D.C.: CQ Press, 1985.
Davis, Morton. *Game Theory.* 2d ed. New York: Basic Books, 1983.
Harsanyi, John C. *Essays on Ethics, Social Behavior, and Scientific Explanation.* Dordrecht: Reidel, 1976.

Rational Behavior and Bargaining Equilibrium in Games and Social Situations. Cambridge: Cambridge University Press, 1977.

Luce, R. D., and Howard Raiffa. *Games and Decisions.* New York: Wiley, 1957.

Peleg, B. *Game Theoretic Analysis of Voting in Committees.* Cambridge: Cambridge University Press, 1984.

Rapoport, Anatol, ed. *Game Theory as a Theory of Conflict Resolution.* Dordrecht: Reidel, 1974.

Roth, Alvin, ed. *Game Theoretic Models of Bargaining.* Cambridge: Cambridge University Press, 1985.

Schelling, Thomas C. *The Strategy of Conflict.* Cambridge, MA: Harvard University Press, 1960.

Shubik, Martin, ed. *Readings in Game Theory and Political Behavior.* New York: Doubleday, 1954.

von Neumann, John, and Oskar Morgenstern. *Theory of Games and Economic Behavior.* 3d ed. Princeton: Princeton University Press, 1953.

Social choice theory

Arrow, Kenneth. *Social Choice and Individual Values.* 2d ed. New York: Wiley, 1963.

Axelrod, Robert. *The Evolution of Cooperation.* New York: Basic Books, 1984.

Barry, Brian, and Russell Hardin, eds. *Rational Man and Irrational Society.* London: Sage, 1982.

Buchanan, J. M., and Gordon Tullock. *The Calculus of Consent.* Ann Arbor: University of Michigan Press, 1962.

Coleman, James Samuel. *Individual Interests and Collective Action: Selected Essays.* Cambridge: Cambridge University Press, 1986.

Collingridge, David. *Critical Decision Making: A New Theory of Social Choice.* New York: St. Martin's Press, 1982.

Dummett, Michael. *Voting Procedures.* Oxford: Clarendon Press, 1984.

Elster, Jon, and Aanund Hylland, eds. *Foundations of Social Choice Theory.* Cambridge: Cambridge University Press, 1986.

Feldman, A. M. *Welfare Economics and Social Choice Theory.* Dordrecht: Nijhoff, 1980.

Fishburn, P. C. *The Theory of Social Choice.* Princeton: Princeton University Press, 1973.

Gottinger, Hans W., and Werner Leinfellner, eds. *Decision Theory and Social Ethics: Issues in Social Choice.* Dordrecht: Reidel, 1978.

Heller, Walter, Ross Starr, and David Starrett, eds. *Essays in Honor of Kenneth Arrow.* 3 vols. Cambridge: Cambridge University Press, 1986.

Kelly, J. S. *Arrow Impossibility Theorems.* New York: Academic Press, 1978.

MacKay, Alfred. *Arrow's Theorem.* New Haven: Yale University Press, 1980.

Margolis, Howard. *Selfishness, Altruism, and Rationality: A Theory of Social Choice.* Cambridge: Cambridge University Press, 1982.

Mueller, D. C. *Public Choice.* Cambridge: Cambridge University Press, 1979.

Olson, Mancur. *The Logic of Collective Action.* Cambridge, MA: Harvard University Press, 1965.

Pattanaik, P. K. *Strategy and Group Choice.* Amsterdam: North-Holland, 1978.

Pigou, A. C. *The Economics of Welfare*. 4th ed. London: Macmillan, 1952.

Russell, Clifford C., ed. *Collective Decision Making: Applications from Public Choice Theory*. Baltimore: Johns Hopkins University Press, 1979.

Schwartz, Thomas. *The Logic of Collective Choice*. New York: Columbia University Press, 1986.

Sen, Amartya. *Collective Choice and Social Welfare*. San Francisco: Holden Day, 1970.

Suzumura, Kotaro. *Rational Choice, Collective Decisions, and Social Welfare*. Cambridge: Cambridge University Press, 1983.

Taylor, Michael. *The Possibility of Cooperation*. Cambridge: Cambridge University Press, 1987.

Index